Contents

IV. Toward an Equitable and Healthy Global System 353

Preface

Medical anthropology is one of the youngest and, some would even boldly claim, the most dynamic of the various subdisciplines of anthropology. It concerns itself with a wide variety of health-related issues, including the etiology of disease, the preventive measures that humans as members of sociocultural systems have constructed or devised to prevent the onset of disease, and the curative measures that they have created in their efforts to eradicate disease or at least to mitigate its consequences. In some ways, the term "medical anthropology" is a misnomer that reflects the curative rather than preventive nature of health care in modern societies. After all, anthropologists who study religious beliefs and practices generally refer to their subdiscipline as the "anthropology of religion" rather than "religious anthropology." Taking their cue from sociologists who speak of the "sociology of health and illness" rather than "medical sociology," some anthropologists interested in health-related issues have suggested substituting the label "anthropology of health and illness" rather than "medical anthropology." Indeed, one of the interest groups (of which Baer and Singer were among the cofounders) of the Society for Medical Anthropology after one year of existence changed its name from the Political Economy of Health Caucus to the Critical Anthropology of Health Caucus. Undoubtedly the preference for the label "medical anthropology" over "anthropology of health and illness" constitutes yet one more example of the powerful influence of M.D. medicine (generally referred to by medical anthropologists as biomedicine) in the modern world. While we will adopt the more common usage of the term "medical anthropology" in this textbook, the perspective that informs our work is far from conventional.

In a long overview of medical anthropology, David Landy (1983:185) observes "that the human group that calls itself by the name medical anthropology is a lively, heterogeneous community, busily engaged in myriad activities, studying, and writing about behaviors of human collectivities and individuals in understanding and coping with disease and injury." In the United States, medical anthropology has grown in recent decades to the extent that the Society for Medical Anthropology constitutes the second largest unit of the American Anthropological Association. While experiencing its most rapid pattern of development in this country, medical anthropology has embarked upon a process of growth in Canada, Britain, Germany, Denmark, Italy, Japan, and South Africa, as well as other countries around the globe. Four journals, *Medical Anthropology, Social Science and Medicine, Culture, Medicine and Psychiatry,* and the *Medical Anthropology Quarterly,* serve as the major forums for anthropologists interested in health-related issues. In addition, many medical anthropologists publish in other anthropological journals as well as sociological behavioral science, medical, nursing, public health, and health policy journals. As should be the case, medical anthropologists have borrowed the frameworks that guide their teaching, research, and applications from a larger corpus of anthropological theory as well as a number of other perspectives that cut across disciplinary boundaries.

Our own perspective has been in large measure, but not exclusively, informed by critical anthropology as well as by other critical perspectives in the social sciences. Relying primarily but not exclusively upon the perspective of "critical medical anthropology" (CMA), *Medical Anthropology and the World System* examines health-related issues in precapitalist indigenous and state societies, capitalist societies, and postrevolutionary or socialist-oriented societies. Although it draws heavily upon neo-Marxian, critical, and world systems theoretical perspectives, critical medical anthropology attempts to incorporate the theoretical contributions of other theoretical perspectives in medical anthropology, including biocultural or medical ecology, ethnomedical approaches, cultural constructivism, poststructuralism, and postmodernism.

Although this textbook is designed primarily for introductory medical anthropology classes at the undergraduate level, it can be used by graduate students as a review of various topics in medical anthropology as well as by health science students and practitioners. Part I ("What Is Medical Anthropology About?") consists of two chapters that discuss central concepts in and the development and scope of medical anthropology, as well as the critical perspective that we employ. Part II ("The Social Origins of Disease and Suffering") consists of a chapter on health and the environment, in societies ranging from foragers to modern states, and several chapters that explore the social origins of specific health problems that Ida Susser and Merrill Singer have explored in their research efforts. Part III ("Medical Systems in Social Context") consists of two chapters that examine the diversity of medical systems created by people in both indigenous, archaic states and modern societies in their efforts to cope with disease. Finally, the single chapter in Part IV ("Toward an Equitable and Healthy Global System") is based upon a premise of critical medical anthropology that argues for a merger of theory and social action that serves indigenous peoples, peasants, working-class people, ethnic minorities, women, gays/lesbians, and others who find themselves in subordinate positions vis-à-vis ruling elites and transnational corporations. As part of an effort to transcend the contradictions of the capitalist world system as well as the remaining socialist-oriented societies, we propose the creation of a democratic ecosocialist world system and the pursuit of health as a human right.

This book is the 2nd edition of *Medical Anthropology and the World System*, which appeared in 1997. While numerous textbooks are now available for introductory undergraduate courses, this is the only one that draws primarily upon critical medical anthropology—a perspective that has achieved some prominence in the subfield over the course of the past twenty years or so. In some ways, this textbook is an expansion of a more theoretical book titled *Critical Medical Anthropology*, which drew heavily upon Singer and Baer's earlier efforts, in collaboration with numerous colleagues (including Susser), to develop a "critical medical anthropology" (Singer and Baer 1995). In that critical medical anthropology (CMA) has now "come of age" and has evolved into one of the major perspectives and a popular one, particularly among younger faculty members and students, we feel that the time is more than ripe for an undergraduate textbook from this perspective.

Philosophically, this volume seeks to contribute to the further development of what we call "critical anthropological realism." In modern analytic philosophy, realism is the perspective that claims that objects, events, and beings in the world exist externally to us and to our experience of them; there is, in other words, an acceptance of a reality independent of our conception of it. As anthropologists, who, by design, seek to have close encounters with the peoples of the world and their ways of being and knowing, it has long been evident in the diversity of worldly conceptions that exist that humans do not ever know the external world directly but only through theory-laden participation and observation. And culture is the source of all theories of the world and hence of all experiences of it. Indeed, even systematic observation, or what we call science (which includes our own systematic observation as anthropologists), is recognized as cultural in origin and function. Additionally, as anthropologists, we have come to appreciate a form of philosophical relativism known as "cultural relativism," which is the notion that beliefs and behaviors must be studied and understood in their natural social context. Ripped from their cultural contexts, behaviors as humane as life-saving surgery or the ritual veneration of one's ancestors, can be ridiculed as practices of inferior beings or fools. Cultural relativism teaches us respect for other ways of being and knowing, as well as humility about our own approaches to worldly knowledge. Nonetheless, as scientists, our work does not stop with the observation and description of peoples and their endless array of beliefs and behaviors, but moves from there to the analysis and explanation of human ways of being, that is to say, to the analysis and explanation of culture (including our own culture, and including science as culture). However, given that, in the words of Cornell West (1999: xv-xvii), our goal as critical scientists is to confront "the pervasive evil of unjustified suffering and unnecessary social misery in our world," we avoid allowing our cultural relativism to "give in to sophomoric relativism ('Anything goes' or 'All views are equally valid')" or "to succumb to wholesale skepticism ('There is no truth')." Rather, we use our anthropological respect and appreciation (indeed, our celebration) of peoples of the world to analytically critique (and, as activist scholars, to publicly oppose) beliefs, behaviors, and social structures that promote structural violence and social suffering.

PART I

What Is Medical Anthropology About?

CHAPTER 1

Medical Anthropology: Central Concepts and Development

Medical anthropology concerns itself with the many factors that contribute to disease or illness and with the ways that various human populations respond to disease or illness. Although the human body is the complex product of at least five million years of a dialectical relationship between biological and sociocultural evolution, it is a system subject to a multiplicity of environmental assaults as well as to the deterioration that inevitably accompanies aging. Its processes are not only shaped by physiological variables but also mediated by culture and by emotional states.

In this chapter, we introduce some key concepts developed in medical anthropology that we use repeatedly in this book. These concepts should enable students to comprehend more clearly the relationship between health-related issues and the sociocultural processes and arrangements of the modern world. We also present a brief history of medical anthropology as a subdiscipline of anthropology—one that has the potential to serve as a bridge between physical anthropology and sociocultural anthropology.

As we show, medical anthropology has drawn from a variety of theoretical perspectives within anthropological theory and social scientific theory. While these perspectives offer important insights into health-related issues, the authors of this volume work within a theoretical framework generally referred to as critical medical anthropology. The authors, with many other medical anthropologists, utilize this critical approach in the belief that social inequality and power are primary determinants of health and health care. Although critical medical anthropology as a theoretical perspective will be discussed in greater detail in chapter 2, along with various other theoretical perspectives within medical anthropology, suffice to say at this point this perspective views health issues within the context of encompassing political and economic forces that pattern human relationships; shape social behaviors; condition collective experiences; re-order local ecologies; and situate cultural meanings, including forces of institutional, national, and global scale. The emergence of critical medical anthropology reflects both the turn toward political-economic approaches in anthropology in general, as well as an effort to engage and extend the political economy of health approach (Baer, Singer, and Johnsen 1986; Morgan 1987; Morsy 1990).

CENTRAL CONCEPTS AND CONCERNS

The concepts that we use frequently in this textbook are key concepts in the discipline of medical anthropology.

Health

The World Health Organization (WHO) defines health as "not merely the absence of disease and infirmity but complete physical, mental and social wellbeing" (WHO 1978). The notion of "wellness" has also become a key concept within the holistic health movement. The human concern with wellness, however, is not a recent one. As chiropractor-anthropologist Norman Klein (1979: 1) so aptly observes, "Well-being is a human concern in all societies—in part because humans, like other life forms, are susceptible to illness." Health, more than merely a physiological or emotional state, is a concept that humans in many societies have developed in order to describe their sense of well being. Many medical anthropologists regard health to be a cultural construction whose meaning varies considerably from society to society or from one historical period to another.

Taking a neo-Marxian perspective, Sander Kelman views health within the context of a system of production (1975). He makes a distinction between "functional health" and "experiential health." The former he defines as a state of optimum capacity to perform roles within society, particularly within the context of capitalism, to carry out productive work that contributes to profit-making. "Experiential health" entails freedom from illness and alienation and the capacity for human development, including self-discovery, self-actualization, and transcendence from alienating social circumstances. Whereas "functional health" is an inevitable component of social life under capitalism, "experiential health" tended to occur in many simple preindustrial societies and could theoretically occur again under modern societies based upon egalitarian social relations. Before casting its attention to state or complex societies, cultural anthropologists focused their research efforts upon indigenous societies. Indeed, anthropologists as well as other visitors to these indigenous societies, including explorers, traders, and missionaries, remarked upon the health and vigor of the people whom they encountered. While such accounts may have often exhibited a certain element of romanticism, epidemiological and ethnographic studies indicate that people in indigenous societies who reach adulthood generally exhibit a general state of good health and vigor. John H. Bodley succinctly captures some of the reasons why health conditions tend to be favorable in indigenous societies:

"[M]ost importantly, the generally low population densities and relative social equality of small-scale societies would help ensure equal access to basic subsistence resources so that everyone could enjoy good nutrition. Furthermore, low population densities and frequent mobility would significantly reduce the occurrence of epidemic diseases, and natural selection—in the absence of the antibiotics, immunizations, surgery, and other forms of medical intervention—would develop high levels of disease resistance. Healthy people are those who survive. Tribal societies, in effect, maintain public health by emphasizing prevention of morbidity rather than treatment. The healthiest conditions would likely exist under mobile foragers and pastoralism,whereas there might be some health costs associated with the increasing densities and reduced mobility of settled farming villages" (Bodley 1994: 124).

From the perspective of CMA, health can be defined as *access to and control over the basic material and nonmaterial resources that sustain and promote life at a high level of satisfaction.* Health is not some absolute state of being but an elastic concept that must be evaluated in a larger sociocultural context. For example, the Gnau, a Sepik Valley group on the island of New Guinea, regard health as an "accumulated resistance to potential dangers" (Lewis 1986: 128). Among the Gnau, these dangers are seen as being primarily malevolent spirits. In capitalist societies achieving health entails struggle against class-dominated powers that do not exist in indigenous societies. While the ultimate character of health care systems is determined outside the health sector by dominant social groups, like heads of insurance companies and other large corporations, significant forms of struggle take place within this sector and help to shape its institutions. Consequently, an examination of contending forces in and out of the health arena that impinge on health and healing becomes an essential task in building a critical approach to health issues.

Disease

Even under the best of circumstances, human beings inevitably find themselves confronted with disease or illness. As it is for biomedicine, a central question for medical anthropology is, What is disease? It is evident why this query is important to biomedicine. As the nature of its importance to medical anthropology is more complex, medical anthropologists have tended to avoid the question altogether by defining disease (i.e., clinical manifestations) as the domain of medicine and illness (i.e., the sufferer's experience) as the appropriate arena of anthropological investigation. From the perspective of CMA, however, the bracketing of disease as outside the concern or expertise of anthropologists is a retreat from ground that is as much social as it is biological in nature. Humans in all societies perceive disease as a disruptive event that in one way or another threatens the flow of daily life. Disease raises moral questions like "Why am I sick?" or "Why am I being punished?" and may serve as a mechanism for expressing dissent from existing sociocultural arrangements.

People around the world struggle with such existential questions, including the etiology of disease. For example, while the Azande of the Sudan acknowledge that misfortunes, including disease and death, may have a variety of causes, they attribute almost all of them to witchcraft, sorcery, or failure to follow a moral rule (Evans-Pritchard 1937). The Azande make a distinction between witchcraft (*mangu*) and magic (*ngua*), the latter term covering not only magical procedures but also herbal and other medicines. Whereas witchcraft may be caused by the unconscious hatred, envy, or greed that an individual may feel, magic functions as a means of counteracting witchcraft through the conscious manipulation of medicines.

Health and disease are conditions that people in a society encounter, depending upon their access to basic as well as prestige resources. Disease varies from society to society, in some part because of climatic or geographical conditions but in large part because of the ways productive activities, resources, and reproduction are organized and carried out. Following in the analytic tradition begun by Friedrich Engels and Rudolf Virchow, it is evident that discussion of specific health problems apart from their social contexts only serves to downplay social relationships underlying environmental, occupational, nutritional, residential, and experiential conditions. Disease is not just the straightforward result of a pathogen or physiological disturbance. Instead, a variety of social problems such as malnutrition, economic insecurity, occupational risks, industrial and motor vehicle pollution, bad housing, and political powerlessness contribute to susceptibility to disease.

In short, disease must be understood as being as much social as it is biological. In this light, the tendency, be it in medicine or in medical anthropology, to treat disease as a given, as part of an immutable physical reality, contributes to the tendency to neglect its social origins. CMA strives, in McNeil's (1976) terms, to understand the nature of the relationship between microparasitism (the tiny organisms, malfunction, and individual behaviors that are the proximate causes of much sickness) and macroparasitism (the social relations of exploitation that are the ultimate causes of much disease). For example, an insulin reaction in a diabetic postal worker might be ascribed (in a reductionist mode) to an excessive dose of insulin causing an outpouring of adrenaline, a failure of the pancreas to respond with appropriate glucagon secretion, etc. Alternatively, the cause might be sought in his having skipped breakfast because he was late for work; unaccustomed physical exertion demanded by a foreman; inability to break for a snack; or, at a deeper level, the constellation of class forces in U.S. society which assures capitalist domination of production and the moment to moment working lives of the proletariat (Woolhandler and Himmelstein 1989: 1208).

Sufferer Experience

Medical social scientists have become increasingly concerned about sufferer experience—the manner in which an ill person manifests his or her disease or distress. Margaret Lock and Nancy Scheper-Hughes (1990), who refer to themselves as critically interpretive medical anthropologists, reject the long-standing Cartesian duality of body and mind that pervades biomedical theory (Lock and Scheper-Hughes 1990). They have made a significant contribution to an understanding of sufferer experience by developing the concept of the "mindful body" (Scheper-Hughes and Lock 1987). Lock and Scheper-Hughes delineate three bodies: the individual body, the social body, and the body politic. People's images of their bodies, either in a state of health or well being or in a state of disease or distress, are mediated by sociocultural meanings of being human. The body also serves as a cognitive map of natural, supernatural, sociocultural, and spatial relations. Furthermore, individual and social bodies express power relations in both a specific society or in the world system.

Sufferer experience constitutes a social product, one that is constructed and reconstructed in the action arena between socially constituted categories of meaning and the political-economic forces that shape daily life. Although individuals often react to these forces passively, they may also respond to economic exploitation and political oppression in active ways. In her highly acclaimed and controversial book *Death without Weeping: The Violence of Everyday Life in Brazil*, Scheper-Hughes (1992) presents a vivid and moving portrayal of human suffering in Bom Jesus, an abjectly impoverished *favela* or shantytown in northeastern Brazil. She contends that the desperate and constant struggle for basic necessities in the community induces in many mothers an indifference to the weakest of their offspring. While at times Scheper-Hughes appears to engage in a form of blaming the victim, she recognizes ultimately that the suffering of the mothers, their children, and others in Bom Jesus is intricately related to the collapse of the sugar plantation, which has left numerous people in the region without even a subsistence income. Most of the residents of Bom Jesus

have not benefited from the development of agribusiness and industrialization sponsored by both transnational corporations and the Brazilian
state.

Medical System

In responding to disease and illness, all human societies create medical
systems of one sort or another. All medical systems consist of beliefs and
practices that are consciously directed at promoting health and alleviating
disease. Medicine in simple preindustrial societies is not clearly differentiated from other social institutions such as religion and politics. The reality of this is seen in the *shaman*, a part-time magicoreligious practitioner
who attempts to contact the supernatural realm when dealing with the
problems of his or her group. In addition to searching for game or lost
objects or related activities, the shaman devotes much of his or her attention to healing or curing. When curing a victim of witchcraft, the shaman
among the Jivaro, a horticultural village society in the Ecuadorian Amazon, sucks magical darts from the patient's body in a dark area of the
house, at night because this is believed to be the only time when he can
interpret drug-induced visions that reveal supernatural reality (Harner
1968). The curing shaman vomits out the intrusive object, displays it to
the patient and his or her family, puts it into a little container, and later
throws it into the air, at which time it is believed to fly back to the be-
witching shaman who originally sent it into the patient.

Even though physicians in industrial societies often purport to practice
a form of medicine distinct from religion and politics, in reality their endeavors are intricately intertwined with these spheres of social life. In his
classic analysis of body ritual among the Nacirema, which has been reproduced in many introductory anthropological books, Horace Miner
(1979) challenges North American ethnocentrism by showing that our
own customs are no less exotic than those of simple preindustrial societies.
Nacirema is simply American spelled backwards and refers to a "magic-
ridden" people whose "medicine men" (physicians) perform "elaborate
ceremonies" (surgery) in imposing temples, called *latipos* (hospitals). The
medicine men are assisted by a "permanent group of vestal maidens [fe-
male nurses] who move sedately about the temple chambers in distinctive
costume and headdress" (Miner 1979: 12). In a somewhat more serious
vein, Rudolf Virchow, the well-known nineteenth-century pathologist and
an early proponent of social medicine declared that politics is "nothing
but medicine on a grand scale" (quoted in Landy 1977: 14). By this, he
simply meant that, just as in government, medicine is filled with power
struggles and efforts to control individuals or social groups. Although
medical anthropologists and other medical social scientists routinely use
the term medicine as a heuristic or analytical device, it is important to

remember that the notion of medicine as a bounded system is a cultural construct. In reality, medicine is intertwined with other cultural arrangements, including kinship, the polity, the economy, and religion.

As noted in Foster and Anderson (1978: 36–38), every medical system embraces a disease theory system and a health care system. The *disease theory system* includes conceptions of health and the causes of disease or illness. Foster and Anderson make a distinction between (1) personalistic medical systems and (2) naturalistic medical systems. The former view disease as resulting from the action of "*Sensate* agent who may be a supernatural being (a deity or a god), a nonhuman being (such as a ghost, ancestor, or evil spirit), or a human being (a witch or sorcerer)" (Foster and Anderson 1978: 53). Naturalistic systems view disease as emanating from the imbalance of certain inanimate elements in the body, such as the male and female principles of yin and yang in Chinese medicine. Personalistic and naturalistic explanations are not mutually exclusive.

The *health care system* refers to the social relationships that revolve around the healer and his or her patient. The healer may be assisted by various assistants and in the case of complex societies may work in an elaborate bureaucratic structure, such as a clinic, health maintenance organization, or hospital. The patient very likely will be supported by what Janzen (1978) refers to as a "therapy managing group"—a set of kinfolk, friends, acquaintances, and community members who confer with the healer and representatives of his or her support structure in the healing process.

Medical Pluralism

Regardless of their degree of complexity, all health care systems are based upon the *dyadic core,* consisting of a healer and a patient. The healer role may be occupied by a generalist, such as the shaman in preindustrial societies or the family physician in modern societies. It may also be occupied by various specialists, such as an herbalist, a bonesetter, or a medium in preindustrial societies or a cardiologist, an oncologist, or a psychiatrist in modern societies. In contrast to simple preindustrial societies, which tend to exhibit a more-or-less coherent medical system, state societies manifest the coexistence of an array of medical systems, or a pattern of *medical pluralism.* From this perspective, *the* medical system of a society consists of the totality of medical subsystems that coexist in a cooperative or competitive relationship with one another. In modern industrial societies one finds, in addition to biomedicine, the dominant medical system; other systems such as chiropractic, naturopathy, Christian Science, evangelical faith healing; and various ethnomedical systems. In the U.S. context, examples of ethnomedical systems include herbalism among rural whites in Southern Appalachia, rootwork among African

Americans in the rural South, *curanderismo* among Chicanos of the Southwest, *santeria* among Cuban Americans in southern Florida and New York City, and a variety of Native American healing traditions.

Various medical anthropologists have created typologies that recognize the phenomenon of medical pluralism in complex societies. Based upon their geographic and cultural settings, Dunn (1976) delineated three types of medical systems: (1) local medical systems, (2) regional medical systems, and (3) the cosmopolitan medical system. *Local* medical systems are folk or indigenous medical systems of small-scale foraging, horticultural or pastoral societies, or peasant communities in state societies. *Regional* medical systems are systems distributed over a relatively large area. Examples of regional medical systems include Ayurvedic medicine and Unani medicine in South Asia and traditional Chinese medicine. *Cosmopolitan* medicine refers to the global medical system or what commonly has been called scientific medicine, modern medicine, or Western medicine. Complex societies generally contain all three of these medical systems. India, for example, has numerous local medical systems associated with its many ethnic groups. In addition to biomedicine, modern Japan has a variety of East Asian medical systems (Lock 1980). The most popular of these is *kanpo*, a form of herbal medicine that was brought to Japan from China in the sixth century. In addition to prescribing herbs, *kanpo* doctors administer acupuncture, body manipulation, and moxibustion therapy. They tend to treat psychosomatic ailments in which the patients' chief complaints are tiredness, headaches, occasional dizziness, or numbness, typical symptoms emanating from the somatization of distress.

Chrisman and Kleinman (1983) developed a widely used model that recognizes three overlapping sectors in health care systems. The *popular* sector consists of health care conducted by sick persons themselves, their families, social networks, and communities. It includes a wide variety of therapies, such as special diets, herbs, exercise, rest, baths, and massage, and, in the case of industrial societies, articles like humidifiers, hot blankets, patent medicines, or over-the-counter drugs. Kleinman, who has conducted research in Taiwan, estimates that 70% to 90% of the treatment episodes on that island occur in the popular sector. The *folk* sector encompasses healers of various sorts who function informally and often on a quasi-legal or sometimes, given local laws, an illegal basis. Examples include herbalists, bonesetters, midwives, mediums, and magicians. In the U.S. context, examples of folk healers include lay hypnotists, lay homeopaths, faith healers, African American rootworkers, *curanderas, espiritistas,* and Navajo singers. The *professional* sector encompasses the practioners and bureaucracies of both biomedicine and professionalized heterodox medical systems, such as Ayurvedic and Unani medicine in South Asia and herbal medicine and acupuncture in the People's Republic of China. Whereas medical sociologists have tended to focus their attention on the professional sector of health, anthropologists have also given much attention to the folk and popular sectors.

Patterns of medical pluralism tend to reflect hierarchical relations in the larger society. Patterns of hierarchy may be based upon class, caste, racial, ethnic, regional, religious, and gender distinctions. Medical pluralism flourishes in all class-divided societies and tends to mirror the wider sphere of class and social relationships. It is perhaps more accurate to say that national medical systems in the modern or postmodern world tend to be plural, rather than pluralistic, in that biomedicine enjoys a dominant status over heterodox and ethnomedical practices. In reality, plural medical systems may be described as dominative in that one medical system generally enjoys a preeminent status vis-à-vis other medical systems. While within the context of a dominative medical system one system attempts to exert, with the support of social elites, dominance over other medical systems; people are quite capable of the dual use of distinct medical systems. Based upon her research among the Manus in the Admirality Islands of Melanesia, Lola Romanucci-Ross (1977) identified a "hierarchy of resort" in which many people utilize self-administered folk remedies or consult folk healers before visiting a biomedical clinic or hospital for their ailments. Conversely, while this sequence is the most prevalent one, more-acculturated Manus often rely upon biomedicine initially or first after home remedies; if these two fail, they may finally resort to folk healers.

Biomedicine

In attempting to distinguish the Western medical system that became globally dominant during this century from alternative systems, social scientists have employed a variety of descriptive labels, including regular medicine, allopathic medicine, scientific medicine, modern medicine, and cosmopolitan medicine. Following Comaroff (1982) and Hahn (1983), most medical anthropologists have come to refer to this form of medicine as "biomedicine." Hahn (1983) argues that in diagnosing and treating sickness, biomedicine focuses primarily upon human physiology and even more specifically on human pathophysiology. Perhaps the most glaring example of this tendency to reduce disease to biology is the common practice among hospital physicians of referring to patients by the name of their malfunctioning organ (e.g., the liver in Room 213 or the kidney in Room 563). A fourth-year chief resident interviewed by Lazarus (1988: 39) commented, "We are socialized to—disease is the thing. Yeah, I slip. We all do and see the patient as a disease." As these examples illustrate, the central concern of biomedicine is not general well being nor individual persons per se but rather simply diseased bodies.

In essence, biomedicine subscribes to a type of physical reductionism that radically separates the body from the nonbody. Hahn notes that bio-medicine emphasizes curing over prevention and spends much more money on hospitals, clinics, ambulance services, drugs, and "miracle cures" than it does on public health facilities, preventive education, clean-ing the environment, and eliminating the stress associated with modern life. Biomedicine constitutes the predominant ethnomedical system of Eu-ropean and North American societies and has become widely dissemi-nated throughout the world.

Within the U.S. context, biomedicine incorporates certain core values, metaphors, beliefs, and attitudes that it communicates to patients, such as self-reliance, rugged individualism, independence, pragmatism, empiri-cism, atomism, militarism, profit-making, emotional minimalism, and a mechanistic concept of the body and its repair (Stein 1990). For example, U.S. biomedicine often speaks of the war on cancer. This war is portrayed as a prolonged attack against a deadly and evil internal growth, led by a highly competent general (the oncologist) who gives orders to a coura-geous, stoical, and obedient soldier (the patient) in a battle that must be conducted with valor despite the odds and, if necessary, until the bitter end. Erwin (1987) aptly refers to this approach as the "medical militari-zation" of cancer treatment. Conversely, according to Hanteng Dai, a Chi-nese physician who has worked with cancer patients in Arkansas, both health personnel and members of the therapy management group in the People's Republic of China tell cancer patients a white lie by referring to their condition as being something less serious in order to spare them from purported mental anguish. Given that cancer constitutes a break-down of the immune system, it is interesting to draw attention to Emily Martin's (1987: 410) observation that the main imagery employed in pop-ular and scientific descriptions of this system portray the "body as nation state at war over its external borders, containing internal surveillance sys-tems to monitor foreign invaders."

It is important to stress that biomedicine is not a monolithic entity. Rather, its form is shaped by its national setting, as is illustrated by Payer's (1988) fascinating comparative account of medicine in France, Germany, Britain, and the United States. He argues that French biomedicine, with its strong orientation toward abstract thought, results in doctor visits that are much longer than in German biomedicine. French biomedicine also places a great deal of emphasis on the liver as the locus of disease, in-cluding complications such as migraine headaches, general fatigue, and painful menstruation. Conversely, German biomedicine regards *Herzin-suffizienz*, or poor circulation, as the root of a broad spectrum of ailments, including hypotension, tired legs, and varicose veins. Both German and French biomedicine relies more heavily than U.S. biomedicine on the ca-pacity of the immunological system to resist disease and therefore de-emphasizes the use of antibiotics. In contrast to U.S. biomedicine, they also exhibit a much greater acceptance of soft medicine or alternative medical systems such as naturopathy; homeopathy; hydropathy (a system that relies on a wide variety of water treatments); and extended stays at spas in peaceful, parklike surroundings. German patients tend on the average to visit the doctor's office more than twice as often as their counterparts in France, England, and the United States. U.S. biomedicine relies much more—than biomedicine in France, Germany, and England—on invasive forms of therapy, such as cesarean sections, hysterectomies, breast cancer screenings, and high dosages of psychotropic drugs. As we saw in the case of cancer treatment, U.S. biomedicine manifests a pattern of aggression that seems in keeping with the strong emphasis in American society on violence as a means of solving problems—a pattern undoubtedly rooted in the frontier mentality that continues to live on in what has for the most part become a highly urbanized, postindustrial society. In this sense, the war on cancer and the war on drugs are symbolic cultural continuations of the war against Native Americans that cleared the frontier for white settlement.

Biomedicine achieved its dominant position in the West and beyond with the emergence of industrial capitalism and with abundant assistance from the capitalist class whose interests it commonly serves. Historian E. Richard Brown argues that the Rockefeller and Carnegie foundations played an instrumental role in shaping "scientific medicine" by providing funding only to those medical schools and research institutes that placed heavy emphasis upon the germ theory of disease. According to E. R. Brown (1979), "The medical profession discovered an ideology that was compatible with the world view of, and politically and economically useful to, the capitalist class and the emerging managerial and professional stratum." Biomedicine focused attention on discrete, external agents rather than on social structural or environmental factors. In addition to its legitimizing functions, the Rockefeller medicine men believed that biomedicine would create a healthier work force, both here and abroad, which would contribute to economic productivity and profit. Biomedicine portrayed the body as a machine that requires periodic repair so that it may perform assigned productive tasks essential to economic imperatives. Even in the case of reproduction, as Martin (1987: 146) so aptly observes, "birth is seen as the control of laborers (women) and their machines (their uteruses) by managers (doctors), often using other machines to help."

Indeed, although the Soviet Union emerged as the first nationwide movement against the capitalist world system, the ideological influence of biomedicine was so strong that Navarro (1977) applied the label "bourgeois medicine" to the "mechanistic" and "curative" orientation of the Soviet medical paradigm. While certain other professionalized medical systems, such as homeopathy, Ayurveda, Unani, and traditional Chinese medicine, function in many parts of the world, biomedicine became the preeminent medical system in the world not simply because of its curative efficacy but as a result of the expansion of the global market economy.

Medicalization and Medical Hegemony

Biomedicine has fostered a process that many social scientists refer to as *medicalization*. This process entails the absorption of ever-widening social arenas and behaviors into the jurisdiction of biomedical treatment through a constant extension of pathological terminology to cover new conditions and behaviors. Health clinics, health maintenance organizations, and other medical providers now offer classes on managing stress, controlling obesity, overcoming sexual impotence, alcoholism, and drug addiction, and promoting smoking cessation. The birth experience, not just in the United States but also in many countries that pride themselves on undergoing modernization, has been distorted into a pathological event rather than a natural physiological one for childbearing women. Aspects of the medicalization of birthing include (1) the withholding of information on the disadvantages of obstetrical medication, (2) the expectation that women give birth in a hospital, (3) the elective induction of labor, (4) the separation of the mother from familial support during labor and birth, (5) the confinement of the laboring woman to bed, (6) professional dependence on technology and pharmacological methods of pain relief, (7) routine electronic fetal monitoring, (8) the chemical stimulation of labor, (9) the delay of birth until the physician's arrival, (10) the requirement that the mother assume a prone position rather than a squatting one, (11) the routine use of regional or general anesthesia for delivery, and (12) routine episiotomy (Haire 1978: 188–94). Fortunately, the women's liberation movement has prompted many women to challenge many of these practices and has contributed to a heavier reliance on home births conducted by lay midwives.

One factor driving medicalization is the profit to be made from discovering new diseases in need of treatment. Medicalization also contributes to increasing social control on the part of physicians and health institutions over behavior. It serves to demystify and depoliticize the social origins of personal distress. Medicalization transforms a "problem at the level of social structure—stressful work demands, unsafe working conditions, and poverty— . . . into an individual problem under medical control" (Waitzkin 1983: 41).

Underlying the medicalization of contemporary life is the broader phenomenon of *medical hegemony*, the process by which capitalist assumptions, concepts, and values come to permeate medical diagnosis and treatment. The concept of hegemony has been applied to various spheres of social life, including the state, institutionalized religion, education, and the mass media. In the development of this concept, Antonio Gramsci, an Italian political activist who fought against fascism under Mussolini, elaborated upon Marx and Engels's observation that the "ideas of the ruling class are, in every age, the ruling ideas." Whereas the ruling class exerts direct domination through the coercive organs of the state apparatus (e.g., the parliament, the courts, the military, the police, the prisons, etc.), hegemony, as Femia (1975: 30) observes, is "objectified in and exercised through the institutions of civil society, the ensemble of educational, religious, and associational institutions." *Hegemony* refers to the process by which one class exerts control of the cognitive and intellectual life of society by structural means as opposed to coercive ones. Hegemony is achieved through the diffusion and reinforcement of certain values, attitudes, beliefs, social norms, and legal precepts that, to a greater or lesser degree, come to permeate civil society. Doctor-patient interactions frequently reinforce hierarchical structures in the larger society by stressing the need for the patient to comply with a social superior's or expert's judgment. Although a patient may be experiencing job-related stress that may manifest itself in various diffuse symptoms, the physician may prescribe a sedative to calm the patient or help him or her cope with an onerous work environment rather than challenging the power of an employer or supervisor over employees.

Syndemics

One effect of the kind of reductionist thinking in health that tends to dominate biomedical understanding and practice is the tendency to isolate, study, and treat diseases as if they were distinct entities that existed separate from other diseases and from the social contexts in which they are found. Critical medical anthropology (as described more fully in the next chapter), however, seeks to understand health and illness from a holistic biological, sociocultural, and political economic perspective (sometimes called critical bioculturalism) that runs counter to the dominant reductionist orientation. This approach attempts to identify and understand the determinant interconnections between one or more health conditions, sufferer and community understandings of the illness(es) in question and the social, political, and economic conditions that may have contributed to the development of ill health. To help frame this kind of big picture dialectical thinking in health, critical medical anthropologists introduced the concept of "syndemic" (Singer 1994, 1996) as a new term in epidemiological and public health thinking. At its simplest level, and as now used by some researchers at the Centers for Disease Control and Prevention (CDC), the term syndemic refers to two or more epidemics (i.e., notable increases in the rate of specific diseases in a population) interacting synergistically with each other inside human bodies and contributing, as a result of their interaction, to excess burden of disease in a population. As Millstein (2001: 2), organizer of the Syndemics Prevention

Network at CDC, notes, "Syndemics occur when health-related problems cluster by person, place or time." Importantly, the term syndemic refers not only to the temporal or locational co-occurrence of two or more diseases or health problems, but also to the health consequences of the biological interactions among the health conditions present. For example, researchers have found that coinfection with HIV and Mycobacterium tuberculosis (MTb) augments the immunopathology of HIV and accelerates the damaging progression of the disease (Ho 1996). If both of these diseases cluster in the same population, opportunities for individuals to be co-infected spiral upward. In fact, HIV and tuberculosis (TB) co-infection is common in U.S. inner city areas as well as in parts of Africa, South America and Asia. Research in the Ivory Coast in Western Africa has shown that co-infection with HIV and MTb reduced the survival time of patients compared to those with just MTb or HIV, suggesting a synergistic interaction with deadly consequence for co-infected individuals.

At the same time, studies have shown that because HIV damages human immune systems, individuals with HIV disease who are exposed to TB are more likely to develop active and rapidly progressing tuberculosis compared to those who are HIV negative (whose immune systems can keep the disease causing tuberculosis bacteria in check and in a dormant state). Again, the important issue is not just co-infection but enhanced infection due to disease interaction. Similarly, research by anthropologist Bryan Page and co-workers (1990) found that individuals infected with human T-lymphotropic virus (HTLV)—a retrovirus originally thought by some to be the cause of AIDS but which actually is associated with the development of leukemia—who were also infected with HIV were three times more likely to die of AIDS then those with HIV disease but not infected with HTLV, suggesting that HTLV adversely affects the course of infection with HIV through synergistic interaction within the human body.

Beyond the notion of disease clustering in a location or population, the term syndemic points to the determinant importance of social conditions in the health of individuals and populations.

"Take tuberculosis, with its persistence in poor countries and its resurgence among the poor of many industrialized nations. We cannot understand its marked patterned occurrence—in the United States, for example, afflicting those in homeless shelters and in prison—without understanding how social forces, ranging from political violence to racism, come to be embodied as individual pathology" (Farmer 1999: 13).

Living in poverty, for example, increases the likelihood of exposure to the bacteria that causes TB because of overcrowding in poorly ventilated dwellings. Research in homeless shelters in New York City, for instance, has shown that they are a focal point of TB transmission among the poor. Once infected, the poor are more likely to develop active TB both because they are more likely to have multiple exposures to the TB bacteria (which may push dormant bacteria into an active state) and because they are more likely to have pre-existent immune system damage from other infections and malnutrition. Finally, poverty and discrimination place the poor at a disadvantage in terms of access to diagnosis and treatment for TB, effectiveness of available treatments because of weakened immune systems, and ability to adhere to TB treatment plans because of structurally imposed residential instability and the frequency of disruptive economic and social crises in poor families. As the case of TB suggests, diseases do not exist in a social vacuum or solely within the bodies of those they inflict, and thus their transmission and impact is never merely a biological process. Ultimately, social factors, like poverty, racism, sexism, ostracism, and structural violence may be of far greater importance than the nature of pathogens or the bodily systems they infect.

As the discussion above suggests, syndemics are not merely co-occurring epidemics in populations that are embodied as co-infections within individual patients, they include the interaction of diseases (or other health conditions, e.g., malnutrition) as a consequence of a set of health threatening social conditions (e.g., noxious living, working or environmental conditions or oppressive social relationships). In other words, a syndemic is a set of intertwined and mutually enhancing epidemics developed and sustained in a community because of harmful social conditions and injurious social relationships.

For example, one of the major threats to health worldwide is malnutrition. The Bread for the World Institute estimates that over 800 million people in developing countries are chronically malnourished and that at least half of the 31,000 children under five years of age who die every day in the world are victims of hunger-related causes. Even in a highly developed country like the United States, over 11 million people cannot afford to adequately feed their families. It is a well-recognized fact that malnourished people tend to have compromised immune systems and are thus particularly vulnerable to infections. For example, influenza can be more harmful (with great lung involvement) and last longer in individuals with nutrient deficiencies. However, recent research has begun to suggest that malnourishment may not only allow pathogens like viruses to flourish, it may contribute to them becoming more lethal. Thus, Dr. Melinda Beck of the University of North Carolina found that the normally harmless virus Coxsackie B3 (which is most commonly associated with light fever and a short-term rash in children) could produce a life-threatening heart disease in malnourished adults (Beck and Levander 2000). In individuals whose diets are deficient in certain key nutrients (e.g., selenium, an anti-oxidant enzyme found in whole grain wheat and vegetables that the body uses to combat oxidative stress) Coxsackie virus may mutate to produce viral strains with deadly potential. Beck was able to demonstrate this effect in animal experiments. According to Beck (BBC

News 2001), "We believe our findings are both important and potentially disturbing because they suggest nutritional deficiencies can promote epidemics in a way not appreciated before. What we found conceivably could be true for any RNA virus—cold virus, AIDS virus [human immunodeficiency virus] and Ebola virus." This type of harmful synergism between Coxsackie virus and malnutrition exemplifies the syndemic process.

A dangerous synergism can also be seen in the relationship between poverty, poor childhood nutrition, and later heart disease. Epidemiological research in England and Wales by Barker and Osmond (1986) demonstrated a close association between geographic areas with current high mortality rates for ischemic heart disease (and previous high rates of infant mortality and other indicators of high rates of poverty and malnutrition) during the period that the adults coming down with heart disease were children. According to these researchers, it appears that exposure to poor nutrition early in life created a high susceptibility for ischemic heart disease later in life as malnourished children grew up and were subsequently exposed to changing dietary patterns (e.g., a diet with heightened levels of dietary cholesterol). As this research affirms, poor diet is one of the direct routes through which social conditions and inequality impact health and contribute thereby to sydemical enhancement of illness and disease. In other research, Evans (1997) and co-workers found an association between severe life stress and early disease progression among individuals with HIV disease. Stress, a common consequence of poverty, discrimination, and other forms of social suffering, appears to be another route through which oppressive social conditions find expression in clinical outcomes.

Another syndemic example involves the interactions among substance abuse, street/domestic violence, and AIDS. Singer (1996) has proposed that the interrelations of these health and social factors constitute a mutually enhancing syndemic, which he calls SAVA (an acronym formed from substance abuse, violence and AIDS). In inner city, low-income communities, he argues (Singer 1996: 99), substance abuse, violence and AIDS "are not merely concurrent, in that they are not wholly separable phenomena. Rather, these three closely linked and interdependent threats to health and well being . . . constitute a major syndemic that already has taken a devastating toll . . . and threaten to wreck further pain and havoc in the future." While the link between substance abuse and AIDS is widely recognized (see chapter 8) other interconnections warrant further study, such as the role of an AIDS diagnosis in enhancing levels of drug use, the impact of violence victimization on subsequent drug use and AIDS risk, and the conditions under which drug use and drug craving lead to enhanced levels of violence. While considerable work has been done on patterns of drug use and on the relationship of AIDS transmission to risk behaviors, violence victimization, which represents a third route for the direct translation of unhealthy social conditions into ill health and suffering, is comparatively understudied. Nonetheless, it is clear that in the lives of the urban poor of the developed world, and, to a noticeably increasing degree in metropolitan areas of developing countries, mind-altering substances, violence and its bio-psychological effects, and HIV disease (as well as other sexually transmitted diseases, hepatitis, and TB) have significant behavioral and biological connections that amplify the dire health consequences of this deadly triad beyond their individual contributions to illness.

These examples point to the importance of understanding how diseases interact with each other and with social conditions to produced excess morbidity and mortality in a population. The appearance of a syndemic points to the existence of breakdowns in the social infrastructure, fragmentation of public health efforts, and gaps in health care delivery. However, as Millstein (2001: 9) points out, recognizing the existence and nature of syndemics "can . . . advance a specific course of social change, one focused on the connection between health and social justice." This is one of the primary goals of critical medical anthropology.

The key concepts discussed in this section were developed as part of an effort on the part of anthropologists to understand better cross-culturally the human confrontation with disease and illness. In the last section of this chapter we sketch the development and scope of medical anthropology as a distinct subdiscipline within anthropology.

A BRIEF HISTORY OF MEDICAL ANTHROPOLOGY IN THE UNITED STATES AND ELSEWHERE

Medical anthropology as a distinct subdiscipline of anthropology did not begin to emerge until the 1950s. Nevertheless, Otto von Mering (1970: 272) contends that the formal relationship between anthropology and medicine began when Rudolf Virchow, a renowned pathologist interested in social medicine, helped to establish the first anthropological society in Berlin. Indeed, Virchow influenced Franz Boas while he was affiliated with the Berlin Ethnological Museum during 1883–1886 (Trostle 1986: 45). Nevertheless, the political economic perspective that Virchow fostered became a part of medical anthropology only beginning in the 1970s. In the course of conducting ethnographic research on indigenous societies, various anthropologists have collected data on medical beliefs and practices along with the usual data on kinship, subsistence activities, religion, and forms of enculturation. W. H. R. Rivers, a physician-anthropologist who conducted fieldwork in the southwest Pacific and one of the first anthropologists to discuss health-related issues cross-culturally, argued in *Medicine, Magic, and Religion* (1924: 51) that "medical practices are not a medley of disconnected and meaningless customs" but rather an integral part of the larger sociocultural systems within which they are embedded. While this observation may appear obvious today, followers of a school of anthropology known as historical particularism tended to view culture as a thing of threads and patches or a byproduct of a complex process of contacts among many social groups.

Forrest Clements (1932) served as another precursor to medical anthropology by attempting to classify conceptions of sickness causation on a worldwide basis. During the 1940s Erwin Ackerknecht (1971) and others wrote papers and articles on topics that would today be considered medical anthropology (e.g. folk nosology and healing). He sought to develop a systematic cultural relativist and functionalist interpretation of what he termed "primitive medicine." Indeed, Rivers, Clements, and Ackerknecht unwittingly contributed to biomedical hegemony by bracketing biomedicine off from ethnomedicine. They accepted biomedicine as science at face value, not as a subject for social science, as do medical anthropologists and medical sociologists today. As Kleinman (1978: 408) aptly observes, biomedical science and care "in fully modern societies were, for a long while, excluded from cross-cultural comparisons, and unfortunately still are even in some fairly recent studies."

After World War II, an increasing number of anthropologists turned their attention to health-related issues, especially applied ones. Indeed, the first overview of what today constitutes medical anthropology, authored by William Caudill (1953), was titled "Applied Anthropology in Medicine." Although Norman Scotch (1963) is often credited with popularizing the term "medical anthropology," it reportedly was first used by a Third World scholar in an Indian medical journal (Hunter 1985: 298). Much of conventional medical anthropology received its initial impetus from two main sources: (1) the involvement of various anthropologists in international health work and (2) the involvement of anthropologists in the clinical setting as teachers, researchers, administrators, and clinicians. Many of these efforts, beginning after World War II and continuing to the present day, have sought to humanize the physician-patient relationship.

Anthropological involvement in the international health field began within the context of British colonialism during the 1930s and 1940s—a period when the delivery of Western health services was seen as part of a larger effort to administer and control indigenous populations. Cora DuBois became the first anthropologist to hold a formal position with an international health organization when she received employment from the World Health Organization in 1950 (Coreil 1990: 5). Later during the 1950s, several anthropologists received appointments to international health posts. They included Edward Wellin at the Rockefeller Foundation, Benjamin Paul at the Harvard School of Public Health, and George Foster and others at the Institute for Inter-American Affairs (the forerunner of the

United States Agency for International Development). Paul (1969: 29) saw anthropologists as being "especially qualified by temperament and training . . . [for] the study of popular reactions to programs of public health carried out in foreign cultural settings." In retrospect, the writings of Paul and many of his contemporaries strike many medical anthropologists, particularly those of a critical bent, as unduly naive about the nature and function of United States-sponsored international health programs. Their work, which was conducted at the peak of the Cold War, exhibited a profoundly Eurocentric ideological cast that included an implicit biomedical bias.

Some anthropologists became involved in efforts to facilitate the delivery of biomedical care to populations in the United States. For example, Alexander and Dorothea Leighton, anthropologists who conducted extensive research on the Navajo, became involved in the Navajo-Cornell Field Health Project, which was established in 1955 (Foster 1982: 190). This project resulted in the creation of the role of "health visitor," a Navajo paramedic and health educator who served as a "cultural broker" or liaison between the Anglo-dominated health care system and his people. As part of the larger effort to deliver biomedical health services and to ensure the compliance of patients, many medical anthropologists turned to ethnomedical approaches that sought to elicit the health beliefs of their subjects.

Clinical anthropology, as a distinct branch of medical anthropology, began to develop in the early 1970s as part of a larger effort to humanize the increasingly bureaucratic and impersonal aspects of biomedical care. Nevertheless, medical anthropologists such as Otto von Mering had been working in clinical settings since the early 1950s (Johnson 1987). Arthur Kleinman (1977), a psychiatrist with an M.A. in anthropology, urged medical anthropologists to assume a "clinical mandate" under which they would help to facilitate the doctor-patient relationship, particularly by eliciting patient "explanatory models" (EMs), or the patient's perceptions of disease and illness, that would help the physician to deliver better medical care. In addition to seeking to reform biomedicine, although certainly not significantly to change it, clinical anthropology has focused attention on searching for alternative health careers for anthropologists during the 1980s and 1990s. The tight academic job market prompted many anthropology students to seek careers in medical anthropology because it held out the hope of providing employment in nonacademic settings, including clinical ones.

A long symbiotic relationship has existed between medical anthropology and medical sociology (Conrad 1997; Good and Good 2000). Various people, such as Peter Kong-Ming New, Ronald Frankenberg, Ray H. Elling, and Meredith McGuire, have served as disciplinary brokers between medical sociology and medical anthropology. Medical anthropologists have often relied upon medical sociological research, particularly in their research on aspects of biomedicine and national health care systems. For instance, in the first medical anthropology textbook ever to be published, Foster and Anderson (1978) drew heavily upon medical sociological research in their chapters on "Illness Behavior," "Hospitals: Behavioral Science Views," "Professionalism in Medicine: Doctor," and "Professionalism in Medicine: Nursing."

A steering committee formed to explore the possibility of establishing a formal organization for medical anthropologists began publishing the *Medical Anthropology Newsletter (M.A.N.)* in 1968. The committee represented a growing coterie of anthropologists interested in "carving out and defining a topical field within anthropology, that was analogous to such other topics as religion, economics, social organization, psychological anthropology, and the like" (Landy 1977: 2–3). Indeed, David Landy began at the University of Pittsburgh in 1960 to teach in the anthropology department a course titled "Primitive and Folk Medicine" and simultaneously, in the School of Public Health, a course titled "Social and Cultural Factors in Health and Disease." At any rate, the Group for Medical Anthropology (GMA) debated whether it should affiliate with either the American Anthropological Association or the Society for Applied Anthropology between 1968 and 1972 (Weidman 1986). GMA evolved into the Society for Medical Anthropology (SMA), which finally became a constituent unit of the American Anthropological Association in 1975. The first doctoral programs in medical anthropology were established at the University of California at Berkeley and Michigan State University. Since that time, many anthropology departments have established master's and doctoral programs in medical anthropology, and some have even established postdoctoral programs in medical anthropology or on specific health issues such as social gerontology.

Over a decade ago, Landy (1983: 193) asserted that medical anthropology "has begun to come of age, or at least to have left its childhood and entered its adolescence." While this dynamic subdiscipline has certainly not yet reached full maturity, one might argue that it has reached late adolescence or even early adulthood. Today, SMA is the second largest unit of the American Anthropological Association. Furthermore, health-related issues have become a major area of study among anthropologists in the United Kingdom, continental Europe, Latin America, South Africa, Japan, and elsewhere.

Outside the United States, medical anthropology has undergone its greatest growth in Great Britain. A session convened by Meyer Fortes at the 1972 annual conference of the Association of Social Anthropologists (A.S.A.) at the University of Kent played a key role in the launching of the subdiscipline in the United Kingdom. The papers presented in this session eventually were published in a volume titled *Social Anthropology and Medicine* (Loudon 1976). The narrow focus of medical anthropology in Britain initially is illustrated by Rosemary Firth's (1978: 244) recommendation that anthropologists interested in health-related issues confine their activity primarily to the translation of symbolic systems and avoid collaboration with other social scientists and also "social engineers and social reformers." Her advice against starting an applied medical anthropology reflects an earlier era during which many sociocultural anthropologists believed that their discipline should focus its research upon simple preindustrial societies in a purportedly pristine or socially isolated form. At any rate, the 1972 A.S.A. conference prompted the founding of the British Medical Anthropology Society in 1976. In contrast to their North American counterparts, however, medical anthropologists in the United Kingdom followed Firth and tended to eschew applied research (Kaufert and Kaufert 1978). In time, medical anthropology in Britain began to emerge from its "tight confinement to ethnomedicine" (Hunter 1985: 1298). The work of Ronald Frankenberg (1974) and that of socially oriented physicians such as Joyce Leeson (1974) at Manchester University served as a precursor to the later emergence of critical medical anthropology in the United States and the United Kingdom. Also important in the development of a critical perspective in British medical anthopologist was the work of the medical sociologist Mervyn, a South African physician who collaborated with anthropologist William Watson during the early 1960s on the *Sociology of Medicine*. While a professor in the Department of Community Medicine at Manchester University in England, Susser participated in discussions of health, medicine, and society with Frankenberg and Leeson.

In the late 1960s, contemporary medical anthropology made its debut in the Federal Republic of Germany when Joachim Sterly established the Arbeitsgemeinschaft Ethnomedizin (Working Society on Ethnomedicine) (Pfeiderer and Bichman 1986). At the same time, he founded a unit for ethnomedicine, since the term medical anthropology already designated earlier medical concerns in the Deutsche Gesellschaft fuer Voelkerkunde (German Society of Ethnography). German cultural anthropology, both in the Federal Republic of Germany and the former German Democratic Republic, has been divided into *Volkskunde* (the study of German populations) and *Voelkerkunde* (ethnology of peoples around the world). The term *Anthropologie* tends to be avoided because it refers to physical anthropology—a field that was employed by the Nazis to support their racial program. After World War II, physical anthropology eventually became rehabilitated in East Germany and, somewhat later, in West Germany.

For a period of time, the Institute of Tropical Hygiene and Public Health at the University of Heidelberg published the journal *Ethnomedizin*. The Arbeitsgemeinschaft Ethnomedizin (the Working Society of Ethnomedicine) publishes the journal *Curae*. Both Heidelberg University and Hamburg University offer course work in medical anthropology, with the latter offering a doctoral degree in medical anthropology. Medical anthropology has become an area of growing interest in various other European countries, including Belgium (Devisch 1986), Italy (Pandolfi and Gordon 1986), the Netherlands (Streefland 1986), and Scandinavia (Heggenhougen 1986), as well as in other parts of the world.

Medical Anthropology and Epidemiology

Toward the close of the twentieth century, the health arena was rocked by the sudden appearance of a host of seemingly new infectious diseases, all of them direly frightening in their sudden appearance, horrific symptoms, and often lethal power (Garrett 1994). Some of these new diseases, like AIDS or Lyme disease, have become widespread and well known to the general public. Others only garner popular attention when an outbreak suddenly occurs. For example, in 1967, the Marburg virus first appeared in the Behring Works company in Germany. Workers came down with fevers, nausea, vomiting, diarrhea, severely bloodshot eyes, rashes, and bleeding mucus membranes. Twenty-five percent of those afflicted died.

Two years later, a group of American nurses in Nigeria were struck by a new disease called Lassa, which produced symptoms similar to Marburg but was found to be caused by a different pathogen. The disease now accounts for at least 5,000 deaths per year in West Africa. The first American case occurred in Chicago in 1989. Seventy percent of those struck by Lassa succumb to the disease.

In 1976, the world first became frighteningly aware of Ebola following a deadly rampage of infection that began at the Yambuku Mission Hospital in western Sudan. Named after the Ebola River, spread of the disease produced widespread fear and anxiety, and helped to spark contemporary global concern about emergent diseases. Families of Ebola victims watched helplessly as their loved ones developed taxing respiratory problems, total loss of appetite, intense headache, chills, abdominal pain, diarrhea, vomiting and massive internal bleeding. As the disease progressed, the blood of victims failed to clot and they bled from injection sites as well as into their gastrointestinal tracts, skin, and internal organs. As body systems collapsed the victims fell into shock and 90 percent died. As described by Preston (1994: 68) in *The Hot Zone*, his best-selling chronicle of this "emergent disease," infection hit the hospital like a bomb. It savaged patients and snaked like chain lightening out from the hospital through patients' families.

The toll mounted as the virus spread to fifty-five villages surrounding the hospital. Especially hard hit were women relatives who prepared bodies for burial. Over three hundred people died in the initial outbreak, including hospital nurses, patients, and the family members of patients. Subsequent outbreaks have occurred in Sudan in 1979, in western Zaire in 1995, in Gabon in 1996, in Uganda in 2000, and Gabon in late 2001 and early 2002. Unlike other the highly contagious hemorrhagic fever viruses, which tend to have an animal or insect vector that spreads the disease, Ebola (for which a vector has not yet been identified) is spread by contact with the blood or other bodily fluids and tissues of an infected person. The Ebola virus has been identified as a member of the virus family called Filoviridae, a group characterized by a thread like appearance. However deadly, these viruses are usually only 800 to 1000 nanometers (nm) long (1nm is equal to one-billionth of a meter). There remains no known cure or vaccine for Ebola.

In 1993, the Four Corners region of the western United States was rocked by the appearance of Hantavirus. Characterized by a mild onset with flu-like symptoms, the disease rapidly progresses to kidney failure with internal bleeding. Victims in the Four Corners outbreak hemorrhaged so badly in their lungs that they suffocated in their own blood. Mortality after infection has been found to be over 60% with the deadliest strains. Over 60 species of birds and rodents have been identified as the vectors for the 70 known strains of the virus.

Each of the cases of the disease outbreaks described above has been of special concern to the public health field of epidemiology. This applied discipline is concerned with understanding the "distribution and deter-minants of disease" (Trostle and Sommerfeld 1996: 253) and using this information to make social, physical, or other changes needed to prevent further illness. Unlike, biomedicine, which primarily focuses on the treat-ment of ailments in specific individuals, epidemiology addresses the larger-level of the population with the intention of preventing new illness. In other words, the goal of epidemiology is assessing the distribution of disease with the intention of identifying "the risk factors that enable in-tervention and, ultimately, control" (Agar 1996: 391). At the first reports of a disease outbreak, epidemiologists, like those who work for the Cen-ters for Disease Control and Prevention (CDC) in Atlanta, Georgia, rush to the scene (often anywhere in the world). Their objectives include de-termining the cause(s) of illness, the incidence rate (numbers over new cases over time), the prevalence (total number of cases relative to the size of the population at risk), the pathways of disease spread, and possible methods for lowering disease morbidity and mortality. Specifically, as Hahn (1999: 34) relates,

In the epidemiological investigation of an outbreak of an infectious disease, the first step is to locate individuals who may be ill and obtain symptom histories. This "case finding" activity allows the epidemiologist to characterize the outbreak and construct hypotheses about the source of the infection.

In the case of the 1976 Ebola outbreak, it was found that the nuns who ran the Yambuku Mission Hospital began their work each day by putting out five syringes for use with the hundreds of patients who would need injections. Occasionally, the syringes were cleaned with warm water to clear blood clots and drying blood that interfered with needle efficiency, but often a syringe was pulled from the arm of one patient, refilled with medicine, and re-injected into another patient without cleansing. In this way, a very effective (if completely unintended) method for viral transmission was created, much like the one that has allowed HIV to move rapidly among illicit injection drug users who are forced to re-use syringes used by others because of a lack of access to sterile syringes. Other routes of Ebola transmission also were identified, including mortuary practices that exposed individuals to the infected body fluids of Ebola victims. Identification of these routes of transmission led to a rapid end to the 1976 Ebola outbreak.

With its focus on observable behaviors and actual social and physical contexts of health and illness, as well as its concern with the population level rather than the individual case of disease, it is recognized that epidemiology shares features with medical anthropology. Indeed, a number of anthropologists and some epidemiologists have pointed out the benefits of close collaboration between the two disciplines. To this union, advocates of collaboration argue, epidemiology brings a rigorous scientific approach, an emphasis on quantitative data collection, and a specifically applied orientation. Anthropology's contribution includes an emphasis on intensive qualitative investigation of behaviors and social relations in context and a keen awareness of the importance of culture (and meaning) in shaping people's behavior as well as their willingness to change behaviors to accommodate public health dictates.

Over the last several decades, collaborations of this sort have become increasingly common, although they do not yet constitute standard practice. Singer, for example, has worked closely with a number of epidemiologists in assessing social context factors that contribute to the extent of HIV risk among injection drug users in three New England cities. Combining anthropological emphasis on direct observation of actual risk settings, social networks, and behaviors with an epidemiological focus on rigorous measurement (e.g., using standardized surveys and the careful structuring of participant sampling), the multi-disciplinary team conducting this study has been able to identify key local context factors at both the neighborhood and city levels that contribute to differences in HIV risk and infection in different social environments. Findings such as this are important in moving the field of AIDS prevention from efforts built on a one-size-fits-all approach to the tailoring of prevention to fit the specific characteristics of local social environments.

Despite the recognized benefits of interdisciplinary collaboration, a number of anthropologists have been critical of epidemiology. Concerns about the types of data that are valued and devalued (e.g., inattention to people's behaviorally motivating beliefs and understandings of disease) and an unquestioned embrace of scientific method without sensitivity to the cultural shaping of scientific understandings have been voiced by a number of anthropologists about epidemiology (True 1996). Further, Digiacomo (1999: 451) has questioned whether genuine collaboration is occurring, noting the tendency of epidemiology to raid the storehouse of anthropological cultural knowledge in search of "bits of information about 'culture' which can then be plugged into a statistical model that generates correlations amenable to being represented as causal . . . " From the critical perspective developed in this volume, the primary concern emerges from the intensely political nature of public health as a social practice. As Moss astutely observes:

As most practitioners know, the comfortable truism about epidemiology that public health schools teach their graduate students—that epidemiology is the basic science of public health—is not actually true. It may be closer to reality to say that politics is the basic science of public health (Moss 2000: 1385).

Politics, not epidemiological findings, tends to dominate social thinking and policy around disease, especially infectious disease, and politics and not misguided cultural behaviors tend to be the determinant force in shaping the conditions for the spread of disease. For example, returning to the 1976 Ebola outbreak, as Farmer (1999: 46) notes, social elites and Europeans did not fall victim because "likelihood of coming into contact with . . . unsterile syringes was inversely proportion to one's social status . . . " High-quality medical care was available to the wealthy, lesser quality care was accessible by subordinate social classes. Similarly, on a global scale, Ebola, an African disease, garnered intense media attention in the West (propelling the very word to Ebola into a symbol of looming darkness and impending danger) despite the relatively small number of individuals that have been infected. Farmer's point is that epidemiological models of disease need to avoid

facile claims of causality, particularly those that scant the pathogenic roles of social inequalities. Critical perspectives on emerging infections [for example] must ask how large-scale social forces come to have their effects on unequally positioned individuals in increasingly interconnected populations; a critical epistemology needs to ask what features of disease emergence are obscured by dominant analytic frameworks (Farmer 1999: 5).

A blindness to the ways in which local behaviors (those found to spread disease) are structured by local and global social inequality has limited the development of broader understandings of disease in epidemiology (Doyal and Pennell 1979). But, this is no less the case for medical anthropology for much of its history. This parallel limitation suggests the potential benefits of the further development of critical epidemiology and critical medical anthropology and of their collaboration in assessing and responding to disease. In this collaboration, strong focus using methodologies that collect both qualitative and quantitative data, and integrate them for purposes of analysis, would be applied to addressing the big questions, such as what are "the precise mechanisms by which such forces as racism, gender inequality, poverty, war, migration, colonial heritage, and even structural adjustment program [such as those imposed by entities like the World Bank and International Monetary fund before monies will be loaned to developing countries] become embodied as [culturally shaped] increased risk" (Farmer 1997: 524).

Today, medical anthropology constitutes an extremely broad endeavor that no single textbook can possibly summarize. Students who are interested in further acquainting themselves with the scope and breadth of medical anthropology as a subdiscipline are advised to consult the following two important anthologies: (1) *Medical Anthropology: Contemporary Theory and Method*, edited by Carolyn F. Sargent and Thomas M. Johnson (1996), and (2) *Training Manual in Applied Medical Anthropology*, edited by Carole E. Hill (1991). At the theoretical level, medical anthropologists are interested in topics such as the evolution and ecology of disease, paleopathology, and social epidemiology; the political economy of health and disease; ethnomedicine and ethnopharmacology; medical pluralism; cultural psychiatry; the social organization of the health professions, clinics, hospitals, national health care systems and international health bureaucracies; human reproduction; and nutrition. At the applied level, medical anthropologists work in areas such as community medicine; public health; international health; medical and nursing education; transcultural nursing; health care delivery; mental health services; health program evaluation; health policy; health care reform; health activism and advocacy; biomedical ethics; research methods in applied medical anthropology; and efforts to control and eradicate a wide array of health-related problems, including malaria, cancer, alcoholism, drug addiction, AIDS, malnutrition, and environmental pollution. In many ways, the work of medical anthropologists overlaps with that of medical sociologists, medical geographers, medical psychologists, medical social workers, epidemiologists, and public health people. In the past, medical anthropologists tended to focus on health problems at the local level and, less often, at the national level.

Physician-anthropologist Cecil Helman (1994: 338) maintains that future research in medical anthropology "will involve adopting a much more global perspective—a holistic view of the complex interactions between cultures, economic systems, political organizations and ecology of the planet itself." He identifies overpopulation, urbanization, AIDS, primary health care, pollution and global warming, deforestation, and species extinction as some of the areas with which medical anthropologists will need to concern themselves. For critical medical anthropologists, the future has already arrived, in that they have for some time been urging making micro-macro connections—ones that link patients' suffering to the global political economy.

CHAPTER 2

Theoretical Perspectives in Medical Anthropology

Since its emergence as a distinct field of research, medical anthropology has been guided by several theoretical perspectives, although their boundaries have not always been neatly delineated. There have been disagreements about what theoretical approaches are the leading ones at any point in time. In his book *Sickness and Healing: An Anthropological Perspective*, Robert Hahn (1995), for example, notes three dominant theoretical perspectives. Byron J. Good (1994), in *Medicine, Rationality, and Experience: An Anthropological Perspective*, identifies four theoretical perspectives in medical anthropology: the empiricist paradigm, the cognitive paradigm, the "meaning centered" paradigm, and the critical paradigm. Finally, in *Medical Anthropology in Ecological Perspective*, Ann McElroy and Patricia Townsend (1996) also discuss four approaches (medical ecological theories, interpretive theories, political economy or critical theories, and political ecological theories) but, as we can see, these are not quite the same as those cited by Good.

Despite these varying ways of grouping medical anthropology's various frames of understanding, it is clear that most medical anthropologists do tend to agree that some reasonably identifiable clusters of theory are guiding work done within the field. This book was written to help students gain a clearer understanding of the issues addressed within medical anthropology from the perspective of one of these clusters: the one labeled *critical* or *political economic* medical anthropology. In this chapter, we first present short introductions to the other two approaches, including discussion of their respective strengths and weaknesses from the critical perspective. This is followed by a more detailed discussion of the critical perspective, which in large part guides this textbook.

It bears noting that critical medical anthropologists sometimes have been accused of being "especially blunt, outspoken critics of other theories in medical anthropology" (McElroy and Townsend 1996: 65) and further, of believing that the critical approach is "superior to other models" (McElroy 1996: 519). We plead guilty to both charges, as should anyone who embraces a theoretical frame of reference. Theory-building in any discipline progresses, in part, through open discussion and debate, including pointing out shortcomings of alternative approaches. Criticism of this sort is a needed and healthy process within a field of study. Indeed, it is the absence of debate that should be cause for concern. Certainly, critical medical anthropology has benefited from critiques framed from other perspectives. Similarly, as a result of the medical ecological framework, McElroy and Townsend (1996: 68) have moved toward a more thoroughgoing political ecological orientation. Moreover, it is likely that the proponents of all perspectives find their own to be superior. After all, why would one embrace a perspective he or she thought to be inferior or even equal to its alternatives? It is the sense that it can better frame important research questions and guide the explanation of research findings that leads to the promotion of a particular perspective. Because the asking of questions and the interpretation of findings is *always* guided by assumptions and prior understandings, having a theoretical perspective is unavoidable. In this light, prior to elaborating upon the perspective of critical medical anthropology, we present two alternatives to it: medical ecological theory and cultural interpretive theory.

MEDICAL ECOLOGICAL THEORY

This approach rests upon the acceptance of the concept of *adaptation*, defined as behavioral or biological changes at either the individual or group level that support survival in a given environment, as the core concept in the field. Indeed, from this perspective, health is seen as a measure of environmental adaptation. In other words, a central premise of the medical ecological orientation is that a social group's level of health reflects the nature and quality of the relationships "within the group, with neighboring groups, and with the plants and animals [as well as nonbiotic features] of the habitat" (McElroy and Townsend 1996: 12). For example, Alexander Alland (1970), the formulator of the medical ecological perspective, pointed out that although the Mano people of Liberia lack a cultural conception or folk disease category for malaria, this disease nonetheless significantly affects Mano well being and their ability to function and reproduce in their local environment. The presence of malaria, he argues, "is known to change gene frequencies, affect the immunological

pattern, produce susceptibility to other pathologies, and lower the efficiency of affected individuals" (Alland 1970: 10). The Mano, to survive,
have had to adapt both biologically and behaviorally to the challenge of
malaria. Biologically, an adaptation to malaria that is commonly cited by
ecologically oriented medical anthropologists is a mutation in the gene
that controls the production of hemoglobin. As a result of this mutation
(which involves a reversal in the order of two amino acids, valine and
glutamic acid, at the sixth position in the genetic instructions for the production of the oxygen-binding blood molecule hemoglobin), red blood
cells are distorted into clumps of needle-like crystals that form a crescent
shape. This change inhibits the production of the malaria parasite, a protozoan of the genus Plasmodium, within human blood and confers protection from the worst symptoms of malaria infection. For individuals
who receive the sickling mutation from both parents, however, the consequence is a life-threatening disease called sickle cell anemia, a condition
that afflicts about two of every thousand African American children in
the United States.

Medical ecologists also point to the importance of behavioral adaptations to health threats. McElroy and Townsend (1996), for example, note
the indigenous development of snow goggles that protect the eyes of arctic
dwellers from the harsh and damaging glare of sunlight reflected off ice
and snow. Also from the medical ecological perspective, behavioral complexes like medical systems, including everything from shamanistic healing of soul loss to biomedical thromboendarterictomy (the reaming out of
the inner layer of a sclerotic or hardened artery) can be viewed as "sociocultural adaptive strategies" (Foster and Anderson 1978: 33).

This way of understanding human biology and behavior, as an interactive set of adaptations to ecological and social challenges, makes a lot
of sense to many medical anthropologists. Yet others have raised questions about this approach. B. Good (1994: 45), an interpretive medical
anthropologist, argues that in ecological studies "[di] sease is often taken
to be a natural object, more or less accurately represented in folk and
scientific thought. Disease is thus an object separate from human consciousness." In turn, medical systems are seen as utilitarian social responses to intrusive natural conditions. B. Good (1994: 46) questions both
parts of this medical ecological equation, asserting that in such formula-
tions "culture is . . . absorbed into nature, and cultural analysis consists
of demonstrating its adaptive efficacy." Lost in such understanding is a
full appreciation of the human cultural/symbolic construction of the
world they inhabit. In other words, human communities do not respond,
even in the ways they get sick and certainly in the ways that they think
about and respond to sickness, to an external material reality that is independent of cultural valuation and signification. AIDS, for example, is a
disease chock-full of cultural conceptions, values, and strong emotions. It

is quite impossible for humans somehow to strip these away and confront AIDS in some kind of raw, culture-free natural state. Humans can experience the external material world only through their cultural frames; and thus diseases, as they are known consciously and somatically by sufferers and healers alike, are packed with cultural content (e.g., believing that AIDS is a punishment from God or, as some people with AIDS have experienced it, an opportunity to turn their lives to more positive ends). Even science is not a route to a culture-free account of the physical world, as it too is a cultural construction.

Critical medical anthropologists agree with much in the interpretive critique of the ecological model. The emphasis in its own critique, however, emerges from critical medical anthropology's focus on *understanding the specific structure of social relationships that give rise to and empower particular cultural constructions,* including medical anthropological theories. Critical medical anthropology asks, "Whose social realities and interests (e.g., which social class, gender, or ethnic group) do particular cultural conceptions express, and under what set of historic conditions do they arise?" Further, critical medical anthropology has faulted medical ecological approaches for failing fully to come to grips with the fact that "it is not merely the idea of nature—the way [external reality] is conceived and related to by humans—but also the very physical shape of nature, including of course human biology, that has been deeply influenced by an evolutionary history of hierarchical social structures—that is to say, by the changing political economy of human society" (Singer 1996: 497).

The problem inherent in conceptualizing the health aspects of the human/environmental relationship, in terms of adaptation, can be illustrated with the case of the indigenous people of Tasmania, an island that lies just off the southeastern tip of Australia. Tasmania was successfully inhabited by aboriginal people for over ten thousand years prior to the arrival of Europeans at the end of the eighteenth century. Yet, building on the work of Robert Edgerton, McElroy and Townsend cite the Tasmanians as a case of maladaptation that led to the dying out of these people by 1876. They note:

In about 12,000 years of isolation from the mainland, the Tasmanians *devolved,* losing the ability to make many tools, to make fire, and to construct rafts or catamarans that would have allowed them to fish and travel. The division of labor between men and women was inefficient, endangering women. Their political ecology emphasized raiding, capture of women, and competitiveness between tribal bands. During the cold season they went hungry, and their clothing and housing were inadequate. . . . [In sum] their way of life was far from ideal, and the society quickly collapsed after Europeans arrived. (McElroy and Townsend 1996: 112; emphasis in original)

The impression given by this account is that the arrival of European settlers on Tasmania in the late eighteenth century played but a small part in the disappearance of a society that was poorly adapted to its environment and paid the ultimate evolutionary price for its maladaptation. A closer examination of the historic political economic events surrounding the nature and impact of European arrival suggests rather different conclusions. Within thirty years of the arrival of the British in Tasmania, the indigenous population, which had been stable at around 4,000–5,000 prior to contact, dropped to a mere eleven. This shocking level of depopulation, which was occurring not just in Tasmania but throughout Britain's Third World colonies, led the British House of Commons to constitute a fifteen-member Select Committee on Aborigines, which published its findings in 1837. The committee concluded that the lands of indigenous people "had been usurped; their property seized; their character debased; European vices and diseases have been introduced." (Quoted in Bodley 1975: 25.) Douglas Oliver, an anthropologist with extensive experience in Oceania, reports the exact nature of these "European vices," noting that the aboriginal peoples of Australia and Tasmania were the victims of playfulness: the sport-loving British pioneers occasionally relieved the boredom of isolation by hunting "abos" in lieu of other game. More frequently, however, these hunts were serious undertakings: now and then aborigines would be brash enough to kill or steal livestock pastured on their horde territories, and that called for systematic drives for extermination by the white owners. Aboriginal men, women, and children would be rounded up and shot; to slay a pregnant woman was accomplished by leaving poisoned food. The tragedy was played to its finish in Tasmania, where all [indigenous people] were wiped out . . . by 1876. One efficient colonial administrator even declared an open season against the Tasmanians, culminating in the infamous "Black Drive" [an open season on the hunting of Tasmanians] of 1830 (Oliver 1961: 161). Quite simply, the disappearance of the Tasmanians was not a consequence of maladaptation to their environment. They were victims of the genocidal extermination that characterized the colonial era.

Medical ecologists respond to such critiques—naively, in the view of critical medical anthropology—by asking: "Should medical ecology be political?" (McElroy 1996). However, if social science is to matter, that is to say, if it is to have any impact on the world other than providing researchers with jobs, then it is *inherently political* (whether we as social scientists like it or not). For those who believe that AIDS is a punishment from God, for example, the scientifically supported statement that syringe exchange programs are effective in protecting drug injectors from the spread of disease is a very political position. Despite the extensive toll of AIDS and multiple studies demonstrating the effectiveness of syringe exchange, a government ban continues to block the use of federal dollars to support this public health measure. Science, including medical anthropology, cannot escape being political if it is to be part of the conflicted world of social policies and actions. It can, however, escape its untenable assertions that its reach for objectivity takes it beyond the influence of social values or that only critical theory has a political agenda (e.g., Hahn 1995: 74).

CULTURAL INTERPRETIVE THEORY

As Byron Good (1994) observes, the emergence of the cultural interpretive or meaning-centered approach in medical anthropology was a direct reaction to the dominance of the ecological perspective on health issues. Whereas ecological medical anthropologists have treated disease as part of nature and hence as external to culture, the fundamental claim of the cultural interpretive model, introduced by Arthur Kleinman, is that disease is not an entity but an explanatory model. Disease belongs to culture, in particular to the specialized culture of medicine. And culture is not only a means of representing disease, but is essential to its very constitution as a human reality (B. Good 1994: 53).

In other words, from the cultural perspective disease is knowable, by both sufferers and healers alike, only through a set of interpretive activities. These activities involve an interaction of biology, social practices, and culturally constituted frames of meaning (e.g., the Western cultural association between obesity and lack of self-control) and result in the construction of clinical realities (e.g., a diagnosis of AIDS or the flu). That different subspecialties of biomedicine sometimes reach quite different conclusions about the same clinical episode affirms to interpretive medical anthropologists the fundamental role of cultural construction in the making of a disease. The training of medical students, for example, as B. Good (1994) points out, does not simply involve teaching students about biology and pathology; more important, it involves enculturating *a way of seeing physical reality.* In anatomy classes, for example, students are taught to see structure where none was obvious. Only with experience [do] gross muscle masses become apparent and recognizable. Veins, arteries, nerves, lymphatic vessels, and connective tissue [are] largely indistinguishable from one another . . . without this training in the clinical construction of "biological reality." (74)

The primary shortcoming, historically, of the interpretive approach from the critical perspective has been its inattention to the role of asymmetrical power relations in the construction of the clinical reality and the social utility of such construction for maintaining social dominance. For example, although B. Good (1994: 62) indicates at the beginning of his book that his intention is to articulate an interpretive approach that is "conversant with critical theory," the fulfillment of this intention seems modest at best in the remainder of the volume. The role of political economy (e.g., class relations) in shaping the formative activities through which illness is constituted, made the object of knowledge, and embedded in experience, for example, is largely ignored in Good's account.

As a result of the clash and exchange between medical ecological theory, cultural interpretive theory, and critical theory, there have been developments in all three of the primary theoretical models within medical anthropology. Medical ecologists have begun to adopt a more political ecological orientation; interpretive medical anthropologists acknowledge and are attempting, and in some cases, succeeding in producing work that is highly sensitive to political economic issues; and critical medical anthropologists have developed a significant level of interest in political ecology (Baer 1996) and the role of political economy in the production of meaning. Nonetheless, there is much work to be done in this regard, and theoretical debate within medical anthropology—which we see as a healthy sign of the vibrancy of the discipline—is likely to continue.

CRITICAL MEDICAL ANTHROPOLOGY: THE BRASH LEFT WING OF MEDICAL ANTHROPOLOGY

It may seem presumptuous to label our approach critical. After all, most medical anthropologists view their subdiscipline as a critical endeavor that challenges the assumptions of the disease model in biomedicine. We contend, however, that this critical perspective is primarily limited to lower levels of analysis and ignores the political economy. Much of this research concerns indigenous societies, peasant communities, and slums, where practitioners of Western biomedicine come into contact with members of a subproletariat or ethnic minority. Although we do not oppose research on social relationships and small communities (indeed, we see it as an essential component of critical medical anthropology), we maintain that it must be conducted with the recognition that disease and its treatment occur within the context of the capitalist world system (Wallerstein 1979). The critical perspective we want to nourish and extend has its taproot in Marx, Engels, the critical theorists of the Frankfurt School and C. Wright Mills (1959). We are concerned with the ways power differences shape social processes, including research in medical anthropology. Like Navarro (1976), Krause (1977), Doyal (1979), Waitzkin (1983), and Foucault (1975), we feel that the dominant ideological and social patterns in medical care are intimately related to hegemonic ideologies and patterns outside of biomedicine. While Baer and Singer were the first to coin the label "critical medical anthropology," in a paper presented at the 1982 American Anthropological Association meeting, others preceded them in the effort to incorporate a critical or political-economic approach into medical anthropology (Frankenberg 1974; Young 1978).

The Precursors of Critical Medical Anthropology

The initial effort to forge a critical redirection for medical anthropology can be traced to the symposium "Topias and Utopias in Health" at the 1973 Ninth International Congress for Anthropological and Ethnological Sciences, which ultimately developed into a volume with the same title (Ingman and Thomas 1975). An explicit turn toward the political economy of health tradition within medical anthropology awaited Soheir Morsy's (1979) review essay titled "The Missing Link in Medical Anthropology: The Political Economy of Health." Morsy's article—as well as an exposure to the political economy of health research, particularly the work of Vincente Navarro, a progressive physician with extensive training in the social sciences—and articles in the *International Journal of Health Services*, prompted Baer (1982) to write a short review of this corpus of literature and its relevance for medical anthropologists. Beginning in 1983, we along with others became involved in the organization of sessions at anthropological meetings and the editing of special issues of several journals on critical medical anthropology.

While a perspective on capitalism is an important starting point for a critical medical anthropology (CMA), it is insufficient for a fully developed approach. CMA attempts to address the nature of health-related issues in indigenous societies as well as in precapitalist and socialist-oriented state societies. It understands health issues within the context of encompassing political and economic forces—including forces of institutional, national and global scale—that pattern human relationships, shape social behaviors, condition collective experiences, reorder local ecologies, and situate cultural meanings. The emergence of CMA reflects both the turn toward political-economic approaches in anthropology in general and an effort to engage and extend the political economy of health approach (Baer, Singer, and Johnsen 1986; Singer, Baer, and Lazarus 1990; Morsy 1990).

Biomedicine as a Starting Point for CMA

The concept of biomedicine serves an appropriate starting point for examining the perspective of critical medical anthropology. CMA seeks to understand who ultimately controls biomedicine and what the implications are of such control. An analysis of the power relations affecting biomedicine addresses questions like (1) Who has power over the agencies of biomedicine? (2) How and in what forms is this power delegated? (3) How is this power expressed in the social relations of the various groups and actors that comprise the health care system? and (5) What are the principal contradictions of biomedicine and associated arenas of struggle and resistance that affect the character and functioning of the medical system and people's experience of it?

Any discussion of the impact of power relations in the delivery of health services needs to recognize the existence of several levels in the health care systems of developed capitalist, underdeveloped capitalist, and socialist-oriented societies. Figure 2.1 presents a schematic diagram of these levels and the social relations associated with them.

The Macrosocial Level

Critical medical anthropology recognizes that the development and expansion of a global economic system represents the most significant, transcending social process in the contemporary historic epoch. Capitalism has progressively shaped and reshaped social life. As a discipline, an-

Figure 2.1
Levels of Health Care Systems

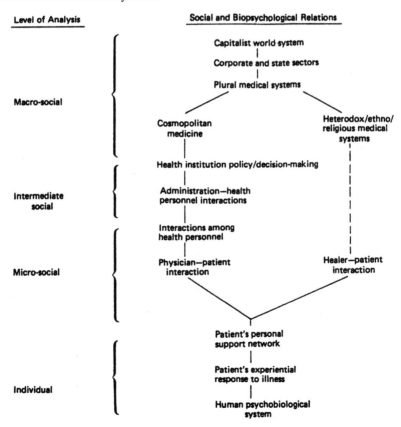

thropology has lagged in its attention to the nature and transforming influence of capitalism. As part of the larger effort of critical anthropology in general to correct this shortcoming, CMA attempts to root its study of health-related issues within the context of the class and imperialist relations inherent in the capitalist world system.

Biomedicine must be seen in the context of the capitalist world system. According to Elling (1981a),

Some of the particular agents of the world-system operating in the health sector include international health agencies, foundations, national bilateral aid programs, all multinationals (especially drug firms, medical technology producers and suppliers, polluting and exploiting industrial firms, agribusinesses, commercial baby food suppliers, purveyors of chemical fertilizers and pesticides, and sellers of population control devices), and a medical cultural hegemony supportive of the activities of these agents on the world scene and in particular nations and locales.

At all levels the health care systems of advanced capitalist nations reproduce the structures of class relations. The profit-making orientation caused biomedicine to evolve into a capital-intensive endeavor heavily oriented to high technology, the massive use of drugs, and the concentration of services in medical complexes. The state legitimizes the corporate involvement in the health arena and reinforces it through support for medical training and research in the reductionist framework of biomedicine. Corporate-controlled foundations simply augment the state, at both international and national levels.

At the international level, the World Bank has become a key player in establishing health policies and making financial loans to health care endeavors. It loaned annually approximately $1.5 billion between 1991 and 1993, which placed it slightly ahead of WHO and UNICEF (cited in Walt 1994: 128). The World Bank has a strong influence on health policy as a result of its practice of cofinancing resources from international and bilateral agencies and matching funds from recipient governments. It also conducts country-specific health sector analyses and makes proposals for health care reform that are compatible with market-driven economies. As a result of this emphasis on capitalist solutions to health problems, Walt (1994: 157) argues, national policy makers sense "that Bank staff [appear to be] more driven by pressure to lend than a desire for successful implementation."

Despite the fact that almost all Third World nations are supposed to be politically independent, their colonial inheritance and their neocolonial situation impose health care modeled after that found in advanced capitalist nations. Paul (1978: 272) argues "medicine has from the beginning functioned in the service of imperialism, supporting logically the voracious search for ever wider markets and profitable deals." The ruling elites that control Third World countries collaborate with international agencies, foundations, and bilateral aid programs to determine health policies (Justice 1986). These elites and the agents they deal with often advocate nationalized and preventive medicine, but their actions favor curative rather than preventive approaches to health care for themselves and even for lower social strata.

Large corporations are involved in the health sector of the Third World not only in pharmaceuticals but also in "hospital construction, development and outfitting, the supply of medical, surgical and diagnostic equipment, and numerous ancillary goods and services" (Doyal 1979: 270). They, of course, ally themselves with Third World elites and, through jobs, favors, and outright bribery, influence health policies.

Despite the global hegemony of biomedicine, our scheme recognizes that complex societies exhibit a pattern of medical pluralism. Ultimately, these systems are dominative in that biomedicine enjoys a dominant status over heterodox and ethnomedical systems. This dominant status is legitimized by laws that give biomedicine a monopoly over certain medical practices and limit or prohibit the practice of other types of healing. Various heterodox medical systems, such as Ayurveda and Unani in India; natural medicine in Germany; and chiropractic and naturopathy in the United States, Canada, and Britain, may have their own professional associations, schools, hospitals, and clinics and thus replicate the organizational structure of biomedicine. Biomedicine systematically attempts to shore up its dominance by progressively subordinating an array of assumed competitors. Nevertheless, alternative practitioners proliferate and even flourish in certain areas, such as the San Francisco Bay Area. In much folk and popular culture, medicine is practiced and learned outside of bureaucratic settings. Especially important to recognize is the role played by class and related social struggle as a breeding ground for medical pluralism. Oppressed populations may attempt to cling to or resurrect traditional ethnomedical practices as an expression of resistance to domination or as a marker of group solidarity/identity, while countercultures may initiate new medical systems for similar reasons. Similarly, the inability of biomedicine to cure the somatized distress and sickness associated with the postmodern world creates a potent source for pluralism. Under such circumstances, it is common for popular health movements, folk healing systems, and heterodox medical traditions to rise up to fill the void. Despite elements of resistance in these alternative medical systems, it is important not to overlook the capacity of biomedicine and its patrons in the capitalist class and the state sector to co-opt them. Nevertheless, it is important to point out that the growth of nongovernmental organizations (NGOs) has come more and more to serve as a counter-hegemonic force challenging corporate and state health policy makers. As Walt (1994: 204) observes, NGOs constitute a "sign of increased civic challenge, which may be translated into new social movements and public protest but may also create debate within existing formal institutions."

The Intermediate Level

At the intermediate level of health care systems, the hospital, which varies in size from a gigantic medical center to a rural hospital, has become the primary arena of social relations. Navarro (1976) has demonstrated the pervasive control that members of the corporate class and the upper-middle class have over both "reproductive institutions" (health foundations and private and state medical teaching institutions) and "delivery institutions" (voluntary and proprietary or profit-making hospitals). The power that hospital administrators and physicians enjoy at this level is in reality a delegated power. As Freidson (1970: 5) observes, the professional dominance of biomedicine is secured by the political and economic influence of the elite which sponsors it—an influence that drives competing occupations out of the same area of work, that discourages others by virtue of the competitive advantages conferred on the chosen occupation, and that requires still others to be subordinated to the profession.

Although physicians exert a great deal of control over their work, because of their monopoly of medical skills and the congruence between their version of disease theory and capitalist ideology, they find themselves subject to bureaucratic constraints in hospitals. Some social scientists have even argued that physicians are undergoing a process of deprofessionalization or proletarianization in their status as employees of health care corporations and health maintenance organizations (HMOs) that seek to increase their profits under the guise of managed care. In addition to a growing number of physicians employed in public agencies, hospitals, medical schools, insurance companies, and HMOs, "even those primarily in office-based practice are dependent on their hospital affiliations to pursue their work, and increasingly face restrictions under the rules of the hospital as a social and legal entity" (Mechanic 1976: 49).

The wide array of other health workers means that the medical hierarchy replicates the class, racial/ethnic, and gender hierarchy. The nurse as a relatively high-status subordinate traditionally was supposed to exhibit docility toward physicians and the top administration, although the impact of the feminist movement had, at least until recently, altered these patterns in certain places to some extent. According to Stein (1967), early in her training the nurse learned to play the "doctor-nurse game," in which "she must communicate her recommendation statement" to the physician. Despite their stereotypic nurturing role, many registered nurses now serve as lower-level managers who must carry out policies made at higher levels. The ironic twist of this development is that the health workers with the lowest status and least power are those persons who come into the most continuous and intimate contact with patients in hospital settings. The medical hierarchies of advanced capitalist countries are replicated in Third World nations, though various accommodations are made to local customs and traditions.

Class struggle has become an explicit aspect of the intermediate social level. While the trend toward unionization in U.S. hospitals first occurred among its underpaid unskilled and semiskilled workers, it has also spread to technicians, nurses, and even physicians. Factors serving to mitigate demands by unionized hospital workers, however, include the shift of costs from higher wages to consumers and the emergence of a "new professional managerial class of hospital administrators" who are sometimes willing to arbitrate with unions in return for disciplined workers (Krause 1977: 68–77). Furthermore, professionalization continues to be seen by many health workers as a more viable approach for socioeconomic advancement, thus preventing them from forming an alliance with lower-status workers. In recent years, many hospitals have turned to downsizing their full-time nursing staffs by utilizing either temporary registered nurses or licensed practical nurses and nurses' aides as cheaper forms of health care providers.

The Microlevel

The microlevel primarily refers to the physican-patient relationship and what Janzen (1978) calls the "therapy management group." The major initial diagnostic task of the physician is heavily mediated by social factors outside the examining room. Similar medical treatment, the other major task of the physician, is not determined solely by the needs of the patient. It also serves the special needs of physicians and other powerful sectors within and outside the health care system. The physician role, in fact, performs two key functions for the encompassing social system and its existing distribution of power: (1) controlling access to the special prerogatives of the sick role and (2) medicalizing social distress. In the first, the physician may limit access to the sick role by judging whether an individual may or may not be excused temporarily from work. It must be noted, however, that his or her power in this area is far from absolute, in that most people adopt the sick role without consulting physicians. They frequently consult with lay members of the therapy management group in arriving at this decision. In the second function, according to the reductionist model of disease in which physicians assign the source of disease to pathogenic or related factors, personal stress emanating from social structural factors such as poverty, unemployment, racism, and sexism is secluded from the potentially disruptive political arena and secured within the safer medical world of individualized treatment. As Zola (1978) argues, the ultimate function of both the gatekeeping and the medicalizing activities is social control. Research and analyses at the microlevel must begin to locate the physician-patient relationship "in the broader political and economic framework" (McKinlay 1976: 155).

The individual level entails consideration of the patient's response to sickness or sufferer experience. Critical medical anthropology is sensitive to what Scheper-Hughes and Lock (1987) term the "mindful body." In their view, an individual's body physically feels the distress that its bearer is experiencing. The critical approach to the individual level begins with the recognition that sufferer experience is constructed and reconstructed in the action arena between socially constituted categories of meaning and the political-economic forces that shape the context of daily life. Recognizing the powerful influence of such forces, however, does not imply that individuals are passive or impersonal objects but rather that they respond to the material conditions they face in light of the possibilities created by the existing configuration of social relations. Medical anthropology needs to generate awareness of the ways in which sufferer experience produces challenges to medical hegemony at both the individual and collective level. For these reasons, the study of sufferer experience and action is an important corrective to the tendency to assume that, because power is concentrated in macrolevel structures, the microlevel is mechanically determined from above. Missing from this understanding of the construction of daily life is an appreciation of the capacity of the microlevel to influence the macrolevel.

Influenced by the argument of Sheper-Hughes and Lock (1987) that human experience is embodied, since the 1980s, the body has become a central topic in the medical anthropology study. Central to this body of work is the realization that we only know the world through our bodies but, in addition, we know ourselves and others not as freestanding minds or personalities, but as personalities within specific bodies. In that illness and disease occur within bodies and are experienced by sufferers as bodily sensations, and, further, in that treatment of illness and disease is focused, at least to some degree depending on the healing system and on changing the body, how we conceptualize the human body is a critical issue for medical anthropology. Yet our bodies are not self-evident; they are not merely biology straightforwardly perceived through an objective, culture-free lens. Rather, they are a focal site for the coming together and entwinement of biology, lived experience, culture, and social relationship.

In other words, the body, as we know and experience it, is culturally and socially constructed. This statement is not intended to deny the material existence and physical properties of the body as a biological system that has a reality separate from human consciousness, but rather to say that: 1) we do not have awareness of our bodies independent of our cultural frames of understanding and valuing; 2) human societies physically shape the human body to conform to cultural expectations; and 3) social relationships are inscribed directly on the body in both intentional and unintentional ways. Each of these aspects of embodiment will be discussed in turn.

All cultures develop an understanding of the human body. Adams (1998: 84), for example, provides the following description of bodily understanding from Tibet within the context of a patient diagnosed as suffering from *rlung* ("heart wind").

"In Tibetan medicine, *rlung* is the most important of the body's humors. Just as with winds outside of the body, winds inside of the body are responsible for any and all movement. . . . As such, winds take a variety of forms . . . Winds are the responsible force that moves the body and substances through and out of the body."

A different conception of the body is found in the Caribbean island of Haiti. According to Brodwin (1996: 86), many Haitians believe that

Certain strong emotions, especially anger and shock, can cause a person's blood to heat, thicken, or rise in the body. Blood can accumulate in the head, causing headaches, stroke, or madness; it can lodge in the throat, causing suffocation; or it can pass into the breast of a nursing mother, spoiling her milk and causing illness to her baby. Blood can change color or become too 'sweet' or 'sour' as a result of unsettling emotional experience as well as exposure to certain 'hot' and 'cold' foods and environmental agents.

As these two accounts suggest, traditional Tibetan and Haitian conceptions of the body differ in marked ways from the body as known in contemporary scientific anatomy or in Western society generally. It should not be assumed, however, that other people's cultural conceptions about the body are misinformed folk notions while our own ideas are rooted in empirical knowledge free of cultural influence. For example, Martin (1996) has analyzed conceptions of the body's immune system in the United States. With reference to the image of the immune system portrayed in the mass media, she found that the body is depicted frequently as a highly defended nation-state with a clear and rigid boundary between the self and the external world, with the latter being described as foreign, hostile, and a constant threat. Always at the ready to fend off a horde of foreign invaders that seek to take over the body, the immune system is visualized in militaristic terms as a hierarchical and well-coordinated army that is always in a state of war. In light of the frequency of U.S. involvement in wars around the globe during the recent evolution of human immunology it is not difficult to identify the source of the body at war imagery that dominates media portrayals. Similarly, hierarchical corporate structures, ruled by decision-making upper class CEOs and boards of directors at the top and populated by working class functionaries carrying out menial tasks at the bottom, would seem to be the model adopted in both professional and popular understandings of the organization of the immune system. In this depiction, smart T cells (lymphocytes) control the immune system, giving biochemical orders to obedient B cells to carry out specific activities, and with dumb macrophage cells at the bottom doing the dirty work of cleaning up the vanquished bodies of foreign invaders and other debris.

Importantly, Martin found the war motif present in the immune system understandings of many immunologists (and immunology textbooks) and among the lay public, although often tempered by other conceptions as well. For many of the physicians, researchers, and representatives of the general public that she interviewed, the military model of the immune system was "not just a metaphor, but 'how it is' " (Martin 1996: 96), that is, not just a useful analogy for describing the immune system but a factual representation of its actual nature. Some immunologists, however, pointed out the problems with this socially dominant conception: a) many "foreign" (i.e., non-human) organisms live in the human body without being targeted for elimination by the immune system, including organisms capable of causing disease; b) newly emergent pathogens, like HIV, could not successfully link-up biochemically, effectively unlock, enter, and reorganize human cells if they were truly foreign; and c) top-down, corporate-like, notions of hierarchy within the immune system do not fit well with the recognized interdependency of the various types of cells that play a role in human immune response. In short, Western understandings of the body, even those held by scientists, are as culturally influenced as any other folk system of bodily knowledge (see Critical Medical Anthropology and Science below).

In addition to images and ideas, cultural influence on our experience of the human body includes the impact of values, that is, beliefs about good and bad, right and wrong. As Freund and McGuire (1991: 4) observe:

Every society has many levels of sharing ideas about bodies: What is defined as healthy, in one society might be considered unhealthily fat and ugly in another; what is seen as thin and lean in one group might be defined as sickly in another. Aging may also be defined as something to be either conquered, feared, accepted, or revered.

As this statement suggests, attitudes about body size and fatness vary considerably across societies. In North America, fatness is seen as both unattractive and unhealthy and is interpreted as a sign of moral laxness if not self-hatred. Studies show that American women who diet have strong concerns about their self-control and associate weight gain with greed (Counihan 1990). By contrast, among the traditionally nomadic Moors of Mauritania, fatness, especially in women, is considered quite attractive. The ability of a man to produce a fat daughter or to sustain a fat wife demonstrates his wealth and secures him highly valued social prestige. Consequently, daughters are force-fed large quantities of fatty camel milk to help them gain weight. Girls generally accept this practice because they know it will enhance their ability to attract a wealthy husband. This sentiment is captured in a Moorish folk saying: "To be a woman of quality, it is necessary to be a woman of quantity" (Cassidy 1991: 197). Hearing about such beliefs and practices, North Americans are quick to raise questions about the health risks of being overweight. As contrasted with Moorish folk sayings, an American quip is that "No woman can be too rich or too thin." However, blanket statements about slimness and health confuse cultural desires with clinical realities in several ways.

First, research shows that from a health standpoint the ideal weight for a specific height increases with age (the best weight for someone at age 25, for example, is too thin for the same person at age 65). Second, while morbidity increases with high weights, it does so for low weights as well. Thirdly, there is a broad range for ideal weight for height ratios, with relatively little change in health risk in increases within a 30–50 pound range. Finally, the key relationship between body fat and morbidity is not degree but distribution (i.e., where body fat is stored), with accumulation of adipose in the abdominal area being notably riskier (for cardiovascular disease, hypertension and cancer) than on the hips and thighs (Ritenbaugh 1991).

The differing ways people conceive and value the human body are evident not only in variations across societies but also within societies. Bourdieu (1984), for example, has analyzed critical differences in ideas about body image across class and gender lines in Western society. Illustratively, he notes (206) that the percentage of women who consider themselves to be below average in beauty or think that they look older than they really are is directly related to social class, with upper class women feeling "superior both in the intrinsic, natural beauty of their bodies and in the art of self-embellishment" with working class women, who have fewer resources and time to invest in cultivating their bodies, being more likely to express alienation from their body image. In that weight is linked culturally in the United States with self control and with personal value, the tendency of upper class individuals to be slimmer than members of the working class (a reversal of nineteenth century weight distribution patterns) serves not only as a visual marker of one's class standing but as an embodied affirmation and constant reminder of the innate superiority of dominant social classes.

The work of culture on bodies is not merely conceptual, it is also physical. Tatooing and body piercing are contemporary illustrations of the ways people actively engage in recreating their physical bodies to conform to desired appearances. While participants often explain these practices as a form of self-expression, their relatively sudden and widespread appearance, especially in certain age and social groups, suggests that cultural forces and not merely individual tastes and values are at work. In fact, throughout history, humans have reconfigured their bodies to conform to cultural standards. Historically, among the Kwakiutl Indians of the northwest coast, babies spent many hours fastened to cradle boards to create a culturally valued flattened head shape. Foot binding of girls—to create a tiny and non-functional foot—as practiced among wealthy families in China traditionally, is another example of culturally dictated body shaping. Other examples, like orthodontia and plastic surgery, indicate that bodies are not only shaped by cultural values, but cultural values about the body can be ensnared by and shaped by for-profit commercial processes. Consequently, body reconfiguring has become big business, generating billions in new wealth for a variety of industries from workout gyms and tanning salons to cosmetics and hair product manufacturers to weight loss programs and dietary supplement distributors. Rather than merely meeting a cultural demand for beauty enhancing products and procedures, critics argue that corporate commodification of body imagery generates feelings of inadequacy and worthlessness resulting in diseases like anorexia and bulimia among vulnerable populations. As critical medical anthropologists Mark and Mimi Nichter observe, promoting

[d]issatisfaction and envy constitute important ingredients in the business of selling transformation. Progress is an ideal basic to the American dream, an ideal exploited by those engaged in marketing by transforming the work ethic from work site to body and from the pursuit of virtue to the pursuit of beauty as commodity fetishism. Being 'self made' has given way to being 'made over' (Nichter and Nichter 1991: 249–250).

Further, as Martin (1990) asserts, medicalization of the body (including the tendency of biomedicine to focus narrowly on individual organs), commercialization of body parts (including the buying and selling of organs for transplant), and commodification by the beauty industry have left people experiencing their bodies not as an inherent component of their immutable selves but as fragmented collections of reworkable organs and improvable appearances imprinted with a public exchange value. We have reached, Martin maintains, the end of the body as we once knew it. In its place, from the standpoint of the capitalist market, is the profitable body, one that can and should constantly be improved through the purchasing of body products, procedures, and activities.

The shaping of bodies is driven not only by cultural notions of ideal appearance but also by class, gender, and other hierarchical social relationships. Social inequalities find direct expression in the shape and appearance of the human body in various ways. One pattern, found in many societies, is that people from upper classes tend to be taller than those from the lower classes in their society, often several inches taller on average. These differences, which are linked to diet, access to health care, and other factors, are first evident prior to birth and are well established by the age of six years (Cassidy 1991).

Work-site exposure to toxic substances produces another type of bodily difference between the classes. Reviewing the literature on this issue, Millen and Holts (1990) note, for example, that half of the workers in factories that produce industrial chromates have been found in both Mexico and South Africa to have perforated nasal septums. Indeed, exposure to toxins in manufacturing, mining, and farming is quite common among workers in developing nations, producing a wide range of disease impacts on lives and bodies. Environmental exposure to toxic substance also differentiates the bodies of upper and lower classes. Dumping of toxins is much more common in the poorer areas of poor countries than in wealthier locations, even if the substances are produced in wealthy countries and shipped for disposal to poorer ones. A wide range of industrial toxins, such as mercury and lead, are dumped into the environment of poor countries each year resulting in a host of damaging effects on the bodies of poor and working class individuals. Similarly, poor neighborhoods are much more likely than wealthy ones to be sited for garbage dumps or other waste disposal locations.

Oths (1999) calls attention to another expression of the embodiment of social relations in her analysis of the folk disease called "debilidad" among highland peasants in Peru. The most common symptom experienced by those who suffer from this culture-specific illness is pain in the brain stem area with pain in the cranium being the second most common complaint. Other symptoms include numbness, dizziness, and fatigue. These discomforts tend to be endured stoically by sufferers without much public complaint. Looking at debilidad in its social context, Oths concludes that it is an expression of the embodiment of life's accumulated hardships. In the highlands of northern Peru, reproductive and productive stresses generated primarily by the pressures of maintaining a living under hard social and economic conditions lead to a culture-specific complaint of debilidad, or exhaustion. . . . Those with debilidad can be shown to have suffered more physically and psychologically over their lifetimes (Oths 1999: 309).

The study of the mindful body in interconnected experiential, cultural, social, and political economic contexts, with particular concern for the ways social inequality is inscribed in bodies and bodies, in turn, are transformed into consumers of self improvement commodities (or themselves become commodities for sale for the improvement of others) are key topics for critical medical anthropology. Implied in this wide range of concerns is the belief that a critical perspective provides the conceptual framework needed to analyze macro-micro connections (e.g., between individual experience, decision-making, and action and powerful social forces like global commodity and labor markets, social stratification, and transnational geo-political domination).

We view CMA as providing a perspective and set of concepts for analyzing macro-micro connections. At the theoretical level, some maintain that critical medical anthropology has developed two contending camps, the so-called political economy/world system theorists and the Foucaultian poststructuralists (Morgan 1987). Scheper-Hughes and Lock (1986: 137), principal proponents of the latter camp, while granting that the political economy of health perspective served as a useful corrective to conventional medical anthropological studies, asserted—perhaps prematurely—that it has "tended to depersonalize the subject matter and the content of medical anthropology by focusing on the analysis of social systems and *things,* and by neglecting the particular, the existential, the subjective content of illness, suffering, and healing as *lived* events and experiences." The orientation of this volume, written from the political economic/world system perspective embraced by its authors, we believe, throws into question the alleged neglect of the individual level of analysis. The study of lived experience, embodiment, social suffering, and individual agency are all-important to the CMA approach. What is distinctive with regard to CMA's approach to the individual level is its recognition of the degree to which issues of power, inequality, oppression, exploitation, and the like create the social environments within which the individual level is actualized and intimately contributes to the social shaping of individual experience, the social construction of human bodies, and the social production of potential pathways of personal action.

More recently, Scheper-Hughes argued for the creation of what she termed a third path between the individualizing, meaning-centered discourse of the symbolic, hermeneutic, phenomenologic medical anthropologists, on the one hand, and the collectivized, depersonalized, mechanistic abstraction of the medical Marxists, on the other hand. To date much of what is called *critical* medical anthropology refers to . . . the applications of marxist political economy to the social relations of sickness and health care delivery (Scheper-Hughes 1990: 189; emphasis in original).

Despite some theoretical differences between the two genres of CMA, they share a commitment to the development of appropriate practical expression. CMA rejects a simple dichotomy between the "anthropology of medicine" and the "anthropology in medicine" that separates theoretical from applied objectives (Foster and Anderson 1978). Rather, critical medical anthropologists seek to place their expertise at the disposal of labor unions, peace organizations, environmental groups, ethnic community agencies, women's health collectives, health consumer associations, self-help and self-care movements, alternative health efforts, national liberation struggles, and other bodies or initiatives that aim to liberate people from oppressive health and social conditions. In sum, through their theoretical and applied work, critical medical anthropologists strive to contribute to the larger effort to create a new health system that will serve the people. This system will not promote the narrow interests of a small, privileged sector of society. Its creation requires a radical transformation of existing economic relationships.

Critical Medical Anthropology and Science

As inscribed in its 1902 Articles of Incorporation, the mission of the American Anthropological Association is to "advance anthropology as the science that studies mankind in all its aspects." Yet in recent years the issue of science in anthropology has become highly contentious. To some degree, this reflects an older debate as to whether anthropology is a science or belongs to the humanities. However, the character of this debate has become more intense, and science is now portrayed by some in increasingly negative terms. Consequently, the question sometimes becomes, "Is CMA science or antiscience?" Those who raise this question are interested to know whether medical anthropologists who embrace a critical perspective believe that their work is conducted within the framework and canons of science or within an alternative, nonscientific mode of understanding reality, such as radical social constructionism, which might be viewed by some as antiscientific in its perspective. Perhaps the starting point for answering this question is to raise another, "What is science?"

It is generally agreed that science views itself as an approach to the discovery of knowledge that adheres to certain rules commonly called the scientific method. Two key rules of the scientific method are *empiricism* (scientific questions are answered through systematic research) and *objectivity* (research must be replicable by others and controlled for bias). The believability of scientific claims to knowledge about the world rests on acceptance that the knowledge it produces is gained through a fair and scrupulous adherence to these rules.

One approach to critiquing science involves showing the high level of bias found in work presented under the banner of scientific objectivity. As an example relevant to the concerns of CMA, there is the book *The Bell Curve: Intelligence and Class Structure in American Life*, by Richard Herrnstein and Charles Murray. This book, one in a long line of books that have attempted to show scientifically that African Americans inherently have lower IQs than whites, created an enormous stir when it was published in 1994. The book was celebrated and embraced by those with a conservative political orientation as strong proof that social programs to redress social inequality are a waste of time and money: Biology is destiny—and the ultimate cause of social disparities. Unfortunately for the authors of

The Bell Curve, as many have pointed out, the book is a case of bad science. For example, Leon Kamin (1995), a professor at Northeastern University, has shown how the book relies on concocted data, research findings contrary to those reported by Herrnstein and Murray, non-IQ data reported as IQ findings, and similar distortions that are made to serve a predetermined set of conclusions about African American inferiority. Based on his analysis, Kamin (1995: 103) concludes, "The book has nothing to do with science." The problem here is not science per se but the rotten apple in an otherwise healthy barrel.

Radical social constructionism takes a different approach in its critique of science. As Haraway (1991: 186) explains, the goal of this perspective is to find "a way to go beyond showing bias in science (that proved too easy anyway), and beyond separating the good scientific sheep from the bad goats of bias and misuse." Instead, social constructionists seek to deconstruct "the truth claims of . . . science by showing the radical historical specificity, and so contestability, of *every* layer of the onion of scientific . . . constructions" (186). In other words, social reconstructionism is concerned with showing that scientific knowledge (including that which falls into the realm of good science) is produced under a particular and influencing set of cultural and historic conditions and that the insights of science are not discovered but socially crafted. As Latour and Woolgar (1986: 243) argue, based on a careful ethnographic study of daily life in a scientific laboratory, "Scientific activity is not 'about nature,' it is a fierce fight to *construct* reality." The underlying objective of science is to create order out of the disorder of experience. But, Latour and Woolgar emphasize, the order of science is constructed by scientists and is not inherent in nature. In this view, the scientific method is a set of rules for constructing an order that is so endowed with an aura of facticity and authority that it is embraced and treated by other scientists as fundamentally true.

In this light, it is the view of CMA that *it is just as problematic not to see the cultural (and political economic) in science as it is to see only the cultural (and political economic) in science.* A failure to see science as an activity that emerged and operates within a given set of cultural circumstances is influenced by the worldview and values peculiar to those circumstances, and serves particular social needs and groups found therein is to treat science as a special case, different from other forms of human activity. There is no justification for this kind of privileging of one form of human endeavor over all others. Conversely, if science is to be treated as nothing but culture, then surely it cannot be brought to bear in discerning the accuracy or validity of any claim to truth. The Nazi claim, for example, that Jews constitute a subhuman group cannot be refuted scientifically if science is deconstructed as culture only. Franz Boas, a leader of modern anthropology during its development in the United States, undertook precisely this kind of work. His books were burned by the Nazis in Germany because he mobilized scientific research to show that Nazi slanders against the Jews and other people whom the Nazis viewed as inferior to Aryans were as full of holes as are the latter-day claims made by Herrnstein and Murray about African Americans.

In sum, CMA views its approach as scientific (and built upon the scientific method), while recognizing that its perspective on reality is no less conditioned by social circumstance and no less open to critical examination and debate than any other perspective. The scientific method is built upon, indeed demands, open and constant critique, and self-examination. This book presents some of the critique developed within CMA of scientific medicine and medical anthropology, the sources of health problems in contemporary society, and a range of other issues pertinent to the field of medical anthropology. To this examination, CMA brings a special concern with the political economic context in which all ideas and behaviors emerge and have impact upon the world.

The Social Origin of Disease

CMA seeks to understand the social origin of disease, all disease. It shares this concern with other critical medical social scientists and public health researchers. Like the latter, critical medical anthropologists endeavor to identify the political, economic, social structural, and environmental conditions in all societies that contribute to the etiology of disease.

CMA views disease as a social as well as a biological product. Friedrich Engels and Rudolf Virchow were nineteenth-century theorists who recognized this reality. In *The Condition of the Working Class in England* ([1845] 1969), Engels, Karl Marx's confidante and frequent collaborator, observed firsthand the conditions of the working class in his position as a middle-level manager in his father's textile mill in Manchester. He maintained that disease in the textile workers was rooted in the organization of capitalist production and the social environment in which they had to live as a result of their meager wages. In contrast to most orthopedists and chiropractors, who generally neglect the social origins of the musculoskeletal problems that their patients experience, Engels recognized that they often derive from the nature of factory work:

The operatives . . . must stand the whole time. And one who sits down, say upon a window-ledge or basket, is fined, and this perpetual upright position, this constant mechanical pressure of the upper portions of the body upon spinal column, hips, and legs, inevitably produces the results mentioned. (Engels [1845] 1969: 190–93)

Rudolf Virchow, a renowned German pathologist and an elected member of the German Reichstag or parliament, also was a pioneer in social medicine—a concern that most biomedical physicians completely ignore. He argued that the material conditions of people's daily life at work, at home, and in the larger society constituted significant factors contributing to their diseases and ailments. Based upon his studies of a typhus epidemic in Upper Silesia, a cholera epidemic in Berlin, and an outbreak of tuberculosis in Berlin during 1948 and 1949, Virchow concluded that these health problems were in large measure shaped by adverse social environmental conditions. He concluded that "[t]he improvement of medicine would eventually prolong life, but improvement of social conditions could achieve this result even more rapidly and successfully" (Virchow 1879: 121–22). In recognition of this insightful medical scientist, the Critical Anthropology of Health Caucus of the Society for Medical Anthropology annually presents the Rudolf Virchow Award for the best article in critical medical anthropology submitted to a panel of three judges.

The study of the social origins of disease is referred to under a number of rubrics, including historical materialist epidemiology, the political economy of illness, and the political ecology of disease. Regardless of its designation, attention to the social origins of disease is an integral part of critical medical anthropology. In keeping with this interest, CMA strives, in McNeil's (1976) terms, to understand the nature of the relationship between microparasitism (the tiny organisms, malfunctions, and individual behaviors that are the proximate causes of much disease) and macroparasitism (the social relations of exploitation that are the ultimate causes of much disease). In the next part of this book, we examine the relationship between health and the environment in general and the social origins of several diseases and forms of suffering, including hunger, malnutrition, homelessness, alcoholism, drug addiction, and AIDS.

PART II

The Social Origins of Disease and Suffering

CHAPTER 3

Health and the Environment: From Foraging Societies to the Capitalist World System

Since their emergence some five million years ago, humans have lived in a delicate interaction with the rest of the natural habitat. Humans, of course, are a part of nature. In contrast to other animal species, however, we engage nature not directly, but through our sociocultural systems. According to Godelier (1986: 28), the natural environment is a "reality which humanity transforms to a greater or lesser extent by various ways of acting upon nature and appropriating its resources." In other words, humans are situated in an environment that entails both a natural dimension and a culturally constructed one. This social environment is an intricate system of interaction between nature and culture, which is created under specific physical limits and imposes various material constraints upon human populations. Experientially, of course, we cannot separate nature and culture. As humans we can only experience nature as we culturally construct it, imbue it with meaning, and interact with it in ways that fit within our particular cultural frames of understanding and emotion.

Technological innovations have enabled humanity to adjust to habitats other than the savannah of East Africa, where it appears that the first bipedal primates or hominids emerged. In the past, most anthropologists believed that the adoption of farming or food production constituted an evolutionary advance: the over foraging or food collection that resulted in an improvement in human health and well being. Research by Richard Lee and Irven DeVore (1976) among the San in the Kalahari Desert of Southwest Africa, however, revealed that people in this desert-dwelling foraging society worked fewer hours per day to provision themselves than most farmers but were better nourished and generally healthier than their horticultural neighbors. As a result of such findings about contemporary foragers, many prehistorians began to revise their theories about living conditions in societies relying upon foraging, horticulture (farming that relies upon simple implements, such as a digging stick or hoe), and agriculture (intensive farming that relies upon more sophisticated implements such as an animal-drawn plow and elaborate techniques such as large-scale irrigation systems and terracing in mountainous areas).

Particularly in foraging societies that lacked contact with civilization or have had minimal contact with it, it appears their members enjoyed good health and long lives while they fulfilled their material desires without endangering the natural environment. As a result of such favorable living conditions, Marshall Sahlins (1972) referred to foragers as the "original affluent society." Conversely, the new interpretation viewed farming as a subsistence strategy necessitated by increasing population densities and declining animal and plant resources among foragers. This new theory argued, "farming permitted more mouths to be fed without necessarily increasing leisure time or lessening the demands of the food quest, while resulting in a general decline in the quality and desirability of food" (Cohen 1984: 2).

Anthropologists and other social scientists have presented a wide array of schemes for delineating the evolutionary trajectory of human societies. In his cultural anthropology textbook, John Bodley (1994) classifies the world's cultures into three broad categories: small, large, and global. Small cultures include nomadic foragers, village horticulturalists, and tribal pastoralists. These societies tend to be relatively egalitarian and to place a great deal of emphasis on reciprocity. Large-scale cultures include both chiefdoms and early states and empires. These societies exhibit a considerable amount of social ranking, or stratification, and centralization of power but lack a developed market economy or industrial production. According to Bodley,

A relatively new scale of organization, [the] global culture has emerged within only the past 200 years. . . . This global system has systematically absorbed large- and small-scale cultures and is itself so homogenous that it could be treated as a single culture. *Industrialization* has enriched, impoverished, and destabilized the world. The global system was created by a *commercialization* process that reversed the relationship between political and economic organization. Political organization is now in the service of ever more powerful economic interests. The global economy is primarily dedicated to the production of profit for the stockholders of corporations. When the costs and benefits of global-scale culture are considered, poverty must be added to inequality and instability, because the global system contains economically stratified nations, which are themselves highly stratified internally. (Bodley 1994: 16)

Following the work of Wallerstein (1979) and others, we prefer, as is apparent in this textbook, to refer to the global culture that Bodley describes as the capitalist world system. At any rate, the evolution of socio-cultural systems has been accompanied, as Bodley (1996: 25) asserts, by "a remarkable increase in the human sector of the global biomass (humans and domestic plants and animals) and a corresponding reduction in the earth's natural biomass" or what environmental scientists refer to as bio-diversity. The advent initially of agrarian state societies and later of cap-italist industrial societies was accompanied by patterns of differential power, social stratification, urbanization, population growth, increasing production and consumption, resource depletion, and environmental deg-radation. Indeed, John Bennett (1974: 403) alludes to an "ecological tran-sition" in sociocultural evolution that entails a "progressive incorporation of Nature into human frames of purpose and action" and evolution from societies that were in relative equilibrium with the natural environment to those that are in disequilibrium with it. According to Bodley (1985: 31), "Social stratification, inequality, urbanization, and state organization . . . set in motion a system that is almost inherently unstable." Agricultural practices in ancient states or civilized societies often were factors in en-vironmental degradation. Large-scale irrigation in ancient Mesopotamia, the area between the Tigris and Euphrates rivers in what is present-day Iraq, resulted in the gradual accumulation of salts in the soil, which in turn contributed to the collapse of Sumerian civilization after 2000 B.C. The development of mercantile and later of industrial capitalism resulted in an expanded culture of consumption that even further strained the environment.

Juergen Habermas describes the destructive impact of capitalism upon the global ecosystem as follows:

The indifference of a market economy to its external costs, which it off-loads on to the social and natural environment, is sowing the path of a crisis-prone eco-nomic growth with the familiar disparities and marginalizations on the inside; with economic backwardness, if not regression, and consequently with barbaric living conditions, cultural expropriation and catastrophic famines in the Third World; not to mention the worldwide risk caused by disrupting the balance of nature. (Habermas 1991: 41)

HEALTH AND THE ENVIRONMENT IN PREINDUSTRIAL SOCIETIES

Critical medical anthropology recognizes that since antiquity human interaction with the environment has created opportunities for the pro-duction of disease. Human health is affected by an environment that is the product of the dialectical interaction of natural and sociocultural forces. According to P. Brown and Inhorn (1990: 190), disease is "not a thing but a process triggered by an interaction between a host and an

environmental insult." Various scholars have argued that people in foraging societies have generally enjoyed cleaner environments and better
health than the majority of peoples in agrarian civilizations (Cohen 1989).
Epidemiological studies indicate that disease became a more rampant and
devastating problem for human populations with the advent of agrarian
state societies or civilization.

Foraging Societies

Ancient foragers appear on the whole to have enjoyed surprisingly
well-nourished and fulfilling lives. Table 3.1 presents data that compare
life expectancies in ancient foraging societies to later, more complex societies.

Although early hominids carried parasitic diseases that had also existed
among their pongid or ape ancestors, their low population densities and
migratory patterns tended to mitigate the disease load of specific foraging
bands. Nevertheless, despite a relative abundance of food and a low incidence of infectious and chronic diseases, it appears that life, in terms of
life expectancy, during the Paleolithic or "Old Stone Age" (the vast period
from the earliest stone tools to the period just prior to the advent of farming) was often precarious. A heavy reliance upon a fluctuating and unpredictable supply of large game and the existence of predators posed a

Table 3.1
Life Expectancies of Various Preindustrial Human Populations

Group	Mean Life Expectancies at Specific Ages		Range in Additional Life Expectancy at 15 Years
	Birth	15 Years	
Paleolithic	19.9	20.6	15.0–26.9
Mesolithic	31.4	26.9	15.0–34.8
Copper Age	28.4	22.2	15.2–34.8
Bronze Age	32.1	23.7	20.4–27.0
Iron Age	27.3	23.4	18.0–32.4
Classical period	27.2	24.7	15.0–34.5
Ancient foragers		16.5	15.0–19.1
Proto-agricultural averages		19.8	15.0–28.7
Urban agricultural averages		25.3	16.9–34.6
Contemporary indigenous averages		26.3	19.2–34.0

Adapted from Kerley and Bass (1978:56).

significant risk for human populations, who had to rely upon handmade weapons and fire as forms of protection. Big game hunting itself was a highly dangerous endeavor that undoubtedly took the lives of many hunters. The retreat of the glaciers of the last Ice Age or Fourth Glacial period (about ten thousand years ago) converted grasslands to forests, thus leading to the extinction of most of the big game animals that had subsisted upon grass and upon which foragers had relied heavily for their food.

These climatic and environmental changes ushered in a period that archaeologists refer to as the Mesolithic, associated with a broad-spectrum revolution that entailed a greater reliance on a wide assortment of small and medium-sized game, such as deer and rabbit (which were far less dangerous to hunt), as well as a wider diversity of plant foods. According to Hunt (1978: 56) and as we can see from Table 3.1, "the evidence from paleopathology indicates a quantum jump in the expectation of human life at birth in the Mesolithic stage of cultural evolution (about ten thousand years ago) followed by a plateau that lasted until medieval times."

Furthermore, ancient as well as contemporary foraging societies lived or continue to live in relative harmony with their respective econiches. Nonetheless, it is important not to romanticize these societies or to believe that we may return to a life of nomadic hunting, fishing, and gathering. Additionally, these societies do leave their footprints on their environments. For example, foragers historically have used fire to clear the landscape of brush and trees in order to hunt game more effectively. This has led to deforestation in many settings. Bison drives on the North American plains, in which the Indians stampeded large herds over cliffs, led to mass deaths of animals. In contrast to later societies, however, the adverse ecological impact of the earliest human societies was minimal. The Mbuti pygmies of the Ituri Forest in Zaire in central Africa, for example, base their tendency to limit the consumption of animal protein upon their belief that eating animals such as deer and elephants shortens their life span. They maintain that in the primeval past they were vegetarians who could have lived forever, but with the adoption of meat eating they embarked upon a path that ultimately led to death.

Epidemiologist Frederick Dunn (1977: 102–3) makes several key generalizations about the health status of foraging populations:

1. Patent malnutrition is rare.
2. Starvation occurs infrequently.
3. Chronic diseases, particularly those associated with old age, are relatively infrequent.
4. Accidental and traumatic death rates vary greatly among hunter-gatherer populations.
5. Predation, excluding snakebites, is a minor cause of death in modern foragers and may have been relatively more important in the past.

6. No generalizations about mental illness among foragers can be made due to lack of sufficient evidence.

7. Ample evidence is available that "social mortality" [homicide, suicide, cannibalism, infanticide, gerontocide, head-hunting, etc.] has been and is significant in the population equation for any foraging society.

8. Parasitic and infectious disease rates of prevalence and incidence are related to the type of econiche.

Dunn's first two generalizations appear to apply better to foragers living in tropical rain forests, savannahs, and even deserts than they do to foragers living in arctic areas. Although starvation was reportedly not a frequent cause of death among the Inuit, McElroy and Townsend (1989: 3) contend "it is certain that mortality increased among old people and small children during serious food shortages."

Humans appear to have inherited various infectious diseases from their primate ancestors. Under certain environmental conditions, infectious diseases are caused by biological agents ranging from microscopic, intracellular viruses to large, structurally complex helminthic parasites. Foragers probably acquired diseases such as head and body lice, pinworms, and yaws from prehominid populations. Livingstone (1958) discounts the likelihood that early hominids had malaria because they lived in savannahs rather than in humid areas in close proximity to still bodies of water. Contemporary primates often carry viral, bacterial, and protozoan infections, including malaria, yellow fever, dysentery, yaws, filariasis, herpes, poliomyelitis, tuberculosis, hepatitis, and rabies (Wood 1979: 42). Humans also became infected by intestinal worms and protozoa carried by hunted animals.

Human susceptibility to disease depends in part upon geography—a reality illustrated in Table 3.2. Whereas groups who live in semiarid or arid conditions, such as the San and the aborigines of the Central Australian desert, encounter few or no species of helminths (intestinal worms) and protozoa (microscopic organisms), those who live in tropical rain forests, such as the Mbuti pygmies and the Semang of Malaysia, encounter numerous species of these parasites.

In the following, "A Closer Look," we explore what lessons the health profile of ancient and contemporary foraging peoples may have for us today.

"A Closer Look"

WHAT DO PREHISTORIC AND CONTEMPORARY FORAGERS TELL US ABOUT EATING AND LIVING RIGHT?

In *The Paleolithic Prescription*, physician S. Boyd Eaton, anthropologist Marjorie Shostak, and physician-anthropologist Melvin Konner propose

Table 3.2
Parasitic Helminths and Protozoa in Four Foraging Groups

	San of Kalahari Desert	Central Australian Aborigine	Semang of Malaysia	Mbuti Pygmy of Zaire
Terrain	savannah	desert	tropical rain forest	tropical rain forest
No. Species				
Helminths	2	1	10	11
Intestinal Protozoa	–	–	9	6
Blood Protozoa	1	–	3	3
Total No. Species	3	1	22	20

Adapted from Dunn (1977:105).

a general plan for healthy living in the modern world by adopting certain dietary and exercise habits from prehistoric and contemporary foraging societies (Eaton, Shostak, and Konner 1988). Indeed, they argue that our biochemistry and physiology are much more in tune with an active nomadic foraging lifestyle than with one in which most people are engaged in relatively sedentary occupations (e.g., repetitive assembly-line work, office work, or attending lectures and studying) and sedentary leisure activities (e.g., spectator sports and television and movie viewing). As part of their program for healthy living, Eaton et al. suggest that modern people adopt a "stone age diet." They contend that among foragers

Dietary quality is generally excellent, providing a broad base of proteins and complex carbohydrates along with a rich supply of vitamins and nutrients. Dietary quantity is occasionally marginal or deficient, but this is true of most agricultural cultures as well—probably even more so. Maintenance of the forager diet is accomplished with a moderate work load, leaving ample time for the pursuit of leisure activities. (Eaton, Shostak, and Konner 1988: 28)

Table 3.3 compares the nutritional content of a late Paleolithic to that of a contemporary U.S. diet. The high level of meat consumption among foragers resulted or continues to result in a high cholesterol intake. According to Eaton et al. (1988: 86), the fact that contemporary foragers seem to "escape cardiovascular complications may be due to their different patterns of fat intake; they eat much less of it, and the fats they do eat— derived from wild game and vegetable foods—have a higher ratio of polyunsaturated to saturated fats." They obtain roughage, or dietary fiber,

Table 3.3
Late Paleolithic and Contemporary U.S. Dietary Compositions

	Late Paleolithic Diet	Contemporary Diet
Forms of Dietary Consumption		
Protein	33	12
Carbohydrate	46	46
Fat	21	42
Polyunsaturated:Saturated Ratio	1.41	0.44
Cholesterol (mg)	520	300–500
Fiber (gm)	100–150	19.7
Sodium (mg)	690	2,300–6,900
Calcium (mg)	1,500–2,000	740
Ascorbic Acid (mg)	440	90

Adapted from Eaton, Shostak, and Konner (1988:84).

from wild plant foods. Foragers drank water as their major and generally only beverage. By and large they began to consume alcohol only after contact with civilized societies. Indeed, alcohol served as an important vehicle used by European societies for conquering not only foragers but also indigenous populations in North America and the Pacific Islands.

Paleontological evidence indicates that prehistoric foragers exhibited strength, muscularity, and leanness on par with outstanding contemporary athletes. Both hunting and gathering demand great stamina. Men track, stalk, and pursue game; and women walk long distances with heavy loads of wild plants, wood, water, and young children. Although blood pressure and blood sugar levels tend to rise with age among contemporary North Americans, they remain low throughout life among foragers, even among those who live to an advanced age. Cholesterol levels typically are much lower among foragers, as well as among horticulturalists and pastoralists, than they are among people in industrial societies. The San of Southwest Africa who are still able to live some semblance of a traditional foraging lifestyle reportedly exhibit a low incidence of hypertension, heart disease, low cholesterol, obesity, varicose veins, and stress-related diseases such as ulcers and colitis (Lee 1979). The life expectancy of San adults exceeds that of adults in many industrial societies. Conversely, they are more vulnerable to infant mortality, malaria, and respiratory infections, as well as to accidents, because of the limited availability of biomedical facilities. In the case of the Inuit, McElroy and Townsend (1989: 28) report that while their diets are high in fat, they exhibit low cholesterol levels, low blood pressure, and low rates of heart disease.

Eaton et al. propose a "discordance hypothesis" as an explanation for many modern illnesses, especially the chronic "diseases of civilization" that account for about 75% of mortality in industrial societies. They contend that modern humans function with a "40,000-year-old model body" that is "essentially out of synch with our life-styles, an inevitable discordance ... between the world we live in today and the world our genes 'think' we live in still" (Eaton, Shostak, and Konner 1988: 43). Conversely, Eaton et al. fully recognize that foragers never lived in the Garden of Eden. They argue,

The late Paleolithic *was* a period when human existence was in accord with nature and when our life-styles and our biology were generally in harmony. . . . [It was also] a time when half of all children died before reaching adulthood, when posttraumatic disfigurement and disability were distressingly common, and when the comfort and basic security of life were orders of magnitude less than they are at present [at least for the majority of people in the middle and upper classes in industrial societies]. (Eaton, Shostak, and Konner 1988: 283)

Although some observers of foraging peoples have reported that they have seen few elderly people in their ranks, others have reported the presence of active, healthy elderly individuals. In contrast, whereas biomedicine has been able to prolong the length of life with medication, surgery, and expensive technology, it has been able to do little for the quality of life in the later years.

Given the paucity of foraging peoples in the world today, Eaton et al. argue that people in industrial societies could also draw insights from the lifestyles of pastoralists, rudimentary horticulturalists, and simple agriculturalists because these populations continue to resemble Paleolithic populations in fundamental ways. In reality, their program for healthy living in the hectic, modern world—or what many describe as the postindustrial, postmodern world with its emphasis on high-tech living and intensive consumption—is easier for affluent and professional people to follow than it is for working-class and, particularly, poor people. The latter generally are much less likely to have the financial resources, time, and educational opportunities that strict adherence to such a regimen dictates. Indeed, health itself has been transformed from a normal dimension of the human condition to yet another commodity. People with disposable incomes invest billions of dollars in diet programs, exercise machines, megavitamin tablets, and even holistic health care, or what in some cases may be termed yuppie medicine.

The program that Eaton et al. call for places the responsibility for good health upon the individual rather than the community or the larger society. While indeed certain foraging dietary practices, such as eating lots of fiber, may counteract the development of various forms of cancer, that program neglects the role that the heavy use of pesticides, preservatives, radioactive materials, various forms of pollution, and other social environmental factors play in the etiology of cancer. Furthermore, we must ask why so many people in modern societies, including physicians and nurses, engage in eating patterns and other forms of behavior, such as smoking, heavy drinking, and overeating, that they know unequivocally contribute to disease. It appears that many unhealthy behaviors constitute mechanisms for coping with modern problems—alienating work, unemployment or the fear of it, social isolation, lack of a sense of personal fulfillment, and the frantic pace of life in which time has become equated with money and in which full membership in a supportive community has been replaced by partial membership in diverse social groups and activities such as churches, hobbies, and self-help organizations.

Horticultural Village Societies

The semi-sedentary encampments of the Mesolithic and the more sedentary villages of the Neolithic provided new breeding places for domesticated animals that harbored infectious diseases (Armelagos and Dewey 1978). The Neolithic refers to an archeological period associated with the domestication of plants and animals. It first appeared in the hilly regions of the Fertile Crescent of the Near East about ten thousand years ago, but it developed either independently or as a result of diffusion in other parts of the Old World as well as the New World. The clearing of land for cultivation, the domestication of animals, and an increase in sedentary living provided ideal conditions for many of the helminthic and protozoal parasites.

Although domesticated animals act as scavengers that remove human waste and recycle garbage, Cohen argues that domestication of animals has probably contributed greatly to human exposure to infectious diseases:

Domestication forces human beings to deal at close range with animals throughout their life cycles and to encounter their body fluids and wastes, as well as their carcasses. Domestic dogs, as well as wild ones, can transmit rabies. In fact, they are the major source of human infection. Domestic cats may harbor toxoplasmosis. . . . Tetanus, one of the most dreaded diseases of recent history, is spread by domestic horses and to a lesser extent by cattle, dogs, and pigs. It can also spread to soil, but soil that has never been grazed or cultivated is generally free from bacteria. (Cohen 1989: 45–46)

In large part, greater susceptibility to disease in sedentary communities results from a higher population density and greater exposure to fecal contamination and household vermin. At any rate, research from Neolithic sites in both the Old and New worlds demonstrates a recurrent pattern of decreased stature, higher infant mortality, and increased physiological stresses associated with malnutrition.

The nutritional quality of food in horticultural village societies tends to be inferior to that of foraging societies. The major foods (e.g., manioc, cassava, sweet potatoes, yams, bananas, plantains, etc.) among slash-and-burn horticulturalists are high in bulk but low in nutrients. Although these starchy tropical crops are good sources of food energy, they are poor sources of protein. As a result, horticulturalists sometimes raise domesticated animals, such as pigs in the case of highland populations in Papua New Guinea. Most horticulturalists, however, lack domesticated animals and rely instead upon hunting or fishing for their supply of animal protein. They also tend to work harder than foragers. Slash-and-burn horticulturalists need considerable time and energy to clear land and plant, tend, and harvest their crops as well as hunt or raise domestic animals.

Agrarian State Societies

The foremost characteristic of state societies—ancient or modern—is a marked pattern of social stratification in which an elite or ruling class dominates economic, political, social, and cultural endeavors. While the ruling class in state societies has generally relied heavily upon ideological or hegemonic methods of social control in order to maintain its domination over subordinate social categories, its monopoly over agencies of coercive force (e.g., the military, the police, legal codes, courts, and prisons) serves to ensure its domination in the event that members or segments of the lower classes resist or revolt against their subjugation.

Because of differential access to resources, including land and food, peasants in agrarian state societies subsist in large part on a limited number of cultivated crops. These crops have historically been highly vulnerable to droughts, floods, and pests. The need for arable land and lumber for building houses, furniture, wagons, tools, and ships induced the inhabitants of agrarian state societies to engage in a large-scale clearing of forests and to develop a world view in which they came to regard nature as a force to be conquered and subdued. Increasing social stratification, resulting from the emergence of a small managerial class in archaic state societies, created the conditions that resulted in a more than adequate food supply for elites and serious and often chronic food shortages for poor urbanites, peasants, and slaves.

The dawn of agrarian states resulted in a significant transformation of societal-environmental relations. The emergence of social mechanisms for harnessing large amounts of energy from the environment produced the emergence of predatory ruling classes. As Hughes (1975: 29) observes, "The rise of civilizations depended upon the increasing ability of people to use and control their natural environment, and the downfall of these same civilizations was due to their failure to maintain a harmonious relationship with nature."

Population density played an even more crucial factor in human susceptibility to disease in agrarian state societies than it did in horticultural village societies. For example, Cohen (1989: 49) contends that measles, which may have come from a virus of dogs or cows, constitutes a "disease of civilization" in that its "origins must be related to the growth of the human population and its coalescence into dense aggregates or widespread and efficient networks." The appearance of the first cities in archaic state societies made access to clean water and the removal of human wastes problematic. Agriculture in many of these early states was based upon large-scale irrigation systems, which often created the conditions for vector-borne diseases such as malaria and schistosomiasis. Unequal access to food supplies contributed to the emergence of malnutrition and, as a consequence, greater susceptibility to disease among the economically exploited masses, particularly in urban areas.

In his classic *Plagues and Peoples,* historian William H. McNeill (1976) demonstrates that epidemics have played a major role in the expansion of agrarian states throughout history, especially in their incorporation of indigenous societies. He suggests that three major waves of disease in the past 2,000 years can be related to three major events of population movements: the formation of trade linkages by sea and land early in the Christian era, the militaristic expansion of the Mongols in the thirteenth century, and European expansion beginning in the fifteenth century. The depopulation of North and South American societies was a by-product of European colonization that introduced alien infections from the Old World. McNeill describes such imperialistic and mercantile processes as expressions of "macroparasitism." Whereas the term microparasites refers to disease organisms, such as viruses, bacteria, protozoa, and helminths, macroparasites are large organisms, including humans, that expropriate food and labor from conquered or low-status groups. Although macroparasitism as a sociocultural phenomenon emerged during the Neolithic period, P. Brown (1987: 160) maintains that it took on its most elaborate form in state societies where it became manifested in "terms of tribute, rent, sharecropping contracts, and other forms of 'asymmetrical economic exchange.'"

Although agriculture served to support an increased population, the rise of civilization also contributed to a net loss of dietary diversity and nutritional quality, particularly among peasants and economically marginal urbanites. As Cohen (1989: 69) notes, the "power of the elite not only affects the quality of food for the poor but may undermine their access to food, their very right to eat." At the very same time that elites came to enjoy sumptuous supplies of food imported from far-flung areas as well as seemingly unlimited luxuries, masses of people were denied fulfillment of their basic subsistence needs—a tragedy of the human condition that historically has contributed to a wide variety of diseases and premature death in the laboring classes. It is no wonder that Stanley Diamond (1974) has argued that ever since the emergence of civilization, humans have been in "search of the primitive"—that is, the ability to satisfy their basic needs for food, clothing, and shelter and a sense of community, all of which are crucial to the maintenance not only of "functional health" but also of "experiential health," a distinction made in chapter 2.

HEALTH AND THE ENVIRONMENT IN THE CONTEXT OF THE CAPITALIST WORLD SYSTEM

Agrarian states, with their patterns of social stratification and urbanization, set in motion an inherently unstable societal-environmental dynamic and the basis for massive malnutrition, susceptibility to infectious diseases, and social mortality resulting from large-scale and systematic warfare. The emergence of capitalism as a world economy—a global network of productive and market activities aimed at profit-making—around the fifteenth century planted the seeds for a global environmental crisis. The dangers of local ecological self-destruction that plagued archaic and feudal state societies became universal with the advent of capitalism.

In the nineteenth century, Karl Marx and Friedrich Engels in a wide array of works presented the most thorough and critical analysis of capitalism ever written. While they did not give a great deal of attention to ecological issues, they were certainly cognizant of the dialectical relationship between sociocultural systems and the natural environment. Colonialism as a mechanism for capitalist expansion in the Americans, Asia, and Africa disrupted traditional farming practices that had achieved some semblance of sustainable adjustment to local environmental conditions. The advent of the capitalist Industrial Revolution in England during the late eighteenth century resulted in increased water and air pollution and, as peasants were pushed off the land and migrated to emerging factory towns seeking work in horribly unsanitary and overcrowded slums. In *The Condition of the Working Class in England*, Engels ([1845] 1969) describes the devastating impact of industrialization on the natural environment. Furthermore, as Merchant (1992: 140) observes, "Marx gave numerous examples of capitalist pollution: chemical by-products from industrial production; iron filings from machine tool industry; flax, silk, wool, and cotton wastes in the clothing industry; rags and discarded clothing from consumers; and the contamination of London's River Thames with human waste."

Capitalist development projects in the Third World in the form of dam construction, land reclamation, road construction, and resettlement of populations have contributed to the spread of infectious diseases such as trypanosomiasis, malaria, and schistosomiasis. The rapid spread of schistosomiasis, which is acquired when larval parasites are released in water from snail vectors, is in large measure a direct consequence of water development projects such as the construction of high dams, artificial lakes and reservoirs, and irrigation canals. It has infected an estimated 200–300 million people worldwide (Inhorn and P. Brown 1990: 98).

As opposed to relatively minor environmental modifications wrought by indigenous societies, the capitalist world system, with its emphasis on ever-expanding production and a culture of intensified consumption, introduced completely new environmental contaminants that interfered with natural biochemical processes. Capitalism has historically assumed that natural resources—not only minerals but also air, water, fertile soil, and trees—exist in unlimited abundance. Moreover, industrial capitalism has expanded into a world system of unequal exchange between developed and underdeveloped countries, with significant implications for global ecological destruction.

Immanuel Wallerstein (1979), a comparative sociologist who incorporates ideas from history, anthropology, and political economy, argues that the capitalist world-system emerged in sixteenth-century Europe and now incorporates the entire globe. He maintains that capitalism "as a system for production for sale in a market for profit and appropriations of this profit on the basis of individual or collective ownership has only existed in, and can be said to require, a world-system in which the political units are not coextensive with the boundaries of the market economy (Wallerstein 1979: 66). Capitalism is an economic system of production and exchange that exploits technology, natural resources, and labor in the pursuit of profit making. Although the contemporary world system consists of some 185 nation-states and several thousand nations or ethnic groups, its economic division of labor consists of three units: (1) the core, (2) the semi-periphery, and (3) the periphery. The core includes very strong stable states characterized by a high degree of bureaucratization and large, technologically sophisticated militaries. It serves as the base for multi-national or transnational corporations owned and managed by a powerful and wealthy capitalist class or bourgeoisie that tends to dominate state policies. The core also has a large professional class, a large working class or proletariat, and a smaller semi-proletariat consisting of semi-skilled, menial workers and unemployed or underemployed people. The core is the site of the most technologically advanced, capital-intensive production and in recent decades has undergone a transformation from heavy industry to information technology. The periphery includes relatively weak, unstable states characterized by inefficient and oftentimes corrupt bureaucracies and unsophisticated and often repressive militaries. Its very small national bourgeoisies and professional classes tend to be closely linked with an international capitalist class. Peripheral countries have small proletariats and large semi-proletariats. The semi-periphery consists of relatively strong states with increasing bureaucratization and relatively technologically sophisticated militaries that are often dependent on core states for arms production. It has relatively small national bourgeoisies and a roughly even mixture of proletarian and semi-proletarian labor force. In keeping with a pattern of unequal exchange, the core exploits the semi-periphery and periphery whereas the periphery is exploited by both the core and the semi-periphery. The periphery and to a lesser degree the semi-periphery serve as sites of cheap raw materials and cheap labor for the core. The semi-periphery is situated in an intermediate status as being exploited by the core and exploiting the periphery.

Scholars disagree as to which countries fit into the three main divisions of the capitalist world-system. Shannon (1996: 87) differentiates between major core countries (e.g., the United States, Japan, Germany, France, and Britain) and minor core countries (e.g., Canada, Australia, Italy, the Switzerland, and the Scandinavian countries). Whereas some scholars classified the Soviet Union as a core country, others viewed it as a member of the semi-periphery. Furthermore, some scholars regard Canada, Australia, and New Zealand as semi-peripheral countries because of their economic subservience to various core countries, particularly the United States and Britain. Examples of semi-peripheral countries include Italy, Spain, Russia, Poland, Mexico, Brazil, Argentina, Saudi Arabia, Israel, Egypt, Indonesia, the Philippines, and South Korea. Examples of peripheral countries include Bolivia, Honduras, Haiti, Zaire, Tanzania, Ethiopia, Afghanistan, and Kampuchea. Whereas some scholars regard China as a semi-peripheral country, others regard it as a member of the periphery. At any rate, over time, countries may move up or down in the division of labor of the capitalist world-system. Over the course of the development of the capitalist world-system, the gap between the rich countries and poor countries has tended to widen. Watkins (1997), an Oxfam policy analyst, says that whereas in 1966, the richest fifth of the world's population earned an income 30 times greater than the poorest fifth, by 1997 the gap had increased to 78:1. As Cohen and Kennedy so aptly observe:

Indeed, a measure of income disparity may not even be the most salient. The significant differences between the global winners and global losers may turn on such basic issues as the provision of clean water, access to shelter and health care and the chances of surviving infanthood. (Cohen and Kennedy 2000: 151)

As Table 3.4 indicates, the capitalist world-system has a strong impact upon the health profiles of its various nation-states. Countries with high gross national products per capita tend to have low infant mortality rates and high life expectancies whereas countries with low gross national products per capita tend to have high infant mortality rates and low life expectancies. Certain post-revolutionary or socialist-oriented countries, such as China, situated in the periphery or semi-periphery exhibit a relatively healthy populace because of the commitments that they have made to eradicate malnutrition, improving sanitation, and providing both preventive and curative health services. Although Cuba remains a relatively poor country and has faced enormous economic difficulties following the collapse of the Soviet Union, it had an infant mortality rate of 7 per 1,000 live births and a life expectancy of 75.7 years in 1999 (United Nations Development Programme 1999)—health statistics that compare favorably with those of the United States, the leading and richest member of the core.

Although globalization has been a feature of the capitalist world-system since its inception, corporate and government policy makers throughout the globe have increasingly relied upon a political-economic perspective referred to as "neoliberalism" that essentially maintains that corporate profit making will result in a trickle-down improvement of socioeconomic and health conditions, with minimal state intervention, to address the health and social needs of the poor. The World Bank's neoliberal policy of "structural adjustment," however, has fostered privatization of social and health services that in turn has adversely affected the poor around the globe. The deleterious impact of neoliberalism upon the poor is documented in *Dying for Growth* (Kim, Millen, Irwin, and Gershman, eds. 2000), an ambitious and encyclopedic project emanating from the collaborative efforts of an interdisciplinary team, which includes several medical anthropologists, based at the Institute for Health and Social Justice in Cambridge, Massachusetts.

Private multinational corporations and state corporations in both capitalist and post-revolutionary or socialist-oriented societies have created not only a global factory but also a new global ecosystem characterized by extensive motor vehicle pollution, acid rain, toxic and radioactive waste, defoliation, and desertification. Anthropologist John Bodley (1996) contends that the environmental crises provoked by "industrial civilization" produces many social problems, including overpopulation, overconsumption, poverty, war, crime, and many personal crises, including a wide array of health problems. Indeed, some analysts, such as Andre Gorz, argue that capitalism is on the verge of self-destruction because of its emphasis on ever-expanding production:

Economic growth, which was supposed to ensure the affluence and well-being of everyone, has created needs more quickly than it could satisfy them, and has led to a series of dead ends which are not solely economic in character: capitalist growth is in crisis not only because it is capitalist but also because it is encountering physical limits. . . . It is a crisis in the character of work: a crisis in our

Table 3.4
A Profile of Health in the Capitalist World-System

	GNP per capita (US$)	Infant Mortality Rate (per 1,000 live births)	Life Expectancy at Birth (years)
Selected Countries			
Core			
Switzerland	43,060	5	78.6
Japan	38,160	4	80.0
Norway	36,100	6	79.0
Germany	28,280	5	77.2
United States	29,080	7	76.7
Australia	20,650	5	78.2
Canada	19,640	6	79.0
Semi-Periphery			
Spain	14,490	5	78.0
Saudi Arabia	7,150	24	71.4
Brazil	4,790	95	66.8
Mexico	3,700	29	72.2
South Africa	3,210	49	54.7
Turkey	3,180	40	69.0
Russian Federation	2,680	20	66.6
Periphery			
Indonesia	1,110	45	65.1
Bolivia	970	69	61.4
China	860	38	69.8
Nicaragua	410	42	67.9
Haiti	380	92	53.7
India	370	71	62.6
Bangladesh	360	81	58.1
Kenya	340	57	52.0
Nigeria	280	112	50.1
Ethiopia	110	111	43.3

Source: Human Development Report 1999. United Nations Development Programme.

relations with nature, with our bodies, with future generations, with history: a crisis of urban life, of habitat, of medical practice, of education, of science. (Gorz 1980: 11–12)

We refer to the approach we find most useful—in considering the complex interaction of political economy and environment, particularly under capitalism—as "political ecology." Conventional biocultural medical anthropology tends to downplay political and economic factors and thus fails to fully "consider the relation of people to their environment in all its complexity" (Turshen 1977: 48). We believe that, on the contrary, critical medical anthropology needs to treat political economy and political ecology as inseparable. As Howard L. Parsons has argued,

Economy is a matter of ecology: it has to do with the production and distribution of goods and services in the context of human society and nature. . . . [It recognizes that] under the ecological practices of monopoly capitalism, the natural environment is being destroyed along with the social environment. (Parsons 1977: xii)

Like critical medical anthropology, *political ecology* is committed to praxis—the merger of theory and social action. In other words, political ecology recognizes that humans not only can comprehend the complexities of their social reality but also ultimately must find a way to end those practices and patterns of social relation that exploit and oppress human populations, causing disease, malnutrition, and injury and destroying the fragile ecosystem of which they are a part. As Turshen (1977: 17) maintains, political ecology "gives central importance to human agency in the transformation of the complex, interacting web that characterizes the environment." As critical medical anthropologists, we seek to contribute to a larger interdisciplinary endeavor that can be termed the "political ecology of health" (Baer 1996; Singer 1998) and to collaborate with various biocultural anthropologists, who in their efforts to incorporate the political economy of health, seek to develop a "critical biocultural anthropology" (Goodman and Leatherman 1998; Singer 2001).

Scholars interested in the political economy/political ecology of health, among whose ranks critical medical anthropologists are increasingly represented, have considered a wide array of political-ecologically induced health problems, including malaria, occupational accidents, and cancer. The social production of black-lung disease among coal miners in eastern Kentucky is the focus of *Harlan County USA,* an excellent documentary film that Hans Baer has found very useful in his medical anthropology course at the University of Arkansas at Little Rock. Fortunately, the miners portrayed in the film became part of a larger black-lung movement that emerged in Southern Appalachia in the late 1960s. The national debate over health and safety conditions in U.S. coal mines, much worse than in countries such as Britain, Germany, and Australia where the labor movement historically has been much stronger, eventually pressured Congress to pass in December 1969 the Coal Mine Health and Safety Act, "which detailed to an unprecedented degree mandatory work practices throughout the industry and offered compensation to miners disabled by black lung and the widows of miners who died from the disease" (Smith 1981: 352).

In the following "Closer Looks," we examine two health problems. The first of these is malaria—a long-standing infectious disease that continues to be endemic in many Third World countries. The second is related to a relatively recent technological development—the motor vehicle—a form of transportation that continues to spread around the globe.

"A Closer Look"

MALARIA IN THE THIRD WORLD: A PERSISTING DISEASE OF POVERTY

Despite repeated campaigns to eradicate or control it, malaria continues to plague massive numbers of people in certain parts of the Third World. Of an estimated 200 million victims of this dreaded disease, some two million people die of it annually (McElroy and Townsend 1989: 84). In Africa alone, an estimated one million people, mostly children under six years of age, die from malaria each year (Mascie-Taylor 1993: 30). The most common form of malaria is transmitted by a protozoan parasite called *Plasmodium falciparum*, which lives in red blood cells and is transmitted from person to person by various species of mosquitoes. The symptoms of malaria include a fever, which sometimes recurs every second or third day, anemia, splenomegaly, headaches, and a wide array of other symptoms. The human host requires many years of repeated infections before he or she becomes more or less immune to the disease. Although malaria appears to be an ancient disease, the environmental conditions for its transmission are greatly enhanced when a human population clears the forest environment to the extent that pools of stagnant water are created.

Frank Livingstone (1958) conducted a now-classic study that demonstrated that malaria became endemic in sub-Saharan Africa about two thousand years ago when Bantu peoples entered the sub-Saharan tropic rain forest and introduced horticulture. The Bantu horticultural villages transformed the African ecology by creating sunlit, stagnant pools of water that allowed mosquitoes to breed. The introduction of horticulture and agriculture in other parts of the world, including South Asia, Southeast Asia, the Mediterranean area, and the Americas, also contributed to endemic outbreaks of malaria. *Falciparum* malaria probably was introduced to the Americas when slave ships transported mosquitoes that followed many of their passengers, most of whom were slated to work on plantations. Malaria is not confined to tropical and semitropical environments. Outbreaks of malaria also occurred in temperate areas, such as southern Canada and New England during the seventeenth century and the frontier of the Pacific Northwest during the nineteenth century.

Initially European colonialists often ignored the impact of malaria upon indigenous populations. Conversely, as indigenous peoples and peasants in conquered state societies were recruited for agricultural work on plantations, colonial powers and corporate-funded foundations came to implement extensive public health campaigns in order to ensure a productive labor force. The Rockefeller Foundation played a key role in malaria and hookworm control in both the U.S. South and China (E. R. Brown 1979). According to Cleaver (1977: 567), such campaigns to control malaria and other infectious diseases in China were part and parcel of an effort to stem peasant uprisings. Conversely, public protests often prompted corporate interests and states to undertake public health projects. Turshen (1989: 57) delineates four basic approaches that corporate interests, states, and, more recently, international health organizations such as the WHO have utilized in their efforts to eradicate or control malaria: (1) the use of drugs or chemotherapy to kill the disease in its human host; (2) the use of insecticides such as DDT to kill the parasite along with its insect vector; (3) the adoption of lifestyle changes such as the proper use of mosquito netting on beds; and (4) an environmental approach—one implemented prior to the invention of DDT—that "deprives the mosquito of its habitat by draining pools of stagnant water, by filling in ditches and open drains where water collects, and by draining or eliminating swamps and marshes." Although constituting a source of profits for the pharmaceutical industry, chemotherapy as a method of malaria control is of limited value because parasites quickly develop resistance to drugs. DDT, which was used in a global malaria campaign undertaken by the WHO and many Third World states beginning in the 1950s, had adverse effects on the environment, created other health problems, and also was counteracted by the development of resistant strains of mosquitoes.

Despite initial success, the international effort to eradicate malaria underwent a reversal in the 1970s, with new outbreaks of the disease occurring in places such as India, Pakistan, Afghanistan, Southeast Asia, Central America, and Haiti. The WHO identified several reasons for the resurgence of malaria, including the increasing resistance of mosquitoes and parasites to pesticides and drugs, the inadequate administration of eradication programs, insufficient medical research on malaria itself, a paucity of adequately trained public health personnel, limited supplies of pesticides and drugs, the lack of malaria-control strategies in hydraulic development projects, and poor health care facilities. Furthermore, the WHO recognized that the overall economic underdevelopment of Third World countries contributed to the eruption of a malaria epidemic.

Critical social scientists have offered a variety of explanations for the upsurge of malaria. Harry Cleaver (1977) maintains that various sectors of business and a number of national governments have allowed malaria to spread in order to counteract the protest efforts of workers who have challenged exploitative economic practices and political oppression. He asserts corporate interests and various governments tried to undercut wage struggles by creating international inflation through shortages, especially in energy and food. The austerity measures used to counteract inflation resulted in cutbacks in public health measures, including those for malaria eradication or control. In 1973 the government of the Philippines, under the notorious dictator Ferdinand Marcos, responded to the demands of Moslem rebels in Mindanao and the Sulu Archipelago by deciding to "stop malaria control spraying on at least one important island in order to help the sickness spread among the insurgent population" (Cleaver 1977: 576).

Chapin and Wassertrom (1981) maintain that the increase of malaria resulted from growth of agribusinesses on a global scale. They conclude that malaria tends to be resurgent or appear in epidemic proportions for the first time in areas where pesticide-intensive cash cropping has occurred. In her study of a long history of campaigns to eradicate or control malaria in the Sudan, a country with a high prevalence of malaria, anthropologist Ellen Gruenbaum (1983) argues the ongoing economic dependence of that poor country on export agriculture for foreign currency serves to trap it in a never-ceasing battle against this debilitating disease. At the global level, as Turshen (1989: 162) so aptly observes, a meaningful antimalarial campaign has to date "come into conflict with overriding political and economic considerations, namely the opposition of urban elites to rural improvements and of agribusinesses to any restraints, such as restrictions on the use of DDT, which would affect the profitable green revolution." Furthermore, pharmaceutical companies and insecticide-producing chemical companies have a heavy investment in conventional approaches to malarial control. Finally, effective malaria eradication requires the existence of adequate national health services, which Third World countries are not in a position to support as long as they are embedded as peripheral political-economic entities of the capitalist world system.

"A Closer Look"

MOTOR VEHICLES ARE DANGEROUS TO YOUR HEALTH

The motor vehicle, with its internal combustion engine, perhaps more than any other machine embodies the ecological contradictions of capitalism. However, as Sweezy notes (1973), the "political economy of the automobile" remains a relatively unexplored topic. The reality that North Americans love their cars is captured in James J. Flink's book *The Car*

Culture. He observes, "During the 1920s automobility became the back-
bone of a new consumer-goods-oriented society and economy that has
persisted into the present" (Flink 1973: 140). By this time, as Barnet and
Cavanaugh (1994: 262) so aptly note, "the car became a primary locus of
recreation, a badge of affluence, a power fantasy on wheels, a gleaming
sex symbol," all images that have been heavily promoted by the automobile industry through intensive advertising. Automobiles constitute
the second most expensive commodity (after homes) that Americans purchase. In 1990, Americans spent 31.3% of their incomes on housing and
18.1% of their income on motor vehicles (Freund and Martin 1993: 16). In
recent decades, automobile firms have been searching for new markets in
the Third World and, with the collapse of the Soviet bloc, in Eastern
Europe.

Motor vehicles have had major impacts upon not only patterns of consumption but also upon energy utilization, the environment, settlement
patterns, social relations, public policy, congestion, and last, but not least,
health. During the Cold War era of the 1950s and early 1960s, General
Motors urged patriotic U.S. citizens to "see the USA in your Chevrolet."
Such advertisements on the part of the automobile industry served to
seduce North Americans away from what was once a relatively well developed mass transportation system, that included passenger trains, numerous intercity bus lines, and extensive urban and interurban trolley
lines. Indeed, a consortium, called National City Lines, consisting of General Motors, Standard Oil of New Jersey, and the Firestone Tire and
Rubber Company, spent $9 million by 1950 to obtain control of street rail-
way companies in sixteen states and convert[ed] them to less efficient GM
buses. The companies were sold to operators who signed contracts specifying that they would buy GM equipment. . . . National City Lines in 1940
began buying up and scrapping parts of Pacific Electric, the world's largest interurban electric rail system, which by 1945 served 110 million passengers in fifty-six smog-free Southern California communities. Eleven
hundred miles of Pacific Electric's track were torn up, and the system went
out of service in 1961, as Southern California commuters came to rely
narrowly on freeways (Flink 1973: 220).

In describing the economic situation in U.S. society during the 1970s,
Sweezy (1973: 7) contended that the "private interests which cluster
around and are directly or indirectly dependent upon the automobile for
their prosperity are quantitatively far more numerous and wealthy than
those similarly related to any other commodity or complex of commodities in the U.S. economy." Automobile advertisements frequently have
promised and continue to promise their target populations that they will
achieve power, prestige, freedom, sexual desirability, and prowess if they
choose to become the proud owners of a highly individualized form
of transportation. In conjunction with automobile driving, Freund and

McGuire (1991: 60) note, "Many young males are socialized into taking lots of risks and into feeling or appearing invulnerable; media messages glorify speed and risk-taking."

Despite the messages conveyed by advertisements promoting its sale as well as by the mass media as a whole, the automobile is not merely a toy or an extension of the male genitalia but a highly lethal machine. Visitors to other countries, particularly Western Europe and Japan, have noted that "automobilization" (Sweezy 1973: 7) has become a global phenomenon. Along with industrial pollution, motor vehicles have transformed many cities around the world, particularly ones in the Third World such as Mexico City, into environmental disaster areas accompanied by a wide array of health problems. Of the estimated 4.4 million tons of human-generated pollutants emitted into the air of Mexico City in 1989, 76% were produced by motor vehicles (Freund and Martin 1993: 67). In contrast, of the 3.5 million tons of human-generated pollutants emitted into the air of Los Angeles—America's most polluted city—in 1985, 63% were created by motor vehicles. The rush-hour motor vehicle speeds have been reported to be 7 miles per hour in London, 12 miles per hour in Toyko, 17 miles per hour in Paris, and 33 miles per hour in Southern California (Freund and Martin 1993: 2). Indeed, Sweezy (1973: 4) compares auto congestion and pollution to the "outward symptoms of a disease with deep roots in the organs of the body." In other words, the automobile has become a major form of assault on the social and ecological body. Motor vehicles also are a major contributor to global warming (Alvord 2000: 70–71).

One of the major by-products of gasoline exhaust is benzoapyrene, a carcinogenic chemical that is suspended in urban air. Motor vehicles emit carbon monoxide, sulfur oxides, and nitrous oxides, which in turn contribute to acid rain and human respiratory complications. The American Lung Association estimated that in 1985 motor vehicle pollution contributed to some 120,000 deaths in the United States (Freund and Martin 1993: 29). Sixty percent of the residents of Calcutta, India, were found to have pollution-related respiratory problems (Freund and Martin 1993: 67).

In addition to their destructive impact on the environment, motor vehicles are a major source of accidents around the world. Freund and McGuire (1991) present the following sobering statistics on auto accidents in this country:

While the death rate due to auto accidents in the United States is by no means the highest among the industrialized countries, some 43,000 to 53,000 Americans die each year in such accidents, producing a death rate of over 26 deaths per 100,000 population. Worldwide, some 200,000 people died in traffic accidents in 1985. There are approximately 4 to 5 million injuries related to motor vehicles in the United States. Of these, 500,000 people require hospitalization. . . . Auto accidents are a leading cause of death for young people between the ages of five and twenty-four; young males between the ages of fourteen and twenty-four are at highest risk. Per passenger mile, cars are more dangerous than trains, buses, or planes. (Freund and McGuire 1991: 59)

Motor vehicles also pose hazards for pedestrians and cyclists. The National Safety Council reported some 6,600 pedestrian deaths and 800 cyclist deaths in 1989 in the United States (Freund and Martin 1993: 102).

Motor vehicle driving, particularly under congested conditions, also induces stress and heightened blood pressure, contributes to medical complications such as lumbar disk herniation, or motorist's spine, and contributes to sedentarization. Truck drivers in particular suffer a high rate of back injuries. Furthermore, auto transportation discourages patterns of sociability that are vital to mental health in that most motorists, especially in First World countries, drive alone. With the decline of public transportation, especially in the United States, mothers in particular function as chauffeurs for their children as they transport them hither and yon in sprawling suburban developments. Low-income people often find themselves without adequate transportation in cities where an increasing number of jobs are located in the suburbs.

Public awareness of some aspects of motor vehicle transportation reached new heights with the publication of Ralph Nader's (1965) book *Unsafe at Any Speed.* Although there have been efforts to reduce motor vehicle accidents with the installation of seat belts and other safety devices and, at least until 1995, a lowering of speed limits, such measures tend to focus on altering individual behavior. Furthermore, the automobile industry lobby has consistently resisted the passage of regulations to require air bags in cars. In reality, as Jacoby (1975: 141) observes, the victim of an automobile accident is a "victim of an obsolete transportation system kept alive by the necessities of profit." Unfortunately, a powerful lobby consisting of the automobile industry, petroleum companies, and trucking companies, poses a power barrier to the development of effective public transportations, especially in most American urban areas. Whereas heavy trucks contribute more than 95% of the highway deterioration in the United States, trucking firms pay only 29% of the country's highway bill (Freund and Martin 1993: 2).

It follows, following Freund and McGuire (1991: 60), that an ecological approach to addressing the health consequences of the automobilization of society requires "changing the social and physical environment (e.g., building safer highways), producing safer cars, and making many alternative ways of traveling available to drivers." Unfortunately, the sanctity of the automobile as an integral component of U.S. culture has virtually gone unchallenged. In contrast, the Green movement in Western Europe has mobilized as a counterhegemonic opposition to the automobilization of society by emphasizing the need for people to rely on other forms of transportation, including cycling. Environmentalists in Germany, for example, attempt to promote cycling as a form of transportation by sponsoring demonstrations consisting of bikers riding through otherwise busy city streets. Conversely, while cycling constitutes an "environmentally friendly" mode of transportation as well a healthy means to provide the body with aerobic exercise, it will remain a highly dangerous activity as long as the streets and highways are filled with fast-moving motor vehicles (increasingly occupied by distracted drivers busily cutting business deals or socializing on car telephones and thus endangering lives even further) and exhaust fumes.

ENVIRONMENTAL DEVASTATION IN POSTREVOLUTIONARY SOCIETIES

Critics of neo-Marxian theory often argue that while capitalism may indeed have had a devastating impact upon the environment, post-revolutionary or socialist-oriented societies have a dismal record of environmental destruction. Indeed, it is essential that critical medical anthropologists and other critical social scientists come to grips with the realities of environmental destruction in these societies. Some of the contributors to journals such as *Capitalism, Nature, and Socialism*; *Society and Nature: The International Journal of Political Ecology*; the *Journal of Political Ecology*; and *EcoSocialist Review* (sources unfortunately rarely cited in the medical anthropology literature) have attempted to grapple with these realities.

Post-revolutionary societies have had, by and large, a poor environmental record. The fast-paced drive for industrialization, in part rooted in the threat posed by the capitalist countries, contributed to serious environmental damage. The managerial objective of producing maximum output at minimum cost resulted in high levels of air, water, and soil pollution and a lack of safety precautions in industrial and nuclear power plants. Feshbach and Friendly (1992: 40) maintain that the "plan and its fulfillment became engines of destruction geared to consume, not conserve, the natural wealth and human strength of the Soviet Union." The Soviet Union exhibited the worst instances of radioactive contamination, the most spectacular being that of the Chernobyl nuclear plant, and Czechoslovakia and Poland had the highest levels of industrial pollution in Europe and perhaps in the world (Commoner 1990: 219–220).

According to Yih, such instances of environmental devastation are rooted in the conditions under which post-revolutionary societies developed:

relative underdevelopment, external aggression, and, especially for the small, dependent economies of the Third World, a disadvantaged position in the international market. The corresponding pressures to satisfy the material needs of the populations, ensure adequate military defense, and continue producing and exporting cash crops and raw materials for foreign exchange, have led to an emphasis by socialist policy-makers on the accumulation by the state, the uncritical adoption of many features of capitalist development, and a largely abysmal record vis-à-vis the environment (although there are exceptions, of course). (Yih 1990: 22)

Furthermore, the weak development of democratic institutions in postrevolutionary societies and bureaucratic suppression of information about the environmental impact of agricultural and industrial practices had until recently inhibited the emergence of an independent environmental movement (O'Connor 1989: 99). Although *glasnost* permitted the emergence of a small Green movement in the Soviet Union, the official policy of *perestroika,* with its emphasis on production, and the serious disruption of the Soviet economy in what proved to be its last days served as impediments to the implementation of environmental protection regulations. The ongoing emphasis on capitalist practices and penetration of foreign capital into the new Commonwealth of Independent States, which encompasses the territory of the former Soviet Union without the Baltic republics and Georgia, may continue to exacerbate environmental problems rather than to resolve them.

CHAPTER 4

Homelessness in the World System

When we look around the cities of the United States in the second millennium, homelessness appears to be a widespread and perhaps unchanging condition. However, in most cities, homelessness reemerged as part of the American experience only in the late 1970s and early 1980s (Dehavenon 1996). In fact, in New York City in 1975 the Governor's Task Force counted only thirty homeless families, whereas by the 1980s this figure had risen to 5,000. The number of families seeking emergency shelter did not begin to drop until the late 1990s and by 2001 homelessness had risen once again to the high levels of the 1980s. In the same period, estimates of the number of homeless individuals in New York City have varied from 35,000 to 100,000.

As many anthropologists have been recruited to conduct ethnographic research in coordination with medical projects concerned with mental illness, tuberculosis, HIV, and other health issues, homelessness and its construction have become controversial issues for medical anthropology. A fundamental question concerns the causes of homelessness. Frequently, there exists an underlying assumption that people may be homeless because of problems with mental health or learned behavior. In the course of their research, anthropologists and other social scientists have consistently found that homelessness is best explained in relation to housing and poverty rather than specific mental problems. Many health problems stem from deprivation or can be found among homeless people, but such problems are not confined to the homeless. In contrast to much media representation and many popular assumptions, mental illness and substance abuse do not define this population, nor do such issues alone account for homelessness.

To understand homelessness, we need to see how it has been created in different historical contexts and in different societies. A brief consideration of the word homeless already shows us some of the issues to be addressed. There are poor people without shelter all over the world. Mexico City, Rio de Janeiro, and many other major cities in Latin America are surrounded by shantytowns or informal settlements outside the formal municipal districts. *Favelas*, squatter communities, have been the subject of much anthropological research in Latin America since the 1960s. Many cities in Africa have been circled by growing squatter settlements for the past thirty years. In Durban, South Africa, hundreds of thousands of Africans moved into informal settlements surrounding the city after apartheid laws restricting the movements of Africans were repealed. None of these populations is usually referred to as homeless.

In the United States, the term homeless came into popular use in the late 1970s as a way to describe the growing numbers of poor people who were sleeping in the streets and public places. Later as many people temporarily found overnight shelter in churches, warehouses, and armories, municipalities began to count homeless populations. The 1990 census contained an institutional recognition of the new homeless population, and anthropologists were called upon to define and count street people for the national statistics. Homelessness has become a predictable aspect of life in American cities, and the fact that the phenomenon is qualitatively new and different from experiences of poverty in the 1950s, 1960s and 1970s has been quickly forgotten (Susser 1996).

In this chapter, we will briefly examine experiences of vagrancy and poverty and their treatment by governments during the emergence of capitalism in Europe and later in the United States. This will give us some background for understanding poverty today and putting homelessness in historical and geographical perspective.

Since Britain was the first country to develop industrial capitalism, we will start there in looking for the roots of modern poverty and homelessness. Vagrants and wandering poor people began streaming into London in the sixteenth and seventeenth centuries. As feudal lords, entering commercial wool production, found it more profitable to keep sheep on wide areas of land, Enclosure Laws were introduced to allow the displacement of serfs from their ancestral cottages and farm plots. As people flocked to towns looking for work and for new ways to survive in an emerging capitalist economy, they were separated from their hereditary ties with the rural villages of Britain.

As many people were freed from agricultural serfdom, the creation of wage labor was accompanied by a new form of insecurity in the form of unemployment. The British government had to introduce a way of coping with the poor, who had previously been tied to and supported by the land of feudal lords. Throughout the sixteenth century in Britain the number of beggars grew; the British government started first to register, license, and count beggars and later to punish and enslave those without licenses. Later, laws were passed that taxed local villages to provide funds to support the poor of their own districts (Piven and Cloward 1971).

In the nineteenth century, with the expansion of agriculture, the taking over of common lands, and the introduction of machinery, many more people found themselves out of work. The poor relief system was greatly expanded to address this issue. In the United States as well as in Britain, poorhouses were created, where people lived and were also forced to work for their living, as the government authorities saw fit. Clearly, under current usage, we would have called such people homeless. It was not until the twentieth century that methods of controlling the destitute through poorhouse residences and work requirements were abandoned and other forms of public assistance were implemented in most industrialized countries.

Based on this brief history, let us now return to consideration of the United States during the twentieth century. New institutions are usually initiated in times of crisis, and the Great Depression was one such period. After the financial crash of 1929, the population of the United States experienced unemployment rates through the 1930s of around 40%. New words became popular, such as hobos, for individuals who crossed the country looking for work, and Hoovervilles, for makeshift settlements set up by families evicted from their homes because unemployment had made it impossible to pay the rent or mortgage. These settlements around the country, like the one in Central Park in New York, were named after President Herbert Hoover, who in the depth of the Great Depression did not believe the government was responsible for solving the unemployment situation. As a consequence he lost the presidency to Franklin Delano Roosevelt.

Anthropologists and sociologists have published studies of the hobos, conceived of consistently as men. Surprisingly little attention was paid to the squatter settlements known as Hoovervilles, where women and children were also to be found. In 1934, President Roosevelt initiated the Social Security Act to provide the first federal public assistance program for widows and orphans: Aid to Dependent Children. No specific provision was outlined for homeless people, but public assistance did include a calculation of the cost of rent and housing. However, having a home was not made into a socially guaranteed right, which might have prevented future homelessness. It was not until the new homelessness of the 1980s that the constitutional right to shelter began to be established in some courts (Hopper and Cox 1982).

From the 1940s to the 1970s, high employment rates and the increasing employment of women combined with entitlement programs and Social Security to keep families in homes and most people from sleeping in the streets. Even Michael Harrington's (1965) famous study of *The Other America*, which reminded Americans that the poor existed, does not mention the word homelessness. Anthropologists studied the poor of Appalachia or the minority populations of the inner cities, but homeless people did not yet exist as a distinct cultural category.

Homelessness again emerged as a public issue in New York City at the end of the 1970s (Baxter and Hopper 1981). In 1975, New York City was declared bankrupt. In response, social services were cut, and tax benefits were allotted for real estate development (I. Susser 1982). Housing costs rose, and poor people began to lose their homes. By 1978, homelessness had begun to emerge as a visible phenomenon in New York City, as individuals sought shelter in railroad stations and other public spaces (Baxter and Hopper 1981). By 1982 homeless families were being housed in rundown hotels around the city (I. Susser 1989). Throughout the 1980s, federal services were reduced, real estate prices rose, and the departure of industry reduced available work; homelessness became a widespread phenomenon across the United States (Dehavenon 1996). Between 1985 and 1987 most cities in the United States reported annual increases of between 15% and 50% in their homeless populations (U.S. Conference of Mayors 1987).

From 1980 to the present, homelessness has been described by anthropologists and sociologists in a variety of settings (for a review see I. Susser 1996). For example, in *Checkerboard Square*, David Wagner (1993) describes in detail the lives of street people in a northern New England city in the 1980s. *Checkerboard Square* challenges stereotypes, in that the homeless population is found in a small New England town and in that most of the homeless people are white, although the homeless population resembles that of large U.S. cities in proportionate size, income, and joblessness.

In contrast to many studies that rely on interviews with individual homeless people, Wagner's is a community study. He describes the social interactions among the people he studies, their shared values and evaluation of U.S. society, and their efforts at collective action. Through the voices of the homeless he convinces us that many people have a clear and rational perception of deindustrialization and the shortage of work. On the basis of their own experiences, homeless people in North City have constructed a critical view of U.S. society. They do not accept explanations of their homelessness put forward by members of the wider society, which blame individuals for their problems without considering the changing economic context.

In the early 1980s, the Coalition for the Homeless was formed in New York City and fought through the courts for the legal right to shelter (Hopper and Cox 1982). New York City was required by law to provide housing for men, women, and families without shelter. Armories were opened up as temporary shelter for homeless men and women; families were housed in a variety of rundown hotels. Since that time, many legal battles have been fought over the lack of provisions for housing homeless people and an entire bureaucracy has been created to address the issue (Gounis 1992; I. Susser 1999).

However, the basic problem of the increasing gap between rich and poor and the difficulty for the poor to find homes or to retain their footing in working class neighborhoods remains (Sharff 1998). In the 1990s, people became homeless when the economy failed to provide work for the growing population of poor people. In 1996, after the welfare laws introduced in the 1930s were replaced by Temporary Assistance to Needy Families (TANF), which required welfare-recipients to find paid work, many people found themselves working in such low-paid jobs that they could not afford rent.

The U.S. media and much of the social science literature have focused on the individual problems of homeless people. Homeless people suffer from many health problems, including mental illness and substance abuse. Some researchers have suggested that the increase in homelessness was precipitated by the closing of state institutions for the mentally ill, which was mandated by the Kennedy administration in the late 1950s. However, large numbers of homeless people did not appear on the streets until twenty years later. Increasing homelessness corresponds directly to changes in the United States such as deindustrialization in the 1980s and globalization since the 1990s, which have resulted in the loss of jobs combined with a shift in public expenditure away from health care, social services and public housing. Reductions in the federal budget for social services, changes in real estate regulation and taxes, and the increasing cost of housing, rather than individual issues such as mental illness and substance abuse make people most vulnerable to homelessness in a worsening economic situation (Hopper, E. Susser, and Conover 1987, Dehavenon 1996, I. Susser 1996).

Since the 1980s, homelessness has become one aspect of life frequently experienced by poor working class people in the United States (I. Susser 2002). For example, it has been estimated that in the 1990s about 5% of New York City's poor population experience homelessness every year. People find themselves doubling up in apartments with relatives long before they end up in public shelters. Later they may pass through the shelter system before they can find an affordable apartment. Many people living in homeless shelters have children living in homes with friends and relatives. In addressing the health problems of the homeless, researchers have found that they must address the problems of access and continuity of care throughout the growing poor population of the United States.

HEALTH ISSUES AMONG U.S. HOMELESS POPULATIONS

While homeless people in the United States suffer from the same health problems as other Americans, the problems are magnified many times by lack of social support, lack of housing, poor nutrition, lack of economic support, and lack of access to medical services. Death rates and rates of disease are all higher among the homeless population, even in comparison to poor people with homes (Weintreb et al. 1998, Gelberg et al. 1997, Barrow et al. 1999).

In a study conducted in a homeless hotel in New York City in 1987, Ann Christiano and Ida Susser (1989) found thirty pregnant mothers. One of the major problems faced by these mothers was the lack of continuity of health care during their pregnancy. Some mothers avoided prenatal care because they feared that their children would be taken away from their supervision because they were homeless. And indeed, in New York City in the 1980s homelessness was one of the main reasons given as to why 50,000 children were in the foster care program. This program increased dramatically during the 1980s, soon after the figures on homeless families began to increase (Christiano and Susser 1989; Susser 1993).

Studies of the health of homeless adults and children find more health problems in general than among a poor population that has housing (Weintreb et al. 1998, Gelberg et al. 1997, Barrow et al. 1999). One study found that 50% of homeless children had immunization delays (Acker et al. 1987) and therefore were subject to infections such as measles from which other children are protected. Once an illness such as measles takes hold among poor children, it is more likely to spread among the homeless population because of the large number of delayed immunizations. Also, homeless children have more respiratory diseases, more ear infections, and more asthma than other poor children (Weintreb et al. 1998). They are many times more likely to suffer from anemia and malnutrition than children with homes. Chronic physical disorders were nearly twice as common among homeless children as among children in the general population (Wright and Weber 1987). In addition, homeless children suffer more emotional and developmental problems than other children, probably precipitated by the insecurity of their lives, the constant changes, and the stresses with which they and their parents have to cope.

Homeless adults as well suffer from an excess of most common illnesses and suffer age-adjusted mortality rates four times that of the general U.S. population (Barrow et al. 1999). They are particularly affected by respiratory illnesses, skin infections, and traumatic injury (including battering, accidents, and other forms of violence). Among adults, many of these problems are exacerbated by mental illness and substance abuse. Mental illness and substance abuse may in some cases have been precipitated by homelessness and joblessness and for other homeless people might be the immediate cause of their current situation. In either case, such problems are common health issues among the homeless population. On many occasions women and their children leave their homes and seek shelter to escape battering and other forms of violence, frequently from their partners (I. Susser 1998). However, as noted above, the causes of homelessness in general must be sought in the lack of available, affordable housing for people, whether or not they are mentally ill or addicted to drugs or alcohol. Historically, in the United States, low rent housing was available for such people. However, in the 1980s and 1990s societal changes and changes in federal funding priorities led to the loss of housing among the poorest groups in the population.

Two of the increasingly serious health problems confronted by the poor and homeless population in the United States of the 1990s were tuberculosis and HIV infection. The two conditions are directly related, as HIV infection undermines the immune system and leaves individuals particularly vulnerable to contracting tuberculosis. In the 1990s, it was estimated that one-half of those individuals with active tuberculosis in New York City were also HIV positive (Landesman 1993). Tuberculosis, which is spread through respiratory secretions, has historically been associated with poor housing conditions and poor nutrition. It should come as no surprise that the problem resurfaced among people deprived of homes and surviving on the margins of the U.S. economy. Crowded conditions, such as those found in shelters and prisons, provide excellent breeding grounds for the tuberculosis bacterium. Exacerbating this situation was the dramatic cutback in clinics and preventive services addressing the problem of tuberculosis in U.S. cities. Between 1960 and 1980 most of the preventive network of clinics and community services constructed over the previous sixty years to combat the tuberculosis epidemics of the nineteenth and early twentieth centuries were dismantled. As a result, between 1979 and 1986, the incidence of tuberculosis in New York City increased by 83%. Twenty to 30% of the people with tuberculosis were homeless (Lerner 1993). As tuberculosis resurfaced, cities had to attempt to rebuild lacerated community prevention networks. New York City implemented monitoring programs to make sure people took their medications. The implications in the media and some of the health literature was that the reason tuberculosis was spreading was that people, particularly poor people like the homeless population, were not taking their medications. This blaming of the victim ignored the systematic causes of the spread of tuberculosis in relation to poor housing conditions and the dismantling of the preventive public health system, which had in previous decades set up clinics in poor areas that provided free x-ray screenings, free medications, and ongoing treatment and evaluation for community residents.

HIV infection/acquired immunodeficiency syndrome (AIDS) is still increasing among poor and minority populations and also among those who have lost their homes. For poor homeless men and women, the sale of sexual services is one avenue through which to earn money. The need for money may also be exacerbated by addiction to substances such as crack cocaine. Among many people in the shelters, beset by violence and hopelessness, attention to the prevention of HIV infection may appear too distant a concern. Many may not envision themselves as living long enough to die of AIDS. Epidemiological research in the shelters of New York City suggests a high rate of HIV infection. Since people usually have sexual relations and share needles and drugs with people in their networks, this puts shelter residents at even higher risk.

Hospitals are required to find adequate housing for people with AIDS and are not supposed to return individuals with an AIDS diagnosis to the streets. However, ethnographers interviewed people in the shelters who were frequently readmitted to hospitals with AIDS complications and some who eventually died while still homeless. Others were in fact housed in special apartments, and some of these chose to return to be with their friends at the shelters (I. Susser and Gonzalez 1992). Just as Wagner documents for a New England town, homeless people in New York developed their own supportive communities around the shelter services, and many chose to return to these social centers after they found other housing.

Ironically, in some cities, shelters have become an opportunity to offer services to which poor people may not have previously had access. For example, public health nurses worked in some homeless hotels in New York City and contacted pregnant mothers to facilitate their access to prenatal care. In one hotel, they also printed a newsletter that discussed issues such as the prevention of HIV infection. Similarly, in other shelters where Ida Susser conducted research some forms of psychiatric evaluation services were offered. Programs such as the Women, Infants, and Children (WIC) program and day-care services were to be found in some shelters, as well as programs to address substance abuse and the search for housing (Christiano and Susser 1989; Susser 1993).

Anthropologists have been particularly involved in interdisciplinary collaboration in such programs as the development of HIV prevention programs in the shelters (Susser and Gonzalez 1992) and in evaluating interventions in community psychiatry. As in the approach to HIV, most anthropologists working with homeless populations have seen themselves both as researchers and as activists concerned with the improvement of conditions faced by the population they serve (M. Singer 1995).

A team approach involving anthropologists with psychiatrists, caseworkers, and epidemiologists proved extremely effective in implementing and evaluating an intervention for mentally ill homeless men in a shelter in New York City (E. Susser et al. 1993). The purpose of the intervention was to assist the homeless men in finding appropriate housing and to continue to maintain contact with and provide assistance to the men in accessing social services for nine months after they had relocated. The aim was to reconnect the men with social services in the community to which they relocated so that they would not be left without supports in the new setting. The men were divided into two groups of approximately one hundred men each. Those who were assigned housing with no follow-up intervention formed the controls. The experimental group received nine months of follow-up transitional services. Working with the research team, two anthropologists were given the task of tracking all the men, from both groups. They were required to meet with each man on a monthly basis to document his housing situation, whether he was taking his medication for mental illness, and other problems.

Working with mentally ill men as they left the shelter system was not easy. In order to be recruited for the study, the men had to have a diagnosis of schizophrenia, schizophrenic personality disorder, or manic depression. Many of the men were not communicative in general and were suspicious of health workers and questionnaires. Since they lived in an environment where illegal activities such as drug dealing took place, they were suspicious of people who were trying to track down lost individuals. Few people had access to telephones or addresses where they received mail. Mentally ill homeless men were often cut off from their families either by their choice or their family's choice. Frequently, calling a family member would not help in finding them. Men also circulated between mental health institutions, shelters, and prison; visiting them or accessing information from these institutions was extremely difficult. Bureaucracies often have strict regulations about not providing information about clients, which, while important for reasons of confidentiality, makes it difficult to keep in touch with people.

The anthropologists began the study by spending time with the men in the large armory where they originally found shelter. They spent several months sitting in the room provided for mentally ill homeless men to socialize and organize group-counseling sessions. They became familiar figures around the shelter and explained to many people that they were conducting an anthropological study of the shelter and the lives of mentally ill homeless men. As men began to be recruited to the study and assigned housing, the anthropologists followed them to their new locales. They visited the men on a monthly basis or arranged for the men to come back to the shelter and discuss their situation there. As the men already knew the anthropologists and had established informal relationships with them, such interviews were not usually regarded as onerous. As interviews were also paid for (at the rate of $15 per interview), the anthropologists encountered requests for unnecessary repeat interviews by men in need of cash.

Over the course of two years, the anthropologists established credibility and trust with mentally ill homeless men and their friends and relatives. In spite of shifting locations from the streets to various sectors of the shelter *unsystem*, institutionalization, and frequent disappearance of clients, the anthropologists were able to maintain a 95% follow-up rate over a period of two years. This was higher than the usually acceptable 80% follow-up rates common to research conducted among educated middle-income populations with permanent addresses and telephones (Conover, Jahiel, Stanley, and Susser 1997). This study clearly shows the significance of an anthropological approach, even in a quantitative epidemiological experimental study. Because of the financial and theoretical support for anthropology in this research, the anthropologists were able to gather important material for an ethnographic description of the lives of mentally ill homeless men, documenting the constantly shifting population as it moved from shelters to hospitals to prisons and back again. At the same time, the anthropological connections provided an excellent research setting for psychiatric epidemiologists.

In a related research project, anthropological researchers in a homeless shelter for men in New York City were involved in a project to assist in the prevention of HIV infection among mentally ill homeless men. They initiated the production of a video to be made by the homeless men themselves for the shelter. Planning this project and filming it in the shelter proved an important experience for the staff and the homeless men in education concerning HIV infection. In addition, the video provided material for anthropological analysis of the perceptions of homeless men concerning sexuality, drugs, and the residents and staff of the shelter (I. Susser and Gonzalez 1992). The video demonstrated the close connections in the lives of the staff and the homeless men, their experiences with drugs and AIDS, and the conflicts between the two groups around these issues. In addition, it documented a problematic perception of women as evil and as purveyors of disease, a further example of arguments which "blame the victim" rather than comprehend the overall situation. In general, the making of the video provided a forum for homeless men to work out conflicts and attitudes concerning sexual orientation, HIV infection, and other issues and to construct ways of addressing one another with respect to AIDS prevention.

HOMELESSNESS IN THIRD WORLD CITIES

In some ways homelessness or informal settlements, squatter settlements, and poor people without shelter in the poorer countries of the world derive from processes akin to those experienced by the wandering poor of early industrial Europe. In other ways, the experiences are very different.

Over the past thirty years, population increases have combined with the development of agribusiness in many poor rural areas to create a population of unemployed wage laborers who are forced to move to the cities in search of work. The development of expensive agricultural technology combined with international corporate investment in agriculture has made it increasingly difficult for small peasants to retain their land. As a result there has been a loss of landholdings among the poorer peasantry and a consolidation of income among corporate investors and peasants with large enough landholdings to withstand the large debts accumulated in bad harvest years. The increasing inequality found in many rural areas has contributed to the creation of a population of landless laborers. In contrast to peasants who own their own land and may scrape a living from the sale of produce, such people have lost their land and have to work for wages like industrial workers. However, accompanying increasing agricultural technology has been the reduced need for rural wage laborers. This in turn has precipitated the waves of poverty-stricken populations that have flooded Third World cities since the 1960s and continue to flow into unserviced areas of major municipalities.

Informal settlements lack major public health foundations. They lack sewage facilities and electricity. They often lack paved roads and transportation as well as running water and drinking water. In addition, they are not easily covered by regulations and make the registration of births and deaths or the tracking of health problems virtually impossible. Even when residents of informal settlements find work and pay taxes, their needs are often ignored in the spending of municipal funds.

Because of the frequent lack of running water and sewage facilities, informal settlements are at risk for cholera and other infectious diseases. In addition, because of the lack of industrial and environmental regulation, informal settlements have been the sites of the some of the world's most tragic industrial disasters in recent history. In Bhopal in 1984, most of the people who died when poisonous gas escaped from the Union Carbide plant that manufactured fertilizers for Indian agriculture were living in an informal settlement between the plant and the city limits. Although regulations stated that the plant could not operate near the resident population, the thousands of people housed in the informal settlements on the outskirts of the city had not been considered by the plant managers or the city government in evaluating safety concerns for the continued operation of the plant.

"A Closer Look"

POLITICAL CHANGE AND HEALTH IN
SOUTH AFRICA

In informal settlements in both poor and wealthy countries, public health measures such as immunizations and medical care follow-up are difficult to implement. For example, in 1992, the clinic that served Alexandra township in Johannesburg, South Africa, introduced a program where a van drove mothers and their newborn babies home after childbirth. In a township without street addresses and where people often had to build their housing from cardboard and scrap metal, the clinic devised this method to help keep in contact with mothers and newborn babies. The reduction of infant mortality depends partly on follow-up care and well-baby visits, which could not easily be implemented in the shifting situations of South African shantytowns.

One approach to public health education in an informal settlement on the outskirts of Durban in Natal, South Africa, was implemented by health researchers and anthropologists concerned with the prevention of HIV infection. In a shifting population with no fixed addresses, where political violence made it difficult for outside health workers to visit or for people to stay in one place, Ida Susser worked with a group of researchers who found that the most effective way to reach the population was through already-structured routes of political mobilization (Preston-Whyte et al. 1995). In a situation where telephones did not exist and shacks were reached by narrow, winding, uphill mud paths, the researchers had to rely on people familiar with the community to contact the residents. The public health situation was made particularly difficult by the fact that this area of Natal was the center of the Kingdom of Kwazulu, where political officials supporting the Zulu king were in competition for power with the African National Congress (ANC), which was not associated with a particular ethnic group. In one part of the settlement that Ida Susser visited in 1992, there were eleven political funerals in one week. For this reason, many people moved quickly from place to place, to escape political reprisals and murder. Shacks were frequently burned down as residents were suspected of being members of opposing political factions. It was virtually impossible for an outside health worker to maintain direct contact with large numbers of people.

In 1992 the researchers met with the local representatives of the ANC, who organized regular meetings in the informal settlements. At that time, the ANC was still struggling for political power in South Africa, and Africans had not yet been permitted to vote. An important woman leader, Dr. Nkosazane Zuma, had mobilized a grassroots women's marketing cooperative in the informal settlement. Through her introductions the HIV prevention team was able to attend meetings and recruit a local community health worker. This local woman, an active and respected leader in her own right, learned about the threat of HIV infection, safe sex, condoms, and female condoms. Using a bullhorn and arranging for space in the back of a local store, she organized meetings where women could learn about HIV infection and discuss methods of prevention.

Three years later, when Ida Susser and the anthropologist Eleanor

Preston-Whyte returned to the informal settlement, they found many women informed about HIV and asking to be trained as community health workers. By that time, the ANC, with Nelson Mandela as its leader, had been elected to form a transitional government in South Africa. One of the researchers from the study, Dr. Nkosazana Zuma later became Minister of Health for South Africa. The ANC had built a large, well-designed meeting hall in the center of the informal settlement. In 1995, meetings were still called together by bullhorn, but the government had paved the mud paths and the meetings were held in the new hall. At the meetings in 1995, local women were demanding housing and employment. They also demanded free distribution of the female condom, which they themselves had decided would be the most effective HIV prevention method for their community. Indeed, partially as a consequence of the previous community work, the national AIDS director, Quarraisha Abdool Karim, who had also been a researcher on the study just described, had ordered female condoms to be distributed free among poor women in South Africa.

One of the most important findings from this anthropological study of HIV prevention in an informal settlement was that it was possible to implement public health education and keep in contact with people over time in a politically violent and shifting community. In spite of the lack of permanent addresses, telephones, and roads, people in the local population were well able to use their own forms of political mobilization to implement health measures when they understood their importance to their own survival. It is also significant that three years later, women's access to information and ability to mobilize around health issues had increased. Public health awareness had increased, despite the fact that the health team had not visited the site in the intervening period, political violence continued intermittently, the population was still shifting, and people still had no permanent housing.

By 2000, the new South African government had built new housing and provided adequate sanitation, community clinics and clean water in the Durban neighborhoods described above. In this case we can see clearly the basic political issues underlying health. With the improvements in democracy in the new South Africa, the potential for a poor population to be healthier also increased.

Public health research demonstrates that the greatest predictor of poor health indicators in any country is the degree of income inequality documented for that country. Absolute poverty is not as accurate an indicator of poor health statistics as inequality. Thus, we can see why homelessness in the United States leads to high levels of mortality, although the per capita income and GNP figures in the United States might lead us to expect better results. Increasing income inequality in the United States has been accompanied by the abandonment of public health standards for immunization, adequate nutrition, and access to health care for the poor and uninsured. Similarly, in poor countries with a small population of increasing wealth and a large population living in worsening poverty—many without adequate housing—we find the breakdown of basic measures of public health and the resurgence of the threat of epidemics of cholera and other more terrifying diseases and high rates of infant mortality and shortened life expectancies.

CONCLUSIONS

Social science research has made important contributions to understanding the lives of the poor and homeless in many parts of the world. From both a theoretical and a practical perspective, critical medical anthropology, which as we have seen takes into account the political and economic circumstances of health and disease, is essential to a clear understanding and documentation of the needs and voices of the majority of the world's population. In addition, in the face of the continuing and increasing inequality we currently confront, the significance of fieldwork to reach the people who do not have direct access to public institutions and an activist approach to this fieldwork, which may assist in addressing their needs, becomes more central all the time.

CHAPTER 5

Legal Addictions, Part I: Demon in a Bottle

INTRODUCTION TO THE SOCIAL SCIENCE OF ADDICTIVE BEHAVIORS

Drinking alcoholic beverages and smoking cigarettes are behaviors that we see everyday. Until the health campaigns of recent years, these behaviors had become so commonplace that they were hardly noticeable. Like swinging our arms when we walk, they seemed to be a natural part of life. Indeed, through a nonstop barrage of TV, radio, billboard, magazine, newspaper, and other advertisements, as well as their frequent presence in movies, drinking and smoking came to be seen as part of the good life, symbols of personal success and achievement. As a result, many adults became smokers and drinkers and, in turn, directly or indirectly (by setting an example) taught these behaviors to their children.

But the health consequences were great. Drinking and smoking came to be major causes of *morbidity* (i.e., disease) and *mortality* (i.e., death) in the United States *and globally*. At this point, drinking and smoking emerged as social problems of concern to health social sciences like medical sociology and medical anthropology. Eventually, some people began to point out that, although legal, alcohol and tobacco should be classified as drugs. Others have difficulty lumping cigarettes and alcohol with cocaine and heroin, because the first two are legal to possess and use and the latter two are illegal. Also, cocaine and heroin commonly are seen as being especially dangerous and a threat to society. As Matveychuk (1986: 8) notes,

if I were to say that I used drugs this afternoon, most people would be either disappointed or amused to find that what I meant is that I drank a glass of beer, smoked a cigarette, and took two aspirin. Though alcohol, nicotine, and aspirin are all psychoactive, they do not fit our stereotype of what a drug is.

But stereotypes are *cultural constructions*. In fact, there is no agreed-upon scientific definition of the word *drug*. Some illegal drugs, like heroin, are addictive (i.e., the body builds up a physical dependence on them and suffers withdrawal symptoms upon discontinuance of their use) and others, like LSD and marijuana, are not. The same can be said of legal drugs. Nicotine (in cigarettes) and caffeine (in coffee) are *quite* addictive. Some illegal drugs, such as cocaine, stimulate the central nervous system, while others depress it. This is also true of legal drugs. Amphetamines are stimulants, and *barbiturates* and alcohol are depressants. In the end, it appears that what drugs have in common is their classification by society. Yet as Matveychuk argues:

That the only commonality among drugs is their label implies that the category "drugs" is an arbitrary definition, a linguistic category that changes overtime. Yet this is not to suggest that this linguistic category of drugs naturally emanates from the voice of the people. We do not equally share in the task of making social definitions . . . What becomes truth and gets accepted as reality benefits some individuals and social groups more than others. (Matveychuk 1986: 9)

In other words, to understand why a particular substance is classified as an illicit drug or a legal commodity, it is important to understand the political and economic interests of groups and the power they are able to exert in society relative to the substance in question.

On the one hand, it is not surprising to find that the alcohol and tobacco industries, groups that have considerable economic and political power, strongly oppose classifying the substances they manufacture as drugs; indeed, they often deny that these substances are harmful for humans to consume. The tobacco industry, for example, has spent millions of dollars trying to counter scientific evidence that links tobacco use to cancer. It would not be surprising, on the other hand, to find that producers of illicit drugs, like marijuana, would oppose their legalization, as this would increase competition by attracting tobacco and other companies to become producers.

Some health researchers, especially those involved in trying to understand the etiology (or development) of addiction have drawn the conclusion that "addiction is a brain disease that develops over time as a result of the initially voluntary behavior" of substance use (Leshner 2001). From this perspective, using psychoactive substances for a (yet to be determined) period of time changes the physical structure of the brain and the functioning therein in fundamental and long-lasting ways that appear to persist even after the individual stops using the substance(s). Argues

Alan Leshner (2001: 75), a former head of the U.S. National Institute on Drug Abuse, "Addiction comes about through an array of neuroadaptive changes and the laying down and strengthening of new memory connections in various circuits in the brain." This reordering of brain anatomy and biochemistry, which is believed to involve an array of cellular and molecular changes, produces an uncontrollable compulsion or craving to acquire and use drugs. It is this intense craving—rooted in the brain's acquired need for the substance(s) that created its new composition—that is the essence of addiction. From this *disease theory of addiction,* compulsive substance use is not a moral failing nor a lack of willpower, it is a consequence of observable (using brain imaging techniques like magnetic resonance spectroscopy) alteration of the brain (e.g., changes in brain chemistry and neuron structure and functioning) that is produced by repeated exposures to powerful, quite literally mind-altering, substances like alcohol, heroin, cocaine, or methamphetamine. Neuroscientists involved in brain studies of addiction generally do not deny the importance of social factors in creating the life conditions that lead some individuals and not others to begin using psychoactive substances, to continue using them steadily over time, and to using them at such regular and high dosages as to produce (unintentionally from the standpoint of the user) the types of brain alteration that transform voluntary use into an overwhelming, biologically driven compulsion. Thus, while "addiction as a brain disease" adherents have concentrated their efforts on understanding the ways brains change as a consequence of prolonged exposure to certain substances, they view addiction as "the quintessential biobehavioral disorder" (Leshner 2001: 76). However, while recognizing that social factors play a role in the development of addiction, they do not tend often to explore the actual interplay between biology and social experience and conditions that underlies obsessive desire. More importantly, they do not fully factor in the issues of social inequality, oppression, and drug dealer profit seeking as key social mechanisms driving the initiation and continuation of substance use for many people. It is precisely this broader, politically and economically informed integration of biological and sociocultural factors that critical medical anthropology seeks to bring to the study of substance abuse research.

In chapter 1, we pointed out that substance abuse is one of a number of health conditions that has been medicalized, meaning it has been defined by society as a disease that requires biomedical treatment. To the degree that the medicalization of substance abuse moves it from the realm of moral blame punishment into the arena of treatment, this may have beneficial outcomes for sufferers. In fact, of course, such movement has never fully occurred and substance users are incarcerated in staggering numbers. Even people who voluntarily enter into drug and alcohol treatment never escape a strong sense of social condemnation and devaluation.

Recognizing that there is a biological component in chemical dependence, is not, as has been stressed, a denial that there is an enormously important social component as well. Consequently, addressing this health and social problem cannot be achieved through narrow medical interventions. This point is most clearly made by looking at what happens to people when they complete alcohol and drug treatment. Most, especially those treated in under-funded publicly supported programs and prison-based interventions, return to social relationships and to social environments that contribute to their relapse into abusive consumption of psychoactive substances and to other behaviors and situations that put them at high risk.

In light of this discussion, in this chapter, we look specifically at alcohol use from the perspective of critical medical anthropology. As indicated in previous chapters, that means we are concerned especially with the health and social consequences of alcohol production and use in terms of class, racial, gender, or other unequal relationships in society. It is our sense, as we will show in the following pages, that these relationships of inequality strongly influence the use of alcohol, both in the United States and elsewhere in the world. Further, because alcohol use can cause significant health problems, more so than many illicit substances, there is a direct connection between inequality and alcohol-related health issues. The ultimate goal of the chapter is to pull together developments in neuroscience, anthropological and related studies of human use of alcohol in social context, and macro-structural social analysis, to lay out a *critical biocultural and political economic model of alcohol use and abuse.*

This chapter is directly tied to the one that follows on the use of tobacco. The unevenness in the size of these two chapters reflects the considerably greater attention medical anthropologists have given to drinking behavior compared to smoking behavior. The point of both chapters, however, is that alcohol and tobacco use, the most commonly used nonmedical legal drugs in U.S. society and beyond, can be understood only in historic context in terms of both sociocultural dynamics (people's culturally constructed beliefs, values, and social patterns) and of special importance to this volume, wider political and economic factors (including relations of inequality between individuals, groups, or nations and the economic interests of dominant individuals, groups, and nations).

DRINKING, DRUNKENNESS, AND DISEASE: AN OVERVIEW

Alcohol is the most widely used *psychoactive* (mind-affecting) drug in the world. Moreover, it is probably the drug with the longest history of use by humans. Fermentation is a relatively simple and quite natural process that occurs fairly quickly in many fruits, vegetables, and grains with adequate concentrations of sugar. Additionally, alcohol is undoubtedly the most versatile drug available, serving at various times and places as a food (providing two hundred calories per ounce, although no vitamins, minerals, or other nutrients), medicine (e.g., for symptomatic relief of pain and insomnia), aphrodisiac, energizer, liquid refreshment, payment for labor, and narcotic. Human use of alcohol is probably as old as agriculture itself; even prior to the rise of Europe as a global world power, alcohol had spread to or had been independently discovered in most parts of the world (except in much of indigenous North America and in Oceania). Some historic researchers have suggested that the oldest intentionally pro-duced alcoholic beverages, dating to 6,000 years ago, were made from the fruit of the date palms of the eastern Mediterranean and Mesopotamia areas. Dates and the sap of date palms have one of the most concentrated levels of naturally occurring sugar, a substance that is needed in adequate levels for fermentation to occur. Beer use is documented from as early as 5,000 years ago in early Sumerian and Akkadia texts and alcohol produc-tion is depicted in Egyptian murals from the Predynastic period.

In all societies in which it is consumed, alcohol is invested with special cultural meanings and emotions, although sometimes, as in the case of the United States, ambiguous and conflicted ones. It is probably not a coincidence that according to the Random House dictionary the word drunk has more synonyms than any other word in the English language; indeed most students are capable of reciting quite a list of such terms. Societal understandings of alcohol are culturally conditioned. Thus, wine is not just a certain type of alcohol made from fruit. The Eucharist wine, the very expensive bottle of imported French wine, and the cheap bottle of rotgut passed around a group of huddled men on skid row may be quite similar chemically but mean very different things culturally. Simi-larly, in Islam drinking alcohol is sacrilegious while in Catholicism it can be a sacramental act. Even within a single religion like Christianity, atti-tudes vary. As anthropologist Genevieve Ames, who has spent much of her career as an alcohol researcher, (1985: 439–40) indicates,

Although the American branches of some large church groups of Europe, such as the Lutherans and Episcopalians, have not opposed moderate drinking, other re-ligious groups, such as Baptists, Methodists, Presbyterians, Congregationalists, and members of small and fundamentalist groups, have a history of strongly op-posing alcohol use and drunkenness as sinful.

That alcohol can be dangerous "has been widely described for as long as we have written records, and elaborate sets of legal, religious, and other norms have been developed to regulate who drinks how much of what, where, and when, in the company of whom, and with what outcomes" (Heath 1990: 265). Alcohol, wherever and in whatever form it is con-sumed, has been subject to cultural rules and regulations that do not apply to other kinds of consumable liquids.

The liver is the body organ most significantly damaged by extensive alcohol consumption. Because the liver oxidizes alcohol and helps eliminate it from the body, it remains longer in contact with ingested alcohol than other body organs. The increased activity in the liver needed to breakdown alcohol causes cell death and hardening of the tissue producing the disease called liver cirrhosis. Cirrhosis is one of the most common diseases associated with alcohol consumption and by 1997 had become the tenth leading cause of death in the United States, accounting for around 25,000 deaths annually, more than half of which were from alcohol-related cirrhosis. Examining the historic rise and fall of cirrhosis rates in the U.S. is instructive. Since national cirrhosis mortality data were first recorded in 1910, the mortality rate due to this disease was highest in 1911 (17 deaths per 100,000 population); the rate then declined steadily to 8 deaths per 100,000 population by 1932. With the repeal of Prohibition in 1933, which had banned alcohol consumption, cirrhosis mortality began a generally steady rise to 14.9 deaths per 100,000 population in 1973, followed by a somewhat steady decrease to 7.4 deaths per 100,000 population by 1997.

Despite this decline, changes have not been uniform and the ethnic distribution of cirrhosis warrants attention. For example, during the 1970s, U.S. researchers observed sharply increased cirrhosis rates among Black men and it was long assumed that this population had the highest rates of cirrhosis and cirrhosis-related deaths. However, in 1989, the U.S. Standard Certificate of Death was revised to include people of Hispanic origin as an ethnic category, which allowed for the study of combed racial/ethnic subgroups, such as white Hispanic, white non-Hispanic, black Hispanic, and black non-Hispanic. As a result of this inclusion, it was soon discovered that while rates of cirrhosis death were in fact high among Black non-Hispanic men and women, they were much higher among white Hispanic men and women. Various factors might account for increased risk for liver cirrhosis among white Hispanic males, including subgroup drinking patterns. It is known that some Hispanic groups, especially those of Mexican and Central American origin, have a drinking style characterized by the periodic consumption of large amounts of alcohol. Other possible factors include socioeconomic status and its component dimensions of income, occupation, and poverty status, all of which directly affect access to medical services, including alcohol treatment. Similarly language and cultural differences with the mainstream population limit access to treatment among Hispanics. What is noteworthy, however, is that until Hispanic was included on death certificates, the very high rate of cirrhosis deaths among Hispanics was not known. Despite this discovery, alcohol-related intervention efforts targeted to Hispanics still do not reflect the fact that they are at greatest risk among ethnic/racial groups in the United States for dying of cirrhosis.

The development of alcohol-related cirrhosis is a complex biological process. When the human liver is exposed continually to alcohol, the body adjusts by increasing the production of the enzymes alcohol dehydrogenase and aldehyde dehydrogenase responsible for breaking down alcohol and allowing it to be metabolized. As a result of this change, the body becomes more efficient at eliminating high levels of alcohol in the blood. The major drawback of this improvement in body efficiency is that it means a person must drink more alcohol to experience the same effects as before (including feeling high, getting drunk, or passing out in a drunk stupor, all of which are effects desired by some heavy drinkers), which commonly leads to more drinking and contributes ultimately to dependence and addiction in some people. Moreover, within the brain, there occurs a marked increase in the pace of normal chemical and electrical functions of nerve cells in order to compensate for the inhibitory effects of constant exposure to alcohol. While this heightened nerve activity helps people to function while under the influence of alcohol, adaptation to increased nerve activity makes heavy drinkers cranky when they are not drinking. Habituation to increased nerve activity also may have the effect of causing abusive drinkers to crave alcohol. Additionally, the increased nerve activity contributes to hallucinations and convulsions (as seen in delirium tremens) when blood alcohol levels drop, making it difficult to recover from alcohol abuse and dependence. If alcohol abuse continues, cells in various brain centers die, reducing the total brain mass. Other health problems and diseases associated with abusive alcohol consumption include:

- Stomach and intestinal ulcers can develop because constant alcohol use irritates and degrades the linings of these organs.
- Blood pressure goes up as the heart compensates for a reduction in blood pressure caused by alcohol, resulting in an increase in heart problems and strokes.
- Male reproductive cell (i.e., sperm) production goes down because of decreased sex-hormone secretion from the hypothalamus/pituitary.
- Poor nutrition associated with regular inebriation decreases levels of iron and vitamin B leading to anemia.
- Driving while under the influence of alcohol is a major cause of traffic accidents, injuries and fatality. Alcohol impaired driving affects one in three Americans during their lifetime. During 2000, almost 17,000 people in the U.S. died in alcohol-related motor vehicle crashes, representing 40% of all traffic-related deaths
- Because alcoholics lose balance and fall more often, they suffer regularly from bruises and broken bones, especially true as they get older.
- Other significant diseases associated with alcohol use are fetal alcohol syndrome, bone disease, weakening of the immune system and cancers of the mouth, tongue, esophagus, and larynx.

Finally, alcohol abuse and dependence commonly lead to emotional and social problems. As a result of the effects of alcohol on emotional centers in the limbic system, alcoholics often are anxious, depressed and even suicidal. These emotional states frequently contribute to marital and family problems, including domestic violence, as well as work-related problems, such as excessive absences and poor or even risky performance. Overall, the National Institute on Alcohol Abuse and Alcoholism estimates a $185 billion annual economic cost to the U.S. associated with alcohol misuse comprised of lost work productivity and medical, legal, and property damage. In terms of human lives and suffering, the actual cost is far greater.

Despite the considerable array of health and social problems associated with abusive drinking, it is well known that, "most people throughout the world who drink do so without suffering any deleterious consequences" (Heath 1991: 364).

Indisputably, alcohol is an unusual substance that has played a significant role in human history and in contemporary societies around the globe. Understanding its role in social groups is of considerable importance, although, as will be emphasized below, this has not always been clear within the field of anthropology, even though anthropologists have been describing drinking behavior in different societies for many decades.

Drinking among Youth

It has been estimated that there are over three hundred thousand adolescent alcoholics in the United States. Problem drinking in the adolescent population clearly is widespread. As Estrada et al. (1982: 348) note, "Alcohol abuse may be reaching epidemic proportions across all segments of the nation's youth." The American psyche is wracked increasingly by the fear that adolescent drinking and illicit drug use, be it in the ghetto, the barrio, the suburbs, or the small town, is overwhelming and out of control.

National studies have found that the onset of drinking among many U.S. adolescents occurs prior to high school and that the percentage of drinkers grows with age. By high school graduation, the majority of adolescents have tried alcohol, and many not only drink frequently but also have already experienced at least short-term negative consequences of that consumption. For example, a national study of drinking and drug use found that in 1991 over half (51%) of high school seniors reported drinking alcoholic beverages during the last thirty days, and about 3% reported drinking everyday (National Institute on Drug Abuse 1994). Rachal et al. (1980) in their longitudinal study identify five types of negative consequences associated with drinking among adolescents: (1) trouble with teachers and school, (2) conflicts with friends and peers, (3) driving while under the influence, (4) criticism by a date, and (5) trouble with the police. Importantly, the results of a large nationwide survey show that more than 40% of people who began drinking before their 15th birthday were diagnosed as alcohol dependent at some point in their lives. Rates of lifetime dependence declined to approximately 10% among those who began drinking at age 20 or older, regardless of gender (Grant and Dawson 1997). Moreover, youth who start drinking before age 14 are 3 times more likely to be injured than those who begin drinking at or after age 21.

In February 2001, Dr Gro Harlem Brundtland, the Director-General, of the World Health Organization (WHO), summarized the current state of the global problem of drinking among youth at the WHO European Ministerial Conference on Young People and Alcohol held in Stockholm Sweden. She noted that, worldwide, 5% of all deaths of young people 15–29 are caused by alcohol use. In Europe, she pointed out, among males in this age group, the rate of alcohol-related mortality is one of every four deaths. In parts of Eastern Europe, where drinking rates among youth are particularly elevated, the figure may be as high as one in three deaths. Over 55,000 young people in Eastern Europe died from alcohol-related causes in 1999. Data from around the world indicate that, what Brundtland referred to as "a culture of sporadic binge drinking among young people," involving drinking large quantities of alcohol until intoxication, is spreading both in technologically advanced and developing countries. The cost of under-age drinking in the United States alone, she stressed was estimated by the U.S. Department of Justice at nearly $53 billion in 1996. To counter this trend, Brundtland urged the adoption of strictly enforced policies that reduce access to alcohol, including a minimum legal drinking age, restrictions in the number of hours per day or days per week that alcohol can be purchased, and limitations on the kind of outlets that are licensed to sell alcohol. Also, she emphasized, restrictions on alcohol advertising have been shown to be effective in lowering consumption. Countries with a ban on alcohol advertising have a 16% lower level of alcohol intake and a 23% lower number of traffic fatalities than countries with no advertising limitations. For young people, research shows that watching five additional minutes of alcohol advertising on television per day is linked to an increase in daily alcohol consumption of five grams. In conclusion, Brundtland observed that

Not only are children growing up in an environment where they are bombarded with positive images of alcohol, but our youth are a key target of the marketing practices of the alcohol industry. Over the past 10–15 years, we have seen that the young have become an important target for marketing of alcoholic products. When large marketing resources are directed towards influencing youth behaviour, creating a balanced and healthy attitude to alcohol becomes increasingly difficult. . . . By mixing alcohol with fruit juices, energy drinks and premixed "alcopops," and by using advertising that focuses on youth lifestyle, sex, sports and fun, the large alcohol manufacturers are trying to establish a habit of drinking alcohol at a very young age. Look at most web sites for alcohol products—they are clearly attempting to attract the young, with computer games, competitions and offers of prizes and teenage fashion shows. Go to night clubs and teenage discos and you will often find dangerous marketing techniques. In Great Britain, young people interviewed for a research project told how they were offered deals that include 'buy one, get one free' and even the so-called 'never ending vodka glass': buy one, get unlimited refills (Brundtland February 2001).

In was in this light that the WHO European Charter on Alcohol, adopted in 1995, explicitly states "all children and adolescents have the right to grow up in an environment protected from the negative consequences of alcohol consumption and to the extent possible, from the promotion of alcoholic beverages."

Drinking on Campus

The contemporary North American research approach to measuring drinking in terms of quantity, frequency, and beverage type dates to Bacon's and Straus 1953 book *Drinking in College*. That college drinking should be the starting point for an important historic trend in drinking research seems appropriate given the considerable amount and intensity of drinking that occurs on many college campuses. The "Monitoring the Future" study (L. Johnson, O'Malley, and Bachman 1994), for example, found that 91% of full-time college students report that they have consumed alcoholic beverages. Approximately three-fourths (72%) reported that they drank during the last thirty days (compared to only 63% of young adults of a similar age who were not in college). Most notable are the findings of this study concerning heavy drinking occasions (in which at least five drinks are consumed in a row). Forty percent of college students reported participation in heavy drinking bouts during the last two weeks, compared to only 34% of the noncollege controls. Often this intense drinking occurs at "chugalug" parties and during rapid-consumption drinking contests, common weekend events on many campuses. In his ethnographic study of a Rutgers University dorm, Moffat, for example, notes:

By the early 1980s, alcohol use appeared to be almost out of control in American college-age populations, and the adolescent drunk-driving death rate was very high. Yet the students definitely did not agree with the new laws; or, more precisely, some of them did agree that many of their peers drank too much, but very few of them felt it was fair or just to abridge their own freedom to drink. Drinking, of course, was not the only issue. Drinking was really about partying, and partying was really about sexuality. And sexuality was arguably at the heart of the pleasure-complex that was college life as the students understood it (Moffat 1989: 123–24).

The alcohol industry has invested considerable sums of money in glamorizing heavy drinking and linking it to sexuality. Campus newspapers, with their comparatively inexpensive advertising rates, have been a prime target for the promotion of drinking. One study found that two-thirds of the national product advertising in college newspapers was alcohol advertising. In this study, Breed and DeFoe found 3,732 column inches dedicated to beer ads in college newspapers for every 189 column inches for soft drinks (cited in M. Jacobson et al. 1983). Studies such as these have shown that many of the alcohol ads targeted to college students promote irresponsible drinking and related attitudes, including depicting alcohol as an escape from schoolwork. In these ads, drinking is shown to be cool. Education, by contrast, is portrayed as boring. Beer ads, in particular, are designed to appeal to the average college student who is immersed in striving to establish personal behavioral norms. The objective of much of this advertising appears to be to make drinking the norm, a goal that has largely been achieved.

One subtle form of advertising that targets college students among others is the sponsorship of sporting and other recreational events by the alcohol industry. Sponsorship expenditures by alcohol producing corporations reached $4.7 billion in 1995 with increases the following year, driving the industry's sponsorship budget up to $5.4 billion and rising. Top U.S. alcohol manufacturers involved in sponsorship include Anheuser-Busch Co., Philip Morris Co., and the Coors Brewing Co., all of which pour $10–$15 million a year into their sponsorship budgets. In a similar vein, in Denmark, when the government began considering a law to ban print and cinema advertising of alcoholic beverages, the Carlsberg Co. responded by opening a chain of youth-oriented stores that sell only comic books, sports trading cards, and CDs. While no beer is sold in the stores, they are all decorated with Carlsberg's beer posters.

Women and Alcohol

While men, on average, drink more than women, women appear to be somewhat more vulnerable than men to many of the negative effects associated with this behavior. Additionally, studies show that drinking behaviors, styles of drinking, and expectations associated with drinking are gendered.

Household surveys in the U.S. have found that 34% of women reported consuming at least 12 standard drinks during the previous year compared with 56% of men (National Institute on Alcohol Abuse and Alcoholism 1998). Among drinkers, 10% of women compared to 22% of men reported that they generally consumed two or more drinks per day. Additionally, men are more likely to become alcohol dependent. Although in the past women generally started drinking at later ages than men, more recent survey data show that this difference has nearly disappeared. Women are most likely to be drinkers between 26–34 years of age and drinking is more likely among women who are divorced or separated. Binge drinking, involving the consumption of five or more drinks per occasion on five or more days in the past month, has been found to be most common among women between the ages of 18–25. Problem drinking overall among women is most common between the ages of 21 and 34, in other words beginning during college age and extending into the early middle years.

Importantly, existing research indicates that women's bodies both absorb and metabolize alcohol differently than men's bodies. Generally, women tend to have a lower level of body water than do men of similar body weight. As a result, when they drink alcohol, women achieve higher concentrations of alcohol in the blood than men when they drink the same amounts of alcohol (Frezza et al. 1990). Moreover, it appears that women eliminate alcohol from the blood faster than men. It is believed that this occurs because women have a higher liver volume relative to body mass than do men. Related to these factors, women develop alcohol-induced liver disease over a shorter period of time and after consuming less alcohol than men (Gavaler and Arria 1995). Also, women are more likely than men to develop alcoholic hepatitis and to die from cirrhosis. Animal studies suggest that women's increased risk for liver damage may be tied to some of the physiological effects of the female reproductive hormone estrogen. Enhanced risk of alcohol-induced impairment among women also includes brain damage. Brain scan data show that an area of the brain that is active in multiple brain functions is significantly smaller among alcoholic women compared with both nonalcoholic women and alcoholic men. Similarly, research on the heart has found that among heavier drinkers similar rates of heart muscle disease (i.e., cardiomyopathy) for both men and women, despite the fact that women had a 60% lower level of lifetime alcohol use. Finally, a number of studies report that moderate to heavy alcohol consumption increases the risk for breast cancer among women.

Beyond disease, women who drink heavily also are at enhanced risk for violence victimization. One survey of female college students found a significant relationship between the weekly drinking levels and the likelihood they would suffer sexual victimization. Another study found that female high school students who used alcohol during the past year were more likely than nondrinking students to be the victims of date-related violence (e.g., shoving, kicking, or punching) (Gross and Billingham 1998, Malik, Sorenson, and Aneshensel 1997). A history of heavy premarital drinking by both partners is a known predictor of first-year aggression among newlyweds. In some studies, problem drinking by wives has been found to be associated with husband-to-wife aggression regardless of the husbands' drinking levels. Finally, although women are less likely than men to drive after they have been drinking and to be involved in fatal alcohol-related car crashes, they have a higher relative risk of driver fatality than men at similar blood alcohol concentrations. Laboratory research on the effects of alcohol on response to visual cues and other driving-related tasks suggests that there may be gender differences in how alcohol affects driving, with task performance levels lower for women than men with similar levels of blood alcohol. Women's overall lower rates of drinking and driving probably stem from generally lower levels of risk taking compared with men. Additionally, women are less likely to believe that drinking and driving is an acceptable behavior. A national household survey conducted in 1990, for example, found that 17% of women, compared with 27% of men, agreed that it was permissible for a person to drink one or two drinks before driving (Greenfield and Room 1997). Despite these differences in belief, the ratio of female to male drivers involved in fatal car crashes is increasing. In 1982, 12% of all drivers involved in alcohol-related fatal crashes were women, by 1986 this figure had risen to 16 percent.

An additional health risk associated with women's drinking is fetal alcohol syndrome (FAS) and related disorders of children. FAS is defined in terms of four criteria: (1) presence of known maternal drinking during pregnancy; (2) a characteristic pattern of facial abnormalities in children; (3) growth retardation; and (4) brain damage, often manifested by cognitive or behavioral problems. When a baby shows signs of brain damage following alcohol exposure during pregnancy but none of the other indicators of FAS, the condition is called alcohol-related neurodevelopmental disorder (ARND). Researchers use both passive and active methods to determine the incidence of FAS and ARND. The former approach uses data collected from existing medical records, which often are based on information recorded at birth, while in the latter approach, investigators use a defined set of diagnostic criteria to screen all members of a selected population for alcohol-related problems. Studies using the active approach have found FAS prevalence levels as high as 40 cases per 1,000 births in a community study of elementary school children in South Africa (May et al. 2000). In the United States, a preliminary active assessment of FAS in a single county in Washington State found a prevalence of 3.1 cases per 1,000 first-grade students (Clarren et al. 2001). The minimum quantity of maternal alcohol consumption required to produce adverse fetal consequences is still unknown, however clinically significant damage is not common in children whose mothers drank less than approximately five drinks per occasion once per week. However, there is considerable diversity in vulnerability to a given level of alcohol consumption during pregnancy, possibly reflecting differences in general health, nutritional status, and social and environmental factors affecting women's well being.

Generally, explaining gender differences in the effects of alcohol has proved to be a challenge for health and behavioral scientists. Some look to genetic causes noting that studies of twins and of children separated from their parents early in life show that close biological relatives are more likely—than would be expected by chance association—to have similar drinking patterns and problems. Nonetheless, all studies of genetic factors show that women's genetic risk for alcohol problems is lower than that of men. Others have pointed to social causes. For example, adopted children (both for males and females) who grow up in a household with a non-biologically related abusive drinker are more likely to develop alcohol-related problems. On a different track, analyzing data from a large general population survey, Wilsnack and co-workers (1997) found that women who reported being sexually abused during childhood were more likely than those who did not report abuse to have experienced alcohol-related problems like family conflict during their life and to exhibit at least one symptom of alcohol dependence. Other research has shown that women in alcoholism treatment were significantly more likely to report childhood sexual abuse as well as father-to-daughter verbal aggression or physical violence than women in the general population. Widom and colleagues (1995) examined court records to identify cases of childhood physical or sexual abuse and found that a history of childhood neglect, but not physical abuse, was a strong predictor of the number of alcohol-related symptoms a woman experienced. Physical abuse experienced during adulthood also has been found to be associated with women's alcohol use and related health and social problems. Significantly more women undergoing alcohol treatment report severe partner violence, including kicking, punching, or threatening with a weapon, compared with women in the general community (B. Miller 1998). The relationship between violence and problem drinking among women is probably bi-directional, with alcohol use among women leading to great vulnerability to violence and violence victimization contributing to women using alcohol to self-medicate as a result of their suffering. A shortcoming of existing research of this sort is that almost all of it has focused on women in traditional marital relationships and nuclear family households, with very limited attention being given to non-traditional arrangements like co-habitating romantic partners or women in lesbian relationships.

In sum, while there may be gender-related biological factors (e.g., hormonal influence) in vulnerability to alcohol abuse and its effects, social relations, including unequal power relations between women and men, are clearly an important part of the puzzle. Other social factors may include less access to alcohol treatment among women, because most treatment programs traditionally have focused on men, and greater emotional burden among women drinkers, because of double standards and more normative restrictions and associated penalties placed on women's behavior. For impoverished women, in particular, and women of color generally, the burdens of subordination are multiplied. As author Audre

Lordes (1984: 129) has written of her experience, "Women of Color in America have grown up with a symphony of anger, at being silenced, at being [neglected], at knowing that when we survive, it is in spite of a world that takes for granted our lack of humanness, and which hates our very existence outside of its service." Reflecting on Lorde's writing, anthropologist Alisse Waterston (1999), whose work has included an ethnographic study of women living at a home for the destitute in New York City, comments that it is no wonder that alcohol and drugs play a role in the "worlds of suffering" of poor women; the only wonder, she asserts, is that it is not more common as a mechanism for self medicating and temporarily relieving the overt and hidden injuries of oppression.

The establishment of norms and their role in shaping behaviors like drinking are topics of considerable interest to anthropology generally, while the impact of normative behavior on health is a question of basic concern to medical anthropology. Yet, as the following discussion suggests, examining other social factors in drinking, such as the role of the alcohol industry in promoting unhealthy drinking patterns, has not been a common topic of anthropological research on drinking.

ANTHROPOLOGY, CULTURE, AND THE STUDY OF ALCOHOL USE

Focused anthropological study of alcohol consumption as a distinct behavior dates to 1940. In that year, Ruth Bunzel published an article entitled "On the Role of Alcoholism in Two Central American Cultures" in the journal *Psychiatry*. The two Indian groups that Bunzel studied were the Chamula of Mexico and the Chichicastenango of Guatemala. Bunzel found that among the Chamula the drinking of an alcoholic beverage called *aguardiente* helped to create a sense of group closeness and conviviality as well as an individual sense of irresponsibility. Interpersonal conflict and sexual promiscuity were rare even when group members became intoxicated. By contrast, among the Chichicastenango, aggression and deviance from group sexual norms were commonly associated with alcohol consumption. Bunzel related these marked differences in group response to alcohol to broader sociocultural differences between these two Indian peoples, including differences in their child-rearing practices and their culturally shaped personality characteristics. Culture, in short, plays a critical role in shaping drinking behavior, including the effect alcohol has on behavior even during intoxication. This insight has been central to anthropological study of drinking ever since.

It is important to note that Bunzel did not go to Central America specifically to study drinking behavior. Her 1940 paper was a by-product of research that had a different purpose. In fact, it was not until the late 1960s that medical anthropologists developed a clear-cut interest in drinking.

Prior to this, anthropologists recorded information on drinking in the societies that they studied but did not single out drinking as a topic worthy of study in its own right. Often this behavior was so striking and so different from experiences anthropologists had had with drinking in their own society that they recorded considerable detail about folk drinking practices in their field notes. As David Pittman and Charles Snyder (1962: 2) noted in their influential book *Society, Culture, and Drinking Patterns,* "Virtually all ethnographers have had something or other to report on the subject of drinking customs, however incidental."

For example, Pittman and Snyder included Ozzie Simmons's account of learning how to drink in the Peruvian community of Lunahuaná, a mestizo village 125 miles south of the capital city of Lima. Simmons found the people of the village to be rather timid, indirect, often at a loss for words, and uncomfortable in group settings. Villagers had a lot of concern about what others might think of them and were cautious lest they be subjects of peer criticism. But the villagers admitted they became "another person" when they drank their homemade wine known as *cachina* (12%–14% alcohol) or a grape brandy called *pisco* (47%–50% alcohol). In the words of one man from the village:

A man passes through four "apparitions" when drinking that represent the following "bloods." Blood of the turkey, when a man is sober and cold. Blood of the monkey, which comes to pass after a man has drunk a little. This is the best state because the body warms up, and one becomes talkative, makes jokes, forgets his worries, and is in condition to make love to a girl. Blood of the lion, which occurs when a man has drunk even more. Now he loses his head, looks for arguments, is easily offended, thinks of people who owe him money and has the courage to go and ask them for it. Blood of the pig, which comes to pass if a man has drunk too much. He cannot stand up and control himself, but can only fall down and sleep like a pig. (Simmons 1962: 40)

Also included in the Pittman and Snyder volume is Walter Sangree's description of beer drinking among the Tiriki people of Kenya. The Tiriki traditionally believed in the continued importance of ancestor spirits in everyday life and in the need to supplicate these spirits to maintain social order and health. When it was time for a man to honor the spirits of his ancestors at his ancestral shrine, he had some banana beer brewed, usually by his first wife, and a chicken was slaughtered. A ritual elder put several drops of blood from the chicken on each of the ancestral stones that comprised the shrine followed by a few drops of beer. The elder would say:

Our forefathers, drink up the beer!
May we dwell in peace!
Everyone is gathering; be pleased, oh ancestor spirits,
And may we be well; may we remain well. (quoted in Sangree 1962: 11)

The elders then ate the chicken and drank the beer from a pot that was placed between the ancestor stones. After the beer drinking was over, a small pot of the remaining beer was left for the ancestors. While ancestor supplication was only one of many occasions for drinking among the Tiriki, as indeed beer was the lubricant of all social interaction and relationship building among them, its use in this ritual context exemplifies the socially structured nature of the drinking event in this society.

Despite richly detailed early accounts like these, drinking behavior was not seen as an acceptable or valued topic for anthropological research during this period, a stigma that has not completely disappeared even today. This attitude is but one example of many that could be cited about how the culture of anthropology shapes the issues that come to be seen as legitimate topics of research within the discipline. Similarly, the discipline has tended to adopt certain theoretical perspectives while avoiding others. These patterns are not peculiar to anthropology, as they are found in all fields of study. But this issue is of considerable importance to critical medical anthropology, which is an approach that asks questions that traditionally have been avoided, especially in medical anthropology, including questions about the use of alcohol. Pushing the field to explore issues that have been neglected in the past is one of the goals of critical medical anthropology.

During the 1940s, another development had a significant impact on subsequent work on drinking by anthropologists. Interestingly, this was a study carried out by a student. His name was Donald Horton, and he was a student of sociology. Horton believed that "The strength of drinking response in any society tends to vary directly with the level of anxiety in that society" (Horton 1943: 293). Using data on fifty-six societies described by anthropologists, he conducted a statistical test of association and found statistically significant support for his hypothesis. In one of the most widely quoted passages in cultural studies of alcohol, he concluded: "The primary function of alcoholic beverages in all societies is the reduction of anxiety" (Horton 1943: 223).

This was a bold assertion that attempted to explain why alcohol had become such a widely (although not universally) used substance. Not surprisingly, others questioned Horton's conclusion and offered alternative theories to explain alcohol consumption. Peter Field (1962), for example, in a restudy of Horton's fifty-six cases, argued that drunkenness in prestate societies is related less to the level of anxiety within individuals than it is to the presence or absence of certain types of relations that bind together the social group. Nonetheless, Horton's work stands as an important methodological advance in answering questions about drinking behavior cross-culturally (an approach that today is called *hologeistic analysis*). This type of large-scale comparison across populations to arrive at generalizations about human behavior is one of the few distinct methods of alcohol research that is specifically rooted in anthropology. Beyond method, Horton's work was important because it was theoretical. He was not specifically concerned with describing what people do but rather with explaining why they do it.

Several developments occurred during the 1960s that contributed to the emergence of a distinctive anthropological focus on alcohol. The first and probably most important was the publication by Dwight Heath of a paper entitled "Drinking Patterns of the Bolivian Camba." Not only did this paper help to launch the career of an anthropologist who has written continually and effectively on the topic of anthropology and drinking, it also began a pattern of treating drinking as a topic that merited anthropological attention.

A mestizo people engaged in slash-and-burn horticulture, the Camba drink alcohol (186-proof rum!) only during group festivals and rites of passage (e.g., weddings). Most participants spend several days drinking (in fact, running out of alcohol is a primary reason for ending a celebration). Because of the frequency of drinking occasions, most adult Camba drink and become intoxicated at least twice each month. For the Camba, drunkenness is a highly valued state, and it is the goal of alcohol consumption. However, Heath (1991: 68) argues that despite "frequent and gross inebriety, alcoholism, in the sense of addiction, does not occur." Further, as with Chamula, drinking among the Camba does not lead to conflict or aggression, and neither is there sexual disinhibition or increased sexual activity during drinking occasions. Rather, Heath (1991: 76) maintains,

Alcohol plays a predominantly integrative role in Camba society, where drinking is an elaborately ritualized group activity. . . . The anxieties often cited as bases for common group drinking [e.g., Horton] are not present. . . . Drinking parties predominate among what are [otherwise] rare social activities, and alcohol serves to facilitate rapport between individuals who are normally isolated and introverted.

In other words, according to Heath and many other anthropologists who have directly studied drinking in prestate societies and in peasant communities, alcohol consumption and even frequent drunkenness should not automatically be viewed as a social or health problem.

As an alternative to a disease model of heavy drinking, Heath embraces a *sociocultural model*. This model is derived from anthropology's *culturological approach*, which asserts the importance of culture (i.e., a local population's set of shared and integrated beliefs, values, and expectations) in shaping individual and group behavior. With reference to alcohol consumption, the approach includes several components.

First, drinking is understood as a culturally patterned and meaningful behavior, and a wide range of variation is seen in human interaction with and experience of alcohol across cultural groups. Part and parcel of the cultural patterning of consumption is the cultural loading of drinking behavior and particular beverages with social meaning. For example, writing of the place of whisky in Scotland, Macdonald (1994: 125) notes:

Whisky, as far as Scotland is concerned, is much more than a drink, or a means of getting drunk. . . . It is also a vital ingredient in various rituals, and a symbolic distillation of many images of Scottishness, especially hospitality, camaraderie, joviality and masculinity.

Second, in keeping with an argument developed by Craig MacAndrew and Robert Edgerton (1969: 165), the way the Camba, the Chamula, the Chichicastenango, or the people in any other society "comport themselves when they are drunk is determined not by alcohol's toxic assault upon the seat of moral judgment, conscience, or the like, but by what their society has taught them" about how to act when under the influence of alcohol. Drunken behavior, no less than drinking behavior itself, is socially learned behavior and thus is culturally generated and varies across social groups. This tenet is used by anthropologists to refute stereotypes about drinking, such as the long-standing firewater myth that asserts that Native Americans have an unusually strong craving for alcohol and that they are unable to engage in controlled drinking. Anthropologists have marshaled observations made in various Indian communities to argue that alcohol addiction is absent in many Indian groups (cf. Leland 1976). For example, Joseph Westermeyer (1974: 30) has written that "with regard to both alcohol and alcohol-related problems, an extremely wide variation exists among individual tribes, among subgroups within tribes, and among individual Indians." Moreover, social attitudes about drunkenness vary across cultures. Thus, Hendry (1994: 187) notes that in Japan there is "considerable tolerance for behaviour attributed to the consumption of alcohol." In other societies, by contrast, tolerance is minimal.

Third, as Mac Marshall (1979: viii) has argued, "The state of alcohol inebriation is at all times and in all places surrounded by [cultural] limits, even though these limits are usually more lax than those regularly permitted." This lowering (but not eliminating) of the controls on behavior has been referred to by MacAndrew and Edgerton (1969) as the "time out" function that alcohol commonly serves. For example, it has been noted that in Japan "almost any foolish behavior under the influence of alcohol can be overlooked" (Sargent 1967: 711).

Finally, drinking and even drunkenness, in particular social contexts, may help to integrate rather than tear apart the social fabric by increasing people's sense of solidarity. Thus asserts Heath (quoted in L. Bennett 1988: 117):

If alcoholism is a disease, Heath argues, it is a most unusual one inasmuch as an individual can often bring an end to it by modifying his/her behavior even in the absence of any other interventions. Moreover, he asserts that most of the reasons commonly given for calling it a disease are fallacious: e.g., it is not progressive, not of known etiology, and does not have clearly recognized diagnostic features.

In opposition to the disease model, Heath stresses (as do other anthropologists) the positive aspects of drinking, including the role it plays as a *social reinforcer*, that is, drinking offers a means of enhancing intragroup sociability and bonding, expressing a group's self-image, and marking group boundaries. For example, in reviewing anthropological analyses of American Indian drinking, Spicer (1997: 306) observes, that anthropologists usually

argue for the important functions that it serves. Whether it be the articulation of social and cultural values . . . , the assertion of an ethnic identity . . . , or a means of escaping the feelings of inadequacy engendered by social and cultural changes . . . , the impulse has nearly always been to delineate the reasons that Indian people drink as they do. . . .

Moreover as Heath notes,

Many an anthropologist has, rightly or wrongly, felt that an important hurdle in terms of rapport had been passed when native drinking companions expressed approval that the anthropologist "drinks like us." Inclusion with a group where drinking is a focal activity is often a mark of social acceptance, just as exclusion from such a group may well signal rejection. (Heath 1990: 270)

Not all anthropologists completely share Heath's perspective on alcoholism. Some, for example, accept that it is a real disease of a certain type and that it shares many features with other diseases (e.g., hypertension is strongly influenced by sufferer behavior (e.g., diet and exercise), as are many forms of cancer). Further, the etiology of alcoholism is becoming clearer, as noted at the outset of this chapter. Nonetheless, Heath's views are important and they have been quite influential. Further, he has played an important role in centering anthropological attention and work on the topic.

The second event that occurred during the 1960s that helped confirm legitimacy on alcohol research in anthropology was the article "Alcohol and Culture" by David Mandelbaum and co-workers. This article signaled a change in anthropology's neglect of drinking behavior. In subsequent years, the number of anthropologists conducting alcohol research and intervention grew appreciably, and the anthropological literature on the topic continued to double about every five years until some time in the mid-1990s when this expansion slowed considerably. Growth also led to the creation of the Alcohol and Drug Study Group of the Society for Medical Anthropology in 1979. Now over twenty years old, the Society continues to be a forum for networking and the sharing of ideas among anthropologists involved in alcohol and drug use research. Further, the evolution of the anthropology of drinking contributed to a definable impact of anthropology on the broader multidisciplinary field of alcohol research, sometimes referred to as *alcohology*.

Anthropologists bring a range of perspectives to the study of drinking, but, as the discussion presented thus far suggests, the three features that best distinguish traditional anthropological studies of alcohol use are (1) the use of naturalistic study methods like ethnography that (2) allow for an understanding of drinking within an encompassing sociocultural context and in terms of the views of the people whose drinking patterns are being studied so as (3) to suggest social policy and/or programs that are appropriate for the population in question. For example, in describing his research on drinking among Mexican Americans in South Texas, Trotter (1985: 285) states, "The general thrust of the [ethnographic] research . . . has been to determine culturally normative drinking patterns, to discover emic [i.e., insider] views of and values toward alcohol use and abuse, and to make recommendations about the development of culturally appropriate treatment of alcohol-related problems." In the view of Mac Marshall, an anthropologist who has devoted much of his career to the study of substance use in Oceania, "The most important contribution anthropology . . . made to the alcohol field was in demonstrating to nonanthropologists the importance of sociocultural factors for understanding the relationship between alcohol and human behavior" (cited in L. Bennett 1988: 100).

CHALLENGES TO THE SOCIOCULTURAL MODEL

A significant and pointed criticism of the types of anthropological studies of drinking that have been described thus far has been made by a well-known alcohol researcher, Robin Room. In 1984, Room published a major article arguing that health and social problems associated with drinking have been systematically underestimated in the ethnographic literature. This article launched a scholarly debate that continues today. The ultimate product of this debate has been an admission by a number of anthropologists (although not all) that Room's criticisms often are warranted.

Room (1984) labeled the systematic bias he detected "problem deflation." His basic point is that in their effort to understand drinking in social context anthropologists have gone overboard in describing the positive aspects of drinking while minimizing its health and social costs. First, agreeing with Spicer, he observes that much of the anthropological literature on drinking behavior has been written explicitly or implicitly from a *functionalist* perspective. In the view of functionalism, the parts of a sociocultural system are highly integrated and mutually reinforcing, much like the organs that make up a living body or the mechanical parts that comprise an electric engine. Remove one key part, and the whole system shuts down. From this standpoint, anthropologists have tended to portray alcohol consumption as an integral (and, by implication, necessary) part of a cultural way of life. For example, among the Tiriki people of Kenya described earlier, alcohol was shown to be closely intertwined with religion and group social organization, including playing a vital role in shaping interpersonal relations among group members. While Room does not challenge this assertion, his argument is that by focusing so much attention on the benefits that drinking confers on the maintenance of a cultural lifeway, anthropologists have been somewhat blind to the real damage drinking may be doing, that is, the *dysfunctional* aspects of drinking.

An example of this shortcoming can be seen in Marshall's book *Weekend Warriors*, an account of drinking on Moen in the Truk Islands of Micronesia. In the preface to this book, Marshall reports that there is a near-universal agreement among foreigners familiar with Micronesia as well as among many Micronesians themselves that alcohol abuse is a major problem in Truk. Certainly, Marshall witnessed a considerable amount of drinking and drunkenness there. Marshall presents an explanation of this behavior in terms of traditional Truk culture. Heavy drinking and drunkenness are not viewed by him as an indication of problems in Truk, such as the anomic response to the disruption of traditional culture caused by the island society's incorporation within the world economic system. Rather, he (1979: 125) argues:

A major part of the bacchanalian life-style of young men is given over to public displays of drunken bravado. These displays are a basic part of growing into manhood in Truk; they do not represent psychopathic or sociopathic behavior. They are expected and accepted parts of contemporary Trukese life, just as warfare and "heathen dancing" were regular parts of Trukese life a century ago.

Drinking by young Trukese men, from this perspective, can be understood as "a modern substitute for traditional warfare," which was banned by colonial powers (Marshall 1979: viii). Consequently, Marshall (1979: 119) maintains that "drunkenness may be looked upon as a psychological blessing for young men in Truk from the standpoint of their overall mental health. Rather than bottling up much of their aggression, they could now express it in a socially sanctioned way."

This is typical of functionalist arguments, in maintaining that heavy drinking is a *functional replacement* for banned warfare, allowing the siphoning off of otherwise dangerous aggression. It is unclear, however, just what would have happened to Truk men or Truk society had this particular alternative to warfare *not* been adopted. Would the society have fallen apart? Would aggression have exploded into island-wide fratricide? Or would the people of Truk have found less harmful venues for expressing pent-up hostility (e.g., through sports).

Acknowledging the value of Room's critique, more recently some anthropologists have begun to articulate a more complex model of drinking. Spicer (1997), in his assessment of American Indian drinking, for example, has sought to present an understanding that matches the contradictory functional/dysfunctional nature of this phenomenon. Says, Spicer (1997: 307):

The American Indian experience with alcohol is profoundly ambiguous, drinking is at once recognized as a means of articulating core cultural values *and* vilified as an alien and degrading influence; it is simultaneously something to which people are drawn *and* by which they are repelled; and it is associated with some of the best *and* some of the worst in contemporary American Indian life.

In his interviews with Indian drinkers, Spicer found many who were quite concerned and troubled by their drinking, and regularly expressed the kind of tolerance-build up and craving suggestive of the disease model of addiction. Similarly, Garrity (2000: 252) points out that with an alcohol-related death rate seven times the national level, Navajo Indian leaders "consider alcohol abuse to be the most serious problem now facing the Navajo people." Although quite variable among Indian tribal groups, alcohol abuse is a factor in five of the leading causes of death for American Indians nationally, namely motor vehicle crashes, alcoholism, cirrhosis, suicide, and homicide. Death rates for crashes and alcoholism are 5.5 and 3.8 times higher, respectively, among American Indians than in the general U.S. population. Among those tribes with high rates of alcoholism, it is estimated that as many as 75% of all accidents, which are the leading cause of death among American Indians, are alcohol-related.

Turning to the sociocultural component in drinking behavior, Spicer (1997: 308–309) rightfully stresses a very critical point that is easily lost in undersocialized explanations of addiction:

An overly narrow focus on the physiological dimensions of alcohol use obscures what makes the situation so troubling to the people involved, chiefly the way in which their drinking is implicated, for both good and bad, in their relationships with others. . . . In order to understand people's ambivalence, we need to understand not only why they want to quit, but also why they continue drinking.

The primary reason for continued drinking among American Indians *who wanted to quit*, Spicer (1997: 317) found, was the *social cost of abstinence*: "Since the use of alcohol had become an integral aspect of proper social relationships, to quit drinking was often perceived as an attempt to elevate oneself above others," an impression that the American Indians interviewed by Spicer wanted desperately to avoid because of their cultural values. In short, cultural factors—very specific cultural factors rooted in particular cultural traditions—were every bit as important as physiological ones in driving continued abusive drinking patterns. As this example suggests, where cultural values, beliefs and practices support frequent heavy drinking, and thus continual brain exposure to alcohol, alcohol addiction can be said to be co-determined by biological and cultural factors. The particular expression of this condition will be determined locally by sociocultural promoters of and constraints on behavior.

Additionally, it must be stressed, the type of functionalist model that traditionally found expression in anthropological studies of drinking has difficulty in addressing the issue of social change. Thus, at the point of actual ethnographic observation of drinking in most prestate societies the transforming effects of colonial and postcolonial political and economic domination were already centuries old. British rule of Tiriki territory, for example, was established in the 1890s, sixty years before Sangree arrived to begin his fieldwork. Similarly, European vessels began bringing alcohol to Micronesia from Europe at about the same time. In both places, the local impact of the expansion of the capitalist world system was even older still. But descriptions of drinking in terms of local culture imagine that cultures are isolated local phenomena. In Eric Wolf's (1982: 114) phrase, they "assume the autonomy and boundedness" of local social groups rather than "take cognizance of processes [like colonialism] that transcend separate cases."

Room continues his critique of anthropological studies of drinking by pointing to a shortcoming of *ethnography*, the touchstone method of anthropological data collection. Indeed, anthropology often has been defined in terms of this research method. Without doubt, the strength of ethnography is that it puts the anthropologist "on the ground," living with the group under study and participating in their day-to-day activities, including, if it is local custom, drinking alcoholic beverages with them. This allows the anthropologist to see and describe the fabric of social life in all of its complexity and to glimpse the interconnections between various domains of behavior and cultural belief. Room (1984: 172) argues that the problem is that ethnography is "better attuned to measuring the [frequent] pleasures than the [less frequent] problems of drinking"; ethnography, he asserts, notices what is regular but misses whatever is hidden or unusual. As various anthropologists who have responded to Room have pointed out, this criticism lacks merit, as many anthropologists have studied social problems, including abusive drinking, in the field. If there is anything ethnography is good at, in fact, it is learning about *backstage* or socially hidden behavior. Based usually on firsthand, immersion-based data collection techniques that are deployed in natural settings in which the researcher(s) directly observes and, at least to some degree, participates in the everyday life activities of members of the group under study, anthropological research has proven its metal in identifying both usual and unusual behaviors.

There is, nonetheless, a weakness of ethnography that Room fails to mention, namely, that the intensive nature of ethnographic fieldwork tends to focus the researcher's attention on what is immediate and local, while the influence of outside forces can easily be overlooked, unless you are inclined to look for it. As Ellen Gruenbaum (1981: 47) points out, "Anthropologists get lost in the fascinating minutiae of experiences in the field." Anthropology's concentration on the intricacies of individual ethnographic cases, while a necessary and useful method for appreciating the rich detail of cultural variation and insider understandings, has caused field workers to miss the importance of uniform processes underlying global social change, including changes in drinking patterns (e.g., the effect of alcohol advertising and the social status accorded imported alcoholic beverages on increases in local drinking patterns). In short, the anthropological examination of drinking has failed to consider systematically the world-transforming effects of the global market and global labor practices associated with the capitalist mode of production.

Room's (1984: 173) third point is, "However much he or she strives to understand and present the culture under study from the inside, the ethnographer brings to the field perceptions and values formed in his or her own culture." Of special importance in this regard, according to Room, is that many of the ethnographers who wrote the early cultural accounts of drinking were members of a "wet generation," by which he means a generation favorably disposed to drinking, tending to view it as a form of liberation from societal constraints on individual behavior. This favorable attitude toward alcohol, he argues, tended to lead them to see the positive sides of drinking in the peoples they studied and to overlook the negative consequences of alcohol consumption. Room's larger point about the impact of the anthropologist's culture (which tends to be Western, middle class, and intellectual) on what he or she concentrates on and pays attention to in the field is of considerable relevance (although sociologists, psychologists, physicians, and all others who study alcohol are no less burdened by cultural baggage). Concern about the impact of cultural blinders with reference to the full impact of the world economic system on local beliefs and practices is central to the worldview of critical medical anthropology and its critique of conventional medical anthropology. Thus, in 1986, Merrill Singer published an article entitled "Toward a Political-Economy of Alcoholism: The Missing Link in the Anthropology of Drinking." The purpose of this article (M. Singer 1986: 114) was "to encourage transcendence of the narrow boundaries of inquiry and perspective characteristic of many anthropological and related studies of drinking behavior: life in a world system demands a global view." For example, in 1988 Heath published a review of the dominant anthropological theories and models of alcohol abuse and alcoholism. He cites the following nine theories/models, some of which have already been discussed:

Sociocultural model (see above)

Single distribution model (asserts that the rate of alcoholism in a population is determined by the general level of per capita consumption of alcohol in that population)

Anxiety model (developed by Horton)

Social organization model (developed by Field)

Socialization and social learning models (children learn to drink by watching adults)

Functional interpretation (see above)

Power model (people are motivated to drink by the desire to feel more in control)

Conflict-over-dependency model (dependency feelings generated in childhood promote alcohol consumption and associated unrealistic fantasies of personal success)

Symbolic interactionist model (human behavior is viewed as dramatic social performance)

As this lists suggests, the dominant models of alcohol abuse and alcoholism in anthropology are sociocultural or psychological in nature. The politics and the economics of drinking, including the role of social inequality, social power to coerce, and the endless search for profit were not on the agenda of the anthropology of drinking until the emergence of critical medical anthropology.

Finally, Room raises two last points: (1) There is a tendency among anthropologists to downplay alcohol problems so as to differentiate themselves from missionaries, colonialists, and other ethnocentric Europeans found in Third World settings; and (2) anthropologists fail to recognize alcoholism as a culture-bound syndrome (i.e., a condition peculiar to the presence of cultural attitudes about individual self-control and responsibility) and therefore do not see other kinds of health and social problems associated with abusive drinking.

Perhaps the true importance of Room's critique can be seen in Marshall's rethinking of his account of drinking patterns in Truk. In retrospect, Marshall (1988: 362) came to recognize that the explanation offered in *Weekend Warriors* "was essentially a functionalist one" and that he was motivated by a desire to "debunk what [he] perceived as an overemphasis on the problems associated with alcohol use in Truk." He also realized (Marshall 1990: 363) that he had "underplayed the extent of alcohol-related problems in Truk because [he] did not find evidence for much 'alcoholism' of the sort discussed under the rubric of the disease model of alcoholism." Most important, with further research, Marshall came to realize that while men in Truk may not view their drinking as problematic, women certainly do! Women, in fact, effectively organized and pushed the government to implement a prohibition law. Marshall (1990: 364) concluded, "It became necessary to rethink Trukese alcohol use from a feminist perspective. To have failed to do so would have been to offer a skewed view of Trukese society in which the opinions and attitudes of half the population went unrepresented."

That there has been much skewing of this sort is precisely the issue from the perspective of critical medical anthropology. It is from this insight that this alternative perspective seeks to fill in the missing link in anthropological studies of drinking and to build a political economy of alcoholism and alcohol abuse. This is not to say, however, that heavy drinking and frequent drunkenness necessarily lead to alcohol-related problems. Additional visits to the Camba by Heath over the last thirty-five years, for example, have convinced him that his original observations were correct. He still can detect no indication that the Camba suffer from "any of the so-called 'drinking problems' that are so deplored in many cultures today, such as spouse- or child-abuse, homicide, suicide, injurious accidents, . . . aggression of any sort, job-interference, psychological distress (on the part of the drinker or close relatives), social strain in the family, trouble with legal authorities, or even physical damage that differs in any significant way from that suffered by others in the area, who drink less or abstain" (Heath 1994: 360).

Elsewhere, however, changes in a community's way of life brought on by changes in the dominant economic and political system or the community's place in that system, in conjunction with efforts by alcohol manufacturers to promote the sale of alcohol, have had definite and telling effects. Before turning to examine this issue in greater detail through a presentation of the critical medical anthropology perspective on alcohol, we first present a somewhat lighthearted (but not unserious) "Closer Look" at the way noncritical conventional views of alcohol problems come to be perpetuated in society.

"A Closer Look"

ALCOHOLISM IN COMIC BOOKS: INDIVIDUALIZING ALCOHOL ADDICTION

Superhero comic book characters, figures like Superman, Spider-Man, the Hulk, and the X-Men, have been likened on occasion to the bigger-than-life culture heroes who populate the colorful myths of preliterate societies. Nonetheless, while considerable energy is expended on the collection and analysis of non-Western folklore, a popular culture medium like comic books traditionally has been dismissed by scholars as being a childish endeavor not worthy of academic study. However, as Les Daniels emphasizes in his book *Marvel* (1991: 14), comics "are—paradoxically—childlike in the best sense: they display uninhibited inventiveness and a sometimes startling capacity for candor. Comics are about what we are thinking, whether as children or adults. . . . The comics show us ourselves and our attitudes in a funhouse mirror, the images exaggerated but still recognizable. The books record angry rebellion at the end of the Great Depression, a surge of self-confident patriotism and purpose in World War II, and then the confusion, disillusionment and search for suitable enemies that characterized the postwar era. The 1960s brought introspection and a quest for identity and meaning, while the 1970s felt nostalgia for the popular culture of the past, undercut by modern skepticism. The 1980s pushed the boundaries with wild self-parody and a frank acknowledgement of the human capacity for cruelty."

Comics, in short, can be understood as an artful reflection on the wider society. But in a society that is sharply divided across class, racial, and gender lines, as is the case in the contemporary United States, the question must be asked, whose truth do comic books or any other element of popular culture reflect? Does the truth of one class or ethnic group dominate in the various popular media?

Examining the portrayal in comic books of a contemporary problem like alcoholism provides a context for answering these questions. This is because the popular writer, including the writer of comic books, has at his or her disposal a very wide variety of culturally meaningful professional and folk models to choose from in presenting alcoholism and its causes. The creator of a comic book in which alcoholism is intended as a theme or important plot element, therefore, must make choices about how to represent the phenomenon to his or her readers. Take for example the comic book called *Iron Man*, which in issue #128 of an ongoing series featured a classic story called "Demon in a Bottle." Written by David Micheline in 1979, the story depicts the nature and underlying causes of alcohol addiction in the title character, a metal-clad superhero whose life is devoted to making the world safe from evil.

It would probably be useful to provide some background information on the hero of this comic, since Iron Man, unlike Superman, Batman, Spawn, and a few other comic book stars, has never quite risen to the level of a cultural icon. Among superhero comic book fans, however, Iron Man is seen as a major character and central pillar of what is fondly referred to as "the Marvel universe." As a character, Iron Man dates to 1963, when he first appeared in issue #39 of the comic book *Tales of Suspense*. Five years later, in recognition of his growing popularity, Iron Man was awarded his own comic book. So who is Iron Man? He is the superhero persona of the millionaire industrialist, genius inventor, and dashing play-boy Anthony Stark. Stark first came to the attention of comic book readers when he was wounded in Southeast Asia and, with the help of a Viet-namese inventor named Yin Sen, constructed a suit of shiny yellow and red metal armor that not only sustains Stark's life but confers upon him powers of flight, great strength, advanced weaponry, and a few other nifty abilities that would no doubt be popular among students trying get through another round of seemingly endless final exams. Having become "one of the Earth's mightiest men," the Golden Avenger (so called because he was a founding member of the superhero team the Avengers) acknowl-edged his responsibilities and devoted himself to fighting evil.

But life as the ultimate heavy-metal superhero isn't necessarily all that it's cracked up to be. Not only is Stark the victim of heart problems and a mysterious nerve disease, but constantly battling against overwhelming odds can tend to get you down. After years of loyal power-packed service in the name of justice, Iron Man was unfairly indicted for the murder of the Carnelian Ambassador to the United States. Moreover, because he refuses to allow it to continue making armaments for the Pentagon, Stark's manufacturing company, Stark International, becomes the target of a hos-tile stock buyout by more patriotic types. To make matters worse, things get pretty shaky in Stark's social support system. First, the Avenger super-hero team disbands. Then Jarvis, Stark's butler of twenty years, resigns. Finally, his romantic relationship falls apart.

Feeling increasingly sorry for himself and out of control in his life, Stark turns to alcohol. Mulling over his problems in a drunken stupor, he de-cides that he will just stop being Tony Stark and will assume his costumed identity as Iron Man full time (and thereby give up all human frailties). Stark concludes, "I don't know why people say alcohol dulls the brain, it's cleared things up real swell for me" (Micheline 1979: 3). Whereupon he proceeds to jump impulsively out of his office window and fly into the sky, except that he forgets to open the window first and causes quite a crash. Zooming over the countryside, he spies a wrecked train and flies boastfully to the rescue, only to accidentally cause a potentially disastrous and clearly embarrassing chlorine leak on the wrecked train.

Thoroughly convinced he can do nothing right, Stark heads back to his office and to his whiskey bottle. But his pouring hand is stopped by Beth-any, his heretofore-lost love, who has decided dramatically not to leave him after all. But Stark rejects Bethany's offer of help (in a way that cul-tural analyses of drinking have shown is a typically individualistic Amer-ican response) by saying, "Thanks Beth. But no thanks. I can handle things myself" (Micheline 1979: 11).

Not easily deterred, Bethany goes on the offensive and lays out for Stark how he is destroying himself and holding all his problems inside. Finally, Stark (in confirmation of the ideology of Alcoholics Anonymous) is portrayed as giving up his control needs and asking Bethany for help. As Bethany and Stark embrace, Stark drops his whiskey glass, which crashes symbolically on the floor. Stark then proceeds to begin repairing his alcohol-shattered relationships (following Step 9 of the Alcoholics Anonymous twelve-step plan). While his resolve to quit drinking almost dissolves as he faces subsequent disappointments, Stark avoids relapse and remains on the wagon. Tellingly, in *Iron Man* #129, he passes up an offered glass of whiskey for a glass of mineral water. By giving up control (through testimonial confession and leaning on others) Stark regains control (over his drinking and his life), although he can never return to moderate social drinking again (or face immediate relapse) because he suffers from a disease called alcoholism. So ends Stark's confrontation with the Demon in a Bottle.

This depiction of the nature of alcoholism is a culturally meaningful one in contemporary U.S. society. Yet it is only one way of thinking about the problem. Most notably, it is a very atomized portrayal, one that emphasizes alcoholism as a problem *at the level of the individual person.* Faced with personal life problems, Stark turns to alcohol as a crutch, as an escape, as a boost to a threatened ego. Unable to handle life's challenges, Stark also is unable to control his drinking. No mention is made of the alcohol industry and its constant encouragement through advertisement to escape life's problems with a few relaxing brews with the guys. No reference is included concerning the way U.S. culture teaches people to think of life as a game (sometimes called the rat race) of individual success and failure, in which all responsibility for achievement lies within the individual, or the way the alcohol industry in its advertisements uses this cultural theme to associate success with drinking in general or with the drinking of particular brands of alcohol. Moving away from the level of the individual using a somewhat limited culturological approach to look at alcohol addiction in light of these wider socioeconomic forces is the goal of the next section of this chapter.

FROM CULTUROLOGY TO THE POLITICAL ECONOMY OF DRINKING AND ALCOHOLISM

The attempt to understand the relationship between drinking and wider political and economic factors traces to Friedrich Engels's seminal study entitled *The Condition of the Working Class in England,* originally published in 1845. In this classic book, Engels explored the causes of illness and early death among working-class men, women, and children during the era of industrialization in terms of the class relations of emergent industrial capitalism and its accompanying social and physical environments. Unlike numerous medical, psychological, social scientific, and popular culture writers who were to follow, Engels did not locate his explanation for the emergence of alcoholism and alcohol abuse within the genes, personality, character, morality, family life, or culture of drinkers but rather within the oppressive structure of class relations and their harmful social consequences for the working class. In doing so, he identified a number of key ideas that have been adopted in the development of a critical medical anthropology of alcohol abuse.

According to Engels, for the members of the working class in England in the early decades of the industrial revolution

Liquor is almost their only source of pleasure, and all things conspire to make it more accessible to them. . . . [Drunkenness provides] the certainty of forgetting for an hour or two the wretchedness and burden of life and a hundred other circumstances so mighty that the worker can, in truth, hardly be blamed for yielding to such overwhelming pressure. Drunkenness has here ceased to be a vice. . . . Those who have degraded the working man to a mere object have the responsibility to bear. (Engels [1845] 1969: 133–34)

In this passage, Engels also draws attention to the social dimension of drinking, noting that for the working man "his social need can be gratified only in the public-house, he has absolutely no other place where he can meet his friends" (Engels [1845] 1969). In subsequent pages, he discusses the Beer Act of 1830, which eased restrictions on the sale of this commodity and in his opinion "facilitated the spread of intemperance by bringing a beerhouse, so to speak, to everybody's door" (156). Engels also mentions the profitability of alcohol sales, observing that the working class of mid-nineteenth-century England was spending 25 million pounds a year on its procurement. Finally, he describes, in dramatic detail, the health, family, and societal damage wrought by abusive drinking.

In sum, Engels' political-economic insights on alcoholism include the following six points, to be examined more fully on the following pages:

1. Abusive drinking is a health and social problem of tremendous magnitude.
2. Abusive drinking develops under identifiable social conditions that are the product of class relations.
3. Given class conflict, heavy drinking may help build in-group social solidarity.
4. The extent of drinking and alcohol-related problems, however, is tied to the availability of alcohol.
5. A key role in the facilitation of availability is played by the state.
6. The other major role in facilitation is played by the social class that controls and profits from alcohol production and distribution.

Drinking as a Social Problem

Engels pointed out the devastating health and social consequences of abusive drinking for the British working class in the nineteenth century.

This pattern has continued from Engels' day into the present. Between 1971 and 1981 in England, death attributed to cirrhosis rose by 25%, and hospital admissions for alcoholism jumped by 50%.

According to the National Institute on Alcohol Abuse and Alcoholism (1998), in 1997, Americans on average drank 2 gallons (7.57 liters) of alcohol per person a week. This translates into about one six-pack of beer, two glasses of wine and three or four mixed drinks per week. However, over one-third of adults do not consume alcohol, so the weekly consumption levels among drinkers are actually higher. Moreover, 53% of all the alcohol that is consumed in the United States occurs during very heavy drinking bouts (i.e., on occasions when more than five drinks are consumed) and another 25% is consumed during fairly heavy drinking occasions (i.e., when three to four drinks are consumed). The 10% of heaviest drinkers in the U.S. are estimated to consume as much as 60% of the alcohol Americans drink. Each year, approximately 8% of people in the U.S. aged 18 and older suffer from alcohol abuse and/or dependence. Moreover, 18% of adults are estimated to experience at least one lifetime episode of alcohol abuse or dependence. It is estimated that annually approximately 15% of children under age 18 (about 10 million children) are exposed to familial alcohol abuse or dependence. Further, 43% of children under age 18 (more than 28 million children) live at some point in households in which one or more adults were drinking abusively.

A comprehensive study of the national economic costs of alcoholism in Sweden found 50 billion Swedish kronor, or about 10% of the GNP, was spent on alcoholism treatment, social services, and preventive efforts or was lost from production because of alcohol-related problems during the 1980s. The extent of health and social costs in European countries is understandable, given that Europe accounts for only one-eighth of the world's population but consumes about half of all recorded alcohol produced internationally (M. Singer 1986).

A particularly interesting European case is that of France, a country in which drinking is known to be very well integrated with family and social life, children begin drinking wine early in life, and drinking is frequent (e.g., with many meals), but, in which, according to popular belief, health consequences of drinking are limited. Indeed, studies show that the French drink one-and-a-half times more per person than Americans. However, what is often not as well known is the fact that the French death rate from liver cirrhosis is also one-and-a-half times greater than that in the United States. According to the World Health Organization, France has the sixth highest adult per capita alcohol consumption level in the world and alcohol is involved in nearly half of the deaths from motor vehicle accidents, half of all homicides, and one-quarter of suicides. Compared to other countries in Europe, French men have a high premature death rate, which primarily is a consequence of alcohol consumption. It is estimated that the health and social cost of alcohol for France is $18.5 billion (U.S.) each year.

Although there is no shortage of studies, reports, documents, and descriptions detailing the alcoholism problem of advanced or middle-range capitalist countries, the impact of the importation and sale of Western alcoholic beverages in underdeveloped countries has been underreported if not totally ignored, by anthropologists among others. Yet the World Health Organization (WHO) estimates that in many underdeveloped countries between 1% and 10% of the population can be classified as either heavy drinkers or alcoholics. Cirrhosis has become a leading cause of death for adults in a number of such nations. A case with particular poignancy is that of the San people of southwestern Africa, long a focus of interest within anthropology because of their retention of a social formation suggestive of prestate society. Prior to the fall of its apartheid government, South Africa occupied the home territory of the San. Cultural Survival, Inc., described the consequence for one group of San, the Ju/wasi:

Ju means person; /wa means correct or proper. They call themselves "the well-mannered people," but today their lives are marred by misery and violence. Crowded together in makeshift settlements and unlivable housing projects around the administrative town of Tshumkwe, and at police and army posts, Ju/wasi live idle, debilitated lives. . . . Drunkenness unleashed jealousies and hatreds that arise from being thrust into a cash economy where only a few get work [primarily as soldiers for the South African army]. Shattered values and collapsing self-esteem encourage drinking. Traditionally, Ju/wasi drank no alcohol, but when a liquor store opened in Tshumkwe with a government loan [from the South African Bantu development fund], drunkenness exploded. (Cultural Survival 1984)

Commercialization of alcohol production also has had a major impact among many peoples, like the Tiriki of Kenya, for whom alcohol consumption was a traditional, socially controlled practice. As Mwanalushi (1981: 13) notes for Zambia,

Despite widespread use of alcohol in various spheres of social and cultural life of traditional Zambian society, drunkenness was infrequent and alcohol problems unknown. With the advent of colonialism, the alcohol scene changed considerably. First, the availability of alcohol was no longer confined to periods of the year when grain was in abundance, nor was brewing now a family affair confined to the domestic setting. Secondly, due to ready availability and increased outlets for alcohol beverages, alcohol became a major commercial enterprise. . . . Changing drinking habits gave rise to a number of alcohol related problems, including alcoholism, road traffic accidents, and social and economic difficulties.

Similarly, for Mexico, William Taylor (1979: 69) argues that early commercialization "contributed to social stratification, as individual entrepre-

neurs acquired personal fortunes in the liquor trade, and may have
weakened the sacred and ritual significance of the drink." Generally
speaking, in places where commercially produced and distributed alcohol
has come to be the dominant drink and traditional regulation of locally
produced alcohol has diminished, "more solitary drinking and more disrupted and violence [are] associated with the drunken state" (57).

The precise process of transition from traditional to commericialized
drinking has been described in some detail by Robert Carlson (1992) for
the Haya of Tanzania. The Haya are a Bantu-speaking people whose staple
food crop is the banana. Prior to European intrusion into Haya territory
during the nineteenth century, the Haya began making a fermented
banana-sorghum beer that they referred to *amarwa*. A special kind of banana is grown for beer making. After harvesting, these bananas either are
buried in a pit or hung over the hearth to transform the starch they contain
into fermentable sugar. When the bananas are ripe, they are laid in a dug
out wooden trough where they are stomped into a pulp. Water, dried
grass, and sorghum are added to the mixture, and the trough is covered
with banana leaves and left to ferment for twenty-four hours. This process
produces a drink that consists of about 4.5% alcohol by weight. The Haya
recognize four levels of physical effects caused by beer drinking:
(1) *okwehoteleza* is marked by the absence of altered perception and refers
to drinking for refreshment to quench a thirst; (2) *okushemera* refers to
feeling happy or hilarious as a result of being full with banana beer;
(3) *okushaagwa amarwa* means being overcome by banana beer and losing
control of oneself; and (4) *okutamiila* is the word for being quite drunk,
staggering, and possibly getting violent while under the influence. Drinking properly in Haya culture means never going beyond the second of
these four levels. Maintaining self-control is highly valued by the Haya.
Symbolically, restricting drinking to the first two levels expresses a key
Haya cultural value: subordination of individual desire to the rules of the
social group through self-control. With European contact the contexts,
quantities, and consequences of drinking have changed, however. Bars
are now operated in Haya territory, and people talk of drinking to forget
their problems. Most Haya interviewed by Carlson report that heavy
drinking and drunkenness are much more common than in the past. As
alcohol becomes a commodity that can be purchased in an impersonal
commercial exchange, the traditional cultural meanings activated by
drinking are diminished. In the process, the individual "is alienated from
his or her ability to articulate creatively the relationship between the natural and the symbolic orders; commodities take on a life of their own, and
the symbols that order their production are controlled by the economy
itself" (Carlson 1992: 57). By disrupting cultural constraints on alcohol
consumption, commercialization contributes to increased levels of drinking and the potential for alcohol-related health and social problems.

Social Conditions That Shape Drinking Behavior

Engels drew attention to the influence of social relations, including social inequality, on alcohol consumption. This concern has been validated by several lines of contemporary research. Based on a series of community and national studies, Cisin and Cahalan (1970: 807) conclude that "lower-status men at any age tend to be considerably more prone to have various types of drinking problems than is true for upper-status men." As Robins points out, the social correlates of alcohol problems are "being poor, male, undereducated, and in low-status ethnic groups" (Robins 1980: 89). Moreover, he notes that in different countries different low-status groups are involved. This conclusion is supported by numerous studies in industrialized countries. With reference to Truk, for example, Marshall now recognizes the importance of the recent growth of a social-class hierarchy. Young men of the lower class, he now believes, "are turning to alcoholic beverages as a solace for failure and as a means of partially coping with this added life stress" (M. Marshal 1979: 123).

This is true, in part, because the industrial ruling class has played a major role in shaping the drinking habits of the poor and working classes. For example, there was the truck system developed during the nineteenth century. In this system, workers were paid a portion of their salary in goods rather than cash, with alcohol being a common item given to workers as a substitute for their paycheck. Thus, white farmers in South Africa, concerned with profitably disposing of wine unmarketable in Europe because of its poor quality, developed the custom of partially compensating their black laborers in tots of wine five or six times a day. For the same reason, in rural areas of Germany during the nineteenth century, many workers became heavy drinkers, a pattern that helped to make alcohol production a profitable enterprise. For urban industrial workers in Germany, more subtle mechanisms were utilized.

Industrial workers rarely received hard liquor as part of their wage payment. Until 1846, however, it was usual to pay the workers in saloons or to make them apply for work there, in places that were under the commission of factory owners and entrepreneurs. The arrangement was deliberately set up in order to make workers drink as much as they could afford. The profit went to the commissionaire and the entrepreneur who installed the saloon for the purpose of making workers drink, even if they desperately needed their money for other goods (Vogt 1984: 556).

Another important line of research has shown that the extent of drinking-related problems in a population correlates with changes in the economic cycle. Thus Brenner has shown that increases in wine and beer sales occur during periods of economic recession and rising unemployment. As a result, national recessions in personal income and employment "are consistently followed in 2 or 3 years by increases in cirrhosis mortality rates" (Brenner 1975: 1282). Brenner contends that economic disruptions create conditions of social stress, which in turn stimulate a heightened rate of anxiety-avoidance drinking and consequent health problems, a finding consistent with Engels's interpretation.

Class Solidarity

Although Engels clearly understood the harmful effects of heavy drinking, he also realized that social drinking can be an act of group solidarity in the working class and, by extension, other oppressed groups as well. For example, in his book *A Shopkeeper's Millennium*, Paul Johnson (1978) analyzed the role of drinking in the formation of the industrial working class and working-class solidarity in Rochester, New York, during the early 1800s. Rochester was the first of the important inland American cities created by the commercialization of agriculture. By 1803, Rochester had grown into a major marketing and manufacturing center serving a surrounding agricultural area. Industrialization introduced a radical change in the nature of work and social life in the city. Before industrialization, production occurred in cottage industries in which employers and workers toiled together in production and gathered together after work to share a convivial drink to mark their day's accomplishment. However, as cottage industries grew into full-blown factories, employers "increased the pace, scale, and regularity of production and they hired young strangers with whom they shared no more than contractual obligations" (P. Johnson 1978: 51). With the profits gained from the shift from cottage to factory capitalism, employers built new mansions in new wealthy enclaves at a distance from their factories and the considerably more modest homes of their workers. Through these changes, distinct class boundaries emerged, and the previously narrow gap in the social fabric widened into a remarkable abyss.

In the barrooms and taverns that dotted their neighborhoods, working men and women forged an independent social life, shaped at every turn by the capitalist maelstrom restructuring their world. Heavy drinking, a feature of Western social life since the introduction of inexpensive distilled spirits in the seventeenth century, became "an angry badge of working-class status" (P. Johnson 1978: 60). Why drinking? According to Johnson:

The drinking problem of the late 1820s stemmed directly from the new relationship between master and wage earner. Alcohol had been a builder of morale in household workshops, a subtle but pleasant bond between men. But in the 1820s proprietors turned their workshops into little factories, moved their families away from their places of business, and devised standards of discipline, self-control, and domesticity that banned liquor. By default, drinking became part of an autonomous working-class social life and its meaning changed. (P. Johnson 1978: 60)

A direct parallel exists between the social role played by drinking in the formation of working-class identity and its function in the maintenance of Indian identity among certain Native Americans. According to Lurie, who studied the Winnebago and Dogrib peoples, getting drunk is "a very Indian thing to do when all else fails to maintain the Indian-white boundary" (Lurie 1979: 138). A somewhat similar argument has been made for the role of drinking among the indigenous peoples of Australia (Becket 1965). These examples suggest a contradictory dimension of alcohol consumption in class relations. While the dominant social class, for political and economic reasons, may promote and help to fashion abusive drinking patterns in exploited classes, the collective and segregated nature of such drinking in these classes may, on occasion, help to facilitate some degree of group unity necessary for effective struggle with the dominant social group.

Alcohol may also play a central role in the creation of new social classes. Although world-system theorists have outlined many of the important features of the growth and spread of capitalism, the local strategies utilized to create, retain, and discipline labor have not been issues of primary regard. However, Leslie Doyal has called attention to the use of alcohol as labor-control device. With reference to East Africa, she points to the parallel transformation of traditional modes of social production and traditional modes of alcohol consumption following the penetration of capital. Like their predecessors in the slums of nineteenth-century Manchester and London, Doyal found that African migrant workers drink to alleviate personal suffering and escape the monotony of their labor. However, she notes that many employers actually encourage drinking despite its negative effect on labor productivity. These employers believe that the presence of a local brewery is a "useful mechanism for stabilizing the workforce" (Doyal 1979: 115). Further, she argues that by absorbing a worker's wages, alcohol ties him more firmly to the capitalist mode.

Hutchinson's account of the tremendous disorganizing effects of European liquor on life in southern Africa reveals an additional aspect of this issue. These effects included a general breakdown of traditional social and political life. Describing a perpetually inebriated tribal leader, for instance, he remarks (1979: 332) "the business of the tribe was necessarily brought to a standstill, for reasons which weakened if they did not disable the prestige of the chiefdomship." But Hutchinson fails to note that destruction of the tribal system was a top administrative priority! Discussing "Native Policy," Lord Selborne, British High Commissioner for Southern Africa and Governor of the Transvaal and Orange River Colony from 1905 to 1910, proposed that a major objective of the colonial government was "to ensure the gradual destruction of the tribal systems, which is incompatible with civilization. An important feature of this policy will be teaching Natives to work" (quoted in Magubane 1979: 11). Since Great Britain did not seize southern Africa for the purpose of extending civilization, as picturesque a rationale as that may be, but rather to extract wealth, the High Commissioner got things a bit twisted. At any rate, it is evident that alcohol contributed greatly to the administration's objectives.

Of note in this regard is Harry Wolcott's comprehensive study of colonial control of indigenous drinking in Bualaway, Rhodesia (now Zimbabwe). Wolcott reports that the white-settler regime organized municipal beer gardens for use by urban black workers. According to Wolcott (1974: 34), beer garden drinking "facilitated some pent-up hostility and frustration; it enhanced gaiety and exuberance; and it contributed to accepting things as they were." In short, he argues, white control of black drinking "contributed nobly to maintaining the status quo in the relationship between Africans and Europeans" (Wolcott 1974: 19). This fact was recognized by the colonial settler government. Thus, the white major of Salisbury could proudly report: "The Rufaro Brewery has been an important contributory factor to the level of happiness which we have been able to maintain in recent times" (Wolcott 1974: 224).

Availability

Engels described a causal chain linking alcohol availability to consumption rates and consumption rates to the prevalence of health and social drinking-related problems. In part, his perspective on the causes of alcoholism has been restated by Kendell (1979: 367), "what determines whether a person becomes dependent on alcohol is how much he drinks for how long rather than his personality, psychodynamics or biochemistry." As opposed to many other human activities that have been labeled social problems or deviant behavior, abusive drinking is not disjunctive with socially acceptable patterns; it is merely an exaggeration of normal behavior. In many social settings, not only is drinking tolerated, it is socially sanctioned and rewarded. Consequently, "the difference between an alcoholic and a 'normal' heavy drinker is quantitative, not qualitative" (Robins 1980: 195), and availability therefore is an issue of investigative concern.

Several researchers have examined the relationship among availability, consumption rates, and health consequences. Bruun et al. (1975) have reported a definite association between increased availability and increased consumption. Likewise, several anthropologists have noted that high incidence areas for drinking and cirrhosis among Native American populations are associated geographically with off-reservation sources of supply.

Political Factors

In explaining availability, Engels, in part, discussed the role of the state. Historical research suggests that state interest in alcohol consumption has undergone at least three identifiable phases. Preindustrial attention was primarily fueled by a fiscal motivation, alcohol being viewed as taxable commodity. With industrialization and the emergence of laborers as a distinct social class, this attitude was joined and eventually superseded by a concern with temperance. Originally, temperance ideology was a feature of self-discipline in the upper class, but at the turn of the twentieth century there emerged a growing concern about the negative impact of drinking on industrial efficiency and employer control of the working class. Not surprisingly, the main target of the prohibition movement was the drinking practices of working people. Johnson's account of the temperance movement in Rochester during the 1820s reveals that an intense class struggle ensued around the issue of alcohol consumption.

Temperance propaganda promised masters social peace, a disciplined and docile labor force and an opportunity to assert moral authority over their men. The movement enjoyed widespread success among the merchants and masters who considered themselves respectable. . . . Temperance men talked loudest in 1828 and 1829, years in which the autonomy of working-class neighborhoods grew at a dizzying rate. . . . Wage earners . . . now . . . drank only in their own neighborhoods and only with each other, and in direct defiance of their employers (P. Johnson 1978: 81–82).

Following World War II, the state position toward alcohol consumption again shifted, a change that can be explained in terms of the emergence of a highly concentrated alcohol industry with the political muscle to strongly influence government policy. The current state approach to alcohol consumption has been summarized recently by Makela et al. (1981), based on a review of the alcohol control policies of eight industrialized nations.

"In general, the State continues to pursue restrictive policies in the non-commercial sector of both manufacture and distribution of alcoholic beverages, whereas the approach toward the commercial segment of the market has become less restrictive and more supportive. In alcohol control, this has taken the form of the opening up of alcohol retail to market pressures and the suppression of non-commercial production" (Makela et al. 1981: 84).

The character of the proindustry state bias has been described in an analysis of the political economy of the California wine industry. The state was found to have played a significant role in the development of monopoly marketing procedures and monopoly-dominated trade associations. By helping to secure the interests of the largest grape growers, state intervention contributed to driving smaller farms out of production: "This new hybrid of private and state power was called agribusiness" (Bunce 1979: 49).

Another glimpse at the role of the state can be seen by examining the activities of the International Center for Alcohol Policies (ICAP). According to its mission statement, the purpose of ICAP is two fold: (1) to help reduce the abuse of alcohol worldwide and promote understanding of the role of alcohol in society, and (2) to encourage dialogue and pursue partnerships involving the beverage alcohol industry, the public health community and others interested in alcohol policy. At first glance, the ICAP would seem to be a nonprofit scholarly association concerned about the problems of alcohol abuse. In fact, ICAP was set up and given its $2 million a year operating budget by eleven giants of the global alcohol industry, including Allied Domecq, Bacardi-Martini, Brown-Forman Beverages Worldwide, Coors Brewing Company, Foster's Brewing Group Ltd., Guinness, IDV (which has since merged with Guinness), Heineken, Miller Brewing Co., Joseph E. Seagram & Sons, and South African Breweries. Many of these companies are well known to public health advocates as pioneers in the targeted marketing of alcohol to the poor, young, and addicted in the developing world and as opponents of public health prevention initiatives. The parent company of IDV, Grand Metropolitan (which owns Burger King, Pillsbury, and Haagen-Dazs), for example, aggressively promoted Jose Cuervo in the Islamic country of Malaysia using its "Lick, shoot, suck" promotion in which male drinkers were encouraged to lick salt from a woman's breasts, take a shot of the tequila, then suck from the lime she holds in her mouth. Bacardi-Martini touted its Benedictine D.O.M. (which is almost 40% alcohol) in Malaysia claiming it had "health-enhancing" powers for new mothers.

In Great Britain, Allied Domecq, Bacardi-Martini and Diageo are all members of The Portman Group, which actively opposed a British attempt to prevent drunk driving by lowering the legal blood-alcohol level for drivers. The Portman Group was found to be offering money to academics to write anonymous critical reviews of the volume *Alcohol Policy and the Public Good,* a book that was written by an international panel of alcohol researchers to provide the scientific foundation for the World Health Organization European Alcohol Action Plan. In Europe, Seagram, Allied Lyons, and Heineken belong to The Amsterdam Group, which sought to take court action against France's policies banning the televising of sports events featuring alcohol advertising. Notably, in 1998, ICAP was able to recruit the U.S. Center for Substance Abuse Prevention (CSAP) to co-issue a report that questions everything from the damaging effects of binge drinking to the causal relationship between alcohol and crime. Public health advocates have criticized CSAP, which in the mid-1990s almost lost its federal budget as a result of heavy alcohol industry lobbying of Congress, for participating in issuing a report that obfuscates the scientific fact that alcohol is a drug. Some interpreted CSAP's action as caving in to Big Alcohol. ICAP also issued a policy statement recommending that governments should join with the alcohol industry and private foundations in researching the relationship between drinking, pleasure and good health (Abramson 1998).

Economic Factors

Engels appreciated that producers view the alcohol market as an expandable arena for profit making. It is probably on this topic that the anthropology of drinking has been the weakest, despite the by-no-means-recent influence of market forces in shaping drinking behavior in populations of traditional anthropological interest. For instance, Doyal (1979) notes that in the late 1800s farmers in the mining areas of South Africa, anxious to put grain surpluses to profitable use in distilleries, recognized that achieving this objective "depended in greatly raising the level of alcohol consumption amongst blacks" (115). As this case suggests, drinking behavior must be understood in terms of a wider field of social relationships and, since the rise of capitalism, in light of capitalist relations of production, processes of commodification and the dynamic, expansionary, and oligopolistic arrangement of the capitalist market.

Since World War II, the major economic forces on the wider alcohol scene have been: (1) an increasingly dominant transitional corporate sector; (2) a near-stampede to consolidate the almost $200 billion a year commercial alcohol market; and (3) a well-financed and quite successful promotional drive to expand consumption on a world scale, with changes of enormous proportion carried out by powerful actors, with far-reaching consequences.

The impact of these forces can be illustrated with the case of the U.S. wine industry. In his analysis of California viticulture previously referred to, Bunce points to the pivotal role played by the Bank of America, in promoting its ascendancy in banking by securing a dominant position as financier of the California wine producers. Along with the state, the Bank of America was a prime mover in the shift to monopoly marketing. Significantly, consolidation was not achieved smoothly nor always through gentlemanly agreement. To discipline growers outside of its control, the bank used "threats of credit withdrawal and when that failed, violence and intimidation" (Bunce 1979: 45). Through these tactics, a high degree of concentration of control ultimately was attained.

The four largest companies in 1947 controlled 26% of U.S. wine and brandy shipments. By 1963 that figure was 44%, and in 1972 the four largest firms had increased their share to 53% of the U.S. total. Similarly the eight largest companies increased their hold over the market from 42% in 1947 to 68% in 1972.

With concentration largely secured, the focus of industry attention shifted toward capital investment in vineyards ($1 billion between 1969 and 1973) and stimulation of the domestic market. Under the influence of intense promotional efforts (see below), U.S. wine consumption doubled during the 1970s, and the industry projected a similar goal for the future. The potential of the domestic market was calculated by reference to European standards; U.S. per capita consumption of wine in 1980 was eight liters compared to seventy for Portugal, ninety-three for Italy, and ninety-five for France (Cavanagh and Clairmonte 1983). A longer-range objective of U.S. corporate wine producers is encroachment on the global wine market, now dominated by Italy, France, and Spain.

A major development in the U.S. wine industry in recent years has been the entrance of major corporations that produce diverse products. However, the level of corporate concentration in the wine industry pales by comparison with distilled spirits and beer (although it becomes increasingly inappropriate to separate these markets as multiple beverage conglomerates become the norm). Concentration "is most dramatic in the brewing industry, which emerged from a small-scale, local activity with significant regional variation into a capital-intensive industry, controlled at national or even international levels, that markets a product that is increasingly uniform" (Makela et al. 1981: 34). In the United States, three phases of the evolution of the brewing industry are identifiable: (1) the founding of the first commercial breweries during the colonial era and the subsequent proliferation of small-scale, labor-intensive, local producers; (2) the decline in the number of local breweries and rapid concentration of the market following World War II, accompanied by enormous increases in production and consumption; and (3) the emergence of oligopolistic dominance by the 1980s. The ten biggest producers now control almost all of the domestic consumption. Expansion has not been confined by national boundaries. The dwindling number of alcohol conglomerates has made strong moves to gain a major share of foreign distilleries, bottling plants, and retail outlets. Among major capitalist counties, interpenetration is extensive, while expansion into and domination of alcohol markets in underdeveloped nations is advancing swiftly. Between 1972 and 1980, underdeveloped countries increased their alcohol imports fourfold, from $325 million to $1.3 billion per year (Selvaggio 1983). Imports of wine more than tripled during this period, with the Ivory Coast, Guadeloupe, and Brazil absorbing one-fifth of the total. Underdeveloped nations now comprise one of the fastest-growing import regions for both hard liquor and beer, with 15% to 25% of the global import totals.

In alcohol, as with other commodities, emergence of the global corporation has been accompanied by the formulation of a corporate worldview that flies in the face of the anthropological use of that term. As defined by Redfield (1953) for anthropology, *worldview* refers to the conception of reality developed within a particular society. Increasingly, corporate leaders eschew the concern with cultural variation inherent in this conception and instead embrace a view of the world in which diverse peoples, lands, and societies are lumped together to form a global market, a set of raw materials, and a multisectorial labor force. Even the nation-state becomes an insignificant feature of this global cognitive map. As summed up by one corporate spokesperson: "The world's political structures are completely obsolete" because they impede "the search for global optimization of resources" (Barnett and Müller 1974).

The alcohol industry has been able to help recreate the world to fit its own view by employing its enormous profits in an extensive advertising campaign, estimated to cost over one billion dollars a year in the United States and two billion worldwide. While industry representatives and their hired scholars maintain that alcohol advertising is primarily geared toward convincing existing drinkers to switch brands and that advertising does not affect consumption rates, the findings of independent researchers suggest otherwise.

A glimpse at some of the giants of the global alcohol industry affirms this conclusion. Anheuser-Busch, the largest beer producer in the United States., with control of about 48% of the national market, is also the world's largest brewer with 10.7% of the world market. The company produces many brands of beer, including Budweiser, Bud Light, Busch, Michelob, Red Wolf Lager, ZiegenBock Amber, and O'Doul's (a nonalcoholic beer). The company is truly global with investments or licensing agreements in Asia, Europe, and Latin America and beer sales in more than 80 countries. Anheuser-Busch also operates recreational theme parks like Busch Gardens and SeaWorld, and water parks like Water Country USA and Adventure Island. In 1999, the company had net profits from alcohol sales of just under $10 billion and an advertising budget just over $650 million, $20 million of which was specifically targeted to U.S. Hispanics.

The third largest producer of hard liquor in the United States in 1999 was Joseph E. Seagram & Sons. The Seagram Spirits and Wine division of the company made and distributed popular liquor brands like Chivas Regal, Glenlivet, and Crown Royal in more than 190 countries and territories around the globe, with just under 7% of the world market. The Seagram Beverage Company division produced low-alcohol beverages like Seagram's Coolers and Mixers. In 1999, Seagrams had just under $5 billion sales of its alcoholic beverages (which only comprised about 30% of its total sales; much of the rest of its business being in the entertainment and music industries with ownership of the contracts for performers like Elton John, Sheryl Crow, Rob Zombie, Shania Twain and Jay-Z). Reflecting the constant drive toward consolidation, Vivendi Universal bought out the Seagram Company and in 2001 sold its beverage units to liquor giants Diageo and Pernod Ricard for over $8 billion.

The privately owned E & J Gallo Winery, the world's largest wine maker, produces approximately 25% of all wine sold in the United States., in no small part as a result of its inexpensive jug brands, Carlo Rossi and Gallo and its fortified bottom-drawer brand Thunderbird. Gallo cultivates over 3,000 acres of vineyard land in Sonoma County, California, manufactures its own bottle labels and bottles, and is the leading U.S. wine exporter. At the same time, Gallo imports and sells the Italian wine Ecco Domani and is a leading brandy producer. Early in its history Gallo only marketed wine in the low-to-moderate price range, but ultimately was able to expand into premium wines such as Turning Leaf and Gossamer Bay (which intentionally do not include the Gallo name on the label). With an annual U.S. advertising budget of about $50 million, Gallo is able to promote its products coast to coast.

CONCLUSION

We began this chapter with a discussion of "What is a drug?" and pointed out that there is no clearly agreed-upon definition. However, societies make choices and have legalized and even supported the consumption of some mood-altering substances, while others have been banned and those who possess, use, or distribute them are often punished, sometimes severely. Alcohol is a drug that has broad use in human societies, and its consumption goes back to ancient times. Anthropologists who have studied alcohol consumption in prestate societies have found that its use is well integrated into the cultural fabric and generally is not conceived of as presenting either a health or a social problem. Indeed, anthropologists commonly have found beneficial consequences of drinking in these kinds of societies. Studies of this sort have led to the formulation of the sociocultural model of drinking within anthropology.

However, there have been challenges to the adequacy of the sociocultural model. One type of challenge has come from alcohol researchers who assert that anthropologists have not paid adequate attention to the negative consequences of drinking in the societies they have studied. Another challenge incorporates this concern but argues as well that there is a need to examine drinking behavior within a political economic model. The latter challenge is raised by critical medical anthropologists concerned about the international transformation of drinking from a socially controlled, culturally meaningful behavior in local communities into one that is driven by the external political and economic interests of dominant groups in the global economy. Viewed in this light, a set of questions and issues about drinking emerge that have not tended to be asked by anthropologists in the past. Building on the early insights of Friedrich Engels, critical medical anthropology seeks to broaden our understanding to include an awareness of the ways drinking and its effects are shaped by interactions between human biology (including brain neurochemistry and physiology) and relations of social inequality locally, nationally, and internationally. In other words, CMA seeks to combine: (1) socially aware ethnographic study of drinking (or other substance use) that situates observable microcontexts, on-the-ground behaviors, and the cultural construction of meaning within wider politicoeconomic structures; (2) with a holistic framework that conceptualizes humans as complex biocultural and social beings; in order, (3) to develop a "critical biocultural" understanding of human health (M. Singer 1999; 2001).

Alcohol, as we noted at the onset of this chapter, is not the only widely legalized drug. Tobacco is another. In the next chapter we turn our attention to smoking behavior and its health consequences in terms of both conventional and critical analytic approaches within medical anthropology.

CHAPTER 6

Legal Addictions, Part II:
Up in Smoke

SMOKING, CULTURE, AND HEALTH:
AN OVERVIEW

The English word tobacco was derived from the Spanish *tabaco*, which in turn was taken directly from the Arawak word for cigar. The Arawak were the indigenous people that Christopher Columbus encountered in the Caribbean on his first and subsequent voyages to the New World. In his log, Columbus recorded his impressions of the Arawak: "They . . . brought us parrots and balls of cotton and spears and many other things, which they exchanged for the glass beads and hawks bells. They willingly traded everything they owned. . . . They were well-built, with good bodies and handsome features" (quoted in Zinn 1980: 1). Among the items that the Arawak brought to Columbus were the dried leaves of a cultivated plant that the Europeans had never seen before. Members of Columbus' crew observed the Arawak people smoking huge cigars made from this plant. The Arawak told the Europeans that smoking tobacco soothed their limbs, helped them not to feel weary, and eased the passage into sleep. Columbus and his crew brought tobacco back with them to Portugal. From there it diffused, first to France in 1560 and to Italy in 1561. By the turn of the century, it was being grown in Europe and had become a widely used substance on the European continent. Europeans, in turn, carried tobacco to much of the rest of the world, even to areas of the New World where it was unknown prior to Columbus's voyage (e.g., the subartic and artic regions).

The exact origin of tobacco use is still unknown. However, botanical study has demonstrated that the cultivated forms of the tobacco plant (several different species have been domesticated) all have their origin in South America. The wild ancestors of domesticated tobacco species are not indigenous to the Caribbean area but are found in Peru, Bolivia, Ecuador, and Argentina. Very likely, the tobacco plant and the knowledge for both cultivating and consuming it diffused from South America to the Caribbean (perhaps through Mexico) along with various cultivated food plants many years before the arrival of Columbus.

Other species of tobacco were indigenous to North America, and these came to be among the most widely cultivated plants grown by the Indians of what was to become the United States. Commonly, North American Indian peoples mixed tobacco with other plants such as sumac leaves and the inner bark of dogwood trees. In fact, the Indians of the Eastern United States and Canada referred to the substance they smoked in their pipes as *kinnikinnik,* an Algonquian word meaning "that which is mixed" (Driver 1969). Different tribal groups consumed tobacco in different ways. Among the Indians of the Northwest Coast, tobacco was chewed with lime but not smoked. Among the Creek, it was one of the ingredients of an emetic drink. The Aztecs ate tobacco leaves and also used it as snuff. Distinct cigarettes with cornhusk wrappings were smoked in the Southwest (although this may not have been an indigenous means of consumption). Smoking tobacco in pipes also was widespread.

Among Indian peoples, tobacco had both religious and secular uses. Shamans, or indigenous healers, used tobacco to enter into a trance state and communicate with spirit beings so as to diagnose the nature of a health or social problem. It also was commonly used in rites of passage to mark changes in an individual's social status. Smoking tobacco communally often was done to mark the beginning or continuation of an alliance between tribes or to make binding an agreement or contract.

As this description suggests, tobacco was deeply rooted in the indigenous cultures of many peoples of the New World. Given the ceremonial controls on the frequency of consumption and the diluted form in which tobacco was consumed, as well as the fact that inhalation of tobacco smoke into the lungs was not emphasized, tobacco may not have been a significant source of health problems among Indian people prior to European contact.

However, with the diffusion of tobacco to Europe and with the rise of industrial capitalism, tobacco was transformed from a sacred object and culturally controlled medicament into a commodity sold for profit. With the emergence and development of the tobacco industry and the intensive promotion of cigarettes, the per capita consumption of tobacco increased dramatically (especially in the early and middle decades of the twentieth century), with significant health consequences. As Barnet and Cavanagh

(1994: 184) observe, "The cigarette is the most widely distributed global consumer product on earth, the most profitable, and the most deadly."

Indeed, tobacco, it has been said, is the one product that if used as directed by the manufacturer will lead to certain disease and death. The significant negative health consequences of smoking are now widely known. Three commonly lethal diseases, in particular, have been closely linked to the use of tobacco: coronary heart disease, lung cancer, and chronic obstructive pulmonary disease. Other fatal or disabling diseases known to be caused by or made worse by smoking include peripheral vascular disease, hypertension, and myocardial infarction. Smoking also causes cancer of the mouth, throat, bladder, and other organs. As anthropologists Mark Nichter and Elizabeth Cartwright (1991: 237) argue, smoking damages the health of families in three additional ways:

First, smoking leads to and exacerbates chronic illness, which in turn reduces adults' ability to provide for their children. Smoking also daily diverts scarce household resources which might be used more productively. And third, children living with smokers are exposed to smoke inhalation [i.e., passive smoking] and have more respiratory disease.

In 1989 the World Health Organization estimated that worldwide 2.5 million people die each year from diseases caused by tobacco use. This had risen to 3 million deaths by 1994. By the year 2000, tobacco is expected to be the leading cause of death in underdeveloped nations (Barnet and Cavanagh 1994). In the United States, tobacco products were the cause of 434,000 deaths in 1992 (Barnet and Cavanagh 1994). This amounts to the death of one person each thirteen seconds (Ile and Kroll 1990; Peto 1990). Smoking is now a factor in over one-fifth of all deaths in the United States, far greater than the death toll caused by automobile accidents, drug use, homicide, AIDS, airplane crashes, and suicide *combined*! (Chandler 1986). The Environmental Protection Agency issued a 1992 report attributing 3,000 deaths a year and prevalent lung disease in children to passive smoking (cited in Barnet and Cavanagh 1994).

There are other costs of smoking as well. Smoking costs the United States approximately $440 billion each year in medical expenses and lost days from work. By smoking one pack a day, a smoker adds an average of 18% to his or her medical bills each year and shortens life expectancy by six years (Resnick 1990). Despite these costs, tobacco is a legal drug, readily sold by supermarkets, vending machines, gas stations, and convenience shops in every community in the United States and worldwide.

Knowledge about the dangerous health effects of smoking is not new. The first study showing the deleterious side of smoking was conducted by Raymond E. Pearl of Johns Hopkins University in 1938. His research demonstrated a clear association between smoking and shortened life span in the 6,813 men included in his sample. A flood of medical reports with similar findings has followed ever since. Oftentimes, this information does not reach the general public because of the influence of the tobacco industry and its advertising dollar on the mass media. Several studies have shown that magazines that carry a lot of cigarette advertising tend not to include news items and articles on the negative health consequences of smoking (Smith 1978; Tsien 1979). As Weis and Burke (1963: 4) note, "The tobacco industry has a history of exerting financial pressure on publishers to suppress the printing of information which would impair tobacco sales. [When questioned,] one reason editors give for the lack of media coverage of smoking is that health effects from smoking are not 'newsworthy.'" Billboard companies similarly are reluctant to carry antismoking messages because they depend on the tobacco companies for half of their advertising income. These companies have refused to sell space to the American Cancer Society for this reason. Even the 1970 legislation passed by Congress banning radio and television advertising of tobacco products did not have a major effect. Tobacco advertising dollars for other forms of promotion, such as ads in women's magazines, quickly increased fivefold.

All of this was money well spent by the tobacco industry, which has been described as a cash cow by industry analysts. Cigarette income enabled R. J. Reynolds to buy up Nabisco, Del Monte, and Hawaiian Punch. Philip Morris used its tobacco dollars to acquire Miller Beer, Seven Up, and General Foods. American Brands turned tobacco profits into ownership of the Pinkerton guard company, sporting goods manufacturers, and various other businesses. Through subsidies paid to tobacco growers and the distribution of large quantities of tobacco to Third World Nations through the Food for Peace program, the federal government has played an important role in supporting the profitability of tobacco production.

Critical to the effort to keep the dollars flowing into the coffers of the tobacco barons has been their effort to find new markets. Women have been high on the advertising hit list, as have ethnic minorities and the populations of developing nations. Another important and vulnerable market is youth.

Smoking and Youth

In light of the publicity that has been given to the health consequences of tobacco use, you might "assume that cigarette smoking is a 'dying' custom that will soon self-terminate" (Stebbins 1990: 228). But this does not appear to be the case. About 1,000 packs of cigarettes are sold in the United States alone every second of everyday. Insuring future sales, 4,000 teenagers begin the smoking habit each day! In the last ten years, the number of smokers between the ages of twelve and fourteen years has increased by 8,000% (Fischer 1987). In fact, teenagers, especially girls, are the only population group in the country that has not reduced its rate of smoking. The National Institute on Drug Abuse has monitored teenage smoking for the years 1991 through 1994 in its "Monitoring the Future" study. In 1991, 14.3% of eighth graders, 20.8% of tenth graders, and 28.3% of twelfth graders reported smoking in the thirty-day period prior to participating in the study. By 1994, these percentages had climbed to 18.6%, 25.4%, and 31.2% for these three grades respectively (National Institute on Drug Abuse 1994). Also, the study found steady increases in the percentage of teenagers reporting that they smoked at least half a pack of cigarettes a day for all three grade levels. For example, among high school seniors, the frequency of smokers of half a pack a day increased from 10.7% in 1991 to 11.2% by 1994. The study also monitored changes in the percentage of students using smokeless tobacco (i.e., chewing tobacco). In 1994, 7.7% of eighth graders, 10.5% of tenth graders, and 11.1% of twelfth graders reported using smokeless tobacco during the last thirty days. Tobacco manufacturers have found that smokeless tobacco has a strong market in this underage population. Among teenagers who drop out of school, smoking rates are notably high, with one study finding that 70% of high school dropouts are smokers (Pirie et al. 1988).

Because nicotine, one of the key products of tobacco burning, is a highly addictive drug, only 15% of teenagers who experiment with tobacco smoking will be able to quit. Almost 60% of all smokers become addicted to tobacco while they are adolescents. The health consequences of this addiction will not show up until later in their lives. Worldwide, it is estimated that two hundred million people who are now under twenty years of age will die from tobacco use (Peto and Lopez 1990).

THE ROAD TO TOBACCO PROFITS

If it is so dangerous, how did tobacco come to be a legal drug? You might at first think that tobacco was always legal, but this is not true. In fact, there was a time when a number of national governments saw tobacco as a dangerous drug that threatened the fabric of society, much as heroin or cocaine are seen today. The reason that this view of tobacco became obsolete and that tobacco came to be a drug approved for production and sale by governments around the world is a very instructive tale.

As we noted earlier, tobacco was one of the items Columbus acquired in the New World and brought back with him to Europe to demonstrate to his benefactors the economic value of his voyage. Tobacco was introduced as a medicinal drug, and it was at first cultivated in Europe for this purpose. European physicians of the sixteenth century became convinced that tobacco could be used to cure a wide assortment of diseases. Before long, however, people who were treated with tobacco, and probably their physicians realized as well that tobacco was a powerful mood-altering drug that had recreational value. By 1600, smoking was a common practice of working people in the port cities of England and Ireland (Brooks 1952).

The shift from medicinal to recreational, mood-altering use of tobacco by the poor and working classes of Europe (which, in fact, as we shall explain below, was a kind of self-medication) produced a backlash against smoking by the dominant classes and the church. Mintz (1985: 100), an anthropologist who has studied the consumable commodities ensnared in colonial trade, suggests that the reason for this hostile response lay in the distinct "visible, directly noticeable" physical reaction that smoking produces, especially for the new user. Mintz (1985: 100) draws a contrast here with sugar, another colonial commodity that became extremely popular in Europe.

In all likelihood, sugar was not subject to religion-based criticisms like those pronounced on tea, coffee, rum, and tobacco, exactly because its consumption did not result in flushing, staggering, dizziness, euphoria, changes in the pitch of voice, slurring of speech, visibly intensified physical activity, or any of the other cues associated with the ingestion of caffeine, alcohol, and nicotine.

These changes in comportment in working people appear to have been threatening to the wealthier classes, who preferred a more passive, controlled demeanor in socially dominated groups. Mintz also points out that unlike tobacco, tea, coffee, and rum, all of which are dark in color, refined sugar is white, the symbolic color of purity in Europe since ancient times. Racialist symbolism of this sort (toward mood-altering products that come from foreign lands with threatening dark-skinned peoples), argues Mintz, may have been an underlying cultural influence on the moralistic opposition to tobacco as well as to tea, coffee, and rum.

In 1602, the first known antismoking tract was printed and distributed in English cities. Entitled "Work for Chimney-sweepers: or A Warning for Tobacconists," it helped to launch a high-minded crusade against tobacco use. The class character of this crusade became clear two years later when another tract, entitled "A Counterblaste to Tobacco," appeared. Although published anonymously, it was widely known to have been produced by James I, the British king (Best 1983). In James's view, smoking tobacco was "A custome lothesome to the eye, hatefull to the Nose, harmefull to the braine, dangerous to the Lungs, and in the blacke stinking fume thereof, neerest resembling the horrible Stigian smoke of the pit that is bottomelesse" (quoted in Eckholm 1978: 6–7). The moral tone of the growing antitobacco effort, an approach later adopted as well by the alcohol temperance movement, can be seen in the text of another tract produced in 1616:

For imagine thou beheldes there such a fume-suckers wife most fearfully fuming forth very fountaines of bloud, howling for anguish of heart, weeping, wailing, and wringing her hands together, with grisly lookes, with wide staring eies, with mind amazed. . . . But suppose withall thou shouldest presently heare the thundring eccho of her horrible outcries ring the clouds, while she pitifully pleades with her husband thus: Oh husband, my husband, mine onely husband! Consider I beseech thee, thy deare, thy loving, and they kind-hearted wife. . . . Why doest thou so vainely preferre a vanishing filthie fume before my permanent vertues; before my amourous imbracings; yea before my firme setled faith & constant love?" (quoted in Best 1983: 175)

Smoking also was criticized at this early moment in its use by Europeans for being harmful to health, causing insanity, sterility, birth defects, and diverse other diseases. Moreover, critics began to taint smoking as a lower-class habit, "of ryotous and disordered Persons of meane and base Condition" (quoted in Best 1983: 175). Finally, in England, which at this point depended on Spain as a source of tobacco, smoking was attacked because it made the country dependent on one of its rivals in the imperial struggle for empire.

Extending these efforts to build a moral argument against smoking, King James in England began to enact policies to restrict tobacco consumption. In 1604, he imposed an additional duty on imported tobacco, raising the existing state tax by 4,000%. Through this dramatic step, he hoped to put tobacco out of the reach of most people. James did not ban tobacco completely for two reasons. First, because it was still being used as a medicine, and second, because (contrary to the antismoking propaganda of the era) addiction to the drug appears not to have been limited to the lower classes. James sought to avoid the wrath of "Persons of good Callinge and Qualitye," that is to say, members of the wealthy classes and nobility, who would have opposed a total ban on tobacco importation (quoted in Best 1983: 175).

By contrast, a number of other northern countries and even one southern European country, including Austria, Denmark-Norway, France, Bavaria, Cologne, Saxony, Württemberg, Russia, Sicily, Sweden, and Switzerland, adopted criminal penalties to punish smokers. Usually the penalties involved a small fine. However, Russia, at various times, adopted quite harsh legislation that called for whippings, slit noses, torture, deportation to Siberia, and even death (Brooks 1952). Despite these efforts, smoking continued to be popular. Thus, for example, in 1670 the Swiss National Assembly issued an official degree stating "Although the injurious habit of smoking has been everywhere prohibited by order, we recognize that these orders have been met by a spirit of opposition which is not easy to suppress" (quoted in Corti 1931: 124). Similarly, King James's tobacco tax led to a drop in the quantity of legal tobacco entering England but not to a drop in smoking. Rather, smugglers filled the demand and an untaxed black market in tobacco emerged.

In the end, government and moralist efforts to limit or prohibit smoking collapsed. By the end of the seventeenth century, the drug was legal throughout Europe. Underlying this radical shift was a reevaluation of smoking. What had been defined as a growing social problem came to be seen as an important source of revenue for an expanding state structure. In England, this transition began as early as 1608, when James significantly lowered his import tax so as not to lose tax revenue to the black market. As a result, tobacco imports rose quickly, as did the taxes collected on the drug. Tobacco was now on the road to full legalization throughout Europe as governments began to view popular craving for tobacco as a useful source of income for the state.

In the English case, colonization of North America played an important role in this process. James had invested considerable sums to launch the British colony in Virginia. The objective was to reap the same kinds of benefits that Spain had in its successful exploitation of the resources of Mexico, the Caribbean, and South America. However, while Spain extracted over seven million pounds of silver from its New World colonies between 1503 and 1660 (Wolf 1982), in Virginia no precious metals were found, nor was the colony able to produce other desired sources of wealth such as iron, potash, or silk. Nonetheless, the colonists did find one item they could produce successfully and export to England in large quantities, and it was tobacco. The soil of Virginia proved to be a good medium for tobacco growth, dried tobacco was lightweight and therefore could be shipped across the ocean at comparatively low cost, and the demand for it in England meant that it would bring a sale price far above the production cost. As Zinn (1980: 24) notes, "Finding that, like all pleasurable drugs tainted with moral disapproval, it brought a high price, the [Virginia] planters, despite their high religious talk, were not going to ask questions about something so profitable." Consequently, from an initial export of 2,500 pounds to England in 1616, Virginia was shipping over a million and a half pounds of tobacco less than fifteen years later. By 1668, the Virginia and Maryland colonies together shipped fifteen million pounds of tobacco to England, and by the end of the century this amount had doubled again (Price 1964). Tobacco emerged as North America's first cash crop.

While both King James and his successor King Charles sent repeated instructions for the Virginia colonists to find other sources of revenue, they did not attempt to stop the growing tobacco imports. During this period, the British government, like its rivals throughout Europe, was attempting to expand its scope of authority. This "gave the king an economic interest in the tobacco trade" (Best (1983: 178). Eventually, however, the influx of tobacco from the colonies was so great that it even overwhelmed the substantial English demand, causing a slump in the market.

The English turned to the other countries of Europe as potential new markets for their surplus colonial production. By the latter part of the seventeenth century, re-exporting came to account for the largest portion of the British tobacco trade. To open up these new markets, the British government send delegations to other nations to convince them that it would be profitable to remove existing bans on smoking, import British tobacco, and then tax it. In this way, the tobacco trade became a force in England's foreign policy. Ironically, "the English, who at the start of the seventeenth century led Europe in an anti-tobacco crusade, came to profit immensely by taxing and trading in the drug, and closed the century serving as missionaries of smoking to the other governments of Europe" (Best 1983: 180). There is, in fact, a double irony here. While the British helped to open the French market to tobacco imports, during the Revolutionary War against England, Thomas Jefferson and Benjamin Franklin put up American tobacco as collateral for French war loans. These loans helped to provide the rebellious colonists with the supplies they needed to defeat the British. Russia, which had imposed the most stringent antismoking laws, was one of the last European countries to remove all penalties. In 1697, Peter the Great, the Russian czar, issued a decree permitting the open sale and consumption of tobacco, although the government imposed high taxes on the lucrative trade.

In this way, tobacco was transformed from an illegal and widely condemned drug into a legal and economically important force in European history, a source of revenue accumulation that helped to fund the transformation from feudalist to capitalist production. In Best's (1983: 182) assessment, "Tobacco was vindicated, not because there was a revolution in morality, but because governments discovered that it provided an economic foundation for colonialism and a new source of tax revenue." Tobacco, in short, gained acceptance because of the role it came to play in an emergent global economic system.

Mintz (1985) offers an additional reason for the vindication of tobacco as a socially accepted and widely used drug. He lumps tobacco, coffee, tea, chocolate, and sugar together as the "drug foods" that came to serve as low-cost food substitutes for the laboring classes of Europe with the rise of colonialism and industrial capitalism. As "drug foods" like tobacco were adopted into the European diet, other more nutritious but more costly food items diminished in importance. Further, increasing "the worker's energy output and productivity, such substitutes figured importantly in balancing the accounts of capitalism" (Mintz 1985: 148) by lowering the cost of supporting a manual labor force while increasing production.

"The substances transformed by British capitalism from upper-class luxuries into working-class necessities are of a certain type. Like alcohol or tobacco, they provide respite from reality, and deaden hunger pains. Like coffee or chocolate or tea, they provide stimulus to greater effort without providing nutrition. Like sugar they provide calories, while increasing the attractiveness of these other substances when combined with them. There was no conspiracy at work to wreck the nutrition of the British working class, to turn them into addicts, or to ruin their teeth. But the ever-rising consumption of [drug foods] . . . was an artifact of intraclass struggles for profit" (Mintz 1985: 186).

This argument is tied also to the recognition that with the rise of capitalist factory production, the lives of laboring people were significantly transformed. Work shifted from personal involvement in craft production or production for personal consumption into segmented, often boring, mass production under conditions that were alienating for most workers. Under these circumstances, tobacco, and the other items that formed the complex of "drug foods" were so welcomed by workers they were hard to legislate against. As we have seen, legal bans failed, resulting in the emergence of an intertwined and spiraling political economic system: Cheap food substitutes and production enhancers like tobacco were readily sought after by workers to provide relief from the drudgery of work. These purchases helped an emergent capitalist class to increase profits. These profits, in turn, could be used to penetrate new arenas of production, which in turn produced new layers of alienated workers vulnerable to the appeals of mood-altering drugs.

Ironically, one of the arenas of production that ultimately came to be penetrated by a capitalist mode of industrial production was cigarette manufacture itself. Prior to 1881, cigarettes were rolled one-by-one by hand. However, in that year, James A. Bonsack introduced the cigarette machine, which was capable of producing more than 200 cigarettes per minute (Tennet 1950). A problem smokers still faced, however, concerned how to get their cigarettes lit. A common practice was for smokers to go to tobacco stores to light their cigarettes from a gas or oil lamp. But in 1912, a safe match finally was invented. As Sobel (1978: 67) points out, "Matches altered the way cigarettes were smoked, encouraging their consumption during odd moments in the day; in effect, they transformed cigarette use from a thoughtful exercise into an almost unconscious habit." These inventions significantly contributed to a major jump in cigarette consumption, from half a billion in 1880 to 2.2 billion in 1888, 18 billion in 1914, and 54 billion in 1919 (Sobel 1978). By this point, smoking had become an acceptable and socially unremarkable habit, a considerable change from the days of the antismoking crusades of the early 1600s.

In 1991, the largest distributor of cigarettes, Philip Morris, was operating a bank of rapid-fire automatic rollers that together were turning out 17,000 cigarettes a second, twenty-four hours a day. Philip Morris produced 11% of the 5.5 trillion cigarettes sold that year and controlled almost half of the U.S. market. Though still based in the United States, Philip Morris had become a transnational corporation with operations around the world. However, the largest cigarette manufacturer is the state tobacco monopoly of China, which produces more than 1.5 trillion cigarettes a year, all of them consumed in China. At this pace, it is projected that two million people in China will be dying each year of tobacco-related diseases by the end of the century.

Despite the expenditure of millions of dollars by the tobacco industry to counter its appeal, in recent years a new antismoking movement has emerged on the social scene and has had a considerable degree of success. While in 1964 over half of the adults in the United States smoked, by 1991 the proportion had fallen to 26% (Barnet and Cavanagh 1994). Bans on smoking in indoor public and private spaces are becoming commonplace. The class membership and motivations of the contemporary antismoking movement, however, are in marked contrast with the earlier effort. The concerns driving antismoking forces in the present are seen in the following "A Closer Look" profile, which examines the effort of the tobacco industry to recruit new markets for tobacco sales.

"A Closer Look"

MARKETING OF DISEASE TO MINORITIES: THE TOBACCO INDUSTRY TARGETS HISPANICS AND AFRICAN AMERICANS

While he was Surgeon General of the United States, C. Everett Koop, M.D., called attention in a press conference to the fact that "Two of the six leading causes of excess deaths observed among blacks and other minorities are cancer and cardiovascular disease, both of which are smoking-related, and a third is infant mortality, to which cigarette smoking contributes." Consequently, in his capacity as the chief guardian of the health of Americans, Koop concluded, "I submit that no public or private effort aimed at improving the health of blacks and other minorities can omit the reduction of cigarette smoking as one of its major goals."

Reducing cigarette smoking among Hispanics was the goal of the Hispanic Smoking Cessation Research Project in San Francisco. The project attempted several strategies, including putting up educational messages on billboards located in Hispanic neighborhoods of the city and on advertisement cards posted in buses. But in 1989 the project ran into trouble.

All of the advertising space in the Hispanic community and on local buses had been bought up by RJR Nabisco to use to advertise Newport cigarettes. "Newport is everywhere," said Barbara Marin, director of the smoking-cessation project. "We had a lot of trouble getting space because of the Newport campaign in the community" (quoted in Maxwell and Jacobson 1989).

There is good reason for concern about the difficulty of reaching Hispanics with smoking-cessation education. According to Bruce Maxwell and Michael Jacobson of the Center for Science in the Public Interest and the authors of *Marketing Disease to Hispanics,* a number of indicators show that rates of smoking are increasing markedly among Hispanics, as well as among African Americans and other ethnic minorities, and that these communities are being targeted by the tobacco industry. In the past, smoking among Hispanics and African Americans tended to be lower than in the general U.S. population, although rates among men from these communities has been rising for several decades. The data for Hispanics, for example, are telling. The 1982–83 Hispanic Health and Nutrition Examination Survey (HHANES), the most comprehensive study of Hispanic health conducted in the United States in recent years, shows that 43.6% of Mexican-American men were smokers, as were 41.8% of Cuban men and 41.3% of Puerto Rican men. Among Hispanic women, Puerto Ricans had the highest rate of smoking, 32.6%, with the rates for Mexican-American and Cuban women being 24.5% and 23.1% respectively. In her study of smoking among Puerto Rican adolescents in Boston, McGraw (1989: 166–167) found that "Puerto Rican males had higher rates of current smoking than any of the [adolescent] populations studied [by other U.S. researchers] and lower quit rates than most." These findings show that while most population groups in the United States have been lowering their smoking in recent years, rates have not been dropping for Hispanics; and among women in the Hispanic community rates have been rising noticeably. Currently, the HHANES data show that "Hispanic smoking rates are substantially higher than those for Whites" (Haynes et al. 1990: 50).

The consequences are identifiable: "There is a big increase in lung cancer rates among Hispanic males," reports Al Marcus of the UCLA Jonsson Comprehensive Cancer Center. "There is an epidemic out there," says Marcus, "and it hasn't received a lot of attention. There aren't a lot of people studying cancer in Hispanics" (quoted in Maxwell and Jacobson 1989: 17).

Other studies support Marcus's conclusions. Between 1970 and 1980, the Colorado Tumor Registry reported a 132% jump in the rate of lung cancer among Hispanics males, compared to a 12% increase for white males (cited in Marcus and Crane 1985). Another study in Colorado found an increase in lung cancer rates among Hispanic males that was several times the increase among white males (Savitz 1986). Similarly, data from New Mexico for the period from 1958 to 1982 show that deaths due to lung cancer tripled for Hispanic males but only doubled for white males, while the death rate for chronic obstructive pulmonary disease increased six fold for Hispanic males but increased less than four fold for white males (Samet et al. 1988). These increases in cigarette-related mortality are connected to increases in smoking among Hispanics beginning in the 1960s. For example, a three-generation study of smoking among Mexican-Americans in Texas by anthropologist Jeannine Coreil and coworkers (Markides, Coreil, and Ray 1987), found rising rates of cigarette consumption among Hispanics. Because there is about a twenty-year incubation period between the beginning of smoking and the development of cancer, it is expected that in coming years rates of tobacco-related diseases will show marked increases for Hispanic males, and eventually for Hispanic females as well.

The existing data on African Americans show a similar pattern. The 1985 Health Interview Survey found that among all American males thirty-five to sixty-four years of age, African-American males were the most likely to be smokers. Similarly, African-American females between the ages of thirty-five and seventy-four were more likely than similar-age women of other ethnicities to be smokers. Were it not for very high rates of smoking among Puerto Rican women twenty-five to thirty-four years of age, African-American women would have had the highest smoking prevalence rates in that age group too (Haynes et al. 1990). Currently, approximately 30% more African Americans smoke than whites (Horan 1993).

Why are smoking rates going up among U.S. ethnic minorities, especially at a time when the public has been exposed to a lot of information about the serious health risks of smoking? Suzanne Haynes of the National Cancer Institute and her coworkers (1990: 49) conclude the following:

One factor that may be responsible for the high rates of smoking in the Hispanic populations is the impact of advertising on these populations. It is well recognized that cigarette manufacturers are now targeting Hispanics and other minority populations with increased expenditures to distribute their message.

So intense is cigarette (and alcohol) advertising in Hispanic and African American newspapers and magazines that industry experts question whether many of these publications could stay in business if this source of funding disappeared. In addition, according to Al Marcus of UCLA, minority magazines and newspapers fail to "come out with criticisms of the tobacco industry, they don't come out with positions that advocate either abstinence or cessation." The question is raised by Marcus as to whether editorial policy is being influenced by advertisement income. A survey of advertising in black magazines like *Ebony, Jet, Black Enterprise, Modern Black Man,* and *Dollars & Sense* found that 40% was for tobacco, alcohol, or cosmetic products (Prevention File 1990). For example, the R. J. Reynolds Tobacco Company advertises in more than 200 minority magazines and newspapers. It also gives scholarships to minority journalism students.

Beyond advertisements in the print media, tobacco companies spend millions of dollars to purchase billboards in minority neighborhoods. In fact, since the 1970s, the tobacco industry has been the leading advertiser on billboards. According to *Advertising Age,* one-third of all billboard revenues come from ads for either tobacco or alcohol. Minority communities are one of the big targets for these advertisement dollars. A 1987 survey conducted by the city of St. Louis found twice as many billboards in African American neighborhoods as in white neighborhoods. Moreover, the survey found that almost 60% of all the billboards in African American neighborhoods were for cigarettes and alcoholic beverages. A parallel study in Baltimore found that 70% of the billboards in African American neighborhoods were for alcohol or tobacco (Scenic America 1990). In the assessment of Dr. Emilio Carrillo, a faculty member of Harvard Medical School,

If you look at the billboard advertising in the Hispanic community, you will find that they all portray young, happy people who appear affluent, who appear very light-skinned. Basically, it's setting up billboards in poor, devastated communities showing pictures of wealth and well-being that are absolutely false in terms of what the billboards are advertising. (quoted in Maxwell and Jacobson 1989: 38)

As this statement suggests, many of the billboards in minority neighborhoods target youth. As Jane Garcia of La Clinica de la Raza states, "I think it's a very vulnerable population. And it's being promoted as a very hip and cool thing to do" (quoted in Maxwell and Jacobson 1989: 38).

Efforts to win minority smokers do not stop with direct advertising. Another strategy is to court favor with minority organizations. Patricia Edmonds, a journalist, wrote a detailed exposé of this practice for the *Detroit Free Press* on July 23, 1989. This is what she found. The makers of Kool cigarettes, Brown and Williamson Tobacco Company, reported that they had $74 million in insurance coverage purchased from minority-owned companies and had established a $10 million line of credit with fifteen African American-owned banks. This tobacco company donated a quarter of a million dollars in four years to inner-city community organizations and has contributed to the United Negro College Fund, the Congressional Black Caucus, and the Joint Center for Political Studies, a think tank concerned with black issues. Philip Morris, the maker of Marlboro,

Benson & Hedges, and Virginia Slims, was supporting one hundred African American organizations with more than $1.3 million in donations. R. J. Reynolds, maker of Winston, Salem, More, and Camel cigarettes, was the largest single contributor to the United Negro College Fund schools.

Reynolds also sponsors minority golf, bowling, and softball tournaments, another strategy that is common among tobacco manufacturers for winning friends and influencing people. An article in the May 1985 issue of the tobacco trade journal *Tobacco Reporter* indicates that Reynolds also underwrites numerous Hispanic festivals across the country. Ignoring the health effects of cigarettes, a company official is quoted in the article as saying, "Our efforts reflect a growing practice of local groups and private enterprises joining hands to preserve a heritage and, at the same time, improve life in the communities in which Hispanics live" (p. 62). Promotional expenditures of this sort by cigarette companies doubled between 1980 and 1983 and had reached $1 billion by 1986. Kenneth Warner (1986: 58), a University of Michigan School of Public Health professor notes, "Perhaps the least well-defined but potentially most important institutional impact of cigarette companies' promotions is their contribution to creating an aura of legitimacy, of wholesomeness, for an industry that produces a product that annually accounts for about a fifth of all American deaths."

Like the Hispanic Smoking Cessation Research Project of San Francisco mentioned earlier, a number of minority communities have attempted to counter the effects of the smoking promotion efforts of the tobacco industry. For example, the Washington Heights-Inwood Healthy Heart Program in New York has developed activities to educate Hispanic children about the dangers of smoking and deception employed by cigarette companies in their advertising campaigns. Targeted to fifth and sixth graders, these activities include:

The World without Smoke Advertising Contest, an annual contest in which students develop posters, poems, songs, and skits that show the truth about smoking. Winners are honored at a ceremony attended by community leaders.

The Burial of Joe Camel, a mock funeral procession and service in which students debunk the glamorous image of this youth-oriented symbol of the tobacco industry.

Knock Down the Lies in Cigarette Ads, a game in which students compete to expose the deceptions of cigarette advertisements.

Similarly, the Heart, Body, and Soul Project in Baltimore used spirituality and pastoral leadership to assist members of twenty-two African American churches to quit smoking. These efforts show that it is possible to fight back against the tobacco industry, but the billions of dollars spent on promoting smoking far outweigh the potential effects of small, poorly funded community-based antismoking projects.

While he was Surgeon General, C. Everett Koop supported a total ban on tobacco promotion and advertising. At a meeting held a number of years ago in the Non-Smokers Inn, a Dallas, Texas motel, Koop reiterated his support of an advertising ban and remarked, "But, don't anyone weep over the future of American cigarette manufacturers, because they are exporting disease, disability and death to the Third World as fast as they can" (quoted in Resnick 1990: 78).

ANTHROPOLOGY AND THE STUDY OF SMOKING BEHAVIOR

Anthropological studies of tobacco use are relatively rare, and the topic is not common in medical anthropology texts. Even in general ethnographic accounts written by anthropologists about the social life and behavior of people around the world, smoking often is mentioned only in passing and then most frequently with respect to people's (sometimes constant) requests for tobacco from the anthropologist. The reason for this neglect of smoking behavior is not entirely clear. Black (1984) has suggested that tobacco use is understudied by anthropologists because of the way smoking is handled in Western cultures. For the most part, smoking, unlike drinking alcohol, is not a highly symbolic or heavily ritualized behavior in the West (at least, not since the invention of prerolled cigarettes and the safety match). This means that in Western cultures smoking tends to be an individual act, tied to internal states of mind and mood, that does not communicate a lot of cultural information. This is not to say that the act of smoking is devoid of symbolic content. For example, as portrayed in numerous movies, a film character may light a cigarette to convey various states of mind or character to those around him or her, including alienation from conventional society, independence from traditional role constraints, an air of mystery and daring, or sexual interest or satisfaction. The defiance theme associated with smoking may, in fact, be intensified in coming years as a result of the popular movement to ban smoking in public places because of the health consequences of passive or secondary smoke inhalation. Yet symbolic valences are known to change overtime, and deviance was not always a theme linked by popular culture to smoking. Earlier in the twentieth century, during World War I, in fact, cigarettes were "associated with the positive values of quiet dignity, courage, and dedication of the model soldier and became an essential part of the soldier's life" (Resnick 1990: 135). This connection was a product of a massive contribution of cigarettes to the U.S. military by the tobacco industry and the subsequent cognitive connection of smoking with soldiering.

Robb (1986) has suggested that currently smoking in the West acts symbolically as an *anticipatory rite of passage* for members of subordinated social groups such as youth, women, and ethnic minorities. Unlike socially approved rites of passage, such as a wedding or graduation, in an anticipatory rite of passage members of the subordinate group seek to unilaterally claim passage to a higher status even though this has not been sanctioned by the dominant group. In a somewhat different vein, Eckert (1983) has suggested that smoking may be used by some youth to symbolically express their membership in particular adolescent peer groups. Several studies show that smoking among adolescents, for example, is associated with perceived approval for smoking in a valued peer network (Green 1979; Mittlemark et al. 1987). In her ethnographic study of smoking among Puerto Rican adolescents in Boston, McGraw (1989: 392) strongly emphasizes an important cultural dimension of this behavior:

Smoking [was found to be] a social behavior governed by cultural rules. It was more than lighting a cigarette and inhaling its smoke. For many of the adolescents who smoked, in fact, the physical results of smoking may have been the least rewarding aspect of their use. Smoking was most often done with friends or others, and infrequently alone. The sharing of a cigarette was an opportunity to create new, or reaffirm old, social ties.

These examples notwithstanding, smoking still does not appear to be a behavior especially fraught with complex cultural meanings, especially for adults. Rather, its primary message in everyday life in Western culture appears to be symbolic marking of either a time-out in the middle of a course of action or work, especially one that may be stressful or demanding (i.e., an equivalent to a coffee break or because of feeling uptight), or to mark the completion of a task or segment of the day (e.g., to mark transition into a period of relaxation). Consequently, to follow Black's argument, anthropologists working in other cultures often have not thought to look at smoking as a topic of interest or one that can be tapped to reveal rich cultural information. Of course, in some settings smoking may be quite loaded symbolically and a topic worthy of interest on these grounds, but it does not appear that many anthropologists yet have explored this possibility. This is not to say anthropologists have ignored smoking completely, but only that they rarely have made it the center of the research projects.

Probably the first anthropological examination of tobacco use in cultural context was carried out by Alfred Kroeber, a (pipe-smoking) founder of American anthropology. In 1939 he published an article subtitled "Salt, Dogs, and Tobacco." This essay explored the distribution of tobacco and tobacco use among several Indian groups in the American West. Keenly interested in the relationships among the parts of a cultural system, Kroeber noted that tobacco was used as a ritual offering to the spirit world among those tribes who cultivated the plant. However, among tribes who did not plant tobacco but only gathered wild species of the tobacco family, it was not offered to the spirits. Similarly, he found that tobacco was used by shamans for healing purposes only in those tribes who smoked it but not among peoples who chewed or ate tobacco. It was Kroeber's (1939) contention that tobacco and particular patterns of consumption tended to diffuse together as cultural packages among Indian groups, thus accounting for the distribution patterns that he found.

Using the same type of functionalist model described in the last chapter for alcohol use, Black (1984) conducted an ethnographic study of the role of tobacco use on the Tobian Islands of Micronesia. Prior to European contact, the Tobian Islanders did not use tobacco. It was introduced to them during the 1800s by trade vessels searching the Pacific for wealth to bring home to Europe. In time, tobacco came to be incorporated socially and symbolically into the web of Tobian culture. Tobacco is highly valued on the islands and heavily smoked. But it still is not grown locally. Cigarettes still are obtained through trading with visiting ships, including U.S. Navy vessels or Asian fishing boats. On the islands, tobacco is an important marker of an individual's social status. Because tobacco is highly sought after and must come from off-island sources, those individuals who control a supply reap the social benefits of becoming centers of social attention. These individuals are noted for having "considerable skill, immense social knowledge, and a good deal of self-control, forethought and social autonomy" (Black 1984: 483). When tobacco supplies on the islands become especially low, social gatherings, such as communal meals, diminish in frequency. One reason for this loss of sociability, according to Black, is that individuals become increasingly irritable and antisocial as they withdraw from their nicotine addiction. To avoid social conflicts, they stay to themselves as much as possible and wait as patiently as possible for the next shipment of their drug of choice.

In a related study, Marshall (1979) examined the role of tobacco on the Pacific islands of Truk. Like the people of the Tobian Islands, the Trukese did not have tobacco prior to the arrival of European vessels. Nonetheless, this lack of experience did not prevent the Trukese from avidly seeking tobacco early in the contact period. The date at which tobacco first reached Truk is unknown, but, like many other Pacific Islanders, the Trukese seemed willing to do almost anything to obtain it. This weakness was of course exploited by the traders who eventually moved into the area (Marshall 1979: 36).

By the last of the 1870s, Marshall (1979: 36) reports, the Trukese were "hopelessly addicted" to tobacco, holding it to be dearer than food or drink. Christian missionaries who arrived in the area in the late 1800s made giving up tobacco a symbol of Christian conversion.

In the modern period, Marshall notes, beginning at about eighteen or nineteen years of age all young men in the village he studied begin smoking. Girls, who are more apt to be involved in the church, are much less likely to smoke. In a 1985 survey of, 1,000 adults in Truk, Marshall found that only about 10% of women were current smokers, compared to over 70% of men (Marshall 1990). In Marshall's (1979: 130) assessment,

Alcohol and tobacco have been thoroughly incorporated into the exclusive male domain, so much so today that they have become primary symbols differentiating young men from young women. Young men are under tremendous pressure to use these substances; young women are under just as much pressure to avoid them.

In another paper, Marshall (1987) describes similar cultural incorporation for the wider Micronesian area of the Pacific.

Elsewhere in the Pacific, anthropologists have described tobacco use in passing in the course of studies on social organization, political conflict, and ecological adaptation. For example, on the Palau Islands of Micronesia, Barnett's (1961: 27) brief account of tobacco use shows a pattern similar to Truk (which lies about a thousand miles to the east):

The tobacco grown in Palau undoubtedly was introduced by the Europeans long ago. Despite the demand for it, only a few men know how to cultivate and treat it successfully today. It is easier to buy imported plugs, twists, and cigarettes—if one has the money—than to raise the local variety. Because of the demand, American cigarettes have become the leading import of the islands. Unlike betel chewing, smoking is a man's vice. A few young women furtively puff a cigarette when they can get one, but men frown on this brashness, as do older women.

By contrast, in Melanesia, to the south, smoking among women is common. A striking example is found in Roger Keesing's (1983) book entitled 'Elota's Story, a life-history account of a local leader in the Solomon Islands. While Keesing gives little mention of tobacco use in the written text, the book is well illustrated with numerous photographs of men, women, and children smoking pipes as they go about their day-to-day activities. Douglas (1955: 35), who also conducted research in the Solomon Islands, affirms that these people "smoke almost continually." In the Trobriand Islands, collective cigarette smoking is customary at social events. For example, at the birth of a baby, Weiner (1988: 51), an anthropologist who has done fieldwork in the Trobriands, observed people breaking off a piece of thick trade-store tobacco, separating it into tiny pieces, and rolling the pieces in newsprint to make long, funnel-shaped cigarettes. These were passed around the group to smoke. At the same time, the Trobrianders view tobacco as a powerful substance that sorcerers use to attack their victims. Indeed, almost all deaths are believed to be the work of a sorcerer who has managed to chant magic spells into the victim's betel nut (a mild stimulant that is commonly chewed in the Pacific and in parts of Asia) or tobacco. Weiner (1988: 40) recorded the following account of tobacco-related sorcery.

Vanoi once told me about Leon, a villager who joined the [Methodist] church and, renouncing his belief in magic, openly mocked Vanoi's legendary knowledge of sorcery. One day the two met at a trade store where many villagers congregate to gossip. Leon brashly told Vanoi that he was unafraid of his magic. Vanoi offered Leon a cigarette and told him that if he doubted his, Vanoi's, magic powers he should smoke it. With everyone watching, Leon lit the cigarette and calmly inhaled it to the end. That night he became violently ill. A week later he died.

Not surprisingly, people in the Trobriands are very cautious about accepting tobacco from powerful individuals who have knowledge of sorcery. Among friends and relatives, however, smoking together is a common social activity.

Among the Sambia of New Guinea, the largest island in Melanesia, Herdt (1987: 71) notes the psychosocial role of tobacco at the end of a day of toil in the gardens: "Smoking and betel-chewing relax people, who turn to gossip, to local news, to stories—the old men always ready to spin tales of war and adventures of the past, the children always ready to hear the ghost stories that make them wide-eyed and giggly with excitement."

Communal smoking is not peculiar to the islands of the Pacific. Shostak (1983) describes in some detail the strong desire for tobacco she encountered among the Kung! San of southern Africa, the frequent requests they made of her for the substance, and the predominant method of consumption. On the latter, she (Shostak 1983: 25–26) describes a typical smoking occasion:

Bo filled an old wooden pipe, one he must have received in trade, with only the bowl section intact. The mouthpiece is rarely used, even in new pipes. He opened a small, worn cloth pouch where he had put the tobacco and filled the bowl. He lit the pipe and inhaled deeply four or five times, trying to hold as much smoke as he could, puffing his cheeks and holding his breath with each inhalation. With the exhalation, he turned, spat in the sand, and handed the pipe to Nisa. She smoked the same way and gave it to Kxoma and Tuma, who each did the same. . . . The four of them were talking, exchanging news of their villages.

In an unpublished study in South India among subsistence farmers of the Sudra and Harijan castes, Mark Nichter (cited in Nichter and Cartwright 1991) found that tobacco is consumed in almost every household in a variety of ways, including smoking and snuff, and in conjunction with the chewing of betel nut. Among males over twenty-five years of age, 65% reported smoking cigarettes. People explained that smoking increased relaxation, contributed to sociability, helped to reduce the pain of hunger and toothache, enhanced digestion, and assisted with regular defecation. He estimated that tobacco purchases consumed 7% to 10% of household income. In another unpublished study from the Middle East, Marcia Inhorn (cited in Nichter and Cartwright 1991) examined tobacco consumption in Alexandria, Egypt. She found that 151 of the 190 (79%) lower-class male heads of household in her sample had smoked, and 53% of these were smoking at least one pack of cigarettes a day. This expense consumed between one-third and one-half of disposable family income and was seen by many women as hurting the family's ability to properly feed their children. Addicted to cigarettes, most men were unable to quit, having begun smoking when they were in late adolescence.

As these accounts reveal, tobacco use is ubiquitous in the Third World and is integrated with wider cultural complexes. In Micronesia, smoking is a culturally constituted male activity; in Melanesia smoking is not gender-typed. Similarly, in some places smoking is continuous, while in others it is limited to particular times and contexts. In either case, many local smokers have become dependent on the international tobacco market and on supplies of cigarettes from the West. Contrary to Western images of traditional primitive peoples leading pristine lives in exotic lands, as these accounts suggest, through their consumption and their labor peoples of the Third World are locked into the global economic system.

Critical Medical Anthropology Studies of Tobacco

Since its emergence in the early 1980s, critical medical anthropology has developed a keen interest in the social origin of disease. This concern has focused critical theoretical attention on the manufacture and promotion of consumer products like tobacco that are known to be harmful. Several critical medical anthropologists have studied the tobacco industry. Foremost in this regard is Kenyon Stebbins, who has undertaken studies of smoking in Mexico and of the impact of transnational tobacco companies on the health of underdeveloped nations. In addition, he was, prior to his retirement, an anti-industry activist in the heart of tobacco country for a number of years (Stebbins 1994).

Of special concern to Stebbins's work has been the effort of the tobacco industry to make up for stagnating sales in the United States by developing markets in underdeveloped nations that are already struggling with infectious, nutritional, and other diseases. He notes that

transnational tobacco corporations have found the Third World to be a much more favorable political and social climate in which to do business, as compared to developed countries. Third World governments, lacking currency, are quick to embrace the revenues that come with tobacco sales, including bribes . . . and are reluctant to enact restrictions against this source of revenue. Furthermore, low levels of awareness of the health risks of cigarette smoking and the scarcity of anti-smoking campaigns further enhance the sales potential for tobacco products. (Stebbins 1990: 229)

Under such conditions, Stebbins argues, tobacco industry advertising can be quite effective in recruiting new smokers, especially given the prestige that often is accorded imported items from the West. Thus, a handful of superrich transnational tobacco corporations have moved ahead quickly to capture new Third World markets, while expending about $12.5 billion annually on advertising. As a result, worldwide tobacco consumption is increasing at the rate of 1% a year, with Brazil, India, and Kenya leading the way. In underdeveloped nations, sales are growing at least three times faster than elsewhere. In some Third World settings smoking is ubiquitous, Stebbins points out, even among physicians. For example, in some parts of Nepal "84.7% of males and 71.5% of females smoke. . . ."

In areas of Bangladesh, China, and Senegal between 55 and 80% of the males are reported to be smokers" (Stebbins 1990: 229–30). As a result, rising rates of lung cancer and related disease have been identified in heavy smoking countries like Pakistan, among South African blacks, and in Malaysia, Bangladesh, and Brazil. Stebbins also cautions about the serious environmental costs associated with tobacco cultivation and curing, especially from deforestation, erosion, and desertification.

Despite these recognizable dangers, Stebbins' analysis of the actions, power, and monetary resources of transnational tobacco corporations does not leave him optimistic about the ability of the Third World to avoid a smoking epidemic. To do so will require a level of political will by Third World governments that

has thus far not been demonstrated among Western governments either. Western governments, already well aware of the health consequences of tobacco use, could potentially prevent a repetition of such tragedies in the Third World by pressuring the international tobacco companies to reduce and even halt their exports to the Third World. . . . Given the capitalist world economy in which Third World countries are embedded, the possibilities for avoiding a smoking epidemic are all the more clouded. (Stebbins 1990: 233-34)

Also involved in the critical medical anthropology analysis of smoking and the impact of the tobacco industry on health are Mark and Elizabeth Nichter (Nichter and Cartwright 1991; Nichter and Nichter 1994). The Nichters note that the United States has played an important role in fostering child-survival (e.g., oral rehydration and immunization) and safe-motherhood programs on a global scale. Unfortunately, the benefits to human health and survival gained through these large-scale efforts will be for naught, they argue, because of the complicity of the U.S. government in promoting cigarette sales in the Third World.

We maintain that the disease focus of child survival programs, like the individual responsibility focus of antismoking campaigns, diverts attention away from the political and economic dimensions of ill health. Saving the children, the symbols of innocence, puts the United States in a favorable light in a turbulent world and competitive international marketplace, but it also deflects attention from other issues. One such issue is that families with young children represent a huge potential market for American products, such as tobacco, which undermine household health. While U.S. support of child survival programs received significant positive press coverage, tobacco quietly became the eighth largest source of export revenue for the United States in 1985–86. (Nichter and Nichter 1994: 237)

The U.S. government, the Nichters point out, has exerted its influence in developing a world market for tobacco in three identifiable ways. First, since the 1930s, hundreds of millions of dollars of Commodity Credit Corporation loans and price supports have gone to tobacco growers, enlisting them to grow more tobacco. Because of these subsidies, an acre of tobacco brings in sixteen times the profit from an acre of soybeans. Second, in the twenty years following World War II, the government spent one billion dollars buying up surplus tobacco from U.S. distributors and supplying it to Third World countries, thereby helping to develop a craving for tobacco. Third, U.S. trade policy is designed to assist American tobacco companies overseas. Countries like Japan, South Korea, and Thailand have all been intensely pressured by the U.S. government to begin importing tobacco or face stiff trade sanctions. In fact, the pressure on Asian countries to increase tobacco consumption has been called "a new opium war" (Ran Nath 1986).

Additionally, noting that 75% of tobacco cultivation occurs in the Third World, the Nichters point out that international lending programs like the World Bank and the Food and Agriculture Organization of the United Nations actively make loans, extend advice, and provide seed and pesticides to small farmers to help them enter into tobacco growing. Ostensibly committed to the development of Third World nations, these programs will, in the long run, help the Third World to develop a significant health problem. Tragically, because of the limits on what these nations will be able to spend on health care, most Third World victims of tobacco-caused diseases will not benefit from advances in the medical treatment of these conditions.

Contributing to this outcome will be the fact that the manufactured cigarettes marketed by transnational tobacco corporations often have much higher tar (the chemical source of health problems in cigarettes) and nicotine (the chemical source of addiction to tobacco) levels than those sold in the West. For example, the Nichters point out, the median tar level in cigarettes sold in the United States is twenty milligrams per cigarette, while in Indonesia it is almost double this level.

Consequently, the Nichters argue for the development of an anthropology of tobacco use that does not limit itself to the narrow confines of studying the motivations or behaviors of individual smokers but rather pays attention to the actions of governments, international organizations, and the tobacco industry in shaping smoking behavior. They argue as well for the study of the social relations of consumption and the semiotics of consumables (i.e., the social meanings invested by people in consumed items and the communication of meanings enacted through their consumption behavior) within a broader political-economic framework. In other words, it is the Nichters' view that it is important to understand how the tobacco industry acquires new markets and with whose help, at the same time that we analyze how people come to infuse tobacco products with particular cultural meanings and to respond to these cultural meanings as if they had the same material reality as the products themselves. Building this type of integrated study of political economy and cultural meaning, along with the study of the interaction of these factors with biology, is the purpose of critical medical anthropology.

CONCLUSIONS

In this chapter, we have analyzed tobacco as a legal mood-altering drug. We have attempted to show that tobacco is certainly as dangerous as, if not more dangerous than any drug that currently is illegal. In fact, as we have indicated through a historical analysis, tobacco itself was once illegal in much of the Western world. However, particular historic, political, and economic factors overwhelmed moral efforts to ban tobacco consumption. Like other mood-altering consumables that Mintz has termed the "drug foods" of the take-off phase of capitalist development, tobacco helped to control the working class by providing brief chemical respite from the grinding pressures and boredom of capitalist production. At the same time, because of its broad appeal to working people and others, tobacco offered a generous source of revenue to pay for the shift from feudal to capitalist modes of production. The product of this *historic coincidence* was the legalization of tobacco and the emergence of a highly profitable and increasingly international tobacco industry, an industry with sufficient profits to pour billions of dollars into advertising and promotion to specific market segments in the West and to all other countries around the globe. The consequence, unfortunately, has been an enormous toll in human misery and death. As Stebbins (2001: 151) stresses, "Fighting Big Tobacco is entirely different from combating most public health problems. Unlike cigarettes, most infectious diseases and maternal and child health problems do not provide profits to transnational corporations and governments. Similarly, most public health problems are not exacerbated by extensive advertising campaigns that promote the cause of the health problems." Fully understanding how all of the historic processes, social relations, distribution and use of power, cultural meanings, and health factors mentioned in this chapter interrelate is the task of critical medical anthropology in its study of tobacco.

CHAPTER 7

Illicit Drugs: Self-Medicating the Hidden Injuries of Oppression

ILLICIT DRUGS: AN INTRODUCTION

In this chapter, we continue our examination of mind-altering substance use in cultural and political-economic context with an exploration of the illicit side of this phenomenon. Illicit substances are those that society has come to define as being unacceptable for use and, within the context of the modern state structure, made illegal. Today, the term "drug" is used widely to refer to illicit consumable substances, although this was not always the case. Prior to the First World War, before the U.S. and other countries began defining substance use as a problem, the term generally was not linked with the notion of illicit consumption, nor with the concepts of abuse or addiction. The original edition of the Oxford English Dictionary (published in 1897) defined the noun *"drug"* as a "simple medicinal substance" without any reference (as is now found in all dictionaries) to narcotics. In fact, after the First World War, pharmacists (who in time stopped calling themselves druggists) fought a losing battle to convince newspapers to not use the term drugs in referring to non-medicinal substances used for their mind-altering effects. The 1930 annual meeting of the American Pharmaceutical Association (APA), in fact, passed a resolution urging the press to use the term narcotic (a term derived from the Greek word *narke* which means stiffness) to refer to drugs like marijuana, heroin, and cocaine. Ultimately, pharmacists gave up this struggle and in 1987 the APA urged its members to use the terms medicine and medication and to avoid the term drug to label pharmaceutical products. Of course, the earlier medical meaning of the term drug did not go out of existence, contributing to the broader terminological/conceptual jungle that surrounds this topic (e.g., use vs. abuse, addiction vs. dependence, recreational vs. ritual use). More recently, there have been public health efforts to expand the term drug to include legal substances like alcohol, creating increasing use of the acronym AOD (alcohol and other drugs) in professional discourse.

All regions of the world have their own particular histories with mind-altering substances. Notably, in Europe, for example, unlike many other parts of the world, drug ingestion did not develop as a central part of religious ritual. Beginning at least as early as the Middle Ages, mood-altering drugs were banned, and the herbalists who created and used them were punished. Today, illicit drug abuse is commonly seen as a significant health and social issue throughout Europe as well as many other countries around the world. Indeed, drug abuse is known to be an international phenomenon, with the plants that produce mood-altering chemicals being grown in one country, processed into useable form in another, and consumed primarily in a third country. With the development of an extensive international system of illicit drug production, smuggling, and sales, addiction itself has become internationalized. In an ironic twist, a quick glance reveals that drugs are one of the things that brings the world together to form, in Louis Lewin's (1964: 4) apt if overly amiable phase, "a bond of union between men of opposite hemispheres." *Globalization*, the term used with growing frequency to describe an ever more intertwined world economy, the so-called new world order, is nothing new in the realm of mind-altering substances. The reason for this is that drug use is and has been for a long time big business, and, in fact, many big businesses, from illicit drug smuggling organizations to legal financial institutions are involved in the action. In recent years, for example, a number of otherwise austere and seemingly proper banking firms have been exposed as important sources for the laundering of illicit drug dollars (i.e., hiding the source of great sums of money to avoid taxation through outright seizure by legal authorities). In 1985, money laundering was found to be an $80 billion-a-year industry, with the majority of the money coming from illegal drug sales and involving major banks and brokerage houses throughout the United States. Curiously, as the result of the extensive money-laundering operations involving Miami banks and with the widespread use and trafficking of cocaine in that city, virtually every piece of U.S. currency handled in South Florida is contaminated with microscopic traces of cocaine (Inciardi 1986: 196).

Illicit drug abuse is an international phenomena involving especially North America, Europe, Asia, and Latin America (and increasingly in most other parts of the world as well). However, for our examination of use patterns we will focus especially on the United States. Not only is the

United States by far the largest consumer of illicit drugs, it also has tended to set international direction in responding to illicit drug use both in the areas of interdiction (trying to stop the drug trade) and treatment/prevention efforts. However, cross-cultural comparison and contrast, as well as a keen awareness of significant differences that operate at the local level, distinctive hallmarks of the anthropological approach to understanding human behavior, also will guide this exploration.

The specific consciousness-changing substances of concern in this chapter can be classified into four subtypes (Embodden 1974) based on their reported effects on users (while recognizing that the same drug can have varied effects on different users or the same user at different times or during different phases of a single occasion of use):

- *Inebriants*—substances that cause intoxication, including temporary diminished control over physical and mental capacities, marked in the case of some inebriative substances by initial exhilaration and disinhibition and, with sufficient dosage, loss of consciousness. Alcohol is the widest known inebriant, but its legality in many settings has warranted separate examination in Chapter 5; other inebriants include ether, chloroform, benzine, and other inhaled solvents like glue or volatile chemicals like gasoline.

- *Hallucinogens*—substances that cause visual, auditory or other artificial sensory experiences, including LSD, peyote, various kinds of mushrooms, cannabis, mescaline, and tropical plants like Banisteriopsis.

- *Hypnotics*—substances that cause tranquility, sleepiness, lethargy and stupor, including tranquilizers, narcotics (e.g., heroin), kava, and mandrake.

- Stimulants—substances that cause a heightened sense of wakefulness and the experience of enhanced cognitive and bodily pace, including coffee, tea, tobacco (examined in Chapter 6), cocaine, amphetamines, qat, and betel.

Some of the specific substances listed above have locally confined use within specific regions (e.g., kava in Oceania), others have moved beyond regional use to international popularity. Commonly, drugs that come to have global patterns of consumption (e.g., coffee, tobacco, cocaine, heroin) have been incorporated into licit or illicit large-scale production, distribution, and promotion systems driven by profit seeking. Another characteristic that differentiates various kinds of drugs, one that is of primary interest to medical anthropology, is their impact on the health of users (or others, such as family members of users or victims of drug-influenced violence or accidents). The capacity of specific drugs to cause harm varies, often depending on the concentration, dosage, method and social context of consumption. The presence of adulterants and the mixing of different kinds of drugs also can produce harm.

The social scientific literature on drug use is vast, with numerous books as well as specialty journals like *Addiction Research and Theory, The Journal of Drug Issues,* and the *American Journal of Drug and Alcohol Abuse.* One of the key themes that marks this literature is the constant process of *change in drug use patterns.* This topic is particularly important from a health perspective on mind-altering drugs because, as the AIDS epidemic reveals, modifications in drug use or the contexts in which drugs are consumed can dramatically impact the health risks involved.

EMERGENT AND CHANGING DRUG USE PATTERNS

Like the social world around it, a world of rapidly changing technologies, mobile populations, frequent market-driven introductions of newer and better consumer goods, and a fluctuating array of global producers and distributors, the underground world of illegal drug use is in constant and consequential flux. As Inciardi, Lockwood, and Pottieger (1993: 1) accurately observe,

If anything has been learned from the history of drug use . . . it is that "drug problems" are ever-shifting and changing phenomena. There are fads and fashions, rages and crazes, and alternative trends in drugs of choice and patterns of use.

In a similar vein, Ouellet, Weibel, and Jimenez (1995: 182) remark:

Illicit drug use is dynamic. Within neighborhoods and across the United States the popularity of any one drug waxes and wanes, a drug's availability fluctuates, the forms and modes of ingestion of drugs change, new drugs are introduced, and people vary in their willingness to try and continue using various types of drugs.

Notable kinds of change in the drug scene, all of which have potential health implications, include the following: 1) the introduction of brand new drugs, such as the mid-1960s appearance of d-lysergic acid diethalamide (LSD or Acid); 2) the diversion of pharmaceuticals to street use, such as the mid-1970s adoption of phencyclidine (PCP or Angel Dust), an animal tranquilizer, among youthful drug users, or the appearance of both street methadone (diverted by methadone patients who spit out their medication and sell it on the street) and street Ritalin (methylphenidate, a stimulant used to treat attention deficit disorder); 3) the marketing of new forms of older drugs, such as the early 1980s appearance of crack cocaine (powder cocaine hydrochloride mixed with water and sodium bicarbonate and heated until a smokable rock is formed) or the late 1980s spread from Asia to the U.S. of ice (a potent, more crystalline and smokable type of methamphetamine); 4) the mixing of new drug combinations, such as the lacing of methamphetamine drugs like Ecstasy with heroin among youthful after-hours club dancers or the older shift to speedballing (mixing heroin and cocaine) among drug injectors; 5) the transition in a user population from focus on a single drug to the regular incorporation of one or more additional drugs, such as the 1980s movement from thoroughbred heroin injection to the contemporary polydrug use pattern; 6) the adoption of specific drugs because of their enhancing effects on other activities, such as the use of poppers during club dancing; 7) the use of new substances to cut or adulterate drugs in order to increase profits from drug sales, such as the occasional use of toxins like strychnine to cut heroin; 8) adoption of new drug use equipment, such as the use of plastic alcohol nip bottles and a plastic straw to construct crack cocaine pipes, the earlier shift from homemade syringes or glass syringes with disposable needles to plastic diabetic syringes with fixed needles; 9) the discovery of new ways to consume existing drugs, such as the mid-1990s advent of crack cocaine injection (through a chemical procedure to re-liquefy the crack cocaine rock), the 1930s initiation of intravenous drug injection, the switch to liquefying heroin without heating that followed the introduction of purer dope in the 1990s, or the recent appearance of alcohol injection in Latin America; 10) the emergence of new drug use settings, such as the anonymous shooting gallery among drug injectors or the medically controlled injection room in parts of Europe; 11) the appearance of new behaviors linked to drug use, such as the development of crack house sex-for-drugs transactions or the use of vaporous rubs among Ecstasy users; 12) the restructuring of drug production and distribution networks or market competition among distributors leading to changes in drug purity, drug price, drug distribution patterns, or drug-related street violence; 13) the development of new populations of drug users, such as homeless street youth in America's cities or the growing pattern of heroin use among suburban teens; and 14) the sudden risk enhancement of established drug-related behaviors, such as the spread of HIV associated with syringe transfer and re-use (including syringe sharing, lending and selling, and re-use of discarded syringes).

The ever changing world of drug use always has had public health ramifications, but the reasons for paying closer attention to drug use trends have multiplied by several fold with the recent emergence of a new set of infectious pathogens like HIV, and the rapid global spread of older diseases like hepatitis among drug injectors. Other recent shifts in drug use patterns, such as increased frequency in drug user overdoses due to intensified drug purity, increases in drug use among pregnant women, and the rapid adoption of a wide range of so-called club drugs among youth, underline the growing need for close monitoring of changing drug use. Ethnography, because it is conducted in real life settings and has the ability to detect changing behaviors and contexts (without having to wait to know which are the right questions to ask, a limitation of survey research), is an especially useful tool for tracking emergent drug use patterns and for assessing some of their health implications. To learn about the exact behaviors and material culture (i.e., drug paraphernalia) of drug users, drug ethnographers routinely visit shooting galleries, get-off houses, crack houses, abandoned buildings, homeless encampments, wooded areas in otherwise urban settings, alleyways, drug user's homes, roof tops, and other illicit drug use locations, as well as drug copping (acquiring) sites, homeless shelters, soup kitchens, street corners, and other places where active drug users can be found, observed, and engaged in conversation. In the course of this work, these ethnographers are able to spot new drug-related behaviors, recently created or introduced drug equipment, and the consumption of new (or newly combined or packaged) mind-altering substances.

While they are lumped under a common label as drugs, substances differ considerably, not just in their chemical composition, but also in the ways they have been constructed (i.e., thought of and responded to) within society and in terms of the risks to health (if any) that their use creates at any point in time or within particular social contexts. For example, while tea and coffee were introduced to Europe during the same period (late 16th to early 18th centuries) and under similar circumstances, the former acquired a culturally constructed image as a therapeutic drink (which it retains) but the latter did not. In England, tobacco at first was thought of by some people as a cause of moral corruption and vanity, and was even linked with sorcery (resulting in punishments handed down by the Inquisition), while coffee was believed to cause idleness and political unrest among the working classes. In time, these constructed images were replaced by others no less cultural in their shaping than the original conceptions. While tobacco came (for a time) to be thought of as sophisticated and even sexual, coffee and tea never achieved such a colorful reputation. We begin an examination of some specific drugs and their changing health and social significance by focusing on marijuana, the most widely used psychotropic substance, after alcohol, among young people. Marijuana has held quite differing culturally constructed images in different times and among different groups, from a demon drug that caused madness to an enhancer of social accord.

DRUG USE AMONG YOUTH: MARIJUANA

During the 1960s, marijuana emerged as a popular hallucinogen among adolescents and young adults, including college students, in the United States and elsewhere in the Western world. Between 1962 and 1980, for example, the percentage of young adults (aged eighteen to twenty-five) in the United States who used marijuana on a daily basis doubled, from 4% to 8% (L. Johnson et al. 1982). Between 1971 and 1982, the percentage of those twelve to seventeen years old who had *ever* used marijuana doubled from 14% to 28%, while among those eighteen to twenty-five years old the increase was from 39% to 64%. By 1982, almost one-third of those eighteen to twenty-five years old reported using the drug in the one-month period prior to being interviewed (Miller 1983). While inner-city youth had been using marijuana for many years, the relatively sudden rise in use among economically and socially privileged youth led to widely voiced concern about a growing drug problem. Social concern about marijuana was not new, but marijuana's rapid rise to being the illicit drug most commonly used by all social sectors in American society, including adolescents, significantly intensified the attention it received in the media and elsewhere.

The contemporary field of drug prevention emerged in the late 1960s in response to the increased rate of use of marijuana and other hallucinogenic drugs like LSD among young people. This led to a series of studies designed to understand why adolescents use such drugs. These studies found that regular marijuana users tend to value nonconventionality and sensation seeking but did not find evidence of greater psychopathology among adolescent heavy users. Also, these studies did not identify a single factor—like pursuit of pleasure, relief of boredom, psychic distress, peer influence, or family problems—that could account for the widespread experimentation with marijuana (Jessor 1979).

Indeed, the appeal of marijuana has caused considerable frustration for those in the substance abuse field because while experimentation with it may serve as a gateway to the use of so-called harder drugs (like heroin and cocaine) for some adolescents, for most adolescents this is not the case. Indeed, the history of marijuana reveals that it has served different roles in society at different times and been perceived in radically different ways as a result. During the colonial era, marijuana or hemp was a cash crop grown to provide material used in the production of both clothing and rope, and it is still grown for these purposes. By the turn of the twentieth century, marijuana was being sold as an over-the-counter medicine for the relief of various minor aches and ailments. It appeared primarily as an ingredient in corn plasters, in nonintoxicating medicaments, and as a component in several veterinary medicines. Its status as a medicinal was affirmed in the Pure Food and Drug Act of 1906, which required that any quantity of marijuana be clearly indicated on the label of drugs or other consumables sold to the public.

Then, during the 1920s, marijuana began to be used as a recreational drug for its mood-and mind-altering effects. This phase began with the transport of increasing quantities of marijuana from Mexico into the United States after World War I. As the popularity of marijuana grew, a significant social reaction occurred. The drug soon was labeled a dangerous narcotic and attempts were made to institute severe penalties for its use. Attempts to criminalize marijuana use did not go unopposed. During 1911 hearings on a federal antinarcotic law by the House Ways and Means Committee, for example, the National Wholesale Druggists' Association protested the inclusion of marijuana as a dangerous drug. Efforts by the drug industry to block federal legislation outlawing the sale of marijuana were successful until 1937, when the Marijuana Tax Act was passed. This legislation was directly linked to an effort to stop the flow of Mexican workers into the American Southwest. While these workers had been welcomed in the 1920s to fill the demand for farm labor, during the Great Depression of the 1930s they came to be seen as an unwelcome labor surplus. Nationalistic anti-Mexican immigration groups began to form and to paint marijuana as an insidious narcotic used and distributed by an unwanted group of foreign residents. As the editor of the Alamosa, Colorado, *Daily Courier* expressed this unabashedly racist sentiment in an editorial published in 1936, "I wish I could show you what a small marijuana cigarette can do to one of our degenerate Spanish-speaking residents. That's why our problem is so great: the greatest percentage of our population is composed of Spanish-speaking persons, most of whom are low mentally" (reprinted in Musto 1987: 223). This campaign to block Mexican immigration contributed to the marijuana scare of the 1930s and to the federal inclusion of marijuana as a narcotic despite its clear chemical differences from narcotizing substances.

Following passage of the Marijuana Tax Act, popular use of the drug and general social concern about it began to flag. Penalties for marijuana use were increased periodically, but its use stabilized among certain social sectors. For the most part, marijuana disappeared from the front pages of newspapers and from other forums of popular discussion. All of this changed again with the sudden reemergence of marijuana in the 1960s.

Researchers have had a difficult time understanding and classifying the effects of marijuana or of cannabis, its primary pyschoactive component. Effects appear to vary based on the local setting and set of cultural expectations. Among working-class Jamaicans, for example, among whom use is widespread, hallucinogenic reactions to *ganja,* as marijuana is known on the island, are not the goal of use and are not regularly reported. Rather, in Jamaica marijuana use is linked culturally with values of endurance, energy, problem solving, invigoration of appetite, and relaxation. As the anthropologists Vera Rubin and Lambros Comitas (1983: 214) indicate,

ganja use is integrally linked to all aspects of working-class social structure; cultivation, cash crops, marketing, economics; consumer-cultivator-dealer networks; intraclass relationships and processes of avoidance and cooperation; parent-child, peer and mate relationships; folk medicine; folk religious doctrines; *obeah* and gossip sanctions; personality and culture; interclass stereotypes; legal and church sanctions; perceived requisites of behavioral changes for social mobility; and adaptive strategies.

Among participants in the *ganja* subculture, affording and acquiring the drug, anticipating the next use, efforts to avoid detection by the police, and the sense of community among fellow users all contribute to the importance of *ganja* at the individual and small-group levels. Moreover, regular users strongly dispute allegations that use leads to crime, violence, apathy, health and mental health problems, or an antisocial attitude. Based on their field study in Jamaica, Rubin and Comitas (1983: 217) conclude, "There is no evidence of any causal relationship between cannabis use and mental deterioration, insanity, violence or poverty; or that widespread cannabis use in Jamaica produces an apathetic, indolent class of people." In the United States, by contrast, despite widespread use at various times by diverse sectors of the population, all of these assertions about the alleged effects of marijuana remain central to ongoing public discourse about the drug.

Indeed, this controversy was renewed during the 1990s. The source again was a notable rise in the popularity of the drug among young people. After the marked increases in marijuana use of the 1960s and 1970s, its use began to diminish during the 1980s. According to the National Household Survey on Drug Abuse (Substance Abuse and Mental Health Services Administration 1996), use of marijuana reached a low point in 1992, with only 5% of those twelve to seventeen years old reporting use during the previous month, compared to over 15% in 1979. However, after 1992 the popularity of marijuana in this age group began to grow once again. By 1995, 11% of those twelve to seventeen years old were reporting at least monthly use of the drug. In a survey of high school seniors in Maryland, 30% of those who had ever used marijuana reported that they first used the drug before fifteen years of age (Maryland State Department of Education 1994). Moreover, the National Center on Addiction and Substance Abuse at Columbia University (1996) found in a national telephone survey that teenagers fourteen to seventeen years old reported that marijuana was easier to buy than beer, and the majority (68%) of seventeen-year-olds said they would have no trouble buying marijuana within a day if they so desired.

Contributing to the continued appeal of marijuana among youth (and adults as well) is the increased availability of high potency marijuana (i.e., with tetrahydrocarbinol—the main psychoactive ingredient—levels that are as much as 5 times higher than in the 1980s). Schensul and co-workers (2000) have studied the subculture of what they refer to as "new marijuana" among inner city youth. Their research points to several factors, all of which have important political, economic, and social dimensions, that contribute to the appeal of new marijuana, including the ability of youth to make fast money through participation in marijuana distribution and sales (many times more than would be possible at the low-levels jobs sometimes available to inner-city youth) and the entwinement of new marijuana use and other arenas of the corporation-driven contemporary youth subculture (e.g., the highly profitable rap and hip hop music industry). One insight of their study is that new marijuana use among inner city youth does not occur in a vacuum isolated from the wider economy, rather, despite anti-drug laws, new marijuana is no less an important economic commodity in the global market and no less shaped by political economic factors than the production and sale of baseballs, designer jeans, Hollywood movies, or fast food hamburgers.

The 1996 passage of legislation in both California and Arizona legalizing marijuana use for medical purposes has further heated up public debate. Opponents argue that marijuana has no proven medical use. Patients suffering from various diseases or injuries, however, counter this argument based on their own personal experiences. For example, Mark Mathew Braunstein, an art librarian at Connecticut College in New London, Connecticut, and a paraplegic following a diving accident in 1990, has written about the relief from spinal-cord injury spasm and pain (SCI) provided by smoking marijuana. He notes,

As a paraplegic from SCI, I sought alternatives. I learned about [use of marijuana] first from the [paraplegic] grapevine, then from testimonies of doctors and patients that were shelved 10 years ago by the U.S. Drug Enforcement Administration, and finally from animal experimentation, the animal being me. I learned that marijuana relaxes SCI spasms more effectively then do tranquilizers and relieves SCI pains more safely than do [medically prescribed] narcotics. (Braunstein 1997)

Those who oppose the medical use of marijuana for cases like Braunstein's argue that those who support medical use are really seeking general legalization of marijuana. However, results from a statewide survey in Maryland of adults eighteen years of age and older shows that while the majority (87%) of Maryland residents surveyed believe that doctors should be allowed to prescribe marijuana for medicinal reasons, only 27% of those people also believe that possession of small amounts of marijuana for personal recreational use should be legal (Center for Substance Abuse Treatment 1997). It is likely that controversy over marijuana use will continue, as will the relationship between using marijuana and other harder drugs like heroin and cocaine.

CHRONOLOGY OF HARD DRUG USE: THE OPIATES AND COCAINE IN HISTORIC, POLITICAL, AND ECONOMIC CONTEXT

The two most significant hard drugs throughout U.S. history have been the opiates (including heroin) and cocaine. Each of these drugs has a long and colorful history of use. Western interest in their use began with the discovery of quinine as a treatment for malarial fever. That a substance derived from a plant could be used with great effect in the treatment of a specific health problem generated an intense concern with discovering other new drugs (i.e., medicines). As we saw with the use of marijuana, placing the history of heroin and cocaine in historic perspective reveals important insights about the political economy of drug use. While drug use commonly is portrayed as either an individual problem (e.g., personality disorder or inadequate socialization) or perhaps a reflection of collapsing family values, a historic account shows that politics, economics, and class and racial relationships play central roles in changing patterns of drug consumption. Consequently, the political economic approach taken in this volume tends to emphasize placing health issues in a historic framework.

The Opiates

The opiates are a set of drugs derived from the flowering Oriental poppy plant (*Papaver somniferum*), specifically from the white sap that forms in the large bulb at the base of the flower. Opiates have an analgesic effect; they inhibit the central nervous system's ability to perceive pain. In addition, they relieve anxiety, relax muscles, cause drowsiness, and produce a sense of well-being or contentment. Continued use produces tolerance, so that increased doses must be administered to achieve the initial euphoria. The best-known consequence of continued use is the development of physiological dependence or addiction. Once a user is dependent, consumption is driven primarily by the desire to avoid withdrawal symptoms such as chills, cramps, and sweats. Other than dependence, opiates in and of themselves are not known to produce other bodily damage (Chien et al. 1964).

The use of opium as a mood altering substance is known to date back at least to ancient Middle Eastern Sumerian civilization, over 6,000 years ago. The Sumerians used a form of picture writing in which the symbol for the poppy plant represented the idea "joy" or "rejoicing" (Lindesmith 1965). Opium was used as a medicine in classic Greek civilization. Galen, the last of the great Greek physicians of the classic period, for example, described multiple beneficial uses of opium in medical treatment in some detail, including relief from snakebites, deafness, asthma, and women's troubles. In addition, he commented on its popular use in the preparation of cakes and candies that were sold by vendors in the streets. In Homer's *Odyssey*, it was a key ingredient that Helen of Troy used in her potion "to quiet all pain and strife, and bring forgetfulness of every ill" (Homer's Odyssey). There is even speculation that the vinegar mixed with a substance called gall that according to *Matthew 27:34* was offered to Christ on the cross contained opium (Inciardi 1986). In more recent times, opium "was one of the products Columbus hoped to bring back from the Indies" (Scott 1969: 11).

When the use of opiates began in the United States is not entirely clear, but it is known to have begun during the colonial period. Critical to its introduction was the work of one of the best-known British doctors of the seventeenth century, a man named Thomas Sydenham. A founder of clinical medicine, Sydenham advocated the use of opium as "one of the most valued medicines in the world [which] does more honor to medicine than any remedy whatsoever" (quoted in Musto 1987:69). In his view, without opium, "the healing arts would cease to exist" (Scott 1969: 114). A student of Sydenham, Thomas Dover, developed a form of opium known as Dover's Powder, which he prescribed especially for the treatment of gout. It contained equal parts of opium, ipecac, and licorice and lesser parts of saltpeter, tartar, and wine. Dover put his product on the market for over-the-counter sale to the public in 1709. Interestingly, this was the same year that Dover, an enthusiastic adventurer, rescued the castaway Alexander Selkirk from the secluded Juan Fernandez Islands off the coast of Chile, an event that inspired Daniel Defoe's famous book *Robinson Crusoe*. Dover's powder was shipped from London to the British colonies and became the most widely used opiate preparation for many decades. Its lengthy popularity has resulted in its specific mention under the general listing for "powder" in Webster's dictionary. Defoe's book was not the only meeting point between opium and British literary developments during this era. Samuel Taylor Coleridge, for example, composed his famous poem *Kubla Khan* under the influence of opium, while Elizabeth Barrett Browning, also a poet, was an avid opium user.

Despite its considerable popularity, Dover's Powder was not without competition. Introduction of the drug helped to launch the patent medicine business in the New World. By the end of the eighteenth century, patent medicines containing opium were readily available and widely used. They were available in pharmacies, grocery stores, and general stores and were touted widely by traveling medicine shows. In addition, they could be purchased from printer's offices or through the mails. These so-called medicines were marketed under a host of personalized labels, such as Ayer's Cherry Pectoral, Mrs. Winslow's Soothing Syrup, McMunn's Elixer, Godfrey's Cordial, Hooper's Anodyne, the Infant's Friend, Scott's Emulsion, and of course, Dover's Powder. The titles of these medicines appear to reflect a period before mass industrial capitalism depersonalized the relationship between products and their producers.

These potions were said to be good for a host of health problems, including body pain, cough, nervousness, TB cures, diarrhea, dysentery, cholera, athlete's foot, baldness, and cancer. Many were marketed as "women's friends," drugs used to calm women who were seen during this period as inherently unstable because of the deleterious effects of having a uterus. For the most part, until the Revolutionary War, these medicinals were shipped from England to its colonies, very likely coming back to the colonies on same ships that had transported tobacco to England.

The British got heavily into the opium business as part of their conquest of India, where poppies had been grown for centuries. By 1773 the British East India Company, a colonial trading firm, had gained a monopoly over opium sales in all of India, and by 1797 it had control over production. As colonial rulers, the British reoriented Indian agricultural production to two main cash crops: cotton and opium. The British colonial empire turned to opium production as a way of overcoming its balance of trade deficit with China. The British wanted a lot of things the Chinese produced, especially tea, but they had trouble finding something to sell to China in turn. The Chinese did not look favorably on European foreigners or their goods. Consequently, from 1839 to 1842, Britain went to war with China to gain the right to export its Indian opium for use as a smokable drug by the Chinese people. The Chinese government resisted this attempt at drug imperialism, but it was defeated in what has since been called the First Opium War (1839–42). Fifteen years later, Britain went to war against China again in the Second Opium War, in order to extend its distribution of opium. In this way, the Chinese were "literally 'force fed' opium, and the supply continued to create its own demand" (Conrad and Schneider 1980: 113). By the end of the nineteenth century, it is estimated that one out of every ten Chinese was addicted to opium smoking (Kittrie 1971).

A primary promoter of opium use during this era was biomedicine. For example, the standard British medical textbook, *The Elements of Materia Medica and Therapeutics* (1854), lauded opium as "undoubtedly the most important and valuable remedy in the whole Materia Medica" (quoted in Musto 1987: 70). Similarly, a leading American medical textbook, *Treatise on Therapeutics* (1868), praised opium for conferring "tranquillity and well being" (quoted in Musto 1987: 74). The widely read practical handbook entitled *Domestic Medicine,* by William Buchan, prescribed the use of poppy leaves and opium for the treatment of coughs. This was the era of heroic medicine, when biomedical cures often were more painful than the diseases they treated. There was widespread suspicion of biomedicine, the prestige of doctors was low, and people leaned heavily on patent miracle cures. Physicians competed intensely with pharmacists, folk healers, and others in the treatment of sickness. One goal that biomedicine set out ultimately to achieve, which was to have a significant impact on future federal legislation, was control over drug distribution.

The Revolutionary War disrupted the importation of opium medicinals. But the patent medicine market was large enough to inspire a homegrown industry. The growth of this industry was closely tied to the expansion of the American newspaper enterprise. The medicinal manufacturers were among the first to seek a national market by advertising in newspapers. Setting a trend that we still live with today, the medicinal companies used psychological lures to entice customers to buy their opium-based wares. By the latter part of the 1800s, some of these companies were spending hundreds of thousands of dollars on advertising. For example, Hamlins Wizard Oil Company of Chicago actively advertised its opium-based oil as "the Great Medical Wonder—There is no sore it will not heal, no pain it will not subdue" (in Inciardi 1986: 5), while the makers of Scott's Emulsion were spending over $1 million a year on advertising by the 1890s.

While medicinals were widely used, the public did not have any clear idea what they were consuming. For one thing, the so-called patent medicines that were so popular during this era were, in fact, unpatented because the "patenting of a drug required revealing its ingredients so that all might know its composition" (Inciardi 1986: 4). The patent medicine companies kept the contents of their elixirs secret; and the Proprietary Medicine Manufacturers and Dealers Association, their trade association, fought for three decades to keep it that way against the few lawmakers who believed in disclosing the contents of consumer products.

A study done in 1888 of the contents of prescriptions purchased from pharmacies in Boston found that of the 10,200 prescriptions filled that year, 15% contained opiates and that opiate-based proprietary drugs had the highest sales (Eaton 1888). The end result was that during the 1800s, opium use was widespread in the United States; it was treated as a normal behavior that was both legal and integrated into everyday life. People of all walks of life became addicted, especially a large number of urban middle-class housewives who, as noted, were often the targets of advertising efforts. Addiction, however, was usually not recognized as such, since the drug was readily available and widely used (and those who were addicted could easily treat their withdrawal symptoms through more drug consumption). Thus, regular use of opium in powder or tincture form was not defined socially as a problem. Users were not labeled criminals or deviants.

Indeed, the only behavior that was labeled as a drug problem was the smoking of opium in so-called opium dens, generally located in the Chinese sections of cities, although not used only by Chinese clients. Thus, the first anti-opium law in the nation was passed in San Francisco in 1875, home to a large Chinese population. Smoking was labeled deviant and debilitating, but the real problem appears to have been racism. The primary concern was not drug use but *who* was using the drugs. This interpretation is supported by a case tried in Oregon and reviewed in an Oregon district court. The defendant in the case was a Chinese man convicted of selling opium. In the review, the district court noted:

Smoking opium is not our vice, and therefore, it may be that this legislation proceeds more from a desire to vex and annoy the "Heathen Chinese" in this respect, than to protect the people from the evil habit (quoted in Bonnie and Whitebread 1970: 997).

From this moment on, U.S. societal reactions to drug use and attitudes about particular racial/ethnic groups have been closely intertwined.

In the case of Chinese opium smoking, a major underlying factor in social condemnation was the depression that began in the 1860s and the resulting redefinition of the Chinese as surplus labor. Originally, imported to build the national railroad system and to work the mines, labor that was unappealing to many U.S. workers, the Chinese later became scapegoats of class frustration as the economy collapsed. This example reveals an important aspect of U.S. experience with illicit drugs that is often hidden behind well-publicized events like so-called wars on drugs or media hype about crack babies. As Helmer (1983: 27) has argued, "the conflict over social justice is what the story of narcotics in America is about."

The place of opium use in American society took a dramatic turn in 1803 with the discovery of morphine. The discoverer was Frederick Serturner, a twenty-three-year-old German pharmacist's assistant. Serturner, who was attempting to isolate the chief alkaloid of opium, named the substance morphine, after Morpheus, the Greek god of sleep. Ten times more potent than raw opium, morphine was quickly realized to have tremendous powers as a painkiller; morphine, in fact, remains the strongest chemical pain reliever available. This fact became significant during the American Civil War, a massively bloody conflict that threatened to overwhelm the capacity of the mid-nineteenth century biomedical system. Physicians turned to morphine as a means of handling the incredible number of war-inflicted wounds and amputations. This process was facilitated by the invention of the hypodermic needle, which allowed the rapid introduction of the drug.

The book entitled *The Hypodermic Injection of Morphia*, published in 1880 by H. H. Kane, described the benefits and deficits of the popularity among doctors of morphine treatment

There is no proceeding in medicine that has become so rapidly popular; no method of allaying pain so prompt in its action and permanent in its effect; no plan of medication that has been so carelessly used and thoroughly abused; and no therapeutic discovery that has been so great a blessing and so great a curse to mankind than the hypodermic injection of morphia. (Kane 1880: 5)

A product of widespread morphine use during and after the Civil War was the emergence of a new medical condition called either "soldier's disease" or "army disease." Its primary symptom was morphine craving by those who had been medically treated with the drug. The treatment adopted by physicians was to continue morphine injections for those who presented with this disease. The frequency of morphine injection created a market for needles. The 1897 edition of the Sears Roebuck catalogue responded to this need and advertised a hypodermic kit that included a syringe, two needles, two vials, and a carrying case for $1.50 (Inciardi 1986).

The success of Serturner in isolating a marketable product from opium prompted additional research on the several dozen other alkaloids found in opium. One of these that has come into common medical use is codeine, discovered in 1831. In the 1870s, a British chemist named C.R.A. Wright conducted a series of experiments involving mixing morphine with various acids. One of the chemicals he discovered in this way is called diacetylmorphine. Twenty-four years later, a German pharmacologist named Heinrich Dreser, who worked for the Bayer pharmaceutical company, used diacetylmorphine in a series of experiments and reported that it proved very effective in the treatment of coughs, chest pains, and discomforts associated with various other respiratory diseases. Antibiotics were unknown at the time, and respiratory diseases were a major cause of death in the Western world. Dreser found that diacetylmorphine was more effective than morphine, and he (incorrectly) believed that a fatal overdose was not possible (Inciardi 1986).

The Bayer laboratory began to market this new wonder drug under the trade name of Heroin, derived from the German word for heroic (*heroisch*). Before long, heroin was being touted as a nonaddictive cure for morphine addiction. As a Bayer advertisement from this era stated: Heroin is "free from unpleasant after effects" (in Inciardi 1986: 10). The *New York Medical Journal* added,

Habituation has been noted in a small percentage . . . of the cases. . . . All observers agreed, however, that none of the patients suffer in anyway from this habituation, and that none of the symptoms which are so characteristic of chronic morphinism have ever been observed. (quoted in Ray 1978: 308)

This mistake grew out of the fact that morphine addicts going through withdrawal stopped experiencing withdrawal symptoms when they were given heroin. At the time, people did not understand the phenomenon we now call cross-addiction (i.e., addiction to one opium product produces addiction to all opium products). As a result of its alleged attributes, heroin use was strongly promoted in the over-the-counter pharmaceutical market and became a very popular legal drug. Importantly, as P. Conrad and Schneider (1980: 116) indicate,

For those of us who are accustomed to thinking of the typical modern-day opiate addict as young, male, urban, lower-class, and a member of a minority group, 19th century addicts provide a sharp contrast. From all the data we have . . . it appears that the typical 19th century addict was middle-aged, female, rural, middle-class, and white.

Cocaine

During the late 1800s, another kind of drug also began to be popular and widely sold in the legal market. Derived from the leaves of the coca plant (Erythroxlon coca), the drug, called cocaine, had long been chewed among the Indians of the Andes as a mild stimulant that eased breathing at high altitudes and produced no health or social consequences. The ancient Inca revered coca and worshiped a god named Mother Coca (Antonil 1978). The Spanish invaders attempted to eliminate the chewing of coca leaves, probably more because of its pagan religious connection than because of antidrug sentiment.

Toward the end of the century, however, a Corsican wine maker, Angelo Mariani, began to import coca leaves from Peru to add to a new wine that he produced called Vin Coca Mariani. The wine was an instant success and was publicized as capable of lifting the spirits and eliminating fatigue. Pope Leo XIII, an avid wine drinker, awarded Vin Coca Mariani a medal of appreciation (Inciardi 1986), and a thirteen-volume set of books was published to compile the testimonials of all the prominent figures who praised Mariani's famous wine (Andrews and Solomon 1975).

Eventually, the Vin Coca Mariani came to the attention of John Styth Pemberton of Atlanta, who was in the patent medicine business. In 1885, Pemberton developed a medicinal drink he registered as French Wine Coca, which he asserted was a nerve stimulant. The following year, he added additional ingredients and began to market it as a soft drink called Coca-Cola. Eventually, over forty different soft drinks included cocaine.

By the 1890s, the patent medicine industry also began marketing the drug for everything from alcoholism to venereal disease and as a cure for addiction to opiate-based patent medicines. At the same time, several researchers were attempting to isolate the stimulant in the coca leaves. This was achieved in the 1860s by Albert Neimann. This pure form was of interest to the armies of several countries as a means of getting soldiers to work harder and was actually administered to Bavarian soldiers in the 1880s. The Parke-Davis Company, "an exceptionally enthusiastic producer of cocaine, even sold coca-leaf cigarettes and coca cheroots to accompany their other products, which provided cocaine in a variety of media and routes such as a liqueurlike alcohol mixture called Coca Cordial, tablets, hypodermic injections, ointments, and sprays" (Musto 1987: 7).

These developments caught the attention of a Viennese neurologist named Sigmund Freud. As a sufferer from chronic fatigue, depression, and other complaints, Freud became very interested in the stimulant effects of the new drug. He began to administer it to himself and to others. Freud concluded that cocaine was a wonder drug and wrote three medical papers on it in the 1880s. Interestingly, for a time he believed that a ten-day course of hypodermic injections of cocaine could cure alcoholism. In a letter to his fiancée, whom he later supplied with cocaine, Freud wrote:

If all goes well I will write an essay on it and I expect it will win a place in therapeutics by the side of morphium and superior to it. I have other hopes and intentions about it. I take very small doses of it regularly against depression and against indigestion, and with the most brilliant success. In short it is only now that I feel that I am a doctor, since I have helped one patient and hope to help more. (Quoted in Inciardi 1986: 7.)

Freud gave the drug to his friends, his sisters, and his fiancée and continued to use it himself for several years, although he ultimately became aware of potential problems with cocaine and ceased his involvement with it. He was not, however, the only famous doctor to become involved with the drug at this time. Another was William Stewart Halsted, one of the founders of the Johns Hopkins Medical School, the prototype of the modern American medical school. He became addicted to cocaine while discovering its properties as an anesthetic. Similarly, William Hammond, former surgeon general of the U.S. Army, pronounced cocaine as the official remedy of the Hay Fever Association.

As with heroin, attitudes about cocaine were colored by racism. Throughout the South, there was a fear that if blacks had access to cocaine they "might become oblivious of their prescribed bounds and attack white society" (Musto 1987: 6). Thus, in 1903, the *New York Tribune* quoted Colonel J. W. Watson of Georgia asserting "many of the horrible crimes committed in the Southern States by colored people can be traced directly to the cocaine habit" (quoted in E. Goode 1984: 186). Similarly, the *New York Times* published an article entitled "Negro Cocaine Fiends Are a New Southern Menace" that described blacks as "running amuck in a cocaine frenzy" (quoted in E. Goode 1984:186). That African Americans were on the receiving end of most of the racially motivated horrible crimes committed in the South during this period was of little consequence. As Musto (1987: 7) notes,

The fear of the cocainized black coincided with the peak of lynchings, legal segregation, and voting laws all designed to remove political and social power from [blacks]. . . . One of the most terrifying beliefs about cocaine was that it actually improved pistol marksmanship. Another myth, that cocaine made blacks almost unaffected by mere .32 caliber bullets, is said to have caused southern police departments to switch to .38 caliber revolvers. These fantasies characterized white fear, not the reality of cocaine's effects, and gave one more reason for the repression of blacks.

Ironically, these politically motivated fears were not only misguided with respect to cocaine's effects, they were motivated by erroneous ideas about African American access to cocaine. In fact, the cost of the drug (twenty-five cents per grain in 1910) prohibited most African Americans in the South, the majority of whom were sharecroppers and notably poorer on average than whites, from purchasing the drug during this period. A study by E. M. Green (1914), who examined admissions to Georgia State Sanitarium at the time, showed that rates of cocaine use by blacks in the South were significantly lower than rates of white use. Nonetheless, to insure that cocaine in any form did not reach African Americans, it was dropped as an ingredient in Coca-Cola in 1903 and replaced by another stimulant, caffeine.

SOCIAL CONTROLS: THE MAKING OF ILLICIT DRUGS AND CRIMINAL DRUG USERS

Ultimately, however, the great American legal drug party came to sudden halt. Beginning in the late 1800s, voices began to be raised against the legal sale of the opiates and cocaine. Among the first voices raised were those of Karl Marx and Fredrick Engels in England.

In 1845, Engels published his book *The Condition of the Working Class in England*. As noted in our discussion of alcoholism in Chapter 5, in this book Engels described the rampant consumption of opium among the working class as clear evidence of capitalist oppression. Decrying a widely used patent medicine, Engels ([1845] 1969: 135) wrote,

One of the most injurious of these patent medicines is a drink prepared with opiates, chiefly laudanum, under the name of Godfrey's Cordial. Women who work at home, and have their own and other people's children to take care of, give them this drink to keep them quiet, and, as many believe, to strengthen them. They often begin to give this medicine to newly-born children and continue, without knowing the effects of this "heart's ease," until the children die.

In 1909 and 1911, the United States convened an international opium conference, which produced a document called the *Hague Convention of 1912*, aimed at restricting international traffic in opium. Under the leadership of William Jennings Bryan, Congress followed this up with the passage of The Harrison Narcotic Act of 1914, which placed restrictions on the sale of over-the-counter narcotic preparations. Congressional debate around passage of this bill did not center on the negative health effects of opium and cocaine or on the rising rate of addiction in the U.S. population, but rather on issues of international relations and profit. In particular, the discussion focused on the fact that the British were gaining an economic windfall from their ability to press opium sales on China and thereby gaining a competitive edge against U.S. businesses globally.

The ultimate social effect of the new federal law was to label the drug user a criminal. In the aftermath of this labeling, drug use came to be synonymous with deviance, lack of control, violence, and moral decay. As Erich Goode (1984: 218) has written in his book *Drugs in American Society,* "by the 1920s the public image of the addict had become that of a criminal, a willful degenerate, a hedonistic thrill-seeker in need of imprisonment and stiff punishment." By this time, it is estimated that there were over 200,000 addicts in the United States, possibly as many as half a million (McCoy, Read, and Adams 1986; E. Goode 1984).

Physicians were exempt from the Harrison Act, and they continued to treat their addicted patients with opium and cocaine; as a result, thousands of people continued legal drug use in this way for five years after passage of the Harrison Act. Drug issues aside, the Harrison Act is of importance in our understanding of health issues because it was an important step in the long-time effort of physicians to gain control over the distribution of medicines and thereby secure their status as the dominant force in U.S. health care. The Harrison Act granted "almost a monopoly for physicians in the supply of opiates to addicts" (Musto 1971: 60).

In the aftermath of the Harrison Act, physicians set up clinics around the country to dispense mood-altering drugs to addicted patients. In the New York clinic, which was the one best known to the public, drugs were handed out widely to those who claimed addiction. Some people eventually began to take their dose plus additional doses for resale on the street to other addicts. Thus began the underground narcotics industry, a pattern that later was repeated in New York with the mishandling of methadone (and avoided elsewhere by strictly managing the distribution of both drugs).

Before long the U.S. Treasury Department, which was assigned to enforce the Harrison Act, began to press against the legal prescription of psychoactive drugs even by doctors. Central to this drive was the growing concern that drug use would spread from the working class "into the higher social ranks of the country" (Helmer 1983: 16). In 1919, in the Supreme Court case of *Webb v. United States,* it was decided that a physician could not prescribe a narcotic to an addict simply to avoid the pain of withdrawal. In 1922, in a second Supreme Court case, *United States v. Behrman,* the court ruled that narcotics could not be prescribed even as part of a cure. The effect was to make it now impossible for addicts to gain legal access to drugs: "The clinics shut their doors and a new figure appeared on the American scene—the pusher" (A. McCoy, Read, and Adams 1986: 110).

At first, physicians resisted these new legal developments. In the twelve years after passage of the Harrison Act, at least 25,000 physicians were arrested on narcotics-selling charges, and 3,000 served time in jail as a result. Thousands more had their licenses revoked. By 1923, all of the drug clinics, even those that had been fairly successful in weaning addicts off drugs, were shut down. By 1919,there were 1,000 addicts brought up on federal drug charges. By 1925,there were 10,000 arrests per year. At this critical juncture, the Mafia, under the direction of Salvatore "Lucky" Luciano, made the decision to replicate its success in the illegal alcohol trade and enter into the heroin business. While older Mafia figures had looked down on drug dealing, Luciano saw a lucrative market. By 1935, he controlled two hundred New York brothels and twelve hundred prostitutes, many of whom were addicted to the heroin Luciano provided to pacify his illicit workforce.

The end result of these developments was the emergence of an underground drug subculture that functioned to enable addicts to gain access to drugs and drug injection equipment and to avoid arrest. Alfred Lindesmith (1947), who studied addicts in 1935 in Chicago, was already able to describe features of this "subculture" in some detail. In the period between 1925 and 1930, intravenous drug injection became standardized as the preferred method of drug use. The origin of this technique of drug use has been traced by O'Donnell and Jones (1968). Interviews with old-time drug users suggest that intravenous injection was discovered several times by individuals who were attempting intramuscular injection and hit a vein accidentally. Some individuals who made this mistake (and who were using large quantities of uncut heroin) paid for it with their lives in the resulting drug overdose. However, others (who were using less or less-pure heroin) found that an intravenous shot "was more enjoyable, and . . . [there followed] a very rapid spread of the technique among addicts" (128).

The drug subculture thrived through the 1930s, until World War II. As various observers have noted, "It was the criminalization of addiction that created addicts as a special and distinctive group and it is the subcultural aspect of addicts that gives them their recruiting power" (Goode 1984: 222).

The drug subculture and illicit drug use were significantly disrupted by the war. Channels of drug smuggling were blocked during this period, and the flow of drugs into the United States dropped to a trickle. Consequently, by the early 1940s, recorded rates of drug addiction in the United States took a sudden drop. However, the decline was short-lived. Soldiers who had used drugs overseas began to bring their addictions and knowledge of drug use home with them. And it was in the ghettos and barrios along the East and West coasts that drug injection found a new home after the war, especially among young men whose hopes, raised by a war against totalitarianism, were smashed by racism and the postwar economic downturn.

In addition to the press of social conditions, the postwar U.S. inner-city drug epidemic was the end result of several events, including the 1949 retreat of defeated Kuomintang Nationalist Chinese forces into eastern Burma and their takeover of opium production in the Golden Triangle poppy-growing region of Southeast Asia, the emergence of Hong Kong and Marseilles as heroin-refining centers, and the reestablishment of Mafia controlled international drug-trafficking networks (Inciardi 1986; Schultheis 1983; M. Singer et al. 1990). The individual responsible for the latter was none other than Lucky Luciano. Arrested in 1936 on drug charges, from his jail cell he sent messages to Sicily directing the Mafia to support the U.S. Army during World War II. It is widely believed that in return for helping the Allied conquest of Sicily and for violently opposing the rise of communism in Italy after the war, the Mafia was made various promises by the U.S. government, including the return of weapons confiscated by Mussolini's Fascists. In addition,

In 1946 American military intelligence made one final gift to the Mafia—they released Luciano from prison and deported him to Italy, thereby freeing the greatest criminal talent of his generation to rebuild the heroin trade. . . . Luciano was able to build an awesome international narcotics syndicate soon after his arrival in Italy. . . . For more than a decade it moved morphine base from the Middle East to Europe, transformed it into heroin, and then exported it in substantial quantities to the United States—all without ever suffering a major arrest or seizure. (A. McCoy, Read, and Adams 1986: 114)

Two other factors, one involving unrestricted production and the other unfettered sales, also were critical in reestablishing the drug trade. On the production end, Schultheis (1983: 237) reports that from "the 1950s through the Vietnam War era, the Nationalist Chinese in the Golden Triangle were supplied, even advised, by the CIA; the involvement of the Chinese in the opium and heroin business was excused because of the fact that they carried out paramilitary and intelligence activities along the Burma-Chinese border and elsewhere in the Triangle." Of importance on the marketing end of the heroin trade, Musto (1987: 236) notes, was "[p]olice collusion with drug suppliers in communities like Harlem."

Throughout the 1950 and 1960s, drug use continued to spread among inner-city poor. However, societal response was minimal, as long as most addicts were African American, Puerto Rican, Mexican American, or Native American. Beginning in the late 1960s, however, the number of white drug users and drug addicts began to grow rapidly, as part of a general rise in injection drug use in the United States. While it has never been possible to know exactly how many drug addicts there are in the country, all indirect measures point to a rapid increase in the number of regular drug injectors just prior to the beginning of the AIDS epidemic. David Musto, whose book *The American Disease* (1987) is a classic in the drug field, estimated that the number of heroin injectors soared from around

fifty thousand in 1960 to at least a half million in 1970. This number continued to escalate between 1970 and the late 1980s, with a slight decline
for a while during the mid-1970s. By 1987, based on aggregated data from
state alcohol and drug agencies, the National Association of State Alcohol
and Drug Abuse Directors, Inc. (NASADAD), concluded that there were
about 1.5 million drug injectors in the United States (reported in Turner,
Miller, and Moses 1989). About the same time, the Centers for Disease
Control and the National Institute on Drug Abuse both estimated that
there were approximately one million drug injectors in the country (Spencer 1989).

In the drug field, this sizeable increase in the number of injectors, now
called injection drug users (IDUs), is seen as a consequence of several
factors: (1) there was a general population surge during these years, especially among teenagers and young adults, the age group (15–24 years)
most susceptible to drug involvement (C. McCoy et al. 1979); (2) an expansion of the gross national product created an increase in disposable
cash and "an unparalleled market for consumer goods and anything else
that promised to make a person feel comfortable, including drugs" (Musto
1987: 253); (3) the Vietnam War contributed to widespread alienation
among youth, leading to a weakening of traditional values and social
control mechanisms; (4) during the late 1970s, there was a considerable
jump in the availability of heroin and cocaine; and (5) the pre-Depression
generation's experience with the harmful effects of drugs was not effectively conveyed to the baby boom generation because the intervening
mid-century generation had little firsthand exposure to mood-altering
substances other than alcohol (Musto 1987). However, while it is likely
that all of these factors contributed to the widespread growth in and tolerance (in some social sectors) of drug use during the 1970s, they do not
fully account for the "graduation" (Page and Smith 1990) from noninjec-
tion gateway drug consumption (e.g., marijuana smoking) to injection
drug use, a transition that occurred disproportionately among urban minority youth during this period.

Examination of the available sources of information make it clear that
the 1-1.5 million IDUs in the United States are not evenly dispersed across
the national landscape; most are concentrated in cities. Further, they are
not evenly dispersed across the urban landscape, as most are concentrated
in particular neighborhoods. Although nonmedical injection drug use appears to have begun in the American South (O'Donnell and Jones 1968),
today there is a disproportionate concentration of IDUs in the northeastern states. It is estimated, for instance, that between one-fourth and one-
half of all IDUs in the United States live in New York City (Turner, Miller,
and Moses 1989). Notably, African Americans and Latinos are over-
represented among IDUs. In New York City, the center of Northeast drug
use, the proportion of African Americans in the IDU population has been

going up steadily since World War II (Chambers and Moffitt 1970). The last National Institute on Drug Abuse nationwide drug abuse treatment survey found that "New York had the highest combined percentage of black and Hispanic enrollees in drug treatment" (L. Brown and Primm 1989: 5). These findings suggest the need to broaden the focus of attention from the psychological characteristics of drug abusers and develop an understanding of the social conditions that produce drug use and abuse. This is what Singer has tried to do (reported on later in this chapter) in his studies of drug use among Puerto Ricans in the United States.

ETHNOGRAPHIC STUDIES OF DRUG USE: RIPPING, RUNNING, AND WRITING

A review of anthropological and other ethnographic writings suggests that there have been three identifiable eras in the qualitative study of drug use: 1) premodern studies carried out by interested amateur observers (e.g., explorers, missionaries, travelers, and colonial officials); 2) modern studies conducted by trained field researchers who viewed their work as objective social science; and 3) postmodern studies conducted by professional ethnographers whose intellectual and emotional worlds had been severely disrupted by the twin forces of the AIDS epidemic and the postmodern challenge to scientific authority and cross-cultural representation. Each of these phases, examined individually below, was conditioned by particular understandings and worldviews inherited from the general and intellectual cultures of the wider society at the time.

Almost Ethnography: Premodern Observational Accounts of Drug Use. As suggested by H. Feldman and Aldrich (1990), the first quasi-ethnographic account of drug use was authored by Christopher Columbus and Friar Ramon Pane, the man assigned by Columbus to record New World native customs. Based on conversations with Taino Indians on the Caribbean island of Hispaniola (which today is parceled between the countries of Haiti and the Dominican Republic), Pane described their experience with a drug they called cohoba, which is now known to be a hallucinogenic extract (containing dimethyltryptamine and bufotenine) from the bean of the tree *Anadenanthera peregrina*. Pane's account of indigenous use of a hallucinogenic snuff—one of at least 100 different snuffs that have been identified among New World peoples—dates the beginning of observational drug studies to over 500 years ago. He also provided a description of tobacco use among the Taino, a drug they smoked in huge cigars to comfort the limbs, induce sleep, and lessen weariness. Not surprisingly, like other accounts of the pre-modern era, Pane's description was not based on the kind of systematic assembly, comparison, and validity checking of carefully recorded data that characterizes ethnography as a social scientific research method. However, he did base his description on direct observation and informal interviewing of participants, hallmarks of the ethnographic approach.

In the period after Columbus, other explorers and European invaders (and their fellow travelers) provided additional accounts of New World drug use. Amerigo Vespucci, for example, first described coca chewing in South America at the turn of the sixteenth century. Drug use among the Aztecs, a behavior observed and recorded by a number of Spanish colonialists and clerics, included several substances. Jimsonweed (*Datura meteloides*) was used by the Aztec for both religious and medicinal purposes according to post-contact descriptions. Healers consumed Jimsonweed mixed with peyote to determine appropriate treatments for their patients. Patients also were given the drug as medication for some ailments.

Harvey Feldman and Michael Aldrich (1990) credit Thomas De Quincey as being the first writer to produce a book length work that could fairly be called a premodern "drug ethnography." Although an adventurer and not a trained social scientist, De Quincey, who spent a number of years living among the urban poor, was a keen observer of the significant upsurge in opium and alcohol use in the working class districts of London during the Industrial Revolution. He also was interested in drug use among prominent individuals, such as the poet Samuel Taylor Coleridge. His book, *Confessions of An English Opium-Eater* (original 1822), records his personal experiences with and observations of opium use across social classes. Unlike in Asia where it was smoked, the opium users observed by De Quincy drank it in liquid form, a practice that continued until the introduction of the hypodermic needle.

Another astute observer of street drug use in England during this era was Friedrich Engels, who, as noted in Chapter 5, recorded his first-hand observations of the city of Manchester in 1845 in his book *The Conditions of the Working Class*. Engels, who was led through the polluted and heavily crowded back streets and alleyways of Manchester by his working class Irish girlfriend Mary Burns, was repulsed by the harsh and degraded living conditions of the urban poor and of the social practices, supported by dominant institutions, that sustained inner city life during the take-off years of the Industrial Revolution. Engels saw etched in the unhealthy faces of overworked and harshly treated men, women, and children of the laboring classes of Manchester the embodied expression of inequality and the many scars of what we would today call structural violence (i.e., brutal social inequality in every sphere of life). Wherever he was led by Mary Burns around the smoky, crumbling streets and darkened hovels that served as worker residences, Engels witnessed great pain and intense suffering brought on by the greed of those who owned the factories and possessed the deeds to the mines.

Engels ([1845] 1969: 133) saw in the use of substances by the urban working class, a population which he believed to be in need of "forgetting for an hour or two the wretchedness and burden of life," an example of what he called "social murder," a term intended to convey somewhat the same meaning as the contemporary use of structural violence in medical anthropology, namely the creation by dominant social institutions of an oppressively toxic social environment characterized by enduring societal inequality.

As this brief review suggests, over the centuries a scattered array of early nonscientific descriptive accounts of drug use were produced by lay observers. Like much descriptive ethnography, these accounts serve primarily to document the rich diversity of life patterns found across place and time, affirming that drug use is an ancient, varied, widespread, and often socially integrated practice. Inherent in such description is the insight that drug use should not be conceived as an example (nor, as is often the case, as the epitome) of social deviance, rather it must be understood in social context.

Ethnography Realized: Modernist Field Studies of Drug Use

The era of the modern ethnographic drug research, consisting of systematic field observation and careful description of actual behaviors in social context, began in the late 1930s with two seminal studies. Anthropologists often consider Weston LaBarre's (1938) field examination of ritual peyote use among Native Americans to be the first full-fledged drug study by a professional ethnographer. Sociologists, by contrast, point to Bingham Dai's study of opium addicts in Chicago (1937) as the grandfather of modern drug ethnographies. Together, these two studies constitute the starting points of modern field research on drug use. Since then, primarily anthropologists and sociologists have produced a long series of studies of drug use, often carried out in major U.S. urban settings like New York, Chicago, and Philadelphia (but including a growing range of research sites over time, especially in Europe, Australia, and Canada, but increasingly global in their range), using observation and/or open-ended, in-depth interviewing within a quasi- or full ethnographic approach.

In 1935, LaBarre began his research on peyote use with an examination of the Kiowa for his doctoral dissertation. Over the next year, he conducted field observations of ritual peyote consumption with 15 different Native American tribes. The first edition of the book based on his dissertation research, *The Peyote Cult* (LaBarre 1938), was published during a period of growing anthropological interest in Native American incorporation of the small hallucinogenic peyote cactus into a set of social revitalization rituals. True to the distinctly anthropological orientation to substance use, LaBarre's work on peyote emphasized the cultural context of consumption. In the case of American Indian peyote use, this was not a difficult task given its highly ritualized and richly symbolical construction. Less ritualized and socially marginal drug use, such as that found among the urban poor, tended not to attract anthropological attention during this era. Thus, Bennett and Cook (1990: 231) could conclude, "as of the early 1970s, anthropology had not yet developed an explicit drug research tradition, especially with respect to abuse of drugs."

Sociology, by contrast, did develop an explicit drug research tradition, and its origin is found in the work of Bingham Dai (1937: 645), who was concerned with understanding addicts "as a group and the world they live in." His work fits within the tradition of "drug use as social deviance" perspective, an approach that developed in the department of sociology at the Chicago School during the 1930s (although, Dai himself also received a year of anthropological training at Yale University in 1932–33). The Chicago School viewed modern urban dwelling as a new way of life that was best understood through the direct field observation of the numerous small social settings (like particular work sites or neighborhoods) and subgroups (e.g., street gangs, petty thieves, musicians) that comprise sectors of the urban whole. Methodologically, the Chicago School utilized a mixed approach that included naturalistic study in local community context and a focus on insider perspectives, strategies that form important components of the ethnographic method. Indeed, the Chicago fieldwork tradition all but mandated that considerable focus be placed on learning the point of view of the people under study, a sentiment that it shared with the Malinowskian research tradition in anthropology. Additionally, the Chicago School saw the city as a stressful environment that produces a breakdown of social bonds, disorganization, individual isolation, depersonalization, and deviance behavior. In short, life in cities is pathological and the behavior of urban dwellers, especially inner city populations, reflects the urban social crisis. Drug abuse, consequently, is seen as a direct expression of the deeply damaging effects of urban life.

In his quite formal and ecologically based account, in the book *Opium Addiction in Chicago,* Dai (1937: 190–91), who spent most of his career as a psychotherapist, expressed a view of drug addicts typical of his day:

If one were emotionally self-sufficient, it seems very unlikely that one would readily accept the suggestion of a drug user and enchain one's self to a practically lifelong habit. By whatever name we may call it, the feeling of inferiority or inadequacy, this predisposing factor found in all of the addicts we have interviewed when they first began the drug habit must not be ignored.

As H. Feldman and Aldrich (1990: 18) note, given Dai's psychotherapeutic orientation it is not surprising that his observations were "cast in terms like 'infantile' personalities, excessive dependence on other, and a tendency to withdraw or escape from social responsibility." Use of these constructs was further reinforced through the recruitment of many respondents through the Psychopathic Hospital in Chicago.

As noted above, Dai helped to usher in the social deviance approach to drug studies. This understanding, which is suggested although never fully developed in Dai's work, depicts the addict as someone caught up in an all-consuming lifestyle or total way of life. Some researchers have referred to the existence of a "deviance syndrome" among impoverished inner city drug users. Thus, Dai (1937: 136), in discussing the link between drug use and prostitution, wrote: "That the pimp in his attempt to entice a girl to his service not seldom 'dopes' her and makes her an addict so that she will have to depend on him for her drug ... " Once addicted, from the perspective of the deviance model, drug users come to view "themselves as culturally and socially detached from the life style and everyday preoccupations of members of the conventional world" (Rettig, Torres and Garret 1977: 244). From the deviance perspective "Addicts become addicted not only to drugs but to a way of life" (Lindesmith, Strauss and Denzin 1975: 571).

In these examples, as Hills (1980: 12–13) observes, " the label 'addict' ... typically conjures up a picture of a strung-out, dirty, furtive, lower-class street junkie—but does not readily bring to mind the millions of middle-class alcohol- and barbiturate-addicted housewives." Consequently, later ethnographic drug researchers questioned the deviance model, arguing that it "leads to an exaggerated picture of [drug] users' lives, as well as an overstatement of differences between users and non-users.... " (Waterston 1993: 14–15.). Importantly, one of the researchers—a social psychologist named Alfred Lindesmith—who worked with Dai, helping him to select and recruit his sample, went on to make his own contribution to ethnographic drug research as well as to the broader drug use and addiction field. As Feldman and Aldrich (1990: 18) point out, Lindesmith "used qualitative interviewing techniques to develop definitions of addiction—probably the first in the world derived from ethnographic research," and during the post-World War II years helped move professional thinking about addiction toward a medical model. Lindesmith proposed a social theory of addiction. In doing so, he rejected explanations of addiction that were based solely on the alleged pharmacological and dependence-producing characteristics of drugs, arguing instead that when drug users seek to stop using drugs they often are attracted back to familiar social settings, relationships, and behavioral patterns. Lindesmith argued for an *emic* or insider definition of addiction and stressed that addiction is not simply a physical need for a particular drug but also a body of shared cultural knowledge about the drug and its effects. In seeking to understand the nature of addiction, Lindesmith's work reflects the primary question driving the work of both qualitative and quantitative drug researchers of this era: why do people use drugs?

With some of the key questions about the nature of addiction settled—at least for the time being—the focus of ethnographic drug research shifted in the years after Lindesmith began to publish his research. However, the body of ethnographic research on drug use that was beginning to develop during the 1930s came to an abrupt halt with the Second World War. Not only did the war block the flow of many drugs into the United States— leading to a significant drop in the frequency of drug use and the number of users—it also pulled potential drug researchers out of the field and into the war effort. Ethnographic research on drug use did not begin to re- gather momentum again until the late 1950s and early 1960s.

In the immediate post-World War II years, a period during which heroin began to flow back into the United States in increasing quantities and the number of inner city drug users began to rise quickly, one must turn to a number of autobiographies penned by drug users (or former drug users) to gain a socially contextualized and quasi-ethnographic account of drug use during this period. Several books, including *The Autobiography of Mal- colm X*, *Manchild in the Promised Land* by Claude Brown, *Down These Mean Streets* by Piri Thomas, and *Manny: a Criminal-Addict's Story* by Richard Rettig, Manual Torres and Gerald Garret, are particularly important re- sources in this regard. For Claude Brown, for example, heroin had become such a power attract that by age 13 he could hardly contain his desire to try it. He was introduced to drug use by his friends, especially a group of older boys whom he greatly admired. They first taught him to use mari- juana. When they moved on to heroin, which, among other names was called "horse" at that time, he intensely wanted to join them. For several months during 1950 all he could think about was his desire for heroin:

Horse was a new thing, not only in our neighborhood but in Brooklyn, the Bronx, and everyplace I went, uptown and downtown. It was like horse had just taken over. Everybody was talking about it. All the hip people were using it and snorting it and getting this new high. . . . I had been smoking reefers and had gotten high a lot of times, but I had the feeling that this horse was out of this world (C. Brown 1965: 111).

During these same years, in nearby Spanish Harlem, Piri Thomas, a boy of mixed Puerto Rican and African American heritage, was a member of the younger post-war generation that was coming of age and coming into contact with drugs. He recalled one of his earliest encounters with mari- juana at age 13. Drinking whiskey with several friends, one of them pro- duced a "stick" of marijuana and asked if he would like some.

I put it to my lips and began to hiss my reserve away. It was going, going, going. I was gonna get a gone high. I inhaled. I held my nose, stopped up my mouth. I was gonna get a gone high . . . a gone high . . . a gone high . . . and then the stick was gone, burnt to a little bit of a roach (P. Thomas 1967: 58).

Within a few years Thomas was not only regularly using but also selling marijuana. Although his initial reaction to heroin, which was becoming widely used among his friend, was negative Thomas' resolve to avoid heroin was overcome by his need to prove he was not a punk. When a peer thrust a dollar cap of heroin and a folded matchbook to use in sniffing the powder at him, Thomas felt compelled to prove himself a worthy companion: "All for the feeling of belonging, for the price of being called 'one of us.'" (P. Thomas 1967: 204). The ability of heroin to take away all pain, misery, and rejection made the drug instantly appealing to Thomas: "All your troubles become a bunch of bleary blurred memories . . . " (200). Before long, Thomas' life came to center on the drug. He'd "go to bed thinking about [heroin] and wake up in the morning thinking about it" (207).

The four autobiographical accounts noted above and related material (e.g., Burroughs 1953) clearly reveal the development of the post-war drug scene in the inner city. Building on the image of the cool marijuana user of the depression and war years, the close of the Second World War ushered in a period of significant increase in heroin use and heroin addiction. The street addict became a common sight on inner city streets, as each new generation of youth, boys and girls alike, sought to prove themselves to their peers by adopting the valued image of a fearless drug adventurer. Other options and role models were few, and none seemed to offer as much opportunity to impoverished youth who felt they had to prove their worth to their peers or face rejection in the one arena—the streets—that offered any potential life validation. However, in the wake of the heroin plague, Harlem and other U.S. inner cities changed. The sense of community that somehow had managed to survive the migration of African Americans from the South and Puerto Ricans from the Island, the grinding poverty they encountered in their new northern and Midwestern homes, and the fierce racial discrimination that undercut self-esteem and self-worth, now fell victim to widespread drug addiction among impoverished individuals who had no where to turn for drug money except robbery, burglary, prostitution and other crimes against themselves, their families, and their neighbors.

Nonetheless, rampant drug use in the inner city after World War II did not attract much attention or real concern from the dominant society or its social scientists, except to the degree that drug users were mentioned as either psychologically damaged or as criminal deviants in need of harsh punishment. In the later part of the 1950s, however, an alternative to this reigning view of drug users began to appear. Its source was the qualitative, interactive study of drug users. One of the first qualitative studies to mark this turning point was conducted by sociologist Harold Finestone (1957) among African Americans in Chicago. Though not based on field ethnographic research per se, Finestone's office-based qualitative interviews with approximately 50 African American heroin addicts helped to focus social scientific attention on the existence of a world view and a subculture among drug addicts. In this work, Fine-stone sought to describe the emically ideal African American drug user role (the "cat"), the often illegal income generating activities needed to sustain drug use (the "hustle"), and the use of drugs (the "kick"). As H. Feldman and Aldrich (1990: 19) note, with Finestone drug studies began a shift in emphasis away

from asking why people used drugs [and towards] asking how they went about getting involved in drug use and how they remained involved ... [E]thnographers began to find their search for etiological influences in the social world rather than the internal [psychological] world of experimenters.

In other words, as a result of open-ended qualitative interviewing of drug users, there began a move away from psychoanalytic and psychiatric thinking, as seen in the work of researchers like Dai, toward a more socio-cultural and meaning-centered approach to drug use. Interestingly, even the title of Finestone's (1957) most important paper, "Cats, Kicks, and Color," reflects this shift toward a concern with drug user experience of "the life," the details of insider speech, and the contours of the subculture(s) of drug users. The change is further evidenced in two of the other seminal papers that ushered in the new orientation: Alan Sutter's "The World of the Righteous Dope Fiend" (1966), based on three years of field work with addicts and non-addicts in Oakland, and, especially, Preble and Casey's classic "Taking Care of Business" (1969), based on research in New York.

The primary goal of much of this new literature was the holistic de-scription of the people for whom drug use was said to be the central organizing mechanism of their lives. For example, in an effort to counter simplistic stereotypes of drug users, Preble and Casey (1969: 2) argued:

Their behavior is anything but an escape ... They are actively engaged in mean-ingful activities and relationships seven days a week. The brief moments of eu-phoria after each administration of a small amount of heroin constitute a small fraction of their daily lives. The rest of the time they are actively, aggressively pursuing a career that is exacting, challenging, adventurous, and rewarding. They are always on the move and must be alert, flexible, and resourceful.

In constructing their description, ethnographic researchers of this pe-riod tried to understand and represent the world as it is actually seen, lived, and experienced by hardcore drug users. To a large degree, this literature consists of fascinating and detailed accounts of the survival strategies used to sustain a drug-focused lifestyle, the underground econ-omy of drug acquisition, processes of socialization into drug use social networks, the social settings that comprise drug users' social environments, the folk systems used to classify drug users based on their social status within the subculture, and the special argot or language system developed to communicate issues of concern to drug users (and to hide information from outsiders including the police). In short, emphasized in the ethnographic literature on drug use from the 1960s onward was the assertion that the lives of drug users are not without considerable cultural order and socially constructed meaning. Drug getting and use as social activities provide the framework for this order. As Preble and Casey (1969: 2–3) comment:

The heroin user walks with a fast purposeful stride, as if he is late for an important appointment—indeed, he is. He is hustling (robbing and stealing), trying to sell stolen goods, avoiding the police, looking for a heroin dealer with a good bag (the street unit of heroin), coming back from copping (buying heroin), looking for a safe place to take the drug, or looking for someone who beat (cheated) him—among other things. He is, in short, taking care of business, a phrase which is so common with heroin users that they use it in response to words of greeting, such as "how you doing?" and "what's happening?"

In addition to structured behaviors and shared social meanings, researchers identified a set of distinctive values operative among hard-core drug users. For example, Alan Sutter (1969: 195) noted that within the drug subculture "[p]restige in the hierarchy of a dope fiend's world is allocated by the size of a person's habit and his success as a hustler." Heroin users positioned at the top of the drug status hierarchy were observed by Sutter to work hard to maintain their position and their lifestyle. More broadly, on the street, H. Feldman (1973: 38) found that heroin users were seen as having

positive qualities of creativity, daring and resourcefulness that provide the impetus for the top level solid guys (persons of established status) to rise to the top of the street hierarchy . . . Their use of heroin solidifies a view of them as bold, reckless, criminally defiant—all praiseworthy qualities from a street perspective.

These accounts, shaped by an emergent "drug use as subculture" paradigm, took researchers a long way from earlier psychopathological conceptions of drug users. As summarized by Friedman et al. (1986: 385) with reference to drug injectors:

In contrast to views that see IV drug use as simply a matter of individual pathology, it is more fruitful to describe IV drug users as constituting a "subculture" as this term has been used within sociological and anthropological research. . . . This calls our attention to the structured sets of values, roles, and status allocations that exist among IV drug users . . .

In short, ethnographers of drug use working in the period just before the appearance of AIDS tried to show that even under difficult circumstances—or more precisely, because of difficult circumstances—a subculture can emerge that is as meaningful and dear to its participants as it is alien and repugnant to outsiders. Further, they attempted to counter earlier images of the drug user framed by the paradigms of psychopathology and the sociology of criminal deviance. Often, in so doing, however, they turned their attention away from the wider social context that fosters drug use and the intense social suffering it often expresses, and instead emphasized the microsocial world of the drug users in holistic culturalist terms.

Components of the drug use as subculture tradition were carried on by a second generation of researchers whose drug research careers often began just before but extended into the era of the AIDS epidemic. Several seminal ethnographic studies were produced by this second generation, including Michael Agar's *Ripping and Running*, Dan Waldorf's *Careers in Dope*, Bill Hanson, George Beschner, James Walters and Elliot Bovelle's *Life With Heroin*, the volume by Bruce Johnson and co-workers tellingly titled *Taking Care of Business: The Economics of Crime and Heroin Abuser*, and Harvey Feldman, Michael Agar, and George Bechner's *Angel Dust: An Ethnographic Study*. Each of these books, primarily written from the drug user subculture perspective, made important ethnographic contributions to the drug field. In so doing, however, as is common in scientific research, they produced findings that called into question aspects of their guiding paradigm.

Agar's study, a formal or ethnosemantic ethnography of the categories of cognitive organization of everyday events in the lives of heroin addicts, was based on two years of fieldwork with patients at the NIMH Clinical Research Center in Lexington, Kentucky, a federal drug treatment hospital. He describes his approach (Agar 1980: 137–38) as follows:

I would spend time hanging around in the patients' areas of the institution, listening and trying to learn how they viewed the world by attending to how they talked about it. . . . After doing this for several months, and after conducting several informal interviews and assembling a dictionary of slang, I began to worry about being more systematic. So I worked up three interlinked methods to help me display my understanding of the junkie world view.

These methods, which were suggested by a wider anthropological turn toward viewing culture as a *shared cognitive template* for enacting socially appropriate behavior, were the simulated situation (tape recording drug user enactments or simulations of real street drug-related behaviors like "copping" [buying] drugs and "getting off" [using drugs]), frame elicitation (a fill-in the blanks approach in which the study participant was handed a card or read a statement about some aspect of street drug use life and asked to use his experience to complete the sentence), and the hypothetical situation (in which the participant was told about a life situation drawn from prior data collection and asked to select from possible courses of action). Based on these methods (both formal and informal), Agar was able to construct an "experience near" account of key scenes, concepts, relationships, artifacts, activities, and experiences that comprise the street drug user's life. Later, Agar was able to test the validity of some components of his understanding of this lifestyle using street ethnography and sociological survey in New York City. Another component of Agar's study was an attempt to understand the lives and behaviors of drug users as patients in drug treatment. In other words, in addition to eliciting information about life on the streets, he also was concerned with the experience of life in an institution. Here, Agar was able to ethnographically address some of the issues he encountered as he learned about staff attitudes and assessments of patients. One of his insights in this regard was that some of the very behaviors (e.g., strong skepticism, constant suspicion, and testing of dependability) that staff cited as evidence that patients were maladapted and lacked appropriate values, goals, and rules of proper behavior, were in fact appropriate to (and acquired to insure) survival on the streets, where the threats are multiple and often come in human form.

Using a somewhat different starting point, Dan Waldorf's *Careers in Dope* was based on a concept introduced into the Chicago research tradition by Everett C. Hughes and first applied to drug use by Howard Becker in his seminal study of the pathway to becoming a marijuana user and the social contexts and relations that perpetuate drug use. The "career" concept in drug research implies that, like a professional in a field of employment (like becoming an anthropologist), it is possible to identify somewhat standardized stages and transitions in the processual development of a drug user's life. The heroin drug-use career in the inner city, argues Waldorf (1973: 6), begins early in life:

Heroin is seemingly everywhere in Black and Puerto Rican ghettos and young people are aware of it from an early age. They know of heroin and addicts through close scrutiny—they see the endless trade of money for white power; they see the user nodding on the front stoop; they watch him "get off" in the communal bathroom . . . ; they see his theft of the family TV set.

Waldorf noted that large numbers of youth from disadvantaged households have few experiences of legitimate employment upon which to build a straight lifestyle. Instead, they develop intricate deviant identities and belief systems centered around drug use. Waldorf examined the survival strategies and established subcultural roles in the drug use world upon which these alternative identities and ideologies are based. He observed that street drug users had to spend many hours each day planning and carrying out some form of income generating hustle. Drug dealing, he noted, was considered one of the better hustles available to street drug users, although the primary career path open them in the drug trade was as a low-level street juggler who sold small quantities of drugs to fellow addicts.

At the terminal end of the "dope career," Waldorf examined untreated natural recovery from heroin addiction, a transition out of drug use, or "retirement" in the career model, that many have assumed is not possible or at least extremely rare. He found that many former heroin users "drifted out" of drug use without significant problems because they had never been highly committed to the drug or the drug user lifestyle. Waldorf also led one of the first modern ethnographic studies of cocaine use and later used an ethnographic approach to study longer term careers among cocaine users. One of the important findings of the later study was the identification of a protracted career path among some cocaine users that involves continuous controlled consumption.

The Heroin Lifestyle Study (HLS) that lead to the writing of *Life With Heroin*, was carried out in the inner city areas of Chicago, New York, Washington, D.C., and Philadelphia. Study participants consisted of 124 African American men. All were regular heroin users and most had "never received or wanted any form of drug treatment" (Hanson et al. 1985: 1). This disinclination to enter treatment was a primary focus of the study. Specifically, the study was designed to "accurately pass on the rich, descriptive firsthand accounts of the daily lives of Black heroin users . . . ; and second, to search for and analyze emergent patterns which reveal the complex social and psychological mosaic that comprises the contemporary Black inner-city heroin lifestyle" (Hanson et al. 1985: 2). Ironically, one of the important findings of the study concerns the validity of assuming that there is a distinctive heroin lifestyle that is separate from the basic lifestyle pattern of the surrounding inner city community. As two members of the HLS research team note:

An unexpected finding is that the HLS men live rather structured lives in which successive daily time periods are spent engaging in a variety of fairly predictable and even conventional activities. Like men in straight society, they arise early in order to spend many of their waking hours "on the job"—but in their case, this usually means hustling in pursuit of the wherewithal to maintain their once-a-day, relatively controlled heroin habits (Bovelle and Taylor 1985: 175–76).

Importantly, it was the pursuit of normalcy (under conditions of marked social inequality and lack of opportunity) rather than escape or exhilaration that was found to drive the continued use of heroin among study participants. Also noteworthy was the control participants exercised over their drug habits, a refutation of the common assertion that regular heroin users "have an insatiable and uncontrollable appetite for heroin and that they therefore shoot up as many times as possible each day" (Bovelle and Taylor 1985: 177). In short, as Waldorf and co-workers had done among cocaine users, the HLS identified a strata of heroin users who did not fit reigning stereotypes about this population nor even ethnographic descriptions of other inner city heroin users, revealing both the changing nature of the heroin scene and a notable heterogeneity of drug using populations. Ironically, the Heroin Lifestyle Study ended up questioning the distinctiveness of the life styles of hard-core drug users.

One of the insights of the Preble and Casey (1969) study was that street drug users are key players in a street economy that involves the redistribution of goods that are stolen from stores, warehouses or other locations and sold on the streets or to local stores and restaurants at discount prices. Bourgois (1995: 3), in fact, credits this "enormous, uncensored, untaxed underground economy" with being one of the main factors that allows the poor to avoid rampant malnutrition and even higher rates of morbidity and mortality in oppressed inner city areas. Ethnographically exploring the drug user role in the underground economy was the focus of the research presented by B. Johnson et al. (1985) in *Taking Care of Business: The Economics of Crime and Heroin Abusers*. Working from field research stations set up in East Harlem (Spanish Harlem) and Central Harlem in New York City, the project staff, composed of researchers and recovering drug addicts, recruited 201 active drug users and interviewed them concerning income generating and spending patterns. Each participant was interviewed for five consecutive days and then once a week over the next month (with additional follow up interviews at the East Harlem site). Specific issues of concern were legal and illegal sources of income, types of illegal activities, arrest record, and daily expense information. The study produced a massive amount of data, which was synthesized by Johnson and his team to clarify the size, scope, and character of the underground economy and its interrelationship with the aboveground economy. These researchers performed various calculations to assess the economic impact of the drug use-driven informal economy. Unlike other researchers who have sought to demonstrate only negative effects of drug-related crime, benefits to the community were identified. For example, they assess the economic impact involved in a drug user stealing a $400 color television from someone's home and selling it to a merchant (who, in turn, sells it to a customer) for money to use in buying drugs. According to B. Johnson et al. (1985: 117), one person—the individual victim—had a substantial loss, but that loss was offset by the direct and immediate gains to four other parties: the burglar, the purchaser of the stolen television, the retail merchant, and the drug seller.

Central to this argument is the idea that even when an item like a TV is stolen that does not mean that it disappears from the economy, it is merely redistributed (even if most of the monetary profits of drug sales are extracted rather than recirculated in poor neighborhoods). Importantly, this study revealed how the underground and the aboveground economies are, in fact, one economy, just as the HLS study showed that mainstream culture and drug user culture were not terribly different.

Angel Dust: An Ethnographic Study, the last of the books mentioned above, was a particularly important contribution for a number of reasons. The edited volume was a product of a collaborative multi-sited ethnographic study carried out simultaneously in four cities (Miami, Philadelphia, Chicago and Seattle) using a common research protocol. The study was initiated because of reports that PCP (phencyclidine, an animal tranquilizer with hallucinogenic properties) was becoming popular among some youth as a regularly consumed psychoactive drug. However, little was known about recreational use of PCP. Agar (1980: 200) casually describes the origin and evolution of the study in the following terms:

A NIDA staff member with ethnographic tendencies (he had been a street worker in New York) decided to try an ethnographic study. He asked that a small team of ethnographers be assembled to get some preliminary feel for the situation . . . [F]our ethnographers were selected who had done good ethnography with drug users in the past. Further, because of their ongoing work, they all had rapport so that they could begin work immediately. . . . The group met for 2 days to work out a strategy for doing the ethnographies. Informal interviews were to be the focus. In addition, the group came up with a four-page guide to specific items of information that would be easy to get from each informant.

The study found that PCP had entered youth drug networks in all four target cities in 1973, increased in popularity through 1974, and begun to lose its appeal the following year (although it never completely disappeared from the youth drug scene and continues to have periods of renewed popularity). An examination of NIDA's annual national survey of drug use among high school seniors for the mid-1970s, however, did not include findings on PCP use. As Feldman and Aldrich (1990: 22) remark, "the PCP phenomenon entered the world of youth and diminished without the national data system ever identifying it." When questions about PCP were finally added to the Monitoring the Future Study in 1979, lifetime prevalence for use among 12th graders was found to be 2.4% (falling over the years to 1.4% by 1991).

The Angel Dust study also found that exclusive PCP use was rare and that its greatest appeal was among especially restless youth who found life to be generally boring and uninteresting. The participants in the study appeared to be quite familiar with the drug's effects and how to modulate them by controlling dosage levels. Of special concern to regular PCP users was a state they referred to as "burn out" in which the users exhibits memory loss and incoherent thoughts. Cutting back on consumption of PCP emerged as a folk strategy for controlling burn out.

One consequence of the PCP study was the realization that ethnography, a method commonly seen as a requiring a protracted period of rapport-building and ever-more-penetrative data collection, was found to be especially useful for the rapid assessment of emergent drug trends. As Weibel (1990: 4–5), who carried out the Chicago arm of the 4-city PCP study, has noted:

Generally speaking there appear to be two factors that contribute to the importance of qualitative methodologies in the field of substance abuse research. First, continually evolving patterns and trends of substance abuse . . . foster a fluid situation in which emergent and novel phenomena are integral facets of today's drug scene. . . . When attempting to construct meaningful data collection instruments for drug-related research, the researcher must gain sufficient a priori familiarity with the topic to frame appropriate, meaningful questions. Such knowledge is the province and product of qualitative methodologies. . . . The second factor confirming the value of qualitative methods in the substance abuse field relates more to the types of information required of research. . . . Clearly, qualitative research is often the only appropriate means available for gathering sensitive and valid data from otherwise elusive populations of drug abusers.

Bourgois (1995: 13) argues that the productivity of ethnography in drug use research stems from the fact that the reason drug users are elusive is that they "live on the margins of a society that is hostile to them." By design, ethnography is a methodology that incorporates rapport-building, self-disclosure, nonjudgemental sensitivity, genuine concern with the insider's perspective and experience, and involvement in the lives of study participants into its approach to data collection. These features of ethnography provide a basis for the establishment of "relations based on trust . . . [that allow the researcher] to ask provocative personal questions, and expect thoughtful, serious answers" from individuals who have learned to be extremely wary (Bourgois 1995: 13). In addition, ethnography offers a means of reaching hard-to-reach populations of drug users and providing background information on them that is useful in the construction of good surveys, by taking the researcher into the world of the drug user it fosters the development of important hypotheses and research questions and empowers the researcher to produce interpretations of findings that are grounded in the social, cultural, and experiential realities of the study population.

Entering the Postmodern: AIDS and Contemporary Drug Use Ethnography

Since the late 1980s, the ethnography of drug use has been propelled especially by the study of AIDS risk and prevention (although broader social concern about the health and economic toll of drug abuse is another push factor). The result has been a significant expansion in the quantity of studies (as well as an improvement in ethnographic methods and sampling procedures), especially in terms of the development of fine-grained examinations of the actual technologies and processes of drug use; the structure of the interpersonal networks and social relations of drug users; the immediate contexts of street drug consumption; the interrelationship between drug use and a range of health risks; cross-site variation among drug users including focused investigation of various drug user subgroups (e.g., drug injectors, crack users, women, minorities, adolescents, and gay men and lesbians); and the political economic structures, policies, and dominant social practices that foster drug use behaviors. Also on the agenda of ethnographic research during this period was the study of prevention and intervention programs, like syringe exchange and drug treatment, targeted to addressing the health of drug users as well as patterns and effects of drug user incarceration.

Much of the new ethnographic work, often supported by the National Institute on Drug Abuse, the Centers for Disease Control and Prevention or other public health institutions, was designed to elucidate AIDS (and other health) risks among drug users (see Chapter 8). As funding in this arena increased during the 1990s, a comparatively large number of ethnographers (many without prior histories in the street ethnography of drug use or much awareness of prior field work with street drug users) were recruited into the field. Often this new wave of neophyte drug researchers worked in close collaboration with (and often under the supervision of) epidemiologists, psychologists, sociologists and researchers from other disciplines. Drug ethnography, as a result, moved from the independent task of an individual qualitative researcher immersed in a local drug scene, usually in a major metropolitan area, into a team initiative involving one or more ethnographers working in close concert with quantitative researchers from other disciplines as well as with street outreach workers and survey interviewers. While demonstrably productive, cross-discipline collaboration did not come without pains and frustrations, with ethnographers sometimes feeling their work did not receive due recognition. As a result, a number started as or moved on to become the directors of their own multi-disciplinary, multi-method drug studies. At the same time, they advocated successfully for the expanded inclusion of ethnographers on the peer review committees established by the National Institutes on Health and other funders to assess the scientific merit of research grant applications.

Ironically, at the very moment that the contributions of ethnography to drugs and AIDS and other public health research were gaining recognition, the ethnographically oriented social sciences were undergoing an intense internal questioning concerning issues of researcher authority and representation. The source of this re-thinking lay in a series of events and transitions and their impact on the life experiences and mood of people living in the developed world in the late twentieth century, an era and a social attitude that came to be called postmodern. Some saw the key event in the rise of postmodernism being a reduction in the relative position of American power and influence in the years after the War in Vietnam, while others pointed to the lose of faith in the ability of the liberal welfare state to create a meaningful, satisfying way of life. Among intellectuals and scholars, the reigning array of broad, order-affirming social theories about human behavior began to lose their explanatory appeal. In addition, in anthropology in particular, a significant change occurred as the peoples of traditional interest (i.e., those living in small communities and neighborhoods scattered throughout the developing world) began increasingly to speak out on their own behalf, sometimes in sharp criticism of the ways in which they had been depicted in anthropological texts. Some anthropologists somberly expressed doubt (recorded in an explosion of postmodern anthropological publications) that they had the ability (as outsiders) or the right (as members of dominant societies) to accurately depict other ways of life and experience, the very objectives that had driven the development of drug ethnography. Some wondered if field studies, like capitalist penetration and re-ordering of traditional economies, were "unwarranted intrusions in the lives of vulnerable and threatened peoples" (Scheper-Hughes 1992: 27). At their annual meetings, anthropologists began to "hear of anthropological observation [described] as a hostile act that reduces . . . 'subjects' to mere 'objects' of [anthropology's] discriminating, incriminating, scientific gaze" (Scheper-Hughes 1992: 27–28). In time, as this questioning and self-doubt gained steam, the very future of ethnography as a legitimate approach to knowledge about the social Other seemed in doubt (M. Singer 1990). Following Derrida's famous postmodern dictum: "There is nothing outside the text," postmodern anthropologists began shifting their focus of attention from the lives and social worlds of peoples around the globe to the social processes involved in the construction of anthropological texts, the writing conventions that shaped textual uniformity, and the place of the author (and the voice of research subjects) in the creation of the ethnographic text.

Drug researchers during this period were cognizant and concerned about the issues and arguments of those expressing the postmodernist critique of anthropology. In the face of the AIDS epidemic, which rapidly was decimating the health and lives of injection and other drug users, however, most ultimately choose

to suspend or ignore the academic issues surrounding their method in order to respond quickly to a pressing public health problem. Thus the issue of whether ethnography can arrive at the "truth" about people's everyday ways of life . . . [was] largely . . . waived in favor of the practical goal of achieving the particular kinds of truths needed to establish programs to save people's lives. (Kotarba 1990: 260)

The goal became not flawless ethnography but "good enough" ethnography (Scheper-Hughes 1992), ethnography that, however partial, however shackled by dominant culture influences on anthropological understandings, was accurate and insightful enough to make useful contributions to efforts to respond to the multiple real perils facing at-risk populations. Researchers who opted to walk this path were able to gain new ethnographic awareness about the complex relationship between drug use and health risk around the world. Interestingly, the anthropologists who spearheaded the critique of ethnography not only stuck with the methodology but also came eventually to privilege the kind of multisited ethnographic research that had been common in the study of drug use since the examination of marijuana use in various Latin American countries and the PCP and HLS studies.

While at times over the years the ethnographic approach has not been always particularly popular in the world of drug research, the approach proved its value in public health research in the time of AIDS. Ethnographers demonstrated that they can gain access to otherwise clandestine groups and can describe variations and patterns of behavior in rich detail. They commonly are able to reach the most active, hard-core drug users (as well as dealers and other players in the drug trade from street syringe sellers to those who cook cocaine to make crack in underground laboratories), the very people who are the most likely to suffer from a broad spectrum of drug-related health problems, including overdose, HIV, other STDs, TB, hepatitis, abscesses, and various other infections.

Early in the period of ethnography and AIDS risk studies, Friedman, Des Jarlais and Sterk et al. (1990: 104) asserted, "[t]hese contributions show the value of ethnographic and other field research techniques in social and epidemiological investigation, and may well establish these previously derogated techniques as legitimate tools of science." Over the course of the next decade, this expectation was realized. Critical events in the validation of drug ethnography included a conference held in Chicago in 1979 that led to the volume *Ethnography: a Research Tool for Policymakers in the Drug and Alcohol Fields*, the National AIDS Demonstration Research project, which incorporated ethnography in a nationwide multi-sited epidemiological study among drug injectors and their sex partners; the Cooperative Agreement for AIDS Community-based Outreach/Intervention Research, another National Institute on Drug Abuse funded multi-site study that emphasized combined ethnographic/epidemiological collaboration (sometimes called ethnoepidemiology); and the Needle Hygiene Study, which illustrated the utility of ethnography in the identification of previously unrecognized risk behaviors among drug users. In the study of hidden behaviors like illicit drug consumption, accompanying drug users into shooting galleries, crack houses, abandoned buildings, homeless shelters, soup kitchens, drug coping sites, treatment centers and similar locations where drug users live out their daily lives proved to be a productive approach to knowledge generation and led to various public health recommendations and programmatic efforts to lower AIDS and related risk among drug users (e.g., expansion of syringe exchange and reworking of prevention education messages to include focus on the risks of indirect forms of sharing such as multiple person use of drug cookers).

Beyond AIDS-related studies, researchers during the third historic phase of ethnographic drug studies extended their focus to include a variety of new issues, including: the spread, in the late 1990s, of heroin to suburban youth; the use of so-called club drugs like ecstasy, GHB, ketamine and Rohypnol, in and out of youth-oriented dance clubs and raves, and increasingly on the street; mixing of drug cocktails (e.g., crack with marijuana, cocaine with club drugs); the emergence and diffusion of new street drugs like illy (embalming fluid) or new consumption methods, like crack cocaine injection; the nature and ideologies of drug treatment; and the spread of injection drug use to developing countries that previously had little or no drug injection. This new wave of studies, to a fair degree, represent the products of drug research careers that began with AIDS and have now expanded to include a growing range of other drug-related topics.

CRITICAL STUDIES IN THE POLITICAL ECONOMY OF ILLICIT DRUG USE

A number of critical anthropologists became involved in the analysis of illicit drug *use* during the postmodern era of ethnographic research. Building on the work of conventional medical anthropology, these researchers have challenged popular stereotypes and politically motivated explanations of the causes and nature of substance abuse, seeing this behavior not as an expression of individual psychopathology, lack of moral fortitude, or even subcultural values but rather as a consequence of social oppression. Findings from some of the studies carried out by critical medical anthropologists on *drug use* are described below.

Street Addicts in the Political Economy

One of the most extensive efforts to develop a critical approach to illicit substance abuse is Allise Waterston's book entitled *Street Addicts in the Political Economy.* In this volume, which is based on the analysis of an extensive set of interviews conducted with active drug users in New York

City, Waterston disputes many of the conventional truisms about street drug addicts and the causes of their behavior. While recognizing the achievements of the early ethnographic studies of the daily life and system of cultural meanings embraced by street addicts, she (1993: 27) ultimately is critical of the tendency in these studies to portray addicts as if they constituted "distinct and autonomous social phenomena." By exoticizing addicts as a distinct group with their own unique and insulated subcultural system of behaviors and beliefs, the early studies, she believes, failed to examine the "basic social forces, such as economic activities, class conflict, and labor-market composition" (Waterston 1993: 29) that drive behavioral patterns as well as the web of meanings and beliefs said to be part of the drug subculture. It is Waterston's critical anthropology argument that the "drug scene" described by the early ethnographers is, in fact, not an independent cultural development at all, but rather is a product of a particular stage in the evolution of a particular type of political economic system, one that many writers have referred to as "late capitalism." In this political economy, street addicts serve identifiable roles and functions. First, they form a pool of cheap, expendable, and highly disorganized laborers, taking odd jobs as they can for minimal pay and without health benefits or occupational safety protections. Second, they serve an ideological role as a "scapegoat of the bourgeoisie, always ready to feed the fires of xenophobia and racism" (Castells 1975: 33). Addicts, in other words, represent an example of what sociologists call a "negative reference group," a group that can be pointed to as an example of what happens to those who do not embrace conventional values and behavior. Moreover, by having addicts to point to as a primary source of social problems and community fear, the larger system of extreme social inequality and unequal distribution of wealth is shielded from public scrutiny or concern. Finally, she argues, drug addiction pacifies unrest in the most oppressed sectors of society. Illustrating this point, Waterston (1993: 233) cites the following comment by a drug addict she called Carl:

"I was willing, able, and ready to fight any I felt powerful, and I wouldn't allow anyone to put a damper on that." But once he discovered tranquilizer, narcotic-type drugs, [Waterston observed] Carl's violence ended, and he was back in the womb—warm, protected—and numb to the world emotionally.

Any resistance by drug addicts to the structures of dominance in society is "highly individualistic, privatized and self-destructive" (Waterston 1993: 244). While many of their activities are illegal, and they, to some degree, enjoy being outside of the law, ultimately addict subculture accommodates rather than challenges the status quo. It could also be argued that because many addicts engage in various property crimes, including shoplifting, burglary, and mugging, and because some of what they steal is taken from the middle class and sold below market value to poor and working people, they serve to control social unrest by redistributing social wealth.

Applying the insights of the critical anthropologist Anthony Leeds (1971: 15–16), Waterston concludes that so-called drug subculture should not be viewed as a "bounded and self-perpetuating design for living," but rather as a set of social "responses to adversity as it is structured within a particular social system."

The Spread of Injection Drug Use among Minorities

An effort to situate drug use within its encompassing historic and political economic contexts can also be found in the work of Merrill Singer, who has been involved in the study of drug use (with a special emphasis) in the Puerto Rican community of Hartford, Connecticut, since 1988. One of the goals of this ongoing research project has been developing an understanding of the sociopolitical origin and spread of injection drug use among Puerto Ricans, and the particular pattern that marks Puerto Rican drug injection. According to Singer (1995), Puerto Rican illicit drug use dates to the late 1940s and early 1950s, as large numbers of Puerto Ricans were migrating to the United States from the island. As U.S. citizens, a status conferred on them in 1917 so that they could be drafted to fight in the U.S. armed services during World War I, Puerto Ricans were free to travel to and relocate to the mainland. After the war, many were attracted to the United States by the loss of jobs brought on by industrialization of agriculture on the Island and the appeal of U.S. agribusiness seeking cheap labor. What they encountered upon arrival in the United States was a society that did not understand or respect them. Trapped by racism, a shifting economy, and other structural forces plaguing the American underclass, Puerto Ricans found themselves "limited to the poorest-paying jobs and to the most dilapidated housing and with only limited access to education and other public services" (Meier and Rivera 1972: 257). These conditions created sharp tensions that were multiplied by overcrowding; being forced by low income to dwell in high-crime, inner-city areas; and facing daily rebuke from the dominant society. In addition to the trauma born of severe economic disadvantage, Puerto Ricans endured a number of other stressful life experiences, including pressure to learn a new language; cultural differences with the dominant society; intergenerational conflict as parents and children come to have differing values and beliefs; and a sense of failure produced by an inability to fulfill traditional role obligations (such as being good family providers for men and protective, nurturing mothers and wives for women). In addition, they encountered heroin, a wonder drug that appeared to offer relief from their daily misery.

Merrill Singer (1995b) reports that during the nine-year period between 1941 and 1950, only twenty adolescents were admitted to Bellevue Hospital in New York as drug addicts (six of them in 1950). However, in January and February of 1951, sixty-five boys and nineteen girls were admitted with this diagnosis. A study conducted in the early 1950s of twenty-two of these youth, most of whom were Puerto Ricans and African Americans, found that they "suffered psychologically from the discriminatory practices and attitudes directed against their racial groups. They feel more keenly than other national minorities that they live in an alien, hostile culture. . . . They suffer almost continuous injuries to their self-esteem" (Zimmering et al. 1951).

These youth were similar to Ramon Colon (pseudonym), a Puerto Rican man interviewed by Singer in the late 1980s in Hartford, Connecticut. Born in East Harlem in 1939, Ramon recalled that he first began to hear about heroin from his friends in about 1947. He stated,

When heroin came into our neighborhood, we were 13 or 14 years old, in middle school. Latinos, African Americans, and Italians all started using at the same time. We would play stick ball in the street and pass a bag around to get loaded. We didn't know anything about addiction. Heroin was as easy to get as candy then, it was everywhere and it was pure. One time the baseball player, Frankie Robinson, came to our school to talk and I bet every kid in that room had a bag of dope in his pocket. I learned about it first from a neighbor who lived upstairs in our building. I began to dip into his stuff. We frowned on guys that were shooting up then. For the first six months it was just snorting. My brother put it up his nose for four years before he started shooting. My cousin snorted for seven years. But I told them they were wasting their dope and got them into shooting. I watched some older boys shoot up on the roof at first. They would skin pop me. People in our building would stash "works" [syringes and cookers] in the basement of the building. I would find them. That was how I got my first set of works. Before dope, it was really a nice neighborhood, nobody locked their doors. But with drugs, everything deteriorated, it became mean. (quoted in M. Singer and Jia 1993: 231)

Characteristics of the youth who formed the first generation of Puerto Rican drug injectors suggest a pattern that Singer argues has typified many Puerto Rican addicts ever since. First, most of these youth appear to suffer from a condition that Singer and his colleague Elizabeth Toledo (1994) have labeled *oppression illness*. They use this term to refer to the chronic traumatic effects of experiencing racism, classism (i.e., disdain and mistreatment of the poor and working class), and related oppression over long periods of time (especially during critical developmental periods of identity formation), combined with the negative emotional effects of intense self-disparagement associated with being the enduring target of social bigotry. Oppression illness, in other words, is a product of the impact of suffering from social mistreatment and, at some level, believing one does not deserve *anything better*. Individuals who suffer from oppression illness not only have very low self-*regard*, they also tend, to some degree, to accept the prevailing negative social stereotypes about their ethnic group, social class, gender, or sexual orientation. In other words, they have internalized their oppression and blame themselves for being poor and socially ostracized or for other *allegedly* personal shortcomings. Consequently, among Puerto Ricans suffering from oppression illness, Singer has described a pattern of feeling that they do not deserve to be respected while, nonetheless, intensely desiring respect (*respeto*) and dignity (*dignidad*), core values in Puerto Rican culture. For example, Singer cites the cases of four Puerto Rican boys from Chicago studied by Glick. All came from troubled homes and were gang members, and all four became addicted to heroin. In trying to explain why they became involved in drug abuse, they talked about "depression, their anger at others, and almost certainly themselves for having been found so worthless, as their principal reason for addiction" (R. Glick 1990: 88).

Second, these youth grew up in a somewhat isolating social environment in which drugs were readily available. For the most part, there were few life options open to these youth. For them, the American dream could not be found in a prestigious job, material comfort, or social recognition in mainstream society, for all of these were denied to them by deteriorating schools that failed to teach and produced large number of school dropouts, discriminatory practices in hiring, and a changing economy that no longer required large numbers of unskilled laborers but did not provide training that would have allowed inner-city youth to find skilled jobs. Drugs, on the other hand, and the kind of dreams they offered were available, alluring, and easily acquirable.

Third, for the most part, these youth were initiated into drug use and drug injection through preexisting social relations, especially by significant social others (like older brothers) who were role models for them or by similar aged peers. As Gamella (1994: 139) notes with reference to the spread of injection drug use in the working class of Madrid, Spain, the transmission of drug injection knowledge in the Puerto Rican community tended to flow within "groups of equals, in a climate of trust, emulation, and peer influence." As with early injectors in the neighborhood studied by Gamella, curiosity and a desire for social approval among peers motivated the initial involvement of Puerto Rican youth. Singer cites various data to show that throughout the 1950s and early 1960s, injection drug use continued to spread widely among Puerto Rican youth in New York City. And yet, there was little in the way of government recognition or response. By the mid-1960s (1964–68), of all the individuals reported to the Narcotics Register in New York City, 24.6% were Puerto Ricans. By the mid-1970s, Puerto Ricans had the highest percentage of admissions to

New York correctional facilities for drug-related offenses of any ethnic group; included in this group was a significant number of admissions for Puerto Rican women. By 1978, one in every fourteen Hispanics in New York, most of whom were Puerto Ricans, was involved in illicit drug use, and drugs were the second leading cause of death among Puerto Ricans aged fifteen to forty-four. Twelve percent of all Puerto Rican deaths in New York in this age group was related to drug use. Among Puerto Ricans the death rate due to drugs was 37.9 per 100,000, compared to 23.2 per 100,000 in the total New York population (M. Singer 1995b).

According to Ronald Glick (1983: 286), "one function of the . . . Puerto Rican community has been to assume the heavy risks and absorb the social costs of supplying drugs to higher status White outsiders." M. Singer (1995b) has noted this pattern in Hartford as well, where police sting operations (i.e., undercover purchases of drugs) net large numbers of white buyers coming into the inner city from near and distant suburbs to purchase drugs from Puerto Rican and African American street suppliers. The latter, usually called pagers or runners, often are youth who serve as the middlemen between customers and gates, which are apartments, commonly controlled by gangs that serve as distribution centers for neighborhood drug sales.

In his research on Puerto Rican drug users, Merrill Singer (1999) observed the existence of a distinctive pattern of drug injection, namely the highest frequency of injection among drug using populations. Consistently in studies of drug injection frequency (e.g., number of injections per month), Puerto Ricans injectors have been found to inject more often than other injectors from other ethnic groups. In one study, drug injectors in Puerto Rico were found to have an average of eight injections per day compared to an average of one injection every other day among injectors in Houston, Texas. More frequent injection means that Puerto Rican IDUs potentially are more often put at risk for blood-borne infectious diseases than are others IDUs. In explaining this pattern, Singer analyzes the role of interacting cultural and political-economic factors, specifically he agues that the types of oppressive social conditions described above subject Puerto Ricans to continuously painful and degrading experiences that clash and contradict with their sense of national pride and culturally constituted expectations about gender roles (i.e., hardworking, family supporting males and nurturing, family sustaining females). Under these conditions

Puerto Rican drug users lean to inject drugs . . . and they learn to inject frequently. Frequent injection among Puerto Rican IDUs . . . has evolved as a form of *defensive structuring* . . . against the constant external threat of oppression (encountered as experiences of injustice, discrimination, mistreatment, disrespect, and insult) and the ever-present internal threat of experiencing painful somatized symptoms of oppression illness like guilt and shame. . . . Daily experience of somatized symptoms [i.e., the experience of emotional distress as physical manifestations], and [Puerto Rican] cultural beliefs about rapidly eliminating them, provide motivation for frequent [distress relieving] injection. (M. Singer 1999: 49)

In sum, the heart of this critical medical anthropology argument is that understanding health-related behavior, including risk behaviors like frequent illicit drug injection, requires an examination of the specific cultural beliefs and values of the target population, an analysis of the socially constructed day-to-day experiences of target group members, and an assessment of the ways hierarchical social inequalities and conditions impact experience and resulting behavior and health.

Risky Behavior and the Law

It is widely known, including among drug users, that drug injection is a primary cause of the spread of AIDS. The critical factor in this transmission is not drug use per se, but the reuse of a syringe that has been used by someone else (who is infected with AIDS and transmits the virus to the syringe during the injection process). But why do drug injectors reuse previously used needles? Prior to the AIDS epidemic, some of the ethnographers who studied street drug use wrote about "rituals of drug injection." These writings implied that the reuse of needles, a behavior that came to be referred to in the literature as needle-sharing, was an integral and important feature of a ritualized act that bound drug users together as peers in an otherwise hostile world. By sharing needles, this literature maintained, drug users were symbolically expressing their shared condition, and this behavior, in turn, helped to reaffirm feelings of social support within a drug injection subculture. As Robert Battjes and Roy Pickens (1988: 178) of the National Institute on Drug Abuse summarize:

Needle sharing . . . occurs for social reasons. Within small groups, it may reflect a sense of camaraderie and trust. Sharing beyond one's intimates reflects an ethic of cooperation among addicts. Thus, needle sharing has become one of the well-entrenched social mores of addiction subcultures, supporting ready access to needles.

During the third phase of ethnographic drug studies, a number of anthropologists initiated ethnographic studies of so-called risk behaviors like needle sharing among drug users. One of these, Stephen Koester, began studying injection drug users in Denver, Colorado, in 1988 through a National Institute of Drug Abuse-funded research project. He describes his research methodology as follows: "Direct observation was carried out in the neighborhoods targeted for intervention, and open-ended interviews were conducted with a sub-sample of injectors who were also recruited as subjects for the survey instrument designed to assess HIV risk behavior" (Koester 1994: 288).

Like other ethnographers working in the AIDS epidemic (e.g., Carlson, Siegal, and Falck 1994), Koester (1994: 289) found that the notion of "sharing" is a misnomer because it "implied that the exchange of a syringe between users is conscious and deliberate, and that it occurs as an act of reciprocity." In fact, long-term injectors have several motivations not to share needles. Many have contracted hepatitis B from previously used needles and are aware of the risks involved. Moreover, the needle on a standard diabetic syringe further loses its sharpness with each subsequent use, making it harder and more painful to penetrate a vein. Additionally, used needles clog up, which slows the relief that drugs offer the addicted individual. Also, because using a previously used needle means possibly injecting the blood of another individual into your body, there is a potential for "an unpleasant experience called a 'bone-crusher'" (Page, Smith, and Kane 1991: 71) if the two blood types are not compatible. Despite these multiple disincentives, Koester (1994: 292–93) argues that drug injectors still use previously used needles because

> "Sharing" syringes and injecting in high risk environs like shooting galleries are not maladaptive rituals of a vast drug subculture, and they do not necessarily occur because of poor planning on the part of street-based injectors. On the contrary, these high-risk activities often continue as deliberate responses to what drug injectors perceive as a more immediate threat than HIV infection. Laws criminalizing syringe possession have made drug injectors hesitant about carrying them, especially during the times they are trying to obtain drugs. As a result, users are frequently without syringes when they are ready and eager to inject.

In other words, needle reuse is a product of a set of laws and a set of practices among law enforcement agencies. As long as laws against purchasing needles or possessing needles without a prescription exist and are enforced by the police, drug injectors are forced to make use of previously used needles if those are the only needles they can get their hands on. There is no evidence that laws that regulate injection equipment prevent drug abuse. However, they do, Koester maintains, promote the spread of AIDS. Thus, in Glasgow in Scotland, where the police do not enforce needle possession laws, the rate of HIV infection among drug injectors is 5%. In nearby Edinburgh, where needle possession laws are strictly enforced, the rate of infection among injectors is 50% (Conviser and Rutledge 1989).

Why do ineffective and even counterproductive laws stay on the books and why are laws that promote disease and death in one sector of the population enforced, often intensely so? Why do societies have unhealthy health policies? (Castro and Singer 2004). As Michael Parenti (1980: 120–21), a critical political scientist, has written,

Since we have been taught to think of the law as an institution serving the entire community and to view its representatives—from the traffic cop to the Supreme Court justice—as guardians of our rights, it is discomforting to discover that laws are often written and enforced in the most tawdry racist, classist and sexist ways. . . . Far from being a neutral instrument, the law belongs to those who write it and use it—primarily those who control the resources of society. It is no accident that in most conflicts between the propertied and the propertyless, the law intervenes on the side of the former.

While there are doctors and lawyers who are drug addicts (indeed, those in demanding, stressful professions tend to have comparatively high rates of substance abuse), the individuals who are most subject to needle prescription and possession laws tend to be poor and African American or Hispanic. These individuals have little in the way of status, wealth, or power and hence little influence on lawmakers. Klein (1983: 33), a criminologist, in fact, argues that a review of the enactment of drug policies shows that they are "part of a larger state project of social control." Similarly, the enforcement of possession and prescription laws is not automatic. Indeed, "Nonenforcement of the law is common in such areas as price fixing, restraint of trade, tax evasion, environmental and consumer protection, child labor and minimum wage" (Parenti 1980: 123). A study by the New York court system (reported in Parenti 1980) found that individuals arrested for small-time drug dealing receive harsher sentences than those convicted of big-time security fraud, kickbacks, bribery, and embezzlement, so-called white-collar crimes that tend to be committed by comparatively wealthy white males. As these examples suggest, risk behavior among drug users unfolds within a sociopolitical context; and the nature of class, race, and other relations that comprise this context may be of far greater importance in determining risk than the rituals or values of the subculture of drug users.

The Cultural Misconstruction of the Injection Drug User

Since early in the twentieth century, following the passage of the Harrison Act, injection drug users have been portrayed in the media and in public policy discourse as abhorrent members of a dangerous netherworld. This intensely negative portrayal has grown even darker and more loathsome during the AIDS epidemic and the rapid spread of the disease among drug injectors. Nina Glick Schiller, a medical anthropologist who became involved in AIDS research through her studies in the Haitian community, has challenged this image as a cultural misconstruction that serves political rather than public health or social science ends. While working for the New Jersey Department of Health, Glick Schiller was part of a team that conducted a survey of a random sample of 107 people with AIDS. In this sample, injection drug use and homosexual contact without a condom were the two dominant routes of HIV infection. An examination of the sociodemographic characteristics of the sample relative *to* these two risk behaviors is noteworthy in light of society's dominant images of gay men and injection drug users.

In the sample, 64% of the African Americans and 63% of the whites reported injection drug use. Prior to diagnosis with AIDS, 32% of the drug users earned less than $10,000 a year, compared to 15% of the gay men in the sample. However, 33% of both the drug injectors and the gay men fell into the middle income category, between $10,000 and $20,000 year, and about one-third of the drug injectors and half of the gay men had incomes over $30,000 year. While 40% of the gay men had finished college compared to only 3% of the drug injectors, 28% of the drug injectors and 23% of the gay men had not gone beyond a high school level of education. Very few individuals in the sample, regardless of route of infection, reported professional occupations. Among gay men, over half reported white-collar jobs, but mostly at lower levels such as clerks or data-entry workers, and about a quarter reported blue-collar jobs. Among the injection drug users, about one-fifth reported having white-collar jobs, with seven holding supervisory or skilled employment. About half of the drug injectors had held blue-collar jobs, and only 13% had been unskilled workers. Also, only a few of the drug injectors reported illegal activities as their primary source of income. The drug users did not differ greatly from the gay men in terms of stability of residence.

Based on these findings, Glick Schiller and coworkers (1994: 1343) conclude that

the assumed sharp differences between gay men and drug injectors could not be found in their sample. The drug injectors did not stand out as a distinct group in terms of their sociodemographic characteristics. Moreover, In their educational, occupational, and residential histories, the intravenous drug users do not emerge as a homogeneous group of hustlers or street people with a particularized subculture. The data collected on their use of shooting galleries and sharing of needles also do not substantiate a picture of homogeneous drug using subculture. . . . We found that almost all respondents had ongoing ties with their families. This similarity cut across risk group, racial and other demographic distinctions.

In deconstructing the "drug subculture," Glick Schiller and her coworkers (1994: 1338) argue that identifying entire subgroups as being at risk "provided the foundation for a view that groups at risk could be . . . differentiated from the 'general population' by their shared culture." Not only did this approach reinforce negative cultural stereotypes about devalued subgroups, it implied to those not in one of these "groups" that they were not at risk for AIDS.

What are the practical implications of insights like these developed by critical medical anthropologists concerning the nature of drug addiction and risk behavior? How can the political economic perspective of critical medical anthropologists be put to use in addressing the drug problem? One way is suggested in the Closer Look section presented below.

"A Closer Look"

A CRITICAL APPROACH TO DRUG TREATMENT: PROJECT RECOVERY

Substance abuse during pregnancy represents a major health threat to both women and their infants. Medical complications associated with drug use during pregnancy include anemia, cardiac disease, cellulitis, edema, hepatitis, phlebitis, pneumonia, cystitis, urethritis, and pyelonephritis. Major effects on the fetus include intrauterine death, overwhelming infection, chorioamnionitis, premature rupture of the membranes, poor fetal growth, and low birth weight with associated complications. Infants born to drug-abusing parents are at heightened risk for physical abuse and neglect, learning disabilities, and behavioral problems. Two recent hospital studies in Hartford, Connecticut, suggest high levels of drug involvement among low-income women. In the first study, urine screening for, 1,000 consecutive maternity patients at the city's largest hospital found that while 2% of private patients were positive for drug exposure, 13% of clinic patients had used drugs within three days of screening. A study of meconium samples (the first bowel movement of a newborn) at another inner-city hospital in Hartford also found a 13% rate of cocaine exposure among clinic patients. Clinic patients tend to be of poor and working-class background relative to private patients. In Hartford, the majority of poor and working-class women are either African American or Puerto Rican.

Because of the potential serious consequences of drug and alcohol abuse during pregnancy, some people in the substance abuse field, including at least one anthropologist, have suggested the need for drastic measures. Michael Dorris (1990: xvii), a Native American anthropologist who adopted an Indian boy who suffered from the painful effects of alcohol exposure while in his mother's womb, has come to believe that because of the "slashing of alcohol and drug treatment and prenatal care programs, the situation has grown so desperate that a jail internment during pregnancy has been the only possible answer in some cases." Others have emphasized the need for targeted treatment programs that are specially designed to address the particular issues and needs of chemically dependent pregnant women.

An example of this type of focused treatment program is called Project Recovery (Singer 1993). Project Recovery was founded in 1990 with funding from the Center for Substance Abuse Treatment as the first specialized treatment program for pregnant women in Hartford (and redesigned and refunded in 2000). Implemented through a citywide consortium of community-based organizations, drug treatment providers, and a general hospital, Project Recovery was designed as a comprehensive, multiorganizational coordinated program that integrates an intensive women's ambulatory day treatment program, strengthened by six interlocking sets of services: (a) intensive client-centered case management, (b) therapeutic child care, (c) transportation to services, (d) developmental assessment and intensified prenatal and well-baby medical care; (e) counseling for male partners; and (f) after-hours support, education, and crisis intervention. Project Recovery serves primarily impoverished, undereducated, inner-city women, most of whom are African American or Puerto Rican. These women have serious polydrug dependencies and limited resources or limited social support. Many have been subject to domestic violence or have attempted suicide. Given the multigenerational pattern of substance abuse, Project Recovery assists these women not only to take the road to a drug-free life but also to break the pattern of intergenerational transmission of chemical dependency.

According to M. Singer (1993), who, along with other members of the Hispanic Health Council staff, helped to design Project Recovery, of the first 140 women admitted to the program, 110 have been discharged (dropped out or completed treatment). At discharge, 16% had been drug-free (based on urine testing) for at least three months. Among women still enrolled in the program, 31% have been drug free for at least three months (reflecting the improving impact of the program as it has developed and implemented new or refined intervention components). In addition, the project has helped to reunite five families (in which children had been removed for abuse or neglect). Among currently enrolled participants, 43% have a partner or other family member(s) participating in the therapy family sessions, all of the pregnant women are in prenatal care, and all of the infant children of clients are in pediatric care.

Critical to the treatment approach used in Project Recovery is a concern with culturally and socially appropriate intervention. Awareness of the need for this type of targeted drug treatment and the parallel need for matching clients to particular treatment modalities has grown considerably in recent years. However, this mounting concern has not produced a clear-cut understanding of what constitutes targeted treatment. Efforts to design such programming have been hampered by a lack of adequate data about what works with particular populations. It is important to stress that there are a number of ways in which treatment programs can be said to be culturally targeted (M. Singer 1991).

Culturally sensitive programs attempt to be aware of and sensitive to the cultural background of their clients (so as not to cause them any unnecessary offense), but they do not necessarily implement any specific treatment modalities, institutional protocols, or environmental elements that are based on the sociocultural backgrounds of their clients.

Culturally appropriate programs attempt to both know about and to use knowledge about client cultural heritages to create a culturally familiar treatment setting and hire a culturally matched program staff. Such programs may identify particular cultural values or practices and actively reinforce them during the treatment process. For example, a number of alcohol and drug treatment programs that serve Native Americans have incorporated use of the sweat lodge, a traditional ritual element for Indian peoples, as part of the treatment program. Similarly, Gilbert (1987) reports on a California substance abuse treatment program targeted to Mexican American women. In this program, because "active participation in discussions [is] not pushed or urged, women [are] able to develop *confianza* (trust) [a traditional Mexican American cultural value] and take part in group sessions at their own pace."

Culturally innovative programs not only incorporate cultural elements in their treatment program but also attempt to actively rework these elements so that they support the therapeutic process. Identified elements are not treated as rigidly fixed and unchanging, but rather as fluid and adaptable frames that potentially can be molded to meet new contingencies. For example, Alasuutari (1990: 117–38) discusses the revamping of a Finnish working-class drinking ritual as part of the intervention program of the A-guild, an alcohol treatment program:

The first thing that attracts the attention of a newcomer in the guild meetings is the importance of the coffee drinking ritual. When the first participants of the morning meeting show up around ten o'clock, making coffee is the very first thing they pay attention to. . . . Meanwhile, other guild members will show up one after another, and the first comment they often utter is whether coffee is available or whether it is being made. Men may also converse about the amount of coffee they have already drunk during the morning, and compare the numbers of cups each has consumed. . . . As in any ritual, there are rules which the participants follow. . . . The particular importance of the coffee ritual . . . stems from [a] replacement logic. The social setting of the meetings has a remarkable resemblance to that of a male drinking group. In that way, those coming to the guild from such groups do not give up the spirit of male camaraderie found in the drinking group which, it appears, is part and parcel of the desire for alcohol.

Finally, *socioculturally empowering* programs, such as Project Recovery, follow the approach of the Brazilian educator Paulo Freire and seek to assist clients to use their culture as a critical consciousness-raising tool for understanding the historical, political, and social sources of substance abuse in their communities and in their lives. Socioculturally empowering treatment, for example, sees intervention for ethnic minority populations in the United States as needing to address simultaneously both the drug addiction and the oppression illness symptoms (e.g., low self-esteem, internalized racism, internalized sexism) of clients rather than subordinating all other treatment needs to the effort to stop substance use. The intervention approach seeks to involve clients in an active participatory effort to transform "privatized emotional experiences into a collective social process of healing" (Zavala-Martinez 1986: 125).

In targeting treatment to client populations, it is necessary to consider the implications of these alternative approaches, as each requires different institutional commitments. Culturally appropriate and innovative programs, for example, require a good awareness of the target culture, while an empowering program, in addition, requires a readiness to link treatment to the wider social and political context of clients (e.g., examining the causes of poverty or the nature of sexism) to address the emotional damage caused by self-anger and self-blame. In Project Recovery, the key mechanism for making this linkage is community-based intensive case management.

Various studies have indicated the difficulties of maintaining low-income, minority women in substance abuse treatment. Social stigmas attached to female substance use combined with multiple life stresses and survival problems, such as lack of child care, limited available transportation, and household crisis render it especially difficult to enroll in and follow through with treatment. The designers of Project Recovery sought to overcome these obstacles by making culturally sensitive, supportive case management the central component of the project. Experience with women in the project suggests that many substance-abusing women are motivated by pregnancy to desire a life change but lack the type of social and emotional support in their home and neighborhood environments that would enable a movement to a drug-free life (M. Singer 1993). Case management in Project Recovery provides this support as well as offering a gateway to a range of available resources and services.

In addition, case managers in the project seek to assist the women in the development of a positive ethnic identity and a positive identity as women. All of the case managers are Latino or African American and many, being in recovery themselves, are quite familiar with the life experiences common to project participants. Not only have the case managers overcome blaming themselves for the pain that they have suffered in their lives (or at least made significant progress in this regard), but they use this knowledge to assist participants in the project in the critical consciousness-raising, empowering transition they themselves have made. As Freire (1974: 51) notes,

As long as the oppressed remain unaware of the causes of their condition, they fatalistically "accept" their exploitation. Further, they are apt to react in a passive and alienated manner when confronted with the necessity to struggle for their freedom and self-affirmation. Little by little, however, they tend to try out forms of rebellious action.

From the empowerment perspective, these actions are signs of healing.

The designers of Project Recovery, after working with drug-dependent women for many years, have come to the conclusion that many such women suffer from a condition the designers have come to call *oppression syndrome*. As noted earlier, this term refers to the enduring traumatic effects of experiencing intense social bigotry and the internalization of this prejudice. In attempting to overcome the symptoms of oppression syndrome (e.g., self-defeating attitudes and behavior, lack of hope, a tendency to relapse into known patterns of risk and substance abuse, interpersonal violence), Project Recovery staff have sought to build a sense of community involvement and responsibility, to counter self-blame and demoralizing fatalism, and to model a hopeful, committed attitude. Furthermore, they have tried to help project participants escape other damage wrought by enduring poverty and discrimination. New research on the relationship between poverty and IQ, for example, shows that while genetics may account for differences in the IQ of people from the middle or upper class, among those living in poverty, especially among African Americans living in poverty, social class overwhelms genetics as a determinant of IQ. Without even broaching the issue of how accurate IQ scores are as measures of innate intelligence across ethnic and other social divides, it is evident that poverty robs children of their ability to achieve and to succeed. Addressing chemical dependence, which serves to chain families into a cycle of poverty, in other words, addresses a range of issues involving the health and well-being of women, men, and children. However, American society is ambivalent about investing resources in drug treatment. Such existing programs are often underfunded and inadequate for the scale of the problem at hand. One goal of Project Recovery, as a result, has been to help empower participants to serve as advocates for community needs like enhanced gender- and culturally-appropriate drug treatment.

CONCLUSIONS

In this chapter, we have attempted to situate illicit drug use in a historic understanding of its development and in terms of key *cultural and political economic* factors that have influenced the nature of this behavior. As a result, the account provided here differs from that commonly found in the popular press or in the pronouncements of policy makers. We have tried to show that illicit drug use is not a pathology of poor people per se, but rather an unhealthy condition that is shaped by the implementation and enforcement of laws, by the character of class and racial relations in society, and by the effort of the oppressed to cope with the hidden and overt injuries of racism, classism, and other forms of social bigotry *and structural violence*. In this context, drug use may function as a form of self-medication for the psychosocial injuries of oppression. At the same time, there should be no denying that substance use can be self-destructive and damaging to communities. Effective social response must address the underlying factors (e.g., poverty, discrimination, social ostracism, toxic living and working conditions, breakdowns in community social life) that lead to widespread chemical dependency, as well as treat the internalization of those social factors in the individuals whose lives are swallowed up in the search for chemical relief.

CHAPTER 8

AIDS: A Disease of the Global System

AN OVERVIEW OF THE AIDS CRISIS

It has been said that as AIDS has spread "along the fault lines of . . . society and becomes a metaphor for understanding . . . society" (Bateson and Goldsby 1988: 2) it has exposed the "hidden vulnerabilities in the human condition" (Fineberg 1988: 128). In other words, while certainly a biological phenomenon, AIDS cannot really be understood only in biological or clinical terms. AIDS, the disease, interacts with human societies and the social relationships that constitute them to create the global "AIDS pandemic," that is, the global distribution of the disease and the social response to it in particular groups and populations. By referring to AIDS as a metaphor for society, Bateson and Goldsby draw attention to an issue that will be of central concern in this chapter, namely, the way in which the AIDS crisis and the disturbing pattern of AIDS distribution expose the nature and consequences of social inequality within and between nations and groups in the contemporary world. Glaring disparities in the distribution of AIDS have inspired a hunt for co-factors that facilitate the spread of HIV in groups with disproportionate rates of infection. For example, genital ulcerative diseases like chancroid and syphilis, because they cause open wounds in the genital area that might allow the movement of body fluids and the pathogens they might contain, have been explored as prompters of the person-to-person spread of HIV infection. However, notes Farmer (1999: 51–52):

To date, not a single one of these associations has been convincingly shown to explain disparities in distribution or outcome of HIV disease. The most well-demonstrated co-factors are social inequalities, which structure not only the contours of the AIDS pandemic but also the nature of outcomes once an individual is sick with complications of HIV infection.

Farmer's assertion is validated by existing studies of the relationship of AIDS to economic deprivation and poverty. These studies (conducted by different groups of researchers in the United States in Philadelphia, Newark, Los Angeles, New York state, and Massachusetts and outside of the United States in Spain, Canada, and Australia) consistently show that HIV infection occurs disproportionately and at a growing rate of disproportion among the poor and socially deprived. For example, Zierler (2000) and her co-workers in Boston found that neighborhood levels of economic deprivation and population density are strong predictors of incidence of AIDS in Massachusetts. Comparing the least and most economically deprived street blocks in the state, they found that poorest neighborhoods had an excess of 309 AIDS cases per 100,000 population. Similarly, the most densely populated blocks had an excess of 333 AIDS cases per 100,000 compared to the least densely populated blocks. The highest rates of AIDS were found among non-Hispanic African American men who lived in the most densely populated areas. The group with the second highest rate of AIDS was composed of non-Hispanic Black men and Hispanic men who lived in the most impoverished areas. The lowest rate of AIDS in Massachusetts was among white women who lived in the wealthiest neighborhoods. In short, the greatest risk factors for AIDS are being poor and being an oppressed ethnic minority; notably these are not behavioral factors (of the sort that commonly are linked to AIDS) but, instead, are reflections of the health effects of the reigning structures of social inequality.

In exploring the relationship between AIDS and social structure, it is important to begin by emphasizing that the AIDS crisis is of considerable and growing magnitude. AIDS is now a leading cause of death among men and women in the U.S. between the ages of twenty-five and forty-four. On a global scale, Jonathan Mann, director of the International AIDS Center of the Harvard AIDS Institute, and his coeditors of *AIDS in the World* report:

In the first decade of response to AIDS, remarkable successes in some communities contrast dramatically with a sense of threatening collective global failure. The course of the pandemic within and through global society is not affected—in any serious manner—by the actions taken at the national or international level. . . . As we enter the second decade of AIDS, it is time to ask: Is the AIDS pandemic now out of control? (Mann et al. 1992: 1)

As we move into the 21st century, and the third decade of AIDS, there are almost 6 million new HIV infections every year in the world. While the death rate from AIDS in developed countries has been dropping, it must be remembered that in the United States alone there are 40,000 new HIV infections each year. Approximately 850,000 people in the U.S. are living with HIV infection; about 450,000 have died from AIDS. It is estimated that as many as 300,000 people in the U.S. are infected and do not know it. While some people misguidedly think that the AIDS epidemic is nearly over, in fact, we are still at the beginning of the epidemic. By the end of the year 2000, there were approximately 40 million people in the world living with HIV infection and another 22 million had already died of the disease (8,000 per day). Over 13 million children have been orphaned by AIDS, with 95% of AIDS cases appearing in the world's poorest countries. HIV/AIDS is now the leading cause of death in sub-Saharan Africa (the southern 46 of the 54 countries in Africa) and the fourth biggest killer worldwide. To take but one example, in South Africa, 24% of pregnant women are HIV infected. AIDS is also spreading rapidly in Asia. In Cambodia, for example, 2.5% of adults in the population are living with HIV infection. According to the Joint United Nations Programme on HIV/ AIDS, AIDS is the most devastating disease ever faced by humankind. The inability of nations, individually and collectively, to respond effectively to the threat of HIV infection and AIDS suggests underlying dimensions of the global system that will be examined in this chapter.

Certainly the sudden appearance of AIDS in the early 1980s was a profoundly unexpected occurrence, "a startling discontinuity with the past" (Fee and Fox 1992: 1). Global public health efforts that date to the period before the beginning of the AIDS pandemic, such as the successful smallpox eradication program, "reinforced the notion that mortality from infectious disease was a thing of the past" (McCombie 1990: 10). Consequently, whatever the actual health needs of particular populations, the primary concerns of the biomedical health care system had been the so-called Western diseases, that is, chronic health problems, such as cancer and cerebrovascular problems, common in a developed society with an aging population. This surely has been the case in the United States comments Brandt (1989: 367): "The United States has relatively little recent experience dealing with health crises. . . . We had come to believe that the problem of infectious, epidemic diseases had passed—a topic of concern only to the developing world and historians." However, with the appearance and spread of AIDS and a growing number of other so-called "emergent infectious diseases," like Ebola, Lyme Disease, or Brazilian purpuric fever, there has been a complete re-thinking of disease risk globally.

As a result of AIDS, in particular, but other diseases as well, the term *epidemic* has been thrust back into the popular vocabulary in recent years. Many definitions of this term exist. Marks and Beatty (1976), in their history of the subject, adopt a broad approach and include both communicable and noncommunicable diseases that affect many people at one time.

Epidemics (a word formed by joining *epi* or in with *demos* the people) are conceptually linked to other words in the demic family of terms, including endemics (from *en* or on), which are nonexplosive, entrenched diseases of everyday life in particular communities, and "pandemics" (from *pan* or all of), which are epidemics on a widespread or global scale.

AIDS in this sense is best described as a *pandemic*. It is now found in every nation on the planet. Further, it has spread to people of every age, race, class, ethnicity, gender, sexual orientation, and religion. However, as noted in chapter 1, another useful term in thinking about AIDS is *syndemic* in that AIDS is best understood in light of its bio-cultural and political economic contexts. Unfortunately, to date no country or community that has been struck by AIDS has been successful in stopping the spread of the disease.

With the transmission of the virus to diverse new populations through a number of routes of contagion tied to a range of behaviors, the pandemic becomes ever more complex and can be said to be composed "of thousands of smaller, complicated epidemics" in local settings and populations (Mann et al. 1992: 3). These local epidemics reveal that in each setting somewhat different subgroups are put at risk, but almost always it is those who have the least power in society or are otherwise subject to social opprobrium and public disparagement who are the most likely to be infected.

Throughout its known history, HIV "has repeatedly demonstrated its ability to cross all borders: social, cultural, economic, political," but this often has not brought people closer together to appreciate their common plight and their shared needs as human beings (Mann et al. 1992: 3). Rather, the pandemic generally has led to increased conflict and social contestation, usually on preexisting lines of tension. Indeed, AIDS has become probably the most political affliction visited upon the human species in modern times. The disease caused by this "strange virus of unknown origin" (Leibowitch 1985) reminds us, in fact, just how political are all facets of health, illness, treatment, and health-related discourse. This is an important point! Public health is never merely a medical issue, it is always shaped and molded by structures of power and struggles over power locally, nationally and internationally.

In sum, AIDS has revealed itself as a disease of social relationship—not merely a social disease, but a disease of society as it is constituted as a markedly stratified and widely oppressive structure. This occurs locally within communities, nationally within the social systems of individual countries, and internationally within the global system of nations. The social features of the AIDS pandemic as it reflects and reveals aspects of the global system, as well as social features of some of the local epidemics that comprise the larger AIDS crisis, are explored in this chapter. To help clarify the social dimensions of the AIDS pandemic as a disease of the world system, we begin with a Closer Look at AIDS within a country generally seen as being one of the poorest in the world, and, in part, as a result, one with a well-developed AIDS epidemic.

"A Closer Look"

THE HEALTH CONSEQUENCES OF BEING A PERIPHERAL NATION IN THE GLOBAL SYSTEM: AIDS IN HAITI

As the second New World colonial creation to successfully overthrow European political dominance and the world's first independent black republic, Haiti has long held a special place in Eurocentered global politics and political discourse. This place was defined early in Haitian history. Absorption of the Caribbean island of Hispaniola that Haiti shares with the Dominican Republic into the world system began on December 5, 1492, with the arrival of Columbus. Over the next ten years, the indigenous population of island Arawak and Carib peoples was enslaved and decimated by forced work in Spanish gold mines. To replace this lost workforce, in the 1520s the Spanish began importing kidnapped Africans to serve as slaves. The wealth and pivotal position of the island attracted French pirates and buccaneers, who seized the tiny neighboring island of La Tortue in 1629 and made it their base for preying on the sea trade, hauling the extracted wealth of the New World back to the colonial centers of Europe. Based on this foothold, the French were able to claim sovereign control of the western third of Hispaniola in 1697, known officially as Saint-Domingue. The French colloquially referred to their New World colonial possession as La Petite France (the Little France) or Grande Isle á Sucre (the Great Sugar Island). By the last years of the eighteenth century, the colony, which was seen as a great source of wealth and productivity, accounted for two-thirds of France's foreign trade. At the time, the population was composed of 40,000 white settlers, 28,000 mulattoes of mixed ancestry, and 450,000 black slaves.

Following on the heels of the American revolution, and certainly inspired by the American victory over British colonialism, a general slave rebellion was launched in Saint-Domingue in 1791. A little over a decade later, rebellious forces under Jean-Jacques Dessalines proclaimed independence from France and adopted the indigenous Indian name of Haiti (mountainous land) for their new nation. The character of its distinctive role in core-periphery relations in the global system was established early in Haiti's history as a free nation. In the first decades after the Haitian revolutionary victory over French hegemony in 1804, a U.S. senator from South Carolina described U.S. policy toward its sister New World republic, saying, "We never can acknowledge her independence . . . which the peace and safety of a large portion of our union forbids us even to discuss" (quoted in Metraux 1972: 9). Fearful of the lessons of a triumphant slave rebellion, the West condemned Haiti to the status of an international pariah state, a position that was sustained through the projection onto the former colony of an image of dangerous and bizarre Otherness (e.g., Loederer 1935; Seabrook 1929). In the Western imagination, Haiti was constructed as "another world far from what they know as ordinary" (Barry, Wood, and Preusch 1984: 337). Thus, voodoo, the indigenously formed syncretic religious system of Haiti, became synonymous in the West with evil, the epitome of so-called black magic, zombiism, strange trances, unearthly feats, and unbridled animalistic sexuality.

With the appearance of AIDS, this distorted portrayal was generalized and Haitians themselves were represented as dangerously infectious and life threatening by their very nature. By 1982, within a year of the identification of the first cases of what was to be termed AIDS (see below), Haitians were labeled as a risk group by the U.S. Centers for Disease Control. As a consequence, it was not long before being a Haitian "meant that you were perceived as an AIDS 'carrier'" and "the fact that AIDS was found among heterosexuals in Haiti . . . [was read as] evidence that Haiti was the *source* of the disease" (Gilman 1987: 102). The U.S. press carried stories quoting Dr. Bruce Chabner of the National Cancer Institute, who reported, "We suspect that this [disease] may be an epidemic Haitian virus" (quoted in Farmer 1992: 2). The politico-ideological context for these developments lay in the well-established constructed images of Haiti.

The link between AIDS and Haiti, strengthened in innumerable articles in the popular press, seemed to resonate with what might be termed a North American "folk model" of Haitians. . . . The press drew upon readily available images of squalor, voodoo, and boatloads of "disease-ridden" or "economic" refugees. One of the most persistently invoked associations related the occurrence of AIDS in Haitians to voodoo. Something that happened at these ritual fires, it was speculated, triggered AIDS in cult adherents, presumed to be the quasitotality of Haitians (Farmer 1990: 416).

The link with voodoo was asserted or suggested in both medical and social science texts. In the October 1983 issue of *Annals of Internal Medicine*, for example, two physicians from the Massachusetts Institute of Technology suggested that it was "reasonable to consider voodoo practices a cause of the syndrome" (Moses and Moses 1983: 565). Other bizarre or weird features alleged to be characteristic of Haiti also were implicated.

Some U.S. researchers proposed that AIDS began with an outbreak of African swine fever in Haitian pigs, and the swine virus had been passed to humans. Others suggested that a Haitian homosexual may have contracted the swine virus from eating undercooked pork, and then passed it on to homosexual partners from the United States during acts of prostitution. . . . Others proposed that Haitians may have contracted the virus from monkeys as part of bizarre sexual practices in Haitian brothels (Sabatier 1988: 45).

As the critical medical anthropologist Paul Farmer notes (1990: 438), "Even cannibalism, the most popular nineteenth-century smear, was resuscitated during discussions of Haiti's role in the AIDS pandemic." In the dark light cast by such linkages, in 1990 the U.S. Food and Drug Administration banned Haitians from donating blood.

All along, Haitian physicians studying the disease had produced evidence to support an alternative, more mundane, although no less politically significant explanation of the high prevalence of AIDS among Haitians. Research by these physicians found that most early cases could be traced to Carrefour, a red-light prostitution center on the southern end of the Haitian capitol of Port-au-Prince. Testing of stored blood samples that were drawn from Haitian adults during an outbreak of dengue fever in 1977–79 found that none carried antibodies to HIV. These data were consistent with the hypothesis that HIV was not indigenous to the country but had been introduced into Haiti in the late 1970s or early 1980s either by tourists or by returning Haitians coming from the United States or Europe (Pape et al. 1986). In addition to seeking an opportunity to purchase inexpensive ethnic curiosities, acquire value-gaining primitivist paintings, and take pictures of barefooted women balancing large bundles on their heads as they walked passed traditional-looking thatched huts, it is well known that many foreigners came to Haiti during the 1970s tourist boom seeking sex. Thus, a Club Méditerranée was established in Port-Au-Prince in 1980, and erotic accounts of available fun in the brilliant Haitian sun were common in tourist guides of this period. Not surprisingly, admitting to exchanging sex for desperately needed tourist dollars was quite frequent among early Haitian AIDS patients.

Driven by poverty that was itself the product of Haitian subordination to external economies and internal stratification, prostitution became a means of survival for some rural migrants to Haiti's crowded capitol city. In short, the politics of AIDS among Haitians and other Caribbean peoples are the politics of political-economic domination and, as a result, "the map of HIV in the New World reflects to an important degree the geography of U.S. neocolonialism" (Farmer 1992: 261). But this set of political relations was successfully submerged in more exotic accounts of Haitian AIDS, images that exuded racism while they mystified hegemony. The mundane and age-old tale of political-economic domination leading to sexual domination, which is a good piece of the real story of Haitian AIDS, remained hidden behind buried newfangled renditions of the master's fear of the rebellious subordinate. And, in various guises, this is a significant part of the history and politics of AIDS everywhere, from the preoccupation with discovering the African origins of the epidemic to the effort to construct AIDS as a disease peculiar to the bodies of gay men and people of color (see below), a disease of the distant and diminished Other.

Behind efforts to see AIDS as a product of Haiti is a depiction of the island as isolated, insular, and mired in ancient ritualistic beliefs and practices; a backward world cut off from scientific, technological and social progress. In fact, Haiti has long-standing intimate economic and political ties with the United States, notes Farmer (1999: 125–26), of all the independent nations of the Caribbean:

The country with the largest number of [AIDS] cases, was also the country most fully dependent on U.S. exports. In all the Caribbean basin, only Puerto Rico is more economically dependent on the United States. And only Puerto Rico has reported more AIDS cases to the Pan American Health Organization. . . . AIDS in Haiti is a tale of ties to the United States . . . ; it is a story about unemployment rates greater than 70 percent and tax-advantaged "free trade" zones. AIDS in Haiti is about steep grades of inequality, both local and transnational.

Ironically, Haitians have their own theory of how AIDS, or *sida* as it is known in Creole, came to their island and how it spread to large numbers of individuals living throughout Haiti, especially among those in urban areas from the poor and working classes. This theory, while no less a cultural creation than other popular ideas about AIDS, nonetheless reflects a clearer understanding of the global system than is commonly found among North Americans and is an example of the fact that those at the bottom often have a somewhat better and less mystified understanding of the actual nature and structure of oppression than those higher up the ladder of social power.

Dieudonné [a Haitian AIDS patient] tended to cast things in sociological terms. . . . Dieudonné "wondered whether *sida* might not have been sent to Haiti by the United States. That's why they were so quick to say that Haitians gave [the world] *sida*." When asked why the United States would wish such a pestilence on Haitians, Dieudonné had a ready answer: "They say there are too many Haitians over there now. They needed us to work for them, but now there are too many over there" (quoted in Farmer 1992: 242).

The social history of AIDS as an identified disease in epidemiology and biomedicine, the topic examined in the next section, reveals additional dimensions of the politics of AIDS.

THE HISTORY AND BIOLOGY OF AIDS: CONTROVERSIES IN SCIENCE AND SOCIETY

In the highly controversial world of AIDS, and despite it being one of the best studied diseases that afflict humankind, there remains much about which we still are uncertain. The beginning of the AIDS pandemic—not the point at which the virus began to spread in human populations, but the point at which people began to recognize this was happening—is not in dispute, however. During 1980, fifty-five young men in the United States, primarily self-identified gay men, were diagnosed with various diseases that ultimately came to be linked with AIDS. The health problems of these men were noticed because they sought medical care; their physicians, in turn, unable to halt the infection with standard remedies, sought approval to use a second-line antibiotic (pentamidine) from the Centers for Disease Control. The first report of an emergent health problem suggested by the diseases of these men appeared on June 5, 1981, in a widely read public health publication, the Centers for Disease Control's *Morbidity and Mortality Weekly Report (MMWR)*. This article, which focused on five cases from Los Angeles, did not mention that the people who were coming down with an unusual form of pneumonia were gay men. On July 4, 1981, however, the same publication carried a second article entitled "Kaposi's Sarcoma and *Pneumocystis* Pneumonia among Homosexual Men—New York and California." This linkage of a rare cancer with a rare pneumonia (caused by a harmless parasite for those with healthy immune systems) in a geographically dispersed population defined by sexual orientation was startling. The story was picked up immediately in both the *New York Times* and the *Los Angeles Times*, and soon found its way into the mass media throughout the country.

But epidemiologists and other health researchers were puzzled by the epidemic that appeared to be breaking out around them. While it was clear that the disease was linked to a breakdown in the body's natural defense system, the immune system, the cause of immunosuppression (i.e., a breakdown of the immune system) was unclear. Was it the result of environmental conditions, dietary practices, a promiscuous fast-lane gay lifestyle, or the inhalation of amyl or butyl nitrite poppers to enhance sexual or dance-floor arousal? No one was sure. There was less uncertainty, or so it seemed, about who was becoming ill. In December 1981, David Durack wrote an editorial for the *New England Journal of Medicine* proposing a multifactorial disease model that centered on the interaction between recurrent sexually transmitted disease and popper use as the cause of immunosuppression in gay men. Before long, the term *gay plague* had made its way into popular discourse. The new disease complex appeared to single out and attack only gay men, particularly those with a promiscuous lifestyle. Ultimately the term gay-related immune deficiency (GRID) was suggested to label the new syndrome descriptively. In short order, San Francisco, especially the heavily gay-populated Castro Street area, came to be thought of as "AIDS City, U.S.A." (Shilts 1987: 268) in the popular imagination.

In this way, gay lifestyle became an intensified object of mainstream social derision; not only was it seen by many as being immoral, but now it could be said to be life-threatening as well. Some people began to see the new disease complex as divine punishment for violating religious prohibitions against homosexuality. In time, the same language of blame and punishment would be applied to illicit drug users infected with HIV and Haitians as well. In this way—involving the social linkage of disease with denigrated behaviors or identities—AIDS came to be a heavily *stigmatized disease*. The extent of the stigmatization of AIDS was evident in the findings of a nationally representative public opinion Internet survey in which nearly one in five U.S. respondents (19%) agreed with the statement "People who got AIDS through sex or drug use have gotten what they deserve." The stigmatizing attitude was found more often among men, whites, individuals aged 44 years of age and older, people without a high school diploma, and individuals who have annual incomes of less than $40,000. Additionally, those who were less knowledgeable about HIV were almost twice as likely to agree with the stigmatizing statement as those who were correctly informed. Thus, 25% of those who answered *incorrectly* that "it is likely for HIV to be transmitted from sharing a glass with someone who is HIV-infected" or "by being coughed or sneezed upon by an HIV-infected individual" were in agreement with the stigmatizing statement, while only 14% of those who knew that HIV cannot be transmitted in these ways agreed with the stigmatizing statement (Centers for Disease Control and Prevention 2000a).

As a result of stigmatization, people living with AIDS often come to experience what has been called "a damaged sense of self." Arliss (1997: 56) encountered an ethnographic example of this process during an interview with Jack, an AIDS nurse who himself is infected with HIV:

I felt unclean like a leper or something, and the sort of prevailing attitude that comes through from different people, particularly who should know better, who don't know better because they haven't the disease yet, and you feel unclean.

Jack's analogy to leprosy is telling. Leprosy historically has fallen into the category of chronic diseases that medical anthropologist Sue Estroff (1993: 257) calls "I am" diseases, meaning diseases that by the very way they are talked about ("He is a leper") are marked as "more mysterious and more stigmatized" and "where attributions of blame for the condition rest with the individual" sufferer. By contrast, "I have" diseases are not seen as embedded in the personhood of the sufferer and who is absolved of blame for his condition. For example, one says, "he has arthritis" not "he is arthritis"; with the term arthritic being reserved for delimited body parts not the whole person. Arthritis, in turn, is generally not stigmatized and sufferers are not blamed for causing their own sickness through immoral beliefs or deeds. While in public discourse AIDS came to be talked of as an "I have" disease (reflecting, according to Estroff, the effort of organized AIDS sufferers and their supporters to destigmatize AIDS and to counter punitive efforts to blame victims of the disease for their own suffering), in actual street conversation, the "I am" usage is common. Thus, in his ethnographic work with African American and Latino drug users, Singer has found that infected individuals often say "I am HIV" rather than "I have HIV," suggesting the experienced stigmatization of people with AIDS. Typical, is a study participant referred to as Carlos who was interviewed by Singer (1998: 69) shortly after learning of his HIV status. "The questions just came into my head again and again; am I good, am I bad? Back and forth. I used drugs. I have problems. I ain't a kid who cares. And now she [his wife] is in jail [on a drug charge that Carlos avoided by leaping from his bedroom window]."

As Lindenbaum (1998: 51) points out, "The notion that AIDS punishes socially marginal people for deviant behavior echoes widely held nineteenth-century American views that the 'vicious poor' and lower orders rightly suffered most during the cholera epidemic of 1832 ... The moral view that established or governing groups have better health by dint of their position in society ... thus has a long history in Western thought and experienced." Such views of disease, in fact, can be seen as part of the ideological support system that helps maintain the existing structure of society. In effect, the stigmatizing of AIDS or other diseases reflects the effort to corral biology in the service of the politics of inequality.

As noted, enforcement of AIDS stigma did not go unchallenged, nor did a moralist or religious interpretation of AIDS as divine punishment. That the disease appeared to target gay men but largely avoid lesbian women *who were not otherwise at other risk* also created a dilemma for the divine punishment argument. The rapid appearance of the disease among blood-transfusion patients, individuals who seemingly were not guilty of any known moral transgression, further undercut but has never fully eliminated the appeal of a punitive view of the disease. Of special note is the response to HIV infection among individuals from groups that hold higher social status and are not otherwise marked by stigma. In a study of white, middle class women with HIV infection in San Diego, Stanley (1999) found that many woman adopted a spiritualized view of AIDS seeing it as a higher calling (e.g., to become an AIDS educator or community activist), as redemption (saving them from a life of sin), or even as a blessing (and personal re-birth). One interpretation of these findings is that people with adequate access to resources are able to minimize the experience of AIDS stigma through "moral management strategies ... [that] facilitate reconnection to an ideal, pre-HIV representation of self to which their self-esteem is intimately linked" (Stanley 1999: 119). Ironically, as a result, it appears that it is not only AIDS that is unequally distributed in society but the social suffering that is a consequence of AIDS stigma as well.

The study of AIDS stigmatization has proceeded slowly and as yet we do not have a full understanding of the toll it takes on the lives and well-being of people living with AIDS, although it is clear that the social damages of stigmatization are equal to if not more painful than the medical consequences of the disease. Slowing our progress, according to anthropologist Gilbert Herdt, is a unified and cross-culturally applicable conception of "harm." Indeed rectifying this short-coming in our conceptual framework would be useful more generally in efforts to understand the role of inequality and oppression in health. To address this dilemma, Herdt (2001: 146), building on the classical study of stigma by Goffman (1963), offers the following definition:

Harm . . . constitutes the state of being vulnerable to scapegoating, shame, and silence, to being the object of accusation and unwarranted, displaced fear, anxiety, and contagion. Harm includes the loss of social status and community belongings . . . but even more, it suggests the loss of basic personhood, of existence itself.

To this definition might be added the loss of health and well-being as a consequence of blame and mistreatment, subordination, and denial of equal access to items, places, and statuses of value or basic need.

The narrow focus on gay lifestyle during the early years of the pandemic overlooked a growing body of evidence that immunodeficiency diseases like Kaposi's sarcoma (KS) and especially pneumocystis carinii pneumonia (PCP) also were showing up in increasing numbers among heterosexual drug injectors, their lovers, and their children, especially in New York and New Jersey. In December 1981, for example, when Arye Rubinstein, Chief of Albert Einstein's medical college Division of Allergy and Immunology, submitted a paper to the annual conference of the American Academy of Pediatrics suggesting that the African American children he was treating in the Bronx, New York, were suffering from the same disease as immunodeficient gay men, he was rebuffed.

Such thinking . . . was simply too farfetched for a scientific community that, when it thought about gay cancer and gay pneumonia at all, was quite happy to keep the problem just that: gay. The academy would not accept Rubinstein's abstract for presentation at the conference, and among immunologists, word quietly circulated that [Rubinstein] had gone a little batty (Shilts 1987: 104).

The same pattern occurred among inner-city adult drug injectors, who began exhibiting immunodeficiency disorders in the early 1980s. Consistently, health officials "reported them as being homosexual, being strangely reluctant to shed the notion that this was a gay disease; all these junkies would somehow turn out to be gay in the end, they said" (Shilts 1987: 106).

By 1983, however, intravenous drug users (IDUs) constituted the majority of immunodeficiency cases in the Northeast. Still, among epidemiologists focused on the gay-lifestyle explanation, "There was a reluctance to believe that intravenous drug users might be wrapped into this epidemic" (Shilts 1987: 83). Nonetheless, the first clinical description of immunosuppression and opportunistic infection among injection drug users appeared in *MMWR* in December 1981, followed by a second report in June 1982 that indicated that 22% of new patients with KS and PCP were heterosexuals, the majority IDUs. Crimp (1988: 249), in fact, has suggested that "the AIDS problem did *not* affect gay men first, even in the United States. What is now called AIDS was first *seen* in middle-class gay men in America, in part because of [their] access to medical care. Retrospectively, however, it appears that IV drug users—whether gay or straight—were dying of AIDS in New York City throughout the 1970s and early 1980s, but a class-based and racist health care system failed to notice, and an epidemiology equally skewed by class and racial bias failed to begin to look *until* 1987."

In fact, IDUs continued not to be counted accurately in the AIDS statistics for several years after 1987 (at least until 1993, when the CDC definition of AIDS changed), and, because they often are not well served by the health care system, are probably still not being counted fully today. As Friedman, Sufian, and Des Jarlais (1990: 47–48) note "a large proportion of the deaths among HIV-infected intravenous drug users in New York City occurs through diseases that are not classified as AIDS under the Center for Disease Control criteria [for defining AIDS]. . . . Many intravenous drug users die of 'non-AIDS' HIV-related disease before they develop the specific opportunistic infections that qualify as AIDS, such as pneumocystis carinii pneumonia."

The actual term *acquired immunodeficiency syndrome* (AIDS) was introduced in 1982, when the growing number of blood transfusion cases made it clear that GRID or other gay-specific terms were problematic. But the cause of acquired immunodeficiency was still not clear. A number of scientists on both sides of the Atlantic became committed to finding the common cause of AIDS among gay men, IDUs, blood-transfusion recipients, and, in Africa, large numbers of non-drug-using heterosexual women and men. Many were now sure that a distinct pathogen had to be involved because AIDS patients did not share a common lifestyle or set of environmental conditions. Blood transfusion cases made it clear that the pathogen in question had to be found in the blood. Cases of sexual transmission suggested that other body fluids harbored the pathogen as well. Then, on April 23, 1984, Margaret Heckler, Secretary of the Department of Health and Human Services, held a press conference to announce that what she referred to as the long honor roll of American medicine and science had recorded another miracle; the virus that caused AIDS had been discovered. Flushed with confidence and enthusiasm, she also added that a vaccine to stop the virus would be ready for testing in two years, and, by implication, ready for human inoculation a few years after, an achievement that over 25 years later has yet to be added to the "honor roll" of medicine and science. The Heckler announcement created an international stir. For several subsequent years a *debate raged* over whether HIV was first isolated in France at the Pasteur Institute laboratory of Luc Montagnier or in the United States at the National Cancer Institute laboratory of Robert Gallo. Both labs were working feverishly on discovering the pathogenic cause of AIDS. Heckler's press conference, in fact, was designed to cut off the French and patriotically to claim American credit for the discovery of HIV as well as the profits to be gained by designing a blood test to detect the virus. Anthropologically, these events are of interest because they reveal the underlying political-economic nature of scientific work. No less than disease, itself, the treatment of disease is far more than a clinical issue, it is at the same time a very lucrative economic one and a political one as well. Ultimately, Gallo and Montagnier agreed to share credit for the discovery, but tension continued for years.

The April 11, 1983, issue of *Newsweek* magazine, which carried a cover story labeling AIDS the "Public Health Threat of the Century," signified a new era in AIDS media coverage. Notes Shilts (1987: 267):

In the first three months of 1983, 169 stories about the epidemic had run in the nation's major newspapers and newsmagazines, four times the number of the last three months of 1982. Moreover, from April through June, these major news organs published an astonishing 680 stories.

AIDS was coming to be recognized as a major health problem, one that was not narrowly limited to any specific population subgroup. With this recognition, the level of public hysteria about AIDS began to grow enormously. These might be thought of as the panic years in the AIDS pandemic, a period when a growing list of well-known actors, sports stars, and other performers either died of AIDS or publicly shared their HIV status. A sense of mounting vulnerability developed in the general public, as did growing political pressure for massive government action to respond to the AIDS crisis. Political activism around AIDS was successful during this period in significantly increasing the level of government spending on AIDS research, prevention, and treatment.

As a result of significantly increased funding for AIDS, a lot has been learned about HIV. Numerous scientific debates notwithstanding, it is clear that infection by HIV causes a severe crippling of the body's natural defense capacity, allowing an array of available viruses, fungi, bacteria, protozoa, bacilli, and other microbial parasites to attack several bodily systems. This destruction, *without treatment*, leads for many—but for not all—to death within about ten years from the point of infection (with the course of infection being conditioned by the viral strain, prior health of the host, living conditions of the infected individual, and a variety of other known and unknown factors). It is clear that HIV thrives in certain body fluids and that the "exchange" of these between people—directly or indirectly (e.g., during sex or through the reuse of hypodermic needles)— is the route of transmission in human populations. There is a range of cofactors, such as prior STD infection, that many researchers believe might influence the likelihood of HIV infection should an individual engage in what have come to be labeled risk behaviors (i.e., behaviors that allow the exchange of certain body fluids, particularly blood, semen, or vaginal secretion). It also appears that certain powerful drugs alone or, especially, in combination hamper the reproductive efficacy of HIV, at least for a period of time. The first of these drugs, AZT (Azidothymidine) was introduced in 1987. HAART (highly active antiretroviral therapy), a mix of several drugs, became widely available in the developed world as the standard in AIDS treatment by 1996. It is also certain that rates of HIV infection, opportunistic diseases, the duration of symptom-free vitality after infection, lengths of survival with infection, and routes of transmission vary across social categories, classes, and groups, as well as geographic regions. Indeed, as has been noted, as the pandemic has progressed it has become increasingly clear that AIDS disproportionately is a disease of the impoverished, subordinated social classes, ethnic minorities, and those who otherwise suffer from social inequality. Internationally, it is also becoming a disease of youth, with more than half of new cases appearing among young people.

Science, in fact, has produced more knowledge about HIV than any other known virus. Because of AIDS, we now realize that "infectious diseases are not a vestige of our premodern past; instead, like disease in general, they are the price we pay for living in the organic world" (Morse 1992: 23). But, because of AIDS we also know that the price of living in an organic world is not paid equally by all of those who live in that world. Indeed, while the virus is a product of the organic world, the AIDS pandemic (i.e., who is likely to become infected and who is not, and what happens to people after they are infected) is a social creation. In other words, as William McNeill (1976) suggests in his book *Plagues and Peoples*, it is important to differentiate between *microparasitism* and *macroparasitism* and to examine interrelations between the two.

Microparasites are tiny organisms like HIV that find the resources for sustaining their vital processes in human tissues and in the process may cause sickness or even death. In the case of HIV, it appears that the virus needs host-cell proteins to be able to transcribe its RNA genome (i.e., its genetic code for making copies of itself), synthesize its glycoprotein outer coat that shields the genome, and assemble new infectious virons that can, in turn, seek out new host-cells for continuing the process of replication.

As it invades a host-cell, HIV harvests proteins that it finds there, including cyclophilin A, actin, and ubiquitin. Without these stolen proteins, HIV would not be able to reproduce itself or successfully avoid destruction by the body's immune system (e.g., it is thought that by covering itself in the type of proteins found on the surface of human cells HIV virons may evade the immune system by masquerading as human blood cells).

Macroparasites, by contrast, are larger organisms that prey on humans, "chief among which have been other human beings" (McNeill 1976: 5). In the course of human history, macroparasitism has become ever more important in determining human health.

In early times, the skill and formidability of human hunters outclassed rival predators. Humanity thus emerged at the top of the food chain, with little risk of being eaten by predatory animals. Later, when food production became a way of life for some human communities, a modulated macroparasitism became possible. A conqueror could seize food from those who produced it, and by consuming it himself become a parasite of a new sort on those who did the work. In especially fertile landscapes, it even proved possible to establish a comparatively stable pattern of this sort of macroparasitism among human beings.

The emergence of a class structure, as McNeill shows, institutionalized macroparasitism. Moreover, as the case of HIV suggests, *microparasitism and macroparasitism interact,* an interaction we have referred to as a syndemic. As a consequence of the effects of macroparasitism some human beings—those who have less power and resources in society—are put at greater risk for exposure to and infection by various microparasites like HIV. This interconnection explains why poorer, less powerful classes in society and nations in the global system suffer more from disease than their richer, more powerful counterparts.

During the mid-to-late 1990s, the era of the "AIDS panic," particularly in the developed world, came to a close. Because of improved treatments, the death rate for AIDS in wealthy nations began to drop rapidly. Newspapers started carrying stories about individuals who were at death's door only to be swept back to reasonable health and activity as a result of available medical treatments. People who were preparing to die suddenly found themselves going back to their old lives, to their prior jobs, and to their remaining social relationships. A report released in March 2001 noted that U.S. AIDS patients diagnosed in 1984 lived an average of 11 months after diagnosis, compared to almost four years for those diagnosed in 1995. For those diagnosed in 1997, 90% were still alive two years later. One effect of this dramatic change was that AIDS came for some to seem like less of an important problem for society; just another chronic disease among many. HIV-negative men interviewed in a San Francisco study reported seeing AIDS as more of an "inconvenience" than a killer, while HIV-positive men said that they were no longer spending as much time warning their friends to be careful about AIDS.

In response, in wealthy nations, by the late 1990s a kind of "AIDS fatigue" set in, with people no longer wanting to hear or think about the disease. This attitude seemed to be particularly strong among young gay men, some of whom began to see condom use as unnecessary or even oppressive. Avoiding condoms, a practice that came to be called barebacking, developed a set of vocal advocates. The consequence was a notable rise in risk behavior in this population with expectable consequences. By 2001, the U.S. Centers for Disease Control and Prevention reported that the new infection rate for 23–29 year old white gay men in the United States had almost doubled since 1997, going from 2.5% per year to 4.4%. Public health officials began warning that if this rate continued, in five years, approximately 25% of young gay men would be HIV positive. Even more alarming, among Black young gay men, the rate was more than 14%.

Among people living with AIDS and their loved ones, AIDS activists, researchers and others still strongly focused on the epidemic, the fear began to grow that AIDS programs would begin to face significant cutbacks. The height of this fear was reached in the weeks after September 11, 2001, in the wake of the brutal terrorist attack on the World Trade Center in New York City and on the subsequent bioterriorist anthrax assault using the U.S. postal system. As a result, the U.S. government initiated a massive budget restructuring, pouring billions of dollars in a war against Afghanistan and in a radical beefing up of what came to be called homeland security. The subsequent war on Iraq, and intensely challenged federal effort to link the war to the fight against terrorism, became another military drain on federal dollars. The prevailing fear among those concerned about the ever rising number of people living with AIDS was that terrorism would become "the new AIDS" in terms of federal spending and public attention. Further dampening enthusiasm were reports of growing drug resistance, as the virus mutated and became immune to some of the best medicines available.

A GLOBAL PICTURE OF AIDS

AIDS, as we have seen, is a global disease. It is found on every continent and probably in every country in the world. It is believed that the worldwide spread of HIV began in the mid-to-late 1970s. In North America, over a million people had become infected with HIV by 1992. Many were still symptom-free, while others had progressed through one or more stages in the deterioration of their immune system, allowing opportunistic infection by various progressively lethal pathogens. At the time, there were over 250,000 diagnosed cases of AIDS in North America, about 10% of the world's cases, according to *AIDS in the World* estimates (Mann,

Tarantola, and Netter 1992). Across the Atlantic, there were over 100,000 diagnosed cases in Western Europe, while sub-Saharan Africa was rapidly moving toward recording its two-millionth case, over 70% of the diagnosed cases in the world. Latin America accounted for 7.5%, and the Caribbean 2%; Southeast Asia, a locus of new infection at the time, reported about 3% of the world's AIDS cases. Even on the dispersed islands of Oceania, there were about 5,000 AIDS cases. By 1992, AIDS cases had been reported to the World Health Organization (WHO) from 164 countries, including 52 countries in Africa, 45 in the Americas, 28 in Asia, 28 in Europe, and 11 in Oceania. Between 1985 and 1990, there was a sevenfold increase in the number of new AIDS cases reported to WHO (Mann, Tarantola, and Netter 1992). Given the fact that it is generally recognized that WHO only receives partial data from many areas of the world, the number of AIDS cases may have been even higher by 1992 than in those figures, and the numbers continued to climb.

Thus, globally over 60 million people had been infected with HIV by the end of the year 2001. AIDS is now the fourth biggest cause of death in the world, with 24 million deaths attributed to the pandemic. Around the world there are over 35 million people living with HIV disease. Each year, another four million people are infected. The majority of these new infections are among young, reproductive-age adults, with young women being particularly vulnerable. About one-third of those currently living with HIV/AIDS are 15–24 years of age, that is, in their early child-bearing years. Most do not know that they have been infected. Many millions more in the world have only limited knowledge about HIV including how to protect themselves from infection. Projecting to the year 2005, the World Health Organization estimates that 100 million people will be infected around the world. Importantly, the largest health and social impacts of the pandemic are yet to come.

A measure of these impacts can be seen by examining differences in AIDS rates between highly developed and developing nations. In sub-Saharan Africa, where the pandemic has been particularly harsh and widespread, there have been 17 million deaths due to AIDS since the beginning of the epidemic, another 25 million people are infected. The average prevalence of HIV infection in sub-Saharan Africa is 8.8% among those 15–49 years of age. However, in 16 countries on the continent, 10% of people in this age range are infected. Notably, 172 children under the age of five die of AIDS for every 1,000 births in the region. By contrast, in the developed world the percentage is six per 1,000 births. If the prevalence of HIV disease goes up by 10% in a country, the Gross Domestic Production will drop by 1% (Quinn 2001). Thus, it is estimated that by the year 2010, sub-Saharan Africa will be 17% less productive than it would have been had the AIDS pandemic never materialized. Some countries in the region, like Botswana, have long surpassed the point of severe impact.

By the end of 2001, 36% of the adult population in the country was already infected. In southern Africa, the lifetime risk of being infected and dying of AIDS is greater than 60% for those who are now adolescents. In the hardest hit areas of the continent, life expectancy has already gone down by 15 years and over the next 30 years may fall another 15 years. Given the age group it is most likely to strike, AIDS has contributed to a tremendous jump in the number of orphans. It is estimated that over 12 million children in Africa have lost one or both parents to the epidemic. Significantly, 30%–50% of Africans dying with AIDS are co-infected with tuberculosis (Quinn 2001).

One brighter spot on the African AIDS scene is Uganda. Based on a program designed to engage religious, traditional, and civic leaders in a full public discussion on AIDS as well as a coordinated effort that includes prevention education in schools, community counseling for people living with the disease, and widespread condom distribution (e.g., putting condoms next to bibles in hotel rooms), Uganda has been able to slow the spread of HIV disease in its population. In the capital city of Kampala, for example, the proportion of people with HIV fell from 31% in 1990 to 14% eight years later. However, the AIDS picture in Uganda is not all rosy. The majority of Ugandan people living with AIDS cannot afford effective treatment. With the pharmaceutical industry producing and setting prices in order to make significant profit, the price of existing medications is too high even for those AIDS drugs that have had their prices slashed because of competition from generic medications manufactured in the developing world.

This account of AIDS in Africa makes it clear that we are far closer to the beginning of the history of the AIDS pandemic than we are to its end. On a global scale, how are we to understand this history? Elizabeth Fee and Nancy Krieger (1993: 323) have argued that

the history of AIDS does not simply present itself as a chronological succession of events. It is a history that necessarily is constructed and that cannot simply be inferred from the biological properties of HIV or the pathological realities of the disease.

The dynamic, still-evolving world AIDS picture, in fact, can only be understood in light of a wide range of cultural practices and in terms of global, national, and local political-economic relations. This is so because *the key dimensions in the spread of AIDS are human behavior and human relations.* Factors that shape the collective patterns of human behavior, from inegalitarian class or gender relations to particular cultural beliefs about reproduction or sexual pleasure, therefore, constitute critical promoters or inhibitors in the spread of HIV. The role played by some of these factors can be seen by examining a few of the local epidemics that comprise the larger global AIDS pandemic.

India and Thailand

There was a dramatic increase in the number of AIDS cases in Southeastern Asia during the late 1980s and early 1990s. Previously, countries in Asia had been labeled "Pattern III." In one of the early epidemiological efforts to organize the global AIDS picture, this meant that rates of HIV infection were quite low and usually were a consequence of recent extensive contact with higher infection "Pattern I" countries (those with high rates of transmission through drug use and homosexual contact) or "Pattern II" countries (those with high rates of transmission through heterosexual contact). Today, these patterns no longer hold, and this classification system has been dropped. Southeast Asia is one of the reasons for this change. In India, HIV prevalence among STD clinic patients in the city of Bombay jumped from 4.3% in 1989–90 to over 30% in 1991. Professional sex workers in Bombay (i.e., those who sell sex for money or other items of desire), a group estimated to be between 100,000 to 150,000 in number, had an HIV seroprevalence (i.e., rate of infection) rate of 1.3% in 1987. A few years later, some studies were reporting rates of infection of 60% in this population. In the east Indian state of Manipur, HIV prevalence among IDUs was found to be minimal in 1986. Four years later, over half of IDUs tested in Manipur were seropositive (i.e., infected with HIV). Overall, during the 1990s India experienced a rapid increase in the estimated number of HIV infections, from a few thousand in the early 1990s to a working estimate of about 3.8 million children and adults living with explosive HIV/AIDS in 2001 (World Bank 2001). With a population of one billion, the HIV epidemics in India have the potential to have a major impact on the spread of HIV in Asia. Most of the Indian states have populations that are greater than a majority of the countries in Africa. Without successful intervention, HIV infection could grow to at least 5% of the adult population—more than 37 million people—by 2005. India is an extremely diverse country, with significant regional variation in ethnicity, behaviors, and social organization. As it has spread, the HIV epidemic in India has come to reflect this diversity, and thus it is best described as comprising a number of separate epidemics, which, in some places, occur within the same state. The epidemics vary from states with primarily heterosexual transmission to states in which injection drug use is the dominant pathway of HIV diffusion. Both tracking the epidemic and implementing effective programs has posed a serious challenge to health officials in India.

With the Prime Minister calling AIDS "India's most important public health problem," in 1992 India established the National AIDS Control Organization (NACO). Its mission was to implement the National AIDS Programme, including policy formation and prevention and control efforts. The same year that NACO was established, the Indian government launched a Five-Year Strategic Plan for HIV/AIDS prevention. The Project established state AIDS agencies in 25 states and 7 union territories and was able to make a number of important improvements in HIV prevention, such as increasing the safety of the country's blood supply. Although the overall HIV prevalence rate in India is comparatively low (0.7%), the actual number of people with HIV disease is high. Weaknesses in the county's HIV surveillance system, bias in the targeting of groups for HIV testing, and the lack of availability of testing services in several parts of the country suggest that there has been considerable underreporting of the extend of the epidemic. Given India's large population, a mere 1% jump in the prevalence rate would increase the number of adults living with HIV/AIDS by over half a million people. As the pandemic moves into its third decade, HIV infection in India remains concentrated among poor, marginalized groups, such as commercial sex workers, truck drivers, and migrant laborers, men who have sex with men, and injection drug users. Transmission of HIV within these groups is driving the epidemic, but infection is spreading rapidly to the general population. Increasingly, the epidemic is shifting towards women (25% of all new cases) and young people. In the Indian state with the highest infection rates, Maharashtra, the rate of HIV infection is now 60% among sex workers, 14%–16% among patients at sentinel STD clinics, and over 2% among women attending anti-natal clinics. Elsewhere (in Namakkai in Tamil Nadu state and Churachanpur in Mainipur state), infection rates have topped 5% among anti-natal clinic patients, suggesting the extent to which the epidemic has spread beyond so-called high risk groups to the general Indian population (World Bank 2001).

A recent study by the United Nations AIDS program found significant levels of AIDS discrimination and stigmatization in India, including negative labeling and stereotyping and a lack of health care for people living with AIDS. Stigmatizing was found to be highly gendered, with women being blamed by their parents for infecting their husbands or for not controlling their partners' desires to have sex with other women. Children of HIV-positive parents, whether positive or negative themselves, were often denied the right to go to school or were kept separate from other children at school. People in marginalized social groups, including female sex workers, *hijras* (transgendered individuals), and homosexual men, were highly stigmatized not only because of their HIV status but also because of being members of socially devalued groups.

Elsewhere in Asia, other patterns have occurred. Thailand, for example, has been the site of both a rampant epidemic and a notable national response to AIDS. The first AIDS case in the country was identified in 1984. The initial response of the Thai government was limited, with policymakers viewing AIDS as foreign and only a threat to a small number of individuals in pre-defined high-risk groups like men who have sex with men and injection drug users. However, as elsewhere, the epidemic did not accommodate wishful thinking about its ability to spread. By 1988–89, the country was facing what it would later see as the first wave of a major epidemic, with rates of infection rising to 40% among those engaged in known high risk behaviors such as IDUs. The second wave of the epidemic hit commercial sex workers. Testing among sex workers in the city of Chiang Mai, a city in the north of the country, in 1989 found HIV infection prevalence at 44%. By 1994, 31% of sex workers in the rest of the country were also HIV-positive. At the time, it was estimated that there were over half a million people with HIV infection in the country. Studies in northeast Thailand confirmed that the primary means of HIV transmission was through prostitution. In the provincial capital of Khon Kaen, for example, four hundred professional sex workers, all women, were identified. These women, who worked out of a variety of sites, including massage parlors, brothels, barbershops, night clubs, restaurants, and short-stay hotels, were found to have high rates of HIV infection. Research in Thailand suggests that between a quarter and a half of Thai men have frequented professional sex workers. Nonetheless, a community study of married women in twelve villages in Khon Kaen Province showed that most women did not believe themselves to be at risk for HIV infection. The reason most frequently given by women for not believing they were at risk was that their husbands never frequent professional sex workers (Maticka-Tyndale et al. 1994). As these data suggest, gender relations and gender inequality can be critical factors in AIDS transmission. Thailand, in fact, is one of a number of sites in Asia where not only local level prostitution is common but where international prostitution or sex tourism flourishes. The practice involves individuals or groups of foreign male visitors booking holiday vacations that include numerous visits to local brothels, x-rated clubs, and massage parlors. These businessman's holidays have created a lucrative income for those who run the sex trade business. Girls and young women who wind up in the sex trade often are duped into coming to urban areas from the countryside through bogus offers of legitimate employment or access to education. Additionally, the sex trade industry recruits and transports thousands of girls and women across national boundaries, a process that is global in its reach. Cut off from personal networks of social support, those caught in the cross-border sex trade industry are particularly vulnerable to forced involvement in risky sex and HIV infection.

Ultimately, the magnitude of the growing AIDS epidemic pushed the Thai government into action beginning in the early 1990s. A nationwide campaign was launched to reduce HIV transmission involving the promotion of condom use during commercial sex. Led by the National AIDS Prevention and Control Committee, chaired by the Prime Minister, and involving active community participation by non-government organizations, the aggressively implemented campaign led to a drop in the number of men going to houses of prostitution, a dramatic increase in the frequency of condom use during commercial sex, and a 90% reduction in the number of client visits to clinics that treat sexually transmitted diseases. The first sign of the effects of this effort on HIV transmission was seen in the HIV testing of new army recruits. Within a few years of the start of the prevention initiative the rate of infection among new conscripts had fallen by half. Assessment of the Thai situation suggests that the height of the epidemic among commercial sex workers and their clients peaked in the 1990s and that there are 200,000 fewer infections in the country than there would have been without the prevention campaign. In the global AIDS pandemic, which has been marked by governments usually doing too little too late, this is a remarkable achievement. Thailand's response to AIDS has been widely heralded as one of the few examples of an effective national AIDS program.

Nonetheless, because HIV had been firmly established in the Thai population prior to government action, HIV has continued to spread. By 1999, it was estimated by the United Nations Programme on HIV/AIDS (2000) that 2.15% of the Thai population was infected with HIV disease, with over 750,000 living with HIV infection and another 65,000 people already dead due to AIDS-related causes. Research suggests that however effective the focus on the commercial sex industry, the Thai prevention campaign overlooked other routes of HIV transmission. Throughout the 1990s HIV continued to spread rapidly among IDUs as a result of the sharing of syringes and among men who have sex with men. In one study in 1995 of men drafted into the Thai army from a region with particularly high rates of infection, for example, 6.7% reported participation in homosexual sex, with almost all of these men also reporting sex with women. HIV testing showed that those who engaged in sex with other men were almost three times as likely to be infected with HIV. As a result of the changes in the primary routes of HIV transmission in Thailand, the composition of newly infected individuals has changed dramatically. In 1990, more than 80% of infections were among commercial sex workers or their clients. Today almost half of new adult infections are among women who were infected by their husbands or non-commercial sex partners, a quarter are among IDUs, and only 20% are among sex workers and their clients. Importantly, since 1997, as a result of a national economic crisis, there has been a drop of almost 30% in public expenditure on AIDS prevention. However, the Thai government has launched a new National Plan for the Prevention and Alleviation of HIV/AIDS in Thailand that does focus on IDUs and men who have sex with men, as well as on renewed efforts among commercial sex workers (17% of whom are HIV-positive) and other populations with high levels of risk (e.g., male sex workers, prisoners, and fishermen). As part of this renewed effort, the government has announced that it would begin selling subsidized condoms at five baht (or 11 cents in U.S. currency) for a pack of two, compared with the standard price of 20 baht. The subsidized condoms will be sold through vending machines at public facilities, such as factories, police stations and military barracks, to address the embarrassment men report experiencing when buying condoms at a pharmacy. Another priority of the new policy is to ensure that people with HIV/AIDS have access to cost-effective prevention and treatment for opportunistic infections, the most important of which in Thailand is tuberculosis.

Overall, the case of Thailand affirms the popular public health slogan that "HIV is a Preventable Disease." However, it also demonstrates that success against the spread of AIDS requires a sustained, large-scale, community and research-based effort with strong support from policymakers.

The Caribbean

Permanently impacted by its post-contact history of colonialism and slavery, the Caribbean has produced a collection of over 25 island societies that differ in their political structures, ethnic compositions, dominant languages, and social histories. The islands also vary considerably by geographic and population size. Generally, rates of infection have risen dramatically in the nations of the Caribbean during the 1990s, although there is considerable diversity in the extent of the epidemic among the islands. It is estimated that over 350,000 people in the Caribbean are infected with HIV disease, with the average adult HIV prevalence rate reaching 2% by the end of the 20th century. However, as has been seen, the epidemic has been particularly harsh in some places, such as in Haiti, which has an adult HIV prevalence rate of 5%, putting it among the top ten countries in the world in HIV prevalence. Elsewhere in the Caribbean there has been a slower but steady increase year by year in the rate of new AIDS cases as the epidemic has progressed. For example, in Trinidad and Tobago, there were 198 new AIDS cases in 1990, rising steadily to 677 new cases in 1999. In Jamaica, the rate of increase in AIDS cases has been steeper in recent years, rising from 62 new cases in 1990 to 892 in 1999. By contrast, the islands of the Bahamas have demonstrated considerable success in responding to the epidemic. In 1994, the Bahamas recorded 719 new cases of HIV infection, by 1999 the annual number of new cases had fallen to 343. Similarly, while 280 died of AIDS in the Bahamas in 1995, in 1999 only 120 deaths were attributed to the epidemic. Other contrasts are also noteworthy. Cuba, which launched an early and aggressive effort to contain the spread of AIDS, including, temporarily, the quarantining of infected individuals, has a comparatively low number of AIDS cases. Thus, while Haiti (population: 7 million) had a seroprevalence rate (percentage of HIV infections in the population) of 9% in 1990, in Cuba (population: 11 million) the rate at the time was only .01% (and is currently estimated at .03%). Overall there are probably 10 times as many AIDS cases in Haiti compared to Cuba. As Chomsky (2000: 339) stresses, the effectiveness of Cuba's prevention and education effort has made AIDS "one of the least important health problems on the island." Another important contrast in Caribbean AIDS profiles is between Cuba and Puerto Rico, which lies to the east and, with Cuba, forms part of the Greater Antilles islands separating the Atlantic Ocean from the Caribbean Sea. While Cuba and Puerto Rico share many linguistic and cultural patterns rooted in their common histories under Spanish colonial rule, unlike Cuba, which has long been an independent nation, Puerto Rico is a territory that has been politically and economically tied to the U.S. since 1890. Currently, particularly because of infection through injection drug use, Puerto Rico ranks among the top ten U.S. states or territories with the highest cumulative AIDS cases among residents.

For the most part, the primary factors driving the AIDS epidemic in the Caribbean have been poverty, inequitable income distribution, population migration (often in search of employment), and lack of employable skills in lower education population segments. Poverty, for example, has pushed both women and men as well as many children into commercial sex work. Studies of rates of HIV infection among commercial sex workers in the Caribbean have found rates ranging between 3%–45% (Camara 2000).

The Former Soviet States

Until the mid-1990s, most of the countries formed following the collapse of the Soviet Union appeared to have escaped the worst of the HIV pandemic. Screening of blood samples from people who were engaged in high-risk behaviors showed extremely low levels of HIV until 1994. At that time, all of Eastern Europe had about 30,000 known HIV infections in a population that totaled 450 million people. By contrast, Western Europe had over 15 times as many cases, while sub-Saharan Africa had over 400 times as many people living with HIV infection. Since then everything has changed.

The countries that comprise the Russian Federation of former Soviet states now have one of the fastest-growing AIDS epidemics in the world, with the number of new HIV infections rising rapidly. In 2001, the World Health Organization estimated that there were 250,000 new infections in the region, bringing to one million the number of people now living with HIV disease. The rate of new infections in 2001 was believed to be as much as 15 times the rate of 1999. High rates of commercial sex, sexually transmitted infections, and injection drug use among young people, developments that are driven by socio-economic instability, suggest that the epidemic will continue to expand at a rapid pace in the 21st century.

As of 1999, Russia reported 130,000 people living with HIV infection, with an adult infection prevalence rate of 18% and an estimated 850 deaths due to AIDS. Between 1994 and 1997, the number of people with HIV infection jumped from 1,052 (with 2% infected through injection drug use) to 6,000 (with 80% of cases among known IDUs). Russia's first HIV epidemic among injection drug users was identified in 1996 in the port city of Kaliningrad. Four years later the epidemic had spread to over 30 cities across Russia. By 1999–2000, a number of new HIV outbreaks among injection drug users occurred in major urban areas, including Moscow, St. Petersburg and Irkutsk. More than 82 of the Russian Federation's 89 regions have now reported HIV cases. The Russian Federation Ministry of Health has reported that the number of drug users in the country jumped from 28,000 in 1990 to 88,000 six years later. However the Russian Ministry of Internal Affairs reports much higher numbers of drug users, estimating as many as 250,000 in 1997 (Khodakevich and Dehne 1998). Others have estimated the actual number of drug users in Russia to be between 1–2.5 million, or more than 1% of the total Russian population. These figures suggest just how widespread drug use—particularly the injection of opioid solution—has become in Russia since the fall of the Soviet Union.

All indications are that there has been a massive increase in the supply of opiates in Russia in recent years, with border controls reporting the smuggling of huge amounts of drugs into the country. In Russia and other former Soviet states, drug users often use imported substances like opium straw to produce injectable opioids in their homes using crude preparation techniques that may contaminate the drugs with HIV. Thus, there are some reports from Russia, Ukraine, Belarus, and Kazakhstan that human blood may be used as a clarifying agent (to absorb toxins) in the preparation of *kompot*, a homemade derivative of opium. If the blood used in this process is infected with HIV, all those who inject the drug will become infected. Additionally, there are indications that large-scale dealers commonly use slaves to test drugs. These individuals draw a dose from the drug solution, inject it, and then report on the quality of the solution. As compensation, these individuals are then allowed to draw another full dose, generally using the same unsterilized syringe. This practice represents another behavior that can introduce the virus into drugs that are subsequently sold to and injected by many people, contributing to the rapid dissemination of HIV among IDUs (United Nations Programme on HIV/AIDS 2000). Increasingly researchers in these countries are turning to ethnographic research methods to carefully observe and document actual drug preparation and injection patterns and assess the nature of risk for HIV infection (Ball 1998).

Beyond Russia, there are rapidly developing AIDS epidemics in the

Ukraine, Belarus, and Moldova. In the Ukraine, for example, sexual transmission was the primary route of infection until the end of 1994. In the early months of 1995, however, rates of infection among IDUs in cities like Odesa and Kikolayev began to skyrocket, jumping from 1,000 cases to as many as 100,000 cases by 1997. Soon high rates of infection among IDUs were being reported in all 25 regional capitals of the Ukraine. From the cities, the epidemic spread to the countryside, following the diffusion of injection drug use to rural areas. Within a year and a half of the spread of HIV to IDUs in the Ukraine, HIV prevalence reached 31% in Odessa and 57% in Nikolayev. Research in Odessa on risk behaviors among IDUs that could account for such rapid transmission found that ready-filled syringes provided by drug dealers and frontloading (removing the needle from the syringe to inject drug solution from one syringe to another) from a drug dealer's syringe to the customer's syringe were common practices. Both of these behaviors could readily contribute to rapid HIV transmission among IDUs if dealers' syringes are infected. Another study in the Ukrainian city of Poltava found that 68% of IDUs reported drawing up their drug solution from shared containers, a known risk practice. (Ball et al. 1998). The result in many parts of the former Soviet Union has been dramatic. For example, during the month of May 1996 over 750 new cases of HIV infection were identified in the small Belorussian city of Svetlogorsk, about 1% of the total population of the city (Ball et al. 1998).

China

While the first AIDS case in China was diagnosed in 1985, the HIV epidemic in China remains a sleeping giant that is just beginning to stir. While there is, as yet, no large-scale HIV epidemic in China, existing epidemiological data affirm the potential for the rapid spread of infection. Over the last 15 years, identified AIDS cases in China have gone from zero to about 20,700. Currently, it is estimated that as many as 10 million people may be infected with HIV by the year 2010 if no prevention is effectively implemented. Injection drug use has been identified as a significant factor in the spread of HIV/AIDS in China. While drug use was widespread in China prior to the establishment of the existing government in 1949, injection drug use was rare. The recent resurgence of drug use, and the appearance of injection drug use, began in the early 1980s in rural areas of the southwestern sector of the country, and have spread from there to other regions and to urban areas. The Chinese Ministry of Health (1997) has identified three primary phases in the spread of AIDS in the country. During phase 1 (1985–88), there were a small number of cases, mostly among individuals who had lived outside of China. During phase II (1989–93), a period of limited HIV spread, a number of indigenous rural drug users were diagnosed with HIV in Yunnan province. During phase

III (1994–), HIV spread beyond Yunnan, with infection being most common initially among IDUs and plasma donors (whose blood has been packed with the donations of others and then returned to donors with the plasma extracted). Currently, China may be entering a fourth phase, involving multiple local epidemics that vary by province and county, with differing epidemiological profiles, in which injection drug use (which has become an increasingly common method of illicit drug consumption) remaining a significant source of new infections, including urban infection (Sun, Nan and Guo 1994, Wu 1998).

Eleven of China's 31 provinces now report more than 10,000 registered drug users each, and it is now estimated that there are six million drug users in the country, creating a significant pool for HIV infection and transmission. Growing numbers of drug users, the spread of injection drug use, increasing numbers of younger drug users, increasing numbers of female drug users, the appearance of urban drug use, and raising rates of HIV infection among drug users are the key characteristics of recent drug use trends in China. To assess the extent of injection drug use and HIV exposure through drug use, and to control these health risks, China has implemented policies and sentinel surveillance studies. This body of research shows that the sharing of drug injection equipment is widespread and that HIV as well as hepatitis infection are spreading rapidly among IDUs. To date, research on HIV and related health risks among drug users in China has emphasized survey and surveillance methods that effectively reveal the extent of many key behaviors of concern. However, thus far there has been only limited qualitative and ethnographic assessment of HIV risk among IDUs in China. This fact results in a narrow base upon which to assess actual on-the-ground risk behaviors; specific contexts of risk and risk promotion, pathways of risk diffusion; and the precise nature of the social, environmental, structural and cultural factors that promote or retard risk behaviors among Chinese IDUs. In recent years a number of anthropologists have been working in China with the expressed purpose of providing ethnographic insight on the growing AIDS epidemic in the country.

Since the early 1980s, controlling illicit drug use has been one of the priorities on the agenda of Chinese leaders throughout all levels of government. A number of regulations regarding the use of drugs were issued during the 1980s and 1990s. These new laws included harsh punishment of drug smugglers and mandatory treatment for users. The latter involves four stages of involvement in the treatment process. The first stage is called "voluntary home-based assistance to quit." If the first stage does not prove effective, the user is then referred to a "voluntary community-based treatment center." The third level of response is the "compulsory treatment service" operated by narcotics control agencies and the strictest stage, "mandatory treatment," is operated by law enforcement agencies. Despite these efforts, it is estimated that the average relapse rate is about 95% for drug users who received compulsory or mandatory treatment. Needle exchange programs and methadone maintenance programs have not been implemented to control HIV infection among IDUs in China. Providing needles and syringes to drug users is interpreted by many officials as helping drug users to use drugs, and therefore, is seen as illegal behavior. However syringes can be legally purchased over-the-counter from pharmacies without restrictions on quantities. Until recently it was illegal to set up a methadone maintenance program to treat heroin addiction because methadone is defined as an illegal drug in China. In 2003, however, the Chinese began preparing for the implementation of methadone treatment in light of consistent findings showing its effectiveness as a means of dramatically lowering HIV risk and new infection among injection drug users.

AIDS, Crack, and Sex: The Second AIDS Drug Epidemic

The impact of gender inequality on the transmission of AIDS is not peculiar to Asia. The spread of crack cocaine use during the 1980s in the United States, for example, contributed to a significant increase in sex-for-drugs exchanges that has caused a notable rise in HIV infection among poor women. Commonly, these exchanges include sexual behaviors that place women at high risk for HIV infection. Often, in addition, they involve women in behaviors that violate their values and leave them feeling dehumanized and defeminized. In a National Institute on Drug Abuse funded ethnographic study of sex-for-crack exchanges in seven metropolitan areas in the United States, researchers found the driving force behind trading sex for a chance to smoke crack was desperation. Because of their intense craving for crack, they are only "minimally able to negotiate the terms of the encounter and are readily exploited and degraded" (Ratner 1993: 13). As Lowen and coworkers (1993: 97) report,

There is a critical element of coercion involved in the degradation associated with crack addiction. This has parallels with rape and torture, where the victim has been forced to perform acts that violate personal standards for human behaviour. . . . In the case of women driven by crack addiction, the . . . source of their stigmatization is the loss of "womanliness" as defined by cultural ideals.

Lown and coworkers (1993: 101) attribute the rise in crack addition, particularly in the African-American community, to radical changes in the economic infrastructure of inner-city communities: "Previously, blacks could compete for unskilled jobs but such employment has all but disappeared from the inner city." As, anthropologist Stephen Koester (Koester and Schwartz 1993: 193), who has studied crack use in Denver, observed,

Poor women with limited marketable skills trade sex-for-crack because they are addicted and because they have no other means of supporting their habit. Their powerlessness and marginality fuel the sex-for-crack phenomenon. The position of women in the underground economy mirrors their location in the mainstream economy. . . . Drug-using male members of the underclass have a greater variety of possible economic strategies than women.

Sterk (1999: 48) who studied inner-city crack-using women in Atlanta found the same pattern, with the women in her study reporting significant economic problems prior to getting involved in drug use and facing "limited opportunities to earn sufficient money through legal means." She (1999: 49) observed that among the 149 active crack using women she interviewed in depth, "few intended to pursue a job since none were available, anyway." Additionally, Sterk found that the women suffered from considerable stigmatization as drug users, indeed "harsher disapproval from society than their male counterparts seem to do" (Sterk 1999: 4). This opprobrium only served to increase desire for a crack high and its temporary self-medicating relief from guilt, shame, disappointment, low self-esteem and hopelessness. Caught in this endless cycle, and realizing they lacked bargaining power in the wider society or even in the drug underground, many of the women in Sterk's study turned to readily available sex-for-crack exchanges, thereby putting themselves at great risk for HIV infection.

It has been argued that the crack industry emerged in the mid-1980s as an arena of employment and economic opportunity for individuals cut off from the legitimate labor market. Certainly, some of the women in Sterk's study found jobs in the drug trade, including as cookers responsible for transforming powder crack into the hardened grey-white rocks smokable with a crack pipe. Some researchers have even described the underground crack industry as a form of ethnic enterprise among those who are blocked by racism and other structural barriers from legal business ventures. As discussed further below, marketing crack to the poor and to women, however, has contributed significantly to the inner-city AIDS crisis and to a second wave of drug-related HIV infection.

AIDS AND URBAN POLICY

Roderick Wallace (1990) has analyzed the social distribution of AIDS in New York City in terms of the social disorganization of poor neighborhoods caused by changes in social policy, such as the withdrawal of essential municipal services like fire protection, implemented with the intention of lowering population densities and achieving planned population shrinkage in targeted neighborhoods. Without public services, areas begin to deteriorate. Fires, of both intentional and accidental origin, destroy building after building, and none are repaired. After service withdrawal by the City Planning Commission and other government agencies, Wallace has documented a subsequent mass migration of people from burned-out areas into nearby neighborhoods, which themselves become overcrowded and are targeted for service reduction and subsequent burnout and migration. In areas undergoing this process of "urban desertification," community life, social networks, and other forms of social support are severely disrupted. These changes are associated with heightened rates of substance use and HIV infection. At the heart of one of the most devastated urban zones studied by Wallace, a section of the South-Central Bronx, 25% of emergency-room patients in the local hospital have tested positive for HIV infection. Wallace concludes that social policies, which are fairly direct expressions of social relations among contending social classes (i.e., those selected to sit on government planning commissions versus those who live in impoverished neighborhoods), propelled the urban environmental changes that produced a skyrocketing of HIV morbidity and mortality rates in parts of New York City.

LOW-INTENSITY WARS AND THE SPREAD OF AIDS

While most attention on the spread of AIDS has been focused on individual psychological factors, social conflicts, including war, have been shown to have a significant impact on AIDS risk. Wars disrupt established patterns of social support and subsistence. As these patterns break down, as in the urban desertification example discussed above, new behavior patterns appear, which, under highly strained conditions, may increase the opportunities for AIDS transmission. Baldo and Cabral (1991) have called attention to the AIDS impact of one particular kind of war that has raged in a number of areas of southern Africa in recent decades. This warfare has been called low intensity because it involves intermittent periods of open military conflict followed by prolonged periods of economic sabotage, that is, destruction of vital infrastructures like health and education services (e.g., through assassinations of doctors and teachers and the burning of clinics and schools). This type of warfare produces massive numbers of refugees, frequent troop movements through civilian areas, the appearance of bandit groups, forced recruitment of soldiers, and a general impoverishment of the countryside. All of these factors increase the likelihood of prostitution, multiple sexual partners, inability to know about or use safer-sex practices, the spread of STDs and other HIV cofactors, and a lack of medical care. It is important to recognize that low-intensity wars are not sustained without outside economic and political support. In the low-intensity wars that have devastated the southern African countries of Mozambique, Angola, and Zimbabwe, the former apartheid government of South Africa played a critical role in supporting rebel forces. Elsewhere in the world, other governments have supported similar arrangements to promote their political ends. The United States, for example, supported and financed a low-intensity war against Nicaragua during the 1970s and 1980s.

DOMESTIC VIOLENCE AND AIDS

Violence and the threat of violence are common tools used by socially dominant groups to control the behavior of subservient groups. Women's social status relative to men has immediate impact on their exposure to violence, especially in the context of their intimate relations with males. M. Johnson (1995) refers to systematic domestic violence against women by their male partners (measured in terms of frequency, severity, recentness, and duration) as patriarchal terrorism. Studies show that patriarchal terrorism is often accompanied by abusive drinking and drug use. Most research on the relationship between substance abuse and partner violence focuses on the ways in which the perpetrator's drug use contributes to violent activities. Psychological theories on the relationship between substance abuse and perpetrator violence include: disinhibition (drugs interfere with internalized sanctions against violence); learned disinhibition (individuals learn to view drug or alcohol consumption as a time-out from normal controlled behavior); cognitive disruption (psychoactive substances impair functioning by reducing the user's ability to perceive, integrate and process information); and power-seeking (men who are concerned with personal power and control are more likely to drink or use drugs heavily and act aggressively). Whatever the relationship, the emotional effects on women who are victims of domestic violence are significant. Beyond physical violence, particularly sexual assault, which is a significant HIV risk in itself, the fear of partner violence is often sufficient to increase HIV risk by decreasing the victim's "HIV prevention self-efficacy" (i.e., ability to maintain risk reduction behaviors like condom use, or, among drug users, cleaning syringes and not using syringes used by other people). It does not appear that personality is the primary factor in a woman's ability to engage in safer sex or in avoiding a risky partner. Instead, prior sexual history (including violence victimization) and use of drugs/alcohol are primary. Also, whether physical and/or emotional abuse is actual or threatened, and whether it occurs recently or in the past, one common psychological outcome among victims of violence is "learned helplessness," a condition characterized by a diminished sense of personal control over one's life, diminished self-efficacy and—particularly in the case of women—increased incidence of depression (M. Singer and Snipes 1991). While learned helplessness is but one response to partner violence, research suggests that women who are exposed to the type of unpredictable violence that is typical of abusive relationships exhibit learned helplessness in the form of low self-esteem and self-efficacy and a general retarding of coping mechanisms, including their ability to negotiate sexual behavior and to advocate on their own behalf, putting them at great risk of HIV exposure. This risk is enhanced by the use of alcohol and drugs by victims to medicate the physical and emotional pain of domestic violence. As a result, Monti-Catania (1997) asserts, within the coming decade, violence will emerge as the primary factor for HIV transmission to women.

The damaging effects of domestic violence also extend to victimized children. Researchers at the University of California at San Francisco found that gay and bisexual men who take sexual risks are more likely to have been abused as children than other men. Among those who had been abused as children, almost 25% were infected with HIV, compared to 14% of those who had not been abused. Researchers concluded that men who are abused during childhood often turn to drug use and risky sexual practices as a way to cope with painful memories.

As these examples suggest, the causes of AIDS transmission involve *far more than individual psychological factors or intentions*. The nature of the interaction of AIDS with social relations and social conditions is further revealed through an in-depth examination of an individual case. In the discussion above, we noted several cases in which unequal social relations—gender relations, racial relations, and class relations—contributed to the spread of AIDS. We continue that discussion below by looking at AIDS as it interacts with other health and social conditions to *create* the *inner-city AIDS syndemic*. As noted in chapter 1, the term *syndemic* refers to a life-threatening set of synergistic or intertwined and mutually enhancing health and social conditions facing socially subordinated populations like the inner city poor.

"A Closer Look"

THE INNER CITY SYNDEMIC: AIDS AND THE BIOLOGY OF POVERTY

It is widely known that the health status of inner-city communities in the United States is notably worse than that of wealthier population groups. Health in the inner city is a product of a particular set of closely interrelated endemic and epidemic diseases, all of which are strongly influenced by a broader set of political-economic and social factors, including high rates of unemployment, poverty, homelessness and residential overcrowding, substandard nutrition, environmental toxins and related environmental health risks, infrastructural deterioration and loss of quality housing stock, forced geographic mobility, family breakup and disruption of social support networks, youth gangs and drug-related violence, and health-care inequality. Urban minority communities are known to suffer from disproportionately high rates of preventable infant mortality and low birth weight, diabetes, hypertension, cirrhosis, tuberculosis, alcohol and drug-related health conditions, and sexually transmitted diseases. As a result, as McCord and Freedman (1990) have observed, men in Bangladesh have a higher probability of survival after age thirty-five than men in Harlem. More generally, "The death rate in blacks is higher than that in whites, and for many causes of death mortality differentials are increasing rather than decreasing" (Navarro 1990: 1238). However, these differences cannot be understood only in terms of racial inequalities; significant class factors are involved as well. The vast majority of urban-dwelling African Americans, as well as Latinos, "are members of the low paid, poorly educated working class that have higher morbidity and mortality rates than high-earning, better educated people" (Navarro 1990: 1240). Indeed, these mortality differentials are directly tied to the widening wealth and income differentials between the upper and lower classes of U.S. society. To clarify these points, we will examine the interconnections between a number of major health problems in the inner city.

Infant mortality, which is often used in public health and epidemiology as a reflection of the general health of a population, provides a good starting point for this discussion. Infant mortality among inner-city African Americans and Puerto Ricans has been called America's shameful little secret. In 1987, the Children's Defense Fund announced that a child born in Costa Rica had a better chance of surviving beyond its first birthday than an African American child born in Washington, D.C. (Edelman 1987). This pattern is not limited to the nation's capital. Overall,

African American children are twice as likely to be born prematurely, die during the first year of life, suffer low birth weight, have mothers who receive late or no prenatal care, be born to a teenage or unmarried parent, be unemployed as teenagers, have unemployed parents, and live in substandard housing. Furthermore, African-American children are three times more likely than whites to be poor, have their mothers die in childbirth, live in a female-headed family, be in foster care, and be placed in an educable mentally-retarded class. (Hope 1992: 153)

In some inner-city neighborhoods of Hartford, Connecticut, where Singer works, the rate of infant mortality has been found to be between 29 and 31 per 1,000 live births, more than three times the state average.

Similarly, in 1985, Boston experienced a 32% increase in infant mortality, with African American infants dying at two and a half times the rate of white infants. Rising infant mortality in Boston as elsewhere has been linked to a sharp increase in the percentage of low-birth weight babies, which in turn is seen as a product of "worsening housing conditions, nutrition and access to medical care" among inner-city ethnic minorities (Knox 1987: 1). Although these "contributing variables act additively or synergistically," household income stands as the single best indicator of an infant's vulnerability, with poor families having infant mortality rates that are one and a half to three times higher than wealthier families (Nersesian 1988: 374).

Class disparities in mortality rates are not limited to infancy, as substantial differences also have been found among older children. For example, children from inner-city poor families are more likely to die from respiratory diseases or in fires than children from wealthier suburban families. Inadequately heated and ventilated apartments also contribute to death at an early age for poor urban children. Hunger and poor nutrition are additional factors. As Fitchen indicates,

That malnutrition and hunger exist in the contemporary United States seems unbelievable to people in other nations who assume that Americans can have whatever they want in life. Even within the United States, most people are not aware of domestic hunger or else believe that government programs and volunteer efforts must surely be taking care of hunger that does exist here. (Fitchen 1988: 309)

However, several studies have shown that a significant link exists among hunger, malnutrition, and inner-city poverty, especially among ethnic minorities. A study by the Hispanic Health Council of 315 primarily minority households (39% African American, 56% Latino) with elementary-school-age children in eight Hartford neighborhoods found that 41.3% reported experiencing hunger during the previous twelve months (based on having positive answers to at least five of eight questions on a hunger scale), and an additional 35.4% experienced food shortages that put them at risk of hunger (based on having a positive answer to at least one question on the hunger scale) (Damio and Cohen 1990). It should be noted that the 1990 census (as did the 1980 census) found Hartford to be among the ten poorest cities (of over 100,000 in population) in the country (as measured by percentage of people living in poverty). Over 27% of the city's residents fell below the federal poverty line, compared to a Connecticut statewide rate of just under 7%, according to the census. Hartford, however, is not unique. Research conducted through the Harvard School of Public Health found that federal cuts in food assistance programs have contributed to significant drops in the number of children receiving free and reduced-price school lunches, producing growing reports of hunger and malnutrition from pediatricians in cities around the country (Physician Task Force on Hunger in America 1985). The study, for example, found reports of marasmus (protein-calorie deficiency) and kwashiorkor (protein deficiency) in Chicago. Young children are also at great risk of iron deficiency because of rapid growth and increased iron requirements during childhood. Poverty, associated with inadequate dietary iron, is one of the primary factors known to place children at risk for iron deficiency anemia.

Cardiovascular disease commonly has been portrayed as primarily a consequence of either genetic predisposition or "lifestyle choice," including such factors as personal eating or exercise habits. As Crawford (1984: 75) suggests, "Americans have . . . been exposed to a virtual media and professional blitz for a particular model of health promotion: one that emphasizes lifestyle change and individual responsibility." Often these portrayals have had the ring of victim-blaming, implying that individuals personally select their "lifestyle," from a range of equally accessible options. As a consequence, even at the popular level, health comes to be defined "in terms of self-control and a set of related concepts that include self-discipline, self-denial, and will power" (Crawford 1984: 66). Research by David Barker and his colleagues on cardiovascular disease suggests the folly in this line of thinking. These researchers show that the lower the birth weight of a newborn or body weight of a one-year-old infant, the greater the level of risk for developing heart disease or stroke in adulthood. Low-birth weight babies, they report, have higher blood pressure and higher concentrations of the clotting factors fibrinogen and factor VII as well as low-density-liproprotein (LDL) cholesterol as adults, factors associated with susceptibility to cardiovascular disease. Numerous attempts have been made to explain excessive levels of premature morbidity and mortality from cardiovascular diseases, especially heart diseases, stroke, and hypertension. Some have attempted to explain this pattern in terms of racial-genetic predisposition. Research by Barker and others, however, reveals the likely relationship of these diseases to the larger syndemic health crisis and thus to poverty and social inequality. Their work suggests that important factors may be the health status of the mother as well as of the infant during the early years of life, conditions directly tied to the kinds of social forces we have been discussing.

Alcohol and drug-related problems have been discussed in previous chapters, but it bears repeating that these conditions contribute to poor health generally among the urban poor. As Herd indicates with specific reference to drinking among African Americans,

Medical problems associated with heavy drinking have increased very dramatically in the black population. Rates of acute and chronic alcohol-related diseases among blacks, which were formerly lower than or similar to whites, have in the post war years increased to almost epidemic proportions. Currently, blacks are at extremely high risk for morbidity and mortality for acute and chronic alcohol-related diseases such as alcohol fatty liver, hepatitis, liver cirrhosis, and esophageal cancer. (Herd 1991: 309)

While racial and ethnic minorities comprise about 27% of the U.S. population, cumulatively just Blacks and Hispanics alone comprised 55.8% of all AIDS cases diagnosed through the end of the twentieth century. Moreover, these two groups account for more then 66% of new AIDS cases in the country, indicating that the segregation of AIDS as a disease of oppressed minorities is accelerating. The rate of infection among African Americans is eight times greater than the rate for whites. Researchers estimate that about 1 in 50 African American men and 1 in 160 African American women are infected with HIV. Among women, 58% of all AIDS cases are African American, and another 20% are Latina. Among children, African American children represent almost two-thirds (65%) of all reported pediatric AIDS cases. Among heterosexually transmitted cases, Blacks accounted for 73% of new cases in the year 2000 compared to 14% for whites. Similarly, AIDS is more prevalent among African American and Latino gay men than among their white counterparts. Additionally, a high percentage of adolescent AIDS cases occur among minority youth (Centers for Disease Control 2001). The transmission of AIDS, of course, has been closely linked to drug use. Drug injection and sexual transmission linked to crack use have become the primary sources of new HIV infection in the United States. Among drug injectors with AIDS nationally, about 80% are African American or Latino. In response to the worsening AIDS epidemic among minorities, in May of 1998 the Congressional Black Caucus of the United States requested that the Secretary of the Department of Health and Human Services declare the HIV/AIDS epidemic in the Black community a "public health emergency." While this did not happen, the president (Bill Clinton) did initiate new efforts to improve the nation's effectiveness in preventing and treating HIV/AIDS in the African American, Hispanic, and other minority populations. By the end of the twentieth century it was not evident that these new efforts had been sufficient to stop the minority AIDS crisis.

Beginning in the mid-1980s, there was a dramatic rise in the incidence of syphilis in the United States, "attributable to a very steep rise in infection among black men and women" (Aral and Holmes 1989: 63). While rates of infection dropped below 5,000 cases per 100,000 population for white men in 1985 and continued to decline through 1988, for African American men the rate began climbing in 1985 and by 1988 was about 17,000 cases per 100,000 population. Among women, in 1988 there were about 2,000 and 13,000 cases per 100,000 for white and African American women respectively. By 1991, 85% of primary and secondary syphilis cases recorded in the United States were among African Americans (Hahn et al. 1989). In part, this sharp increase has been linked to sex for drugs or money exchanges associated with cocaine use. Blood test data show that low income, urban residence, and lack of education are all associated with positive blood results for syphilis. In 2000, 71% of all cases of primary and secondary syphilis reported to CDC occurred among African Americans. Although the syphilis rate for African Americans declined from 15 to 13 cases per 100,000 persons between 1999 and 2000, the 2000 rate was still 21 times higher than among non-Hispanic whites. Compared with 1999, the 2000 rate of congenital syphilis decreased by 16% among African Americans but increased 12% among Latinos.

Rates of gonorrhea infection also show marked racial differences, and these differences have widened noticeably since 1984, when the incidence among African Americans began a sizeable increase. By 1991, of the 544,057 cases of gonorrhea reported to the Centers for Disease Control and Prevention (CDC), 82% were among African Americans (Hahn et al. 1989). This trend has continued. In 2000, 76.4% of the total number of cases of gonorrhea reported to CDC were among African Americans with an infection case rate of 827 cases per 100,000 persons. Among Latinos, the 2000 reported gonorrhea rate was 78 cases per 100,000 persons. Rate of gonorrhea among African Americans and Latinos are now 30 and 3, times higher, respectively than the rate reported among non-Hispanic whites. Rates are highest for young African Americans 15–24 years of age. Most strikingly, among young African American women (15-19 years of age) the gonorrhea case rate of 3,594.3 cases per 100,000 females in 2000 was 19 times the rate among non-Hispanic white females of the same age. Among African American young men of this age group, the gonorrhea rate was 1,911.6 cases per 100,000 males in 2000, 50 times higher than for young white males (Centers for Disease Control 2000b).

Beginning in 1984, another sexually transmitted disease, chancroid, which produces open lesions and has been associated with HIV transmission in parts of Africa, began to appear in a number of U.S. inner cities. The total number of chancroid cases reported in the United States rose from 665 in 1984 to 4,714 by 1989 (Aral and Holmes 1989). Similarly, African American women report 1.8 times the rate of pelvic inflammatory disease as do white women, while herpes simplex virus type 2 is 3.4 times higher in African Americans, hepatitis B is 4.6 times higher, and cervical cancer with a suspected STD etiology is 2.3 times more common among African Americans than whites (Centers for Disease Control 1992).

As this epidemiologic overview suggests, the diseases and conditions that comprise the inner-city syndemic are not independent of each other; they are closely intertwined and collectively enhancing. Poverty contributes to poor nutrition and susceptibility to infection. Poor nutrition, chronic stress (e.g., due to being the object of overt and covert racist practices and attitudes), and prior disease produce a compromised immune system, increasing susceptibility to new infection. A range of socioeconomic problems, lack of social support, and various stressors (such as unemployment, access to only the lowest-status, most demeaning jobs, or access primarily to illegal work like drug sales) increase the likelihood of substance abuse and resulting exposure to HIV. Substance abuse contributes to increased risk for exposure to an STD, which can, in turn, be a cofactor in HIV infection. HIV further damages the immune system, increasing susceptibility to a host of other diseases. While HIV thereby increases susceptibility to tuberculosis, there is growing evidence that the tuberculosis bacterium, in turn, can activate latent HIV.

Locating and reconceptualizing AIDS as part of the broader syndemic that plagues the inner-city poor helps to demystify the rapid spread of the disease in marginalized populations. In this context, *AIDS itself emerges as an opportunistic disease,* a disease of compromised health compromising social conditions, a disease of poverty and discrimination. It is for this reason that it is important to examine the social origins of disease and ill health, whatever the immediate causes of specific health problems (e.g., in the case of AIDS, a particular pathogen). Conceptually isolating AIDS from its wider health environment has resulted in the epidemiological construction of risk groups and risk behaviors that, rather than unhealthy living and working conditions, discrimination, racism, sexism, homophobia, and related social structural issues, have become the primary focus of public health efforts to halt the epidemic in the inner city. Lost in these public health campaigns is an understanding of AIDS as a disease that is spreading under particular historical and political-economic conditions (Quam 1994). It is for this reason that in this chapter we have called AIDS a disease of the global system. Our intention is to refocus attention on the relationship between the spread of AIDS and the particular set of political economic forces that have contributed to the rapid movement of the virus along particular routes of transmission locally, regionally, and globally. When we bring together our discussion of AIDS in Haiti and elsewhere in the Caribbean, Asia, the countries of the former Soviet Union and southern Africa with our discussion of AIDS in the U.S. inner city, we see that poverty, political domination (e.g., across genders, sexual orientations, classes, and nations), and other expressions of social inequality are the social engines driving the global pandemic.

ANTHROPOLOGISTS AND AIDS: WORK AT THE FRONT LINES OF THE PANDEMIC

Ironically, in the first volume edited by anthropologists about AIDS (Feldman and Johnson 1986), most of the individuals who authored articles were sociologists. Bolton and Orozco (1994: vi) observe:

In the early years of the pandemic, anthropologists were slow to respond to this rapidly emerging health problem. After the mid-1980s, however, this initial neglect was followed by serious engagement with the epidemic on the part of a large number of anthropologists. More than two hundred of our colleagues have joined the AIDS and Anthropology Research Group, a [subgroup] of the Society for Medical Anthropology. It is safe to assert that no topic in the entire field of anthropology commands more attention and more scholarly involvement at the present time.

Indeed, a number of anthropologists see AIDS as a litmus test of the relevancy of the discipline in the modern world. Merrill Singer (1992) has suggested that because HIV infection is spread through socially structured, culturally meaningful behaviors about which there is much still to be learned, the AIDS crisis presents a historic challenge to anthropology to prove its relevance. "How anthropology responds to AIDS," he asserts, "may be one measure of whether anthropology merits survival as a distinct entity" (M. Singer 1992: 94).

Anthropological neglect during the first years of the AIDS epidemic was, at least in part, tied to the lack of funding for social science of AIDS research and applied work. From the beginning of the pandemic, AIDS research dollars have been dominated by biomedical research, while social scientists have been hampered by a limited availability of AIDS funding. For example, at the Hispanic Health Council in Hartford, efforts in the early and mid-1980s by anthropologists on staff to attract federal AIDS funding went unrewarded. As Feldman and Johnson (1986: 261) have noted, "in fiscal year 1985, federal spending for [research on] psychological and social factors of AIDS amounted to a meager 2.1% of the $92.8 million actually spent." With almost all federal AIDS dollars being spent intramurally at the time and no foundation support yet available, funding for community-level AIDS work was scarce. Like all nonprofit agencies that depend primarily on project-specific grants as a source of income, the Hispanic Health Council was constrained in the type and extent of AIDS work it could initiate for several years. Finally, in 1986 the Hispanic Health Council held several meetings with representatives of the Centers of Disease Control (CDC) to develop an AIDS prevention effort targeted to injection drug users. Recognizing that among Puerto Ricans and African Americans injection drug users may not be ostracized from their communities, a preliminary plan was developed for a citywide research and intervention program involving a neighborhood-based system for disseminating AIDS educational information to individuals, families, and local groups. However, two developments delayed and almost derailed the thrust of this initiative. First, the CDC questioned aspects of the fairly ambitious program being proposed. Second, during this period, a shift occurred in CDC funding priorities, with commitment moving from the direct funding of community agencies to state departments of health. Consequently, a series of meetings were initiated with the Connecticut State Department of Health Services. During these meetings, the state's need for information on knowledge and practices relative to AIDS was emphasized. As a result, the character of the proposed effort underwent considerable revision and evolved into several studies of inner-city AIDS knowledge, attitudes, and risk behavior (Singer et al. 1991).

The earliest anthropological publication on AIDS was written by Douglas Feldman (1985). This article presents a pilot study, carried out between August 1982 and April 1983, on social changes in response to the AIDS pandemic in a convenience sample of gay men in New York City. In some ways, this study was a harbinger of many anthropological studies on AIDS that were to follow. First, it reflects the fact that gay anthropologists were the pioneers of AIDS work within the discipline; they have continued to be strong voices promoting AIDS research and applied work using anthropological models. Second, like others who were to follow, Feldman encountered a number of methodological problems carrying out his study, most notably an inability to construct a random sample because the precise size and demographic characteristics of the gay population in New York were not known. Feldman sought creatively to overcome this limitation by using various strategies to construct as broad and diverse a sample as possible. For data collection, he used a questionnaire. Given the sensitive and socially defined private nature of sexual behavior, Feldman could not use traditional ethnographic approaches in his study. This remains a significant problem for anthropologists working in the pandemic. While some innovative and sometimes controversial strategies have been developed (see below), for the most part anthropologists, like other social science researchers, have had to rely on the self-report of study participants for gaining information about sexual practices. However, anthropologists have stressed the importance of conducting open-ended, in-depth interviews with individuals in their natural social contexts rather than always bringing them into unfamiliar office settings for formal structured interviews or the administration of questionnaires. With other kinds of AIDS risk behavior, such as drug injection and crack use, anthropologists have been able to conduct field observations, which have contributed to significant insights about the nature and context of risk.

Bolton and Orozco (1994) have compiled a bibliography of over 1,500 publications and conference presentations by anthropologists (although related items by nonanthropologists are included in these figures). This number indicates the significant attention AIDS received within the discipline during the 1990s. The bibliography, which now contains over 4,000 listings, is maintained by the AIDS and Anthropology Research Group and can be accessed online. As the number of anthropologists working in AIDS during the first and second decades of the epidemic grew, there evolved a considerable diversification in the research problems they tackled and in the ways they came to contribute to AIDS work. Anthropological research on AIDS has included numerous topics such as:

"Symbolic analyses of AIDS discourse; surveys of adolescent attitudes toward sexuality and AIDS; the response of health-care personnel toward AIDS patients; [studies] of general population knowledge, attitudes, and risk behaviors; ethnographies of drug using populations; . . . experimental evaluation of the effectiveness of culturally specific prevention programs; and [analyses] of societal responses to the epidemic among a wide spectrum of other topics" (Bolton and Singer 1992: 1).

This research has been carried out in many locations, including North America, Africa, Asia, Europe, and South America. In the applied arena, anthropologists have filled a number of roles, such as health educators and developers of AIDS education materials; AIDS outreach workers; peer counselors and case managers for people with AIDS, their families, and partners; designers and administrators for prevention programs in community, national, and international organizations; evaluators of AIDS program effectiveness; advocates seeking to set or change social policies related to AIDS services and funding; and advisors to health care organizations and institutes. Applied work by anthropologists has addressed a variety of issues, including the use of needle exchange programs as a means of preventing the spread of AIDS among injection drug users; the development of socially and culturally sensitive approaches to AIDS vaccine testing; the incorporation of indigenous and traditional healers in condom promotion; development of community support structures and activities for people living with AIDS, the design of community-based outreach to out-of-treatment injection drug users; the testing of the female condom in specific populations; policy-based examination of the experiences and challenges of lay care givers to AIDS patients; and the creation of intervention models targeted to changing risk behavior in the social networks of drug injectors and men who have sex with men. Two of the authors of this volume (I. Susser and M. Singer) have been very involved in AIDS prevention work. Ida Susser (I. Susser and González 1992: 182), for example, has worked with shelter residents in New York on a video project designed as a self-help initiative to empower the homeless to reshape "their conscious views of themselves and their potential to confront hazards such a HIV infection along with the numerous other issues with which they are forced to battle." She also has worked on AIDS prevention at the community level in Puerto Rico and among women in southern Africa (I. Susser and Stein 2000).

While anthropologists have made a variety of contributions in the AIDS field, probably the most important have been in the area of understanding AIDS risk. Much of this research has a very significant applied dimension. In other words, it is research designed not only to comprehend the social nature of viral transmission but, in addition, to understand it in a way that will contribute to AIDS prevention. Parker (1992: 226) has pointed out that "if we are to understand the radical differences that seem to characterize the epidemiology of AIDS in different areas, we need data that will allow us to compare and contrast not only distinct societies but also distinct social groups within any given society." Socially grounded data of this sort is needed to design targeted intervention programs that are appropriate for specific populations. Critical to our understanding of risk is an awareness of social context and the larger forces that shape behavior. As Parker and Ehrhardt (2001: 110) emphasize

one of the most important contributions of ethnographic studies related to HIV and AIDS ... has been their ability to capture and highlight the importance of a range of broad, structural or political and economic factors that have increasingly been understood as crucial in shaping the course of the global HIV/AIDS epidemic ... such as underdevelopment, poverty, labor migration and forced population movement, gender inequalities, and sexual discrimination and oppression.

As a result of its demonstrated strengths, ethnographic methods, including extended or rapid field observation, participatory involvement in social life, informal and in-depth open-interviewing, detailed life-history interviewing, social network assessment, and the use of cognitive tools for analyzing cultural frameworks (e.g., pile sorts, free listing) have been integrated into collaborative, multi-disciplinary studies of HIV/AIDS using *multi-method research designs* (usually involving both qualitative methods like ethnography and quantitative methods like surveys but also laboratory analyses of biological markers) and the *triangulation* (i.e. analytic integration) of different kinds of data. Exemplary of this increasingly common approach is a multi-site study of the social geography of AIDS and hepatitis risk among injection drug users co-lead by Merrill Singer and three laboratory and field epidemiologists (M. Singer et al. 2000). Designed to assess factors in the local social environment at the neighborhood and city level that shape IDU access to, use of, and discard of syringes (e.g., presence of a syringe exchange program, pharmacy sale of syringes without a prescription, discrimination, availability of services, and police attitudes and practices), this study collected and analytically integrated a wide range of different types of data, including neighborhood observations and written descriptions, narratives from in-depth interviewing of IDUs, social maps of the key features of neighborhoods drawn by resident IDUs, diaries kept by IDUs, field notes from direct observation of drug injection behaviors, recorded assessment of pharmacy sales practices, laboratory results from the testing for human DNA of syringes sold on the street by underground syringe dealers (to determine prior use of these syringes), laboratory results from the assessment of discarded syringes (for HIV and hepatitis), and forced-choice answers from epidemiological survey of IDUs on behaviors and risks. This type of multi-method, multi-site ethnoepidemiologic approach increasingly has become a standard in HIV/AIDS behavioral research. It is precisely this approach, most researchers recognize, that is needed to expand HIV prevention and intervention efforts beyond the level of individual or even small group beliefs and behaviors to the develop of *structural interventions* capable of impacting AIDS risk and care at the level of larger social groups (e.g., reductions in gender discrimination, increased access to prevention resources, destigmatization campaigns, improved access to health care for the poor) (Blankenship, Bray and Merson 2000, Sumartojo 2000).

Several other examples of anthropological research on HIV/AIDS are described below.

Studying Private Sexual Encounters

Given the importance of sexual behavior in the transmission of AIDS, we need to have a clear understanding of what actually happens when two (or more) people have sex in diverse cultural settings. However, the privacy of sex in most cultures makes it difficult to collect this kind of observational data. One innovative response to this dilemma was undertaken by Ralph Bolton in his study of AIDS risk among gay men in Belgium. He reports,

I spent most of my time, at all hours of day and night . . . in settings where gay men in Brussels hang out: bars, saunas, restaurants, parks, tearooms [public bathrooms where sex occurs], streets, and privates homes. . . . My presentation of self was simple and straightforward: I was a gay man doing research as a medical anthropologist on AIDS and sex. . . . In my casual sexual encounters with men I picked up in gay cruising situations, my approach during sex was to allow my partner to take the lead in determining which sexual practices to engage in. Low-risk activities posed no problem, of course, but to discover which moderate and high-risk behaviors they practiced, I assented to the former (oral sex, for example) while declining the latter (unprotected sexual intercourse). (Bolton 1992: 133–35)

Through this strategy, Bolton was able to determine that high-risk sexual behavior was quite common and quite accepted in the privacy of the bedroom among gay men in Brussels. This finding was of importance because health officials in Belgium had come to the conclusion, based on several surveys, that gay men had significantly curtailed risky sexual behavior and that it was no longer necessary therefore to focus prevention efforts on the gay community.

Another approach for going beyond self-reported sexual practices was developed by Terri Leonard in her study of male clients of street sex workers in Camden, New Jersey. Leonard conducted her research by hanging out at an inner-city "stroll" area (a street where sex workers seek business among pedestrians and the drivers of passing cars).

All men who attempted to solicit my services, assuming I was a sex worker, were invited to participate in a "sex survey." Men initiated contact using several approaches. Some pulled up alongside the curb or onto a side street and, with engines idling, engaged me in conversation. Some men parked alongside the street and got out to make a phone call or have a drink in a nearby bar, initiating conversation en route. Some men "cruised" by several times per day, several days per week, or once every few weeks before approaching. (Leonard 1990: 43)

Leonard found that twenty men out of the forty-nine she was able to interview reported that they used condoms during commercial sex. However, despite this self-report, only five of the men actually had condoms with them at the time they solicited sex with Leonard. Like Bolton's work, Leonard's shows that ethnographic approaches can produce data that reflects actual rather than idealized behavior.

In cross-cultural settings, the study of sexual behavior may be especially problematic, as cultural norms about and experiences with sex vary significantly. For example, the spread of HIV in Africa has been attributed primarily to heterosexual contact, and African male "hyperheterosexuality" has been blamed for the sub-Saharan epidemic. Additionally, homosexuality has been publicly condemned by a number of African leaders as un-African behavior. As a result of this stigmatization, efforts to study sexual practices, including same-sex contact, among African men are stymied by respondent defensiveness and the fear of condemnation. Consequently, Niels Teunis (2001) found in his attempt to study the role of same-sex practices in the spread of HIV among men in Darkar, Senegal, that such behaviors were hidden and their existence denied. Ultimately, Teunis (with the aid of a street youth) learned of a bar with a homosexual clientele. While he was able eventually to interview 42 men who engaged in same-sex contact, as well as to participate with them in various social activities, he quickly realized that these men operate with a code of secrecy and live in fear that their behavior will be exposed with drastic consequences. Under these conditions, Teunis was never able to tape-record his interviews and was otherwise restricted in the methods of data collection he could use (e.g., photography was not possible). Nonetheless, through building relationships and maintaining high ethical standards (e.g., strict confidentiality) he was able to document same-sex practices (e.g., anal sex) and social roles (such as *yauss* men who engage in sex with men but do not identify themselves on the basis of this aspect of their sexuality), and to identify HIV prevention needs in this diverse population. In Teunis's assessment, given the intense secrecy that brackets sexuality in general and same-sex behaviors in particular, in-depth ethnography, based on long-term interaction, social participation, and rapport building, is the preferred research method; other approaches, like public surveys, he argues, are unlikely to break through the protective wall of silence and denial.

Risky Behaviors among Drug Injectors

Ethnography has also been used with noted success to describe AIDS risk among drug users. In the early years of AIDS prevention among drug injectors, primary focus was on providing education about the risks of needle sharing. But other routes of infection in contexts of drug injection often were ignored. Based on ethnography among drug injectors in Miami, Bryan Page has identified several other possible routes of AIDS transmission in this population. For example, Page found that in Miami water that is used to liquify drugs is referred to as "clean water" (as opposed, ironically, to water used to unclog needles, which is referred to as "dirty water"). Liquification usually occurs in a metal container, usually a spoon, a bottle cap, or even a cut-off soda can.

Drawing the desired amount of water from the clean water into the syringe, the user squirts ("skeets") this water into a bottle cap onto the drug powder that has already been dumped into the cap. If the drug is cocaine, the water is then stirred, usually with the tip of the syringe or the plunger. (Page et al. 1990a: 65)

As Page, Smith, and Kane (1991: 76) indicate, so-called clean water may in fact harbor pathogens.

As most Miamian drug injection behavior involves cocaine, which is not "cooked" during the mixing process, whatever microbes are in the clean water will be injected into the shooter. Even if the client uses a new set of works to inject the drug, the water mixed with the drugs could be contaminated by exposure to [other injectors'] contaminated syringes.

Risk for HIV transmission through water also occurs during needle rinsing. Explain Page, Smith, and Kane (1991: 76),

The small, diabetic-gauge disposable syringes and needles preferred by IVDUs [intravenous drug users] inevitably become clogged and inoperable after repeated injections. To forestall this condition, the house rules in all houses [i.e., shooting galleries] observed in Miami dictates that after each use of a set of works [a syringe and needle], the customer must clean the set with "dirty water" (water provided for cleaning purposes) before returning the syringe and needle to the storage container. Every needle returned to the container is supposed to be returned after this kind of "cleaning."

In the process of "cleaning" their needles, injectors, in fact, may be infecting them with virons in the rinse water that has been used by other injectors. Ethnographic studies of drug injectors, like those Page has conducted in Miami and a growing number of anthropologists have carried out in other cities in the United States and in other countries, have identified a range of risks for HIV infection faced by street drug injectors.

The Stories People Tell

In their attempt to identify effective ways of curbing the AIDS epidemic among drug users, public health researchers have been concerned especially with expanding understanding of: 1) the precise nature of risk behaviors among drug-users (i.e., specific acts that increase the chance that a drug-user will be infected with HIV and/or transmit the virus to others); 2) the social contexts that facilitate risk behavior; 3) the social structural factors that contribute to risk taking; and 4) the role of social networks and relationships in promoting or inhibiting risky acts. Anthropologists working in AIDS have attempted to advance our understanding of these issues by directly observing behavior, fully describing the immediate and broader social environments in which risk occurs, and exploring insider drug user perspectives about their lives and behaviors. The latter effort has produced a rich corpus of narrative data of various kinds, including stories told by drug users about their day-to-day activities and adventures, the challenges and suffering they face, and their relations with other people. War stories, as these narratives are known on the street, provide a window into the often hidden worlds of active illicit drug users. Story telling has been recognized by anthropologists and others as central human social activity that functions to help people to work through, organize, and invest meaning in their experiences. Moreover, narratives situate people in "local moral worlds," constructing borders and pathways of valued and devalued conduct. Analysts of narratives have argued that they can be decomposed into a series of mini-events and intermediary states, and that a vast number of different but similar events may be included under a single event label. In this light, in listening to numerous drug user war stories over ten years of HIV research, Singer and his colleagues (Singer et al. 2001) realized that they could be grouped into a number of distinct categories. Using etic event labels (i.e., designations developed by the researcher team), they constructed a typology of drug user stories by twice reading through interview transcripts and field notes from one of their studies and identifying distinct themes, messages or plot elements. Examination of these themes suggested a typological organization of primary (namely: learning the ropes, adventurous experiences, miraculous gains, not like the old days, the power of drugs, and suffering and regret) as well as various secondary and tertiary categories. One subtype of adventurous story, for example, focused on the display of useful survival skills, as depicted in the following narrative told to research team members by Kyle, a middle-aged African American man:

I used to work in the hospital [in prison]. My job was in the hospital. I set up all the stuff for the doctor [e.g., syringes]. So, I was the guy selling the needles [to other inmates]. I had access to needles; they'd tell me to destroy them [after use

with a patient, but] I'd put them [aside instead]. . . . You know . . . they sent you
up on different floors, like guys with low crimes on the first floor. Bigger crimes
on the second floor, bigger crimes on the third floor, highest crimes on the top
floor . . . So, I always went straight to the top floor. Those were the guys that had
the C.O.s [correction officers] running the drugs [in] for them. So, I'd go over to
them and . . . every morning those guys would say, "Look man, I need fresh needles every day." So, that's how I took care of myself [i.e. his drug addiction] in
jail. "You need five set ups [syringes] every morning, you got them. Now grab me
a couple of bags [of drugs]." And they'd give it to you man, no questions, no wait.
When I got there [to the cells of customers], they'd slide that shit [drugs] under
the door . . . I took care of the guys! It's something that you learn. (M. Singer et
al. 2001: 595)

Stories like these invert the socially dominant image of street drug users
as social failures and people lacking the intelligence or skills to succeed
in regular society. Rather, narratives like this one portray efficacious individuals with notable abilities, people who make things happen and get
things done even under trying circumstances. Whatever the veracity of
such stories, they reveal, by the cultural elements they express, that contrary to the assumptions of "straight society," drug users embrace conventional action- and achievement-oriented cultural values. While street
drug-users commonly are seen as socially marginal individuals, their stories appear to give voice to noticeably mainstream concerns and ideas.

Also found among the adventurous narratives of drug users are stories
that tell of close calls, narrow escapes, and heroic rescues. Commonly,
these narratives emphasize the grave threats that drug users face each day
on the street. Oftentimes, narrow escape narratives involve mistaken identities in which the wrong person or, alternately, a substitute (e.g., an accessible friend of the intended victim) is targeted for some form of
retribution stemming from a violation of trust in the drug trade (e.g.,
receiving drugs to sell and not turning in the money).

Great escapes from the police are also common as seen in the following
story told to the field team:

So, we was on the highway. I was smoking [rock cocaine] just looking around. He
was just driving. He was like doing fifty on the highway at night. The next thing
you know the narcs were pulling us over. I rolled down my window, I just shot
the stem [cocaine pipe] right out the thing and the lighter out the window. My
brother, I don't know what he did with the cooker or whatever. I think he slipped
it under the seat or something. The needle, I don't know what he did with it. They
took us out of the car. They searched us and everything. They made us drop our
underwear, lift up our socks, everything. And they didn't find nothing!

The general literature on narratives would certainly suggest that in for-
mulating their tales drug users, like all storytellers, merge their immediate

experiences with culturally constituted imagination, objective fact with colorful fantasy, and the details of real events with rhetorical devices and culturally meaningful themes. In analyzing the narratives in their sample, Singer and his colleagues found that they appear to group around a number of contrastive experiential sets: high (psychotropic effects) vs. low (drug withdrawal), kindness vs. abuse, trust vs. betrayal, success vs. failure and regret, and excitement and surprise vs. burdensome routines (things you have to put up with) and enduring suffering. Whatever the historic truthfulness of any particular narrative, the dynamic and oppositional tension of the narratives seems to very accurately reflects the actual experience of street drug use: drug users both love and hate being on drugs and all that focusing their lives on drugs entails. The intensity of this conflicted involvement enlivens their stories, just as their stories construct and encapsulate *core cultural meanings* in their lives. The research team identified three of these core cultural meanings which they believe have relevance for HIV prevention as well as drug treatment.

First, it is evident from the narratives that acts of generosity and caring are not expected, and hence, when they occur they are seen as a pleasant surprise. The stories underline the degree to which street drug-users expect to be mistreated and abused in their social interactions, producing, as a result, a narrational celebration of unforeseen acts of kindness. One lesson of this realization is that in drug treatment or AIDS prevention work with drug users consistently treating participants in a caring fashion, based on a genuine appreciation of them as fellow human beings, would be warmly received. While all service providers who work with street drug-users come to grow wary of their survival-oriented tendency to engage in manipulation or to be undependable, their narratives reveal both a hunger for acts of patient kindness and a strong valuing of caring behavior.

Second, drug user stories emphasize that they are quite wary of betrayal. Their personal narratives suggest that they expect others to fail them, although it is always, nonetheless, a painful experience. Avoiding actions that can be construed (rightly or wrongly) as betrayal, therefore, should be a critical program element in AIDS prevention.

Finally, the narratives emphasize the skills and abilities of drug users, attributes that fly in the face of their usual denigration as unproductive individuals who lack desirable qualities or useful talents. Reversing the usual course, by treating drug-users as socially resourceful, knowledgeable, and goal-oriented individuals, is a way of engaging drug-users in AIDS prevention. At the same time, the narratives suggest the value of recognizing and appreciating demonstrated acts of generosity and caring by drug-users, traits that similarly are denied by social stereotypes that portray them as aggressively self-focused and completely controlled by their drug dependencies.

Muddles in the Models

In order to track and predict the course of the AIDS pandemic, public health workers attempted to identify groups of people at heighten risk for infection. Various risk groups have been identified and referred to in the AIDS literature. Anthropologists, however, *effectively* have challenged risk group categories based on their ethnographic experiences. For example, one group that commonly is listed in AIDS surveillance reports from city and state health departments and the national Centers for Disease Control and Prevention is referred to as "sex partners of injector drug users." Kane (1991) has emphasized that being the sex partner of a drug injector is not a natural category, it is not a social group, nor is it necessarily part of an individual's identity. Indeed, many people are sex partners of injection drug users and do not know it. Others may suspect but fear knowing the full truth. Needless to say, this makes prevention efforts targeted to individuals at risk in this way very difficult. Moreover, as Herdt (1990: 13) has written, "Though the notion of sexual partner may seem obvious, it varies across cultures and is probably the source of significant error in research design. Whether a partnership is sexual and/or social, culturally approved or disapproved, voluntary or coercive, is of real import."

Similarly, Radliff (1999) has shown some of the problems with using labels like commercial sex worker or prostitute in AIDS prevention. Based on her study of dancers in Philippine "go-go bars," many of whom have sex with bar customers for money, Radliff found that women do not tend to think of themselves as prostitutes because they view their bar sex partners as boyfriends not customers. In fact, the women, almost all of whom came from poor families, viewed often wealthier bar patrons as possible future husbands and were disinclined to adhere to condom promotion messages that could hinder the development of meaningful relationships with patrons.

In questioning the epidemiological categories that have been used for studying AIDS, anthropologists have argued that better and more useful data will be collected if we use natural social categories and actually social identities rather than categories that are constructed by researchers. Ethnography has proved time and again that people rarely accept labels and categories imposed externally, especially when they almost always have meaningful, indigenously developed identities that are not based on the often stigmatizing factors associated with behavioral risk typologies.

Economic Determinants of Sexual Risk

While most of the examples of anthropological work in AIDS discussed above are drawn from Western cases, anthropologist have worked in other parts of the world as well. Janet McGrath, a biological anthropologist, and her colleagues at Makerere University in Uganda, for example, have studied the cultural rules that shape sexual behavior among Baganda women. Uganda is a country that has been hit particularly hard by AIDS. It is estimated that well over a million Ugandans have been infected with the virus, and the highest rates of infection are among women between twenty and thirty years of age. For example, in the capital of Kampala, 28% of mothers attending a prenatal clinic were found to be infected (McGrath et al. 1992). The Baganda are the largest ethnic group in Kampala. To better understand cultural practices associated with Baganda sexual risk behavior, McGrath and her coworkers interviewed sixty-five seropositive and sixty-five seronegative Baganda women. They found that the infected women had more sex partners than uninfected women but that all women reported they are limiting the number of partners they have to avoid AIDS. However,

there are situations, such as economic need, when it is acceptable in Baganda culture for a women to have a partner outside of her primary union. If sexual partnerships involve financial gain or increased financial security, then simply advising them to reduce their sexual contacts without recognizing the potential economic harm that may result is problematic. (McGrath et al. 1992: 158–59)

This case shows the critical importance of understanding pressing economic factors that contribute to AIDS risk. Failure to recognize such factors could doom an AIDS prevention project to failure because people may be unable to heed AIDS prevention information if it puts their economic survival at risk.

AIDS Risk and the Cultural Construction of Sexuality

The sexual identities that have been dominant in the discussion of AIDS, heterosexuality and homosexuality, have not been found to be the dominant categories of sexual identity in many locales. In Brazil, for example, Richard Parker (1987: 160) has found that the structure of sexual life is organized around a distinction between activity and passivity, with males being identified with the former attribute and females with the latter.

The outlines of this cultural configuration emerge clearly in the language that Brazilians use to describe sexual relations—in their verbs, such as *comer* (to eat) and *dar* (to give), as metaphors for forms of sexual interaction. *Comer* describes the act of penetration during sexual intercourse. Used in a variety of context as a synonym for verbs such as *vencer* (to conquer, vanquish) and *possuir* (to possess, own), it clearly implies a form of symbolic domination, as played out in either vaginal or anal intercourse. Just as *comer* suggests an act of domination *dar* implies some form of submission or subjugation.

This model extends to sexual intercourse among men who have sex with other men. The individual who is penetrated during anal intercourse is seen as playing the passive role, while his partner is viewed as fulfilling a masculine role. In Brazilian society, the former are subject to considerable social stigma while the latter are "reasonably free within the context of this system to pursue occasional or even ongoing sexual contacts with both males and females without fear of severe social sanction" (Parker 1987: 161). Similarly, based on his research in Mexico, Joe Carrier (1989: 134) has noted that males who play the penetrative or insertive role

are not stigmatized as "homosexual". . . . The masculine self-image of Mexican males is thus not threatened by their homosexual behavior as long as the appropriate role is played and they also have sexual relations with women. Males playing this role are referred to as *mayates;* and may be called *chichifo* if they habitually do so for money. Although involved in bisexual behavior, they consider themselves to be heterosexual.

By contrast, in the United States, men who have sex with other men are defined by society as being homosexual regardless of the role they play during anal intercourse. Moreover, among self-identified gay men in the United States, mutual penetration is common while distinct active and passive roles, to the degree that they exist, tend to be constructed as personal preferences rather than distinct or enduring sexual identities. These examples show that not only are sexual identities constructed somewhat differently in different societies but that AIDS prevention must be sensitive to these differences if it is to be effective in reaching individuals who— whatever their specific sexual identities—are at risk for HIV infection because of their sexual behaviors.

As seen in the examples described above, in their AIDS-related studies, anthropologists have stressed the importance of (1) gathering data in natural social settings; (2) paying keen attention to the role of culture in shaping behavior; (3) looking at insider understandings and identities; (4) maintaining a holistic approach that recognizes the influence of range of social factors on risk behavior; (5) paying attention to gender issues in social life; and (6) using information gained through ethnographic approaches to build culturally targeted AIDS prevention programs.

To this set of anthropological approaches to AIDS risk research, critical medical anthropology draws attention to the importance of political-economic factors. As seen in the discussion of AIDS risk in southern Africa, oppressive political and economic relations can be seen as macro-parasitic causes of new infection. The failed effort by South Africa to maintain its internal system of apartheid exploitation as well as its regional dominance by promoting a series of low-intensity wars of destabilization against its neighboring countries produced social conditions that significantly increased opportunities for HIV infection. In another African case, that of Zaire, Schoepf notes:

Disease epidemics generally erupt in times of crisis, and AIDS is no exception. Zaire, like most other sub-Saharan nations and much of the Third World, is in the throes of economic turmoil. Propelled by declining terms of trade and burdensome debt service, the contradictions of distorted neocolonial economies with rapid class formation have created what appears to be a permanent, deepening crisis. . . . In Zaire, as elsewhere in the region, economic crisis and the structure of employment inherited from the colonial period shape the current configuration, contributing to the feminization of poverty and consequently to the spread of AIDS [e.g., through prostitution or multiple partner sexual relationships associated with smuggling networks developed to contend with the worsening economic conditions]. (Schoepf 1992: 262)

A number of parallel examples also have been noted in this chapter, including McGrath's study of the role of economic subordination of women in AIDS risk in Uganda, the role of international relations on tourism and commercial sex in Haiti, and the contribution of unequal social relations on the syndemic of the urban poor in the United States. As these examples show, while the human immunodeficiency virus has a material existence independent of social factors, its role and importance as a source of morbidity and mortality among humans cannot be understood in isolation from political economy. Placing emphasis on the social origins of disease does not constitute a denial of the biotic aspects of pathogens, hosts, and environments. Rather, it is an affirmation of the critical importance of adopting a holistic and historically informed biopolitical economic approach to health. In this view, AIDS emerges as a disease of the global system of oppressive political-economic relationships.

The Need for Speed: Working in a Crisis

In response to the spiraling AIDS crisis in U.S. minority communities, the Office of HIV/AIDS Policy within the Department of Health and Human Services initiated a research-based prevention effort to assist cities in identifying hidden AIDS risk and to develop appropriate programs and policies. As part of this effort, a rapid assessment procedure was adopted (Trotter et al. 2001) and a federal crisis response team was formed to provide multidisiciplinary technical assistance (specifically, training in rapid assessment, response and evaluation methodologies) to sites most heavily impacted by HIV/AIDS. The cities declared eligible for federal technical assistance were those with: (1) populations of 500,000 or greater; (2) 1,500 or more African Americans or Latinos living with AIDS; (3) at least 50% of living AIDS cases within the metropolitan area being African American and Hispanic Americans combined; and (4) a chief elected official of the locality (e.g., the mayor), in collaboration with appropriate health officials, being willing to submit a letter to the Secretary of Health and Human Services requesting a crisis response team. Developed originally by anthropologist Susan Scrimshaw and her co-workers, rapid assessment procedures, which involve rapidly implemented ethnographic studies on targeted issues, have a well-documented history of success in public health with a wide range of problems, including malaria, diarrheal disease, dengue fever, water sanitation, and natural disasters. In recent years, the World Health Organization, Joint United Nations Programme on HIV/AIDS, Doctors Without Borders (Medicins sans frontiers), and, the United Nations International Drug Control Programme have conducted rapid assessments on injection drug use and HIV in Eastern Europe, Russia, and the former states of the Soviet Union. In the U.S. initiative, which was titled project RARE (Rapid Assessment, Response and Evaluation), the cities of Detroit, Philadelphia and Miami were the first of 11 U.S. metropolitan areas with large minority populations affected by HIV/ AIDS selected to receive federal assistance. Fieldwork in these three cities began in September and October 1999 in each of the three cities. The Federal crisis team visited each of the cities to consult with a working group (consisting of AIDS service providers, elected officials, public health workers, and AIDS activists) approved by the chief local official to coordinate local participation in project RARE. Local working groups then engaged in a process to guide the assessment in terms of the selection of high risk geographical areas in the city, groups engaged in risk behaviors, and points of intervention that represented the leading edge of the HIV epidemic in that city. The working group also had the responsibility to select a local field team (usually consisting of 8–12 AIDS and other outreach workers, direct service providers, and community activists). The Federal crisis team, consisting of several anthropologists, then provided field team members (few of whom had prior research experience) with three days of training on RARE assessment methodologies, analysis of data, and preparing reports for the working group and chief elected official. Each field team under the supervision of a lead ethnographer who was often an anthropologist or other social scientist, used focus groups, rapid or indepth interviews, field observations, and social mapping to determine what factors had been missed in prior AIDS intervention activities or where unmet intervention needs were contributing to new infections. The focus of data collection included previously unrecognized risk behaviors, newer populations at risk, the role of temporary factors in risk (e.g., night time vs. day time behavioral patterns), and high-risk settings. Given the crisis nature of the AIDS epidemic in minority communities, all data collection, analysis and recommendation develop was designed to be completed in four months time. In the initial three cities, reports and recommendations were presented to the working groups in December 1999, and meetings to present reports to the chief elected official began in early 2000. Based on the success of the first three cities, the program, which is ongoing, was then implemented in two phases in an additional 20 cities around the United States. Significantly, project RARE demonstrated the utility of anthropological techniques in addressing hidden or overlooked aspects of the epidemic and assisted local AIDS workers in developing achievable recommendations for blunting the moving edge of the epidemic. As a result, the project has been implemented in a growing number of locations. Rare, Hartford, for example, conducted in the later part of 2003, focused on middle-of-the-night drug use and sex risk that was rarely, if ever, reached by prior prevention efforts (which tended to end at 5 P.M. when service organizations closed for the evening).

CONCLUSION

As Farmer (1992: 262) notes, "One way to avoid losing sight of the humanity of those with AIDS is to focus on the experience and insights of those who are afflicted." This is an extremely important point. While the thrust of critical medical anthropology is to understand human health issues in their sociohistoric and political-economic contexts, it also has been emphasized in the CMA literature that we must pay close attention to sufferer experience and agency. Sufferer experience, an arena long neglected in the social science of health, increasingly has become a topic of research interest. From the perspective of CMA, sufferer experience is a social product, one that is constructed and reconstructed in the action arena between socially constituted categories of meaning and the political-economic forces that shape the contexts of daily life. Recognizing the powerful role of such forces, however, does not imply that individuals are passive and lack the agency to initiate change, and it certainly does not mean that they are insignificant. Instead, it means that people respond to the material conditions they face in terms of the set of possibilities created by the existing configuration of social relations and social conditions. Within this framework, it is vital that we remain sensitive to the individual level of experience and action so that we never forget that the ultimate goal of critical medical anthropology is to contribute to the creation of a more humane health care system and more humane lives for all people.

CHAPTER 9

Reproduction and Inequality

Patterns of reproduction represent one of the most dramatic indicators of the differences in life conditions of rich and poor populations in the world today. In countries on the periphery of the world system, both maternal and infant mortality have remained much higher than in the core capitalist countries. Maternal mortality, most effectively prevented by the availability of emergency obstetric facilities, remains much greater in countries where women still do not have immediate access to blood transfusions, antibiotics, and cesarean section (Freedman and Maine 1993). In core countries, the maternal mortality rates are about 10 per 100,000 live births, but "in parts of Africa and Asia they are now 100 times higher" (Maine and McGinn 2000: 395). "One in every 21 women in Africa will die from complications of pregnancy or delivery in comparison to only one in every 9,850 in Northern Europe" (Freedman and Maine 1993: 153).

Poverty and inequality also affect the health of women in the centers of the capitalist system. Within the United States, one of the world's wealthiest nations, poor and minority women face dilemmas concerning pregnancy that are different from the higher income populations (Mullings and Wali 2001). The ongoing daily stresses of poorly paid work combined with the long waits for impersonal prenatal care in municipal hospitals, the lack of funds for shelter and good nutrition during pregnancy, and the lack of access to well-baby care for infants are associated with a higher frequency of low birth weight, premature infants with less chance of survival in the first year, and lower life expectancies than babies born in middle income communities (Hogue 2000).

GENDER

Reproduction and the health of mothers and infants cannot be understood separately from the gendered distribution of resources and the division of labor in any society. Women's access to education and employment has a direct effect on patterns of family size and the health of the mother and child. Despite many improvements, women continue to be disadvantaged with respect to men in employment and health and, in general, poorer and minority women suffer poorer health with a direct relationship between degree of disadvantage and the extent of health problems (Hogue 2000: 21). In fact, many women and children are dying from their experience of gendered discrimination (Freedman and Maine 1993). In 43 out of 45 poor countries surveyed, girls were less likely to survive than boys (Heise 1993). Girls are less likely to be taken for treatment should they fall ill and more likely to suffer from malnutrition, which particularly affects their childbearing years (Miller 2000, Merchant and Kurz 1993). Even female fetuses are less valued as, for example, when amniocentesis was introduced in India, most of the fetuses aborted were female (B. Miller 2000). Among poor households, the health effects of gender, as measured in the morbidity and mortality statistics for women in relation to men, are frequently magnified by lifelong nutritional deprivation combined with lack of care in pregnancy and childbirth (Koblinsky et al 1993). Institutional discrimination against women combined with household inequality is also manifest in the high maternal mortality rates and infant mortality rates common in many poor regions (Goldman and Hatch 2000, Koblinsky et al 1993). The World Health Organization estimated that about 500,000 women die every year in childbirth and pregnancy, mostly from preventable causes (Freedman and Maine 1993).

ANTHROPOLOGICAL PERSPECTIVES ON REPRODUCTION

As reproduction is central to human existence, so it has been to the development of anthropology. Beginning with the publication of the *Vindication of the Rights of Women* by Mary Wollstonecraft in 1792, Western social theorists hotly debated values, rites and regulations around sexuality and virginity, marriage, and childrearing practices. In 1877, one of the founders of American anthropology, Lewis Henry Morgan contributed to this discussion in his effort to organize his collected data about rules of kinship and marriage in different societies in relation to the means of subsistence. Karl Marx and Friedrich Engels used Morgan's research to connect women's subordination to the development of capitalism. Inspired by the notion that women were not universally dominated by men, nineteenth century feminists from many parts of the world, such as Olive

Schreiner, from southern Africa, and Alexandra Kollontai, in Russia, delineated women's rights to work and love with greater freedom.

In the early twentieth century, another American anthropologist, Margaret Mead, a student of Franz Boas, entered the fierce public debate concerning the place of women by documenting the flexibility of human sexual behavior and the malleable definitions of masculinity and femininity through her pioneering ethnographies in Samoa and New Guinea. Mead was among a number of independent-thinking women anthropologists of her time, including researchers such as Elsie Clewes Parsons and Ruth Landes, who were critically exploring the roles of men and women, and rethinking gender and reproduction.

Nevertheless, for the first half of the twentieth century, in spite of the internationally renowned writings of such eminent theorists as the anarchist leader and Russian immigrant to the United States, Emma Goldman, and the French existential philosopher, Simone de Beauvoir, most ethnographies although they might well include descriptions of rituals of betrothal and childbirth did not set such discussions squarely within a broader analysis of sexuality and power relations. Indeed, kinship and marriage, or the constitution of the rules for the reproduction of a society, were generally analyzed without attention to the controversial issues of power and autonomy between men and women (Rubin 1975). Later feminist anthropologists insisted that reproduction must be analyzed in the context of varying power relations as well as changing expectations of maleness and femaleness (Rapp Reiter 1975, Lamphere and Rosaldo 1974.) Rather than interpreting sexual difference simply in terms of biological characteristics, analysts began to see people and societies making or performing masculinity and femininity, fatherhood and motherhood. Rules of marriage and reproduction were recognized as intertwined with such issues as colonialism, nationalism and state power as well as family and community expectations. Later research has deconstructed the notion of gender even further, drawing attention to the experience of transgendered and third genders. Recognizing that the situation and power of the researcher affects their work, feminists emphasized the significance of the analyst's position as well as that of informants. As Christine Gailey (1998) has noted, feminist methods in anthropology, require a recognition of the researcher's own position and an understanding of the social construction of gender, but also involve a commitment to working for the empowerment of women (see also Behar 1996, Lamphere et al 1997). Since women suffer inequality in most of the world, it seems particularly important to examine reproductive health within this context. As we shall see, ethnographic analysis has been making significant contributions to our understanding of reproduction in the changing world system, the impact of historical shifts in gender and class relations, government regulations, nationalism, and globalization.

Because reproduction is so crucial to social continuity, both symbolically and biologically, decisions about sexuality, fertility, pregnancy, childbirth and even child rearing have seldom been left solely to the parents involved. Societies have generated rituals, rules and regulations designating the responsibilities for the bearing and rearing of children and the continuation of populations. Frequently, such expectations are deeply embedded in the symbols of kinship as well as perceptions of gender roles (Lindenbaum 1987).

In modern states, political concerns expressed in terms of overpopulation, under-population, nationality, ethnicity, and religious precepts have been translated by governments into regulations about reproduction. We find varying legal restrictions with respect to contraception, abortion and reproductive technologies. Such laws crucially affect men and women's strategies and options with respect to family size and child rearing (Ginsburg and Rapp 1995). Values or laws that do not directly address reproduction, for example, with respect to men and women's inheritance of land, employment, nutrition or public health, may also constrain the sexual and fertility decisions of men and women or affect the mortality of infants in unexpected ways.

Sexuality, marriage and fertility, labor and childbirth will be fundamentally shaped by the class position of a man or woman's family in society and his or her access to resources and power (Whiteford 1996, Lamphere et al. 1999, Schneider and Schneider 1996, Scheper-Hughes and Sargent 1998). Within these contours, contemporary medical anthropologists have looked at reproduction from the point of view of rituals of the life cycle, changing perceptions of the body, negotiations over sexuality, marriage and parental roles between men and women, and the cultural perceptions surrounding men and women's practices (Martin 1987, Ginsburg and Rapp 1995, Browner and Sargent 1990).

In recent decades, reproduction has become a contested issue in global regulation and struggles around international human rights. In world forums and regulatory bodies, such as the United Nations and the 1995 Beijing NGO Forum on Women (Friedlander 1996), people have called for reproductive rights and freedom of sexual orientation to be included in human rights and for rape to be understood as a violation of human rights. Even as many people have organized to promote human rights, religious fundamentalism, incorporating patriarchal values and the subordination of women, has undermined the recognition of sexual and reproductive freedoms (Petchesky 2000). For example, although the U.S. Supreme Court has supported the right of women in the United States to choose to terminate a pregnancy, the U.S. government now denies that right to women served by U.S. funded agencies outside the country, and has recently begun to severely limit their access to education about contraception and reproductive strategies.

In this chapter, in order to highlight different possibilities in the social organization of reproduction, we look first at childbirth and child-rearing patterns in some indigenous societies, such as the San people of southern Africa, and the ways in which the lives of men and women changed as their communities were incorporated into the world system. Then, we consider the changing patterns of reproduction in state societies and the impact of colonization. Finally, we return to an examination of the contrasting contemporary experiences of reproduction in the world system among populations in peripheral as opposed to core nations and the newly emerging encroachments of globalization.

REPRODUCTION IN INDIGENOUS SOCIETIES

As we discussed in chapter 3, in the late 1950s, many of the San peoples of the Kalahari Desert still maintained a foraging way of life, wandering in small bands in search of fruits, nuts, berries and other plants and hunting game (Lee 2002). The San speak many languages and live in many different areas and the group we refer to most often are, in fact, the Ju'/hoansi [Lee 2002], among whom Ida Susser recently conducted fieldwork with Richard Lee with respect to HIV/AIDS prevention. For simplicity we have chosen to use the more general term San throughout this book. They knew where to find water from hidden springs scattered over the dry land, and when the trickles dried up they knew where to dig for roots that stored liquid. They built groupings of shelters from branches or caked mud and shifted these temporary villages as they sought to renew their sources of food.

Over centuries, the San peoples interacted with the surrounding cattle herding populations, living and working with them from time to time and exchanging goods and services. As Dutch, British and German colonial powers established their territories, the San intermittently worked for encroaching farm settlements, raided the encroachers, and were shot and imprisoned for their wanderings (Gordon 1992).

Under these conditions, ethnographers of the San in the 1950s and 1960s described such societies as more or less egalitarian. Women were seen as autonomous, in that women made their own decisions about subsistence activities and the tasks for which they were responsible (Draper 1975, Leacock and Lee 1982, Lee 1979, 2002). (We must make clear, here, that we are discussing San gender relations at a particular moment and under specific historical conditions and do not mean to suggest that their way of life represents all foraging societies nor that the San themselves have no variation in their own history.) Although men predominated as folk healers, both men and women could learn to become practitioners and lead curing rituals. The propensity to trance was often passed down from mother to daughter, and there was a specific drum dance performed by women. Men did most of the hunting. However, contrary to common Western stereotypes, a number of women knew how to set traps and hunt small animals. Women also made poisoned hunting arrows used by the men, although they did not often accompany the men on long hunting trips.

San women gathered food together, usually trailed by young children. Sometimes mothers carried their infants on such daylong expeditions but on other occasions they would leave them behind in the village under the supervision of other women in the band. Sometimes women breastfed one another's children.

Childrearing, shared by both men and women, was an easier task than in many industrialized societies, as, from infancy, children, like adults, were allowed a high degree of independence and autonomy. Children of one band grew up together, almost as brothers and sisters. The young were not forced early into adult labor and children often mimicked adults in their days of play, including games of hunting as well as sexual experimentation (Draper 1975, Lee 1979, 2002).

Among the San at this time, kin often arranged marriage for prepubescent girls to boys a few years older. One incentive for a family to arrange an early marriage for their daughter was that the groom's family was expected to provide gifts for the family of the bride and her new husband would hunt for her family as bride service. To indicate betrothal, a young girl was ritually carried to her future husband's hut, but, in fact, for several years after this ceremony, she might stay with her own family.

In spite of what appears to be a somewhat subordinated or constrained initiation to marriage, a young girl actually had a variety of options. Without being subject to force or other negative repercussions, although certainly subject to teasing by privileged joking members among her kin, she could decide when or even, if, she wanted to interact sexually with her new husband. Indeed, because work and resources were substantially shared with other band members, if a woman wished, she could leave her husband without punishment or much loss of economic resources and he could leave her without subjecting his family to destitution. Much flexibility and freedom for women and men continued through the life cycle. In *Nisa: The Diary of a !Kung Woman* (Shostak 1983), which records one woman's story as a wife, mother, and lover in a foraging society, we see that even after many years of marriage, a woman could leave her husband, taking her children with her to another village, without fear of loss of resources or the physical abuse and social ostracism common in many other societies.

Among the nomadic San, girls tended to begin menstruation in their late teens, in contrast to the earlier onset of menarche in modern industrialized societies (Howell 2000). One reason for this may have been their low fat-diet. Meat was not plentiful and since the foragers of that period did not keep cattle or goats, dairy foods were practically non-existent. In addition, San women were physically active on a daily basis and often walked twenty miles a day with their bands. Among such active women with little excess fat, ovulation might start late and be irregular even among adult women (Howell 2000, Lee 1979).

Since there was little dairy produce to substitute for mother's milk and, as the San did not grow cereals, there were few soft foods or alternate sources of protein, and many foraging women breastfed their babies for four or more years. This too contributed to a lack of excess fat and a reduced likelihood that a woman with a young child would ovulate regularly. In fact, demographic research demonstrated that nomadic women spaced their pregnancies, on average, about four years apart. However, this was not simply a biological or natural consequence of diet, exercise, and breastfeeding. The San adopted a variety of rules and practices which prevented a new child from being an insupportable burden as the small band wandered many miles on foot seeking food and water.

If the cultural strategies that limit fertility failed, foraging mothers faced a tragic dilemma in which their options were limited and shaped by their environment and access to resources. Under conditions of famine and starvation, a San woman had the autonomy to decide how to cope. If a mother did become pregnant again, before her last child could travel long distances without being carried, she might try to abort the pregnancy or not allow the infant to survive. *Nisa* (Shostak 1983) tells a story of a pregnant mother, wishing to save the life of her youngest child, whom she sees as mortally threatened by the future infant in competition for nutrition and resources. The mother gives birth outside the village, accompanied only by her small daughter, and then abandons the new baby.

From the 1960s as vast stretches of foraging land were taken over by cattle ranches and roads built through the desert, the San settled near bore holes built by the local governments, raised a few cattle and goats and received free supplements of grain. As people kept dairy animals and more soft food was available for infants, women did not exclusively breastfeed their babies as long and were more likely to ovulate and become pregnant sooner and more often (Howell 2000). In addition, young girls and women were expected to be more subordinate to men and the learning of gendered sex roles by girls was more obvious, as young girls played with dolls and young women were expected to obey their husbands (Draper 1975).

For the first 70,000 years of human existence, societies survived by foraging and populations remained relatively stable. Since population size is more directly limited by the number of women, anthropologists have suggested that female infanticide was among the strategies used by foragers to maintain small populations, in order not to strain the resources available (Harris and Ross 1987). A man can father any number of children at one time, whereas a woman can only carry a finite number of pregnancies to term.

Populations began to increase with settled agriculture. Possibly, as some researchers have argued, people had to work harder to produce food and resorted to horticulture or herding animals, because they had to feed growing populations. Since subsistence conditions required more intensive labor, kin groups and lineages valued children as future workers.

However, societies still sought to culturally define household and population size. Spacing strategies, such as the separation of the mother and child from the father immediately after birth, and local abortion practices were common in horticultural and pastoral populations.

In many societies, women established power in their descent group by bearing children, and particularly sons, who would represent their interests later (Kabeer 1985, Gammetoft 2000). In contrast to the customary requirements in Mediterranean states for a bride to be a virgin (Schneider and Schneider 1996), women among many other peoples such as the Kadar of Nigeria were highly valued if they had a child before marriage as this demonstrated their fertility to their future husband and his kin, and when the young girl married, the children joined her husband's patrilineage (M.G. Smith 1968: 113).

Barren wives, or women who did not have children, were often penalized in such societies. However, biological fertility does not always limit women's access to influence through children. Mona Etienne (2001) described the way in which barren women among the Baule in Ivory Coast enhanced their political status by migrating to urban areas and adopting children to maintain and later inherit their property in their rural village. Only such connections insured a woman influence while she was alive and a respectable funeral at her death.

Francis Nyamnjoh (2002), a sociologist from Cameroon, describes his own upbringing and adoption by two social mothers besides his biological mother and two men who regarded him as a social son, contributing towards the cost of his education and providing him with land. His social mothers and fathers (his biological mother had passed away and his biological father, whom he did not know well or like) attended his wedding. Nyamnjoh notes that in the grassfields of Cameroon, among a vibrant, changing population trying to negotiate the opportunities of the global marketplace without losing their collective rights, migrants adopt children in an effort to negotiate continuity in their native regions while traveling far afield in their entrepreneurial activities.

Thus, in many pastoral and horticultural societies, in contrast to foragers like the San who had to carry their infants long distances, both men and women had reasons to want a large number of children. As we noted above, as the San settled more permanently around government dug boreholes, they also had more children, spaced closer in age (Howell 2000).

Since children were highly valued, kin groups carefully defined through marriage to which lineage or household they belonged. However, while marriage defined a child's status, sexuality and biological kinship were not necessarily limited by these rules. Among the Nuer, for example, a pastoral society in which people inherited cattle through their patrilineal connections, a woman who had many cattle and whose husband had died, could marry another woman (Evans-Pritchard 1940). This strategy allowed the new wife to find her own partner to bear children for her "ghost" husband's patrilineage. Such offspring would help herd the cattle and generally bolster the position of the first woman. Clearly, the new children would have a biological father, but his status was irrelevant to the status of the children who would belong to the lineage of the "woman-husband" and her wife. Kathleen Gough (1971) demonstrated further that, in the 1930s, a Nuer woman from a high status patrilineage, rather than marrying into another Nuer descent group as prescribed by patrilineal rules, might find a partner among ostensible "strangers" from the nearby Dinka population and thus keep her children attached to her own patrilineage.

Sharon Hutchinson and Jok Madut Jok (2002) have described the tragic contemporary transformations of Nuer and Dinka gender relations in the militarization of an independent state in the Sudan. As the Nuer and Dinka have been drawn into ethnic conflicts over land, tribal allegiance is no longer as flexible as it was and, sadly, women and children, previously interrelated through marriage and off-limits in battle, have become the targets for greater and more brutal assault and killing (Hutchinson and Jok 2002).

In many indigenous societies, while marriage clearly defined the status and lineage of their children, both men and women were allowed a degree of sexual freedom. In other societies, men but not women were allowed such freedoms and in some societies, sexuality outside marriage is heavily sanctioned for both men and women (Scheffler 1991). The relationship between kin terms and customary practice has to be examined rather than assumed (Scheffler 1991). Rules about gender, social reproduction, or the rearing of children, may not necessarily correspond with biological reproduction, or sexuality. Indeed, some anthropologists have suggested that they correspond more closely to rules about the division of labor (Leacock 1972). Frequently, the claims of family, motherhood and fatherhood are negotiated to accommodate patterns of migration, investment and other changes, such as wars and militarization. Differences between rules of marriage and kinship and patterns of sexual behavior and biological links become extremely important in understanding the transmission of genetic traits or sexually transmitted diseases such as HIV/AIDS.

In Richard Lee and Ida Susser's (Lee 2002) research in Botswana and Namibia in the 1990s, they found that, although much has changed among the San and foraging is no longer their fundamental form of subsistence, women still maintained unusual sexual autonomy. In addressing questions about HIV/AIDS, San women said they were able to refuse sexual advances from their San partners or else ask them to use condoms. They were less confident in discussing their sexual relationships with men from other groups. In contrast, Ovambo women, living in farming settlements in Northern Namibia, were more likely to be afraid that they might be beaten if they refused to have sex with their partners or asked them to use condoms (I. Susser and Stein 2000). But, in spite of the San women's history of autonomy, at least in relation to San men, as ecotourism was developing and more roads constructed into the San villages, many road builders, guards, construction workers and other men from the surrounding groups found their way to the villages and along with the new sexual partners, the risk of HIV/AIDS was increasing among the San along with their growing interactions with the global economy.

STATE SOCIETIES: INEQUALITY, MEN AND WOMEN, SEXUAL RIGHTS AND CHILDREN

For more than five thousand years, human populations have lived in various forms of state societies, characterized by different patterns of inequality and class stratification. Rules of marriage and kinship under these unequal state societies often delineated hierarchical relations between men and women. In fact, some anthropologists have suggested that early state societies, in the effort to centrally control households and kin groups, stressed men's rights over women and their children. Women's competing influence over their own children was restricted in this way, and men were also given license to control women's sexuality (Gailey 1987). Others have argued that women's historical subordination represents a Western image of the state and that in other circumstances elite women ruled in parallel to elite men (for a discussion of debates concerning women's inequality in state societies, see Silverblatt 1991). Only historical research will disentangle the particular struggles around gender, power, and resistance fought by men and women in any specific state (Silverblatt 1991).

In settled agricultural states with urban centers, epidemic disease was a frequent occurrence and, under such conditions, infants were then, as now, the most susceptible to infectious diseases. Thus infant mortality rates were high, often one in four died in the first year of life. Maternal mortality was also very high. Many women died in childbirth, and for this reason, women had a shorter life expectancy than men all over the world. A man frequently outlived several wives, as each wife might bear a number of children but not live to see them grow up (M. Susser, Watson, and Hopper 1985). Under these conditions, a man might marry again, in order to find a partner to care for the children, or the oldest child might be expected to care for his or her siblings, or, in fact, children might be reared by adoptive parents.

With the advent of capitalist societies and later industrialization, populations increased dramatically, but for several hundred years, health and life expectancy decreased. In London, in the 1800s, for example, infant mortality rates and the general death rates from disease were surpassing the birth rate. The population would have declined dramatically if thousands of migrants had not streamed into the city. Later, as wages increased and sanitation improved in the new industrial cities, infant mortality rates decreased and epidemics of the plague, cholera and other diseases became less frequent (M. Susser, Watson, and Hopper 1985). However, even as general conditions improved, women continued to die at younger ages than men until the twentieth century (Hogue 2000).

From antiquity, states, like later governments in industrial societies, were much involved in regulating women's sexuality, controlling patterns of reproduction and defining the status of children. In the 1960s, Jane Schneider traced the virgin complex through North Africa and the Mediterranean to the changing relationship between pastoral societies and the state (Schneider 1968). Many anthropologists have tried to understand the strength of this honor and shame complex and the varying significance of the enforcement of virginity before marriage. The Eurasian complex of virginity, dowry, and patrilineality also has been associated with a class system and the control of property as men seek to control women's reproductive capacity in order to insure inheritance in the men's family group (Goody 1976). Although Jack Goody has suggested that we view dowry as woman's property, many of those who have studied the dowry in India have noted that the inheritance is completely controlled by men and the value of the dowry assures only that the woman marry a man of rank as the property passes from the bride's family to the groom (Stone and James 2001). The low value of women's paid work and the reduced value of her domestic role in the rearing of children in recent years has contributed to the importance of the dowry in defining the economic value of the woman and in some instances has led to murder, as men wish to get rid of one wife in order to collect a new dowry from another woman (Stone and James 2001).

Colonial governments, also, regulated marriage and sexual relations (Etienne and Leacock 1980, Lockwood 2001, Stoler 1997). In Indonesia, after 100 years of colonial rule, the Dutch administration legally forbade European settlers to marry members of the local population in their efforts to institutionalize racial divisions and control the colonized. In addition, the transformation of societies under colonization often undermined cooperative organization among women and decreased their political influence while increasing their workload in agriculture and domestic responsibilities (Van Allen 2001, Guyer 1991). From this early period, although there was much variation in the local strategies of men and women and the specific histories of resistance to colonialism, unequal employment opportunities, segregated living conditions, unequal health care provisions and the institutionalized discrimination and regulation of women among colonized populations set the scene for the differences between the maternal and infant survival rates documented between peripheral, often previously colonized, and core countries to this day (for discussions of the issues of women and colonialism see Lockwood 2001).

From the 1940s, in the industrialized Western countries, with improved housing, education and nutrition, the discovery and generalized distribution of penicillin, vaccines, and other medical interventions and the implementation of hospitalized childbirth in sterile conditions, many more women survived labor and childbirth. In fact, World War II had an interesting impact on women in the United States, as it represented the first time the majority of women gave birth in hospital settings, funded by the health insurance payments of soldiers. This shift, represented in the high levels of access to medical care, also contributed to a nationwide lowering of maternal mortality rates. While infant mortality rates dropped dramatically and life expectancy increased for everyone, women actually began to live longer than men (Goldman and Hatch 2000).

Throughout the twentieth century, maternal and infant mortality rates have been decreasing in Western industrialized countries. This was a gradual process and the survival rates for women and children of different age groups varied over the time period. But, the health of poor men and women and infant mortality rates for poor and minority populations did not improve at the same rate as those with more wealth. In the past three decades there has been an increasing gap in the United States between the income, living conditions, and health of the poor and that of the better-off (Pappas et al 1993, Susser 1989).

CLASS AND REPRODUCTION

Although Malthus once argued that the poor have more children and therefore are responsible for overpopulation and subsequent reduction of available resources, the relationship between income, fertility, and resources is much more situationally determined than such an argument suggests. In a historical analysis of fertility shifts in Sicily, Jane and Peter Schneider (1996) documented the changing demographic patterns among different classes that accompanied one hundred years of modernization. Their study, as an anthropological contribution to demography, undermines age-old modernization arguments that rely on ideas that poor people "have less self-control" or fail to plan for the future and so have more children. In contrast, in the nineteenth century the Sicilian aristocracy, healthier and more affluent, reared more children while the impoverished peasants, due to higher rates of mortality, had fewer children surviving to maturity. Later, in order to preserve their wealth, the landed gentry reduced the number of children per family, and, during the Great Depression, the merchant class began to change their household strategies to limit conception and childbirth (for *respectability*). Lastly, in the 1950s and 1960s, as a strategy for upward mobility, poor Sicilian landless laborers also began to implement their own methods to reduce fertility, and, in ideological terms, to demonstrate that they too could control their sexual urges and achieve *respectability*. In a Mexican village in the 1980s, Frances Rothstein (1982, 1999) documented similar historical contingencies among working class households whose members cycled between agricultural labor and factory employment; as possibilities for mobility through education seemed to emerge, families changed their reproductive strategies and fewer children were born.

Household members strategize to achieve culturally defined goals within the constraints of the situation in which they find themselves. We cannot define laws of reproduction, such as to argue that working women always have fewer children or that poor people have more. In the Western industrialized states of the twentieth century, as women entered the workforce in greater numbers, the average number of children per household decreased. However, this was also accompanied not only by the invention of new methods of contraception, which could for the first time in history be controlled by women, but also by increasing levels of education for women of all incomes and, as noted above, improved housing and health and a dramatic decrease in both infant and maternal mortality (M. Susser, Watson, and Hopper 1985).

In Western societies, images of motherhood and fatherhood changed dramatically over the twentieth century. As Louise Lamphere (1987) documented in her research, in Providence, Rhode Island, in the early 1900s, daughters went out to work while mothers worked at home, taking in boarders, sewing or baking or preserving fruits for extra income. By the 1970s, mothers were working outside the home in increasing numbers. In the second millennium, as reflected in the U.S. federal policy, which has dismantled public assistance, women are expected to earn money at paid work whether or not they have to care for infants or young children (I. Susser 1996). Changing government policies also structure family relations. In the 1980s and 1990s, as the alterations in tax laws precipitated a rising cost of housing and the eviction of poor New Yorkers, this process of gentrification led to increased periods of homelessness. When families lost housing, children were often separated from their parents by government officials seeking to put them in institutional housing. Institutional policies also varied by gender, as women were more likely to be able to keep their children than men. Boys were often separated from their mothers at age nine while most girls were allowed to stay with their mothers through their teenage years (Susser 1993).

These family transformations are not a predicable or one-way process. Ruth Milkman (1987), in her historic analysis shows the way American women were encouraged to work outside the home during World War II: day care was provided and the work was glorified in images of the hard-working patriotic "Rosie the Riveter." As servicemen returned after the war, women lost their jobs. Simultaneously, images of motherhood and home dominated the media. Such images were hardly brought into play when the New York City administration was making decisions about homeless children in the 1980s (Susser 1989, 1993).

Thus both individual goals and culturally approved roles for women change at different historical moments, and patterns of reproduction and child rearing reflect these changes.

THE SOCIAL CONTEXT OF REPRODUCTION TODAY

Reproduction today takes place within a global capitalist economy, which affects people at different points in different but interconnected ways. In the following section, we discuss first the changing ways states have framed and regulated reproduction and sexuality within the world system and globalization, next we explore the different interests and control that members of a household may have with respect to the birth and rearing of children. Lastly, we outline the contrasting experiences of reproduction and the contrasting approaches of anthropologists as they examine reproduction in wealthy and poor countries of the world system.

THE CONSEQUENCES OF STATE REGULATION OF POPULATION

Images of women and reproduction have been shaped by projects of nationalism. Many nations have made efforts to limit their populations partly as a symbol of progress and modernization. The state may not necessarily implement the policies in the interests of fulfilling the potential of all women as productive human beings. But, as a component of this modernist project, family planning resources allow women some choice about the responsibilities of motherhood. Women's option to control their own fertility is one step towards greater autonomy in their ongoing struggle against a long history of gendered discrimination in their own homes, education, and the workplace.

Other national projects emphasize images of women as mothers, confined to their role in procreation, as powerful symbols of national or religious continuity. Such an idealization of motherhood in the effort to reinforce nationalist sentiments has not generally resulted in the empowerment of women. To the contrary, an emphasis on women's role as mothers has historically been associated with the subordination of women to their fathers, husbands, and other male kin and to oppressive constraints on women's work, travel, sexual and reproductive rights as enforced by religious institutions or the government (Das 1995, Freedman 2000, Petchesky 2000, Aretxaga 1997, Kligman 1998).

There are also well-documented instances where population control policies were introduced by a racist government wishing to limit undesirable populations. Examples such as the apartheid government of South Africa in the 1980s, and the communist regime in Rumania, which tried to reduce births among the stigmatized Romani group while forcing population growth among other Rumanians (Kligman 1998), remind us that state intervention in population growth or reduction can have destructive rather than liberationist intent.

In the 1960s, international policy makers raised the specter of population growth and connected it to world poverty. Although other explanations for world poverty pointed to the history of colonialism and the unequal distribution of resources within the world system, U.S. foundations began to fund family planning programs internationally. While in many poor countries governments may have been seeking to reduce the population, it became evident that households were strategizing with different aims. In a classic evaluation of a Harvard School of Public Health birth control project, funded by the Rockefeller Foundation, Mahmoud Mamdani (1972), conducting research in one of the Indian villages where the program was in operation, found that only those families who were already limiting their fertility actually made use of the pills they were given. At each income level, families had pressing economic reasons for wanting more children. Among poor peasants, more children meant more laborers to work the land, and among the middle classes, more children meant that the family could train doctors, lawyers, and businessmen and thus hope the variety allowed them security and financial gains in the future. In each situation, girls were less desirable, as they could not hope to earn as much as men. The subordination of women in every sphere led to corresponding poor health, less food, less education and less employment opportunities. Women's continuing inequality undermined efforts to introduce birth control as mothers who might have welcomed contraceptive methods for the purposes of spacing their children and taking control of their own fertility had little power over family planning.

A contrasting set of problems occurred as European industrialized countries began to face declining birthrates and aging populations (M. Susser, Watson, and Hopper 1985). In the 1980s, in Rumania, the communist government banned abortion in their effort to increase the population and build their idea of a successful and powerful nation (Kligman

1998). As a result, many women died from attempting illegal abortions in unsafe circumstances. Many of those who did not risk this dangerous option carried their pregnancy to term but did not have the resources to raise the child. As a result, thousands of children were put into state orphanages, where they suffered from malnutrition and disease. In 1989, when the Rumanian government was overthrown, the conditions in these orphanages came to international attention and it was discovered that many of the children had contracted HIV/AIDS through the sharing of needles for vaccination and the blood transfusions that were apparently given for anemia caused by malnutrition. Thus, the government's efforts to foster population growth had, instead, led to the death of hundreds of mothers from illegal abortions, the mistreatment of infants and the death of thousands of children from disease (Kligman 1998).

The Rumanian experience introduces adoption as another kind of window into the different ways states institutionalize rules of the family in a changing world. The adoption of a child by a middle class American family generally reflects the patterns of class stratification in the United States, such that the child may be most easily legally adopted from a poor household and reared in a household with access to wealth and education (Gailey 1998, 1999). However, as in the case of Rumania, the child may be adopted from a poorer country or a country in political turmoil and the source of such adopted children, as well as their health and the legal regulations binding the adoption, will depend on the particular historical moment and the uneven access to resources between core and periphery in the world system (Ginsburg and Rapp 1995, Kligman 1998, Gailey 1999).

As in India and Rumania, ethnographic research has revealed that government policies which attempt to directly control household reproductive decisions and family structure can have unforeseen and sometimes tragic consequences, often differentiated by gender. But, making options available to men and women to control family spacing and size can also increase the possibilities for women's autonomy. Below, we explore the complex interaction between government policies, changing societal conditions, and household strategies.

MEN, WOMEN AND CHILDREN: DECISIONS IN THE HOUSEHOLD

Carole Browner (2000) tells of contrasting interests among men and women in a rural Mexican household. Women, already exhausted by their multiple responsibilities of housework and agriculture and often suffering from malnutrition and vitamin deficiencies, insisted that more children make more work and that they did not wish for further pregnancies. Men were more likely to want their wives to rear another child. Meanwhile, government concern for population growth precipitated family planning policies, which had little impact on the village households.

A similar case study in Bangladesh notes that, in poor households, men and women may have different perspectives on reproductive decisions: "Women have the responsibility for feeding children, particularly in the early, less productive years of their lives. They cannot walk away from them in times of crisis, the way men can and do . . . " (Kabeer 1985: 105). Once children were grown, however, such poor landless women maintained little authority over their offspring. Under these conditions, most women still expressed a preference for sons, since in the long run, the main position from which a woman could exert power was as a mother-in-law to her adult married son. Nevertheless, as they perceived much drudgery and little advantage from rearing many children a number of "women from landless and near-landless households took advantage of the family planning services offered by the local women's project, often without their husband's knowledge" (Kabeer 1985: 104).

The struggle among the different interests of men and women, daughters and mothers-in-law within the context of shifting state and national policies, will be expressed in family planning choices. As a result, unless gendered inequality is considered and addressed in the local arrangements, the outcome may not necessarily be in the best interests of the health of the women and children.

LABOR AND CHILDBIRTH

In addition to looking at family-planning strategies, anthropologists have described the different ways in which women have experienced childbirth and contributed to our understanding that women can participate in decisions about childbirth and labor (Davis-Floyd 2001, Michaelson 1988).

In pre-industrial Europe and the United States, labor and childbirth were managed and controlled by women in the household, often with the assistance of midwives or their equivalent. In the late nineteenth century, as Western doctors were beginning to conduct scientific experiments and to establish the medical profession, women were still active as midwives. However, in the early twentieth century United States, as the medical profession became more rigorously licensed and depended on an extensive education, women were excluded from such training. Childbirth became less the sphere of midwives and more an arena of professional male doctors. This process, sometimes called the medicalization of childbirth, involved the introduction of anesthetics to reduce the pain of labor, which, also, as the woman lost consciousness, placed labor further under the control of medical authority (Wertz and Wertz 1979).

The conflicting issues related to the medicalization of pregnancy and labor were recently highlighted in controversies among Inuit women in Canada, as they continued to insist on their rights to home births supervised by local women. They resisted being flown to a well-equipped hospital for labor and childbirth, far away from their community support (Kaufert and O'Neil 1993). While science and technology have clearly prolonged the lives of women dramatically, women have lost some of the responsibility and autonomy previously associated with the process of childbirth.

THE ANTHROPOLOGY OF REPRODUCTION
AMONG POOR POPULATIONS TODAY

In poor and especially the vast majority of poor rural populations, medical anthropologists have to consider reproduction within the context of the lack of prenatal care, the distance to the nearest clinic, the expense and consequent unavailability of antibiotics and other medications fundamental to public health, the shortage of immunizations, poor nutrition of the mother and infant, and the lack of clean water to wash food or dilute formula. Anthropologists and public health researchers have noted that, throughout the world, women's health is often neglected in favor of children's health, to the detriment of both.

As in the core countries, we find women on the periphery of capitalism trying all available methods, those of Western science as well as those of other healers. However, in poor countries the lack of doctors, trained nurses, and medical provisions leads to greater dependence on alternative medical models, indigenous knowledge of herbal treatments, and communal rituals of healing. Many ethnographies document folk practices in childbirth and pregnancy, as well as the communal aspects of childbirth in the domestic setting. In such settings, critical medical anthropologists are careful to understand reproduction within the context of the availability of care and resources and also to include both the men's and woman's points of view (Scheper-Hughes and Sargent 1998). What strategies are available to men and women to assure the health and welfare of their families? How do men and women make decisions about family size, the timing of births, the survival of the newborn and the access to resources of boys and girls (Browner 2000, Gammeltoft 1999)?

Tine Gammeltoft's (1999) study, *Women's Bodies, Women's Worries*, of rural women in Vietnam today, provides us with a clear sense of women struggling to maintain their own and their children's health in the context of patriarchal rules and their own recognition of the need for a unified family to build strong economic resources. As one woman says "Women know how to put up [with situations], to endure. Men often flare up so it is mostly women who endure . . . " (Gammeltoft 1999: 201).

However, this does not mean that women do nothing. On the contrary, as another rural Vietnamese woman makes clear, "If you go to a hospital in secret, who will know? If your husband wants more children and you don't, he can't force you. You decide for yourself first. The husband's opinion is only a small part. For women, if you want a child, you have a child. You don't have to say anything to your husband until your stomach is big, and then what can he do? . . . It's all up to you" (Gammeltoft 1999: 187).

Since the 1980s, HIV/AIDS has emerged as a central concern in reproduction. Over the past twenty years, HIV/AIDS has also become a gendered issue, as women worldwide are contracting the virus earlier and at a greater rate than men (Piot 2001, Stein and Abdool Karim 2000). HIV positive mothers can transmit the virus both through pregnancy and labor (perinatally) and through breastfeeding.

Over the past two decades such transmission has become preventable. In 2001, in Western societies, as well as in Brazil, Argentina, and Uruguay, mothers may opt for testing prenatally and also be entitled to treatment for themselves. Mothers in poorer countries who would not go for testing for themselves, since almost always treatment is available for the baby but not for the mother herself, will take the risk of testing for HIV/AIDS knowing that it may save the baby. If the mother tests positive, she often faces ostracism and stigma from her husband and family and a knowledge of certain death. Nevertheless, she will be offered medications in the last few months of pregnancy to take during labor. The baby will be given the medications for a short period after birth. If the baby is exclusively breast-fed or formula-fed, these simple procedures will reduce the perinatal transmission of HIV. Sometimes the mother will continue to receive medications for her own continued health but in most situations in poor countries worldwide the baby may live but no attention will be paid to the courageous mother's survival.

Many poor mothers in southern Africa and other parts of the world do not yet have access to such preventive measures for their babies, nor treatment for themselves, although there are ongoing efforts to improve this situation. As a response to worldwide social movements that demand that pharmaceutical companies provide affordable options for poor countries and that wealthy countries contribute resources for public health in poorer countries, medications are slowly becoming available for free or at lower prices (Farmer, Connors, and Simmons 1996). However, government policies that neglect HIV/AIDS, combined with the domestic subordination of women and the fact that many people do not live near clinics, or cannot afford the transportation, or the clinics do not provide testing or treatment still present challenges to prevention and care.

THE ANTHROPOLOGY OF REPRODUCTION IN THE CENTERS OF CAPITALISM

In wealthy, mostly urban, populations, medical anthropologists have to confront the challenges of high-level technologies that can offer mothers a painless, generally safe, birth. The women's health movement in United States questioned the shift to high-technology births and the accompanying reduction in women's control and community supports, as well as the class and racial inequalities in access to reproductive health care (S. Morgen 1987, 1990). Betty Levin (1990) has studied the dilemmas of doctors, health care workers, and parents faced with medical interventions which can, in fact, save the lives of extremely low birth-weight premature infants, but with no guarantee of their future physical and mental abilities. How are decisions made about extraordinary measures that prolong invasive and expensive procedures when the infant may not benefit from the interventions and the parents may suffer inordinately without saving their child? Others have analyzed the changing perceptions of parents and the commoditization of motherhood as couples who might not otherwise have children are offered assisted conception through in vitro fertilization and surrogate motherhood (Franklin and Ragone 1998). As Rayna Rapp has clearly delineated in her discussion of women as moral pioneers, in the United States, questions arise after amniocentesis results demonstrate that the fetus has the genetic mutation for Down syndrome. Such a diagnosis indicates that if the child were to be born, it might never have full mental capacities. Nevertheless, Rapp's research indicates that the decision to terminate a pregnancy is embedded in the class and institutional realities of the historical moment, including the available services for the parents of Down syndrome children and people with disabilities (Rapp 2000).

Other researchers, such as Lynn Morgan (1998) and Sarah Franklin (Franklin and Ragone 1998), have taught us how U.S. perceptions differ from other cultural constructs of life and the fetus and how Western perceptions have changed over the past fifty years as sonograms and video technology have catapulted representations of conception in the uterus and the developing fetus into our consciousness. In the nineteenth century, quickening, or the first flutter of movement felt by the pregnant woman, generally in the eighteenth week of pregnancy, represented the entry of the soul into the womb. Nowadays, technology and genetic engineering, combined with fundamentalist religious beliefs have precipitated debate about the life of the embryo. Powerful scientific developments with respect to conception and pregnancy have not only made conception more predictable, and childbirth safer but also made the fetus more visible.

Such technologies have obviously broadened choices available to women in core capitalist countries. The morning-after pill, which acts to prevent conception and addresses some of the U.S. cultural constructions concerned with the life of the fetus, is now available in most Western countries. Women, informed through sonograms and laboratory testing that their pregnancy may lead to a mentally disabled child, have the option to terminate the pregnancy. At the same time, the invasion of science into the domain of the woman and her body has in some ways reduced the woman's own decision-making power. Representing the fetus and even the embryo, as a separate legal entity, even though an infant still has to be reared by the parents, or neglected, has, in some ways, reduced the control of women over their own conception.

Through the enlightenment of science, we now understand that certain substances such as benzene, radiation, and nitrous oxide may affect the developing fetus (Lindbohm and Taskinen 2000). Women who may be exposed to such substances in the workplace can protect their future child by requesting to be moved to a safer environment and in the U.S. legal regulations allow her to move at work without losing her job. However, as researchers have pointed out, now that we know that alcohol, smoking, and drugs may affect a fetus (Husten and Malarcher 2000, Russell et al. 2000), women can be limited by state policy in what they do during pregnancy and in the extreme, a mother can be jailed for putting the fetus at risk (Whiteford 1996).

In the United States, violence in the household is a factor in reproduction. Battering by a partner is the number one reason women between the ages of 15–45 arrive in hospital emergency rooms. Homicide is the first cause of death for women of that age group. As medical anthropologists have noted, this is one problem that first world women share with poorer countries where battering, murder, and sexual violence, frequently directly associated with a male partner's unemployment, also reach epidemic proportions (Heise 1993). However, violence against women has to be understood within the context of the world system and the impact of globalization, as men have lost jobs, women have been increasingly employed long hours in low-wage sweatshop conditions and resources available to poor families have been reduced. To quote Lynn Freedman from the Center for Population and Health, Columbia University, "Even domestic violence can not be delinked from the growing impoverishment experienced in vast portions of the world since the 1980s. For example, studies conducted as early as 1988 documented an explicit connection between the implementation of International Monetary Fund and World Bank structural adjustment programs, the upheaval that the resulting impoverishment caused and an upsurge in domestic violence"(2000: 436).

The research of medical anthropologists in countries on the periphery, as opposed to the centers of capitalism, ask fundamentally different questions but in their very difference they raise basic questions of their own. In what light should we view the contrast between the millions of dollars spent on cosmetic surgery among the wealthy countries and the lack of the most elementary prenatal care for women in poorer countries?

As in the nineteenth century, reproduction in the second millennium is still intimately interconnected with the rights of women to autonomy, education, and employment (Freedman 2000; Farmer, Connors, and Simmons 1996; I. Susser 2002). Reproductive health is also crucially determined by the histories of colonialism, the uneven development of the world system and the current impact of globalization. Globalization, which has involved among other shifts, a massive privatization of public resources, has contributed to the increasing gap between rich and poor within the world system, as well as to the undermining of women's autonomy with respect to reproductive options as resources for reproductive choice and education are increasingly limited.

A movement for the reproductive health rights of women must incorporate a recognition of women's own abilities to strategize in any historical situation (Freedman 2000, I. Susser 2002). International agencies or movements can assist local women in creating spaces of autonomy, in countering fundamentalist assumptions which limit access to reproductive choice and in providing the resources for education, the technologies of birth control, the funds for medications and employment opportunities. As we have seen from the historical record, with access to funds, health facilities, employment and education, men and women themselves adapt their reproductive strategies to the changing situations in which they find themselves.

PART III

Medical Systems in Social Context

CHAPTER 10

Medical Systems in Indigenous and Precapitalist State Societies

The conceptions of human existence held by people cross culturally reflect their relationship to the forces of production. Foragers tend to view themselves in a friendly and cooperative relationship with their society and their habitat. The Mbuti Pgymies of the Ituri Forest in Zaire view the forest as their mother and father and the source of all goodness in life. Horticulturists tend to view nature in more precarious terms. The Bantu villagers, who are relative newcomers to the Ituri Forest, view it as a place that has to be transformed and overcome in order to survive. They believe that the forest is filled with malevolent spirits and dangerous animals—a view that probably is reinforced by the Mbuti as a means of keeping the Bantu villagers from encroaching even farther upon their ancient home. Foragers believe that most misfortunes are self-inflicted by careless behavior in their otherwise harmonious relationship with nature but also attribute unexplainable accidents and severe diseases to external forces, particularly supernatural ones. Conversely, horticulturists, who live in larger and more densely populated settlements, believe that misfortune, often in the form of witchcraft or sorcery, emanates from strained relationships with people in their own or neighboring communities. Urban dwellers in agrarian state societies often express their alienation from the natural habitat and their political powerlessness by perceiving misfortune as emanating from the whim of the gods, the constellation of the stars or fate.

Disease or physical injury is one of the misfortunes that may befall people in any society. Humans universally have developed theories of disease etiology and health care systems that reflect their living conditions and resources. As Young (1976: 19) observes, "that while serious sickness is an event that challenges meaning in this world, medical beliefs and practices *organize the event into an episode* that gives it form and meaning." The medical systems devised by various peoples in all societies include healing techniques that may be employed either by ordinary persons or by healers of one sort or another. These healing techniques include a pharmacopoeia as well as at least rudimentary medical techniques. Ari Kiev (1966) has argued that the configuration of healers found in various societies varies according to their economic basis. Whereas shamans tend to prevail in foraging societies, such as the Inuit, Shoshone, Australian Murngin, and Andaman Islanders, horticultural societies manifest the beginnings of a medical division of labor with the appearance of diviners, herbalists, midwives, and medical guild members.

Anthropologists often have used the term "ethnomedicine" to refer to the multiplicity of medical systems associated with indigenous societies as well as peasant communities and ethnic minorities in complex or state societies. Charles Hughes (1978: 151) defines ethnomedicine as "those beliefs and practices relating to disease which are the products of indigenous cultural development and are not explicitly derived from the conceptual system of modern medicine." Yet, there is something implicitly ethnocentric about making a sharp distinction between indigenous medical systems and "modern medicine." Indeed, Hahn (1983) argues that biomedicine emerged as a form of Euro-American ethnomedicine that diffused to many other parts of the world. In the ethnomedical systems of the "little peoples"—indigenous peoples, peasants, working-class people, and ethnic minorities—whom anthropologists typically study, biomedicine constitutes an ethnomedical system of a special sort—one that has undergone a process of professionalization and etiological specificity that makes it acceptable to ruling elites around the world in that it downplays the social origins of disease. Whether we are referring to the indigenous medical system of a foraging society or to biomedicine as it is practiced in a particular national setting, each can be viewed, as Grossinger (1990: 75) so aptly observes, as "an elegant and comprehensive response to social and ecological resources and a patchwork of desperate solutions to an ongoing crisis of health and survival." Conversely each ethnomedical system has its limitations, even biomedicine, whose practitioners regard it as vastly superior to local and regional medical systems.

ETHNOMEDICINE AS A RESPONSE TO DISEASE IN INDIGENOUS SOCIETIES

Ultimately, professionalized medical systems have their roots in the ethnomedical systems of indigenous societies, which intricately combine empirical and magicoreligious beliefs and practices. Grossinger makes a distinction between "practical medicine" and "spiritual medicine," noting that the "later and present schism between healing and technological medicine begins in the occupational distinction between faith healers and surgeons, and shamans, medicine men, and voodoo chiefs, on the one hand, and herbalists, wound dressers, and midwives on the other" (Grossinger 1990: 76). He delineates three forms of pragamatic medicines: (1) pharmaceutical medicine, which consists primarily of a wide variety of herbal remedies; (2) mechanical medicine, which consists of surgical techniques as well as techniques that simulate physiological processes such as bathing, sweat-bathing, shampooing, massage, cupping, emetics, burning, incision, and bloodletting; and (3) psychophysiological healing, which relies on a wide variety of magical and psychotherapeutic techniques such as the classic "sucking cure" (Grossinger 1990: 76–95), in which a shaman orally extracts intrusive objects from a patient body. The distinction between psychophysiological healing and spiritual medicine is blurred. For the most part, however, spiritual medicine emphasizes the spiritual origin of disease and views it as the "primary weapon of the spiritual world" (Grossinger 1990: 99).

Indigenous Theories of Disease Etiology

All medical systems seek to answer ultimate questions, such as, "Why did it happen to *me?*" or, "What meaning does disease have in the larger scheme of things." Indigenous peoples often do not make a sharp distinction between disease per se and other kinds of misfortune. All undesirable events may be lumped together, both in a theory about why they occur and in practices directed at alleviating or preventing them. Indigenous peoples rely heavily, but not exclusively, upon supernaturalistic explanations of disease. This prompted Ackerknecht (1971) to view "primitive medicine" as "magic medicine." Nevertheless, indigenous medical systems contain a strong dose of naturalism in terms of both disease etiology and treatment. The Azande do not resort to oracles as a means of detecting the source of witchcraft except when naturalistic explanations have failed to explain why people experience a misfortune. Indigenous societies generally do not compartmentalize their cognitive systems in the manner that Western societies do. Ultimately, indigenous disease theories generally have major relevance to the moral order of a society. Disease compels people to reflect on certain aspects of the social order.

Forrest E. Clements (1932) proposed the first cross-cultural classification of emic theories of disease etiology. These are sorcery, breach of taboo, intrusion of a foreign object, intrusion of a spirit, and soul loss. Many societies emphasize one or a combination of causes. The San, a foraging society that resides in the Kalahari Desert of Southwest Africa, believe that disease is caused by a specific intruding substance, sometimes placed in the body by spirits or a witch, but often not (Katz 1982).

The spirits involved are sometimes specific ancestors who desire the company of their loved ones or maybe the great god or a lesser god. The Inuit generally attribute disease to soul loss or breach of a taboo. Soul loss also serves as an explanation of disease among many groups in western North America.

Among the Murngin, an Australian aboriginal people located in northeastern Arnhem Land, various forms of witchcraft are considered to be the causes of many serious diseases and of almost all, if not all, deaths (Reid 1983: 44). The Jivaro Indians of the Amazon Basin also believe that witchcraft is the cause of the vast majority of diseases and nonviolent deaths. Many African societies tend to attribute disease to the malevolence of sorcerers or witches. Although disease etiology is important among the Gnau, a horticultural society of the Sepik River region of New Guinea, Gilbert Lewis (1986), a physician-anthropologist, notes that they often merely accept disease as a fact of life, without attempting to explain or treat it. The Gnau explain wounds, burns, and the like in obvious naturalistic terms but generally ascribe most diseases to offended spirits.

Clements concluded that the attribution of disease to soul loss or a magical intrusion of a foreign object had only a single point of origin, from which it spread over the rest of the globe. He argued that attributing disease to violation of a taboo had probably started independently in three different places: Mesoamerica, the Arctic, and southern Asia. More recently, Murdock (1980) argued that regional variations suggest an important influence of diffusion of ancient ideas, noting the failure of some explanations to appear in places isolated from the societies that already share them. He observes that attribution of disease to the action of spirits is almost universal, appearing in all but two of a world sample of 139 societies. Murdock examined the relation between the importance of spirit explanation and several variables of general societal characteristics.

Foster and Anderson (1978) make a distinction between personalistic and naturalistic theories of disease. In a personalistic system, disease emanates from some sort of sensate agent, such as a deity, a malevolent spirit, an offended ancestral spirit, or a sorcerer. Naturalistic theories posit disease in terms of an imbalance among various impersonal systemic forces, such as body humors in ancient Greek medicine or the principles of yin and yang in traditional Chinese medicine. In Greek medicine as delineated by Aristotle, the universe consists of four elements: fire, air, water, and earth. People represent a microcosm of the universe and are composed of four humors with four corresponding personality types: blood is associated with high-spiritedness, yellow bile with bad temper, black bile with melancholia, and phlegm with sluggishness. Disease results from an imbalance of the humors. The physician attempts to restore health by correcting this imbalance.

In Chinese medicine, *yang* is associated with heaven, sun, fire, heat, dryness, light, the male principle, the exterior, the right side, life, high, noble, good, beauty, virtue, order, joy, and wealth. Yin is associated with the earth, moon, water, cold, dampness, darkness, the female principle, the interior, the left side, death, low, evil, ugliness, vice, confusion, and poverty. A proper balance of yang and yin results in health. Excessive yang, associated with heat, produces fever; and excessive yin, associated with cold, produces chills.

While Foster and Anderson do not see the two types of etiological systems as mutually exclusive, they argue that personalistic explanations predominate among indigenous peoples as well as in certain state societies such as West African ones and the Aztecs, Mayans, and Incas. Conversely, naturalistic theories historically have been associated with certain great traditional medical systems, such as traditional Chinese medicine and Ayurveda and Unani in South Asia.

Morley provides a more elaborate typology of indigenous "etiological categories" of disease in the form of a four-cell matrix, illustrated in Figure 10.1.

Supernatural causes ascribe disease etiology to superhuman forces, such as evil spirits, ancestral spirits, witches, sorcerers, or the evil eye. Nonsupernatural disease categories are "those based wholly on observed cause-and-effect relationships regardless of the accuracy of the observations made" (Morley 1978: 2), such as profuse bleeding. Immediate causes follow from nonsupernatural sources and account for sickness in terms of perceived pathogenic agents. Ultimate causes posit the underlying sources of misfortune as it affects a specific individual.

Based upon comparative data from 186 societies listed in the Human Relations Area Files, George P. Murdock (1980) delineated an elaborate typology of "theories of illness," which is summarized in Figure 10.2.

While many of the categories in Murdock's scheme are self-explanatory, others are not. Theories of mystical causation posit illness to "some putative impersonal causal relationship" (Murdock 1980: 17). Theories of animistic causation posit illness to "some personalized supernatural en-

Figure 10.1
Etiological Categories

Supernatural Causes	Nonsupernatural Causes
Ultimate Causes	Immediate Causes

Source: Morley (1978:3).

Figure 10.2
Theories of Illness

A. Theories of Natural Causation

1. Infection

2. Stress

3. Organic deterioration

4. Accident

5. Overt human aggression

B. Theories of Supernatural Causation

1. Theories of mystical causation

a. fate

b. ominous sensations

c. contagion

d. mystical retribution

2. Theories of animistic causation

a. soul loss

b. spirit aggression

3. Theories of magical causation

a. sorcery

b. witchcraft

Source: Murdock (1980).

tity—a soul, ghost, spirit, or god" (19). Theories of magical causation posit illness to the "covert action of an envious, affronted, or malicious human being who employs magical means to injure his victims" (21).

Murdock's scheme of illness or disease etiology has the advantage of illustrating the wide repertoire of explanations that peoples around the globe have devised to explain their maladies and ailments. Conversely, it is much more cumbersome than both Foster and Anderson's scheme and Morley's scheme. At any rate, Murdock's sample draws primarily from indigenous societies but also from some archaic state societies such as the Egyptians, the Babylonians, the Romans, the Japanese, the Aztecs, and the Incas. Many societies rely upon multiple causes of illness or disease. Murdock also reports on the relative frequency of theories of disease etiology in various culture areas. Africa ranks very high in theories of mystical retribution. North America "outranks all other regions in theories of sorcery, which occur in all of its societies without exception and are reported as important in 83 percent of them" (Murdock 1980: 49). Conversely, South America "ranks high in theories of spirit aggression, which are recorded as present in 100 percent of its societies and as important in 91 percent of them" (52).

Horacio Fabrega (1997), a biocultural anthropologist, has posited a rather elaborate discussion of medical systems in various types of societies. He employs the acronym SH for referring to a hypothesized biological adaptation for sickness and healing. Fabrega maintains that chimpanzees exhibit some basic behaviors, such as the use of leaves to wipe themselves and the use of leaf napkins to dab at bleeding wounds, associated with the SH, but also observes that they exhibit some non-SH responses, such as aversion to and exploitation of sick group members. He suggests that many of the SH characteristics of chimpanzees existed in early hominid societies and that SH became more refined during the Neanderthal stage, as is implied by the presence of healed fractures in some Neanderthal remains. Asserting that "SH constitutes the foundational material for the elaboration of medicine as a social institution," Fabrega (1997: 70) posits that the provider of SH in early foraging societies tended to be a relatively insightful individual who possessed an elaborate knowledge of the social organization and culture of his or her society. He introduces the notion of *meme:* a unit of cultural information that is stored in the brains of individuals and passed onto others through enculturation. With regard to sickness and healing, medical memes serve as mechanisms for orienting to, thinking about, and responding to disease and injury. Unfortunately, while the concept of medical meme may be a useful analytical device, Fabrega provides no concrete evidence that it has any physical reality and thus this idea remains within the realm of creative speculation.

At any rate, he characterizes SH in foraging societies as family and small group oriented, based upon "non-systematized knowledge," and focused on immediate restoration of well-being or accommodation to death through ritual activities and social practices. SH in village-level societies is characterized by the presence of specialized healers, elaborate healing ceremonies attended by community members, and an expansion of the sick role—that is exemption from expected work and social obligations, for example, in growing attention to psychosocial needs and sick individuals. According to Fabrega, chiefdom, prestate, and early state societies exhibit the beginnings of the "institution" or "system" of medicine that includes: (1) an elaborate corpus of medical knowledge which continues to embrace aspects of cosmology, religion, and morality; and (2) the beginnings of medical pluralism, manifested by the presence of a wide variety of healers, including general practitioners, priests, diviners, herbalists, bonesetters, and midwives who undergo systematic training or apprenticeships.

Indigenous Healing Methods

In facing any kind of crisis, humans characteristically feel compelled to take some kind of action, if for no other reason than to alleviate their anxiety and sense of powerlessness. Healing is the response that humans characteristically adopt in coping with disease. Hahn (1995: 7) defines healing as "not only the remedy or cure of sickness—that is the restoration of a prior healthy state—but also rehabilitation—the compensation for loss of health—the palliation—the mitigation of suffering in the sick." In reality, most ailments are self-limiting and eventually end with recovery. In their effort to exert control over disease, however, human societies have developed a wide array of therapeutic techniques. Therapies are not only a means of curing disease but also, equally important, a means by which specific diseases are culturally defined. While indigenous medical systems rely heavily upon various forms of symbolic healing, they also exhibit a storehouse of empirical knowledge. Laughlin (1963) argues that the acquisition of anatomical knowledge started at an early stage in human history and was based upon the crucial significance of the meat-eating diet, relating practices of hunting and the processing of animals.

Even Ackerknecht (1971), who we noted earlier viewed indigenous medicine as "magical medicine," recognized the existence of a wide array of "primitive surgical procedures," including wound treatment, the setting of fractures, bleeding, incision, amputation, cesarean section, and trephination. The Masai, cattle pastoralists in East Africa, were master surgeons who operated upon both humans and animals. The indigenous populations of the Aleutian Islands and Kodiak Island off the coast of Alaska developed a sophisticated anatomical knowledge and surgical competence (Laughlin 1963: 130). Various Native American groups, including the Carrier Indians of the Pacific Northwest, the Mescalero Apaches of New Mexico, the Teton Dakota of the Plains, and the Winnebago of the Great Lakes region, sutured wounds with sinews. Wounds were sutured with thorns by the Masai and with the heads of termites by various indigenous peoples of New Mexico, the Azande of West Africa, and the Melanesians, as well as among many other societies around the world. Other empirical techniques associated with indigenous medicine include massage, sweat baths, mineral baths, and heat applications.

All human societies have a pharmacopoeia consisting of a wide variety of materials, including plants, animals (including fish, insects, and reptiles), rocks and minerals, waters (salt and fresh, surface and subterranean), earths and sands, and fossils, as well as manufactured items. An estimated 25% to 50% of the pharmacopoeia of indigenous peoples has been demonstrated to be empirically effective by biomedical criteria. Various biomedical drugs, including quinine and digitalis, were originally derived from indigenous peoples. The older people of northeastern Arnhem Land in Australia reportedly know how to locate and prepare at least a hundred herbal medicines (Reid 1983: 92). Indigenous pharmacy blends together herbal medicine and spiritual medicine. As Grossinger (1990:

105) relates, "A doctor gains full control over pharmacy by making allies of the spirits who control the plants, animals, stones, and springs from which he makes his tonics."

As noted earlier, ritual or symbolic healing constitutes the principal therapeutic technique in indigenous societies. Conversely, as we see in chapter 5, biomedicine and professionalized heterodox medical systems in modern state societies also rely upon the manipulation of a "field of symbols" (Moerman 1979: 60). Dow proposes the possible existence of a universal structure of symbolic healing that consists of the following patterns:

1. The experiences of healers and healed are generalized with culture-specific symbols.

2. A suffering patient comes to a healer who persuades the patient that the problem can be defined in terms of myth.

3. The healer attaches the patient's emotions to transactional symbols particularized from the general myth.

4. The healer manipulates the transactional symbols to help the patient transact his or her own emotions. (Dow 1986: 56)

In other words, symbolic healing occurs when both healer and patient accept the former's ability to define the latter's relationship to the mythic structure of their sociocultural system. As this observation implies, healing by its very nature often entails an element of faith in both healer and patient. Healing rituals, however, have a broader field of concern in that they are designed to mend wounds in the body politic within which the patient is symbolically embedded.

One of the best examples of symbolic healing is the *sing* practiced among traditional Navajo residing in northeastern Arizona and northwestern New Mexico. Conceptions of disease and therapy are central elements in their elaborate cosmology. Indeed, in large part Navajo religion consists of a set of some thirty-six healing ceremonies (often referred to as sings or chants), each lasting from one to nine nights and the intervening days. The Navajo attribute disease to various causes, including sorcery, intruding spirits, and inappropriate actions on the part of the afflicted person. In the singer's hogan (Navajo dwelling), he creates a mythic sand painting and then destroys it with his feet as a symbolic enactment of the restoration of harmony in both the patient and his or her social network. A Navajo sing blends together many elements—ritualistic items such as the medicine bundle, prayer-sticks, precious stones, tobacco, water collected from sacred places, a tiny piece of cotton string, sand paintings, and songs and prayers. Sand paintings exemplify the centrality of symbols to Navajo healing in that they must carefully follow traditional patterns that

recall significant episodes of mythical drama. . . . The patient in his or her plight is identified with the cultural hero who constructed a similar disease or plight in the same way the patient did. . . . From the myth the patient learns that his or her plight and illness is not new, and that both its cause and treatment are known. To be cured, all the patient has to do is to repeat what has been done before. It has to be done sincerely, however, and this sincerity is expressed in concentration and dedication. The sandpainting depicts the desired order of things, and places the patient in this beautiful and ordered world. The patient thus becomes completely identified with the powerful and curing agents of the universe. (Witherspoon 1977: 167–68)

Ultimately, healing is directed toward restoring harmony in the patient's life and in the members of his or her social network present at the chant.

The Shaman as the Prototypical Indigenous Healer

What anthropologists generally refer to as the shaman constitutes the prototypical healer in indigenous societies. Shamanism has been the focus of an extensive corpus of anthropological literature and continues to be a topic of considerable interest, not only among anthropologists (see Hoppal and Howard 1993; Seaman and Day 1994; Jakobsen 1999; Winkelman 2000; Kehoe 2000) but also among certain historians, such as Mircea Eliade (1964), and writers who hope that shamanic traditions can provide spiritual guidance in our own troubled times. Bowie (2000: 192–96) delineates four basic approaches to the study of shamanism: (1) as a widespread form of indigenous ecstatic or trance-like behavior, (2) as a primordial or early form of religion dating back at least to the Upper Paleolithic, (3) as primarily a northern-Arctic phenomenon, and (4) as a revitalized form of religion referred to as neo-shamanism. With respect to the fourth approach, the writings of anthropologists such as Carlos Casteneda, Michael Harner, and Holger Kaiweit as well as numerous proponents of New Age philosophy, as is shown in greater detail in the next chapter, have transformed the shaman into a primordial and existential "culture hero." Within anthropology, shamanism has been for sometime a topic of interest to those interested in either religion or healing or in the interface of these areas.

Ripinsky-Naxon (1993: 67) defines shamanism as a "specialized body of acquired techniques, leading to altered states of consciousness or facilitated ecstatic transformations, with the purposes of attaining mystical or spiritual experiences." Although shamans carry out a number of roles, such as culture hero, entertainer, judge, and repository of cultural values, healing appears to be their primary activity in those societies where they exist. As Harner (1980: 175) observes, shamanism "represents the most widespread and ancient methodological system of mind-body healing known to humanity." While the category of shamanism is being reconstituted and rejuvenated by both academic and popular writers as well as holistic health and/or New Age practitioners, it is being deconstructed within anthropology (Atkinson 1992).

The term *shaman* is derived from the Tungusic-Mongol word *saman* (to know). It has become an etic category for a part-time magicoreligious practitioner who serves as intermediary between his or her sociocultural system and the Cosmic Environment. Mircea Eliade (1964), a renowned historian of religions, defines a shaman as one who has mastery over the "techniques of ecstasy" or the ability to attain or engage in magical flight to the heavens or to the underworld. In her working definition of shamanism, Townsend (1999: 431–432) delineates five "essential criteria" and four "related criteria." The former include direct communication on the part with the supernatural realm, his/her ability to control the spirits, an altered state of consciousness, an emphasis on solving problems in this life, and soul flight. The latter include the functioning of the shaman as a medium for the voices of the spirits, and/or the ability of the shaman to call upon his or her spirits to be present at the séance without actually possessing him; the ability of the shaman to remember at least some aspects of his trance; and the ability of the shaman to cure physical, psychological, or emotional disorders.

With respect to the issue of communication with the spirit world, Rogers (1982: 6–7) delineates two types of shamans: (1) the inspirational or ecstatic shaman who engages in a theatrical battle with the spirits in order to heal the patient and (2) the seer who relays messages from the spirits to the people but in a less intense manner. Whereas the former is sometimes associated with "Arctic shamanism," the latter is associated with the "general shamanism" characteristic of many New World societies. While much ink has been spilled in the past attempting to identify true shamanism in terms of the level of the shaman's consciousness of his or her activities and other criteria, more recent work on shamanism has attempted to understand it as a complex, diverse, and widespread phenomenon.

Much of the literature on shamanism has also focused upon the social and psychological attributes of shamans. Whereas priests as full-time religious practitioners in chiefdoms or state societies generally are males, shamans may be males or females, although this pattern varies considerably from society to society. Whereas male shamans predominated in lowland South American societies, the Yakuts in the Kolmyck district of Siberia had a higher regard for their female shamans than for their male shamans (Rogers 1982: 27). In fact, Yakut male shamans adopted women's clothing and hairstyles. Much of the literature on shamans indicates that many of them assume various unconventional lifestyles, such as homosexuality, bisexuality, or transvestism. Conversely, while transvestism apparently was common among shamans in various Siberian and North American cultures, it reportedly has been uncommon in South American indigenous cultures but did occur among the Mapache of Patagonia during the nineteenth century (Langdon 1992). Shamans in many societies are social recluses who choose not to enter into lasting social relationships with others. As Gaines (1987: 66) observes, shamans are not peripheral or marginal as a social category but rather as individuals.

Anthropologists and other scholars have characterized the psychodynamic makeup of shamans in the following three ways: (1) as pathological personalities, (2) as highly introspective and self-actualized individuals with unique insights about the psychosocial nature of their respective societies, and (3) as individuals who experienced an existential crisis but became healed in the process of becoming a shaman.

Various anthropologists, particularly in the past, have argued that shamans exhibit universally psychotic traits, such as hysteria, trance, and transvestism (Ackerknecht 1971; Devereux 1956, 1957). The Russian ethnographer Waldemar Bogaras characterized Chuckee shamans as on the "whole extremely excitable, almost hysterical, and not a few were half-crazy" (quoted in I.M. Lewis 1989: 161). Weston LaBarre (1972: 265), who made a case for the shamanic origins of religion as a by-product of the use of hallucinogenic drugs, maintained "'God' is often clinically paranoiac because the shaman's 'supernatural helper' is the projection of the shaman himself." More recently, Ohnuki-Tierney (1980) has asserted that Ainu shamanism is often associated with *imu*, a culture-bound syndrome. Aside from the matter of the actual mental status of the shaman, shamanist healing séances often impose considerable strain on the practitioner. A California Indian shaman reported, "The doctor business is very hard on you. You're like crazy, you are knocked out and you aren't in your right mind" (quoted in Rogers 1982: 12).

In contrast to negative portrayals of shamans, anthropologists in more recent times have presented shamanic behavior as a category of universal psychobiological capacities. Shamans are often portrayed as insightful, creative, and stable personalities who, while freely drawing upon indigenous traditions, transcend the limitations of their culture by creating their own responses to new situations. In essence, shamans are viewed as having a capacity to interpret the events of daily life more adequately than the other members of the culture. Kalweit (1992: 222–24) characterizes the shaman as a "spiritual iconoclast" who learns about humanity through solitude and as a "holy fool" who is holy because he or she has been healed. Murphy's portrayal of the mental status of Inuit shamans on St.

Lawrence Island, Alaska, in the Bering Strait bear out this characterization:

The well known shamans were, if anything, exceptionally healthy. . . . As for the shamans who had suffered from psychiatric instability of one kind or another, it has been suggested that shamanizing is itself an avenue for "being healed from disease." Whatever the psychiatric characteristics that may impel a person to choose this role, once he fulfills it, he has a well-defined and unambiguous relationship to the rest of society, which in all probability allows him to function without the degree of impairment that might follow if there were no such niche into which he could fit. (Murphy 1964: 76)

In his study of Henry Rupert, Handelbaum (1977) reports that this Washo shaman exhibited a process of lifelong psychological growth. In his comparison of sixteen shamanistic healers and nonhealers among the !Kung of the Kalahari Desert, Richard Katz (1982) found that the former tended to exhibit a more expressive, passionate, and fluid conception of their bodies as well as a richer fantasy life than the latter. Winkelman adopts a neurophenomenological approach to shamanism and asserts shamanistic healing activates

normally unconscious or preconscious primary information-processing functions and outputs to be integrated into the operations of the frontal cortex. This integrates implicit understandings, socioemotional dynamics, repressed memories, unresolved conflicts, intuitions, and nonverbal—visual, mimetic [imitative], and representational—knowledge into self-conscious awareness. (Winkelman 2000: xiii)

While there is evidence of heightened cognitive and psychic functioning among shamans, this second approach often tends to romanticize shamanism by overlooking the variability among shamans both within a specific culture and cross culturally. Apparently some shamans exhibited exploitative and sadistic tendencies in that they acted as bullies and terrorized their communities to the point that they were killed (Kiev 1966: 110).

A fair number of anthropologists have characterized the role of shaman as a culturally constituted defense mechanism. Whereas Kiev (1966) views some shamans as assuming a mature and integrated "normal" disposition, he also maintains that other shamans use their calling as a method for working out their psychological problems. In a similar vein, Spiro (1967) argues that shamanism provides an opportunity for certain members of a community to satisfy sexual, dependency, prestige, and Dionysian needs. The shaman has been depicted as a "wounded surgeon" (Lewis 1989) or a "'holy fool' who is holy because he [or she] has been healed" (Kalweit 1992: 222). Walsh (1997: 117) asserts that the "shaman may not only recover from the initiation crisis but may emerge strengthened and enabled to help others."

Unlike the schizophrenic, the shaman is not alienated from society and performs a valued social role. Unfortunately, studies that emphasize the therapeutic benefits of shamanism for the practitioner often downplay shamanic practices of manipulation, deception, and, in some instances, destruction. In reality, indigenous people often exhibit an ambivalent view of shamans—on the one hand, holding them in high esteem and being in awe of their abilities and, on the other, fearing and resenting them. The Netsilik Inuit believe that if one can control the universe or its objects for good purposes, one can also use that power for evil designs (Balikci 1963). Hippler (1976: 112) makes an interesting point by asserting that shamanism "could provide a life-style for the insightful observer of his own community who could act easily within its cultural limits and still, on the other hand, provide a necessary identity to the individual who is almost schizophrenic."

Certain scholars have associated shamanism with foraging societies or specific cultural areas, such as Siberia and North America (Walsh 1990: 15–17). More recent research, however, has tended to view shamanism as a "globalizing" and "dynamic cultural-social complex in various societies overtime and space" (Langdon 1992: 4). Despite the voluminous literature on shamanism, most of the research on this topic has tended to be particularistic. From a CMA perspective, shamanism as a form of indigenous healing appears to take different forms depending upon the economic base of the society. Unfortunately, this issue still has not received much systematic attention. Critical medical anthropologists still need to develop an analysis of health beliefs and practices in precapitalist social formations that parallels the general sociocultural analyses that various critical anthropologists have made of such societies. Bearing these thoughts in mind, we present a modest effort to provide a broad perspective on shamanism by examining it in the following contexts: (1) foraging societies, (2) horticultural societies, and (3) indigenous cultures that have come into intense contact with or have been absorbed by state societies.

The role of shaman or healer tends to be a relatively open one in foraging societies, as we will see in the following "Closer Look."

"A Closer Look"

"BOILING ENERGY" AMONG THE !KUNG

Richard Katz (1982), a comparative psychologist, has conducted the most extensive study of shamanistic healing in a contemporary foraging society. His study of indigenous healing among the !Kung of the Kalahari

Desert in Southwest Africa is particularly valuable because it gives us a partial glimpse of what shamanism may have been like under more pristine conditions and also of how the outside world has impacted upon shamanism. Although some fifty thousand San live in Botswana, Namibia, and southern Angola, only about three thousand continue to live primarily as foragers. The !Kung, a subgroup of the San, are a highly egalitarian people whose women contribute from 60% to 80% of the caloric intake, participate actively in decision making, and have been known to engage in hunting.

Katz studied shamanism among the !Kung of the Dobe area of Botswana, an area that embraces nine permanent waterholes. Shamanistic healing constitutes a highly important ritual of solidarity and intensification in !Kung culture. The all-night Giraffe dance, which appears to be an ancient part of !Kung culture and is depicted on rock paintings in South Africa, occurs about four times a month and serves as the central event in the !Kung healing tradition. Several men, who are sometimes joined by women, dance around a fire and a group of singers. The ecstatic dancing stimulates the "boiling" of spiritual energy, or *num*, in the dancers, who begin to *kia* or trance. The healers may ingest plant substances that contain *num*. The fire that illuminates the dance also serves to induce trance in the healers, who may begin to shake violently and experience convulsions, pain, and anguish. The intensity of *kia* has been so great in some cases that it has caused a heart attack in the healer. While in a state of *kia*, healers treat people at the dance by struggling with their ancestral spirits for the body of a sick person. The most powerful healers sometimes travel to the great god's home in the sky. The !Kung believe that the gods originally gave them *num*, which resides in the pit of the stomach and the base of the spine. It boils fiercely within a person when activated and rises up the spine to a spot around the base of the skull, at which point *kia* results.

The !Kung believe that specific diseases are manifestations of some imbalance between an individual and his or her environment. Disease occurs when the gods and ancestral spirits try to take the sick person to their realm. The spirits have various ways of creating mishaps and even death, such as permitting a lion to maul a person. The !Kung believe that the dance may function as a preventive health measure, which keeps an incipient illness from being manifested, or may cure an illness, especially a severe one. Katz (1982: 53) maintains that the !Kung healing dance functions to "reestablish balance in the individual-cultural environmental gestalt." A healing dance may also be performed to celebrate the killing of a large game animal, the return of absent family members, or visits from close relatives or honored guests, such as anthropologists. Other !Kung healing techniques include herbal medicines and massage. Some fifteen medicinal plants are used by healers and nonhealers alike in treating minor ailments and for spiritual protection. They are mixed with charcoal and applied to the skin to alleviate aches and pains, to treat abrasions, cuts, and infections, and even to bring luck in hunting.

Most !Kung males and about a third of adult women seek to become healers at one time or another. More than half of the adult males but only 10% of females succeed in doing so. Women tend to experience *kia* at the Drum dance, at which they only may sing and dance, to the accompaniment of a male drummer. Women assert that *num* endangers the human fetus and therefore often postpone seeking it until after menopause. Most young women expect to learn *kia* for its own sake regardless of whether they will eventually learn to heal. Whereas the healing of the Giraffe is available to all, the healing in the Drum extends only to the dancers and singers but not to the spectators. Although the !Kung are often portrayed as one of the most sexually egalitarian societies in the ethnographic record, the differential access to shamanistic healing between men and women in this society provides some clues as to how healing over time became increasingly a predominantly male preserve. Conversely, Katz (1982: 174) suggests that the Drum may constitute a response to the "greater role differentiation between the sexes and the loss of status for women which accompanies sedentism" in !Kung society as it has come into contact with the outside world.

In contrast to foraging societies, healing appears to be a somewhat more privileged role in horticultural societies. In his generalizations about shamans among the peoples of the tropical rain forests of South America, most of whom are horticulturalists, Metraux observes (see Sharon 1978: 132) that male shamans may play a predominant role, with women shamans, if they exist, exhibiting a modest role in comparison. Among the Culina Indians of western Brazil, only men become shamans (Pollack 1992: 25). Approximately one out of every four Jivaro males becomes a shaman, but no women apparently do (Harner 1968).

Other Healers in Indigenous Societies

In addition to the shaman per se, many indigenous societies have other types of healers. Based upon his cross-cultural analysis of magicoreligious practitioners, Winkelman (1992, 2000) proposes an evolutionary typology of "shamanistic healers" consisting of two main categories: the "healer complex" and the "medium." The healer complex consists of three subtypes: (1) the shaman, (2) the shaman/healer, and (3) the healer. The *shaman* represents the original institutionalization of trancelike behavior or altered states of consciousness (ASC) and is primarily associated with societies that rely on hunting, gathering, and fishing modes of subsistence. Of the societies surveyed, this subtype appears in two Eurasian pastoral societies as well, namely, the Chuckee and the Samoyed. *Shaman/healer* refers to a "group of cases which varied between the Shaman group and the Healer group under different measurement procedures" (Winkelman 1992: 26). This subtype is found primarily in horticultural societies and also occasionally in pastoral societies. Shamans and shaman/healers are predominantly male, but females sometimes occupy this position. The *healer* "shares some similarities with the Shaman role, but lacks major ASC, and occurs predominantly in societies with political integration beyond the local community." *Mediums* are predominantly female and are low in social status. Winkelman's distinction between the relatively high status of the shaman, shaman/healer, and healer and the relatively low status of the medium roughly parallels Lewis's (1989) distinction between "central morality cults" presided over by shamans or priests and "peripheral cults" consisting of mediums and other devotees undergoing possession. Whereas the former play a significant role in upholding the morality of society, the latter tend to involve people who are subject to strong patterns of discrimination, such as women in societies at various sociopolitical levels and ethnic minorities and commoners in rank or stratified societies. In peripheral cults, the sick person being possessed by a spirit receives the attention of a social superior and has an opportunity to ventilate her or his frustrations without directly threatening the established system of social relations.

The healing role appears to undergo a process that Max Weber termed "routinization of charisma" in its evolution from the shaman to the healer. As Winkelman (1992: 65) observes, "While the Shamans are selected for their roles on the basis of ASC experiences labeled as illness, visions, spirit requests, and vision quests, the Healers are selected on the basis of voluntary self-selection, and generally without major ASC experiences." This trajectory appears to parallel the evolution of religious leadership from that of the shaman into that of the priest. Whereas the shaman functions primarily as a medicoreligious practitioner, religion and medicine become increasingly differentiated in chiefdoms and state societies, with the former constituting the domain of the priest and the latter the domain of the healer or physician. Furthermore, shamans and healers "differ with respect to political power, with the Shamans having informal and charismatic political power and the Healers exercising political/legislative power, judicial power, and higher socioeconomic status" (Winkelman 1992: 65).

Wood (1979: 321–326) identified three types of "nonshamanic traditional curers"—spiritualists, diviners, and herbalists. Like the shaman, the spiritualist possesses the ability to communicate with the spirits and to relay messages to the living. Conversely, the spiritualist lacks an ecstatic experience, whereas the shaman purportedly undergoes a dramatic visitation to the supernatural realm and struggles with his or her spirit guides. In reality, as we saw earlier, the distinction between the shaman and the spiritualist or seer is a fine line. Among the Temiar, a horticultural society in the Malay Peninsula, most spiritualists or mediums are males who call upon various spirit guides and sing in their communal healing ceremonies. The wife of the medium serves as the cornerstone of the chorus during healing performances and serves as a "particularly astute foil to the medium's wit during performances" (Roseman 1991: 76). Temiar mediums also heal patients on an individual basis and may call for a spirit séance.

As compared to the shaman and spiritualist, who communicate directly with the supernatural realm, the "diviner interprets symptoms, prognosticates, and prescribes courses of action through mechanical, magical manipulations" (Wood 1979: 323). Whereas in traditional Navajo culture the shaman or singer conducts a healing ceremony, various specialists diagnose disease through a combination of divination and visualization:

There are three ways of determining an illness—gazing at sun, moon, or star, listening, and trembling. Listening is nearly, if not quite, extinct; "motion-in-hand" indicates trembling induced by proper ritualistic circumstances. The diviner is seized with shaking, beginning usually with gentle tremors of arms or legs and gradually spreading until the whole body shakes violently. While in a trembling state, the seer loses himself. Guided by his power, he sees a symbol of the ceremony purporting to cure the person for whom he is divining. Gazing may be accompanied by trembling; usually the diviner sees the chant symbol as an afterimage of the heavenly body on which he is concentrating. (Reichard 1950: 99–100)

According to Wood (1979: 325), the herbalist is "probably the most pragmatic of the traditional healers" in that "he or she frequently relies on the knowledge gained during a lengthy training from an experienced practitioner." Among the Subanum on Mindinao Island in the Philippines, virtually every adult functions as his or her own herbalist.

The shaman and other indigenous healers described in this chapter persist in both archaic and modern state societies. In these settings, however, they tend to serve primarily members of the lowest strata of society.

MEDICAL PLURALISM IN PRECAPITALIST STATES: MEDICINE FOR THE ELITES AND MEDICINE FOR THE MASSES

In contrast to the indigenous societies, where healing tends to be relatively accessible, elite practitioners in state societies attempt to monopolize this role for themselves. Nevertheless, counterparts of indigenous healers persist in state societies. Indeed, a hierarchy of healers that reflects social relations in the larger society was a characteristic feature of precapitalist state societies. According to Fabrega (1997), the sickness and healing system in early civilizations and empires is characterized by an complex pattern of medical pluralism consisting of two tiers: (1) an official, scholarly academic medical system oriented to the care of the elites and (2) a wide array of less prestigious physicians and folk healers who treat subordinate segments of society. The state plays an increasing role in medical care by hiring practitioners for elites and providing free or nominal care for the poor, especially during famines and epidemics. The literate or "great" medical tradition includes the formation of a medical profession, the beginnings of clinical medicine, and the increasing commercialization of the healing endeavor.

In archaic state societies, priests often functioned as physicians or healers of one sort or another. Ancient Sumerian civilization possessed three categories of cuneiform texts that included medical information: (1) therapeutic or medical texts per se, (2) omen collections or "symptom" texts, and (3) miscellaneous texts that included information on ailments and medical practices (Magner 1992: 18). Sumerian physicians reportedly diagnosed symptoms by taking health histories rather than performing direct physical examinations. Conversely, the "conjurer," "diviner," or "priest-healer" conducted a direct physical examination and viewed the patient's symptoms and life circumstances as omens that diagnosed disease (Magner 1992: 19). Sumerian prescriptions included some 250 vegetable and some 120 mineral drugs as well as alcoholic beverages, fats and oils, animal parts and products, honey, wax, and various kinds of milk.

In ancient Egypt, priests of the goddess Sekhmet treated a wide array of diseases, except for eye disorders, which were treated by the priests of Douaou (Ghalioungui 1963: 31). Certain Egyptian temples developed a reputation as healing centers. In the fifth century b.c., Herodotus, the famous Greek traveler, maintained that Egypt had the healthiest population in the world next to the Libyans, because of the state's commitment to health services. Egypt had a medical hierarchy consisting of three categories of practitioners: (1) the priest-physician or *wabw,* (2) the "lay physician" or *swnw,* and (3) the magician. Like the priest-physician, the ordinary physician followed the teachings of various sacred books. Lay physicians apparently functioned as state employees with medical appointments in various areas, including public works, residential areas, the military, burial grounds, religious sites, and royal palaces (Ghalioungui 1963: 106–13). Lay-physicians themselves were organized into a hierarchy consisting of the chief physician of the South and the North, chief physicians, physician inspectors, and physicians per se. The royal palace also had a medical hierarchy consisting of the Chief Physician of the King, the Chief of the Physicians of the Palace, and Court Physicians.

Some of the more influential physicians meddled in state politics. The financial remuneration received by physicians varied widely. In contrast to the palace physicians or physicians with rich clients, many physicians were little more than manual workers who basically earned the bare necessities of life. A few physicians in Egypt were female, and a woman physician known as Pesehet bore the title of "Lady Director of Lady Physicians" (Magner 1992: 28). Although Herodotus contended that among the Egyptians, "Every physician treats one disease, not many" (quoted in Ghalioungui 1963: 149), apparently some physicians specialized as surgeons and veterinarians (quoted in Ghalioungui 1963: 149). In some instances, physicians were assisted by aides, pharmacists, nurses, masseurs, physiotherapists, and bandagists (Nunn 1996: 132). In contrast to Mesopotamian medicine, Egyptian prescriptions were relatively precise. The Ebers papyrus lists about seven hundred drugs, which were made into more than eight hundred formulas (Magner 1992: 31).

Medical pluralism in China can be traced back to the Shang dynasty, which emerged approximately between the eighteenth and sixteenth centuries B.C. along the middle course of the Yellow River and continued into the eleventh century B.C. Unshuld (1985: 25–27) identifies two forms of therapy during this period—*wu* therapy and ancestor therapy. The *wu* petitioned the divine ancestor Ti for good winds and rain for crops and attempted to ward off evil winds, which may have also been viewed as the source of sickness. Under ancestor therapy, the emperor functioned as the physician of his subjects during epidemics and other catastrophes but was assisted in this task by various diviners.

Beginning with the Chou dynasty (1050–256 B.C.), the Chinese system of medical pluralism consisted of two broad categories of healers: state-employed physicians and folk healers. Physicians consisted of two types: court physicians and practitioners of public and street medicine. The rank and salary for government physicians were based upon their success rate. The imperial medical corps during the Chou dynasty included Food Physicians, Physicians for Simple Diseases, Ulcer Physicians, Physicians for Animals, and Chief-of-Physicians (Magner 1992: 52). Although most physicians trained as apprentices, the Chinese state established medical schools in virtually every province of the empire. The Imperial College of Medicine consisted of about thirty physicians attached to the imperial palaces. Ancient China had a stratum of physician-scholars who had access to the Imperial Library's collection of some twelve thousand works, lectured to their junior colleagues on these classic texts, and provided medical care to the elite class. Although physicians with scholarly training or aspirations tried to separate their practices from magicoreligious procedures, they sometimes compromised by resorting to the latter (Magner 1992: 53). Folk healers included surgeons, apothecaries, the *wu* and other magicoreligious practitioners, and fortunetellers.

During the Period of Warring States (481–221 B.C.), Confucianism and Taoism came to influence Chinese medical thought. Confucianism was associated with the "medicine of systematic correspondence"—a syncretic system that incorporated the concepts of *chi*, ying and yang, and the Five

Phases with homeopathic magic (Unshuld 1985: 52–67). This medical system "dominated Chinese medical literature and the approaches of educated practitioners and self-healing private citizens as well, at least among the upper strata" for most of Chinese history until the modern era (Unshuld 1985: 223). Taoism drew upon demonic medicine and pragmatic *materia medica* and introduced macrobiotics. Somewhat later Buddhist monks offered medical treatment to the Chinese people as part of their missionary efforts and as a fulfillment of their ethical obligation to assist human beings (Unshuld 1985: 139).

Medical pluralism in the Greco-Roman world expressed itself in part in the form of various medical sects. These included the rationalist or dogmatists who maintained that physicians should rely upon reason to discern the roots of health, disease, and human physiology; the empiricists who argued that theory is ultimately useless in medical practice; and the methodists who asserted that medical care could be achieved by adhering to a few simple rules that could be mastered in a half a year (Siraisi 1990: 4; Gourevitch 1998: 104–17). Galen, who was born in A.D. 129 in Pergamum in Asia Minor, attempted to rise above the medical sectarianism of the time by asserting that an imbalance of four bodily humors—hot, cold, dry, and moist—resulted in disease (Strohmaier 1998: 139–142).

Medical pluralism was well in place in the agrarian tributary regimes of the Arab world during the period A.D. 660–950 (Gran 1979). Islamic culture combined the Galenic theory of disease and prophetic medicine, which drew upon Mohammed's views of health and disease (Strohmaier 1998: 146–153). Conversely, like earlier Christian mystics, Muslim mystics also distrusted physicians and looked to God or Allah as the source of cures. Islamic culture began to establish hospitals and hospices in the early eighth century. These hospitals appear to have drawn their inspiration from the assistance offered to the poor and sick at Christian monasteries and other establishments. The services of these hospitals were initially subsidized by philanthropy and later by public funds and reportedly were free regardless of age, gender, or social status (Reynolds and Tanner 1995: 249). The Adubi hospital in Baghdad, built in A.D. 981, had twenty-four physicians. The largest hospital in the Islamic world, with a capacity of eight thousand beds, was established in Cairo in A.D. 1286 (Magner 1992: 138).

These hospitals provided their patients with a systematic treatment based upon Greek notions of humoral medicine that included exercises, baths, dietary regimens, and a comprehensive materia medica. Islamic medicine also relied upon manipulation, bone setting, cauterizing, venesection, and minor eye surgery, but devalued major surgery because of the religious prohibition on human dissection. The Al-Faustat hospital, built in A.D. 872, organized its wards on the basis of gender, illness, and the surgical procedure to be conducted. Furthermore, as in contemporary biomedical hospitals, "patients were required to wear special clothes provided by the hospital authorities while their clothes and valuables were kept in a safe place until their discharge" (Reynolds and Tanner 1995: 250). Whereas Islamic or Yunani medicine was sponsored by the courts, mystical medicine served urbanites in the larger towns, and the healing system associated with the Zanj movement catered to slaves, peasants, and some artisans.

CHAPTER 11

Biomedical Hegemony in the Context of Medical Pluralism

The emergence of capitalism in sixteenth-century Europe contributed to the development of a global world economy by the twentieth century. Biomedicine as an outgrowth of this development provided an ideological rationale by downplaying the roles that political, economic, and social conditions played in the production of disease. The emerging alliance around the turn of the century between the American Medical Association, which consisted primarily of elite practitioners and medical researchers based in prestigious universities, and the industrial capitalist class ultimately permitted biomedicine to establish political, economic, and ideological dominance over rival medical systems in the United States. Navarro asserts that the capitalist class came to support a version of medicine in which:

disease was not an outcome of specific power relations but rather a biological individual phenomenon where the cause of disease was the immediately observable factor, the bacteria. In this redefinition, clinical medicine became the branch of scientific medicine to study the biological individual phenomena and social medicine became the other branch of medicine which would study the distribution of disease as the aggregate of individual phenomena. Both branches shared the vision of disease as an alteration, a pathological change in the human body (perceived as a machine), caused by an outside agent (unicausality) or several agents (multicausality). (Navarro 1986: 166)

Biomedicine also achieved preeminence over alternative medical systems such as homeopathy in European societies and eventually throughout the globe. The argument on the part of homeopaths, for example, that disease could be best treated by administering small dosages of drugs that produced symptoms in a healthy person and by altering environmental conditions was incompatible with the reductionist, high-dosage drug treatment of biomedicine.

THE EMERGENCE OF BIOMEDICINE AS A GLOBAL MEDICAL SYSTEM

Historically biomedicine has played a central role in capitalist imperialism in efforts to maintain control of exploited populations. As Arnold (1993: 1396) asserts, "Western medicine was present from the outset and implicated in all the subsequent phases of colonialism: from exploration and conquest, to state formation and the exploitation of human and natural resources." Beginning in the 1880s, the major colonial powers embarked upon a project of political control over much of the world. The British Empire alone at its peak in the 1930s encompassed approximately one-fourth of the world's land area. A tiny European colonial elite dominated the native population with a combination of military might and administrative control. In contrast to the tributary nature of earlier states, the modern colonial state aimed to contribute to the development of productive resources and expanding markets.

Disease as a major obstacle to European expansion in Africa, Asia, and the Americas prompted the attachment of medical personnel to merchant marines and the creation of rudimentary hospital facilities at overseas trading posts. Both British and German colonies in Africa initially were served by a handful of physicians who were directly employed by trading companies and provided medical treatment to the colonizers. Medical missionaries also functioned as early purveyors of health care in the colonies. Christian missionaries, for example, first introduced allopathic medicine into the territory of what today is called Tanzania in the second half of the nineteenth century (Turshen 1984: 140).

Colonial states eventually, however, assumed responsibility for health care. Joseph Chamberlain, the British Secretary of State for Colonies, promoted the establishment of the London and Liverpool schools of medicine in 1899, noting that "the study of tropical disease is a means of promoting Imperial policies" (quoted in Doyal 1979: 240). Schools of tropical medicine were also established in Amsterdam, Paris, and Brussels (Banerji 1984: 258). Germany established colonial medical services in Tanzania initially to serve the army garrison stationed there, in part to counter indigenous resistance during the 1880s and 1890s, and later to provide health care for European settlers.

After World War I, Britain assumed control of colonial medical care in Tanzania. Four types of medical care were created in Tanzania during the period 1919–1961: (1) government services organized on the basis of a three-tiered structure of central, provincial, and district administration; (2) voluntary services, most of them missions; (3) employer-based (sisal plantations, mines, and factory) services; and (4) private practices that tended to be concentrated in urban areas and catered primarily to Europeans and a few privileged Africans. Although the colonial state implemented preventive measures in the form of public health programs, by and large colonial medicine tended to be highly curative in its orientation. In Tanzania, as Turshen observes,

Up to 72 percent of the health budget was spent on expensive curative facilities, as late as 1961. This is in part the origin of the "demand for curative medicine" identified by European physicians. But there were also factors connected with the wage-earning population that helped to determine the type of health service offered. The government adapted colonial medical services to the needs of private enterprise for a productive labor force. . . . Men with chronic diseases were likely to be dropped from the labor force or, if discovered on recruitment, not hired. This was especially true of tuberculosis, for which recruits were x-rayed routinely. (Turshen 1984: 149)

Secular biomedicine did not reach rural African communities in any form in many places until the 1930s, and sometimes even as late as the 1950s and 1960s (Vaughn 1991: 57). The system of indirect rule, whereby native leaders were used to carry out colonial policies at the local level, provided the administrative framework for implementing colonial medicine. As Comaroff (1993: 324) observes, "medicine both informed and was informed by imperialism in Africa and elsewhere. It gave validity of science to the humanitarian claims of colonialism, while finding confirmation for its own authority in the living laboratories enclosed by expanding imperial frontiers." Biomedicine also ascribed the poverty of African peoples to the diseases that they contracted as a result of appropriation of their lands and the exploitation of their labor power. When Tanzania finally gained independence in 1961, its medical services lacked native trained personnel because of the racist educational policies of the colonial government (Turshen 1984: 161).

Despite the fact that Chinese medicine is probably the world's oldest body of medical knowledge and tradition, dating back some four thousand years, Western medicine gained a strong foothold in China with the assistance of European and U.S. colonial powers in the nineteenth and early twentieth centuries. Medical missionaries began to establish allopathic hospitals and clinics in China as early as 1835 (Leslie 1974: 84). The European and North American missionary societies and churches that financed the establishment of hospitals did so more for evangelical reasons than because they aimed to provide "exemplary models of Western healing to China" (Unshuld 1985: 240). John Kenneth MacKenzie, a Scottish physician, established the first allopathic school in China in Tianjin in 1881, and foreign governments followed suit over the course of the next thirty years by establishing several other medical schools (Sidel and Sidel 1982: 23).

Rockefeller philanthropists sponsored medical and public health projects as an alternative means to missionaries and armies for opening up new markets in China. The Rockefeller Foundation took over the Peking Union Medical College from the missionary society that had established it. According to E. R. Brown (1979), Rockefeller campaigns against hookworm in not only China but also the Philippines, Latin America, the West Indies, Ceylon, Malaysia, Egypt, and other countries were "blatantly intended, first, to raise the productivity of the workers in underdeveloped countries, second, to reduce the cultural autonomy of these agrarian peoples and make them amenable to being formed into an industrial workforce, and third, to assuage hostility to the United States and undermine goals of national economic and political independence" (259). As elsewhere, biomedicine in prerevolutionary China tended to be urban-based and curative in its orientation.

The introduction of Western medicine, or what evolved into biomedicine, met with strong resistance in most underdeveloped countries as was made evident by the continued demand for traditional medical care. Christian missionaries in Africa opposed indigenous medicine on the grounds that traditional practitioners were allegedly witch doctors. Western physicians also denied that traditional medicine might have any benefits because "such an admission would run counter to the belief that Victorian civilization was the acme of human achievement" (Turshen 1984: 145). Colonial governments often feared indigenous medical systems because their communal orientation held the potential for local populations to organize opposition movements.

DOMINATIVE MEDICAL SYSTEMS AS REFLECTIONS OF SOCIAL RELATIONS IN THE LARGER SOCIETY

Medical pluralism in the modern world is characterized by a pattern in which biomedicine exerts dominance over alternative medical systems, whether they are professionalized or not. The existence of dominative medical systems in complex societies, however, predates capitalism. As Charles Leslie (1974), an anthropologist who has conducted extensive research on South Asian medical systems, observes,

All the civilizations with *great tradition* medical systems developed a range of practitioners from learned professional physicians to individuals who had limited or no formal training and who practiced a simplified version of the great tradition medicine. Other healers coexisted with these practitioners, their arts falling into special categories such as bone setters, surgeons, midwives, and shamans. However, the complex and redundant relationships between learned and humble practitioners, and between those who were generalists or specialists, full or part-time, vocational or avocational, naturalist or supernaturalist curers, is clarified by professionalization in the great tradition that defined the relative statuses of legitimate practitioners and distinguished them from quacks. (Leslie 1974: 74)

With European expansion, allopathic medicine or what eventually became biomedicine came to supercede in prestige and influence even professionalized traditional medical systems. Third World societies are characterized by a broad spectrum of humoral and ritual curing systems. Some of these, such as Ayurveda and Unani in India and traditional Chinese medicine, are associated with literate traditions and have schools, professional associations, and hospitals. Although the upper and middle classes resort to traditional medicine as a backup for the shortcomings of biomedicine and for divination, advice, and luck, it constitutes the principal form of health care available to the masses. As Frankenberg (1980: 198) observes, "The societies in which medical pluralism flourishes are invariably class divided."

India, the most populated country second only to China, is an outstanding example of a complex society exhibiting a dominative system. Leslie (1977) delineates five levels in the Indian dominative medical system: (1) biomedicine, which relies upon physicians with M.D. and Ph.D. degrees from prestigious institutions; (2) "indigenous medical systems," which have within their ranks practitioners who have obtained degrees from Ayurvedic, Unani, and Siddha medical colleges; (3) homeopathy, whose physicians have completed correspondence courses; (4) religious scholars or learned priests with unusual healing abilities; and (5) local folk healers, bonesetters, and midwives. While approximately 150,000 physicians practiced biomedicine in India in the early 1970s, they were outnumbered by an estimated 400,000 practitioners of the three principal traditional medical systems, namely, "Ayurveda, which is based upon Sanskrit texts; Unani, or Greek medicine, based upon Arabic and Persian texts; and Siddha, a tradition of humoral medicine in South India" (Leslie 1977: 513). In 1972, of some 257,000 state-registered practitioners of traditional medicine, about 93,000 had at least four years of formal training. At the same time, in addition to ninety-five biomedical colleges, India had ninety-nine Ayurvedic colleges, fifteen Yunani ones, and a college of Siddha medicine. Many of the traditional medical schools were small and poorly equipped, but twenty-six of them were affiliated with universities and ten offered postgraduate programs. Modern Ayurvedic medicine is drastically different from the system delineated in its classic texts. Indeed, it has a long tradition of syncretism, which has drawn heavily upon the

Galenic (Unani) concepts of Islamic medicine. Both professionalized Ayurvedic and Unani medicine have incorporated aspects of biomedicine. Many Ayurvedic colleges have been converted into biomedical ones, whereas others are trying to return to a more pristine tradition (Taylor 1976: 290). Although homeopathy entered India as a European import, the opposition to it by the British-dominated biomedical profession spared it association with colonialism (Leslie 1977: 513). Homeopathic practices have become a standard part of Ayurvedic medicine.

During the late nineteenth century, nobles, philanthropists, and caste and religious associations supported the establishment of Ayurvedic colleges and health facilities throughout India. After independence the Indian ruling elite promised to take active steps to make the benefits of health services available to the masses, particularly to peasants and workers. For this purpose they also promised a revival and strengthening of certain traditional medical systems, including Ayurveda (Banerji 1984). As Frankenberg (1981: 124) asserts, however, such elite support for traditional medicine is really only a "surface phenomenon" in that members of the ruling class actively rely primarily upon biomedicine for treatment of their own ailments, and most government funds for health education and services are allocated to biomedicine. It appears that the populist, anti-imperialist rhetoric characteristic of elite support for traditional medicine was primarily intended to deflect popular unrest about oppressive social conditions rather than to try to eradicate the conditions contributing to widespread disease in India and other underdeveloped countries. At any rate, as part of an effort to legitimize the professionalized traditional medical systems, in 1970 the Indian government did establish the Central Council of Indian Medicine as a branch of the Ministry of Health for the purposes of registering indigenous physicians, regulating education and practice, and fostering research (Leslie 1974: 101). Leslie succinctly summarizes the contradictory role that traditional medical systems play in South Asia and elsewhere:

[Traditional] physicians . . . are sometimes painfully aware that cosmopolitan medicine [or biomedicine] dominates the Indian medical system, yet a substantial market exists for commercial Ayurvedic products and for consultations with practitioners. The structural reasons that medical pluralism is a prominent feature of health care throughout the world are that biomedicine, like Ayurveda and every other therapeutic system, fails to help many patients. Every system generates discontent with its limitations and a search for alternative therapies. (Leslie 1992: 205).

Whereas some anthropologists such as Leslie have examined medical pluralism at the societal level, Paul Brodwin (1996) examines medical pluralism in the Haitian village of Jeanty (pseudonym). In addition to access to biomedicine or "metropolitan medicine," the villagers turn to various other practitioners and healing systems in their search for better health. These include herbalists, bonesetters, midwives, the cult of Roman Catholic saints, Voodoo priests, and Pentecostal ministers. Morality and medicine are intricately intertwined in rural Haiti and poses questions of innocence or guilt. Brodwin asserts:

People must constantly choose which gods to worship, and which forms of healing power and moral legitimation to accept, and they know the practical consequences of embracing one over the other. People know that distaining the *lwa* [Voodoo gods] allies them with the centralized Catholic Church: a traditional source of legitimation and advance. They know that fundamentalist conversion leads away from local allegiances and would propel them into a transnational space, politically centered in North America (Brodwin 1996: 199).

In another study of medical pluralism in Haiti, Singer and co-workers (1988) examined the efforts of Haitian women to receive biomedical treatment for folk illness. Knowing Western-trained physicians scoff at folk health beliefs, the women present their symptoms in terms that are meaningful to physicians while still retaining their own beliefs about the sources of their ailment.

Anthropologists have tended to examine medical systems that invariably are directly or indirectly dominated by biomedicine. The U.S. dominative medical system consists of several levels that tend to reflect class, racial/ethnic, and gender relations in the larger society (Baer 1989). In rank order of prestige, these include (1) biomedicine; (2) osteopathic medicine as a parallel medical system focusing on primary care; (3) professionalized heterodox medical systems (namely, chiropractic, naturopathy, and acupuncture); (4) partially professionalized or lay heterodox medical systems (e.g., homeopathy, rolfing, and reflexology); (5) Anglo-American religious healing systems (e.g., Spiritualism, Christian Science, Seventh Day Adventism, and evangelical faith healing); and (6) ethnomedical systems (e.g., Southern Appalachian herbal medicine; African-American ethnomedicines, Hispanic ethnomedicines such as *curanderismo, espiritismo, Santeria*, and Native American healing systems. As a result of financial backing of initially corporate-sponsored foundations and later the federal government for its research activities and educational institutions, biomedicine asserted scientific superiority and clearly established hegemony over alternative medical systems. Although American biomedical physicians continue to exert a great deal of control over their work, some scholars have argued that they have been undergoing a process of "deprofessionalization" or even "proletarianization." Haug (1975: 197) argues that three forces may be contributing to this process: the computerization of diagnosis and prognosis; the emergence of new health occupations, such as physicians' assistants and nurse practitioners, which have assumed many of the task carried out by the physician in the past; and a growing public awareness of health matters and an associated distrust of biomedicine's limited ability to address a wide variety of diseases, particularly chronic ones. McKinlay and Arches (1985) argue that as a result of the bureaucratization that is being forced on biomedical practice by the logic of capitalist expansion, physicians are being "proletarianized" or becoming glorified workers, largely because of their still relatively high incomes. Before World War II, solo practitioners dominated American biomedicine, and the American Medical Association served their entrepreneurial interests well. Berliner (1982) asserts that between 1900 and 1970 biomedicine functioned as an "industrial mode of production" carried out by competing practitioners who produced a commodity purchased by patients.

In the past three decades, the political clout of the AMA has been diffused by various organizations of specialists. The house of biomedicine has been split into two establishments: the AMA and the hospital doctors—those physicians who are employees in high-prestige teaching hospitals, university hospitals, government hospitals, research centers, and health corporations. In other words, an increasing number of physicians are becoming salaried employees of massive medical empires under private or state control, a development that has contributed to the emergence of a "monopoly mode of production" in biomedicine (Berliner 1982: 172). American biomedicine has evolved into a big business in which health care has become increasingly concentrated in large health care corporations and medical centers. Some scholars see biomedicine as embedded within a "medical-industrial complex" (Wohl 1984). The penetration of capital into health care has become a highly contradictory process. As Krause succinctly observes,

Capitalism itself is divided . . . between the few sectors that make money as costs rise—medical technology, drugs, hospital supply—and the majority, which suffer increases in health coverage costs. The state acts with the majority of capitalist sectors and is gradually restricting for-profit medicine. Doctors thriving as owners of for-profit settings are already beginning to lose their advantage as regulation tightens (Krause 1996: 8).

Despite the tendency toward growing monopolization and concentration in biomedicine, other medical subsystems persist and even thrive, although often under precarious conditions. Indeed, biomedicine's dominance over rival medical systems has never been absolute. The state, which primarily serves the interests of the corporate class, must periodically make concessions to subordinate social groups in the interests of maintaining social order and the capitalist mode of production. As a result, certain heterodox practitioners, with the backing of clients and particularly influential patrons, were able to obtain legitimation in the form of full practice rights (e.g., osteopathic physicians, who may prescribe drugs and perform the same medical procedures as biomedical physicians) or limited rights (e.g., chiropractors, naturopaths, and acupuncturists). Lower social classes, racial and ethnic minorities, and women have often utilized alternative medicine as a forum for challenging not only biomedical dominance but also, to a degree, the hegemony of the corporate class in the United States as well as other advanced capitalist societies.

Regardless of the society, biomedicine attempts to control the production of health care specialists, define their knowledge base, dominate the medical division of labor, eliminate or narrowly restrict the practices of alternative practitioners, and deny laypeople and alternative healers access to medical technology. Despite the hegemonic influence of biomedicine, alternative medical systems of various sorts continue to function and even thrive not only in the countryside but also in the cities of the world, including those in the United States. Ultimately, the ability of biomedicine to achieve dominance over competing medical systems is dependent upon support from "strategic elites" (or certain businesspeople, politicians, and high-level government bureaucrats) (Freidson 1970). Biomedicine is unable to establish complete hegemony in part because elites permit other forms of therapy to exist but also because patients seek—for a variety of reasons—the services of alternative healers. Because of the bureaucratic dimensions of biomedicine and the iatrogenic situations or mishaps occurring in the course of biomedical treatment, alternative medicine under the umbrella of the holistic health movement has made a strong comeback even in North America and Western Europe. This eclectic movement incorporates elements from Eastern medical systems, the human potential movement, and New Ageism as well as earlier Western heterodox medical systems.

Alternative medical systems often exhibit counterhegemonic elements that resist, often in subtle forms, the elitist, hierarchical, and bureaucratic patterns of biomedicine. In contrast to biomedicine, which is dominated ultimately by the corporate class or state elites, folk healing systems are more generally the domain of common folk. Unfortunately, according to Elling (1981b: 97), "Traditional medicine has been used to obfuscate and confuse native peoples and working classes." Ethnomedical practitioners in the modern world have shown an increasing interest in acquiring new skills and use certain biomedical-like treatments or technologies in their own work, a process in which they often inadvertently adopt the reductionist perspective of biomedicine. Many Third Word peoples receive regular treatment from injection doctors and advice from pharmacists who indiscriminately sell antibiotics and other drugs over the counter. Many Ecuadorians now purchase natural medicines, which often are advertised on radio programs and commercially prepared in advanced capitalist countries, rather than utilizing indigenous herbal remedies (Miles 1998). In essence, biomedicine, commercialized alternative remedies, and traditional medicine, despite antagonistic relations between them, exhibit a great deal of overlap and even fusion.

The growing interest of corporate and governmental elites in alternative medicine is related to the cost of high-technology biomedicine. Even in countries such as Hong Kong, where explicit financial and/or legal support for traditional medicine is absent, governments often prefer to support traditional medicine because they recognize that it takes some of the strain off Western doctors in dealing with self-limiting diseases or diseases that tend to run their natural course without treatment (Topley 1976). Moreover, in the urban setting, traditional medicine minimizes the trauma of acculturation associated with the familiar cycle of capital penetration, import-substituting industrialization, and rural to urban migration of the peasant population. Singer has found that *espiritismo* often helps its Puerto Rican clients deal with social adjustments associated with migration to the United States and to deal with related conditions such as alcoholism. In essence, traditional medicine is assigned to address many of the stresses associated with capitalist development that are not easily garnered into the diagnostic categories and treatment approaches of biomedicine.

SHAMANISM AND OTHER INDIGENOUS HEALERS' ENCOUNTERS WITH THE WORLD SYSTEM

Whereas the shaman tends to be an integral part of indigenous societies as both a magicoreligious practitioner and a healer, the occupant of this role generally poses a threat to the priest and the physician in state societies, including capitalist ones. The shaman is a representative of an earlier, more egalitarian, and more democratic social order, while the latter two figures tend to function as hegemonic agents of state religion and medicine, respectively. Biomedical practitioners often accuse indigenous healers of perpetuating superstitious behavior and engaging in sorcery. Based upon his examination of medical pluralism in Bolivia, Bastien describes a scenario that resembles the encounter of Western medicine or biomedicine in many other parts of the world:

After the Spanish conquest of Central and South America, ethnomedical practitioners were forbidden to function as such because their curing techniques were considered heretical. Around the middle of this century, doctors and pharmacists in Bolivia pressured the Bolivian legislature to outlaw ethnomedical practices by requiring licenses. Although a few noted middle-class herbalists obtained licenses, others were unable to and were jailed. (Bastien 1992: 19)

In a similar vein, Janzen (1978: 51) reports that colonial authorities as late as 1956 rounded up village healers in the Kibunzi and Mbanza Mwembe region of Zaire when relatives removed a patient in order to receive indigenous medical care.

With the encroachment of the frontier in the United States, shamanism underwent a rapid decline among the Washo Indians of the Intermountain West. Siskin (1984: 171–72) reports that only ten Washo shamans remained in 1939, and in 1956 there was only one, Henry Rupert, who died in 1973. Rupert, who spent much of his life in white society as a printer, hypnotist, farmer, and entrepreneur, incorporated Hindu and Hawaiian personages into his pantheon of spirit guides and was the first Washo to eschew a belief in sorcery. In contrast to Rupert, John Frank, a Washo healer in his nineties in the early 1980s, was never in Siskin's (1984: 201) view a "full-fledged shaman," in large part because he was an elderly man when he began to doctor in 1974 after having watched Rupert cure over the years.

Although shamans and other indigenous healers historically have been suppressed in state societies, they have often adopted entrepreneurial characteristics with exposure to a capitalist market economy. While Siskin (1984: 68) provides no direct evidence to this effect, this may have been what occurred among the Washo when he reports that shamans "knew no lack in a tribe which suffered not infrequent shortage of food and in which paucity of material goods is characteristic." During the contact period, shamans exploited Washo fear of sorcery to the limit. According to Siskin (1984: 180), peyotism, a syncretic, introversionist religion that views peyote as the transformative sacrament of Native American peoples, offered the Washo an escape from their "long-standing antipathy and simmering resentment against shamans."

The matter of fees has also become a controversial issue among the !Kung. As several !Kung shamanistic healers began to receive goods or cash for treating members of other ethnic groups, they came to expect the same from their own people (Katz 1982). Kaw Dwa, a healer who has a reputation of having strong *num*, reportedly gives special attention to patients who pay for his services at "professionalized" dances. Elsewhere in Africa, Anthony Thomas (1975: 271) observes that in Kenya "traditional and illegal practitioners are doing very well financially. Healing for profit is much more lucrative than growing crops and raising livestock." Eduardo Calderon Palomino, a healer representing the north coastal Peruvian tradition of *curanderismo* and the subject of publications and films by anthropologist Douglas Sharon, has become a renowned figure by conducting performances for foreign tourists in his community as well as participating in New Age workshops abroad (Joralemon 1990). As a result of these activities, Calderon has been able to build a restaurant and a tourist hostel across from his home and to better provide for his large family. Lest anthropologists judge this eclectic, postmodern shaman too harshly, Joralemon argues that

it would be hypocritical for anthropology to scorn others for profiting from traditions in other cultures. Our livelihood too is earned on the basis of a Western fascination with other cultures. We, like the tour operator, are in the business of exploiting our informants for profit; the principal difference is that we legitimize our activities by reference to the pursuit of scientific knowledge and produce publications in place of travel opportunities. (Joralemon 1990: 105)

Despite the existence of numerous instances of pecuniary activities on their part, indigenous healers also exhibit counterhegemonic tendencies within the context of the capitalist world system. Michael Taussig (1987) maintains that shamans mediate divisions of caste and class relations in modern societies. In his highly acclaimed *Shamanism, Colonialism, and the Wild Man*, he presents a detailed portrayal of shamanic responses to colonial and neocolonial domination in multiethnic Colombia. Shamanism survives because it recreates the egalitarian and democratic ethos of indigenous society by allowing patients to live in the shaman's home. According to Taussig,

Unlike the situation of a priest or a university-trained modern physician, for example, whose mystique is facilitated by his functionally specific role defining his very being, together with the separation of his workplace from his living quarters, the situation in the shaman's house is one where patients and healer acquire a rather intimate knowledge of each other's foibles, toilet habits, marital relations, and so forth. (Taussig 1987: 344)

As opposed to the biomedical physician, who often is viewed as a demigod, the shaman is a mere mortal who possesses a certain gift or skill, namely, that of healing.

Ayahuasca shamanism refers to a healing system involving the use of ayahuasca, a plant with hallucinogenic properties, which has developed in urban contexts in west Amazonia over the past three hundred years. Gow (1994: 91) maintains that it

evolved as a response to the specific colonial history of western Amazonia and is absent precisely from those few indigenous peoples who were buffered from the processes of colonial transformation caused by the spread of the rubber industry in the region.

Town shamans, who are *mestizos*, insist that they have obtained their knowledge from the forest Indians. Conversely, the forest Indians look downriver for the source of shamanic power, to the cities of Pucallpa and Iquitos and to the *ayahuasca* shamans of the lower Ucayali and Amazon rivers. In contrast to their view that the *ayahuasca* shamans possess the curing power of the forest spirits, they look at their own shamans as relatively impotent. On the surface, *ayahuasca* shamanism appears to function as a hegemonic force in that the forest Indians have adopted a prototypical colonial mentality. Conversely, the counterhegemonic component of shamanism lies in the belief that the forest spirits afflict people with disease as a punishment for environmental damage caused to their domain. Curing entails a mediation of this imbalance through use of ayahuasca—a vine that as both cultigen and wild plant symbolizes the transition from domesticated space to full forest. In essence, as Gow (1994: 104) observes, the "historical sorcery of ayahuasca shamanism is centered on that spatial category that connects the forest and the city: the river."

Shona spirit mediumship constitutes yet another example of how shamanism serves to mediate social tensions in colonial and postcolonial societies. Spirit mediums played an instrumental role in assisting guerrillas belonging to the Zimbabwe African National Liberation Army (ZANLA) to liberate the Shona people from the oppressive rule of the white-dominated Rhodesian colonialist state (Lan 1985). Guerillas lived with a number of spirit mediums in the Zambezi Valley and regularly received advice from their ancestors that was mediated by the mediums who favored the return of appropriated lands to the peasantry. After the revolution, many mediums encouraged women to participate in local politics. Unfortunately, various mediums feel that they were not properly rewarded for their support of the revolution after independence. According to Lan (1985: 221), the Traditional Medical Practitioners Act implemented by the Zimbabwean state "entrenches in law precisely that control over the mediums that political authorities of the past, whether chiefs or district commissioners, attempted to enforce in order to discredit mediums who opposed them."

In the case of another postrevolutionary society, the Soviet Union beginning in the 1930s waged a campaign against shamans among the North Khanty villagers of Siberia, labeling them "deceivers" and *kulaks* (rich peasants) (Balzer 1991). While some shamans went underground or turned to drinking, others rebelled against the repressive tactics of the Soviet state. Whereas in the past Khanty shamanic séances tended to be community events at which the patient received moral support from a large number of people, during the Soviet period they evolved into sessions which generally were conducted in secret or with only a few family members present (Balzer 1987: 1091). In 1990 Vladimir Alekssevich Kondakov, who identifies himself as a Sakha shaman (*oiuun*), established the Association of Folk Medicine as part of a revival of shamanism in Siberia (Balzer 1993).

Taman shamanism or *balienism* in Borneo represents an example of what Winkelman termed the shaman/healer in the context of the capitalist

world system (Bernstein 1997). *Baliens* tend to be women who have re-
covered from some sort of chronic emotional problem. They belong to
healing societies but do not generally associate with one another on an
informal basis. Some *baliens* do not actively engage in healing or attend
other ritualistic events. Shamanism has also become closely associated
with women in other state societies, such as eastern Asia, where, as Vitebsky (1995a: 118) observes, "it has been subordinated to a Buddhist or
Confucian High Culture which is more male-centered."

As noted earlier, many New Agers in advanced capitalist countries,
particularly the United States, are proponents of neoshamanism, a movement that idealizes the shamanistic practices of Native American and
other indigenous peoples around the world. Vitebsky graphically describes the juxtaposition of traditional shamanism and neoshamanism:

In the jungles and the tundra, shamanism is dying. An intensely local kind of
knowledge is being abandoned in favour of various kinds of knowledge which
are cosmopolitan and distant-led. Meanwhile, something called shamanism
thrives in western magazines, sweat lodges and weekend workshops. The New
Age movement, which includes this strand of neo-shamanism, is in part a rebellion
against the principle of distant-led knowledge (Vitebsky 1995b: 182).

Anthropologist Michael Harner, a former professor at the New School
for Social Research, has become a New Age guru as a result of his popular
book *The Way of the Shaman* (1990) and his creation of the Foundation for
Shamanic Studies. He became intimately acquainted with shamanism
among the Jivaro and Conibo Indians of South America and has developed a synthesis of universal shamanic practices, called "core shamanism," which he teaches in workshops. On its website, the Dance of the
Deer Foundation (est. 1979), based in the Santa Cruz Mountains of California, advertises its commitment to maintaining the shamanic traditions
of the Huichol Indians of northern Mexico through seminars, pilgrimages,
and study groups in the United States, Mexico, Europe, and other parts
of the world. Some Native Americans, however, regard New Age dabbling
into shamanism as an illegitimate and imperialist appropriation of their
cultures. In early 1994, the National Congress of American Indians declared war on "non-Indian 'wannabes', hucksters, cultists, commercial
profiteers and self-styled shamans" (quoted in Glass-Coffin 1994: A48) for
exploiting, distorting, and abusing American Indian religious traditions.

In contrast to the traditional shaman who is oriented to serving the
group, New Age neo-shamans focus upon serving the individualistic endeavors of their clients to "journey" to higher states of spiritual consciousness. Kehoe (2000: 33) asserts that neo-shamanism "offers a haven
for educated, middle-class Westerners uncomfortable with conventional
institutionalized congregations and unwilling to limit themselves to

strictly materialistic pursuits." She also argues that neo-shamanistic workshops offer their clients "gregariousness, relief from anxiety, and myths to daydream with" (Kehoe 2000: 34). In his observations of neo-shamanistic workshops in Denmark and England, Jakobsen (1999: 167–203) found that many of the participants were physicians, nurses, social workers, psychologists, counselors, and teachers. Despite its lament that the modern world has lost a sense of community, neo-shamanism has become part and parcel of the capitalist marketplace in which a wide array of religious and healing systems offer people salvation either in the next life or in this life. For the most part, neo-shamans serve clients in group or private settings, but not as members of specific congregations per se. Moreover, in keeping with capitalist market dictates, neoshamanism is sold as a set of consumer items (e.g., tapes, CDs) through mass advertising at a profit.

The "Therapeutic Alliance" in Third World Countries

Despite numerous instances of state hostility to indigenous or traditional healers, many Third World countries have been turning to an increasing reliance on them as a cheap alternative to capital-intensive, high technology biomedicine. Indeed, despite the emergence of biomedicine as a global medical system, indigenous healers reportedly continue to function as the major health care providers for about 90% of the world's rural population (Bastien 1992: 96). Joseph W. Bastien, an anthropologist who has done extensive ethnographic work in Bolivia, presents a relatively favorable report of the efforts to integrate biomedicine and traditional medicine in that country. He asserts that a "dialogue between doctors and shamans would provide doctors with an open-mindedness important to exploring the multifariousness of healing, and it would provide shamans with scientific knowledge in order to be a bit more earthly" (Bastien 1992: 101). In a similar vein, Sharon (1978) maintains that the only realistic solution to health problems in northern Peru rests upon a paramedical program that entails "reciprocity between traditional and modern medicine."

In contrast, Phillip Singer, a critical medical anthropologist, views the "therapeutic alliance" between biomedical and traditional practitioners as a manifestation of a "new colonialism." He contends that under this arrangement, traditional healing functions as a "mediation or 'brokerage' process between the individual and the dominant values, institutions, powers, agencies, etc., that exist and with which he has to cope" (P. Singer 1977: 19–20). Singer also maintains that medical anthropologists who collaborate with biomedical practitioners, particularly psychiatrists, within the context of the "therapeutic alliance" contribute to the status quo by offering symptom relief for patients. He views "good health" as "largely a function of the social and economic conditions that make possible the conditions for good health, i.e., nutrition, housing, water, sewage, etc." (P. Singer 1977: 14). In a similar vein, Velimirovic emphasizes the need for structural changes that complement the utilization of indigenous healers:

There is no need to either copy a Western model or to settle for low-quality care in coping with the health problems of the developing world. Indigenous healers might perhaps be incorporated into a modern health care system in some places, but they are not the only answer to lack of coverage. What is needed is the imagination and the will to institute basic, low-cost health measures appropriate for a particular country's culture and level of socioeconomic development. For these measures to succeed, transformation of the social structure may be a precondition. (Velimirovic 1990: 59)

In essence, an emancipatory "therapeutic alliance" ultimately requires an egalitarian relationship between representatives of various medical systems, one that transcends the hierarchical structure of existing dominative medical systems associated with the capitalist world system.

THE HOSPITAL AS THE PRIMARY LOCUS OF BIOMEDICINE

The modern hospital has become the primary locus for the practice of biomedicine as well as certain alternative medical systems, such as homeopathy in Britain, Ayurvedic medicine in India, and herbal medicine and acupuncture in China. Michel Foucault (1975) views the hospital as a significant site of what he terms the "clinical gaze." He describes how the Hospital Generale, which was constructed in Paris in 1656, served as an institution where the poor, sex workers, vagabonds, and the mentally disturbed were institutionalized and subjected to various medical experiments and surveillance. In the United States at the turn of the century, hospital construction became a favored form of philanthropy on the part of very rich donors such as Johns Hopkins, Cornelius Vanderbilt, Eli Whitney, and John D. Rockefeller. By contrast, the state in many European countries funded the erection and operation of hospitals.

The basic structure of the contemporary hospital had taken shape by the 1920s (Raffel 1994: 125). The hospital is an elaborate social system, interlaced with smaller social systems and a wide variety of other occupational subcultures. Melvin Konner (1993: 29), a prominent physician-anthropologist, describes hospitals as "our modern cathedrals, embodying all the awe and mystery of modern science, all its force, real and imagined, in an imposing edifice that houses transcendent expertise and ineffable technology." Another anthropologist describes the hospital in less glowing terms by referring to it as an institution that views patients as lucrative sources of revenue as well as one that at various times functions as jail, school, factory, or resort hotel (Grossinger 1990: 28). At any rate, the hospital has become the locus of technological biomedicine. It resembles a bureaucratic assemblage of workshops that deliver a labor-intensive form of medical care. According to Georgopoulos and Mann (1979: 298), the authoritarian structure of the hospital "manifests itself in relatively sharp patterns of superordination-subordination, in expectations of strict discipline and obedience, and in distinct status differences among organizational members."

U.S. hospitals fall into one of three categories: (1) private community hospitals, (2) government hospitals, and (3) proprietary hospitals. Despite their purported nonprofit status, the first two types support capital accumulation by acting as "ideal conduits for the profits of drug companies, equipment manufacturers, construction and real estate firms, and financial institutions" (Himmelstein and Woolhandler 1984: 18). Furthermore, private community hospitals frequently share directors with profit-making health industries (Waitzkin and Waterman 1974: 109). These hospitals also provide an arena where physicians may charge high fees to their patients or third-party payers while retaining free access to sophisticated medical equipment that has been paid for at public expense through federal or state dollars.

Unfortunately, social scientific studies of hospitals have not given much attention to their governing boards of trustees. While boards generally do not involve themselves in the day-to-day operations of hospitals, their members, however, do possess control over hospital governing policy. In the United States, hospital boards tend to recruit members from local private elites.

"Analyzing the boards of trustees of these [voluntary community] hospitals, one sees less predominance of the representatives of financial and corporate capital, and more of the upper-middle class, and primarily of the professionals—especially physicians—and representatives of the business class. Even here, the other strata and classes, the working class and lower-middle class, which constitute the majority of the U.S. population, are not represented. Not one trade union leader (even a token one), for instance, sits on any board in the hospitals in the region of Baltimore" (Navarro 1976: 154).

An example of such domination is illustrated by a project that a critical medical anthropologist worked on in 1994. The project was designed to improve the ethnic, gender, and class diversity of the boards and staff of an association of hospitals in a New England city. The effort had the official endorsement of hospital directors, and meetings took place in the hospital association's plush offices with secretarial and staff support provided by the association. Over a several-month period a project that would have moderately changed the hitherto white male dominance of hospital boards of directors and managers while significantly improving hospital sensitivity to the ethnic heritages of patients was developed. The general need for the plan was presented at a daylong workshop with hospital trustees, managers, and leading staff. Publicly these hospital elites, most of whom were white males, gave full support for the effort to improve diversity. Based on this work, a grant proposal was written and submitted to a local community foundation to support implementation of the diversity plan. To the surprise of the project's planners, the community foundation reserved money for the grant but did not award it because they found that in their private conversations hospital elites expressed far less than full support for the proposed project.

The corporate class does not exert as much influence over the policies of hospital boards as it does over those of private health foundations, private medical schools, and even state medical schools. Its interests are represented by middle-level managers and other social actors who agree with the premises of a capitalist economy.

The board of trustees has overall responsibility over the hospital and in turn delegates the day-to-day management of the organization to the hospital administration. The medical staff controls matters concerning patient care and exercises substantial influence throughout the hospital organization. This dual authority lends itself readily not only to conflict between the hospital administration and its physicians, but also to a confusion of roles among other health personnel, particularly nurses. With the growing technological and organizational complexity of hospitals, however, an increasing degree of authority is being delegated to administrators, who all more and more likely to be businessmen rather than physicians.

Indeed, a declining percentage of physicians in the United States are self-employed, and an increasing percentage of them are employees of public agencies, hospitals, medical schools, and health maintenance organizations. Some social scientists refer to this trend as the "deprofessionalization" or "proletarization" of biomedicine. By these terms they do not mean to imply that that biomedical physicians resemble the typical worker. In fact, they continue to "maintain significant power by capitalizing and keeping control of patient recruitment while ceding other market-mediation functions to third parties" (Derber 1983: 591), such as insurance companies. Nevertheless, much of the work of hospital physicians, particularly in the United States, has increasingly become subject to cost controls, audits, and managerial and even patient evaluations (Schiff 2000).

Nevertheless, class struggle has become an overt aspect of the hospital. While the trend toward unionization in U.S. hospitals first occurred among its underpaid unskilled and semiskilled workers, it also spread to technicians, nurses, and even physicians. Indeed, various surveys indicate that physicians and medical students suffer from high levels of emotional distress due to their working conditions in hospitals (Morrow 2003: 67).

Factors serving to mitigate demands by unionized hospital workers, however, include the shift of the cost of higher wages to consumers and the willingness of administrators to arbitrate with unions in return for disciplined workers. Furthermore, professionalization continues to be seen by many health workers as a more viable approach for socioeconomic advancement, thus preventing them from forming an alliance with low-status health workers.

Although surgery continues to remain the focal activity of the hospitals, many U.S. community general hospitals now provide rehabilitation services, home care, and even primary care. In contrast to rural hospitals, urban hospitals have become big businesses that reflect the "segmentation of society into diverse ethnic, religious, occupational, and class groups" (Stevens 1986: 88). Indeed, an increasing percentage of urban hospitals are owned by large health care corporations oriented toward managed care—a form of health care that emphasizes cost-containment procedures that contribute to greater profit making.

Most underdeveloped countries have reproduced the pattern of hospital-based, highly technological, and curative biomedicine. National elites, which constitute the immediate beneficiaries of biomedicine, have worked in conjunction with international financial institutions and health organizations to consolidate the establishment of biomedicine in the Third World. According to Doyal (1979: 270), "Hospital development can . . . distort the whole balance of third world health expenditure and it is not uncommon to find up to half of the recurrent budget consumed by one or two big city hospitals." Ultimately, it could be argued that biomedicine indirectly kills people in rural areas and in urban slums by diverting a large percentage of health care resources from primary care and public health projects.

Despite its centrality as an organization of medical care, the hospital as such has not been the subject of much sociological or anthropological research. Social scientists conducting research in hospitals have tended to focus primarily on more microscopic settings, such as the physician-patient relationship. Much of this research discusses the process by which patients are stripped of their identity, preferences, and decision-making. Fortunately, as recounted in the following Closer Look, various sociologists have conducted ethnographic fieldwork in hospitals in the People's Republic of China. Gail E. Henderson, a sociologist, and Myron S. Cohen, a medical specialist on infectious disease, conducted fieldwork on the Second Attached Hospital of Hubei Provincial Medical College in the People's Republic of China (Henderson and Cohen 1984). The period from November 1979 to March 1980, when they conducted their fieldwork, is treated as the "ethnographic present"—a phrase that anthropologists use to refer to the time frame of a social setting as if it exists at the present moment rather than at the time of actual investigation. Joseph W. Schneider (2001) conducted fieldwork from December 1986 to April 1987 in a hospital in a North China city.

"A Closer Look"

A CHINESE HOSPITAL: A WORK UNIT IN A SOCIALIST-ORIENTED SOCIETY

The Second Attached Hospital complex, its staff dormitories, and various auxiliary buildings are situated on the outskirts of Wuhan, the fifth largest city in China. The medical college is adjacent to the hospital grounds. About two-thirds of the employees at the hospital belong to its attached *danwei* or work unit. The *danwei* functions as a sort of "urban village" that not only provides housing and other services but serves as the center of its members' social, political, and economic life. The hospital *danwei* is the "vehicle through which state and party health policies are implemented, and through which staff may communicate with higher-level authorities" (Henderson and Cohen 1984: 7).

About a third of the approximately 830 hospital workers live outside the complex. Furthermore, some residents of the *danwei* work outside it. The hospital complex includes day-care centers, schools, and businesses. An estimated 70% to 80% of the hospital and medical staff are married to each other. The standard apartment consists of a dining area, two bedrooms, and a small kitchen and bathroom. Access to desirable housing appears to be determined primarily by seniority in the work unit, luck, and a policy that attempts to restore those persecuted during the Cultural Revolution to the equivalent of their previous quarters. In contrast to residential patterns in capitalist societies, physicians often live next door to cooks or maintenance workers.

Personnel in the hospital and associated medical school are divided into three broad occupational categories: cadres, technicians, and workers. Cadres are state administrative and professional personnel and include physicians, nurses, scientists, teachers, and accountants. The category of technicians includes the small number of lab technicians. The category of workers includes cooks, electricians, health aides, plumbers, carpenters, mechanics, laundry workers, construction workers, and unskilled manual laborers. Prior to and particularly during the Cultural Revolution of the 1960s health professionals routinely were sent to work on public health projects in the countryside for extended periods of time. By the late 1970s only about 10% of the health professionals were given such assignments at any given point in time. The hospital is responsible for dispatching health workers for a fifteen-county area. As opposed to the past, when visiting physicians and nurses spent much time in rural communes or brigades, they now concentrate on the county hospitals that provide medical teaching for health workers in the communes and brigades.

The hospital has 580 beds and 830 staff, including some 300 physicians, 300 nurses, and 230 administrators, technicians, and workers. It consists of departments of infectious disease; surgery; internal medicine; pediatrics; obstetrics and gynecology; neurology and urology; radiology; combined Western and traditional medicine; dentistry; and ear, nose, and throat care. The hospital building is

laid out like a giant, three-story X, with a library providing a small fourth-story cap. The legs of the X are the hospital wards; at their intersection are a double staircase, auxiliary offices for radiology and laboratory tests, and a small pharmaceutical factory. Administrative offices are in a separate building. (Henderson and Cohen 1984: 47–48)

A special ward provides medical treatment for high-level cadres. A cancer unit is situated behind the hospital. In contrast to the United States, where hospital stays have been becoming shorter, the average length of stay for inpatients at the Second Attached Hospital is nineteen days. Although the hospital emphasizes biomedical treatment procedures, patients may request admission to the combined Western and traditional Chinese medicine ward. Other than two biomedically oriented physicians, the physicians on this ward are primarily practitioners of traditional medicine.

The hospital operates under the authority of the medical college, which in turn is under the authority of the provincial health and education bureaucracies. The hospital director is a Communist Party member and a physician. Vice-directors head the Departments of Medical Treatment and Medical Education and a third vice-director heads the departments of administration and general affairs. The administration of the medical college parallels that of the hospital. "Ultimately, the Chinese Communist party and its basic-level organizations at the hospital and medical college direct the implementation of all political and economic policies and address local concerns ranging from personnel appointments to teaching and research" (Henderson and Cohen 1984: 69).

Although work units are hierarchical units whose staff are assigned and whose leaders are appointed, some provisions have been made for feedback from *danwei* workers, as described here:

The one most commonly cited is "consultation with the masses" whenever major plans or policies are being considered. These consultations may take place in small work groups such as the infectious disease ward staff. For example, at one morning report the new economic campaign was explained to the staff and their opinions solicited. Strong feelings about the proposed staff-to-bed ratio were freely offered, and the staff planned to request another physician and nurse for the ward. To our knowledge, the ratio was not changed. . . . For decisions on the ward itself, staff members are generally given a chance to participate in discussions about an upcoming change. In addition to group discussions, special days for criticism are regularly scheduled. (Henderson and Cohen 1984: 74)

While the input sought by supervisory personnel from their subordinates hardly fulfills the socialist ideal of "proletarian democracy," it is hardly any less rigid than patterns of authority in U.S. work settings, including in hospitals. Nevertheless, as Henderson and Cohen (1984: 75) aptly observe, "such mechanisms may also conceal manipulation, acting to co-opt people into loyalty to the organization by giving them a sense of participation." Conversely, lower-echelon leaders do not generally frown upon complaints from their subordinates because they in turn can pass responsibility along to their superiors. The doctor-patient relationship follows the same basic hierarchical arrangement found among hospital personnel.

At the ward level, the doctor-nurse relationship is more egalitarian than in Western countries. In fact, with additional training, nurses may become physicians. Furthermore, health aides can become nurses, and technicians can become medical researchers. Virtually all physicians work under the direct supervision of hospital administrators. Their status in the larger society is considerably lower than it is in capitalist societies but has been increasing, because of the modernization policies of the state. Hospital and medical college administrators are generally Communist Party members and physicians, but some are not health professionals. Despite organizational constraints, physicians have a considerable amount of autonomy over their work—a pattern that undoubtedly is related to their knowledge base.

In his fieldwork on another Chinese hospital, Schneider (2001) focused on how family members and friends, referred to as *peibans*, contribute to the care of patients. In contrast to North American and European hospitals, members of the therapeutic management group cleaned patients' rooms, brought food from home, and fetched medicines and other supplies from outside the hospital, placed oxygen tanks in patients' rooms, and even delivered physicians' orders for lab tests to the appropriate places. Moreover, "if a patient was to be taken to another hospital for a special test, the work of contacting that hospital, making an appointment, and arranging transportation by means of some work unit's car all might be taken over by a family member" (Schneider 2001: 358). If the patient does not have enough family members to assist him or her, his or her work unit might send fellow workers to the hospital for this purpose. Such caretaking activities conform to both traditional Chinese familial duties as well as an emphasis on "revolutionary humanitarianism" (J. Schneider 2001: 361).

In contrast to the Soviet Union and the Eastern European countries, which prior to the collapse of Communist regimes had highly centralized ministries of health, the Chinese health care system is a relatively decentralized one in which financing and delivery are left to local political units on the county and village levels.

There is essentially now a three-tiered system with parallel structures in the urban and rural parts of the country. The rural areas' first tier is the Village Doctors (former Barefoot Doctors) and health workers offering primary care but with a major emphasis on preventive and sanitation work; the second tier, township hospitals serving 10 to 30 villages; and the third tier, county hospitals with senior doctors who deliver care for the most seriously ill. The urban counterpart begins with neighborhood and factory doctors, moves to the district hospitals, and then the municipal hospitals offering advanced services. Some of the latter are regional and national specialty centers (Rosenthal 1992: 294).

China has a number of separate insurance programs (Rosenthal 1992: 294-95). Slightly more than 2% of the population receives free medical care as a result of government employment or special status, such as college students and certain disabled veterans. Nearly 10% of the population is covered under labor insurance through national taxpaying enterprises. Whereas 48% of the rural population once received health care as members of medical cooperative plans, only 4.8% are now covered under such plans. The remainder is either enrolled in private insurance schemes or pays out of pocket.

Under Communist rule, the number of hospitals in China increased from 224 to 111,344, and the number of "county and larger hospitals" increased from 19 to 1,485 between 1952 and 1985 (Rosenthal 1992: 306). Economic reforms that began in the 1980s have contributed to the significant socioeconomic and concomitantly health differences between urban and rural areas. The ratio of expenditure in health care per capita between 1981 and the early 1990s increased from 3:1 to 5:1 (Hsiao 1995: 1053). In part due to an increased emphasis on market forces, the Chinese hospital exhibits multiple forms of ownership.

Hospital beds are not owned solely by the government; many are owned by large state enterprises. Among the 1.9 million beds in county or regional hospitals, close to 68% are owned by central and local governments, while the rest are mostly owned by various state enterprises. The Health Ministry and Provincial Health Bureaus have no regulatory jurisdiction over enterprise-owned hospitals (Hsiao 1995: 1051).

Private hospitals, especially as joint ventures with foreigners, have appeared in China and charge much higher fees, sometimes ten to twenty times higher than those charged in public hospitals (Hsiao 1995: 1048). Although peasants in the coastal areas often can afford a fairly high level of fee-for-service health, those in the interior generally cannot, as a result of programs of decollectivization and privatization. As Kleinman (1995: 23) observes, health care in China under the program of economic reform emphasizes "high-technology practice in urban centers and medicine as a business."

While in theory biomedicine and traditional medicine are on an equal footing in China, in reality the former has a considerably higher status and is funded more heavily than the latter. China has about three hundred thousand practitioners, and about 13% of the hospitals in 1986 reportedly focused on Traditional Chinese Medicine (Zheng and Hillier 1995: 1061). At Second Attached Hospital, traditional medicine functioned largely as an adjunct to biomedicine, but it is important to note that China does have hospitals that emphasize traditional medical treatment. Biomedical physicians with some traditional training, however, are in charge. Traditional medicine is more extensively employed in remote rural areas than in urban areas or in rural county hospitals close to urban areas. According to Rosenthal (1992: 302), "Western-style is . . . the major mode of medical practice in Mainland China and dominates health care in the urban areas of the country."

Nevertheless, the PRC government continues to adhere to a policy of combining biomedicine and traditional Chinese medicine. Zheng and Hillier (1995: 1061) report that the number of TCM practitioners and inpatient beds in TCM hospitals continues to rise in China.

As is the case in China, a country that in the process of embarking upon a modernization program has emulated capitalist practices and downplayed social ideals, medical pluralism in complex societies is characterized by a pattern in which biomedicine exerts dominance over alternative medical systems, whether they are professionalized or not. According to Leslie (1976: 512–513), biomedicine, regardless of the society, attempts to control the production of health specialists, define their knowledge base, regulate the biomedical division of labor, eliminate or narrowly restrict the practice of alternative healers, and deny laypeople and alternative healers access to medical technology. Despite biomedical imperialism, traditional medical systems continue to function and even thrive in the Third World. Indeed, many traditional practitioners have adopted various biomedical techniques, such as drug injections, as well as a pecuniary orientation. In his discussion of medical pluralism in Kenya, Thomas (1975: 271) observes "traditional and illegal practitioners are doing very well financially. Healing for profit is much more lucrative than growing crops and raising livestock."

PART IV

Toward an Equitable and Healthy Global System

CHAPTER 12

The Pursuit of Health as a Human Right: Health Praxis and the Struggle for a Healthy World

In what we see as the first phase of its development, critical medical anthropology (CMA) struggled primarily with issues of self-definition within academic medical anthropology. Now that CMA has come of age, its proponents have begun to grapple more seriously with strategies for creating healthier environments and more equitable health care delivery systems. CMA is ultimately concerned with *praxis* or the merger of theory and social action. Critical anthropology as the larger framework of CMA poses the questions of "anthropology for what?" and "anthropology for whom?" It wishes to move beyond an anthropology that all too often has viewed the subjects of its research as museum pieces or populations to be administered by bureaucratic organizations, such as governmental agencies and, more recently, transnational corporations. Critical anthropology strives to be part of a larger global process of liberation from the forces of economic exploitation and political oppression.

As part of this larger endeavor, a panel of critical medical anthropologists examined various actual and potential forms of health activism at the 1994 American Anthropological Association meeting, which had as its theme "Human Rights." This session, organized by Hans Baer and Kenyon Stebbins, was titled "Medical Anthropology in the Pursuit of Human Rights." Papers presented by panelists at this session recognized that critical medical anthropologists have questioned the reformist nature of conventional social science education, the co-optation of clinical anthropology, and the pro-physician bias of many biomedical intervention programs utilizing anthropological insights. The presenters, in so many words, felt that they should not stand idly by until "the revolution" arrives to address health change. Like other critical medical social scientists, many critical medical anthropologists work as health activists for women's health collectives, free clinics, ethnic community health centers, environmental groups, AIDS patient advocacy efforts, antismoking pro-health groups, national health care reform groups, and nongovernmental organizations (NGOs) in the Third World. These socially active critical medical anthropologists view access to a healthy environment and comprehensive and holistic health care as a human right, not a privilege or commodity accessible to only a privileged few.

THE VISION OF DEMOCRATIC ECOSOCIALISM AS THE BASIS FOR CREATING A HEALTHY WORLD

Given the authoritarian nature of Communist regimes in the Soviet Union, its satellites in Eastern Europe, China, North Korea, and other postrevolutionary societies, most North Americans as well as many people in other societies immediately conjure up negative images of the word socialism or find its association with the concept of democracy to be contradictory. Various commentators have interpreted the collapse of Communist regimes in most of these countries as evidence that capitalism constitutes the end of history and that socialism was a bankrupt social experiment that led to totalitarianism, forced collectivization, gulags, ruthless political purges, and inefficient centralized economies. Unfortunately, what these commentators often forget is that efforts to create socialist-oriented societies occurred by and large in economically underdeveloped countries. Russia, for instance, was an agrarian nation ruled by an absolutist czarist monarchy upon the eve of the Bolshevik Revolution in 1917. Indeed, the czarist regime did not abolish serfdom until the 1860s, as part of an effort to stabilize imperial rule in the wake of having lost the Crimean War to Britain. The efforts of Lenin, Trotsky, and other Bolsheviks to develop the beginnings of the process that they hoped would result in socialism occurred under extremely adverse conditions.

In addition to economic underdevelopment and the presence of a tiny trained working class, the new Soviet republic faced a civil war and the military intervention of fifteen foreign powers, including the United States, during the period 1918–1920. Furthermore, Russia at best had only rudimentary experience with parliamentary democracy along the lines of what existed in Western Europe and North America. Although the Bolsheviks, particularly under the dictatorial leadership of Stalin, managed to transform the Soviet Union into an industrial powerhouse by the 1930s, a variety of external factors, such as World War II and the arms race associated with the Cold War, and internal forces, such as a centralized command economy and a political system of one-party rule, prevented the development of socialist democracy in the Soviet Union. According to Schwartz (1991: 68), "in an isolated and relatively backward country, lacking democratic traditions, and where a militant but extremely small working class had been decimated by civil war, the bureaucracy was able to impose Stalinism as a noncapitalist crash modernization programme." With some modifications, the model of bureaucratic centralism was adopted by various other postrevolutionary societies after World War II, starting with China in 1949. The contradictory nature of Leninist regimes imploded first in Eastern Europe in 1989 and in the Soviet Union in 1991. China has embraced capitalist structures to the point that some experts argue that it now constitutes a state capitalist society in which, "though there is a high degree of public ownership, workers and peasants are exploited for the benefit of officials and managers" (Weil 1994: 17). With the loss of Soviet support, Cuba finds itself with a fragile economy that various U.S. businesspeople, including many of Cuban extraction, would like to take over. North Korea has developed into what appears to be an isolated dynastic system that in some ways resembles former archaic states.

Reconceptualizing Socialism

The collapse of Communist regimes has created a crisis for people on the left throughout the world. Many progressives had hoped that somehow these societies, which were characterized in a variety of ways (e.g., state socialism, transitions between capitalism and socialism, state capitalism, and new class societies), would undergo changes that would transform them into democratic and ecologically sensitive socialist societies. Various progressives have advocated shedding the concept of socialism and replacing it with terms such as "radical democracy" and "economic democracy." Stanley Aronowitz, as a major proponent of radical democracy, observes that

In contrast to conventional liberal, parliamentary democracy, radical democracy insists on *direct popular participation* in crucial decisions affecting economic life, political and social institutions, as well as everyday life. While this perspective does not exclude a limited role for representative institutions such as legislatures, it refuses the proposition according to which these institutions are conflated with the definition of democracy. In the workplace, radical democrats insist on extending the purview of participation both with respect to decisions ranging from what is to be made, to how the collective product may be distributed, as well as to how it should be produced. (Aronowitz 1994: 27)

While efforts to replace the term socialism with new ones are understandable given the fate of postrevolutionary or socialist-oriented societies. Therefore, it is our contention that progressive people need to come to terms with both the achievements and flaws of these societies and to reconceptualize the concept of socialism. According to Miliband (1994: 51), three core propositions define socialism: (1) democracy, (2) egalitarianism, and (3) socialization or public ownership of a predominant part of the economy. Although some areas of a socialist society would require centralized planning and coordination, democratic socialism recognizes the need for widespread decentralized economic, political, and social structures that would permit the greatest amount of popular participation in decision making possible. As Miliband (1994: 74) observes,

Socialist democracy would encourage the revolution of as much responsibility as possible to citizen associations at the grass roots, with effective participation in the running of educational institutions, *health facilities* [emphasis ours], housing associations and other bodies which have a direct bearing on the lives of people concerned.

In a similar vein, Boggs (1995: x) maintains that future strategies for change will need to be "more anti-bureaucratic, pluralistic, ecological, and feminist than anything experienced within the vast history of Marxian socialism."

Democratic ecosocialism rejects a statist, growth-centered, or productivist ethic and recognizes that we live on an ecologically fragile planet with limited resources that must be sustained and renewed for future generations. Common ownership, which would blend elements of centralism and decentralism, has the potential to place constraints upon resource depletion. McLaughlin (1990: 80-81) maintains "Socialism provides the conscious political control of those processes of interacting with nature which are left to the unconscious market processes under capitalism." The construction of democratic ecosocialism needs to be based upon a commitment to a long-term sustainable balance between sociocultural systems and the natural environment.

Democratic ecosocialism constitutes a vision that will entail a long-drawn-out process of struggle that will meet with resistance from the corporate class and its political allies globally for sometime to come. The maldistribution of resources on a global scale that capitalism produces is bound to keep alive ideals of equality, democracy, and socialism in oppressed classes. Under the present global economic system, the United States, as Bodley argues, constitutes the leading "culture of consumption."

Estimates vary widely, but it appears that by 1970, although their population contributed only about 6 percent of the world's total annual production, Americans consumed some 40 percent of the world's total annual production and 35 percent of the world's energy. By 1992, after two decades of worldwide economic growth, the United States, with less than 5 percent of the world's population, managed to slightly increase its per capita energy consumption and remained a major global consumer, accounting for 25 percent of the world's commercial energy. . . . In comparison, China virtually reversed the figures, with 20 percent of the world's population consuming 8 percent of the commercial energy. (Bodley 1996: 69)

For the immediate future, a "new socialist movement" needs to "focus on concrete questions of people's welfare, democracy, and survival" (Silber 1994: 266). Needless to say, health and eradication of disease are essential components of survival.

The Concept of Socialist Health

A meaningful discussion of socialist health is ultimately grounded in our ability to define socialism itself. As Segall (1983: 222) argues, "The concept of socialism is of no use to people seeking solutions within capitalism, but it is essential for those interested to see that system transcended." While disease is bound to occur under any mode of production, in that people will continue to be subject to certain hazards and infectious diseases in the natural environment and the physiological degeneration that inevitably accompanies aging, in socialist society it would be possible to resolve the basic tension between providing for human material needs and social psychological needs and for preserving the health of the people. Ultimately, any attempt to create a socialist health system and socialism per se must not, as Wright (1983: 124) so aptly asserts, focus "simply on the provision of various services by the state and various regulations of capital (as is the case under welfare capitalism), but also on the democratization of the forms of delivery of such services." In this process, critical medical anthropology has an important role to play in providing careful analysis of health care systems in the social context and in contributing to the direct application of this information in improving the quality of health care, accessibility of services, and popular empowerment within the health care domain.

TOWARD HEALTH PRAXIS AND A CRITICAL BIOETHICS IN MEDICAL ANTHROPOLOGY

From its beginnings as a subdiscipline of anthropology, medical anthropology has exhibited a strong applied orientation. Indeed, Weaver (1968: 1) defined medical anthropology as "that branch of applied anthropology which deals with various aspects of health and disease." As Lindenbaum and Lock accurately observe,

Often confronted with human affliction, suffering, and distress, fieldwork in medical anthropology challenges the traditional dichotomies of theory and practice, thought and action, objectivity and subjectivity. The very nature of the subject matter forces the researcher to seek out a position of informed compromise from which it is impossible to act. (Lindenbaum and Lock 1993: ix-x)

Whereas various critical anthropologists, such as Wolf (1969) and Stavenhagen (1971), urged the profession during the 1960s and 1970s to direct attention to establishing a theoretical framework for political engagement in the global system, anthropologists interested in health-related issues tended to seek avenues by which their research might be acceptable to mainstream international health agencies and biomedicine. Unfortunately, most applied anthropology historically has been and continues to be sponsored by colonial and neocolonial (e.g., the World Bank, the International Monetary Fund, the U.S. Agency of International Development, etc.) agencies and consequently fosters the maintenance of existing patterns of differential power. Sometime ago, Batalla (1966) asserted that much of the research done in Latin America on problems of public health neglected the social-structural causes of disease and malnutrition by focusing on issues such as ethnomedical beliefs, nutritional practices, and communication barriers between biomedical health providers and the target populations. Elsewhere, in commenting upon research on public health in Africa, Onoge (1975: 221) made a similar criticism of the reductionist tendency of both medical anthropologists and medical sociologists to restrict their analyses to social interaction in small groups.

In contrast to most applied work in medical anthropology, some anthropologists have provided their research skills to community-based health organizations. After working for a few years at the El Barrio Mental Health Center in Chicago (Schensul 1980), Steve and Jean Schensul went on to become two of the founders of the Hispanic Health Council in Hartford. Since Merrill Singer became its deputy director and its director of research, the council has evolved into a leading U.S. site of CMA-inspired health praxis.

Despite their commitment to health praxis, critical medical anthropologists need to develop this notion more fully. As Partridge (1987: 215) observes, praxis "signifies the theories and activities that affect human ethical and political behavior in social life." Various critical medical anthropologists in the past and particularly in recent years have noted the need for CMA to address matters of application. Scheper-Hughes (1990: 196) calls upon medical anthropologists to work "at the margins, questioning premises, and subjecting epistemologies that represent powerful, political interests to oppositional thinking." More recently, she has called upon anthropologists to adopt the "idea of an active, politically committed, morally engaged anthropology" (Scheper-Hughes 1995: 415). Contrary to Gaines's (1991: 232) assertion that critical medical anthropologists believe that "local initiatives can count for naught in the alleviation of human suffering," as has been noted a significant number of them have been and are involved in a wide array of forms of health activism, including ones at the local level.

In ensuring health as a human right, critical medical anthropologists are strong advocates of participatory democracy in the workplace, the body politic, and health care institutions. Regardless of whether their primary work occurs in academia, in a clinical setting, a community organization, or elsewhere, they need to function as proponents of "patient power." Ultimately, as Bolough (1981: 202) states, "the problem of alienated patient cannot be overcome until medical knowledge becomes social property in practice." Under a global system organized on the basis of meeting human needs rather than on profit-making, patients would in essence control the medical means of production and work in cooperation with physicians and other health experts toward the eradication of disease at both the personal and the community levels.

Conventional medical anthropologists often assume that critical praxis begins and ends with the advocacy of global transformation, since anything less would seem to amount to little more than system-maintaining reformism. While the provision of medical care as a welfare function can serve to dampen social protest, it is nonetheless true that by placing pressure on the system real gains can be achieved, such as a cleaner environment, a safer and less alienating workplace, and improved levels of access to socially and culturally more sensitive health care. Following this line of reasoning, a distinction must be drawn between two fundamentally different categories of social and health reform. Gorz (1973) accomplished this task in his differentiation between "reformist and nonreformist reform." He used the term *reformist reform,* or what Merrill Singer (1995a) calls "system-correcting praxis," to designate the conscious implementation of minor material improvements that avoid any alteration of the basic structure in the existing social system. Between the poles of reformist reform and complete structural transformation, Gorz identified a category of applied work that he labeled *nonreformist reform.* Here he referred to efforts aimed at making permanent changes in the social alignment of power. While system-correcting praxis tends to obscure the causes of suffering and sources of exploitation, system-challenging praxis is concerned with unmasking the origins of social inequity. Moreover, this latter form of praxis strives to heighten rather than dissipate social action.

System-challenging praxis that comprises the day-to-day work of critical practice constitutes a means for furthering drastic social transformation and is not an end point in change-seeking behavior. CMA praxis must emerge from recognition of a significant limitation in contemporary globalist approaches to social change. In world system, dependency, and related globalist theories, there is a tendency to assign all causality to the world capitalist system and, in the process, to ignore the impact of local-level actors. Critical medical anthropologists, in seeking to develop meaningful health praxis, attempt to identify opportunities for nonreformist reform ultimately as part and parcel of a long-drawn-out process of furthering global transformation.

As we have seen, medical anthropology has come to incorporate a wide array of concerns such as the role of disease in human biological evolution, paleopathology, indigenous medical systems, the political economy of health, biomedicine, medical pluralism, national health care systems, reproduction, and specific health problems. In addressing these topics, medical anthropologists have not only attempted to forge links between physical and cultural anthropology, but also with medical sociologists, medical psychologists, epidemiologists, physicians, nurses, public health people, and health policy-makers. Despite these efforts at cross-fertilization, medical anthropology has only begun to enter a dialogue with bioethicists—an endeavor which has tended to be dominated by theologians, philosophers, and lawyers. Perhaps the most explicit examples of this recent development are Richard Lieban's (1990) "Medical Anthropology and the Comparative Study of Medical Ethics" and Patricia A. Marshall and Barbara Koening's (1996) review essay titled "Bioethics in Anthropology: Perspectives on Culture, Medicine and Morality." In contrast to other medical anthropology textbooks, Donald Joralemon (1999: 101–17) includes a chapter on "Anthropology and Medical Ethics" in his recent textbook.

From a social scientific perspective, the term *bioethics* is problematic in that it implies a concern with the ethical concerns associated with one particular medical system, namely biomedicine (Fox 1990: 201). Jonsen (2000: 116) contends that "[t]he word *bioethics* had been invented in the late 1960s to designate a vision of the world in which scientific advances were linked to human and environmental values in an effort to create a global community." In keeping with anthropological interest in medical pluralism, Joralemon (1999: 103) employs the term "medical ethics" as a "cross-cultural concept that refers to the rules of conduct and underlying values that guide healing activities in each society" (Joralemon 1999:1 03). Conversely, historically the term *medical ethics* has tended to be associated with the particularistic concerns of the biomedical profession in regulating its own internal affairs and in dictating the nature of its interaction with patients and practitioners of other medical systems, such as homeopathy, osteopathy, and chiropractic. Despite various difficulties with the term *bioethics*, it is an identifier that has become well entrenched.

In this section, in conjunction with our commitment to health praxis, we wish to contribute to the development of a critical anthropological perspective on bioethics. This perspective seeks to transcend a strong tendency in bioethics to focus upon individualistic or familial concerns in a manner that conforms to Western, and perhaps more specifically, American culture. While individual as well as familial rights in the medical arena have their place, both bioethicists and medical anthropologists need to consider the rights of patients and their families as members of social groups, be they nation-states, social classes, racial and ethnic minorities, women, gays and lesbians, disabled people, people with AIDS, etc. A critical bioethics incorporates the concept of "social bioethics" as delineated by Gallagher et al.:

Social ethics links clinical or philosophical bioethics with ethnographically oriented social science. Moreover, social ethics [as does critical medical anthropology] connects microsocial perspectives with macrosocial knowledge. From its linkage of situational with societal factors, social bioethics gains a "political" leverage that clinical bioethics lacks (Gallagher et al. 1998: 169).

Most bioethicists who view health care as a human right tend to do so from a liberal and/or theological perspective that ultimately accepts the parameters of a capitalist political economy (McConnell 1982: 197–217; Churchill 1987; Devine 1996: 230–42; Terney 1999). To date, few U.S. bioethicists situate the struggle for universal health care within the larger endeavor of constructing an authentically democratic socialist world system or even the parameters of the U.S. political economy—one in which health care often is embedded in profit-making endeavors. Susan Sherwin (1997: 393), a feminist bioethicist, seeks to develop a critical bioethical perspective. She he argues that conventional bioethics is closely wedded to the power structures of the larger society:

For instance, work in bioethics is largely defined in terms of what may be characterized as the narrower field of medical ethics; attention is focused on the moral dilemmas that confront physicians, and the doctor's point of view is generally adopted. Problems specific to nurses are encountered far more rarely, and those that might be experienced by occupational or respiratory therapists, pharmacists, social workers, technicians, orderlies, or nursing assistants are seldom dealt with at all (Sherwin 1992: 2–3).

The tendency on the part of bioethicists to eschew a more forceful critique of the embeddedness of biomedicine in a capitalist political economy is rather ironic given the fact that an appreciable number of ethicists, including some in the United States, have relied upon neo-Marxian or socialist premises and ideals in developing their notions of morality (Hodges 1974; Fisk 1980; Geras 1990; Sayers 1998; Wilde 1998). Milton Fisk (2000) is one philosopher who does adopt a critical bioethical perspective. He argues that political morality entails an "element of political advocacy" (Fisk 2000: 1) and calls for a "radical politics of reform" that would require the eradication of "winner-take-all elections," given that the two mainstream parties represent primarily corporate interests, and the creation of single-payer health care system in the United States. Last, but not least, Marcio Fabri dos Anjos, a Brazilian liberation theologian, also calls for what we term a critical bioethics by arguing the following:

> The poor constitute a class of persons who enter into medical encounters encumbered by health problems caused by a mesh of social relationships, including extreme poverty, hunger, lack of opportunity, and poor health care. From this perspective, medical ethics must be concerned with the causes of hunger and the diseases which have become synonymous with particular social classes (dos Anjos 1996: 632).

Various leftist scholars have argued, however, that ultimately an incompatibility exists between capitalism and human rights due to patterns of inequality that it exhibits both internationally and within specific nation-states. Victor Sidel (1978: 348), a progressive physician, in his essay on an international perspective on the right to health care alludes to the "injustice, immorality, and ethical bankruptcy" of a world in which "the people of one country [have] relatively abundant medical care (not to speak of abundance of food, clothing, shelter, and other necessities of life) while the people of many countries have little medical care and indeed little of anything but hunger, illness and despair." Elsewhere, he delineates the following socialist principles that should underlie a national health care system:

1. Health care should be oriented toward improving quality of life rather than profit making;
2. Health care should not engage in the exploitation of its providers;
3. Health care should "enlighten and empower people" (Sidel 1994: 559); and
4. Health care "should be provided in ways that eliminate financial barriers at the time of need, permit the recipients to evaluate their care, [and] to select among alternative services" (Sidel 1994: 558).

Unfortunately, capitalism both internationally and within nation-states is characterized by patterns of social inequality. The United States exhibits the most pronounced maldistribution of wealth of all the advanced capitalist countries. A Federal Reserve research survey reported "in 1992 the richest 1/2 percent of U.S. families owned 22.8 percent of the total net wealth while the top 10 percent owned 67.2 percent" (Harris and Johnson 2000: 206). Furthermore, the gap between the rich and working-class Americans widened appreciably over the course of the last three decades of the twentieth century. Whereas in the 1970s, CEOs earned 35 times what employees earned, by 1995 the former were earning close to 2000 times what the latter were (Harris and Johnson 2000: 207).

Factors that have contributed to the enormous disparity between those at the top and those at the bottom in the United States over the course of the last 30 years, in particular, have been: (1) strong corporate influence over the election of political candidates through massive campaign contributions; (2) a historically weak labor movement compared to other advanced capitalist countries; (3) the absence of relatively strong labor, social democratic, and socialist parties (e.g., such as the New Democratic Party in Canada and the Greens and the Party of Democratic Socialism in Germany); (4) a "winner-take-all" electoral system (as opposed to a system of proportional representation) which makes it extremely difficult for third party candidates to win, particularly in national elections; (5) the existence of a large "underclass" or massive numbers of poor working-class people, particularly among African Americans, Hispanic Americans, and Native Americans; (6) the presence of a racist ideology that makes it difficult for working-class people to mobilize against the corporate class and its political allies; (7) pervasive corporate influence upon hegemonic institutions, particularly the mass media and formal education; and (8) the role of the culture of consumption, organized religion, and spectator sports in deflecting attention from the pervasive corporate control of the corporate economy. At any rate, within the context of U.S. society, we argue that the pursuit of a universal health care system constitutes both a significant venue of health praxis and expression of a critical bioethics.

Indeed, Howard Waitzkin, a critical medical sociologist and biomedical physician, observes that the present U.S. corporate-driven health care system raises significant ethical concerns:

> For instance, there is concern that corporate strategies lead to reduced services for the poor. While some corporations have established endowments for indigent care, the ability of such funds to assure long-term access is doubtful, especially when cutbacks occur in public-sector support. Other ethical concerns have focused on physicians' conflicting loyalties to patients versus corporations, the implications of physicians' referrals of patients for services to corporations in which the physicians hold financial interests, and the unwillingness of for-profit hospitals to provide unprofitable but needed services (Waitzkin 2001: 19).

Ethical Issues in Medical Anthropology

In the course of their work, in: a) *basic research* (i.e., research intended to expand general knowledge about behavior and society); b) *applied research* (i.e., research implemented as part of a social intervention, such as a needs assessment or program evaluation), as well as c) *practice* (i.e., the use of research knowledge in advocacy, policy formation, and program development), medical anthropologists regularly confront significant ethical dilemmas or uncertainties for appropriate moral decision-making and conduct. Work in medical anthropology often puts anthropologists in a position to do both considerable harm and considerable good, and it is necessary, therefore, that there be structures, training, and guidelines in place to minimize any harm and to insure maximum benefit for the lives of people touched by work in our discipline. Consequently, medical anthropologists are not only interested in the development and nature of bioethics and ethical practices in medicine as research topics, but also in the development and application of ethical principles *for* anthropologists in all areas in which they do work. We will consider the role of ethics and ethical challenges in each of the three arenas of anthropological activity mentioned above: basic research, applied research, and practice.

Ethics in Basic Anthropological Research

The field of research ethics that has developed over the last five decades strongly emphasizes the importance of minimizing harm to research subjects. This orientation emerged initially as a reaction to gross and intentional violations of subject agency (i.e., the right to have a say in one's fate) and subject well being by Nazi researchers prior to and during the Second World War. The establishment of generally shared standards for acceptable research with human subjects dates to the post-war Nuremberg War Crimes Trials and the Nuremberg Code. The Helsinki Declaration of 1964 (revised in 1975); the U.S. Department of Health, Education, and Welfare 1974 Guidelines; The Belmont Report on Ethical Principles and Guidelines for the Protection of Human Subjects of Research; public and researcher revulsion over the infamous Tuskegee syphilis study (White 2000); and a range of other incidents, seminal meetings, and documents have all contributed to the consolidation of contemporary thinking about research ethics with human subjects. All of these, in turn, have had an influence on thinking about the ethics of research in medical anthropology.

Traditionally, basic research in anthropology has involved the use of participant-observation ethnographic techniques within a given community, such as a village, a neighborhood, or a particular social group (e.g., patients in a hospital). Importantly, the very nature of ethnography as it defines how anthropologists should behave while conducting research raises several special ethical challenges for the discipline that may not be directly addressed by the various guidelines and discussions of ethics noted above. From the standpoint of ethics in research, ethnography as a research method is distinctive for the following reasons: 1) its *location of performance:* usually ethnography is carried out in the social and geographic domain of the research subjects, on their home turf so to speak, giving the anthropologist access to aspects of the life of study participants that is not found in many other types of research (e.g., people's homes); 2) its *context of realization:* data collection in ethnography is interwoven with everyday and sometimes private and quite intimate or highly emotionally charged activities of research subjects (e.g., illegal activities or secret behaviors); 3) its *investigative goals:* commonly anthropologists seek to grasp the insiders' understanding and world view, to understand their behavior in social context, including what they feel, experience, and believe; 4) its *methods of data collection:* to the degree possible, ethnography involves direct participation in the day-to-day activities of research subjects, as well as quite informal interviewing, and direct observation of behavior in context, activities that put anthropologists in a position to hear, see, and learn about aspects of study participants lives that are much more extensive than other research methods; 5) its *level of personal commitment:* ethnographers often do not go to work, per se, while in the field they live on the job, their work involves a full immersion into the lives of their research subjects and, as a result, during the period of research the personal lives of ethnographers are not, by design, separated from those of research participants; and, finally, 6) its *style of presentation:* as a written document, the ethnography, typically, is a holistic narrative description of behaviors, events, and social meanings, as well as underlying patterns and associations.

One consequence of this unique approach to understanding human lifeways is that anthropologists often spend long periods of time with research subjects and commonly develop very intimate knowledge of and close personal relationships with at least some of them. Not uncommonly, anthropologists have key informants among their research subjects who they define as personal friends, and with whom they maintain a relationship long after the period of research has ended. Conversely, anthropologists can develop enemies or have conflicts with people in the group under study. At the same time, from the research subject's perspective, the ethnographer as a person may be of far greater significance than the ethnographer as a researcher (a role that the subject may not well understand). Finally, a completed ethnographic account stands as a public description and assessment of aspects of the group in question. While anthropologists often attempt to hide the name or the location of the group through the use of pseudonyms, sometimes this is not possible and some members of the group under study may be offended by how their group is portrayed to the word.

As this description makes clear, basic research in anthropology is comparatively intrusive, long lasting, and personal. While in many lines of inquiry researcher responsibility to research subjects falls primarily within the specific context of the risks or burdens generated by the research project, in ethnography the boundaries between research activities and other arenas of research subjects' lives may be blurry. The ethnographer contract with subjects (to protect their confidentiality and minimize harm), may, as a result, be broader than it is in biomedical, epidemiological, or other research.

These features of ethnography create critical challenges to ethical conduct in medical anthropological research. For example, because of the access anthropologists often gain to the "back stage" aspects of study participants' private lives, they are in a position to learn very confidential information. In her study of female surgeons, for example, Joan Cassell (1998) learned about many private aspects of her study participants' lives, thoughts, and emotions, including deep resentments toward superiors and suggestions of improper behavior. To ensure adherence to ethical standards, in 1971 the American Anthropological Association adopted a set of Principles of Professional Responsibility (revised in 1990). These Principles indicate researchers have an ethical responsibility to:

- the people whose lives and cultures anthropologists study (exercised by avoiding deception, ensuring voluntary consent, protecting confidentiality, avoiding exploitation, and avoiding doing harm)
- the general public (demonstrated by communicating honestly and considering consequences of communication, and by using knowledge gained through research for the public good)
- the discipline (maintained by protecting the discipline's reputation, avoiding plagiarism, justly treating colleagues, and showing them proper professional respect)
- students and trainees (shown by treating them fairly, offering appropriate assistance and guidance, giving recognition for their contributions to work, and avoiding taking advantage of them in any way)
- employers, clients, and sponsors (expressed by being honest)
- governments (evidenced by being candid with government representatives and by setting ethical limits on acceptable work assignments)

While these are useful standards, research settings, study populations, and research goals vary considerably, and quite generalized guidelines of ethical practice, like those found in the Principles of Professional Responsibility, may be inadequate for specific research projects. Moreover as Marshall (1991: 215) points out, medical anthropology researchers can be "accountable to individuals and organizations representing diverse interests, including the financial sponsor of the study, the institution or community in which the study is conducted, and the research subjects. In considering the risks and benefits at the individual and the societal level, the anthropologist must explore potential conflicts of interest and determine the most effective way to balance competing claims for allegiance."

The issue of competing claims of researcher allegiance is another arena in which social inequality if of considerable importance. In his study of "urban nomads" (homeless street-corner men) in Seattle, for example, Spradley (2000) found that his study participants were subject to inhumane treatment by the police, prison guards, and court officials. Because Spradley observed and interviewed members of all three of the later groups, they too were his research subjects. Clearly urban homeless men have considerably less power and voice in society than do the other social groups in Spradley's study. Consequently, Spradley had to confront the issue of researcher allegiance in choosing what to do with his research findings, including what to write and how to act in response to them. His choice to fully report and initiate social action to correct the abuses his research uncovered has been acclaimed as a model example of ethical behavior in anthropological research (M. Singer 2000).

Applied Research

All of the issues of concern in basic research are also confronted in applied research, but applied research faces some additional dilemmas. In applied research, there is a conscious commitment to making social change. The researchers involved, in other words, are not simply learning about, describing, and analyzing the world as they find it, they are attempting to use research to respond to a pressing human problem; in effect, they are attempting to use research to help fix something in human society that is deemed to broken. A vitally important question in all applied research, therefore, is: who decides there is a problem in need of correcting, and it is this question that goes to the heart of the critical issues of social inequality of power and decision making. For example, during the late 1970s and early 1980s, because of continued poverty, a number of developing countries began to default on their development loans from the World Bank and International Monetary Fund. A number of economic analysts who hold to what has been termed a neoliberalist philosophy came to the conclusion that the main economic problem facing poor countries is that their national governments are too deeply involved in shaping their economies (e.g., by keeping prices low on basic commodities and health care) and were inhibiting the growth of privatization, free-market activity, and a general rise in production levels that would benefit everyone. Therefore, neoliberal economists and their supporters in the Ronald Reagan administration in the United States, the Margaret Thatcher administration in Great Britain, and the Helmut Kohl administration in Germany called for a total restructuring of the economies of developing nations, involving a reduction in the role of governments in the production, sale and purchase goods, letting prices of goods be determined by the market place, and lifting protective barriers to international trade and investment. What has been the impact of these policies (developed by rich countries) on health in poor countries? Applied medical anthropology researchers at Partners in Health in Boston (Schoepf, Schoepf, and Millen

2000) has drawn the following conclusions about the impact of structural adjustment policies (SAP) on AIDS in developing countries:

Specific SAP measures, such as currency devaluation, not only shrink resources that could improve AIDS prevention and the treatment and care of persons with AIDS; they also precipitate social upheavals that accelerate the rate of HIV transmission. Poverty and SAPs have undermined the viability of rural economies, promoted mass labor migration and urban unemployment, worsened the condition of poor women, and left health systems to founder.

In short, from a critical medical anthropology perspective, applied research and planned social change must always be assessed from the standpoint of understanding who is the group proposing social change and who is the target group to be impacted by the change that is being proposed. This is a crucial question for ethical practice in applied medical anthropology research.

Another important ethical question, especially with reference to the kinds of socially subordinated populations studied by anthropologists, concerns the appropriate extent of the intervention responsibilities of researchers. In other words, when studying disadvantaged, highly at-risk and otherwise vulnerable populations, how broadly should the lines be drawn specifying the obligations of researchers to insure the welfare of the study population, especially with regard to *health and other risks that do not originate with and are not the direct result of participation in research?* While the contemporary discourse on research ethics has tended to focus attention on the risks to human subjects that are directly created or enhanced by research procedures and activities, with highly vulnerable populations, some anthropologists have asked whether research responsibility should be expanded beyond current standards to include additional protective behaviors in light of the intimate knowledge ethnographic researchers gain about study participants.

Merrill Singer and co-workers (2000), for example, raised this question during a study of AIDS risk among injection drug users. During the course of the study, one of the participants, a 26-year-old man of mixed Puerto Rican and Italian heritage, was shot to death by the police in an incident that the police labeled a police-assisted suicide (i.e., the man provoked the police to shoot him, by point a knife at them, because he wanted to die). A re-examination of various interviews conducted with the man prior to his death forced the research team to ask themselves whether, in light of the problematic and suggestive nature of some of his answers, they could have averted his death. Should, for example, they wondered, the study have had in place a mechanism for quickly spotting depressive symptoms among study participants or for querying them about suicidal ideation (and responding accordingly)? Should the project have attempted to help educate the police or other institutions that come into contact with drug users about cultural expression of distress in the Puerto Rican community? Should all research projects that work with marginalized, low income populations of highly at-risk drug users be required to establish a credible system of aggressive, advocated referral into drug treatment and culturally sensitive psychiatric and other medical services for all participants (even for those who do not request such assistance)? These questions, which to some degree go beyond the usual ethical standards that guide research at present, point to potential direction for the development of new standards for research on vulnerable human subjects.

Practice and Application

Almost by definition, the practical application of anthropological knowledge to engineer social change must be guided by high ethical standards. Application demands both a strong commitment to humane decision-making and a keen respect for the rights of agency of the target population. Within applied anthropology, the kind of enhanced concern with professional responsibility noted above is evidenced, especially in discussions of advocacy efforts conducted by researchers. For example, Partridge (1985: 157) maintains that the appropriate level of responsibility of anthropological practitioners "requires a commitment beyond narrow professionalism to take action once analysis indicates a course of action." This "commitment to socially responsible science" is rooted in an ethic of social practice that Partridge (1985: 157) believes "contrasts vividly with the ethic of noninvolvement" (Partridge 1985: 157) characteristic of the work of many basic researchers (e.g., D'Andrade 1995).

At present, work done by anthropologist can be situated along a continuum of advocatorial stances.

At the left end of this continuum . . . lies the use of the ethnographic encounter in the service of anthropologically defined goals (e.g., broadening human understanding, expanding cultural knowledge). . . . At the other end of the continuum is the use of the ethnographic encounter in the service of the Other, including defending the right to self-determination or promoting access to needed resources . . . (M. Singer 1990: 549).

From the perspective of critical medical anthropology, there is no contradiction between science and action, focused research and social responsibility, and morality and adherence to objective standards for knowledge generation. In other words, critical medical anthropologists argue that ultimately the discipline of anthropology must be assessed in terms of its contributions to the enhancement of human welfare broadly defined. As a result, critical medical anthropologists are finding fault with approaches that treat active response to social suffering as beyond the purview of anthropological responsibility. While application is a particularly challenging endeavor, lack of application and social inaction when there is research-supported awareness of human risk and suffering and available courses of social response would be deemed unethical professional behavior by critical medical anthropologists.

A SINGLE-PAYER HEALTH CARE SYSTEM AS A POTENTIAL ARENA OF CMA PRAXIS

From the CMA perspective, the health care model that would be in the best interests of most people in the United States is a single-payer health care system—one in which the government will serve as the primary funding source for health care.

The Thicket of Proposals for Health Care Reform

Proposals for national health care reform have come and gone over the course of twentieth-century U.S. history. As Ginzberg observes,

National health insurance (NHI) has been on and off this country's political agenda since 1912, when Teddy Roosevelt, running for the presidency on the Progressive ticket, first advocated its enactment. Support for NHI has reemerged periodically—in the mid-1930s, the late 1940s, and the mid-1970s—yet it has never come close to winning popular or congressional support. In the 1990s, the defects of the health care system in the United States—costliness, inefficiency, and inequitable provision to the population—have prompted health specialists and the public to turn their attention once again to NHI. (Ginzberg 1994: 51–52)

The problem of access to health insurance is no longer only a concern of the poor and the elderly, who have since the 1960s theoretically been covered under Medicaid and Medicare, respectively, but increasingly one faced by middle-class people as well. Thus, the proportion of workers with fully paid health insurance at companies employing one hundred or more people diminished from 75% in 1982 to 48% in 1989 (Bartlett and Steele 1992: 124).

Aside from the issue of national health insurance in general, various single-payer proposals, all of which were opposed by the American Medical Association, have come and gone since the 1930s. The Wagner-Dingwell bill, introduced in 1943, called for the creation of a universal health care plan that would operate as part of Social Security but was defeated. President Harry Truman proposed the creation of a national health care system that would function independently of Social Security, but the AMA thwarted his proposal on the grounds that it would constitute a form of "socialized medicine" (Fisk 2000: 69). Following the defeat of the Kennedy-Griffiths Health Security Act, "Senator Edward Kennedy and his AFL-CIO [American Federation of Labor-Congress of Industrial Organizations] retreated from the single-payer concept and supported the central role of private insurance companies in paying for health services" (Bodenheimer 1993: 14). Ron Dellums, an African-American congressperson from Oakland and a member of Democratic Socialists of America, prepared in 1972 the most progressive health care reform plan ever introduced before Congress. His bill called for the passage of a Health Service Act that would create a network of community-based prepaid health plans coordinated at the regional level and serviced by salaried health care providers (Rodberg 1994). Community health boards would administer local health facilities. Proponents of the Dellums bill included the American Public Health Association, the Gray Panthers, and the United Electrical Workers.

The Managed Competition Model

During his bid for the presidency in 1992, Bill Clinton inadvertently backed into the national health care reform debate under pressure from the Kerry presidential campaign. Bob Kerry, a Democratic senator from Nebraska and a proponent of a single-payer plan, made health care reform the major issue in his campaign. Although Clinton had never before shown much interest in health care reform, he became convinced that he could not ignore it. In his desire not to offend big business, Clinton turned to the managed competition model for health care reform. Alain Enthoven, a business school professor and former vice president of Litton Industries, initially developed the concept of managed competition. He presented it at a conference in Jackson Hole, Wyoming, attended by executives from the largest managed care corporations, health insurance companies, and pharmaceutical companies.

The Clinton plan called for the creation of regional Health Alliances, which would contract with insurance plans (mainly in the form of health maintenance organizations or HMOs) on behalf of small employers, the self-employed, and the unemployed. Larger employers were to provide insurance for their employees, contract directly with certified plans for coverage, or choose to pay into the Health Alliances. The Health Alliances would impose cost controls upon the insurance companies or HMOs, which would in turn discipline physicians and hospitals by denying contracts to those who would refuse to comply with insurance company cost-cutting directives. Out-of-pocket costs for covered services would be capped at $1,500 per individual and $3,000 per family. One of the positive features of the Clinton plan was a requirement that 50% of all residency slots be allocated to family medicine, general medicine, and general pediatrics. The plan also provided an option for states to pursue a single-payer system.

Under the Clinton plan, it was generally recognized that the big health insurance companies would dominate national health care with an elaborate system of HMOs. Navarro (1994: 207) argues that "Managed competition will mean corporate assembly-line capitalism for the masses and their health care givers and continuing free choice and fee-for-service medicine for the elites." As has been the case for existing managed care operations, heavy reliance upon advertising, marketing, and utilization reviewers would have made managed competition a costly way of providing national health insurance. Chief executive officers (CEOs) would have continued to be compensated extremely handsomely for transforming their companies into profitable enterprises. For example, James Lynn, CEO of Aetna, earned $23 million in 1990. Most analysts maintain that the large insurance companies would be the winners under managed competition, whereas the smaller health insurance companies would go out of business. Indeed, Aetna, Prudential, Cigna, Met Life, and Travelers' formed the Coalition for Managed Competition.

Managed Care Following the Demise of the Clinton Plan

The corporate class and its political allies in the executive and legislative branches of the federal government have pushed serious discussion of some type of national health care plan on the back burner since the demise of the Clinton plan. During the 2000 presidential campaign, George W. Bush completely dismissed the idea of national health insurance and Al Gore promised, if elected, the creation of a national health plan covering all children by 2004. In contrast, Ralph Nader, the Green Party candidate who received about three percent of the popular vote, spoke out in favor of a national health plan. Since the early 1990s, reforms in biomedical health care delivery have consisted of an array of piece-meal managed care arrangements that have left both health care personnel, including physicians, and patients frustrated. Critical medical sociologist Rose Weitz describes managed care as follows:

Managed care refers to any system that controls costs through closely monitoring and controlling the decisions of health care providers. Most commonly, managed care organizations (MCOs) monitor and control costs through *utilization*, in which doctors must obtain approval from the insurer before they can hospitalize a patient, perform surgery, order an expensive diagnostic test, or refer to a specialist outside the insurance plan. Although the terms *HMO* [health maintenance organization] and *managed care* increasingly are used interchangeably, HMOs represent only one form of managed care, and most fee-for-service insurers now also use managed care (Weitz 2001: 230–231).

Other MCOs included preferred physician provider organizations and proprietary health corporations that operate hospitals, clinics, nursing homes, and hospices. Whereas managed care encompassed 29 percent of the health care market in 1988, by the late 1990s it had come to encompass 61 percent of it (Court and Smith 1999: 104). Managed care has become part and parcel of the profit-driven medical-industrial complex. Some 200 corporate takeovers of non-profit hospitals occurred between 1990 and 1996 (Court and Smith 1999: 86). Steve Wiggins (the chairperson and CEO of Oxford Health Plans), Wilson Taylor (the chairperson and CEO of Cigna Corporation), and William McGuire (the CEO of United Healthcare) earned salaries of over $30.7 million, $12.4 million, and $8.6 million, respectively, in 1997 (Court and Smith 1999: 105). Whereas some upper-echelon HMO functionaries may be biomedical physicians, most hold MBAs or PhDs. Nurses have increasingly come to assume position as lower-echelon HMO functionaries. Light (2000: 209) asserts that "[m]ost managed-care corporations . . . so far have principally managed contracts and costs through deep discounting, rather than the more complex of managing patient care." Purchasers of MCOs now include private sector employers, public sector employers, and public sector programs, such as Medicare and Medicaid. Despite the assertion on the part of health insurance companies and health corporations that they would provide a cheaper form of health care than a single payer system would, Fisk observes that:

The debt-laden acquisitions of the late 1990s—like the $8.8 billion Aetna buyout of U.S. Healthcare—called for cost cutting in the delivery of services but, ironically, raised health care costs for employers by adding on the expense of servicing billion-dollar debts. By 1997, less than half of the health insurers made money. Insurance rates then started going up at twice the rate of the years 1993–1996 (Fisk 2000: 278).

In response to such developments, various consumer groups and physician organizations, including unions, have arisen in opposition to managed care (Fuentes 1997; Waitzkin 2000). Unfortunately, numerous U.S. citizens lack any form of health care coverage. Lassey, Lassey, and Jinks (1997: 27) provide figures indicating that about 15 percent of the U.S. population (40–45 million people) are uninsured and that an estimated 50 million are underinsured in that they lack sufficient insurance to "cover serious illnesses or must pay very high deductibles."

The Single-Payer Model

Despite the fact the plan for a managed-competition health care system failed early on in Clinton's first presidential term, growing dissatisfaction with managed care and the failure of the existing system or what some term non-system to provide adequate health care to a significant portion of the American people make it apparent that health care reform will be a major societal concern now that we have begun the twenty-first century. In paraphrasing Mark Twain, Graig (1999: 39) notes, "news of health care reform's demise is greatly exaggerated." Whereas most corporate interests and physician groups oppose the concept of a single-payer health care system, various physician groups, grassroots groups, and legislators favor it—a fact generally downplayed by the mainstream media. The single-payer concept reemerged in January 1989 with the publication of a proposal of the Physicians for a National Health Program (PHNP) in the *New England Journal of Medicine* (Himmelstein and Woolhandler 1989). PHNP, an organization with some 5,000 members in thirty-four chapters in twenty-five states, advocates the creation of a single-payer Canadian-style health care system in the United States. PHNP is not a left organization per se, but much of its leadership is openly leftist and includes progressive physicians such as David Himmelstein, Steffie Woolhandler, and Vincente Navarro. Although the Canadian health care system has shortcomings of its own, it clearly is more equitable than the U.S. health care system.

The United Nations Human Development Report "ranked Canada first in the world with respect to health status, overall quality of life, and socioeconomic status" (Lassey, Lassey, and Jinks 1997: 72). Canada's three major political parties, namely the Progressive Conservatives, the Liberals, and the New Democratic Party, support a single-payer, which was approved in 1968, with strong labor support, in 1968 and fully implemented in 1971 (Coburn 1999). In large part this is due to the fact that Canada exhibits a stronger "collectivist culture" than does the United States (Lemco 1994: 6). In contrast to the United States, the Canadian health care system is, according to Birenbaum (1995: 176), "accepted widely today by Canadian conservatives who oppose state intervention as well as liberals who see the state as the mediator between conflicting classes." The Canadian system is premised on the notion that health care is a right rather than a privilege.

The Canadian system, called Medicare, consists of ten provincial health plans that must abide by certain national standards and that are funded jointly by federal and provincial governments through corporate taxes, personal taxes, property taxes, and taxes on gasoline, tobacco, and liquor. The federal government exerts more control over the health care plans of the Northwest Territories and the Yukon Territory than those of the provinces. All Canadian physicians participate in the provincial or territorial health plans. The federal government prepays each province about 40% of medical costs, provided the provincial health insurance programs are universal, comprehensive, portable (each province recognizes the others' coverage), and publicly administered. Each province devises its own payment system for providers but is required to provide comprehensive medical services in order to obtain federal funding. The provincial governments set hospital budgets, limit the number of specialists, allocate the purchase of medical technology, and restrict costly medical procedures, such as open-heart surgery, to hospitals in large urban areas. The Canadian system charges nominal fees for medication and has administrative costs that are much lower than in the U.S. system (11% versus 25%) (Himmelstein and Woolhandler 1994). Indeed the 1964 Royal Commission on Health Services, the body that designed Canada's Medicare, maintained that private administration of insurance was uneconomical. Whereas about 20% of U.S. physicians are primary care providers, about 50% of their Canadian counterparts are primary care physicians. Patients choose their own physicians, most of whom are not government employees. Furthermore, most hospitals are not owned or operated by the government. Whereas U.S. citizens often feel chained to their jobs because of health care benefits, a Canadian "worker who leaves to take a job in another city or province, or with a different employer, is always completely covered" (Birenbaum 1995:178).

National and local coalitions of health care persuaded some thousand legislators prior to the Republican sweep of Congress in 1994 to cosponsor single-payer legislation. Representatives Jim McDermott (D-Washington) and John Conyers (D-Michigan) proposed a single-payer plan, called the American Health Security Act. Paul Wellstone (D-Minnesota) proposed a single-payer plan in the Senate. A Congressional Budget Office report in 1993 concluded that a single-payer system would trim up to $100 billion a year in administrative costs.

Groups supporting a single-payer system include Public Citizen, Neighbor-to-Neighbor, the Oil, Chemical and Atomic Workers, the AFL-CIO, and many other labor unions, as well as the National Medical Association (an organization of African-American physicians), the Women's Medical Association, the Rainbow Coalition, and the "72 religious organizations that make up the Interreligious Health Care Access Campaign" (Navarro 1994: 211). As part of an effort to retain physician control over working conditions, which would inevitably be considerably eroded under managed competition, the College of Surgeons endorsed the Wellstone-McDermott bill. A single-payer initiative called the Health Security Act of California, which became Proposition 186, sponsored by Neighbor-to-Neighbor, garnered 1,060,000 signatures in California, ensuring a referendum on the November 8, 1994, ballot. The Health Security Act also included coverage for licensed chiropractors, acupuncturists, nurse-midwives, and mental health professionals. Heavy lobbying on the part of the health insurance industry as well as the politics of reaction that resulted in the passage of Proposition 187, which excluded undocumented workers from social and health services, contributed to the defeat of this initiative (Andrews 1995: 103–19). Furthermore, there was no unanimity nationwide among grassroots health reform groups on the issue of a single-payer system. Nevertheless, a Louis Harris poll showed that 66% of those surveyed preferred the Canadian health care system to the U.S. system. Other polls have also shown strong popular support for a single-payer system.

Navarro (1995) offers the following explanation as to why the large corporations oppose a single-payer plan even though they would very likely pay considerably less in fringe benefits for their employees if such a plan were implemented:

[The majority of large employers and their trade associations] most value control over their own labor force, and the employment-based health benefits coverage gives them enormous power over their employees. The United States is the only country where the welfare state is, for the most part, privatized. Consequently, when workers lose their jobs, health care benefits for themselves and their families are also lost. In no other country does this occur. . . . The United States, the only major capitalist country without government-guaranteed universal health care coverage, is also the only nation without a social-democratic or labor party that serves as the political instrument of the working class and other popular classes. (Navarro 1995: 450)

Health Care Reform Plans as System-Correcting and System-Challenging Praxis

At this point, it seems appropriate to view the two principal models for national health care reform just presented with a distinction between *system-correcting* and *system-challenging* praxis. From the CMA perspective, the managed competition health care model constitutes by and large a reformist reform, whereas the single-payer model has a much greater potential to function as a nonreformist reform.

The Clinton plan would have contributed toward the process of concentration in the medical-industrial complex. A Prudential executive described managed competitions as the "best-case scenario for reform— preferable even to the status quo" (quoted in *In These Times,* 18 October 1993: 2). The pharmaceutical industry prefers managed competition over a single-payer system because the purchaser of drugs has much greater power to negotiate for lower prices under the latter.

A single-payer system, including one based on the Canadian health care system, appears to come much closer to system-challenging praxis. The Canadian system operates as a "publicly-funded, privately-provided, universal, comprehensive, affordable, single-payer, provincially administered national program" (Bernard 1990: 35). Canadians see the physician of their choice, 50% of whom are primary care providers, as opposed to the United

States, where primary care providers are in scarce supply. Canada spends about 9% of its GNP on health care, as opposed to the United States, which spends 14%.

Despite its superiority to the U.S. system, the Canadian health care system itself contains contradictions, including a hierarchy in the health labor force as well as in the physician-patient relationship, very little community control over health services or worker self-management within health care settings, and relatively little emphasis on prevention. While all Canadians have access to health care, class-based inequalities persist in terms of its utilization (Schwartz 1998: 540). The Canadian system relies less on medical technology than some other advanced capitalist countries. According to Lassey, Lassey, and Jinks (1997: 85), "there were 0.46 magnetic resonance imaging (MRI) units per one million population in 1987, compared to 3.69 in the United States and 0.94 in Germany." Substantial waiting lists for selected surgical and diagnostic procedures occur. Conversely, it is important to note that many American HMOs require substantial waiting periods for medical appointments. The overall rates of hospital use per capita in Canada exceed those in the United States, and patients are generally cared for in a timely manner.

Unfortunately, the Canadian health care system faces external pressures in large part due to the fact that, like the American system, it is embedded in a capitalist political economy and world system (Armstrong and Armstrong 1996). According to Chernomas and Sepehri,

As a result of economic stagnation and conservative economic policy (e.g., deindexing the per capita grant) the federal contribution, as a percentage of the total public spending on health care, has been declining over time, while per capita health expenditures have been growing. The result is increasing pressure on the provinces and private sector to meet the financial needs of the health care system. The provinces in turn have reduced the number of services covered, and the private sector has begun to take on a larger role (Chernomas and Sepehri 1998: 3).

In that it is reliant upon profit-making operations, such as medical equipment and pharmaceutical companies, the Canadian health care system is not a utopian model. Nevertheless, a Canadian-style single-payer system holds the potential for transformation into a national health service under which the government would provide health services. As Marmor so aptly observes,

Contrary to the message of the AMA and the HIAA [Health Insurance Association of America], the Canadian system not only works reasonably well—it pays for universal access to ordinary medical care, maintains a generally high quality, is administratively efficient, and restrains the growth of health care costs far more effectively than any of the myriad cost containment schemes tried in the United

States—but is as adaptable to American circumstances as one could imagine a foreign model to be (Marmor 1994: 184).

Opposition to a single-payer health care system in the United States does not for the most part stem from the public but rather from a narrow but powerful group consisting of the insurance companies, some providers (particularly proprietary hospitals and highly paid medical specialists), and some small businesses that would be forced to pay a share of health costs for the first time. When Hillary Clinton asked David Himmelstein, a progressive physician-activist who advocates a single-payer system, how to defeat the insurance industry, he replied "With presidential leadership and polls showing that 70 percent of Americans favor [the features of] a single-payer system" (quoted in Marmor 1994: 160). The First Lady reportedly retorted, "Tell me something interesting, David" (quoted in Marmor 1994: 160).

Although the *MacNeil Lehrer Report* on the Public Broadcasting System included single-payer supporters on its health reform panels, the major commercial news programs consistently avoided reports on a Canadian-style single-payer health care plan (Canham-Clyde 1994). On the few occasions that they mentioned the single-payer plan, the major TV networks, the *New York Times,* and the *Washington Post* ridiculed it (Navarro 1995). Despite conservative attempts to implement significant cutbacks in Medicaid and Medicare, the demise of the Clinton plan may have inadvertently created a new opening for serious consideration of a single-payer system among health activists.

Obviously, Americans should not adopt the Canadian or any other single-payer system "lock, stock, and barrel" in creating a national health care system of their own. Various aspects of the Swedish single-payer health care system, such as county and municipal ownership and operation of hospitals, may prove to be amenable to local preferences. The creation of an American single-payer system will have to be coupled with the creation of an authentically holistic and pluralistic medical system—one that integrates biomedicine with a wide array of alternative subsystems, something that the Canadian system has not achieved (Crelin, Anderson, and Connor 1997).

Critical Medical Anthropologists as Advocates for a Single-Payer Health Care System

Despite their interest in the comparative study of national health systems, critical medical anthropologists have not systematically become involved in health reform in the United States. In contrast, Vincente Navarro, a progressive physician with a strong training in the social sciences, served as the principal health adviser to the Rainbow Coalition during Jesse Jackson's 1988 presidential bid and now functions as a strong advocate of a single-payer health care system in the United States (Navarro 1989). Melvin Konner (1993), a physician-anthropologist, has published a short book in which he critiques the Clinton administration's proposed managed competition plan and advocates a single-payer system. As opposed to anthropological and sociological associations, several professional associations, including the American Public Health Association (APHA) and the National Association of Social Workers (NASW), have endorsed the creation of a single-payer system in the United States.

The greater willingness on the part of APHA and NASW to make public endorsements of national health care reform may be related in large part to the high proportion of practitioners as opposed to academics in these two organizations. In contrast to many practitioners of public health and social work, academics often adopt an individualistic orientation that emphasizes career advancement rather than the implementation of social change. Given the dismal academic job market in anthropology since the early 1970s, a large number of anthropologists now work in nonacademic positions as applied or practicing anthropologists. Many of these anthropologists belong to the Society for Applied Anthropology, the National Association of Practicing Anthropologists, and the Society for Medical Anthropology.

The relevance of health care reform as a matter of anthropological concern is attested to by what may have been the first session on this topic presented at an American Anthropological Association meeting. Janet M. Bronstein (University of Alabama at Birmingham) organized a session at the 1994 meeting on "U.S. Health Care Reform: Origins, Development and Impact." Unfortunately, as Hans Baer noted in his comments as a discussant, none of the papers in the session referred to a single-payer system as a potential model for health reform in the United States. Indeed, one of the presenters argued that medical anthropologists should assist health administrators in the implementation of total quality management—a business-oriented approach that emphasizes increased surveillance of health workers as an integral part of supposedly increasing efficiency or, more accurately stated, profit making to an even greater extent that at present in U.S. health care.

Although medical anthropologists have been reluctant to take public positions on health policy to date, the ongoing debate on health care reform provides them with an opportunity to serve as advocates for changes that will benefit many of the populations who have served as subjects of their research within the border of the United States. Despite the demise of the Clinton health plan and the defeat of the California initiative on a single-payer system, health care reform is a topic that will remain in the public spotlight for some time to come. Rather than being divided as they were on the Clinton plan, grassroots organizations, professional associations, and health activists may have a unique opportunity to rally behind a single-payer system and force it onto center stage in the health care reform debate.

As Flacks (1993: 465) argues, "The demand for a universal health-care program . . . has the potential to politically unite very diverse movement constituencies and to link these with middle-class voters." Critical medical anthropologists can serve as a vanguard within the Society for Medical Anthropology and the American Anthropological Association to endorse a single-payer health care system for the United States as a system-challenging action. Such an effort can serve as a mechanism for linking medical anthropologists, critical or otherwise, with a growing coalition of grassroots groups, labor unions, and even professional associations that favor the creation of a single-payer system in the United States. Ultimately, the creation of a single-payer health care system will have to be part and parcel of other non-reformist reforms in U.S. society. In pursuing the creation of a single-payer health care system, Milton Fisk (2000: 187–206) calls for a "radical politics of reform" that would include a system of proportional representation that would make it easier for a labor or socialist-oriented party to win seats in various levels of government as well as an alliance of various working-class groups (including labor unions). At even a more profound level, however, even if the United States manages to implement a national health care program, Waitzkin (2001: 175) asserts that health policies must address social differentials in health statistics that "remain closely linked to social class, racism, gender inequalities, work hierarchies and exposures, and environmental problems." Ultimately, critical medical anthropology, as well as the critical medical sociology that Waitzkin espouses, are committed to the eradication of these inequities not only in this country but internationally.

Bibliography

Abramson, Hilary. 1998. "Big Alcohol's Smokescreen." *Newsletter of the Marin Institute for the Prevention of Alcohol & Other Drug Problems* 13: 1.

Acker, P., A. Fierman, and V. Dreyer. 1987. "An Assessment of Parameters of Health Care and Nutrition in Homeless Children." *American Journal of Diseases of Children* 141(4): 388.

Ackerknecht, Erwin. 1971. *Medicine and Ethnology: Selected Essays.* Baltimore: Johns Hopkins University Press.

Adams, Vicanne. 1998. "Suffering the Winds of Lhasa: Politicized Bodies, Human Rights, Cultural Difference, and Humanism in Tibet." *Medical Anthropology Quarterly* 12: 74–102.

Agar, Michael. 1973. *Ripping and Running: A Formal Ethography of Urban Heroin Addiction.* New York: Seminar Press.

———— 1980. *The Professional Stranger.* Orlando: Academic Press.

Alasuutari, Pertti. 1990. *Desire and Craving.* Tampere, Finland: University of Tampere.

Alland, Alexander. 1970. *Adaptation in Cultural Evolution: An Approach to Medical Anthropology.* New York: Columbia University Press.

Alvord, Katie. 2000. *Divorce Your Car: Ending the Love Affair with the Automobile.* Gabriola Island, BC, Canada: New Society Publishers.

Ames, Genevieve. 1985. "Middle-Class: Alcohol and the Family." In *The American Experience with Alcohol,* ed. Linda Bennett and Genevieve Ames, 435–458. New York: Plenum.

Anderson, Robert. 1996. *Magic, Science, and Health: The Aims and Achievements of Medical Anthropology.* Fort Worth: Harcourt Brace College Publishers.

Andrews, Charles. 1995. *Profit Fever: The Drive to Corporatize Health Care and How to Stop It.* Monroe, ME: Common Courage Press.

Andrews, George, and David Solomon. 1975. *The Coca Leaf and Cocaine Papers*. New York: Harcourt Brace Jovanovich.

Anjos, Marcio Fabri dos. 1996. "Medical Ethics in the Developing World: A Liberation Theology Perspective." *Journal of Medicine and Philosophy* 21: 629–37.

Antonil, T. 1978. *Mama Coca*. London: Hassle Free Press.

Aral, S., and K. Holmes. 1989. "Sexually Transmitted Diseases in the AIDS Era." *Scientific American* 264(2): 62–69.

Aretxaga, Begona. 1997. *Shattering Silence: Women, Nationalism, and Political Subjectivity in Northern Ireland*. Princeton, NJ: Princeton University Press.

Arliss, Robert. 1997. *Against Death: The Practice of Living with AIDS*. Amsterdam: Gordon and Breach.

Armelagos, George J., and John R. Dewey. 1978. "Evolutionary Response to Human Infectious Diseases." In *Health and the Human Condition: Perspectives on Medical Anthropology*, ed. Michael H. Logan and Edward H. Hunt, Jr., 101-6. North Scituate, MA: Duxbury Press.

Armstrong, Pat, and Hugh Armstrong. 1996. *Wasting Away: The Undermining of Canadian Health Care*. New York: Oxford University Press.

Arnold, David. 1993. "Medicine and Colonialism." In *Companion Encyclopedia of the History of Medicine, Volume 1*. ed. W. F. Bynun and Roy Porter, 1393–1416. London: Routledge.

Aronowitz, Stanley. 1994. "The Situation of the Left in the United States." *Socialist Review* 23(3): 5–79.

Atkinson, Jane Monnig. 1992. "Shamanisms Today." *Annual Review of Anthropology* 21: 307–330.

Bacon, Selden, and Robert Strauss. 1953. *Drinking in College*. New Haven, CT: Yale University Press.

Baer, Hans A. 1982. "On the Political Economy of Health." *Medical Anthropology Newsletter* 14(1): 1–2, 13–17.

———. 1989. "The American Dominative Medical System as a Reflection of Social Relations in the Larger Society." *Social Science and Medicine* 28: 1103–12.

Baer, Hans A., ed. 1996. "Critical Biocultural Approaches in Medical Anthropology: A Dialogue." Special issue of *Medical Anthropology Quarterly*, n.s. 10(4).

Baer, Hans A., Merrill Singer, and John Johnsen, eds. 1986. "Towards a Critical Medical Anthropology." Special issue of *Social Science and Medicine* 23(2).

Baldo, M., and A. Cabral. 1991. "Low Intensity Wars and Social Determination of HIV Transmission: The Search for a New Paradigm to Guide Research and Control of the HIV/AIDS Pandemic." In *Action on AIDS in Southern Africa*, New York: Committee for Health in Southern Africa.

Balikci, A. 1963. "Shamanistic Behavior among the Netsilik Eskimos." *Southwestern Journal of Anthropology* 19: 380–396.

Ball, Andrew. 1998. "HIV Prevention among Injecting Drug Users." In *Global Research Network Meeting on HIV Prevention in Drug-Using Populations*. Bethesda, MD: National Institute on Drug Abuse.

Ball, Andrew, Sujata Rava, and Karl Dehne. 1998. "HIV Prevention Among Injecting Drug Users: Responses in Developing and Transitional Countries." *Public Health Reports* 113 (Supplement 1): 170–181.

Balzer, Majorie Mandelstam. 1987. "Behind Shamanism: Changing Voices of Siberian Khanty Cosmology and Politics." *Social Science and Medicine* 12: 1085–1093.

———. 1991. "Doctors or Deceivers? The Siberian Khanty Shaman and Soviet Medicine." In *The Anthropology of Medicine: From Culture to Method*, 2nd ed, ed. Lola Romanucci-Ross, Daniel E. Moerman, and Laurence R. Tancredi, 56–80. New York: Bergin & Garvey.

———. 1993. "Two Urban Shamans: Unmasking Leadership in Fin-de-Soviet Siberia." In *Perilous States: Conversations on Culture, Politics, and Nation*, ed. George E. Marcus, 131–64. Chicago: University of Chicago Press.

Banerji, Debabar. 1984. "The Political Economy of Western Medicine in Third World Countries." In *Issues in the Political Economy of Health Care*, ed. John B. McKinlay, 257–82. New York: Tavistock.

Barker, D. and C. Osmond. 1986. "Infant Mortality, Childhood Nutrition and Ischaemic Heart Disease in England and Wales." *Lancet* 43: 1077–81.

Barnet, Richard, and John Cavanagh. 1994. *Global Dreams: Imperial Corporations and the New World Order*. New York: Simon and Schuster.

Barnet, Richard, and Ronald Müller. 1974. *Global Reach*. New York: Simon and Schuster.

Barnett, Homer G. 1961. *Being a Palauan*. New York: Holt, Rinehart, and Winston.

Barrow, S. M., D. B. Herman, P. Cordova, and E. L. Struening. 1999. "Mortality among Homeless Shelter Residents in New York City." *American Journal of Public Health* 89(4): 529–34.

Barry, T., B. Wood, and D. Preusch. 1984. *The Other Side of Paradise*. New York: Grove Press.

Bartlett, Donald L., and James B. Steele. 1992. *America: What Went Wrong?* Kansas City, MO: Andrews and McNeel.

Bastien, Joseph W. 1992. *Drum and Stethoscope: Integrating Ethnomedicine and Biomedicine in Bolivia*. Salt Lake City: University of Utah Press.

Batalla, G. 1966. "Conservative Thought in Applied Anthropology: A Critique." *Human Organization* 25: 89–92.

Bateson, Mary Catherine, and Richard Goldsby. 1988. *Thinking AIDS*. Reading, MA: Addison-Wesley.

Battjes, Robert, and Roy Pickens. 1988. "Needle Sharing among Intravenous Drug Abusers: Future Directions." In *Needle Sharing among Intravenous Drug Abusers: National and International Perspectives*, ed. Robert Battjes and Roy Pickens, 176–83. Bethesda, MD: National Institute on Drug Abuse.

Baxter, E., and Kim Hopper. 1981. *Public Places, Private Spaces*. New York: Community Service Society.

BBC News Online. 2001. "Poor Diet Boosts Virus Power." [cited 8 June].

Beck, Melinda, and Orville Levander. 2000. "Host Nutritional Status and Its Effect on Viral Pathogen." Supplement to *Journal of Infectious Diseases* 182: S93–S96.

Becker, Howard. 1953. "Becoming a Marijuana User." *American Journal of Sociology* 59:235–42.

Becket, J. 1965. "Aborigines, Alcohol and Assimilation." In *Aborigines Now*, ed. M. Reay, 32–47. Sydney: Angus and Robertson.

Behar, Ruth. 1996. "Introduction: Out of Exile." In *Women Writing Culture*, ed. Ruth Behar and Deborah Gordon, 1–33. Berkeley: University of California Press.

Bennett, John. 1974. *The Ecological Transition: Cultural Anthropology and Human Adaptation*. New York: Pergamon Press.

Bennett, Linda. 1988. "Alcohol in Context: Anthropological Perspectives." *Drugs and Society* 2(3/4): 89–131.

Bennett, Linda, and Paul Cook. 1990. "Drug Studies." In *Medical Anthropology: Contemporary Theory and Method*, ed. Thomas Johnson and Carolyn Sargent, 230–47. New York: Praeger.

Berliner, Howard. 1982. "Medical Modes of Production." In *The Problem of Medical Knowledge: Examining the Social Construction of Medicine*, ed. Andrew Treacher and Peter Wright, 162–73. Edinburgh: Edinburgh University Press.

Bernard, Elaine. 1990. "The Politics of Canada's Health Care System: Lessons for the US." *Radical America* 24(3): 34–43.

Bernstein, Jay H. 1997. *Spirits Captured in Stone: Shamanism & Traditional Medicine Among the Taman of Borneo*. Boulder, CO: Lynne Rienner Publishers.

Best, Joel. 1983. "Economic Interests and the Vindication of Deviance: Tobacco in Seventeenth Century Europe." In *Drugs and Society*, ed. Maureen Kelleher, Bruce MacMurray, and Thomas Shapiro, 173–83. Dubuque, IA: Kendall/ Hunt.

Birenbaum, Arnold. 1995. *Putting Health Care on the National Agenda*. Rev. ed. Westport, CT: Praeger.

Black, Peter. 1984. "The Anthropology of Tobacco Use: Tobian Data and Theoretical Issues." *Journal of Anthropological Research* 40: 475–503.

Blankenship, Kim, Sarah Bray, and Michael Merson. 2000. "Structural Interventions in Public Health." Supplement to *AIDS* 14: 11–21.

Bodenheimer, Tom. 1993. "Health Care Reform in the 1990s and Beyond." *Socialist Review* 23(1): 13–29.

Bodley, John H. 1975. *Victims of Progress*. Menlo Park, CA: Benjamin/Cummings.

———. 1985. *Anthropology and Contemporary Human Problems*. 2nd ed. Palo Alto, CA: Mayfield Publishing.

———. 1994. *Cultural Anthropology: Tribes, States, and the Global System*. Mountain View, CA: Mayfield Publishing.

———. 1996. *Anthropology and Contemporary Human Problems*. 3rd ed. Mountain View, CA: Mayfield Publishing.

Boggs, Carl. 1995. *The Socialist Tradition: From Crisis to Decline*. New York: Routledge.

Bolough, Roslyn W. 1981. "Grounding the Alienation of Self and Body: A Critical, Phenomenological Analysis of the Patient in Western Medicine." *Sociology of Health and Illness* 3: 188–206.

Bolton, Ralph. 1992. "Mapping Terra Incognita: Sex Research for AIDS Prevention—An Urgent Agenda for the 1990s." In *The Time of AIDS*, ed. Gilbert Herdt and Shirley Lindenbaum, 124–58. Newbury Park, CA: Sage Publications.

Bolton, Ralph, and Gail Orozco. 1994. *The AIDS Bibliography: Studies in Anthropology and Related Fields*. Arlington, VA: American Anthropological Association.

Bolton, Ralph, and Merrill Singer. 1992. *Rethinking AIDS Prevention: Cultural Approaches*. Philadelphia: Gordon and Breach Science Publishers.

Bonnie, Richard, and Charles Whitebread. 1970. "The Forbidden Fruit and the Tree of Knowledge: An Inquiry into the Legal History of American Marijuana Prohibition." *Virginia Law Review* 56(6): 971–1203.

Bourdieu, Pierre. 1984. *Distinction: A Social Critique of the Judgment of Taste*. Cambridge, MA: Harvard University Press.

Bourgois, Philippe. 1995. In Search of Research: Selling Crack in El Barrio. Cambridge: Cambridge University Press.

Bovelle, E., and A. Taylor. 1985. "Conclusions and Implications." In *Life with Heroin*, ed. B. Hanson. Lexington, MA: Lexington Books.

Bowie, Fiona. 2000. *The Anthropology of Religion: An Introduction*. Oxford: Blackwell.

Brandt, T. 1989. "AIDS in Historical Perspective: Four Lessons from the History of Sexually Transmitted Disease." *American Journal of Public Health* 78(40): 367-71.

Braunstein, Mark. 1997. "Marijuana Has Worked the Best in Easing Pain." *Hartford Courant*, (12 January): C1, C4.

Brenner, M. Harvey. 1975. "Trends in Alcohol Consumption and Associated Illnesses." *American Journal of Public Health* 65(12): 1279–292.

Brettel, Caroline, and Carolyn Sargent, eds. 2001. *Gender in Cross-Cultural Perspective*. Upper Saddle River, NJ: Prentice-Hall.

Brodwin, Paul. 1996. Medicine and Modality in Haiti: The Contest for Healing Power. Cambridge: Cambridge University Press.

Brooks, Jerome. 1952. *The Mighty Leaf*. Boston: Little, Brown.

Brown, Claude. 1965. *Manchild in the Promised Land*. New York: Penguin.

Brown, E. Richard. 1979. *Rockefeller Medicine Men: Medicine and Capitalism in America*. Berkeley: University of California Press.

Brown, Lawrence, and Benny Primm. 1989. "A Perspective on the Spread of AIDS among Minority Intravenous Drug Abusers." In *AIDS and Intravenous Drug Abuse among Minorities*, ed., 3–23. Rockville, MD: National Institute on Drug Abuse.

Brown, Peter J. 1987. "Microparasites and Macroparasites." *Cultural Anthropology* 2:155-71.

Brown, Peter J., and Marcia C. Inhorn. 1990. "Disease, Ecology, and Human Behavior." In *Medical Anthropology: Contemporary Theory and Method*, ed. Thomas M. Johnson and Carolyn Sargent, 187–214. New York: Praeger.

Browner, Carole. 2001. "The Politics of Reproduction in a Mexican Village." In Caroline Brettel and Carolyn Sargent, 460–70. Upper Saddle River, NJ: Prentice-Hall.

Brundtland, Gro Harlem. 2001. Presentation on Current State Of The Global Problem Of Drinking Among Youth at WHO European Ministerial Conference on Young People and Alcohol, Stockholm Sweden, February.

Bruun, Kettle, et al. 1975. *Alcohol Control Policies in Public Health Perspective*. Vol. 25. Helsinki: Finnish Foundation for Alcohol Studies.

Buchan, William. 1784. *Domestic Medicine: Or, a Treatise on the Prevention and Cure of Diseases by Regimen and Simple Medicines*. Philadelphia: Crukshank, Bell and Muir.

Bunce, Robert. 1979. *The Political Economy of California's Wine Industry*. Toronto: Addiction Research Foundation.

Bunzel, Ruth. 1940. "On the Role of Alcoholism in Two Central American Cultures." *Psychiatry*. 3: 301–87.

Burroughs, William. 1953. *Junkie*. New York: Ace.

Camara, Bilali. 2000. "Eighteen Years of HIV/AIDS Epidemic in the Caribbean." Port of Spain, Republic of Trinidad and Tobago: Caribbean Epidemiology Centre.

Canham-Clyde, John. 1994. "When 'Both Sides' Are Not Enough: The Restricted Debate over Health Care Reform." *International Journal of Health Services* 24: 415–419.

Carlson, Robert. 1992. "Symbolic Mediation and Commoditization: A Critical Examination of Alcohol Use among the Haya of Bukoba, Tanzania." *Medical Anthropology* 15: 41–62.

Carlson, Robert, Harvey Siegal, and Russel Falck. 1994. "Ethnography, Epidemiology and Public Policy: Needle Use Practices and Risk Reduction among IV Drug Users in the Mid-west." In *Global AIDS Policy*, ed. Douglas Feldman, 185–214. Westport, CT: Greenwood Press.

Carrier, Joe. 1989. "Sexual Behavior and the Spread of AIDS in Mexico." *Medical Anthropology* 10: 129–42.

Cassell, Joan. 1998. *The Woman in the Surgeon's Body*. Cambridge, MA: Harvard University Press.

Cassidy, Claire. 1991. *The Good Body: When Big is Better*. Medical Anthropology 13(3): 181–214.

Castells, Manuel. 1975. "Immigrant Workers and Class Struggles in Advanced Capitalism: The Western European Experience." *Politics and Society* 5: 33–66.

Castro, Arochra, and Merrill Singer. 2004. Unhealthy Health Policy: A Critical Anthropological Examination. Walnut Creek, Calif.: Altamera Press.

Caudill, William. 1953. "Applied Anthropology in Medicine." In *Anthropology Today*, ed. Alfred L. Kroeber, 771–806. Chicago: University of Chicago Press.

Cavanagh, J., and Clairmonte, F. 1983. "Corporate Power and Public Health." *The Globe* 4: 9.

Center for Substance Abuse Treatment. 1997. "Most Maryland Residents Who Support Medicinal Use of Marijuana Do Not Support Legalizing the Drug." *Cesar Fax* 6(1): 1.

Centers for Disease Control. 1990. "HIV/AIDS Surveillance: U.S. AIDS Cases Reported through July 1990." Atlanta: AIDS Program, Center for Infectious Diseases.

———. 1992. "Summary of Notifiable Diseases, United States, 1991." *Morbidity and Mortality Weekly Report* 40(53).

———. 2002a. "HIV-Related Knowledge and Stigma." *Morbidity and Mortality Weekly Report* 49(47): 1062.

———. 2002b. "Sexually Transmitted Disease Surveillance." Atlanta: AIDS Program: Center for Infectious Diseases.

Chambers, C., and Moffitt, A. 1970. "Negro Opiate Addiction." In *The Epidemiology of Opiate Addiction in the United States*, ed. J. Ball and C. Chambers, Springfield, IL: Charles C. Thomas.

Chandler, W. 1986. *Banishing Tobacco*. Worldwatch Paper #68. Washington, DC: Worldwatch Institute.

Chapin, Georganne, and Robert Wasserstrom. 1981. "Agricultural Production and Malaria Resurgence in Central America and India." *Nature* 293: 181–85.

Chernomas, Robert, and Ardeshir Sepehri. 1998. "Introduction." In *How to Choose: A Comparsion of the U.S. and Canadian Health Care* Systems, ed. Robert Chernomas and Ardeshir Sepehri, 1–5. Amityville, NY: Baywood Publishing Company.

Chien, Isadore, D. Gerald, R. Lee, and E. Rosenfield. 1964. *The Road to H.* New York: Basic Books.

Chomsky, Aviva. 2000. "The Threat of a Good Example: Health and Revolution in Cuba." In *Dying for Growth: Global Inequality and the Health of the Poor*, ed. Jim Kim, Joyce Millan, Alec Irwin, and John Gershman, 382–390. Monroe, ME: Common Courage Press.

Chrisman, Noel J., and Arthur Kleinman. 1983. "Popular Health Care, Social Networks, and Cultural Meanings: The Orientation of Medical Anthropology." In *Handbook of Health, Health Care, and the Health Professions*, ed. David Mechanic, 569–90. New York: Free Press.

Christiano, A., and Ida Susser. 1989. "Knowledge and Perceptions of HIV Infection among Homeless Pregnant Women." *Journal of Nurse Midwifery* 34: 318–22.

Churchill, Larry R. 1987. *Rationing Health Care in America: Perceptions and Principles in Justice.* South Bend, IN: University of Norte Dame Press.

Cisin, Ira, and Don Cahalan. 1970. "Some Correlates of American Drinking Practices." In *Recent Advances in Studies of Alcoholism*, ed. N. Mello and J. Mendelson, 805–25. Rockville, MD: National Institute of Mental Health.

Clarren, S., S. Rondels, M. Sanderson, and R. Fineman. 2001. Screening for Fetal Alcohol Syndrome in Primary Schools: A Feasibility Study. *Teratology* 63(1): 3–10.

Cleaver, Harry. 1977. "Malaria and the Political Economy of Health." *International Journal of Health Services* 7: 557–79.

Clements, Forrest. 1932. "Primitive Concepts of Disease." *University of California Publications in American Archaeology and Ethnology* 32(2): 185–252.

Coburn, David. 1999. "Phases of Capitalism, Welfare States, Medical Dominance, and Health in Ontario." *International Journal of Health Services* 29: 833–51.

Cohen, Mark Nathan. 1984. "An Introduction to the Symposium." In *Paleopathology at the Origins of Agriculture*, ed. Mark Nathan Cohen and George Armelagos, 1–7. New York: Academic Press.

———. 1989. *Health and the Rise of Civilization.* New Haven, CT: Yale University Press.

Comaroff, Jean. 1982. "Medicine, Symbol and Ideology." In *The Problem of Medical Knowledge: Examining the Social Construction of Medicine*, ed. Peter Wright and Andrew Treacher, 49–68. Edinburgh: University of Edinburgh Press.

———. 1993. "The Diseased Heart of Africa: Medicine, Colonialism, and the Black Body." In *Knowledge, Power & Practice: The Anthropology of Medicine and Every*, ed. Shirley Lindenbaum and Margaret Lock, 305–29. Berkeley: University of California Press.

Commoner, Barry. *1990. Making Peace with the Planet.* New York: Pantheon Books.

Connecticut Department of Health Services. 1990. *AIDS in Connecticut: Annual Surveillance Report.* Hartford, 31 December.

Conover, S., A. Berkman, A. Gheith, R. Jahiel, D. Stanley, P. Geller, E. Valencia, and E. Susser. 1997. "Methods for Successful Follow-up of Elusive Urban Population: An Ethnographic Approach with Homeless Men." *Bulletin of the New York Academy of Medicine* 74(1): 90–108.

Conover, S., R. Jahiel, D. Stanley, and E. Susser. Forthcoming. "Longitudinal Studies with People Who Are Homeless and Mentally Ill: An Ethnographic Approach to Quantitative Studies."

Conrad, Lawrence. 1993. "Arabic-Islamic Medicine." In *Companion Encyclopedia of the History of Medicine, Volume 1.*, ed. W. F. Bynum and Roy Porter, 676–727. London: Routledge.

Conrad, Peter. 1997. "Parallel Play in Medical Anthropology and Medical Sociology." *American Sociologist* 90–100.

Conrad, Peter, and Joseph Schneider. 1980. *Deviance and Medicalization: From Badness to Sickness.* St. Louis: C. V. Mosby Co.

Convisier, Richard, and John Rutledge. 1989. "Can Public Policies Limit the Spread of HIV among IV Drug Users?" *Journal of Drug Issues* 19: 113–28.

Cook, Rebecca. 1999. "Gender, Health and Human Rights." In *Health and Human Rights*, ed. Jonathan Mann, Sofia Gruskin, Michael Grodin and George Annas, 253–65. New York: Routledge.

Coreil, Jeannine. 1990. "The Evolution of Anthropology in International Health." In *Anthropology and Primary Health Care*, ed. Jeannine Coreil and J. Dennis Mull, 3–27. Boulder, CO: Westview Press.

Corti, Egon. 1931. *A History of Smoking.* London: George C. Harrap.

Counihan, C. 1990. *Food Rules, Gender Morality in the United States.* Presented at the Annual Meeting of the American Anthropological Association, New Orleans, LA.

Court, Jamie, and Francis Smith. 1999. *Making a Killing: HMOs and the Threat to Your Health.* Monroe, ME: Common Courage Press.

Cox, Christopher. 1996. *Chasing the Dragon: Into the Heart of the Golden Triangle.* New York: Henry Holt and Co.

Crawford, Rob. 1984. "A Cultural Account of 'Health': Control, Release, and the Social Body." In *Issues in the Political Economy of Health* Care, ed. John McKinlay, 60–103. New York: Tavistock Publications.

Crellin, J. K., R. R. Anderson, and J.T.H. Connor, eds. 1997. *Alternative Health Care in Canada: Nineteenth- and Twentieth-century Perspectives.* Toronto: Canadian Scholars' Press.

Crimp, Douglas. 1988. "How to Have Promiscuity in an Epidemic." In *AIDS: Cultural Analysis, Cultural Activism*, ed. Cambridge, MA: MIT Press.

Cultural Survival. 1984. Fact Sheet on the Ju/Wa People. Cambridge, MA.

Dai, Bingham. 1937. *Addiction in Chicago.* Montclair, NJ: Patterson Smith.

D'Andrade, Roy. 1995. "Moral Models in Anthropology." *Current Anthropology* 36: 399–408.

Damio, Grace, and L. Cohen. 1990. *Policy Report of the Hartford Community Hunger Identification Project.* Hartford: Hispanic Health Council.

Daniels, Les. 1991. *Marvel.* New York: Harry N. Abrams.

Davis-Floyd, Robbie. 2001. "Gender and Ritual: Giving Birth the American Way." In *Gender in Cross-Cultural* Perspective, ed. Caroline Brettel and Carolyn Sargent, 447–60. Upper Saddle River, NJ: Prentice-Hall.

Dehavenon, Anna Lou, ed. 1996. *There's No Place Like Home: Anthropological Perspectives on Housing and Homelessness in the United States.* Westport, CT: Bergin & Garvey.

Derber, Charles. 1983. "Sponsorship and the Control of Physicians." *Theory and Society* 12: 561–601.

Devereux, George. 1956. "Normal and Abnormal: The Key Problem in Psychiatric Anthropology." In *Some Uses of Anthropology: Theoretical and Applied*, ed. Joseph B. Casagrande and Thomas Gladwin, 3–48. Washington, DC: Anthropological Society of Washington.

———. 1957. "Dream Learning and Individual Ritual Differences in Mohave Shamanism." *American Anthropologist* 59: 1036.

Devine, Richard J. 1996. *Good Care, Painful Choices: Medical Ethics for Ordinary People*. Mahwah, NJ: Paulist Press.

Devisch, Renaat. 1986. "Belgium." *Medical Anthropology Quarterly*, o.s., 17(4): 87–89.

Diamond, Stanley. 1974. *In Search of the Primitive: A Critique of Civilization*. New Brunswick, NJ: Transaction.

Di Giacomo, Susan. 1999. "Can There be a 'Cultural Epidemiology?'" *Medical Anthropology Quarterly* 13: 436–457.

Di Leonardo, Micaela, ed. 1991. *Gender at the Crossroads of Knowledge: Feminist Anthropology in the Postmodern Era*. Berkeley, CA: University of California Press.

Dorris, Michael. 1990. *The Broken Cord*. New York: HarperCollins.

Douglas, Oliver. 1955. *A Solomon Island Society*. Boston: Beacon Press.

Dow, James. 1986. "Universal Aspects of Symbolic Healing: A Theoretical Analysis." *American Anthropologist* 88: 56–69.

Doyal, Lesley (with Imogen Pennell). 1979. *The Political Economy of Health*. Boston: South End Press.

Draper, Patricia. 1975. "!Kung Women: Contrasts in Sexual Egalitarianism in the Foraging and Sedentary Contexts." In *Toward an Anthropology of Women*, ed. Rayna Rapp Reiter, 77–109. New York: Monthly Review Press.

Driver, Harold. 1969. *Indians of North America*. Chicago: University of Chicago Press.

Drope, J., and S. Chapman. 2001. "Tobacco Industry Efforts at Discrediting Scientific Knowledge of Environmental Tobacco Smoke: A Review of Internal Industry Documents." *Journal of Epidemiology and Community Health* 55(8): 588–94.

Dunn, Frederick. 1976. "Traditional Asian Medicine and Cosmopolitan Medicine as Adaptive Systems." In *Asian Medical Systems: A Comparative Study*, ed. Charles Leslie, 133–58. Berkeley: University of California Press.

———. 1977. "Health and Disease in Hunter-Gatherers: Epidemiological Factors." In *Culture, Disease, and Healing: Studies in Medical Anthropology*, ed. David Landy, 99–107. New York: Macmillan.

Eaton, S. Boyd, Marjorie Shostak, and Melvin Konner. 1988. *Paleolithic Prescription: A Program of Diet and Exercise and a Design for Living*. New York: Harper and Row.

Eaton, Virgil. 1888. "How the Opium Habit Is Acquired." *Popular Science* 33: 665–66.

Eckert, Penelope. 1983. "Beyond the Statistics of Adolescent Smoking." *American Journal of Public Health* 73(4): 439–41.

Eckholm, E. 1978. *Cutting Tobacco's Toll*. Worldwatch Paper #18. Washington, DC: Worldwatch Institute.

Edelman, M. 1987. *Families in Peril: An Agenda for Social Change.* Cambridge, MA: Harvard University Press.

Eliade, Mircea. 1964. *Shamanism: Archaic Techniques of Ecstasy.* New York: Pantheon Books.

Elling, Ray H. 1981a. "The Capitalist World-System and International Health." *International Journal of Health Services* 11: 25–51.

———. 1981b. "Political Economy, Cultural Hegemony, and Mixes of Traditional and Modern Medicine." *Social Science and Medicine* 15A: 89–99.

Embodden, William. 1974. *Narcotic Plants: Hallucinogens, Stimulants, Inebriants, and Hypnotics—Their Origins and Uses.* London: Studio Vista.

Engels, Friedrich. 1845. *The Condition of the Working Class in England.* Reprint, London: Grenada, 1969.

———. 1972. *The Origin of the Family, Private Property and the* State. Edited by. Eleanor Burke Leacock. New York: International Publishers.

Erwin, Deborah Oates. 1987. "The Military Medicalization of Cancer Treatment." In *Encounters with Biomedicine: Case Studies in Medical Anthropology,* ed. Hans A. Baer, 201–27. New York: Gordon and Breach.

Estrada, Anthony, J. Rabow, and R. Watts. 1982. "Alcohol Use among Hispanic Adolescents: A Preliminary Report." *Hispanic Journal of Behavioral Sciences* 4: 339–51.

Estroff, Sue. 1993. "Identity, Disability and Schizophrenia: The Problem of Chronicity." In *Knowledge, Power and Practice: The Anthropology of Medicine in Everyday Life,* ed. Shirley Lindenbaum and Margaret Lock, 247–86. Berkeley: University of California Press.

Etienne, Mona. 2001. "The Case for Social Modernity: Adoption of Children by Urban Baule Women." ed. Caroline Brettel and Carolyn Sargent, 32–38. Upper Saddle River, NJ: Prentice-Hall.

Evans-Pritchard, E. E. 1937. *Witchcraft, Oracles and Magic among the Azande.* Oxford: Oxford University Press.

——— 1940. *The Nuer: A Description of the Modes of Livelihood and Political Institutions of a Nilotic Peoples.* Oxford, England: Clarendon Press.

Fabrega, Horacio, Jr. 1974. *Disease and Social Behavior: An Interdisciplinary Perspective.* Cambridge, MA: MIT Press.

——— 1997. *Evolution of Sickness and Healing.* Berkeley: University of California Press.

Farmer, Paul. 1990. The Exotic and the Mundane: Haitian Immunodeficiency Virus in Haiti. *Human Nature* 1:415–446.

———. 1992. *AIDS and Accusation: Haiti and the Geography of Blame.* Berkeley: University of California Press.

———. 1997. "AIDS and Anthropologists: Ten Years Later." *Medical Anthropology Quarterly* 11: 516–25.

———. 1999. *Infections and Inequalities: The Modern Plagues.* Berkeley: University of California Press.

Farmer, Paul, Margaret Connors, and Janie Simmons, eds. 1996. *Women, Poverty, and AIDS: Sex, Drugs and Structural Violence.* Monroe, ME: Common Courage Press.

Farquhar, Judith. 1994. *Knowing Practice: The Clinical Encounter of Chinese Medicine.* Boulder, CO: Westview Press.

Farrelly, M. C., D. L. Faulkner, and P. Mowry. 2000. *Cigarette Smoking Among Youth: Results from the 1999 National Youth Tobacco Survey.* Washington, DC: Coordinating Center for Evaluation and Applied Research, American Legacy Foundation.

Fee, Elizabeth, and Donald Fox. 1992. "Introduction: The Contemporary Historiography of AIDS." In *AIDS: The Making of a Chronic Disease,* ed. Elizabeth Fee and Donald Fox, 1–19. Berkeley: University of California Press.

Fee, Elizabeth, and Nancy Krieger. 1993. "Thinking and Rethinking AIDS: Implications for Health Policy." *International Journal of Health Services* 23: 323–46.

Feldman, Douglas. 1985. "AIDS and Social Change." *Human Organization* 44(4): 343–48.

Feldman, Douglas, and Thomas Johnson. 1986. *The Social Dimensions of AIDS.* New York: Praeger.

Feldman, Harvey. 1973. "Street Status and Drug Users." *Society* 10: 32–39.

Feldman, Harvey and Michael Aldrich. 1990. "The Role of Ethnography in Substance Abuse Research and Public Policy: Historical Precedent and Future Prospects." In *The Collection and Interpretation of Data from Hidden Populations,* Elizabeth Lambert, 12–30. Rockville, MD: National Institute on Drug Abuse (NIDA Research Monograph #98).

Feldman, Harvey, Michael Agar, and George Bechner. 1979. *Angel Dust: An Ethnographic Study* Lexington, Mass.: Lexington Books.

Femia, Joseph. 1975. "Hegemony and Consciousness in the Thought of Antonio Gramsci." *Political Studies* 23: 29–48.

Feshbach, Murray, and Alfred Friendly, Jr. 1992. *Ecocide in the USSR: Health and Nature under Siege.* New York: Basic Books.

Fiddle, S. 1967. *Portraits from a Shooting Gallery.* New York: Harper and Row.

Field, Peter. 1962. "A New Cross-Cultural Study of Drunkenness." In *Society, Culture, and Drinking Patterns,* ed. David Pittman and Charles Snyder, 48–74. Carbondale, IL: Southern Illinois University Press.

Fineberg, H. 1988. "The Social Dimensions of AIDS." *Scientific American,* October, 128–34.

Finestone, H. 1957. "Cats, Kicks, and Color." *Social Problems* 5: 39–45.

Firth, Rose Mary. 1978. "Social Anthropology and Medicine—A Personal Perspective." *Social Science and Medicine* 12B: 237–45.

Fischer, P. 1987. "Tobacco in the Third World." *Journal of Islamic Medical Association* 19: 19–21.

Fisk, Milton. 1980. *Ethics and Society: A Marxist Interpretation of Value.* New York: New York University.

———. 2000. *Toward a Healthy Society: The Morality and Politics of American Health Care Reform.* Lawrence: University Press of America.

Fitchen, J. 1988. "Hunger, Malnutrition, and Poverty in the Contemporary United States: Some Observations on Their Social and Cultural Context." *Food and Foodways* 2: 309–33.

Fitzpatrick, Joseph. 1971. *Puerto Rican Americans: The Meaning of Migration to the Mainland.* Englewood Cliffs, NJ: Prentice-Hall.

———. 1990. "Drugs and Puerto Ricans in New York." In *Drugs in Hispanic Communities,* ed. Ronald Glick and Joan Moore, 103–26. New Brunswick, NJ: Rutgers University Press.

Flacks, Richard. 1993. "The Party's Over—So What Is to Be Done?" *Social Research* 60: 445–70.

Flink, James J. 1973. *The Car Culture*. Cambridge, MA: MIT Press.

Foster, George M. 1982. "Applied Anthropology and International Health: Retrospect and Prospect." *Human Organization* 41: 189–97.

Foster, George M., and Barbara Gallatin Anderson. 1978. *Medical Anthropology*. New York: John Wiley and Sons.

Fox, Renee. 1990. "The Evolution of American Bioethics: A Sociological Perspective." In *Social Science Perspectives on Medical Ethics*, ed. George Weisz, 201–17. Dordrecht, Netherlands: Kluwer Academic Publishers.

Foucault, Michel. 1975. *The Birth of the Clinic: An Archaeology of Medical Perception*. New York: Vintage.

Frankenberg, Ronald. 1974. "Functionalism and After? Theory and Developments in Social Science Applied to the Health Field." *International Journal of Health Services* 43: 411–27.

———. 1980. "Medical Anthropology and Development: A Theoretical Perspective." *Social Science and Medicine* 14B: 197–207.

———. 1981. "Allopathic Medicine, Profession, and Capitalist Ideology in India." *Social Science and Medicine* 15A: 115–25.

Freedman, Lyn and Deborah Maine. 1993. "Women's Mortality: A Legacy of Neglect." In *The Health of Women: A Global Perspective*, ed. Marge Koblinsky, Judith Timyan, and Jill Gay, 147–71. Boulder, CO: Westview Press.

Freidson, Elliot. 1970. *Profession of Medicine*. New York: Dodd, Mead and Co.

Freire, Paulo. 1974. *Pedagogy of the Oppressed*. New York: Seabury Press.

Freund, Peter S., and George Martin. 1993. *The Ecology of the Automobile*. Montreal: Black Rose Books.

Freund, Peter S., and Meredith B. McGuire. 1991. *Health, Illness, and the Social Body: A Critical Sociology*. Englewood Cliffs, NJ: Prentice-Hall.

Frezza, M., C. Padova, and G. Pozzato. 1990. "High Blood Alcohol Levels in Women: The Role of Decreased Gastric Alcohol Dehydrogenase Activity and First-Pass Metabolism." *New England Journal of Medicine* 322(2): 95–99.

Friedlander, Eva, ed. 1996. *Look at the World Through Women's Eyes: Plenary Speeches, Beijing '95* New York: NGO Forum on Women.

Friedman, S., D. Des Jarlais, and J. Sotheran. 1986. "AIDS Health Education for Intravenous Drug Users." *Health Education Quarterly* 13: 383–93.

Friedman, Samuel, Don Des Jarlias, Claire Sterk, Jo Sotheran, S. Tross, J. Woods, M. Sufian, and A. Abdul-Quader. 1990. AIDS and the Social Relations of Intravenous Drug Users. *Milbank Quarterly* 68 (Supplement): 85–110.

Friedman, Samuel, Maryl Sufian, and Don Des Jarlais. 1990. "The AIDS Epidemic among Latino Intravenous Drug Users." In *Drugs in Hispanic Communities*, ed. Ronald Glick and Joan Moore, 45–54. New Brunswick, NJ: Rutgers University Press.

Fuentes, Annette. 1997. "White Coats with Blue Collars." *In These Times* (3 March): 17–19.

Gailey, Christine. 1998. "Feminist Methods." In *Handbook of Anthropological Methods*, ed. Russell Bernard, Washington, DC: American Anthropological Association.

Gaines, Atwood. 1987. "Shamanism and the Shaman: Plea for the Person-Centered Approach." *Anthropology and Humanism Quarterly* 12(3&4): 62–68.

———. 1991. "Cultural Constructivism: Sickness Histories and the Understanding of Ethnomedicines beyond Critical Medical Anthropologies." In *Anthropologies of Medicine: A Colloquium of Western and European Perspectives*, ed. Beatrix Pfiederer and Gilles Bibeau, Wiesbaden, Germany: Verlag Vieweg.

Gallagher, Eugene B. et al. 1998. "Enrich Bioethics: Add One Part Social to One Part Clinical." In *Bioethics and Society: Constructing the Public Enterprise*, ed. Raymond DeVries and Jaradan Subedi, 166–91. Upper Saddle River, NJ: Prentice Hall.

Gamella, Juan. 1994. "The Spread of Intravenous Drug Use and AIDS in a Neighborhood in Spain." *Medical Anthropology Quarterly*, n.s., 8:131–60.

Gammeltoft, Tine. 1999. *Women's Bodies, Women's Worries: Health and Family Planning in a Vietnamese Rural Community*. Surrey, England: Curzon Press.

Garrett, Laurie. 1994. The Coming Plague: Newly Emerging Diseases in a World Out of Balance. Penguin Books USA Inc.

Garrity, John. 2000. "Jesus, Peyote, and the Holy People: Alcohol Abuse and the Ethos of Power in Navajo Healing." *Medical Anthropology Quarterly* 11: 306–23.

Gavaler, J. and A. Arria. 1995. "Increased Susceptibility of Women to Alcoholic Liver Disease: Pathology and Pathogenesis." In *Alcoholic Liver Disease: Pathology and Pathogenesis*, ed. P. Hall, 123–33, London: Edward Arnold.

Gelberg L., T. C. Gallagher, R. M. Andersen, and P. Koegel. 1997. "Competing Priorities as a Barrier to Medical Care among Homeless Adults in Los Angeles." *American Journal of Public Health* 87(2): 217–20.

Georgopoulos, Basil S., and Floyd C. Mann. 1979. "The Hospital as an Organization." In *Patients, Physicians, and Illness*, ed. E. Gartley, 296–305. New York: Free Press.

Geras, Norman. 1990. *Discourses of Extremity: Radical Ethics and Post-Marxist Extravagances*. London: Verso.

Ghalioungui, Paul. 1963. *Magic and Medical Science in Ancient Egypt*. New York: Barnes and Noble.

Gilbert, M. Jean. 1987. "Programmatic Approaches to Alcohol-Related Needs of Mexican Americans." In *Mexican Americans and Alcohol*, ed. M. Jean Gilbert and Richard Cervantes, 95–107. Los Angeles: University of California.

Gilman, S. 1987. "AIDS and Syphilis: The Iconography of Disease." In *AIDS: Cultural Analysis, Cultural Activism*, ed. D. Crimp, 87–108. Cambridge, MA: MIT Press.

Ginsburg, Faye, and Rayna Rapp. 1995. "Introduction." *Conceiving the New World Order*, ed. Faye Ginsburg and Rayna Rapp, 1–17. Berkeley: University of California Press.

Ginzberg, Eli. 1994. *Medical Gridlock and Health Reform*. Boulder, CO: Westview Press.

Glass-Coffin, Bonnie. 1995. Anthropology, Shamanism, and the 'New Age'. *Chronicle of Higher Education*. June 15, 1748.

Glick, Ronald. 1983. "Demoralization and Addiction: Heroin in the Chicago Puerto Rican Community." *Journal of Psychoactive Drugs* 15: 281–92.

———. 1990. "Survival, Income, and Status: Drug Dealing in the Chicago Puerto Rican Community." In *Drugs in Hispanic Communities*, ed. Ronald Glick and Joan Moore, 77–102. New Brunswick, NJ: Rutgers University Press.

Glick Schiller, Nina, S. Crystal, and D. Lewellen. 1994. "Risky Business: The Cultural Construction of AIDS Risk Groups." *Social Science and Medicine* 38(10): 1337-46.

Godelier, Maurice. 1986. *The Mental and the Material: Thought Economy and Society.* London: Verso.

Goffman, Irving. 1963. *Stigma.* Englewood Cliffs, NJ: Prentice-Hall.

Goldman, Marlene, and Maureen Hatch, eds. 2000. *Women and Health.* New York: Academic Press.

Good, Byron. 1994. *Medicine, Rationality, and Experience.* Cambridge, England: Cambridge University Press.

Good, Mary-Jo Delvecchio, and Byron Good. 2000. "Parallel Sisters": Medical Anthropology and Medical Sociology. In *Handbook of Medical Sociology*, 5th ed., ed. Chloe E. Bird, Peter Conrad, and Allen M. Fremont, 377–88: Prentice-Hall.

Goode, Erich. 1984. *Drugs in American Society.* New York: Alfred A. Knopf.

Goode, Judith, and Jeff Maskovsky, eds. 2001. *The New Poverty Studies: The Ethnography of Power, Politics, and the Impoverished People in the United States.* New York: New York University Press.

Goodman, Alan, and Thomas L. Leatherman, eds. 1998. *Building a New Biocultural Synthesis: Political-Economic Perspectives on Human Biology.* Ann Arbor: University of Michigan Press.

Gordon, Robert. 1992. *The Bushman Myth.* Boulder, CO: Westview.

Gorz, Andre. 1973. *Socialism and Revolution.* Garden City, NY: Anchor.

———. 1980. *Ecology as Politics.* Boston: South End Press.

Gough, Kathleen. 1971. "Nuer Kinship: A Re-Examination." In *The Translation of Culture: Essays to E.E. Evans-Pritchard*, ed. T. O. Beidelman, London: Tavistock Publications.

Gounis, K. 1992. "Temporality and the Domestication of Homelessness." In *The Politics of Time*, ed. H. Rutz, Washington, DC: American Ethnological Society (Monograph Series # 4).

Gourevitch, Danielle. 1998. "The Paths of Knowledge: Medicine in the Roman World." In *Western Medical Thought From Antiquity to the Middle Ages*, ed. Mirko Grmk, 104–38. Cambridge: Harvard University Press.

Gow, Peter. 1994. "River People: Shamanism and History in Western Amazonia." In *Shamanism, History, and the State*, ed. Nicholas Thomas and Caroline Humphrey, 90–113. Ann Arbor: University of Michigan Press.

Graiz, Laurene A. 1999. Health of Nations: An International Perspective on U.S. Health Reform. Washington, D.C.: Congressional Quarterly Press.

Gran, Peter. 1979. "Medical Pluralism in Arab and Egyptian History: An Overview of Class Structures and Philosophies of the Main Phases." *Social Science and Medicine* 13B: 339–48.

Grant, B. and D. Dawson. 1997. "Age at Onset of Alcohol Use and Its Association with DSM-IV Alcohol Abuse and Dependence: Results from the National Longitudinal Alcohol Epidemiologic Survey." *Journal of Substance Abuse* 9: 103–10.

Green, D. 1979. *Teenage Smoking: Immediate and Long Term Patterns.* Washington, DC: National Institute of Education.

Green, E. M. 1914. "Psychoses among Negroes—A Comparative Study." *Journal of Nervous and Mental Disease* 41: 697–08.

Greenfield, T. and Robin Room. 1997. "Situational Norms for Drinking and Drunkenness: Trends in the US Adult Population, 1979–1990." *Addiction* 92(1): 33–47.

Grinspoon, Lester, and James Bakalar. 1985. *Cocaine: A Drug and Its Social Evolution.* New York: Basic Books.

Gross, W. and R. Billingham. 1998. "Alcohol Consumption and Sexual Victimization Among College Women." *Psychological Reports* 82(1): 80–82.

Grossinger, Richard. 1990. *Planet Medicine: From Stone Age Shamanism to Post-Industrial Healing.* Berkeley, CA: North Atlantic Books.

Gruenbaum, Ellen. 1981. "Medical Anthropology, Health Policy and the State: A Case Study of Sudan." *Medical Anthropology* 7(2): 51–62.

———. 1983. "Struggling with the Mosquito: Malaria Policy and Agricultural Development in Sudan." *Medical Anthropology* 7: 53–62.

Guyer, Jane. 1991. "Female Farming in Anthropology and African History." In *Gender in the Crossroads of Knowledge: Feminist Anthropology in the Postmodern Era,* ed. Micaela di Leonardo, 257–78.

Habermas, Juergen. 1991. "What Does Socialism Mean Today? The Revolutions of Recuperation and the Need for New Thinking." In *After the Fall: The Failure of Communism and the Future of Socialism,* ed. Robin Blackburn, 25–46. London: Verso.

Hahn, Robert A. 1983. "Biomedical Practice and Anthropological Theory: Frameworks and Directions." *Annual Review of Anthropology* 12: 305–33.

———. 1995. *Sickness and Healing: An Anthropological Perspective.* Ann Arbor: University of Michigan Press.

Hahn, Robert A., et al. 1989. "Race and the Prevalence of Syphilis Seroactivity in the United States Population: A National Sero-Epidemiologic Study." *American Journal of Public Health* 79(4): 467–70.

———. 1999. Anthropology and the Enhancement of Public Health Practice. In *Anthropology in Public Health: Bridging Differences in Culture and Society,* 3–26. New York: Oxford University Press.

Haire, Doris. 1978. "The Cultural Warping of Childbirth." In *The Cultural Crisis of Modern Medicine,* ed. John Ehrenreich, 185–200. New York: Monthly Review Press.

Handelbaum, Don. 1967. "The Development of a Washo Shaman." In *Culture, Disease, and Healing: Studies in Medical Anthropology,* ed. David Landy, 427–38. New York: Macmillan.

Hanson, Bill, George Beschner, James Walters, and Elliot Bovelle. 1985. *Life with Heroin: Voices from the Inner City.* Lexington, MA: Lexington Books.

Haraway, Donna. 1991. *Simians, Cyborgs, and Women.* New York: Routledge.

Harner, Michael. 1968. *The Jivaro.* Berkeley: University of California Press.

———. 1980. *The Way of the Shaman: A Guide to Power and Healing.* New York: Bantam Books.

Harris, Marvin, and Eric Ross. 1987. *Death, Sex, and Fertility: Population Regulation in Preindustrial and Developing Societies.* New York: Columbia University Press.

Harris, Marvin, and Orna Johnson. 2000. *Cultural Anthropology.* Boston: Addison-Wesley.

Haug, M. 1975. "The Deprofessionalization of Everyone?" *Sociological Focus* 8: 197–213.

Haynes, Suzanne, et al. 1990. "Patterns of Cigarette Smoking among Hispanics in the United States: Results from HHANES 1982–84." *American Journal of Public Health* 80(12): 47–53.

Heath, Dwight. 1988. "Emerging Anthropological Theory and Models of Alcohol Use and Alcoholism." In *Theories on Alcoholism*, ed. C. Douglas Chaudron and D. Adrian Wilkinson, 353–410. Toronto: Addiction Research Foundation.

———. 1990. "Coca in the Andes: Traditions, Functions and Problems." *Rhode Island Medical Journal* 73: 237–41.

———. 1991. "Drinking Patterns of the Bolivian Camba." In *Society, Culture, and Drinking Patterns Reexamined*, ed. David Pittman and Helene White, 62–108. New Brunswick, NJ: Rutgers Center of Alcohol Studies.

———. 1994. "Agricultural Changes and Drinking among the Bolivian Camba: A Longitudinal View of the Aftermath of a Revolution." *Human Organization* 53: 357-361.

Heggenhougen, Kris. 1986. "Scandinavia." *Medical Anthropology Quarterly*, o.s., 17(4): 94–95.

Heise, Lori. 1993. "Violence Against Women: The Missing Agenda." In *The Health of Women: A Global Perspective*, ed. Marge Koblinsky, Judith Timyan, and Jill Gray, 171–97. Boulder, CO: Westview Press.

Helman, Cecil. 1994. *Culture, Health, and Illness: An Introduction for Health Professionals*. 3rd ed. Oxford: Butterworth Hinemann.

Helmer, John. 1983. "Blacks and Cocaine." In *Drugs and Society*, ed. Maureen Kelleher, Bruce MacMurray, and Thomas Shapiro, 14–29. Dubuque, IA: Kendall/Hunt.

Henderson, G., and M. Cohen. 1984. *The Chinese Hospital: A Socialist Work Unit*. New Haven, CT: Yale University Press.

Hendry, Joy. 1994. "Drinking and Gender in Japan." In *Gender, Drink and Drugs*, ed. Maryon McDonald, 175–190. Oxford: Berg.

Herd, Denise. 1991. "Drinking Patterns in the Black Population." In *Alcohol in America: Drinking Patterns and Problems*, ed. W. Clark and M. Hilton, 308–19. Albany: State University of New York Press.

Herdt, Gilbert. 1987. *The Sambia: Ritual and Gender in New Guinea*. New York: Holt, Rinehart, and Winston.

———. 1990. "Introduction." In *The Time of AIDS*, ed. Gilbert Herdt and Shirley Lindenbaum, 3–26. Newbury Park, CA: Sage Publications.

———. 2001. "Stigma and the Ethnographic Study of HIV: Problems and Prospects." *AIDS and Behavior* 5(2): 141–49.

Hernstein, Richard J., and Charles Murray. 1994. *The Bell Curve: Intelligence and Class Structure in American Life*. New York: Free Press.

Herzfeld, Michael. 1980. "Honour and Shame: Problems in the Analysis of Moral Systems." *Man* 15: 339–51.

Hill, Carole E., ed. 1991. *Training Manual in Medical Anthropology*. Washington, DC: American Anthropological Association.

Hills, Stuart. 1980. *Demystifying Social Deviance*. New York: McGraw-Hill.

Himmelstein, David U., and Steffie Woolhandler. 1984. "Medicine as Industry: The Health-Care Sector in the United States." *Monthly Review* 35(11): 13–25.

————. 1989. "A National Health Program for the United States: A Physician's Proposal." *New England Journal of Medicine* 320: 102–8.

————. 1994. *The National Health Program Book: A Source Guide for Advocates.* Monroe, ME: Common Courage Press.

Hippler, Arthur. 1976. "Shamans, Curers, and Personality: Suggestions toward a Theoretical Model." In *Culture-Bound Syndromes, Ethnopsychiatry, and Alternate Therapies,* ed. William Lebra, 103–13. Honolulu: University of Hawaii Press.

Ho, John. 1996. "The Influence of Coinfections on HIV Transmission and Disease Progression." *The AIDS Reader* 6(4): 114–16.

Hodges, Donald Clark. 1974. *Socialist Humanism: The Outcome of Classical European Morality.* St. Louis: Warren H. Green.

Hogue, Carol J. Rowland. 2000. "Gender, Race, and Class: From Epidemiologic Association to Etiologic Hypotheses." ed. Marlene Goldman and Carolyn Sargent, 15–25. New York: Academic Press.

Hope, K. 1992. "Child Survival and Health Care among Low-Income African American Families in the United States." *Health Transition Review* 2: 151–64.

Hoppal, Mihaly, and Keith D. Howard, eds. 1993. *Shamans and Cultures.* Los Angeles: International Society for Trans-Oceanic Research.

Hopper, Kim. August 1992. "Counting the Homeless: S-Night in New York." *Evaluation Review* 16(4).

Hopper, Kim, and L. Cox. 1982. "Litigation in Advocacy for the Homeless: The Case of New York City." *Development: Seeds of Change* 2: 57–62.

Hopper, K., E. Susser, and S. Conover. 1987. "Economics of Makeshift: Deindustrialization and Homelessness in New York City." *Urban Anthropology* 14: 183–236.

Horan, Michael. 1993. "Are Minority Groups Winning the Fight against CVD and Pulmonary Disease?" In *Minority Health Issues for an Emerging Majority.* Proceedings of the 4th National Forum on Cardiovascular Health, Pulmonary Disorders, and Blood Resources, ed. 22–23. Washington, DC: National Heart, Lung, and Blood Institute.

Horton, David. 1943. "The Functions of Alcohol in Primitive Societies: A Cross-cultural Study." *Quarterly Journal of Studies on Alcohol* 4: 199–320.

Howell, Nancy. 2000. *Demography of the Dobe !Kung.* Hawthorne: Aldine-DeGruyter.

Hsiao, William C. 1995. "The Chinese Health Care System: Lessons for Other Nations." *Social Science and Medicine* 41:1047–55.

Hughes, Charles C. 1978. "Ethnomedicine." In *Health and the Human Condition: Perspectives on Medical Anthropology,* ed. Michael H. Logan and Edward E. Hunt, Jr., 150–58. North Scituate, MA: Duxbury Press.

Hughes, Donald H. 1975. *The Ecology of Ancient Civilizations.* Albuquerque: University of New Mexico Press.

Hunt, Edward E., Jr. 1978. "Evolutionary Comparisons of the Demography, Life Cycles, and Health Care of Chimpanzee and Human Populations." In *Health and the Human Condition: Perspectives on Medical Anthropology,* ed. Michael H. Logan and Edward E. Hunt, Jr., 52–57. North Scituate, MA: Duxbury Press.

Hunter, Susan S. 1985. "Historical Perspectives on the Development of Health Systems Modeling in Medical Anthropology." *Social Science and Medicine* 21: 1297–1307.

Hutchinson, B. 1979. "Alcohol as a Contributing Factor in Social Disorganization: The South African Bantu in the Nineteenth Century." In *Beliefs, Behaviors and Alcoholic Beverages*, Ed. Mac Marshal, 328–41. Ann Arbor: University of Michigan Press.

Hutchinson, Sharon, and Jok Madut Jok. 2002. "Gendered Violence and the Militarisation of Ethnicity: A Case Study from South Sudan." In *Postcolonial Subjectivities in Africa*, ed. Richard Werbner, 84–109. New York: Zed Books.

Ile, Michael, and Laura Kroll. 1990. "Tobacco Advertising and the First Amendment." *Journal of the American Medical Association* 264(12): 1593–94.

Inciardi, James. 1986. *The War on Drugs: Heroin, Cocaine, Crime and Public Policy.* Mountain View, CA: Manfield Publishing Co.

Inciardi, James, Dorothy Lockwood, and Anne Pottieger. 1993. *Women and Crack-Cocaine.* New York: Macmillan.

Ingman, Stanley R., and Anthony E. Thomas, eds. 1975. *Topias and Utopias in Health: Policy Studies.* Hague: Mouton.

Inhorn, Marcia C., and Peter J. Brown. 1990. "The Anthropology of Infectious Disease." In *Annual Review of Anthropology* 19: 89–117.

Institute of Medicine. 1988. *Homelessness, Health and Human Needs.* N.P.: National Academy Press.

Jacobson, Jodi. 1993. "Women's Health: The Price of Poverty." In *The Health of Women: A Global Perspective*, ed. Marge Koblinsky, Judith Timyan, and Jill Gay, 3–33. Boulder, CO: Westview Press.

Jacobson, Michael, George Hacker, and Robert Atkins. 1983. *The Booze Merchants: The Inebriating of America.* Washington, DC: Center for Science in the Public Interest.

Jacoby, Russell. 1975. *Social Amnesia: A Critique of Contemporary Psychology from Adler to Laing.* Boston: Beacon Press.

Jakobson, Merete Demant. 1999. *Shamanism: Traditional and Contemporary Approaches to the Mastery of Spirits and Healing.* New York: Berghahn.

Janzen, John M. 1978. *The Quest for Therapy in Lower Zaire.* Berkeley: University of California Press.

Jessor, R. 1979. "Marijuana: A Review of Recent Psychosocial Research." In *Handbook of Drug Abuse*, ed. R. DuPont, A. Goldstein, and J. McDonnell. Washington, DC: U.S. Government Printing Office.

Johnson, Bruce, Paul Goldstein, Edward Preble, James Schmeidler, Douglas Lipton, and Thomas Miller. 1985. *Taking Care of Business: The Economics of Crime by Heroin Abusers.* Lexington, MA: Lexington Books.

Johnson, Jay. 1990. "Ethnopharmacology: An Interdisciplinary Approach to the Study of Intravenous Drug Use and HIV." *Journal of Contemporary Ethnography* 19: 349-369.

Johnson, Lloyd, Patrick O'Malley, and Jerald Bachman. 1982. *Drugs and American High School Students, 1962–1980.* Rockville, MD: National Institute on Drug Abuse.

———. 1994. *National Survey Results on Drug Use from the Monitoring the Future Study, 1975–1993.* Rockville, MD: National Institute on Drug Abuse.

Johnson, M. 1995. "Patriarchal Terrorism and Common Couple Violence: Two Forms of Violence Among Women." *Journal of Marriage and the Family* 57: 283–294.

Johnson, Paul. 1978. *A Shopkeeper's Millennium.* New York: Hill and Wang.

Johnson, Thomas M. 1987. "Practicing Medical Anthropology: Clinical Strategies for the Work in the Hospital." In *Applied Anthropology in America*, 2nd ed., ed. Edith M. Eddy and William L. Partridge, 316–39. New York: Columbia University Press.

Jonsen, Albert R. 2000. *A Short History of Medical Ethics.* New York: Oxford University Press.

Joralemon, Donald. 1990. "The Selling of the Shaman and the Problem of Informant Legitimacy." *Journal of Anthropological Research* 46: 105–18.

———. 1999. *Exploring Medical Anthropology.* Boston: Allyn and Bacon.

Justice, Judith. 1986. *Policies, Plans, and People: Culture and Health Development in Nepal.* Berkeley: University of California Press.

Kabeer, Naila. 1985. "Do Women Gain from High Fertility?" In *Women, Work, and Ideology in the Third World*, ed. Haleh Afshar, 66–83. London: Tavistock.

Kalweit, Holger. 1992. *Shamans, Healers, and Medicine Men.* Boston: Shambhala.

Kamin, Leon. 1995. "Behind the Curve." *Scientific American* 272(2): 99–103.

Kane, H. H. 1880. *The Hypodermic Injection of Morphia.* New York: C. L. Bermingham.

Kane, Stephanie. 1991. "HIV, Heroin and Heterosexual Relations." *Social Science and Medicine* 32: 1037–50.

Katz, Richard. 1982. *Boiling Energy: Community Healing among the Kalahari !Kung.* Cambridge, MA: Harvard University Press.

Kaufert, Leyland, and J. M. Kaufert. 1978. "Alternative Courses of Development: Medical Anthropology in Britain and North America." *Social Science and Medicine* 12B: 255–61.

Keesing, Roger. 1983. *Elota's Story: The Life and Times of a Solomon Islands Big Man.* New York: Holt, Rinehart, and Winston.

Kehoe, Alice Beck. 2000. *Shamans and Religion: An Anthropological Exploration in Critical Thinking.* Prospect Heights, IL: Waveland Press.

Kelman, Sander. 1975. "The Social Nature of the Definition Problem in Health." *International Journal of Health Services* 5: 625–42.

Kendell, Robert. 1979. "Alcoholism: A Medical or a Political Problem?" *British Medical Journal* 10: 367–75.

Kerley, Ellis R., and William M. Bass. 1978. "Paleopathology: Meeting Ground for Many Disciplines." In *Health and the Human Condition: Perspectives on Medical Anthropology*, ed. Michael H. Logan and Edward E. Hunt, Jr., 43–51. North Scituate, MA: Duxbury Press.

Kiev, Ari, ed. 1966. *Magic, Faith and Healing: Studies in Primitive Psychiatry Today.* New York: Free Press of Glencoe.

Kim, Jim Yong, Joyce V. Millen, Alec Irwin, and John Gershman, eds. 2000. *Dying for Growth: Global Inequality and the Health of the Poor.* Monroe, ME: Common Courage Press.

Kittie, N. 1971. *The Right to be Different: Deviance and Enforced Therapy.* Baltimore: Johns Hopkins University Press.

Klein, Dorie. 1983. "Ill and against the Law: The Social and Medical Control of Heroin Users." *Journal of Drug Issues* 13(1): 31–55.

Klein, Norman. 1979. "Introduction." In *Culture, Curers and Contagion*, ed. Norman Klein, 1–4. Novato, CA: Chandler and Sharp.

Kleinman, Arthur. 1995. *Writing at the Margin: Discourse Between Anthropology and Medicine*. Berkeley: University of California Press.

———. 1977. "Lessons from a Clinical Approach to Medical Anthropological Research." *Medical Anthropology Newsletter* 8: 5–8.

———. 1978. "Problems and Prospects in Comparative Cross-Cultural Medical and Psychiatric Studies." In *Culture and Healing in Asian Societies: Anthropological, Psychiatric and Public Health Studies*, ed. Arthur Kleinman, Peter Kunstadter, E. Russell Alexander, and James L. Gale, 329–74. Cambridge, MA: Schenkman Publishing Co.

Knox, R. 1987. "Hub Infant Deaths Up 32%." *Boston Globe* (9 February):1, 5.

Koblinsky, Marge, Judity Timyan, and Jill Gay, eds. 1993. The Health of Women: A Global Prespective Boulder, CO: Westview Press.

Koester, Stephen. 1994. "Copping, Running, and Paraphernalia Laws: Contextual Variables and Needle Risk Behavior among Injection Drug Users in Denver." *Human Organization* 53: 287–95.

Koester, Stephen and Judith Schwartz. 1993. "Crack, Gangs, Sex, and Powerlessness: A View from Denver." In *Crack Pipe as Pimp: An Ethnographic Investigation of Sex-for-Crack Exchanges*, ed Mitchell Ratner, 187–205. New York: Lexington Books.

Kolata, Gina. 1995. "New Picture of Who Will Get AIDS Is Crammed with Addicts." *New York Times* (2 February): C3.

Konner, Melvin. 1993. *Medicine at the Crossroads: The Crisis in Health Care*. New York: Pantheon Books.

Kotarba, J. 1990. "Ethnography and AIDS." *Journal of Contemporary Ethnography* 19: 259–70.

Krause, Elliot. 1977. *Power and Illness: The Political Sociology of Health and Medical Care*. New York: Elsevier.

———. 1996. *Death of the Guilds: Professions, States, and the Advance of Capitalism, 1930 to the Present*. New Haven: Yale University Press.

Kroeber, Alfred. 1939. "Cultural Elements and Distributions XV: Salt, Dogs, and Tobacco." *Anthropological Records* 6(1).

LaBarre, Weston. 1972. "Hallucinogens and the Shamanic Origins of Religion." In *Flesh of the Gods: The Ritual Use of* Hallucinogens, ed. Peter T. Furst, 261–78. New York: Praeger.

———. 1989. *The Peyote Cult*. 5th ed. Norman: University of Yale Oklahoma Press.

Lamphere, Louise. 1987. *From Working Daughters to Working Mothers: Immigrant Women in a New England Industrial Community*. Ithaca, NY: Cornell University Press.

Lamphere, Louise, Helena Ragone, and Patricia Zavella, eds. *Situated Lives: Gender and Culture in Everyday Life*. New York: Routledge.

Lamphere, Louise, and Michelle Zimbalist Rosaldo, eds. *Women, Culture and Society*. Stanford, CA: Stanford University Press.

Lan, David. 1985. *Guns and Rain: Guerrillas and Spirit Mediums in Zimbabwe*. Berkeley: University of California Press.

Landesman, S. 1993. "Commentary: Tuberculosis in New York City—The Consequences and Lessons of Failure." *American Journal of Public Health* 83(5): 766–68.

Landy, David. 1977. "Introduction." In *Culture, Disease, and Healing: Studies in Medical Anthropology*, ed. David Landy, 1–9. New York: Macmillan.

———. 1983. "Medical Anthropology: A Critical Appraisal." In *Advances in Medical Social Science*, vol. 1., ed. Julio L. Ruffini, 185–314. New York: Gordon and Breach.

Langdon, E. 1992. "Introduction: Shamanism and Anthropology." In *Portals of Power: Shamanism in South America*, ed. E. Langdon, Jean Matteson, and Gerhard Baer, 1–21. Albuquerque: University of New Mexico Press.

Lassey, Marie L., William R. Lassey, and Martin J. Jinks, eds. 1997. *Health Care Systems Around the World: Characteristics, Issues, Reforms.* Upper Saddle River, NJ: Prentice Hall.

Latour, Bruno, and Steve Woolgar. 1986. *Laboratory Life: The Construction of Scientific Facts.* Princeton, NJ: Princeton University Press.

Laughlin, William S. 1963. "Primitive Theory of Medicine: Empirical Knowledge." In *Man's Image in Medicine and Anthropology*, ed. Iago Galdston, 116–40. New York: International Universities Press.

Lazarus, Ellen. 1988. "Theoretical Considerations for the Study of the Doctor-Patient Relationship: Implications of a Perinatal Study." *Medical Anthropology Quarterly*, n.s., 2: 34–59.

Leacock, Eleanor Burke. 1972. "Introduction." In *The Origins of the Family, Private Property and the State*, ed. Eleanor Burke Leacock, 7–69. New York: International Publishers.

Leacock, Eleanor Burke, and Richard B. Lee, eds. 1982. *Politics and History in Band Societies.* Cambridge: Cambridge University Press.

Lee, Richard B. 1979. *The !Kung San: Men, Women and Work in a Foraging Society.* Cambridge, UK: Cambridge University Press.

———. 2002. *The Dobe Ju/'Hoansi.* : Wadsworth.

Lee, Richard B., and Irven DeVore. 1976. *Kalahari Hunter-Gatherers.* Cambridge, MA: Harvard University Press.

Lee, Richard B., and Susan Hurlich. 1982. "From Foragers to Fighters: South Africa's Militarization of the Namibian San." In *Politics and History in Band Societies*, ed. Eleanor Burke Leacock and Richard B. Lee, 327–46. Cambridge: Cambridge University Press.

Leeds, Anthony. 1971. "The Concept of the 'Culture of Poverty': Conceptual, Logical, and Empirical Problems, with Perspectives from Brazil and Peru." In *The Culture of Poverty: A Critique*, ed. Eleanor Burke Leacock, 226–84. New York: Simon and Schuster.

Leeson, Joyce. 1974. "Social Science and Health Policy in Preindustrial Society." *International Journal of Health Services* 4: 429–40.

Leibowitch, J. 1985. *Strange Virus of Unknown Origin.* New York: Ballantine Books.

Leland, J. 1976. *Firewater Myths: North American Indian Drinking and Alcohol Addiction.* New Brunswick, NJ: Rutgers Center of Alcohol Studies.

Lemco, Jonathan. 1994. "Introduction." In *National Health Care: Lessons from the United States and Canada*, ed. Jonathan Lemco, 1–41. Ann Arbor: University of Michigan Press.

Leonard, Terri. 1990. "Male Clients of Female Street Prostitutes: Unseen Partners in Sexual Disease Transmission." *Medical Anthropology Quarterly*, n.s., 4: 41–55.

Lerner, B. 1993. "New York City's Tuberculosis Control Efforts: The Historical Limitations of the 'War on Consumption.'" *American Journal of Public Health* 83(5): 758–66.

Leshner, Alan. 2001. "Addiction is a Brain Disease." *Issues in Science and Technology* 57(3): 75–80.

Leslie, Charles. 1974. The Modernization of Asian Medical Systems. In *Rethinking Modernization*, ed. John Poggie, Jr., and Robert N. Lynch, 69–107. Westport, CT: Greenwood Press.

———. 1976. Introduction. In *Asian Medical Systems: A Creative Study*, ed. Charles Leslie, 1–12. Berkeley: University of California Press.

———. 1977. "Medical Pluralism and Legitimation in the Indian and Chinese Medical Systems." In *Culture, Disease, and Healing: Studies in Medical Anthropology*, ed. David Landy 511–17. New York: Macmillan.

———. 1992. "Interpretations of Illness: Syncretism in Modern Ayurveda." In *Paths to Asian Medical Knowledge*, ed.Charles Leslie and Allan Young, 177–208. Berkeley: University of California Press.

Lessinger, J. 1988. "Trader vs. Developer: The Market Relocation Issue in an Indian City." In *Traders versus the State: Anthropological Approaches to Unofficial Economies*, ed. G. Clark Boulder, CO: Westview Press.

Levin, Betty Wolden. 1990. "International Perspectives in Decision-Making in Neonatal Intensive Care." *Social Science and Medicine* 30: 901–912.

Lewin, Louis. 1964. *Phantastica: Narcotic and Stimulating Drugs—Their Use and Abuse*. London: Routledge and Kegan Paul.

Lewis, Gilbert. 1986. "Concepts of Health and Illness in a Sepik Society." In *Concepts of Health, Illness and Disease: A Comparative Perspective*, ed. Caroline Currier and Meg Stacy, 119–35. Leamington Spa, England: Berg.

Lewis, I. M. 1989. *Ecstatic Religion: A Study of Shamanism and Possession*. 2nd ed. London: Routledge.

Lieban, Richard W. 1990. "Medical Anthropology and the Comparative Study of Medical Ethics." In *Social Science Perspectives in Medical Ethics*, ed. George Weisz, 221–39. Dordrecht, Netherlands: Kluwer Academic Publishers.

Lindenbaum, Shirley. 1987. "The Mystification of Female Labors." In *Gender and Kinship: Essays Toward a Unified Analysis*, ed. Jane Fishburne Collier and Sylvia Junko Yanagisako, 221–43. Stanford, CA: Stanford University.

———. 1998. "Images of Catastrophe: The Making of an Epidemic." In *Political Economy of AIDS*, ed. Merrill Singer, 33–58. Amityville, NY: Baywood Publishing.

Lindenbaum, Shirley, and Margaret Lock. 1993. "Preface." In *Knowledge, Power and Practice: The Anthropology of Medicine and Every*, ed. Shirley Lindenbaum and Margaret Lock, ix–xv. Berkeley: University of California Press.

Lindesmith, Alfred. 1947. *Opiate Addiction*. Bloomington, IN: Principia Press.

———. 1965. *The Addict and the Law*. New York: Mayfield Publishing Co.

Lindesmith, Alfred, Anselm Straus, and Norman Denzin. 1975. *Social Psychology*. Hinsdale, IL: Dryden Press.

Link, B., E. Susser, J. Phelan, R. Moore, and E. Streuning. 1994. "Lifetime and Five-Year Prevalence of Homelessness in the US." *American Journal of Public Health* 84: 1907–12.

Livingstone, Frank B. 1958. "Anthropological Implications of Sickle Cell Gene Distribution in West Africa." *American Anthropologist* 60: 533–62.

Lock, Margaret. 1980. *East Asian Medicine in Urban Japan.* Berkeley: University of California Press.

Lock, Margaret, and Nancy Scheper-Hughes. 1990. "A Critical-Interpretive Approach in Medical Anthropology: Rituals and Routines of Discipline and Dissent." In *Medical Anthropology: Contemporary Theory and Method,* ed. Thomas M. Johnson and Carolyn F. Sargent, 47–72. Westport, CT: Praeger.

Loederer, R. 1935. *Voodoo Fire in Haiti.* New York: Literary Guild.

Lordes, Audre. 1984. *Sister Outsider.* Traumansburg, NY: Crossing Press.

Loudon, J. B. 1976. "Preface." In *Social Anthropology and Medicine,* ed. J. B. Loudon, v-viii. London: Academic Press.

Lown, E. Anne, et al. 1993. "Tossin' and Tweakin': Women's Consciousness in the Crack Culture." In *Women and AIDS: Psychological Perspectives,* ed. Corinne Squire, 90–105. London: Sage.

Lurie, Nancy. 1979. "The World's Oldest On-going Protest Demonstration: North American Indian Drinking Patterns." In *Beliefs, Behaviors and Alcoholic Beverages,* ed. Mac Marshall, 127–45. Ann Arbor: University of Michigan Press.

MacAndrew, C., and Robert Edgerton. 1969. *Drunken Comportment: A Social Explanation.* Chicago: Aldine.

Macdonald, Sharon. 1994. "Whisky, Women and the Scottish Drink Problem. A View from the Highlands." In *Gender, Drink and Drugs,* ed. Maryon McDonald, 125–44. Oxford: Berg.

Magner, Lois N. 1992. *A History of Medicine.* New York: Marcel Dekker.

Magubane, Bernard. 1979. *The Political Economy of Race and Class in South Africa.* New York: Academic Press.

Maine, Deborah, and Thomas McGinn. 2000. "Maternal Mortality and Morbidity." In, ed. Marlene Goldman and Maureen Hatch, 395–404. New York: Academic Press.

Makela, K., et al. 1981. *Alcohol, Society and State, Vol. 1: A Comparative Study of Alcohol Control.* Toronto: Addiction Research Foundation.

Malik, S., S. Sorenson, and C. Aneshensel. 1997. "Community and Dating Violence Among Adolescents: Perpetration and Victimization." *Journal of Adolescent Health* 21(5): 291–302.

Mandelbaum, David. 1965. "Alcohol and Culture." *Current Anthropology* 6(3): 281–88.

Mann, Jonathan, Daniel Tarantola, and Thomas Netter. 1992. *AIDS in the World.* Cambridge, MA: Harvard University Press.

Marcus, Alfred, and Lori Crane. 1985. "Smoking Behavior among US Latinos: An Emerging Challenge for Public Health." *American Journal of Public Health* 75: 169–72.

Markides, Kyriakos, Jeannine Coreil, and Laura Ray. 1987. "Smoking among Mexican Americans: A Three Generation Study." *American Journal of Public Health* 77 (6): 708–11.

Marks, G., and Beatty, W. 1976. *Epidemics.* New York: Charles Scribner's Sons.

Marmor, Theodore R. 1994. *Understanding Health Care Reform.* New Haven, CT: Yale University Press.

Marshall, Mac. 1979. "Introduction." In *Beliefs, Behaviors and Alcoholic Beverages,* ed. Mac Marshall, 2–11. Ann Arbor: University of Michigan.

———. 1987. "Tobacco Use in Micronesia." *Journal of Studies on Alcohol* 42: 885–93.

———. 1990. Problem Deflation and the Ethnographic Record: Interpretation and Introspection in Anthropological Studies of Alcohol. *Journal of Substance Abuse* 2(3): 353–67.

Marshall, Patricia. 1992. "Research Ethics in Applied Medical Anthropology." In *Training Manual in Applied Medical Anthropology*, ed. Carole Hill, 213–35. Washington, DC: American Anthropological Association.

Marshall, Patricia A. and Barbara A. Koenig. 1996. *Medical Anthropology: Contemporary Theory and Method*, rev. ed., ed. Carolyn F. Sargent and Thomas M. Johnson, 349–73. Westport, CT: Praeger.

Martin, Emily. 1987. *The Woman in the Body: A Cultural Analysis of Reproduction.* Boston: Beacon Press.

———. 1990. "Toward an Anthropology of Immunology: The Body as Nation State." *Medical Anthropology Quarterly*, n.s., 4: 410–26.

———. 1992. "The End of the Body?" *American Ethnologist* 19: 120–38.

———. 1996. *Flexible Bodies.* Boston: Beacon Press.

Maryland State Department of Education. 1994. *Maryland Adolescent Survey.* Annapolis: Maryland State Department of Education.

Mascie-Taylor, C.G.N. 1993. "The Biology of Disease." In *The Anthropology of Disease*, ed. C.G.N. Mascie-Taylor, 1–72. Oxford: Oxford University Press.

Maticka-Tyndale, Eleanor, et al. 1994. "Knowledge, Attitudes and Beliefs about HIV/AIDS among Women in Northeastern Thailand." *AIDS Education and Prevention* 6(3): 205–18.

Matveychuk, Wasyl. 1986. "The Social Construction of Drug Definitions and Drug Experiences." In *Culture and Politics of Drugs*, ed. Peter Park and Wasyl Matveychuk, 7–12. Dubuque, IA: Kendall/Hunt.

Maxwell, Bruce, and Michael Jacobson. 1989. *Marketing Disease to Hispanics.* Washington, DC: Center for Science in the Public Interest.

May, Philip, L. Brooke, and J. Gossage. 2000. "Epidemiology of Fetal Alcohol Syndrome in a South African Community in the Western Cape Province." *American Journal of Public Health* 90: 1905–12.

McCombie, S. 1990. "AIDS in Cultural, Historic, and Epidemiologic Context." In *Culture and AIDS*, ed. D. Feldman, 9–28. New York: Praeger.

McConnell, Terrence C. 1982. *Moral Issues in Health Care: An Introduction to Medical Ethics.* Monterey, CA: Wadsworth.

McCord, C., and H. Freedman. 1990. "Excess Mortality in Harlem." *New England Journal of Medicine* 322: 173–75.

McCoy, Alfred, Cathleen Read, and Leonard Adams. 1986. "The Mafia Connection." In *Culture and Politics of Drugs*, ed. Peter Park and Wasyl Matveychuk, 110-18. Dubuque, IA: Kendall/Hunt.

McCoy, Clyde, et al. 1979. "Youth Drug Abuse." In *Youth Opiate Use*, ed. G. Beschner and A. Friedman, 82–97. Lexington, MA: Lexington Books.

McElroy, Ann. 1996. "Should Medical Ecology Be Political?" *Medical Anthropology Quarterly*, n.s., 10: 519–22.

McElroy, Ann, and Patricia K. Townsend. 1979. *Medical Anthropology in Ecological Perspective.* Boulder, CO: Westview Press.

———. 1989. *Medical Anthropology in Ecological Perspective*. 2nd ed. Boulder, CO: Westview Press.

———. 1996. *Medical Anthropology in Ecological Perspective*. 3rd ed. Boulder, CO: Westview Press.

McGrath, Janet, et al. 1992. "Cultural Determinants of Sexual Risk Behavior for AIDS among Baganda Women." *Medical Anthropology Quarterly*, n.s., 6: 153–61.

McGraw, Sarah. 1989. "Smoking Behavior among Puerto Rican Adolescents: Approaches to Its Study." Doctoral Dissertation, Department of Anthropology, University of Connecticut.

McKinlay, John B. 1976. "The Changing Political and Economic Content of the Patient-Physician Encounter." In *The Doctor-Patient Relationship in the Changing Health Scene*, ed. Eugene B. Gallagher, 155–88. Washington, DC: U.S. Government Printing Office (DHEW Pub. No. (NIH) 78–183).

McKinlay, John B. and Joan Arches. 1985. "Towards the Proletarianization of Physicans." *International Journal of Health Services* 15: 161–95.

McLaughlin, Andrew. 1990. "Ecology, Capitalism, and Socialism." *Socialism and Democracy* 10: 69–102.

McNeill, William H. 1976. *Plagues and Peoples*. New York: Anchor Books.

Mechanic, David. 1976. *The Growth of Bureaucratic Medicine*. New York: John Wiley and Sons.

Meier, Matt, and Feliciano Rivera. 1972. *The Chicanos*. New York: Hill and Wang.

Merchant, Carolyn. 1992. *Radical Ecology: The Search for a Livable World*. New York: Routledge.

Merchant, Kathleen, and Kathleen Kurz. 1993. "Women's Nutrition Through the Life-Cycle: Social and Biological Vulnerabilities." In *The Health of Women: A Global Perspective*, ed. Marge Koblinsky, Judith Tinyan, and Jill Gay, 63–91. Boulder, CO: Westview Press.

Mering, Otto von. 1970. "Medicine and Psychiatry." In *Anthropology and the Behavioral and Health Sciences*, ed. Otto von Mering and Leonard Kasdan, 272–307. Pittsburgh: University of Pittsburgh Press.

Metraux, Alfred. 1972. *Voodoo in Haiti*. New York: Schocken Books.

Michaelsen, Karen L., ed. 1988. *Childbirth in America: Anthropological Perspectives*. South Hadley, MA: Bergin & Garvey Publishers.

Miles, Anne. 1998. "Science, Nature, and Tradition: The Mass-Marketing of Natural Medicine in Urban Ecuador." *Medical Anthropology Quarterly* 12: 206–25.

Miliband, Ralph. 1994. *Socialism for a Skeptical Age*. London: Courage Press.Verso.

Millen, Joyce and Timothy Millen. 2000. "Dying for Growth: Transnational Corporations and the Health of the Poor." In *Dying for Growth: Global Inequality and the Health of the Poor*, ed. Jim Kim, Joyce Millen, Alec, Irwin, and John Gershman, 177–224. Monroe, ME: Common Courage Press.

Miller, B. 1998. "Partner Violence Experiences and Women's Drug Use: Exploring the Connections." In *Drug Addiction Research and the Health of Women*, ed. C. Wetherington and A. Roman, 407–16. Rockville, MD: National Institute on Drug Abuse.

Miller, Barbara D. 2000. "Female Infanticide and Child Neglect in Rural North India." In *Gender in Cross-Cultural Perspective*, ed. Caroline Brettel and Carolyn Sargent, 492–507. Upper Saddle River: Prentice-Hall.

Miller, Judith. 1983. *National Survey on Drug Abuse: Main Findings*. Rockville, MD: National Institute on Drug Abuse.

Mills, C. Wright. 1959. *The Sociological Imagination*. New York: Grove Press.

Millstein, Bobby. 2001. *Introduction to the Syndemic Prevention Network*. Atlanta: Syndemic Prevention Network, Centers for Disease Control and Prevention.

Miner, Horace. 1979. "Body Ritual among the Nacirema." In *Culture, Curers and Contagion*, ed. Norman Klein, 9–14. Novato, CA: Chandler and Sharp Publishers.

Mintz, Sidney. 1985. *Sweetness and Power*. New York: Penguin Books.

Mittlemark, Maurice, et al. 1987. "Predicting Experimentation with Cigarettes: The Childhood Antecedents of Smoking Study (CASS)." *American Journal of Public Health* 77(2): 206–8.

Moerman, Daniel E. 1979. "Anthropology of Symbolic Healing." *Current Anthropology* 20: 59–80.

Moffat, Michael. 1989. *Coming of Age in New Jersey*. New Brunswick, NJ: Rutgers University Press.

Monti-Catania, D. 1997. "Women, Violence, and HIV/AIDS." In *The Gender Politics of HIV/AIDS in Women: Perspectives on the Pandemic in the United States*, ed. N. Goldstein and J. L. Manlowe, 442–251. New York: New York University Press.

Moore, Lorna G., Peter W. Van Arsdale, JoAnn E. Glittenberg, and Robert A. Aldrich. 1980. *The Biocultural Basis of Health: Expanding Views of Medical Anthropology*. Prospect Heights, IL: Waveland Press.

Morgan, Lynn M. 1987. "Dependency Theory in the Political Economy of Health: An Anthropological Critique." *Medical Anthropology Quarterly*, n.s., 1(2): 131–55.

Morgan, Myfanwy. 1997. "Hospitals, Doctors and Patient Care." In *Sociology as Applied to Medicine*, ed. Grahman Scambler, 63–76. London: W.B. Saunders.

Morgen, Sandra. 1987. "The Women's Health Movement." In *Women and the Politics of Empowerment*, ed. Ann Bookman and Sandra Morgen, Philadelphia: Temple University Press.

Morley, Peter. 1978. "Culture and the Cognitive World of Traditional Medical Beliefs: Some Preliminary Considerations." In *Culture and Curing: Anthropological Perspectives on Traditional Medical Beliefs and Practices*, ed. Peter Morley and Roy Wallis, 1–18. Pittsburgh: University of Pittsburgh Press.

Morrow, Carol Tupperman. 2003. Sick Doctors: The Social Construction of Professional Deviance. In Health and Health Care as Social Problems. Peter Conrad and Valerie Letter, eds., 297–316. Canada, Ont.: Rowann and Lexington.

Morse, Stephen. 1992. "AIDS and Beyond: Defining the Rules for Viral Traffic." In *AIDS: The Making of a Chronic Disorder*, ed. Elizabeth Fee and Daniel Fox, 23–48. Berkeley: University of California Press.

Morsy, Soheir. 1979. "The Missing Link in Medical Anthropology: The Political Economy of Health." *Reviews in Anthropology* 6: 349–63.

———. 1990. Political Economy in Medical Anthropology. In *Medical Anthropology: Contemporary Theory and Method*, ed. Thomas M. Johnson and Carolyn F. Sargent, 26–46. New York: Praeger.

Moses, Peter, and John Moses. 1983. "Haiti and the Acquired Immune Deficiency Syndrome." *Annals of Internal Medicine* 99(4): 565.

Moses, A. R. 2000. Epidemiology and the Politics of Needle Exchange. *American Journal of Public Health* 90(9): 1385–96.

Mullings, Leith, and Alika Wali. 2001. *Stress and Resilience: The Social Context of Reproduction in Central Harlem.* New York: Kluwer Academic Press.

Murdock, George Peter. 1980. *Theories of Illness: A World Survey.* Pittsburgh: University of Pittsburgh Press.

Murphy, Jane. 1964. "Psychotherapeutic Aspects of Shamanism on St. Lawrence Island, Alaska." In *Magic, Faith, and Healing,* ed. Ari Kiev, 53–83. New York: Free Press.

Musto, David. 1971. "The American Anti-Narcotic Movement: Clinical Research and Public Policy." *Clinical Research* 29(3): 601–05.

———. 1987. *The American Disease: Origins of Narcotic Control.* New York: Oxford University Press.

Mwanalushi, M. 1981. "The African Experience." *World Health,* 14 August.

Nader, Ralph. 1965. *Unsafe at Any Speed: The Designed-in Dangers of the Automobile Industry.* New York: Grossman.

National Cancer Center. 1999. *Health Effects of Exposure to Environmental Smoke: The Report of the California Environmental Protection* Agency (Smoking and Tobacco Control Monograph # 10). Bethesda, CA: US Department of Health and Human Services, National Institutes of Health, National Cancer Institute (NIH Publication No. 99–4645).

National Center on Addiction and Substance Abuse. 1996. *National Survey of American Attitudes on Substance Abuse II: Teens and Their Parents.* New York: Columbia University.

National Institute on Alcohol Abuse and Alcoholism. 1998. "Drinking in the United States: Main Findings from the 1992 National Longitudinal Alcohol Epidemiologic Survey (NLAES)." *U.S. Alcoholc Epidemiologic Data Reference Manual, Volume 6.* 1st edition. Bethesda, MD: NIAAA.

National Institute on Drug Abuse. 1994. *Monitoring the Future Study: Trends in Prevalence of Various Drugs for 8th-Graders, 10th-Graders, and High School Seniors.* Washington, DC: U.S. Department of Health and Human Services (NIDA Capsules).

Navarro, Vincente. 1976. *Medicine under Capitalism.* New York: Prodist.

———. 1977. *Social Security and Medicine in the U.S.S.R.: A Marxist Critique.* Lexington, MA: Lexington Books.

———. 1986. *Crisis, Health and Medicine: A Social Critique.* New York: Tavistock.

———. 1989. "The Rediscovery of the National Health Program by the Democratic Party of the United States: A Chronicle of the Jesse Jackson 1988 Campaign." *International Journal of Health Services* 19: 1–18.

———. 1990. Race or Class versus Race and Class: Mortality Differentials in the United States. *Lancet* 336:1238–1240.

———. 1994. *The Politics of Health Policy: The US Reforms, 1980–1994.* Oxford: Blackwell.

———. 1995. Enact Health Care Reform. *Journal of Health Politics, Policy and Law* 20(3):455–462.

Navarro, Vincente, David U. Himmelstein, and Steffie Woolhandler. 1989. "The Jackson National Health Program." *International Journal of Health Services* 19: 19–44.

Nersesian, W. 1988. "Infant Mortality in Socially Vulnerable Populations." *Annual Review of Public Health* 9: 361–77.

New York Department of Social Services. 1988. *Annual Report to the Government and Legislature.* Albany: Homeless Housing and Assistance Program.

Nichter, Mark, and Elizabeth Cartwright. 1991. "Saving the Children for the Tobacco Industry." *Medical Anthropology* 5: 236–56.

Nichter, Mark, and Mimi Nichter. 1991. "Hype and Weight." *Medical Anthropology* 13: 249–84.

Nichter, Mimi, and Mark Nichter. 1994. "Tobacco Research in the US: A Call for Ethnography." Paper presented at the annual meeting of the American Anthropological Association, Atlanta, GA.

Nielsen, Kai. 1989. *Marxism and the Moral Point of View: Morality, Ideology, and Historical Materialism.* Boulder, CO: Westview Press.

Nunn, John Francis. 1996. *Ancient Egyptian Medicine.* Norman: University of Oklahoma Press.

Nyamnjoh, Francis. 2002. "'A Child is One Person's Only in the Womb': Domestication, Agency and Subjectivity in the Cameroonian Grassfields." In *Postcolonial Subjectivities in Africa*, ed. Richard Werbner, 111–39. New York: Zed Books.

O'Connor, James. 1989. "The Political Economy of Ecology of Socialism and Capitalism." *Capitalism, Nature, Socialism* (3): 93–127.

O'Donnell, John, and Judith Jones. 1968. "Diffusion of Intravenous Techniques among Narcotic Addicts in the U.S." *Journal of Health and Social Behavior* 9: 120–30.

Ohnuki-Tierney, Emiko. 1980. "Shamans and *Imu* among Two Ainu Groups: Toward a Cross-Cultural Model of Interpretation." *Ethos* 8: 204–28.

Oliver, Douglas. 1961. *The Pacific Islands.* Garden City, NY: Anchor Books.

Ong, E., and S. Glantz. 2001. "Constructing 'Sound Science' and 'Good Epidemiology': Tobacco, Lawyers, and Public Relations Firms." *American Journal of Public Health* 91: 1749–57.

Onoge, Omafume F. 1975. "Capitalism and Public Health: A Neglected Theme in the Medical Anthropology of Africa." In *Topias and Utopias*, ed. Stanley R. Ingman and Anthony E. Thomas, 219–32. The Hague: Mouton.

Oths, Kathryn. 1999. Debilidad: A Biocultural Assessment of an Emodied Andean Illness. *Medical Anthropology Quarterly* 13(3): 286–315.

Ouellet, Lawrence, Wayne Wiebel, and Antonio Jimenez. 1995. Team Research Methods for Studying Intranasal Heroin Use and Its HIV Risks. In *Qualitative Methods in Drug Abuse and HIV Research.* Elizabeth Lambert, Rebecca Oshery, and Richard Needle, eds. 182–211. NIDA Research Monograph 157. Rockville, Maryland: National Institute on Drug Abuse.

Page, J. Bryan, and Prince Smith. 1990. "Venous Envy: The Importance of Having Functional Veins." *Journal of Drug Issues* 20: 291–308.

Page, J. Bryan, et al. 1990a. "Intravenous Drug Use and HIV Infection in Miami." *Medical Anthropology Quarterly*, n.s., 4: 56–71.

Page, J. Bryan, et al. 1990b. "HTLV-1/11 Seropositivity and Death from AIDS among HIV-1 Seropositive Intravenous Drug Users." *Lancet* 335: 1439–41.

Page, J. Bryan, Prince Smith, and Normie Kane. 1991. "Shooting Galleries, Their Proprietors, and Implications for Prevention of AIDS." *Drugs and Society* 5(1/2): 69-85.

Pandolfi, Mariella, and Deborah Gordon. 1986. Italy. *Medical Anthropology Quarterly*, o.s., 17(4):90.

Pape, J., et al. 1986. "Risk Factors Associated with AIDS in Haiti." *American Journal of Medical Sciences* 29(1): 4–7.

Pappas, Gregory, S. Queen, W. Hadden, and G. Fisher. 1993. "The Increasing Disparity of Mortality Between Socio-Economic Groups in the United States, 1960–86." *New England Journal of Medicine*.

Parenti, Michael. 1980. *Democracy for the Few*. New York: St. Martin's Press.

Parker, Richard. 1987. "Acquired Immunodeficiency Syndrome in Urban Brazil." *Medical Anthropology Quarterly*, n.s., 1: 155–75.

———. 1992. "Sexual Diversity, Cultural Analysis, and AIDS Education in Brazil." In *The Time of AIDS*, ed. Gilbert Herdt and Shirley Lindenbaum, 225–42. Newbury Park, CA: Sage Publications.

Parker, Richard and Anke Ehrhardt. 2001. "Through and Ethnographic Lens: Ethnographic Methods, Comparative Analysis and HIV/AIDS Research." *AIDS and Behavior* 5(2): 105–14.

Parsons, Howard L., ed. 1977. *Marx and Engels on Ecology*. Westport, CT: Greenwood.

Partridge, William L. 1987. "Toward a Theory of Practice." In *Applied Anthropology in America*, ed. Elizabeth M. Eddy and William L. Partridge, 211–33. New York: Columbia University Press.

Paul, Benjamin. 1969. "Anthropological Perspectives on Medicine and Public Health." In *Cross-Cultural Approach to Health Behavior*, ed. R. Lynch, 26–42. Madison, NJ: Fairleigh Dickinson University Press.

Paul, James A. 1978. "Medicine and Imperialism." In *The Cultural Crisis of Modern Medicine*, ed. John Ehrenreich, 271–86. New York: Monthly Review Press.

Payer, Lynn. 1988. *Medicine and Culture: Varieties of Treatment in the United States, England, West Germany and France*. New York: H. Holt.

Petchesky, Rosalind P. 2000. "Sexual Rights: Inventing a Concept, Mapping an International Practice." In *Framing the Sexual Subject: The Politics of Gender, Sexuality, and Power*, ed. Richard Parker, Regina Maria Barbosa, and Peter Aggleton, 81–104. Berkeley: University of California Press.

Peto, Richard. 1990. "Future Worldwide Health Effects of Current Smoking Patterns. Paper presented at WHO Workshop, Perth, Australia.

Peto, Richard, and A. Lopez, eds. 1990. *Proceedings*. Perth, Australia: Seventh World Conference on Tobacco and Health.

Pfeiderer, Beatrix, and Wolfgang Bichman. 1986. Germany. *Medical Anthropology Quarterly*, o.s., 17(4): 89–90.

Physicians' Task Force on Hunger in America. 1985. *Hunger in America: The Growing Epidemic*. Boston: Harvard University School of Public Health.

Pirie, P., D. Murray, and R. Luepker. 1988. "Smoking Prevalence in a Cohort of Adolescents, Including Absentees, Dropouts, and Transfers." *American Journal of Public Health* 78(2): 176–78.

Pittman, David, and Charles Snyder. 1962. *Society, Culture, and Drinking Patterns*. Carbondale, IL: Southern Illinois University Press.

Piven, Frances, and Richard Cloward. 1971. *Regulating the Poor.* New York: Vintage.

Pollack, Donald. 1992. "Culina Shamanism: Gender, Power, and Knowledge." In *Portals of Power: Shamanism in South America,* ed. E. Langdon, Jean Matteson, and Gerhard Baer, 25–40. Albuquerque: University of New Mexico Press.

Preble, Edward, and J. Casey. 1969. "Taking Care of Business: The Heroin User's Life on the Streets." *International Journal of the Addictions* 15: 329–37.

Preston, Richard. 1994. The Hot Zone. New York: Random House Publishers.

Prevention File. 1990. "Are Alcohol and Tobacco Companies Buying Their Way into Black Communities?" *Prevention File* (Winter): 9–10.

Price, Jacob. 1964. "The Economic Growth of the Chesapeake and the European Market, 1697–1775." *Journal of Economic History* 24: 496–511.

Quam, Michael. 1994. "AIDS Policy and the United States Political Economy." In *Global AIDS Policy.* ed. Douglas Feldman, 142–59. Westport, CT: Bergin and Garvey.

Quellet, Lawrence, Wayne Weibel, and Antonio Jimenez. 1995. "Team Research Methods for Studying Intranasal Heroin Use and Its HIV Risks." In *Qualitative Methods in Drug Abuse and HIV Research,* ed. Elizabeth Lambert, Rebecca Ashery, and Richard Needle, 182–211, Rockville, MD: National Institute on Drug Abuse (NIDA Research Monograph #157).

Quinn, Thomas. 2001. "Response to the Global AIDS Pandemic: The Global AIDS Fund—Will It Be Enough and Will It Succeed?" *The Hopkins HIV Report* 13(5): 12–15.

Rabkin, Judith, Robert Remien, and Christopher Wilson. 1994. *Good Doctor, Good Patient.* New York: NCM Publishers.

Rachal, J. Guess, et al. 1980. *Drinking Behavior,* vol. 1. Research Triangle Park, NC: Research Triangle Institute.

Raffel, Marshall W., and Norma K. Raffel. 1994. *The U.S. Health System: Origins and Functions.* 4th edition. Albany, NY: Delmar Publishers.

Ran Nath, Uma. 1986. *Smoking: Third World Alert.* Oxford: Oxford University Press.

Rapp, Rayna. 2000. *Testing Women, Testing the Fetus: The Social Impact of Amniocentesis in America.* New York: Routledge.

Radliff, Eric. 1999. "Women as 'Sex Worker,' Men as 'Boyfriends': Shifting Identities in Philippine Go-Go Bars and Their Significance in STD/AIDS Control." *Anthropology and Medicine* 6: 79–102.

Ratner, Mitchell. 1993. "Sex, Drugs, and Public Policy: Studying and Understanding the Sex-for-Crack Phenomenon." In *Crack Pipe as Pimp: An Ethnographic Investigation of Sex-for-Crack Exchanges,* ed. Mitchell Ratner, 1–36. New York: Lexington Books.

Ray, O. 1978. *Drugs, Society, and Human Behavior.* St. Louis: C. V. Mosby Co.

Redfield, Robert. 1953. *The Primitive World and Its Transformations.* Ithaca, NY: Cornell University Press.

Reichard, Gladys. 1950. *Navaho Religion: A Study of Symbolism.* New York: Stratford Press.

Reid, Janice. 1983. *Sorcerers and Healing Spirits: Continuity and Change in an Aboriginal Medical System.* Canberra: Australian National University Press.

Reiter, Rayna Rapp, ed. 1975. *Toward an Anthropology of Women.* New York: Monthly Review Press.

Resnick, Hank. 1990. *Youth and Drugs: Society's Mixed Messages.* Rockville, MD: Office of Substance Abuse Prevention (OSAP Prevention Monograph #6).

Rettig, Richard, Manuel Torres, and Gerald Garrett. 1977. *Manny: A Criminal-Addict's Story.* Atlanta: Houghton Mifflin Co. Review Press.

Reynolds, Vernon, and Ralph Tanner. 1995. *The Social Ecology of Religion.* New York: Oxford University Press.

Ripinsky-Naxon, Michael. 1993. *The Nature of Shamanism: Substance and Function of a Religious Meta.* Albany: State University of New York Press.

Rittenbaugh,Cheryl. 1991. "Body Size and Shape: A Dialogue of Culture and Biology." *Medical Anthropology* 13: 173–80.

Rivers, W.H.R. 1924. *Medicine, Magic, and Religion.* London: Kegan, Paul, Trench, Trubner and Co.

Robb, J. 1986. "Smoking as an Anticipatory Rite of Passage: Some Sociological Hypotheses on Health Related Behavior." *Social Science and Medicine* 23: 621–27.

Robins, Lee. 1980. "Alcoholism and Labelling Theory." In *Readings in Medical Sociology,* ed. David Mechanic, 188–98. New York: Free Press.

Rodberg, Leonard S. 1994. "Anatomy of a National Health Program: Reconsidering the Dellums Bill after 10 Years." In *Beyond Crisis: Confronting Health Care in the United States,* ed. Nancy F. McKenzie, 610–15. New York: Meridian.

Rogers, Spencer L. 1982. *The Shaman: His Symbols and His Healing Power.* Springfield, IL: Charles Thomas.

Romanucci-Ross, Lola. 1977. "The Hierarchy of Resort in Curative Practices: The Admiralty Islands, Melanesia." In *Culture, Disease, and Healing: Studies in Medical Anthropology,* ed. David Landy, 481–87. New York: Macmillan.

Room, Robin. 1984. *Alcohol and Ethnography: A Case of Problem Deflation.* New York: Plenum.

Roseman, Marina. 1991. *Healing Sounds from the Malaysian Rainforest: Temiar Music and Medicine.* Berkeley: University of California Press.

Rosenthal, Marilynn M. 1992. "Modernization and Health Care in the People's Republic of China: The Period of Transition." In *Health Care Systems and Their Patients: An International Perspective,* ed. Marilynn M. Rosenthal and Marcel Frenkel, 293–315. Boulder, CO: Westview Press.

Rothstein, Frances. 1982. *Three Different Worlds: Women, Men and Children in an Industrializing Community.* Westport, CT: Greenwood Press.

Rubin, Gayle. 1975. "The Traffic in Women: Notes on a 'Political Economy' of Sex." In *Toward an Anthropology of* Women, ed. Rayna Rapp Reiter, 157–210. New York: Monthly Review Press.

Rubin, Vera, and Lambros Comitas. 1983. "Cannabis, Society and Culture." In *Drugs and Society: A Critical Reader,* ed. Maureen Kelleher, Bruce Mac-Murray, and Thomas Shapiro, 212–18. Dubuque, IA: Kendall/Hunt.

Sabatier, Renee. 1988. *Blaming Others.* Philadelphia: New Society Publishers.

Sahlins, Marshall. 1972. *Stone Age Economics.* Chicago: Aldine.

Samet, Jonathan, et al. 1988. "Mortality from Lung Cancer and Chronic Obstructive Pulmonary Disease in New Mexico, 1958–1982." *American Journal of Public Health* 78(9): 1182–86.

Sangree, Walter. 1962. "The Social Functions of Beer Drinking in Bantu, Tiriki." In *Society, Culture, and Drinking Patterns,* ed. David Pittman and Charles Snyder, 6–21. Carbondale, IL: Southern Illinois University Press.

Sargent, Carolyn, and Thomas M. Johnson. 1996. *Medical Anthropology and Contemporary Theory and Method.* Rev. ed. Westport: Praeger.

Sargent, M. 1967. "Changes in Japanese Drinking Patterns." *Quarterly Journal of Studies on Alcohol* 28: 709–22.

Savitz, David. 1986. "Changes in Spanish Surname Cancer Rates Relative to Other Whites, Denver Area, 1969–71 to 1979–81." *American Journal of Public Health* 76(10): 1209–14.

Sayers, Sean. 1998. *Marxism and Human Nature.* London: Routledge.

Scenic America. 1990. *Fact Sheet: Alcohol and Tobacco Advertising on Billboards.* Washington, DC: Scenic America.

Schensul, Jean, Christina Huebner, Merrill Singer, Marvin, Snow, Pablo Feliciano, and Lorie Broomhall. 2000. "The High, the Money, and the Fame: The Emergent Social Context of 'New Marijuana' Use among Urban Youth." *Medical Anthropology* 18: 389–414.

Schensul, Stephen L. 1980. "Anthropological Fieldwork and Sociopolitical Change." *Social Problems* 27: 309–19.

Scheper-Hughes, Nancy. 1990. "Three Propositions for a Critically Applied Medical Anthropology." *Social Science and Medicine* 30: 189–97.

———. 1992. *Death without Weeping: The Violence of Everyday Life in Brazil.* Berkeley: University of California Press.

———. 1995. "The Primacy of the Ethical: Propositions for a Militant Anthropology." *Current Anthropology* 36: 409–20.

Scheper-Hughes, Nancy, and Margaret Lock. 1986. "Speaking 'Truth' to Illness: Metaphors, Reification, and a Pedagogy for Patients." *Medical Anthropology Quarterly*, o.s., 17(5): 137–40.

———. 1987. "The Mindful Body: A Prolegomenon to Future Work in Medical Anthropology." *Medical Anthropology Quarterly*, n.s., 1: 6–41.

Schiff, Gordon. 2000. "Fatal Distraction: Finance Versus Vigilance in U.S. Hospitals." *International Journal of Health Services* 30: 739–43.

Scheffler, Harold. 1991. "Sexism and Naturalism in the Study of Kinship." In *Gender at the Crossroads of Knowledge: Feminist Anthropology in the Postmodern Era*, ed. Micaela di Leonardo, 361–83. Berkeley, CA: University of California Press.

Schneider, Jane. 1971. "Of Vigilance and Virgins: Honor, Shame and Access to Resources in Mediterranean Societies." *Ethnology* 9: 1–24.

Schneider, Jane, and Peter Schneider. 1996. *Festival of the Poor: Fertility Decline and the Ideology of Class in Sicily, 1860–1980.* Tucson: University of Arizona Press.

Schneider, Joseph W. 2001. "Family Care Work and Duty in a 'Modern' Chinese Hospital." In *Readings in Medical Sociology*, ed. Duanne A. Matcha, 354–71. Boston: Allyn and Bacon.

Schoepf, Brooke. 1992. "Women at Risk: Case Studies from Zaire." In *The Time of AIDS*, ed. Gilbert Herdt and Shirley Lindenbaum, 259–86. Newbury Park, CA: Sage Publications.

Schoepf, Brooke, Claude Schoepf, and Joyce Millen. 2000. "Theoretical Perspectives, Remote Remedies: SAPs and the Political Ecology of Poverty and Health in Africa." In *Dying for Growth: Global Inequality and the Health of the Poor*, ed. Jim Kim, Joyce Millen, Alec Irwin, and John Gershman, 91–126. Monroe, ME: Common Courage Press.

Schultheis, Rob. 1983. "Chinese Junk." In *Drugs and Society*, ed. Maureen Kelleher, Bruce MacMurray, and Thomas Shapiro, 234–41. Dubuque, IA: Kendall/Hunt.

Schuart, Donald. 1998. The Limits of Health Insurance. In *Health and Canadian Society: Sociological Perspectives*, David Coburn, Carl D'Arcy, and George M. Torrance, eds., 536–48. Toronto: University of Toronto Press.

Schwartz, Justin. 1991. A Future for Socialism in the USSR. In *Communist Regimes— The Aftermath: The Socialist Register 1991*, ed. Ralph Miliband and Leo Panitch, 67–94. London: Merlin.

Scotch, Norman. 1963. "Medical Anthropology." In *Biennial Review of Anthropology*, ed. Bernard J. Siegel, 30–68. Stanford, CA: Stanford University Press.

Scott, J. 1969. *The White Poppy*. New York: Harper and Row.

Seabrook, W. 1929. *The Magic Island*. New York: Harcourt Brace and Co.

Seaman, Gary, and Jane S. Day. 1994. *Ancient Traditions: Shamanism in Central Asia and the Americas*. Niwot, CO: University Press of Colorado.

Segall, M. 1983. "On the Concept of a Socialist Health System: A Question of Marxist Epidemiology." *International Journal of Health Services* 13: 221–25.

Selik, Richard, Kenneth Castro, and Marguerite Pappaioanou. 1988. "Racial/Ethnic Differences in the Risk of AIDS in the United States." *American Journal of Public Health* 79: 1539–45.

Selvaggio, K. 1983. "WHO Bottles Up Alcohol Study." *Multinational Monitor* 4(9): 9.

Sharon, Douglas. 1978. *Wizard of the Four Winds: A Shaman's Story*. New York: Free Press.

Sherwin, Susan. 1992. *No Longer Patient: Feminist Ethics and Health Care*. Philadelphia: Temple University Press.

———— 1997. "Gender, Race, and Class in the Delivery of Health Care." In *Bioethics: An Introduction to the History, Methods, and Practice*, ed. Nancy S. Jecker, Albert R. Jonsen, and Robert A. Pearlman, 392–401. Boston: Jones and Bartlett Publishers.

Shannon, Thomas R. 1996. *An Introduction to the World-System Perspective*. 2nd ed. Boulder, CO: Westview Press.

Sharff, Jagna. 1998. *King Kong on 4th Street: Families and the Violence of Poverty on the Lower East Side*. Boulder, CO: Westview Press.

Shilts, Randy. 1987. *And the Band Played On*. New York: St. Martin's Press.

Shostak, Marjorie. 1983. *Nisa: The Life and Words of a !Kung Woman*. New York: Vintage.

Shrivastava, P. 1987. *Bhopal: Anatomy of a Crisis*. Cambridge, MA: Ballinger Publishing Company.

Sidel, Victor. 1978. "The Right to Health Care: An International Perspective." In *Bioethics and Human Rights: A Reader for Health Professionals*, ed. Elsie L. Bandman and Betram Bandman, 341–50. Boston: Little, Brown, and Company.

————. 1994. "Health Care for a Nation in Need." In *Beyond Crisis: Confronting Health Care in the United States*, ed. Nancy F. McKenzie, 559–73. New York: Meridian.

Sidel, Victor W., and Ruth Sidel. 1982. *The Health of China*. Boston: Beacon Press.

Silber, Irwin. 1994. *Socialism: What Went Wrong? An Inquiry into the Theoretical and Historical Sources of the Socialist Crisis*. London: Pluto Press.

Silverblatt, Irene. 1991. "Interpreting Women in States: New Feminist Ethnohistories." In *Gender at the Crossroads of Knowledge: Feminist Anthropology in the*

Postmodern Era, ed. Micaela di Leonardo, 140–75. Berkeley: University of California Press.

Simmons, Ozzie. 1962. "Ambivalence and the Learning of Drinking Behavior in a Peruvian Community." In *Society, Culture, and Drinking Patterns*, ed. David Pittman and Charles Snyder, 37–47. Carbondale, IL: Southern Illinois University Press.

Singer, Merrill. 1986. "Toward a Political-Economy of Alcoholism: The Missing Link in the Anthropology of Drinking." *Social Science and Medicine* 23: 113–30.

———. 1990. "Postmodernism and Medical Anthropology: Words of Caution." *Medical Anthropology* 12: 289–304.

———. 1991. "Confronting the AIDS Epidemic among Injection Drug Users: Does Ethnic Culture Matter?" *AIDS Education and Prevention* 3: 258–83.

———. 1992. "AIDS and U.S. Ethnic Minorities: The Crisis and Alternative Anthropological Responses." *Human Organization* 51: 89–95.

———. 1993. "Project Recovery: A Substance Abuse Treatment Program for Hartford Women." Report submitted to the Hartford Foundation for Public Giving, Hartford, CT.

———. 1994. "AIDS and the Health Crisis of the Urban Poor: The Perspective of Critical Medical Anthropology." *Social Science and Medicine* 39: 931–48.

———. 1995a. "Beyond the Ivory Tower: Critical Praxis." *Medical Anthropology Quarterly*, n.s., 9: 80–106.

———. 1995b. "Providing Substance Abuse Treatment to Puerto Rican Clients Living in the Continental U.S." In *Substance Abuse Treatment in the Era of AIDS*, vol. 2, ed. Omowale Amuyleru-Marshal, 93–114. Rockville, MD: Center for Substance Abuse Treatment.

———. 1996. "Farewell to Adaptationism: Unnatural Selection and the Politics of Biology." *Medical Anthropology Quarterly*, (n.s., 10(4): 496–575.

———. 1996. "A Dose of Drugs, A Touch of Violence, A Case of AIDS: Conceptualizing the SAVA Syndemic." *Free Inquiry in Sociology* 24(2): 99–110.

———. 1998. "Articulating Personal Experience and Political Economy in the AIDS Epidemic: The Case of Carlos Torres." In *The Political Economy of AIDS*, ed. Merrill Singer, 61–73. Amityville, NY: Baywood Publishing.

———. 1999. "Why Do Puerto Rican Injection Drug Users Inject So Often?" *Anthropology and Medicine* 6: 31–58.

———. 1999. "Toward a Critical Biocultural Model of Drug Use and Health Risk." In *Cultural, Observational, and Epidemiological Approaches in the Prevention of Drug Abuse and HIV/AIDS*, ed. Patricia Marshall, Merrill Singer, and Michael Clatts, 26–50. Bethesda, MD: National Institute on Drug Abuse.

———. 2000. "Introduction." *You Owe Yourself a Drunk*, ed. James Spradley, xiii–xxvii. Prospect Heights, IL: Waveland Press.

———. 2001. "Toward a Biocultural and Political Economic Integration of Alcohol, Tobacco, and Drug Studies." *Social Science and Medicine* 53: 199–213.

Singer, Merrill, and Hans A. Baer. 1995. *Critical Medical Anthropology*. Amityville, NY: Baywood Press.

Singer, Merrill, and Maria Borrero. 1984. "Indigenous Treatment for Alcoholism: The Case of Puerto Rican Spiritualism." *Medical Anthropology* 8: 246–73.

Singer, Merrill, Lani Davison, and Gina Geddes. 1988. "Culture, Critical Theory and Reproductive Illness Behavior in Haiti." *Medical Anthropology Quarterly* 2: 370–85.

Singer, Merrill, Else Huertas, and Glen Scott. 2000. "Am I My Brother's Keeper: A Case Study of the Responsibilities of Research." *Human Organization* 59: 389–400.

Singer, Merrill, and Zhongke Jia. 1993. "AIDS and Puerto Rican Injection Drug Users in the U.S." In *Handbook on Risks of AIDS: Injection Drug Users and Their Sexual Partners*, ed. Barry Brown and George Beschner, 227–55. Westport, CT: Greenwood Press.

Singer, Merrill, and Elizabeth Toledo. 1994. "Chemical Dependency and Pregnancy: Building a Community Based Treatment and Research Consortium." Paper presented at a meeting of the Society for Applied Anthropology. Cancun, Mexico.

———. 1995b. "Oppression Illness: Critical Theory and Intervention with Women at Risk for AIDS." Paper presented at the American Anthropological Association Meeting, Washington, DC.

Singer, Merrill, Hans A. Baer, and Ellen Lazarus, eds. 1990. "Critical Medical Anthropology: Theory and Research." Special issue of *Social Science and Medicine* 30(2).

Singer, Merrill, Glen Scott, Wilson Scott, Delia Easton, Margaret Weeks. 2001. "War Stories: AIDS Prevention and the Street Narratives of Drug Users." *Qualitative Health Research* 11(5): 589–602.

Singer, Merrill, et al. 1991. "Puerto Rican Community Mobilizing in Response to the AIDS Crisis." *Human Organization* 50: 73–81.

Singer, Merrill, et al. 2000. "The Social Geography of AIDS and Hepatitis Risk: Qualitative Approaches in Sterile-Syringe Access Among Injection Drug Users." *American Journal of Public Health* 90(7): 1049–56.

Singer, Merrill, and Charlene Snipes. 1991. "Generations of Suffering: Experiences of a Pregnancy and Substance Abuse Treatment Program." *Journal of Health Care for the Poor & Underserved* 3: 325–39.

Singer, Philip. 1977. "Introduction: From Anthropology and Medicine to 'Therapy' and Neo-Colonialism." In *Traditional Healing: New Science or New Colonialism*, ed. Philip Singer, 1–25. London: Conch Magazine Limited.

Siraisi, Nancy G. 1990. *Medieval and Early Renaissance Medicine: An Introduction.* Chicago: University of Chicago Press.

Siskin, Edgar E. 1984. *Washo Shamans and Peyotists: Religious Conflict in an American Indian Tribe.* Salt Lake City: University of Utah Press.

Smith, Barbara Ellen. 1981. "Black Lung: The Social Production of Disease." *International Journal of Health Services* 11: 343–59.

Smith, M.G. 1968. "Secondary Marriage Among Kadera and Kagoro." In *Marriage, Family, and Residence*, ed. Paul Bohannon and John Middleton, 109–30. Garden City, NJ: Natural History Press.

Smith, R. 1978. "The Magazine's Smoking Habit." *Columbia Journalism Review* (January/February): 29–31.

Sobel, R. 1978. *They Satisfy: The Cigarette in American Life.* Garden City, NY: Doubleday.

Spencer, B. 1989. "On the Accuracy of Current Estimates of the Number of Intra-
    venous Drug Users." In *AIDS: Sexual Behavior and Intravenous Drug Use*, ed.
    C. Turner, H. Miller, and L. Moses, 429–46. Washington, DC: National Re-
    search Council.
Spicer, Paul. 1997. "Toward a (Dys)functional Anthropology of Drinking: Ambiv-
    alence and the American Indian Experience with Alcohol." *Medical Anthro-
    pology Quarterly* 11: 306–23.
Spiro, Melford. 1967. *Burmese Supernaturalism*. Englewood Cliffs, NJ: Prentice-Hall.
Stanley, Laura. 1999. "Transforming AIDS: The Moral Management of Stigmatized
    Identity." *Anthropology and Medicine* 6: 103–20.
Stavenhagen, Rodolfo. 1971. "Decolonizing Applied Social Science." *Human Or-
    ganization* 30: 333–57.
Stebbins, Kenyon. 1987. "Tobacco or Health in the Third World? A Political-
    Economic Analysis with Special Reference to Mexico." *International Journal
    of Health Ser* 17: 523–38.
———. 1990. "Transnational Tobacco Companies and Health in Underdeveloped
    Countries: Recommendations for Avoiding a Smoking Epidemic." *Social
    Science and Medicine* 30: 227–35.
———. 1994. "Clearing the Air: Introducing Smoking Restrictions in West Virginia,
    America's Leading Consumer of Cigarettes Per Capita." Paper presented
    at the American Anthropological Association Annual Meeting, Atlanta,
    GA, November.
———. 1997. "Clearing the Air: Challenges to Introducing Smoking Restrictions
    in West Virginia." *Social Science and Medicine* 44: 1395–1401.
———. 2001. "Going Like Gangbusters: Transnational Tobacco Companies 'Mak-
    ing a Killing' in South America." *Medical Anthropology Quarterly* 15: 147–70.
Stein, Howard. 1990. *American Medicine as Culture*. Boulder, CO: Westview Press.
Stein, Leonard I. 1967. "The Doctor-Nurse Game." *Archives of General Psychiatry*
    16: 699–703.
Sterk, Clare. 1999. *Fast Lives: Women Who Use Crack Cocaine*. Philadelphia: Temple
    University Press.
Stevens, Rosemary. 1986. "The Changing Hospital." In *Applications of Social Science
    to Clinical Medicine and Health Policy*, ed. Linda H. Akin and David Me-
    chanic, 80–99. New Brunswick, NJ: Rutgers University Press.
Stoler, Ann Laura. 1991. "Carnal Knowledge and Imperial Power: Gender, Race,
    and Mortality in Colonial Asia." In *Gender at the Crossroads of Knowledge:
    Feminist Anthropology in the Postmodern Era*, ed. Micaela di Leonardo, 51–
    102. Berkeley: University of California Press.
Streefland, Pieter. 1986. "The Netherlands." *Medical Anthropology Quarterly*, o.s.,
    17(4): 91.
Strohmaier, Gotthard. 1998. "Reception and Tradition: Medicine in the Byzantine
    and Arab World." ed. Mirko Grmek, 139–69. Cambridge: Harvard Univer-
    sity Press.
Substance Abuse and Mental Health Services Administration. 1996. *Preliminary
    Estimates from the 1995 National Household Survey on Drug Abuse*. Washing-
    ton, DC: Office of Applied Studies.
Sumartojo, Esther. 2000. "Structural Factors in HIV Prevention: Concepts, Exam-
    ples, and Implications for Research." *AIDS* 14(Supplement): 3–10.

Sun, X., J. Nan, and Q. Guo. 1994. "AIDS and HIV Infection in China." *AIDS* 8 (Supplement 2): 55–59.

Susser, E., E. Valencia, and S. Conover. 1993. "Prevalence of HIV Infection among Psychiatric Patients in a Large Men's Shelter." *American Journal of Public Health* 83: 568–70.

Susser, Ida. 1991. "The Separation of Mothers and Children. "In *The Dual City*, ed. J. Mollenkopf and M. Castells, 207–25. Newbury Park, CA: Sage Publications.

———. 1993 "Creating Family Forms: The Exclusion Men and Teenage Boys from Families in the New York City Shelter System, 1987–91." *Critique in Anthropology* 13: 267–83.

———. 1996. "The Construction of Poverty and Homelessness in U.S. Cities." In *Annual Reviews in Anthropology* 25: 411–25.

———. 1998. "Inequality, Violence and Gender Relations in a Global City". New York. *Identities* 5: 219–47.

———. 1999. "Creating Family Forms: The Exclusion of Men and Teenage Boys from Families in the New York City Shelter System, 1987–91." In *Theorizing the City: The New Urban Antheropology Reader*, ed. Setha Low, 67–83. New Brunswick, NJ: Rutgers University Press.

———. 2002. "Losing Ground: Advancing Capitalism and the Relocation of Working Class Communities." In *Time and Space: Global Restructurings, Politics, and Identity*, ed. David Nugent, 274–90. Stanford, CA: Stanford University Press.

Susser, Ida, and M. Alfredo González. 1992. "Sex, Drugs and Videotape: The Prevention of AIDS in a New York City Shelter for Homeless Men." In *Rethinking AIDS Prevention*, ed. Ralph Bolton and Merrill Singer, 169–84. Philadelphia: Gordon and Breach Science Publishers.

Susser, Ida, and Zena Stein. 2000. "Culture, Sexuality, and Women's Agency in the Prevention of HIV/AIDS in South Africa." *American Journal of Public Health* 90(7): 1042–48.

Susser, Mervyn. 1993. "Health as a Human Right: An Epidemiologist's Perspective on Public Health." *American Journal of Public Health* 83: 418–26.

Susser, Mervyn, William Watson, and Kim Hopper. 1985. *Sociology in Medicine.* New York: Oxford.

Sutter, Alan. 1966. "The World of the Righteous Dope Fiend." *Issues in Criminology* 2: 177–222.

———. 1969. "Worlds of Drug Use on the Street Scene." In *Delinquency, Crime and Social Process*, ed. Donald Cressey and David Ward, 802–29. New York: Harper and Row.

Swartz, Donald. 1998. "The Limits of Health Insurance." In *Health and Canadian Society: Sociological Perspectives*, 3rd ed., ed. David Coburn et al., 536–48. Toronto: University of Toronto Press.

Sweezy, Paul. 1973. "Cars and Cities." *Monthly Review* 24(11): 1–18.

Taussig, Michael. 1987. *Shamanism, Colonialism, and the Wild Man.* Chicago: University of Chicago Press.

Taylor, Carl E. 1976. "The Place of Indigenous Medical Practitioners in the Modernization of Health Services." In *Asian Medical Systems: A Comparative Study*, ed. Charles Leslie, 285–99. Berkeley: University of California Press.

Taylor, William. 1979. *Drinking, Homicide and Rebellion in Colonial Mexican Villages.*
    Stanford, CA: Stanford University Press.
Tennet, R. 1950. *The American Cigarette Industry: A Study in Economic Analysis and
    Public Policy.* New Haven, CT: Yale University Press.
Terney, Robert M. 1999. "Challenge to Universal Access to Health Care with Lim-
    ited Resources." In *The American Medical Ethics Revolution: How the AMA's
    Code of Ethics Has Transformed Physicians' Relationship to Patients, Profession-
    als, and Society,* ed. John B. Baker et al., 252–59. Baltimore: Johns Hopkins
    University Press.
Teunis, Niels. 2001. "Same-Sex Sexuality in Africa: A Case Study from Senegal."
    AIDS and Behavior 5: 173–82.
Thayer, Millie. 2000. "Traveling Feminisms: From Embodied Women to Gendered
    Citizenship." In *Global Ethnography: Forces, Connections, and Imaginations in
    a Postmodern World,* ed. Michael Burawoy, 203–35. Berkeley: University of
    California Press.
Thomas, Anthony E. 1975. "Health Care in *Ukambani* Kenya: A Socialist Critique."
    In *Topias and Utopias,* ed. Stanley Ingman and Anthony E. Thomas, 266–81.
    The Hague: Mouton.
Thomas, Piri. 1967. *Down These Mean Streets.* New York: Knopf.
Topley, Marjorie. 1976. "Chinese Traditional Etiology and Methods of Cure in
    Hong Kong." In *Asian Medical Systems: A Comparative Study,* ed. Charles
    Leslie, 243–65. Berkeley: University of California Press.
Townsend, Joan B. 1999. "Shamanism." In *Anthropology of Religion: A Handbook,*
    ed. Stephen D. Glazier, 429–69. Westport, CT: Praeger.
Trostle, James. 1986. "Early Work in Anthropology and Epidemiology: From Social
    Medicine to the Germ Theory, 1840 to 1920." In *Anthropology and Epidemi-
    ology: Interdiscplinary Approaches to the Study of Health and Disease,* ed. Craig
    R. Janes, Ron Stall, and Sandra M. Gifford, Dordrecht, Netherlands: D.
    Reidel.
Trostle, Jim and Johannes Sommerfeld. 1996. Medical Anthropology and Epide-
    miology. *Annual Reviews in Anthropology* 25: 253–74.
Trotter, Robert. 1985. "Mexican-American Experience with Alcohol: South Texas
    Examples." In *The American Experience with Alcohol,* ed. Linda Bennett and
    Genevieve Ames, 279–96. New York: Plenum Press.
Trotter, Robert, Richard Needle, Eric Goosby, Christopher Bates, and Merrill
    Singer. 2001. "A Methodological Model for Rapid Assessment, Response,
    and Evaluation: The RARE Program in Public Health." *Field Methods* 13(2):
    137–59.
True, William. 1996. Epidemiology and Medical Anthropology. In Medical An-
    thropology: Contemporary Theory and Method, 2nd ed., 325–46. Carol Sar-
    gent and Thomas Johnson, eds. New York: Praeger.
Tsien, A. 1979. "The Smoking Habits of Three News Magazines." Master's Thesis,
    School of Journalism, Southern Illinois University.
Turner, C., H. Miller, and L. Moses. 1989. *AIDS: Sexual Behavior and Intravenous
    Drug Use.* Washington, DC: National Academy Press.
Turshen, Meredith. 1977. "The Political Ecology of Disease." *Review of Radical Po-
    litical Economics* 9: 45–60.
———. 1984. *The Political Ecology of Disease in Tanzania.* New Brunswick, NJ: Rut-
    gers University Press.

———. 1989. *The Politics of Public Health*. New Brunswick, NJ: Rutgers University Press.

United Nations Development Programme. 1999. *Human Development Report 1999*. New York: Oxford University Press.

United Nations Programme on HIV/AIDS. 2000. *UNAIDS Report on the Global HIV/AIDS Epidemic*. Geneva, Switzerland.

Unshuld, Paul U. 1985. *Medicine in China: A History of Ideas*. Berkeley: University of California Press.

U.S. Conference of Mayors. 1987. *Status Report on Homeless Families in America's Cities: A 29-City Survey*. Washington, DC: U.S. Conference on Mayors.

Vaughn, Megan. 1991. *Curing Their Ills: Colonial Power and African Illness*. Stanford, CA: Stanford University Press.

Velimirovic, Boris. 1990. "Is Integration of Traditional and Western Medicine Really Possible?" In *Anthropology and Primary Health Care*, ed. Jeannine Coreil and J. Dennis Mull, 51–78. Boulder, CO: Westview Press.

Vitebsky, Piers. 1995a. *The Shaman*. Boston: Little, Brown and Company.

Vitebsky, Piers. 1995b. From Cosmology to Environmentalism: Shamanism as all Knowledge in a Global Setting. In *Counterworks: Managing the Diversity of Knowledge*. Richard Farah, ed., 182–204. London: Routledge.

Virchow, Rudolf. 1879. *Gesammelte Ahandlungen aus dem Gebeit der Oeffentlichen Medizin under Seuchenlehre*. Vol. 1. Berlin: Hirschwald.

Vogt, Irmgard. 1984. "Defining Alcohol Problems as a Repressive Mechanism: Its Formative Phase in Imperial Germany and Its Strength Today." *International Journal of the Addictions* 19: 551–69.

Wagner, D. 1993. *Checkerboard Square*. Boulder, CO: Westview Press.

Waitzkin, Howard. 1981. "The Social Origins of Illness: A Neglected History." *International Journal of Health Services* 11: 77–103.

———. 1983. *The Second Sickness: Contradictions of Capitalist Health Care*. New York: Free Press.

———. 2000. "Choosing Patient-Physician Relationships in the Changing Health-Policy Environment." In *Handbook of Medical Sociology*, 5th ed., ed. Chloe E. Bird, Peter Conrad, Allen Fremont, 271–83. Upper Saddle River, NJ: Prentice-Hall.

———. 2001. *At the Front Lines of Medicine: How the Health Care System Alienates Doctors and Mistreats Patients and What We Can Do about It*. Lanham, MD: Rowman & Littlefield Publishers

Waitzkin, Howard, and Barbara Waterman. 1974. *The Exploitation of Illness in Capitalist Society*. Indianapolis: Bobbs-Merrill.

Waldorf, Dan. 1973. *Careers in Dope*. Englewood Cliffs, NJ: Prentice-Hall.

Wallace, R. 1990. "Urban Desertification, Public Health and Public Order: 'Planned Shrinkage,' Violent Death, Substance Abuse and AIDS in the Bronx." *Social Science and Medicine* 31: 801–13.

Wallerstein, Immanuel. 1979. *The Capitalist World-Economy: Essays*. New York: Cambridge University Press.

Walsh, Roger N. 1990. *The Spirit of Shamanism*. New York: G. P. Putnam's Sons.

———. 1997. "The Psychological Health of Shamans: A Reevaluation." *Journal of the American Academy of Religion* 45: 101–20.

Walt, Gill. 1994. *Health Policy: An Introduction to Process and Power.* London: Zed Books.

Warner, Kenneth. 1986. *Selling Smoke: Cigarette Advertising and Public Health.* Washington, DC: American Public Health Association.

Warren, C. W., et al. 2000. "Tobacco Use by Youth: A Surveillance Report from the Global Youth Tobacco Survey Project." *International Journal of Public Health* 78: 890–920.

Waterston, Alisse. 1993. *Street Addicts in the Political Economy.* Philadelphia: Temple University Press.

———. 1999. *Love, Sorrow, and Rage: Destitute Women in a Manhattan Residence.* Philadelphia: Temple University Press.

Weaver, Thomas. 1968. "Medical Anthropology: Trends in Research and Medical Education." In *Essays in Medical Anthropology,* ed. Thomas Weaver, 1–12. Athens: University of Georgia Press.

Weibel, Wayne. 1990. "Identifying and Gaining Access to Hidden Populations." In *The Collection and Interpretation of Data from Hidden Populations,* ed. Elizabeth Lambert, 4–11. Rockville, MD: National Institute on Drug Abuse (NIDA Research Monograph #98).

Weidman, Hazel H. 1986. "Origins: Reflections on the History of the SMA and Its Official Publication." *Medical Anthropology Quarterly,* o.s., 17(5): 115–24.

Weil, Robert. 1994. "China at the Brink: Contradictions of 'Market Socialism,' Part I." *Monthly Review* 46(7): 10–35.

Weiner, Annette. 1988. *The Trobrianders of Papua New Guinea.* New York: Holt, Rinehart, and Winston.

Weinreb, L., R. Goldberg, E. Bassuk, and J. Perloff. 1998. "Determinants of Health and Service Use Patterns in Homeless and Low-income Housed Children." *Pediatrics* 102(3 pt 1): 554–62.

Weis, W., and C. Burke. 1963. "Media Content and Tobacco Advertising: An Unhealthy Addiction." *Columbia Journalism Review* (Summer): 6–12.

Weissman, P. et al. 1999. "Maternal Smoking during Pregnancy and Psychopathology in Offspring Followed to Adulthood." *Journal of the American Academy of Child and Adolescent Psychiatry* 38: 7.

Weitz, Rose. 2001. *The Sociology of Health, Illness, and Health Care: A Critical Approach.* 2nd ed. Belmont, CA: Wadsworth.

Werbner, Richard, ed. *Postcolonial Subjectivities in Africa.* New York: Zed Books.

Wertz, Richard, and Dorothy Wertz. 1979. *Lying-In: A History of Childbirth in America.* New York: Schocken Books.

Westermeyer, Joseph. 1974. The Drunken Indian: Myths and Realities. *Psychiatric Annals* 4(11): 29–36.

White, Robert. 2000. "Unraveling the Tuskegee Study of Untreated Syphilis." *Archives of Internal Medicine* 160(5): 585–98.

Whiteford, Linda. 1996. "Political Economy, Gender and the Social Production of Health and Illness." In *Gender and Health: An International Perspective,* ed. Carolyn Sargent and Caroline Brettel, 242–56. Upper Saddle River: Prentice-Hall.

Whiteford, Linda, and M. Poland, eds. 1989. *New Approaches to Human Reproduction: Social and Ethical Dimensions.* Boulder, CO: Westview Press.

Widom, C., T. Ireland, and P. Glynn. 1995. "Alcohol Abuse in Abused and Neglected Children Follow-Up: Are They at Increased Risk?" *Journal of Studies on Alcohol.* 56(2): 207–17.

Wilde, Lawrence. 1998. *Ethical Marxism and Its Radical Critics.* New York: St. Martin's Press.

Williams, Dennis. 1991. "A New State, a New Life: Individual Success in Quitting Smoking." *Social Science and Medicine* 33: 1365–72.

Wilsnack, S., N. Vogeltanz, and A. Klassen. 1997. "Childhood Sexual Abuse and Women's Substance Abuse: National Survey Findings." *Journal of Studies on Alcohol* 58: 264–71.

Winkelman, Michael James. 1992. *Shamans, Priests and Witches: A Cross-Cultural Study of Magico-Religious Practitioners.* Tempe: Arizona State University (Anthropological Research Papers # 44).

———. 2000. *Shamanism: The Neural Ecology of Consciousness and Healing.* Westport, CT: Bergin & Garvey.

Witherspoon, Gary. 1977. *Language and Art in the Navajo Universe.* Ann Arbor: University of Michigan Press.

Wohl, Stanley. 1984. Medical Industrial Complex. New York: Harmony Books.

Wolcott, Harry. 1974. *The African Beer Gardens of Bul.* New Bruswick, NJ: Rutgers Center for Alcohol Studies.

Wolf, Eric. 1969. "American Anthropologists and American Society." In *Concepts and Assumptions in Contemporary Anthropology,* ed. Stephen Tyler, 3–11. Athens: University of Georgia Press.

———. 1982. *Europe and the People without History.* Berkeley: University of California Press.

Wood, Corinne Shear. 1979. *Human Sickness and Health: A Biocultural View.* Palo Alto, CA: Mayfield Publishing.

Woolhandler, Steffie, and David Himmelstein. 1989. "Ideology in Medical Science: Class in the Clinic." *Social Science and Medicine* 28: 1205–9.

World Bank. 2001. *World Bank Reports, India HIV/AIDS Update.* Washington, DC.

World Health Organization. 1978. *Primary Health Care.* Geneva.

Wright, Erik O. 1983. "Capitalism's Future." *Socialist Review* 13(2): 77–126.

Wright, J. D., and E. Weber. 1987. *Homelessness and Health.* New York: McGraw-Hill.

Wu, Zunyou. 1998. "Recent Trends of Injection Drug Use and Relative HIV Infection in China." In *Global Research Network Meeting on HIV Prevention in Drug Using Populations,* ed. Bethesda, MD: National Institute on Drug Abuse.

Yih, Katherine. 1990. "The Red and the Green." *Monthly Review* 42(5): 16–27.

Young, Allan. 1976. "Some Implications of Medical Beliefs and Practices for Medical Anthropology." *American Anthropologist* 78: 5–24.

———. 1978. "Rethinking the Western Health Enterprise." *Medical Anthropology* 2(2): 1-10.

Zavala-Martinez, Iris. 1986. "En La Lucha: Economic and Socioeconomic Struggles of Puerto Rican Women in the United States." In *For Crying Out Loud: Women and Poverty in the United States,* ed. R. Letkowitz and A. Withorn, 111–24. New York: Pilgrim Press.

Zheng, Xiang, and Sheila Hillier. 1995. "The Reforms of the Chinese Health Care System: County Level Changes: The Jiangxi Study." *Social Science and Medicine* 41: 1057–64.

Zierler, Sally, et al. 2000. "Economic Deprivation and AIDS Incidence in Massa-
    chusetts." *American Journal of Public Health* 90: 1064–73.
Zimmering, Paul, et al. 1951. "Heroin Addiction in Adolescent Boys." *Journal of
    Nervous and Mental Diseases* 114: 19–34.
Zinn, Howard. 1980. *People's History of the United States*. New York: Harper and
    Row.
Zola, Irving Kenneth. 1978. "Medicine as an Institution of Social Control." In *The
    Cultural Crisis of Modern Medicine*, ed. John Ehrenreich, 80–100. New York:
    Monthly Review Press.

INDEX

About the Authors

HANS A. BAER is in the Department of Sociology, Anthropology, and Gerontology at the University of Arkansas, Little Rock.

MERRILL SINGER is Associate Director and Chief of Research at the Hispanic Health Council in Hartford, Connecticut.

IDA SUSSER is Professor of Anthropology at Hunter College, City University of New York.